TRUSTS:
A comparative study

This is the first attempt ever to deal with trusts on a comparative law basis. It covers three models of trust: the English, the international and the civilian. It examines more than thirty countries, and submits a unified theory of trusts. The effects of the Hague Convention of 1985 are discussed, as well as its implementation in ratifying civil-law countries, where it is now possible to form trusts under a foreign law. Academics will find this book a novel approach to the English-model trust, and practitioners will find it gives a wealth of information on foreign legal systems.

CAMBRIDGE STUDIES IN INTERNATIONAL AND COMPARATIVE LAW

This series (established in 1946 by Professors Gutteridge, Hersch Lauterpacht and McNair) is a forum for studies of high quality in the fields of public and private international law and comparative law. Although these are distinct legal subdisciplines, developments since 1946 confirm their interrelationship. Comparative law is increasingly used as a tool in the making of law at national, regional and international levels. Private international law is increasingly affected by international conventions, and the issues faced by classical conflicts rules are increasingly dealt with by substantive harmonization of law under international auspices. Mixed international arbitrations, especially those involving state economic activity, raise mixed questions of public and private international law. In many fields (such as the protection of human rights and democratic standards, investment guarantees, international criminal law) international and national systems interact. National constitutional arrangements relating to 'foreign affairs', and to the implementation of international norms, are a focus of attention.

Professor Sir Robert Jennings edited the series from 1981. Following his retirement as General Editor, an editorial board has been created and Cambridge University Press has recommitted itself to the series, affirming its broad scope.

The Board welcomes works of a theoretical or interdisciplinary character, and those focusing on new approaches to international or comparative law or conflicts of law. Studies of particular institutions or problems are equally welcome, as are translations of the best work published in other languages.

General Editors	James Crawford
	Whewell Professor of International Law, University of Cambridge
	David Johnston
	Regius Professor of Civil Law, University of Cambridge
Editorial Board	Professor Hilary Charlesworth *University of Adelaide*
	Mr John Collier *Trinity Hall, Cambridge*
	Professor Lori Damrosch *Columbia University Law School*
	Professor John Dugard *Director, Research Centre for*
	International Law, University of Cambridge
	Professor Mary-Ann Glendon *Harvard Law School*
	Professor Christopher Greenwood *London School of*
	Economics
	Professor Hein Kötz *Max-Planck-Institut, Hamburg*
	Dr Vaughan Lowe *Corpus Christi College, Cambridge*
	Professor D. M. McRae *University of Ottawa*
	Professor Onuma Yasuaki *University of Tokyo*
Advisory Committee	Professor D. W. Bowett QC
	Judge Rosalyn Higgins QC
	Professor Sir Robert Jennings QC
	Professor J. A. Jolowicz QC
	Professor Eli Lauterpacht QC
	Professor Kurt Lipstein
	Judge Stephen Schwebel

A list of books in the series can be found at the end of this volume

TRUSTS:
A comparative study

Maurizio Lupoi
Translated by Simon Dix

PUBLISHED BY THE PRESS SYNDICATE OF THE UNIVERSITY OF CAMBRIDGE
The Pitt Building, Trumpington Street, Cambridge, United Kingdom

CAMBRIDGE UNIVERSITY PRESS
The Edinburgh Building, Cambridge CB2 2RU, UK   http://www.cup.cam.ac.uk
40 West 20th Street, New York 10011–4211, USA   http://www.cup.org
10 Stamford Road, Oakleigh, Melbourne 3166, Australia

Originally published in Italian as *Trusts* by Giuffrè Editore 1997
and © Dott. A. Giuffrè Editore, S.p.A. Milano
First published in English by Cambridge University Press 2000 as *Trusts: a Comparative Study*
English translation © Cambridge University Press 2000

First published 2000

Printed in the United Kingdom at the University Press, Cambridge

Typeset in Swift Regular 9.75/13pt [VN]

A catalogue record for this book is available from the British Library

Library of Congress cataloguing in publication data

Lupoi, Maurizio.
  [Trusts. English]
  Trusts: a comparative study / Maurizio Lupoi; translated by Simon Dix.
    p.   cm. – (Cambridge studies in international and comparative law)
  Includes index.
  ISBN 0 521 62329 4 (hardback)
  1. Trusts and trustees. I. Title. II. Series.
K795.L8713 1999   346.05′9 – dc21   99–24171   CIP

ISBN 0 521 62329 4 hardback

Contents

Texts cited in abbreviated format	*page* xi
Abbreviations of journals and law reports	xiv
Table of cases	xix

1 Introduction 1

Preliminary aspects 1
Layout of the book 5
    'Trust' or 'trusts'. The English and international models 5
    The purpose of the individual chapters 8
Regulae, knowledge of foreign law, comparisons 10

2 The heart of the trust 14

Introduction 14
    Systematic and structural data 14
    Terminology 16
    Statutory trusts 19
    Equitable notion of fraud 20
Trusts arising out of rules of equity (constructive trusts) 22
    Improper benefits obtained from a fiduciary relationship 22
    Transfer of trust property 26
    Participation in a breach by a trustee: 'knowing receipt' and
    'knowing participation' 29
    Trustee de son tort 34
    A seller of land not yet transferred 34
    Donatio mortis causa 36
    Benefits deriving from the commission of a crime 38
    Undue payment 38

Undue influence or awe 39
Influence over the will of a testator 41
Mutual wills 41
Agreements void because of a defect in form, regarding the
benefits due to the transferor of real property 43
Transfer to a purchaser of the obligations of a seller towards
a third party, notwithstanding the lack of form 45
Oral agreement with equitable effect 45
Rights in the family home 46

Returning or residual trusts (resulting trusts) 50

Lack of completeness or ineffectiveness of transfers 50
Delivery of a sum for a specific purpose 51
Making over assets in the name of third parties 53
Purchase of property in common 55
Westdeutsche v. Islington (1996) 56

The maxims and protection of equity 57

Equity follows the law 57
Tracing 58
Fraud and legal requirements 65
Equity and the form of the trust instrument 66
'Equity looks at that as done which ought to have been done' 69
'Equity acts *in personam*': the injunction 70
'Equity acts *in personam*': specific performance 73
The receiver 73

Equity and non-express trusts 74

Express and non-express trusts: how they differ 74
Expressly and non-expressly established trusts:
how they are alike 75
Theoretical basis of constructive and resulting trusts 77
Applications and enhancements of the theory 84
The constructive trust between substantive law and
remedy; unjust enrichment 86

3 The traditional English model 95

The creation of a trust 95

The trust instrument and its form 95
The settlor as trustee 99
Powers to consent; powers of appointment 100
Revocable trusts; 'grantor trusts' 103
The notion of 'estate' and the duration of trusts 104
The secret trust 110
The half-secret trust 114

Trustee and personal representative 116
The *actio pauliana* 117
Reasons for nullity 119

Typology of trusts 122

Business trusts 122
Purpose trusts 123
Charitable trusts 126
Discretionary trusts 130
Protective trusts 133
Asset-protection trusts 135
The mortgage and the *pactum commissorium* 136
Trusts for business activities 138
Trusts for financial operations 145
Family-interest trusts 149
Applicable law and non-resident trusts 149

The notion of trust 156

The bare trustee and double-taxation treaties 156
The legal position of the settlor: the emerging
contractual element 162
The office of trustee 166
The trustee 178
The beneficiary 183
Webb v. Webb 193
Trust, entrusting and segregation 195

4 The international trust model 201

Introduction 201

Overview of legal systems 205

Anguilla 205
Antigua and Barbuda 206
The Bahamas 206
Barbados 207
Belize 207
Bermuda 208
The British Virgin Islands 209
The Cayman Islands 209
Cyprus 210
Cook Islands 211
Gibraltar 212
Guernsey 213
Hong Kong 214
The Isle of Man 215
Jersey 215

Malta   217
Mauritius   218
Nauru   218
Nevis   219
Niue   219
Saint Vincent   220
Seychelles   220
Turks and Caicos   221
Vanuatu   221
Western Samoa   222

Structural elements of the model: consolidation of
English *regulae*   223
    Acceptance of the trustee   223
    The juridical position of the trustee   224
    The juridical position of the beneficiary   225
    Obligations of trustees   228
    Unanimity among trustees   228
    Delegation of trustee powers   229
    Responsibilities of the trustee   229
    Third parties contracting with a trustee; participants
    in a trustee's breach   232
    Constructive trusts and the form of the trust
    instrument   233
    Tracing   235
    Cy-près in charitable trusts   235
    Protective trusts   236
    Resulting trusts   236
    Bringing forward the date of termination of a trust   237
    Definition of trust   237

Structural element of the model: new *regulae*   239
    Applicable law of the trust   240
    The applicable law of the creation of the trust   242
    The applicable law of the transfer to the trustee   243
    Limits of application of foreign laws or judgments   245
    The revocatory action   248
    Trusts for purposes, charitable or otherwise   252
    Duration of the trust   255
    Protector   257
    Letter of wishes   262
    The emerging contractual element   264

5 **Trusts in civil-law or mixed legal systems**   267

Comparative data   267
    Early misunderstandings   267

The *fideicomiso* in Latin America 269
Basic comparative data 269

Overview of legal systems 273

Argentina 273
Colombia 274
Ecuador 275
Ethiopia 276
The Philippines 277
Japan 277
Israel 279
Liechtenstein 280
Louisiana 281
Luxembourg 283
Mauritius 283
Mexico 284
Panama 285
Peru 286
Quebec 287
Russia 288
The Seychelles 289
St Lucia 290
Venezuela 290

Two special cases 292

Scotland 292
South Africa 297

Comparative considerations 301

Limits of these considerations and the exportation of
the trust 301
The transfer to the fiduciary 303
The segregation of the trust assets 308
Entrusting and powers retained by the settlor 310
Fiduciary components and conflicts of interest 313
Peculiarities of civil-law systems 315
Conclusion: open and closed systems 325

6 **The Hague Convention, 1985** 327

The general framework of the shapeless trust 327

The convention and civil-law systems 327
The purposes of the Convention 329
The motives behind the shapeless trust 331
The shapeless trust (article 2) 333
Voluntary and involuntary trusts (articles 3 and 20) 341

Conclusions   345

The applicable law   346

Negotium of creation and *negotium* of transfer:
the law of the trust (article 4)   346
The unlimited freedom to choose the
applicable law (article 6)   348
Other questions of private international law
(articles 7, 5, 9, 10 and 8)   350
The 'domestic' trust (article 5)   352

Recognition and its effect   353

The 'foreign' trust and the universality of the
Convention (article 21)   353
The minimum effects of recognition   354
The minimum effects of recognition and the form
(articles 3 and 12)   356
Optional recognition (article 13)   358
Limits to recognition (article 15)   362
Limits of the Convention (articles 16, 18 and 19)   364
Conclusion: articles 14 and 15.2, and article 13 as a
closing provision   366

7   **Trusts in Italy**   368
The civilian approach to trusts   368
Introduction   368
Fiducia, *fideicommissum* and trust   369
Separation, autonomy and segregation   377
Conclusions   384

Index   387

Texts cited in abbreviated format

Actes
Conference de La Haye de droit international privé – Hague Conference on private international law, Actes et documents de la Quinzième session – Proceedings of the Fifteenth Session, II, Imprimerie Nationale, The Hague, 1985

Atti Milano
I. Beneventi (ed.), *I trusts in Italia oggi*, Milan, 1996

Béraudo, *Trusts*
J.-P. Béraudo, *Les trusts anglo-saxons et le droit français*, L.G.D.J., Paris, 1992

Birks, *Restitution*
P. Birks, *An Introduction to the Law of Restitution*, revised edition, London, 1989

Commissione
A. E. von Overbeck, *Rapport de la Commission spéciale/Report of the Special Commission*, in Actes, 172

Explanatory report
A. E. von Overbeck, *Rapport explicatif/Explanatory Report*, in Actes, 370

Fratcher, *Trust*
W. F. Fratcher, *Trust*, in *International Encyclopedia of Comparative Law*, vol. VI, ch. II (1973)

Gambaro, *Proprietà*
A. Gambaro, *Il diritto di proprietà*, Milan, 1995

Gardner, *Introduction*
S. Gardner, *An Introduction to the Law of Trusts*, Oxford, 1990 (paperback, 1993)

Glasson
J. Glasson (ed.), *International Trust Laws*, London, 1992–1995 (periodically updated)

Goff and Jones, *Restitution*
Goff, Lord of Chieveley and G. Jones, *The Law of Restitution* (4th edition), 1993

Graziadei, *Diritti nell'interesse altrui*
M. Graziadei, *Diritti nell'interesse altrui. Undisclosed agency e trust nell'esperienza giuridica inglese*, Università degli Studi di Trento, 1995

Hanbury, *Equity*
Hanbury and Martin, *Modern Equity* (14th edition), J. E. Martin (ed.), London, 1993

Hayton, *Trusts*
D. J. Hayton, *The Law of Trusts* (2nd edition), London, 1993

Honoré, *Trusts*
Honoré's *South African Law of Trusts* (4th edition), T. Honoré and E. Cameron (eds.), Cape Town, 1992

Jacobs, *Trusts*
Jacobs' *Law of Trusts in Australia* (5th edition), R. P. Meagher and W. M. C. Gummow (eds.), Butterworths, 1986

Johnston, *Roman Trusts*
D. Johnston, *The Roman Law of Trusts*, Oxford, 1988

Lupoi, *Appunti*
M. Lupoi, *Appunti sulla real property e sul trust in diritto inglese*, Milan, 1971

Matthews and Sowden
P. Matthews and T. Sowden, *The Jersey Law of Trusts* (3rd edition), London, 1993

Megarry, *Real Property*
R. Megarry and M. P. Thompson, *Megarry's Manual of the Law of Real Property* (7th edition), London, 1993

Pettit, *Trusts*
P. H. Pettit, *Equity and the Law of Trusts* (7th edition), London, 1993

Report
A. Dyer and H. van Loon, *Report on trusts and analogous institutions/Rapport sur les trusts et institutions analogues*, in Actes, 7

Restatement, *Restitution*
Restatement of the Law of Restitution, Quasi Contracts and Constructive Trusts, St Paul, MN, 1937

Restatement, *Trusts*
Restatement of the Law Second, Trusts, St Paul, MN, 1959; Appendix, 1987

Scott, *Trusts*
A. W. Scott and W. F. Fratcher, *The Law of Trusts* (4th edition), Boston, MA, 1989 (12 vols.); update 1995

Snell, *Equity*
E. H. T. Snell, *Principles of Equity*, P. V. Baker and P. St-John Langan, London, 1990

Underhill, *Trusts*
Underhill and D. J. Hayton, *Law Relating to Trusts and Trustees*, D. J. Hayton (ed.), London, 1995

Waters, *Trusts*
D. W. M. Waters, *Law of Trusts in Canada* (2nd edition), Toronto, 1984

Waters, *Cours*
D. W. M. Waters, *The Institution of the Trust in Civil and Common Law*, Academy of International Law, *Recueil des cours*, vol. 252, Dordrecht, 1995

Wilson and Duncan
W. A. Wilson and A. G. M. Duncan, *Trusts, Trustees and Executors* (2nd edition), Edinburgh, 1995

Abbreviations of journals and law reports

AC	Appeal Cases
Actalur	*Acta Iuridica*
AfcP	Archiv für civilistische Praxis
AllER	All England Law Reports
AJCL	*American Journal of Comparative Law*
Alberta Rep	Alberta Reports
ALR	Australian Law Reports
AmJIL	*American Journal of International Law*
AmJLH	*American Journal of Legal History*
ArchPhilDr	Archives de philophie du droit
Atk	Atkinson, Quarter Sessions Records (in English Reports, vol. 26)
Banca, Borsa	Banca, Borsa, *Titoli di credito*
BCLC	Butterworths Company Law Cases
Beav	Bevan (in English Reports, vols. 48–55)
BIDR	Bullettino dell' Istituto di diritto Romano
Bli NS	Bligh, New Series (in English Reports, vols. 4–6)
BLR	Barbados Law Reports
Bollet. tribut di informazione	Bolletino tributario di informazione
Bro CC	Brown (in English Reports, vols. 28–9)
Cal	California Reports
CBR	Canadian Bar Review
Ch	Chancery Reports
ChApp	Appeals in Chancery
ChD	Chancery Division
Chron	Dalloz, Chronique
CILR	Cayman Islands Law Reports

CJQ	*Civil Justice Quarterly*
CJTL	*Columbia Journal of Transnational Law*
CLJ	*Cambridge Law Journal*
CLP	*Current Legal Problems*
CLR	Commonwealth Law Reports
CoLLR	*Columbia Law Review*
Cont. e imp.	Contratto e impresa
Conv	*The Conveyancer and Property Lawyer*
Corriere giur.	Il Corriere giuridice
Cox Eq Cas	Cox, Chancery Reports (in English Reports, vols. 76–7)
CrimLR	Criminal Law Reports
D	*Dalloz*
De GF & J	De Gex, Fisher & Jones (in English Reports, vol. 45)
De GM & G	De Gex, Magnagcten & Gordon (in English Reports, vols. 42–4)
Dick	Dickens (in English Reports, vol. 21)
Dir. del comm. int.	Diritto del commercio internazionale
Dir. fam.	Rivista del diritto di famiglia e delle persone
DLR	Dominion Law Reports
Dyer	Dyer (in English Reports, vol. 73)
EGCS	Estates Gazette Case Summaries El & Bl
El & Bl	Ellis & Blackburn (in English Reports, vols. 118–20)
FLR	Family Law Reports
Foro. it.	Foro italiano
Foro. pad.	Foro padano
FSR	Fleet Street Reports
Giur. Comm.	Giurisprudenza commerciale
Giur. it.	Giurisprudenza italiana
Giust. Civ.	Giustizia civile
GLR	Guyana Law Reports
HarvardLR	*Harvard Law Review*
HL	House of Lords
ICLQ	*International and Comparative Law Quarterly*
IndLJ	*Indiana Law Journal*
IR	Irish Reports
IsrLR	*Israel Law Review*
IurRev	*Iuridical Review*
JBL	*Journal of Business Law*
JcompL	*Journal of Comparative Legislation*

JCP	*Juriclasseur périodique*
JdrInt	*Journal de droit international*
JIntPl	*Journal of International Planning*
JlegH	*Journal of Legal History*
JLR	Jersey Law Reports
JR	*Juridical Review*
Kay & J	Kay & Johnson's Vice-Chancellor's Reports (in English Reports, vols. 69–70)
KB	King's Bench
Leggi civ. comm.	Le nuove leggi civili commentate
LlR	Lloyd's Reports
LouisianaLR	*Louisiana Law Review*
LQR	*Law Quarterly Review*
LR	Law Reports
LRBG	Law Reports of British Guiana
LT	Law Times Reports
M&S	Maule & Selwyn (in English Reports, vol. 6)
Macq	Macqueen (in English Reports)
MALR	Manx Law Reports
Mass.	Massimario del Foro italiano
McGillLJ	*McGill Law Journal*
Mer	Merivale (in English Reports, vol. 35–36)
MichLR	*Michigan Law Review*
MissouriLR	*Missouri Law Review*
MLR	*Modern Law Review*
MR	Mauritius Reports
Nels	Nelson (in English Reports, vol. 21)
NILQ	*Northern Ireland Law Quarterly*
NSWLR	New South Wales Law Reports
Nuova giur. civ. commentata	Nuova giurisprudenza civile commentata
NZLR	New Zealand Law Reports
NZULR	*New Zealand Universities Law Review*
OI	*Offshore Investment*
OJLS	*Oxford Journal of Legal Studies*
OTPR	*Offshore Tax Planning Review*
P	*Pacific Reporter*
P Wms	Peere Williams (in English Reports, vol. 24)
Ph	Phillips (in English Reports, vol. 41)
Plowd	Plowden (in English Reports, vol. 75)

PLR	Pension Law Reports
QB	Queen's Bench
Qd	Queensland
R	Scotch Session Cases, 4th Series
RabelsZ	Rabels Zeitschrift für ausländisches und internationales Privatrecht
Rass. dir. farmaceutico	Rassegna di diritto farmaceutico
RBQ	*Revue du barreau de Québec*
RDIDC	*Revue de droit international et de droit comparé*
RevCrit	*Revue critique de droit international privé*
RevFDer	*Revista de la Facultad de Derecho*
RevNot	*Revista del Notariado*
RevNotB	*Revue du notariat belge*
Riv. dir. civ.	Rivista di diritto civile
Riv. dir. comm.	Rivista del diritto commerciale
Riv. dir. int. priv. proc.	Rivista di diritto internazionale privato e processuale
Riv. dott. comm.	Rivista dei dottori commercialisti
Riv. not.	Rivista del notoriato
Riv. soc.	Rivista delle società
Riv. trim. dir. proc. civ.	Rivista trimestrale di diritto e procedura civile
RLR	*Restitution Law Review*
RTDC	*Revue trimestrielle de droit civil*
RTDComm	*Revue trimestrielle de droit commercial et économique*
S	Scotch Session Cases, 1st Series
SA	South African Law Reports
SALJ	South African Law Journal
Sask R	Saskatchewan Reports
SC	Session cases
Sel Cas CH	Select Cases in Chancery
SIZ	*Schweizerische Juristen-Zeitung*
SJIR	*Schweizerisches Jahrbuch für internationales Recht*
SLR	Singapore Law Reports
SLT	*Scots Law Times*
So	*Southern Reporter*
Società	Le società
Sol	*The Solicitor*
SS	Selden Society

STC	Simon's Tax Cases
Swans	Swanston, Chancery Reports (in English Reports, vol. 36)
SydneyLR	*Sydney Law Review*
T&E	*Trust & Estates*
T&T	*Trusts & Trustees and International Asset Management*
TCM	*G. Kodilinye, Trusts. Text, Cases, Materials, London, 1996*
TLI	*Tolley's Trust Law International*
TulLR	*Tulane Law Review*
Turn & R	Turner & Russell (in English Reports, vol. 37)
UBCLR	*University of British Columbia Law Review*
UnChLR	*University of Chicago Law Review*
UnSWLJ	*University of South Wales Law Journal*
UNSWLR	*University of New South Wales Law Review*
VAJIL	*Virginia Journal of International Law*
Vern	Vemon (in English Reports, vol. 23)
Ves Er	Vesey Senior (in English Reports, vols. 27–8)
Ves	Vesey Junior, chancery Reports (in English Reports, vols. 30–4)
Vita not.	Vita notarile
VR	Victoria Reports
WIR	West Indian Reports
WLR	Weekly Law Reports
WTR	*World Tax Report*
WWR	*Western Weekly Reporter*
YaleLJ	*Yale Law Journal*
ZfsR	*Zeitschrift für schweizerisches Recht*

Table of common law cases cited

Abbey National v. Moss (1994) 1 FLR 307 50n.

Abbot of Bury v. Bokenham (1535) 1 Dyer 7b 184n., 185n.

Abbot Fund Trusts, Re (1900) 2 Ch 326 51n., 125n.

Aberdeen Railway v. Blaikie Brothers (1854) 1 Macq 461 168n.

Acro v. Rex Chainbelt (1971) 1 WLR 1676 71n.

A-G v. Peacock (1676) 73 SS n. 440 130n.

A-G v. Webster (1875) LR 20 Eq 483 130n.

A-G. of the Bahamas v. Royal Trust Co (1986) 3 AllER 423 128n.

A-G for Hong Kong v. Reid (1993) 3 WLR 1143, (1994) RLR 57,
(1995) in 50 MLR 87 24n., 25n., 26n.

Agip (Africa) v. Jackson (1990) Ch 265, (1991) Ch 547, 3 WLR 116 30n., 60n.

Air Canada, Re (1993) 108 DLR (4th) 593 32n.

Allan's Trustees v. Inland Revenue (1971) SLT 62 295n.

Allen v. McCrombie's Trustees (1909) SC 710 7 294n.

Allen v. Snyder (1977) 2 NSWLR 685 18n., 47n., 49n.

Alsop Wilkinson v. Neary (1995) 1 AllER 43 168n.

Aluminium Industries v. Romalpa (1976) 2 AllER 552 139n.

American Cyanamid v. Ethicon (1975) AC 396, (1975) 1 AllER 504 72n.

Andrews v. Ramsay (1903) 2 KB 635 24n.

Armour v. Thyssen (1990) 3 AllER 481 139n.

Ashburn Anstalt v. Arnold (1988) 2 AllER 147, (1988) 2 WLR 706,
(1989) 43n., 45n., 48n.

Astor's Settlement Trust, Re (1952) Ch 534 127n.

Attorney General (in Recueil, 1994, I-1717) 194n.

Augustus v. Permanent Trustee (1971) 124 CLR 245 152n., 153n., 154n.

Austin v. Austin (1978) 31 WIR 46 53n., 54n.

Austin v. Bailey (1962) MR 113 284n., 322n.

Australian Elizabethan Theatre Trust, Re (1991) 102 ALR 681 52n.

Avondale *v.* Haggie (1979) 2 NZLR 124   88n.
Baden and Others *v.* Société Générale (1983) BCLC 325   29n., 32n.
Bank of Credit (1994) MaLR 272   172n.
Bankers Trust *v.* Shapira (1980) 1 WLR 1274, 3 AllER 353   32n.
Bannister *v.* Bannister (1948) 2 AllER 133   43n., 44n.
Banque Belge *v.* Hambrouck (1921) 1 KB 321   59n.
Barclays Bank *v.* O'Brien (1992) 3 WLR 593   137n.
Barclays Bank Ltd *v.* Quistclose Investments Ltd (1968)
    3 AllER 651   51n., 52n.
Barlow Clowes *v.* Vaughan (1992) 4 AllER 22   62n.
Barnes *v.* Addy (1874) LR 9 ChApp 244   29n.
Barret *v.* Hartley (1866) LR 2 Eq 789   168n.
Bartlett *v.* Barclays Bank (1980) Ch 515, 1 AllER 139   30n., 177n.
Bateman, Re (1970) 3 AllER 817   114n.
Baumgartner *v.* Baumgartner (1987) 164 CLR 137   47n.
Beatty *v.* Guggenheim (1919) 225 NY 380   90n.
Beatty, Re (1990) 1 WLR 1503   114n.
Belmont Finance *v.* Williams Furniture (1980) 1AllER 393   24n., 30n.
Bennet *v.* Bennet (1879) 10 ChD 474   54n
Berchtold, Re (1923) 1 Ch 192   154n.
Binions *v.* Evans (1972) 2AllER 70   43n., 45n.
Birch *v.* Treasury Solicitor (1950) 2 AllER 1198   37n.
Birmingham *v.* Renfrew (1937) 57 CLR 666   41n., 42n., 112n.
Bishopgate *v.* Homan (1995) Ch 211, 1 AllER 347   62n.
Black *v.* Freedman (1910) 12 CLR 105   38n.
Blackwell, Re (1929) AC 318   114n.
Blesbok *v.* Cantamessa (1991) 2 SA 712   87n.
Boardman *v.* Phipps (1967) 2 AC 46; (1968) 84 LQR 472   23n.
Booth *v.* Ellard (1980) 1 WLR 1443   147n.
Borden *v.* Scottish Timber Products (1981) Ch 25   61n., 140n.
Boscawen *v.* Bajwa (1995) 4 AllER 769   59n., 64n.
Boyes, Re (1884) 26 ChD 531   110n.
Bridgeman *v.* Green (1755) 2 Ves Sr 627   40n.
Brinks *v.* Abu-Saleh (1996) CLC 133   30n.
Bristol & West Building Society *v.* May May & Merrimans (a firm)
    (1996) 2 AllER 801   175n.
Bristol & West Building Society *v.* Mothew (t/a Stapley and Co)
    (1996) (Court of Appeal) The Times, 2nd August 1996   175n.
British Petroleum *v.* Hunt (No 2) (1982) 1 AllER 295   87n.

British Steel Coal Corporation *v.* British Steel Coal Staff (1993)
PLR 303   169n.
Brown *v.* IRC (1964) 3 AllER 119   23n.
Burns *v.* Burns (1984) Ch 317, AllER 244   48n.
Burton *v.* Winters (1993) 1 WLR 1077   71n.
C. Corporation *v.* P (1994) CILR 189   32n.–33n.
Caborne, Re (1943) Ch 224   120n.
Calverley *v.* Green (1985) 59 ALJR 111   47n.
Campbell *v.* Walker (1800) 5 Ves 678   168n.
Canadian Aero Service *v.* O'Malley (1973) 40 DLR (3rd) 371   24n.
Carl Zeiss Stiftung *v.* Herbert Smith (No 2) (1969) 2 Ch 276   34n.
Carreras Rothmans *v.* Freeman (1985) Ch 207, 1 AllER 155   51n., 52n.
Chamberlain, Re (1976) 126 NLJ1034   102n.
Chan *v.* Zacharia (1984) 53 ALR 417   24n.
Charles *v.* Federal Commissioner of Taxation (1954) (609)
90 CLR 598   147n.
Chase Manhatten *v.* Israel-British Bank (1979)3 AllER 1025
(1981) 1 Ch 105   93n.
Cheong Kim Hock *v.* Lin Securities (1992) SLR 349   24n., 41n.
Christ's Hospital *v.* Grainger (1848) 16 Sim 83   129n.
Cigna *v.* Westpac Securities (1996) 1 NZLR 80   31n.
Citro, Re (1991) Ch 142   50n.
Clarke *v.* Heathfield (No 2) 1985   74n.
Clayton's Case (Devaynes *v.* Noble) (1816) 1 Mer 529   62n.
Cleaver *v.* Mutual Reserve (1892) 1 QB 147   38n.
Cleaver, Re (1981) 2 AllER 1018, 1 WLR 939   41n., 112n.
Cochrane's Settlement Trusts, Re (1955) 2 WLR 267   51n.
Cohen *v.* Cohen (1985) 60 Alberta Rep 234   54n.
Coleman *v.* Bucks (1897) 2 Ch 243   28n.
Commissioners for Special Purposes *v.* Pemsel (1891) AC 531   127n.
Commissioners of Stamp Duties *v.* Livingston (1965) AC 694   116n.
Continental Trust Company (1991) JLR 83   260n.
Cook *v.* Fountain (1676) 3 Swans 585, 73 SS No 500   15n., 19n., 184n.
Cook-Bodden *v.* Kirkconnell (1994) CILR 27   34n., 35n.
Cooke *v.* Head (1972) 2 AllER 38   49n.
Cowan *v.* Eagle Trust (1992) 4 AllER 700   28n., 31n., 32n.
Cowan *v.* Scargill (1985) Ch 270   146n.
Cox, Re (1948–57) 1 Barb LR 26, TMC 246   168n.
Crippen, Re (1911) P 108   38n.

Cunningham v. Harrison (1973) QB 942, 3 AllER 463   86n.
Cunningham v. Montgomerie (1879) 6 R 1333   294n.
Cupid v. Thomas (1985) 36 WIR 182   48n.
Curtis, Re (1885) 52 LT 244   53n.
Cutter v. Powell in JlegH (1987)   89n.
Dale, Re (1993) 3 WLR 652, 4 AllER 129, Ch 31   42n., 43n.
David Securities v. Commonwealth Bank of Australia (1992)
   175 CLR 353   47n., 88n.
Davies v. Otty (No 2) (1865) 35 Beav 208   43n.,68n.
Davis v. Richards & Wallington (1990) 1 WLR 1511   120n.,145n.
De Bussche v. Alt (1878) 8 ChD 310   24n.
De Falco v. Crawley (1980) 1 AllER 913   72n.
Denley's Trust Deed, Re. (1968) 3 AllER 65, 3 WLR 457, (1969)
   1 Ch 373   121n.,124n.
Dennis, Re (1992) 3 WLR 204, (1995) 3 WLR 367   20n.,119n.
Densham, Re (1975) 3 AllER 726   43n.
Dillon v. Freine (1589–95) 1 Co Rep 120a   184n.
Diplock, Re (1948) 2 AllER 318   39n., 61n., 63n., 78n., 79n.
Director General of Fair Trading v. Buckland (1990) 1 WLR 920 71n.
Dixon v. Olmius (1795) 1 Cox Eq 414   139n.
Doering, Re (1949)   127n.
Drake v. Whipps (1995) The Times 19 December   49n., 55n.
Drexel Burnham, Re (1995) 1 WLR 32   24n., 145n., 169n.
Drury v. Drury (1675) 73 SS n. 292   53n.
Duffield v. Elwes (1827) 1 Bli NS 497   37n.
Dufour v. Pereira (1769) 1 Dick 419   42n.
Duke of Beaufort v. Berty (1721) 1 P Wms 703   117n.
Duke of Norfolk's Settlement, Re (1982) Ch 61   169n.
Duo v. Osborne (1992) 1 WLR 611   71n.
Duxbury's Settlement, Re. (1995) 1 WLR 425   167n.
Dyer v. Dyer (1788) 2 Cox Eq Cas 92   53n.
Eagle Trust v. SBC Securities (1993) 1 WLR 484   30n.
Earl of Chesterfield v. Janssen (1751) 2 Ves Sr 125   203n.
Earl of Egmont v. Smith (1877) 6 ChD 469   35n.
Eaves v. Hickson (1861) 30 Beav 136   29n.
El Ajou v. Dollar Land Holdings (1993) 3 AllER 717, (1994) 2
   AllER 685, (1995) 2 AllER 213   31n., 33n., 64n., 82n., 188n.
Ellerson v. Westcott (1896) 148 NY 506   38n.
Emery's Settlement Trusts, Re (1959) Ch 410, 1 AllER 577   54n.
Endacott, Re (1959) 3 AllER 562   123n.

Equity & Law Home Loans *v.* Prestidge (1992) 1 WLR 137   49n.

Eves *v.* Eves (1975) 3 AllER 768, 1 WLR 1338   8n., 48n., 49n.

EVTR Ltd, Re (1987) BCLC 646   53n.

Express Newspapers *v.* Keys (1980) IRLR 247   71n.

Eykyn's Trusts, Re. (1877) 6 ChD 115   53n.

Featherstonaugh *v.* Fenwick (1810) 17 Ves 298   24n.

Federated Pension Service *v.* Midland Bank (1995) in
    (1996) PLR 179   216n., 231n.

Finers *v.* Miro (1991) 1 WLR 35   30n.

Fordyce *v.* Bridges (1848) 2 Ph 497   154n.

Freevale Ltd *v.* Metrostore (1984) 1 AllER 495, Ch 199   35n.

Gardner, Re (No 1) (1920) 2 Ch 523   43n.,112n.

Gardner, Re (No 2) (1923) 2 Ch 230   113n.

Garner *v.* Bermuda Trust Company (1992) JIntPl 51, 133   246n.

Gartside *v.* IRC (1968) AC 553, 2 WLR 277   131n.

Gartside *v.* Isherwood (1788) Bro CC 558   22n.

Gascoigne *v.* Gascoigne (1918) 1 KB 223   54n.

Gates, Re (1933) Ch 913   168n.

Gibbon *v.* Mitchell (1990) 1 WLR 1304   134n.

Gibbons, Re (1917) 1IR 448   124n.

Gidrxsleme *v.* Tantomartransportes (1995) 1 WLR 299   73n.

Gillies *v.* Keogh (1989) 2 NZLR 327   47n., 83n., 88n.

Gillingham Bus Disaster, Re (1958) Ch 300, 1 AllER 37   51n.

Gilmour *v.* Coates (1949) AC 426   128n.

Gissing *v.* Gissing (1970) 2 AllER 780; (1971) AC 886, (1996) in
    112 LQR 378   47n., 48n., 50n.

Gold *v.* Rosenberg (1995) 129 DLR (4th) 152   31n.

Goldcorp Exchange, Re (1995) 1 AC 74   22–3n., 62n.,80n., 91n., 140n.

Goodchild *v.* Goodchild (1996) 1 AllER 670   42n., 112n.

Gorman, Re (1990) 1 WLR 616   55n.

Gourju's Will Trusts, Re (1942) 2 AllER 605   133n.

Grant *v.* Edwards (1986) Ch 638, 2 AllER 426   48n.

Grant's Will Trusts, Re (1980) 1 WLR 360   124n.

Greasley *v.* Cooke (1980) 1 WLR 1306   83n.

Green *v.* Smith (1738) 1 Atk 572   35n.

Green, Re (1951) Ch 148   41n.

Greenidge *v.* Bank of Nova Scotia (1984) 38 WIR 63   37n.

Griffith *v.* Griffith (1981) 16 BLR 291   53n.

Grison, Re (1980) 101 DLR (3d) 728   41n.

Guinness plc *v.* Saunders (1988) 1 WLR 863   25

Gulbenkian's Settlements, Re (1970) AC 508   132n.
Hagger, Re (1930) 2 Ch 190   41n.
Haig v. Kaye (1872) LR 7 ChApp 469   68n.
Halifax Mortgage Services v. Stepsky (1995) 4 AllER 656   28n.
Hallett, Re (1880) 13 ChD 696   60n.
Hambro v. Duke of Marlborough (1994) 3 WLR 347   175n.
Hammond v. Mitchell (1991) 1 WLR 1127, (1992) 1 AllER 109   47n., 48n.
Harries v. Church Commissioners (1992) 1 WLR 1241   174n.
Hay's Settlement Trusts, Re (1981) 3 AllER 786   121n., 132n.
Hayward v. Giordani (1983) NZLR 246   47n.
Helvering v. Clifford (1940) 309 US 331   99n.
Henry v. Hammond (1913) KB 515   172n.
Heritable Reversionary Co v. Millar (1891) 18 R 1166   293n.
Heseltine v. Heseltine (1971) 1 AllER 952   53n.
Hetherington, Re (1989) 2 AllER 129   128n.
Higgins v. Wingfield (1987) VR 689   48n.
Hillingdon Estates Co v. Stonefield Estates Ltd (1952) Ch 627,
    1 AllER 853   70n.
Howard v. Harris (1683) 1 Vern 190   138n.
Howe v. Earl of Dartmouth (1802) 7 Ves 137   174n.
Hubbard v. Pitt (1975) 3 AllER 1   71n.
Hunt v. Severs (1994) 2 AllER 385, 2 WLR 602   86n.
Hunter v. Moss (1994) 1 WLR 452, 3 AllER 215   99n.
Huntingford v. Hobbs (1993) 1 FLR 736   49n.
Hussey v. Palmer (1972) 1 WLR 1286   48n., 92n.
Ideal Bedding v. Holland (1907) 2 Ch 157   168n.
ILG Travel, Re (1995) 2 BCLC 128   141n.
Imperial Group Pension Trust v. Imperial Tobacco (1990)
    1 WLR 589   145n.
Inche Noriah v. Shaik Allie bin Omar (1929) AC 127   40n.
Industrial Development Consultants v. Cooley (1972) 1 AllER 162   23n.
Ingram v. IRC (1995) STC 564, (1997) Court of Appeal 4 AllER 395,
    (1999) House of Lords 1 AllER 297   158n.
Invercargill City Council v. Hamlin (1996) 1 AllER 756   6n.
Inwards v. Baker (1965) 2 QB 29   83n.
IRC v. McMullen (1980) 1AllER 884   128n.
IRC v. Stype Investments (Jersey) Ltd (1982) 3 AllER 419   34n.
Jaffray v. Marshall (1993) 1 WLR 1285   175n.
Jewish National Fund v. Royal Trust Company (1965) 53 DLR (2nd)
    577   151n.

Johnson, Re (1967) Ch 387, 1 AllER 553 — 120n.

Karak Rubber *v.* Burden (No 2) (1972) 1 WLR 602 — 24n.

Katharine, Duchess of Suffolk *v.* Hevenden (1560) 93 QLR (1977) 33, at 37 — 66n.

Kayford, Re (1975) 1 WLR 279 — 51n., 99n., 141

Keech *v.* Sandford (1726,1817) Sel Cas Ch 61 — 22n., 24n.

Keen, Re (1937) Ch 236 — 110n., 114n.

Kelly, Re (1932) IR 255 — 109n.

Kemp, Estate *v.* MacDonald's Trustee (1915) AD 491 — 299n.

Khan *v.* Khan (1994) TCM 95 — 84n.

Kitchen *v.* R.A.F. Association (1958) 1 WLR 563, 3 AllER 241 — 203n.

Kleinwort Benson Ltd *v.* Lincoln City Council (1998) 3 WLR 1095 — 78n.

Knight *v.* Knight (1840) 3 Beav 148 — 119n.

Krubert, Re (1996) The Times 16 July 1996 — 365n.

Kumar, Re (1993) 1 WLR 224 — 119n.

Kunja *v.* Bruce (1984) in G. Kodilinye, *The Law of Trusts in the West Indies, Cases and Commentary*, Barbados, 1991, 20 — 68n.

Kuwait Asia Bank *v.* National Mutual Life Nominees Ltd (1990) 3 WLR 297 — 169n.

Lac Minerals *v.* International Corona Resources (1989) 61 DLR (4th) 14 — 90n., 93n.

Laidlaw, Re (1985) 13 DLR (4th) 491 — 128n.

Leahy *v.* A-G for New South Wales (1959) AC 457 — 123n.

Learoyd *v.* Whiteley (1887) 12 App Cas 727 — 167n.

Le Cren Clarke, Re (1996) 1 AllER 715 — 128n.

Lee Hiok Woon *v.* Lee Hiok Ping (1993) 3 SLR 148 — 172n.

Leigh's Will Trust, Re (1970) Ch 277 — 116n.

Lemos, In the matter of (1993) CILR 291, CILR 26 — 168n., 263n.

Lemos *v.* Coutts (1993) CILR 5; (Court of Appeal) 560 — 263n.

Liggett *v.* Kensington (1993) 1 NZLR 257 — 62n., 79n.

Lim Teng Huan *v.* Ang Swee Chuan (1992) 1 WLR 113 — 83n.

Lipkin Gorman *v.* Karpnale (1987) 1 WLR 987; (1991) 2 AC 548; (1992) 4 AllER 512 — 59n., 63n., 88n., 89n.

Lister *v.* Stubbs (1890) 45 Ch D 1 — 25n.

Lloyds Bank, Re (1931) 1 Ch 289 — 40n.

Lloyds Bank *v.* Carrick (1996) The Times 13 March 1996 — 35n.

Lloyds Bank *v.* Duker (1987) 3 AllER 193, 1 WLR 1324 — 110n.

Lloyds Bank *v.* Rosset (1990) 1 AllER 1111, (1991) 1 AC 107 — 81n., 82n.

Locobail International *v.* Agroexport (1986) 1 AllER 901, 1 WLR 657 — 72n.

Locker's Settlement, Re (1977) 1 WLR 1323 — 132n.

London Wine Shippers, Re (1975) 126 NLJ 977 — 99n.
Londonderry's Settlement, Re (1965) Ch 918 — 131n.
Lonrho v. Fayed (1992) (No 2) (1992) 1 WLR 1 — 79n.
Lord Cable (deceased) (1976), Re 3 AllER 417 — 152n.
Lord Napier v. Kershaw (1993) 1 LlR 10 — 51n.
Lord Nottingham's Chancery Cases, London, 1961 (SS No 79), II — 26n.
Lumley v. Gye (1853) 2 El & Bl 216 — 29n.
Lupton v. White (1808) 15 Ves 432 — 172n.
Lyus v. Prowsa Developments (1982) 1 WLR 1044 — 45n.
M v. Home Office (1992) 2 WLR 73 — 71n.
McBride, Re (1980) 107 DLR (3rd) 233 — 120n.
McCormick v. Grogan (1869) LR 4 H 82 — 90n., 113n.
McGovern v. A-G (1981) 3 AllER 493 — 128n.
McKendrick v. Sinclair (1972) SLT 110 — 66n.
McPhail v. Doulton (1970) 2 AllER 228 — 131n.
Mahadai v. Ragabir (1967) GLR 535 — 54n.
Malsbury v. Malsbury (1982) 1 NWSLR 226 — 50n.
Mara v. Browne (1896) 1 Ch 199 — 34n.
Marchant v. Onslow (1994) 3 WLR 607 — 51n.
Martin v. Martin (1963) 110 CLR 297 — 54n.
Mercier v. Mercier (1903) 2 Ch 98 — 53n.
Metall v. Donaldson (1989) 3 WLR 563 — 27n.
Mettoy Pension Trustees v. Evans (1990) 1 WLR 1587 — 146n.
Middleton v. Middleton (1980) 110 DLR (3rd) 497 — 152n.
Midland Bank v. Cooke (1995) 4 AllER 562 — 49n., 50n.
Midland Bank v. Dobson (1986) 1 FLR 171 — 48n.
Midland Bank v. Federated Pension Services (1994)
    Royal Court, Jersey, 4 August 1994, (1995) — 178n., 203n., 216n., 231n.
Midland Bank v. Green (1980) Ch 590 — 35n.
Midland Bank v. Wyatt (1994) EGCS 113 — 99n.
Milroy v. Lord (1862) 4 De GF & J 264 — 96n.
Ministry of Health v. Simpson (1951) AC 251 — 79n.
Mitchner, Re (1922) St R Qd 252 — 154n.
Montagu's Settlement Trusts, Re (1983–5) (1987) Ch 264, 2
    WLR 1192 — 28n., 31n.
Moody v. Stevenson (1992) Ch 486 — 365n.
Morice v. Bishop of Durham (1804) 9 Ves 399 — 123n.
Moss v. Cooper (1861) 1 John & H 352 — 110n.
Mothercare v. Robson Books (1979) FSR 466 — 72n.
Mucklestone v. Brown, cf. Scott, *Trusts*, §498.2 — 41n.

Murdoch v. Murdoch (1974) 41 DLR (3rd) 367   88n.
Muschinski v. Dodds (1985) 160 CLR 583   47n., 51n.
Nanwa, Re (1955) 1 WLR 1080   148n.
National Anti-Vivisection Society v. IRC (1948) AC 31   129n.
National Provincial Bank v. Ainsworth (1965) 2 AllER 472   78n.
National Westminster Bank v. Morgan (1985) 1 AC 686   21n., 24n.
Neblett v. Bentham (1984) TCM 41   37n.
Nelson v. Nelson (1995) 70 ALJR 47   54n.
Nestlé v. National Westminster Bank (1993) 1 WLR 1260 (1994)
    1 AllER 118   167n., 174n. 176n.
Neville v. Wilson (1996) 3 AllER 171   18n., 46n., 68n., 98n.
Neville Estates v. Madden (1962) Ch 832   128n.
Newey, Re (1994) 2 NZLR 590   43n., 88n.
Nisa v. Khan (1946) LRBG 170   41n., 111n.
Nottage, Re (1895) 2 Ch 649   128n.
Ojjeh Trust (1994) CILR 118   263n.
Oldham Borough Council v. A-G (1993) 2 WLR 224   175n., 176n.
Oppenheim v. Tobacco Securities (1951) AC 297   127n.
Orakpo v. Manson (1978) AC 95   87n.
Ottaway v. Norman (1972) Ch 698   112n.
Oughtred v. IRC (1966)   46n.
Pasi v. Kamana (1986) NZLR 603   47n.
Pass v. Dundas (1880) 43 LT 665   231n.
Paul v. Constance (1997) 1 AllER 195, 1 WLR s527   16n., 99n.
Pavey v. Paul (1987) 162 CLR 221, 69 ALR 577, (1988) 104 LQR 12   88n.
Pavlou, Re (1993) 1 WLR 1046   55n.
Peachdart, Re (1984) Ch 131   140n.
Persad v. Persad (1979) TCM 249   22n.
Peso Silver Mines (1965) 56 DLR (2nd) 117, (1971) 49 CBR 80   24n.
Pettit v. Pettit (1970) AC 777   48n., 53n., 54n.
Pettkus v. Becker (1980) 117 DLR (3rd) 257   47n., 88n.
Poh Siew v. Chong Poh Heng (1995) SLR 135   35n.
Polly Peck v. Nadir (No 2) (1992) (per Scott LJ 242), 2 Ll R 238,
    4 AllER 769   31n., 71n., 73n.
Porter v. Hubert (1672-3) Nels 150   137n.
Powell v. Thompson (1991) 1 NZLR 597   88n., 90n.
President of the Conference of the Methodist Church (1993)
    2 SA 697   130n.
Pye, Ex parte (1811) 18 Ves 140   53n.
Quinn v. Executive Director (1981) 5 WWR 565   131n.

R, Re (1994) 1 WLR 487   71n.
R v. Clerkenwell Metropolitan Stipendiary Magistrate (1992)
    2 WLR 233   71n.
R v. District Auditor (1986) RVR 24   121n.
R v. Kensington Borough Council (1989) 2 WLR 90   72n.
R v. Palmer (1992) 1 WLR 568   71n.
R v. Shadrokh-Cigari (1988) CrimLR 465   39n.
R v. Tower Hamlets (1988) AC 858   63n.
Rahman v. Chase Bank (1991) JLR 103   164n., 166n., 166n., 216n., 265
Ramsden v. Dyson (1866) LR 1 HL 129   83n.
Randall v. Russell (1817) 3 Mer 190   24n.
Rasmanis v. Jurewitsch (1970) NSWR 650   38n.
Reading v. A-G (1951) AC 507   24n., 87n.
Regal v. Gulliver (1941) 1 AllER 378   24n.
Regier v. Campbell-Stuart (1939) Ch 766   24n.
Registered Securities (1991) 1 NZLR 545   62n.
Renard, Matter of (1982) 56 NY2d 973, 453 NYS2d 625, 439
    NE2d 341   152n.
Reynolds v. Reynolds (1980) 388 So 2d 1135   282n.
Richards v. Dellbridge (1874) LR 18 Eq 11   100n.
Richardson's Will Trusts, Re (1958) Ch 504   134n.
Riffel, Re (1988) 64 Sask R 190   113n.
Rolled Steel Products (Holdings) Ltd v. British Steel Corpn
    (1986) Ch 246; (1985) 2 AllER 52   24n.
Rouchefoucauld v. Boustead (1897) Ch 196 (Court of Appeal)
    in CLJ (1984) 306   15n., 68n.
Rover International Ltd v. Cannon (1989) 1 WLR 912   63n., 92n.
Royal Brunei Airlines v. Tan (1995) 3 WLR 64, 3 AllER 97   32n., 175n.
Sainsbury v. IRC (1970) Ch 712   131n.
Saipem Spa v. Rafidain Bank (1994) CLC 253   142n.
Saunders v. Vautier (1841) 4 Beav 115   110n.
Scott v. Miller (1832) 11 S 21   296n.
Scottish Burial v. Glasgow (1968) AC 138   127n.
Seale's Marriage Settlement, Re (1961) Ch 574, 3 WLR 262   102n.
Sealy v. Sealy (1990) TCM 94   84n.
Selangor United Rubber v. Cradock (No 3) (1968) 2 AllER 1073,
    1 WLR 1555   24n., 29n.
Sen v. Headley (1991) 2 AllER 636, Ch 425, 2 FLR 449   36n.
Shabinsky v. Horwitz (1973) 32 DLR (3rd) 318   16n.
Sharp v. Thomson (1995) SLT 837   13n., 36n., 82n., 140n., 188n., 295n.

Shaw, Re (1957) 1 AllER 198   127n.

Shaw v. Foster (1872) LR 5 HL 321   35n.

Silver v. Silver (1958)1 AllER 523   54n.

Simplex v. Van de Merwe (1996) 1 SALR 111   298n.

Sinclair v. Brougham (1914) AC 398   39n., 64n.

Sitti Kadija v. De Saram (1946) AC 208   192n.

Smith, Re (1928) 1 Ch 915   107n.

Snook v. London & West Riding (1967) 2 QB 786   166n.

Snowden, Re (1979) 2 AllER 172   113n.

Sociedad Financiera Sofimeca v. Kleinwort Benson (1992) Royal
    Court, Jersey, 13 July 1992   260n.

Sorochan v. Sorochan (1986) 29 DLR (4th) 1   47n., 88n., 90n.

South Orange Grove Owners Association v. Orange Grove
    Partners (1995), High Court of the Cook Islands 208/94   250n.

Space Investments v. Canadian Imperial Bank (1986) 34 WIR 8,
    3 AllER 75   62n., 172n.

Springette v. Defoe (1992) 2 FLR 388   48n.

Springfield Acres v. Abacus (1994) 3 NZLR 502   30n.

State v. Levi Strauss & Co (1986) 41 Cal 3rd 460,715 P 2d 564   146n.

Stephens Travel Service v. Qantas (1988) 13 NSWLR 331   141n.

Steele v. Paz Limited OI (May 1996) 33   259n.

Stevenson v. Wilson (1904) 14 SLT 743   36n.

Stokes v. Anderson (1991) 1 FLR 391   48n.

J. T. Stratford v. Linley (1964) 3 AllER 102 ,(1965) AC 269   72n.

Stratulatos v. Stratulatos (1988) 2 NZLR 424   83n.

Street v. Mountford (1985) AC 809   44n.

Strickland v. Aldridge (1804) 9 Ves 516   41n., 112n.

Stump v. Gaby (1852) 2 De GM & G 623   40n., 79n.

Swain v. Law Society (1981) 3 AllER 797, (1982) 1 WLR 17
    (1983) AC 598   25n.

Target Holdings v. Redferns (1994) (Court of Appeal)1 WLR 1089,
    2 AllER 337; (1995) (House of Lords) 3 WLR 352,
    3 AllER 785   6n., 23n., 159n., 175n.,176n.

Taylor v. Plumer (1815) 3 M & S 562   61n.

Tee v. Ferris (1856) 2 K & J 357   110n.

Tharp v. Tharp (1916) 1 Ch 142   41n.

Thomson, Re (1930) 1 Ch 203   168n.

Thrupp v. Collett (1858) 26 Beav 125   120n.

Thwaites v. Ryan (1984) VR 65   47n.

Tinker v. Tinker (1970) 1 AllER 540   54n., 118n.

Tinsley *v*. Milligan (1992) 2 WLR 508, (1993) 3 WLR 126   56n.
Tito *v*. Waddell (No 2) (1977) Ch 106, 3 AllER 129   168n.
United States Surgical Corporation *v*. Hospital Products (1983–4)
    2 NSWLR 157, 58 ALJR 587   23n.
Universal Thermosensors *v*. Hibben (1992) 1 WLR 840   71n.
Vandervell's Trusts (No 2), Re. (1974) Ch 269   51n., 55n.
Villiers *v*. Villiers (1994) 1 WLR 840   71n.
Von Knieriem *v*. Bermuda Trust Company (1994) reference in
    (1995) JIntPl 31   261n.
Walshingham's Case (1579) 2 Plowd 547   106n.
Walton Stores *v*. Maher (1988) 164 CLR 387   83n.
Wayling *v*. Jones (1995) 2 FLR 1029   83n.
Webb *v*. Webb (1992) 1 WLR 1410, High Court , Chancery Division
    (1994) 3 WLR 801   53n., 193-5
Weir's Settlement, Re (1969) 1 Ch 657   131n.
West *v*. Lazard Brothers (1993) JLR 165   203n., 204n., 216n.
Westdeutsche *v*. Islington (1996) 2 AllER 961   18n., 38n., 39n., 55n.,
                                    56-7, 65n., 66n., 77n., 79n., 80n.,
                                    84n., 90n., 92n., 93n.,140n., 175n.
Weston's Settlements, Re (1968) 1 WLR 786, 3 AllER 338   102
Westpac Banking Corporation *v*. Savin (1985) 2 NZLR 41   31n.
West Sussex Constabulary's Widows , Re. (1970) 1 AllER 544,
    (1971) Ch 1   51n.
White *v*. Jones (1993) 2 WLR 187   42n.
Williams and Glyn's *v*. Bowland (1980) 2 AllER 408, (1981)
    AC 487   50n.
Willis *v*. Barron (1902) AC 271   40n.
Willis Faber *v*. Receiver of Revenue (1992) 4 SA 202   78n.
Woodward *v*. Woodward (1991) 1 FLR 399   37n.
Woolwich *v*. IRC (No 2) (1992) 3 AllER 737, 3 WLR 366   78n., 89n.
Worth Library, Re (1994) 45 NILQ 364   130n.
Wright *v*. Atkyns (1832) Turn & R 143   119n.
Wright *v*. Carter (1903) 1 Ch 27   40n.
Young, Re (1950) 2 AllER 1245, (1951) Ch 344   113n.
Zamet *v*. Hyman (1961) 1 WLR 1442   40n.

1   Introduction

1. Preliminary aspects

A civilian who wishes to understand trusts must try to immerse himself in them more than is normally necessary under the current comparative law tenets. He must also take unusual pains to avoid making immediate, and almost instinctive, comparisons with institutions of the legal system with which he is familiar. He must try to forget any ideas which he may already have on the topic, because there is an extremely high likelihood that the limitations in comparative analysis which have often distinguished the civil-law approach to trusts have rendered these ideas imprecise, and, therefore, misleading.

I shall now lay out a few propositions as a preparatory mental exercise. They relate to the traditional English model of trusts, and I do not propose to explain them at this stage. Some may appear to be incorrect if traditional concepts are used as a starting-point, but each will be illustrated in the appropriate section of this book.

1. *Trusts are not only 'voluntary'.*
   Voluntary trusts (or expressly established trusts, as I prefer to call them) are not the only type of trust; on the contrary, it is my belief that the 'heart of the trust' lies elsewhere, in those trusts which are created when equitable principles are applied independently of a valid declaration of intent to form a trust.

2. *There need not be three persons involved.*
   It is not true that a trust involves three persons. As the classic basic configuration would have it, these persons are:
   (1) The settlor, who transfers an asset to the trustee;
   (2) The trustee, who acquires 'legal' ownership of the asset (or rather, a

right of 'ownership' protected by common law)[1] in favour of the beneficiary;

(3) The beneficiary, or *cestui que trust*,[2] who acquires equitable ownership of the asset (or rather, a right of 'ownership' protected by equity).

A person may establish a trust of which he is both trustee and beneficiary, or only the trustee or only the beneficiary. The three persons in the basic configuration may therefore be reduced to two, or even only one.[3] Furthermore, charitable trusts and, where they are permitted, trusts for purposes, do not have a beneficiary at all. In order to preserve the theory of trusts, it is often said that in these cases the purpose, or even society as a whole, is the beneficiary of the trust. Finally, as I will explain below, where a trust is not expressly established, there is by definition no settlor.

3. *There need not be a transfer of the property to the trustee.*

It is not even true that the establishment of a trust is the consequence of a transfer in favour of the trustee. In addition to the instance mentioned above, in which the settlor is himself the trustee (and therefore no transfer takes place), the very nature of constructive and resulting trusts prevents there being any transfer to the trustee, because there is no settlor.

Furthermore, the element which characterizes those trusts which are not expressly established is not a transfer to the trustee, but the existence of an *act of disposition*: even a settlor who appoints himself as trustee carries out an act of disposition, by which he changes his legal standing.

4. *There is no splitting of ownership.*

It is not true to say that the rights of the beneficiary of a trust fall within the notion of 'ownership' (as that term is understood in civil-law cultures), thereby standing in contrast with the rights of the trustee, which also represent an 'ownership' position. The splitting of ownership rights between trustee and beneficiary, and the existence of two ownership rights in the same asset ('legal ownership' and 'equitable ownership'), represent misunderstandings which the time has now come to explain and overcome. In charitable trusts and trusts for purposes, on the other hand, where there are no beneficiaries, there cannot be an equitable owner.[4]

---

[1] It has become fashionable for writers in Romance languages to employ the term 'common law' in the masculine (see most recently R. C. van Caenegem, 'Le jugement sous l'angle historico-comparatif', in [1995] ArchPhilDr 125, note 6). Giovanni Criscuoli troubled Lord Denning for his opinion (G. Criscuoli, *Introduzione allo studio del diritto inglese. Le fonti* (2nd edition), Milan, 1994, p. x) and obtained his *placet*. My mentor, Gino Gorla, has always used the term common law in the feminine, and that is enough for me.

[2] There are various plurals of this expression. These days, *cestuis que trust* is the preferred form.

[3] The settlor may also be the trustee and one of the beneficiaries. When no beneficiary has an actual interest until the death of the settlor, in the practical life of the trust only one person derives benefits from it. This does not mean that he may abuse his rights.

[4] This point was made in F. W. Maitland, *Selected Essays*, edited by H. D. Hazeltine, G. Lapsley and P. H. Winfield, Cambridge, 1936, p. 138.

To combat other current theories, I have nevertheless been obliged to use, and will continue to use, the term 'equitable ownership' in the remainder of these preliminary discussions.

5. *What does identify trusts is a lack of equitable fullness of ownership on the part of the trustee.*
The different types of trust, including constructive and resulting trusts, can be brought together by taking the position that the trustee's ownership position is distinguished by a lack of equitable fullness, and that what is lacking in order to obtain that fullness does not necessarily belong to another person.

6. *The beneficiaries need not be 'equitable owners'.*
It is not true that where a trust calls for the existence of beneficiaries they need necessarily be 'equitable owners'. Many modern trusts fall within the category of discretionary trusts, where it is the duty of the trustee to decide from time to time to whom to distribute income or rights, or indeed whether to make a distribution at all. The discretionary trust does not create any entitlement in the beneficiaries, except that they have the right to expect that the trustee will exercise his discretionary powers and will administer the assets of the trust in a proper manner.
It is the notion of the beneficiary which needs to be reviewed, and associations with the concept of *'equitable ownership'*, which are not applicable in all cases, must be done away with: the equitable entitlement which is lacking in the trustee is not necessarily in the possession of others.

7. *The trust may have purely 'equitable' interests as its subject matter.*
Furthermore, it is not the case that the trustee must necessarily have a legal status which is recognized by common law, so that the position of the beneficiary would be recognized by equity:[5] the subject matter of the trust may perfectly well be an *equitable right*, as in the case where the beneficiary of a trust declares that he will in turn place the rights to which he is entitled as beneficiary (and which therefore belong exclusively to equity) into a trust. More generally, one might say that any kind of entitlement is capable of forming the subject matter of a trust.

8. *The trust is not a* negotium *which may be compared to the* fiducia.
It is not true that the trust is a fiduciary *negotium*, as the concept is

---

[5] I do not believe it is appropriate in these introductory pages to explain what is meant by equity. In various parts of the book, as the need arises, I shall make some observations (see, in particular, §§4 and 5 of chapter 2). I prefer that the reader should enter into the understanding of equity in this way rather than by general pronouncements which would of necessity be limited in nature. As will also be seen with reference to the notion of the trust, which will not be discussed until the end of chapter 3, I have chosen an inductive method for the book. The reader will probably have to work harder to get to the heart of the issues without the benefit of introductory definitions, but at least he will not be misled. I hope that in the end he will thank me.

understood in civil-law legal systems. The trust is a form of 'confidence', either in favour of specific parties or to attain a purpose. It is not necessarily voluntary in origin, and in no cases does it naturally attribute any rights to the person who 'confides' with respect to the person in whom his 'confidence' is placed.

9. *The trust is not born out of a contract.*
    It is not true that, as many civilians believe, the basis of the trust is a contract between the settlor and the trustee. One needs only to recall that in many cases, as we have already seen, there is no settlor, while in others the basis of the trust is a will. Moreover, in the limited area of trusts expressly established *inter vivos*, there are two transactions which underlie the trust, not one: the creation of the trust and the transfer of the right to the trustee. The former, which actually gives life to the trust, is a unilateral act.

10. *Trusts and innovations in case law.*
    It is not true that the law of trusts is a specialized and archaic field which has become rigid in the formulation of its rules.[6] The rules governing the area of trusts which have their origin in case law are in evolution, and show notable flexibility in adapting to modern society. Good examples may be found in the area of property rights among persons who live together, or in the area of responsibilities of a fiduciary (not necessarily a trustee) who may have obtained improper benefits from his position.

11. *Equity, common law and statute law.*
    It is not true that the supplementary or complementary function of Equity is a historical legacy because for more than a century Equity and common law have been one. Precedents from the most recent decades illustrate how equitable obligations are introduced to give effect to precepts of conscience which contrast with precepts of statute law in cases where application of the latter would permit the perpetration of a fraud (within the special meaning which Equity gives to that word). It is the traditional concept of Equity as a mere supplement to common law which should be discussed and re-examined; it is an idea which appears today to be extremely limiting and outdated.

12. *Trusts also exist in legal systems which do not belong to the common-law world.*
    It is not true to say that the trust is a legal device which is found exclusively in common-law systems. Numerous civil-law or mixed-law systems have institutions which, although they may not make use of the distinction between common law and Equity (which is unknown in these systems), perfectly reflect the legal structure of trusts created according to the traditional English model.

---

[6] The accusation that equity is *functa officio* was first discussed and rejected by H. G. Hanbury, 'The Field of Modern Equity', in 45 LQR (1929) 199, at 209–11.

2. Layout of the book

a 'Trust' or 'trusts'. The English and international models

The French title of the Hague Convention of 1 July 1985 on the law applicable to trusts and on their recognition[7] is *Convention relative à loi applicable au trust et à sa reconnaissance*, while the English title is *Convention on the Law Applicable to Trusts and on their Recognition*. In French, as is customary in Italian, the singular is used. In English, on the other hand, the word is used in the plural.[8] Does this different linguistic use have any significance?

The determination of whether to speak of the trust in the singular or in the plural is a matter of no small significance,[9] and I will state from the outset that I personally lean towards the second alternative. Of course, if we reach a high level of abstraction it is possible to propose a notion of trust (in the singular) which, in an effort to take account of the different varieties of the institution, would be so technical and highly articulated that it would become difficult for the civilian to comprehend. It would also be misleading, given that the civilian does not know how to place a value on the role of definitions and classifications in common law, leading to the birth of errors and the adoption of false premises. Attempts to be intelligible to those unfamiliar with the myriad practical applications of the institution too easily result in an adoption of obvious and generalized positions: a sure way to hinder the development of awareness of and increase the ignorance of foreign law. Nevertheless, as we shall see, this was the path chosen by the authors of the Hague Convention, who in the end found themselves confronted by a shapeless and ill-defined creature.

---

[7] It was ratified in Italy by L. 16 ottobre 1989 n. 364, and came into force on 1 January 1992. The Convention has also been ratified by Australia, Canada (by nearly all the Provinces), Malta, the Netherlands and the United Kingdom. The law by which it was adopted by the United Kingdom (Recognition of Trusts Act 1987) has extended the Convention to a number of British Colonies and other territories, as we shall see in chapter 4. One must, however, take account of the special method by which the Convention has been adopted by the United Kingdom, by transcribing some, but not all, of the articles of the Convention: for example, articles 13, 19, 20 and 21, and the second and third sub-sections of article 16 are omitted.

The Convention has been signed, but not ratified, by France, Luxembourg and the United States.

[8] Legal texts in the area of trusts also follow this practice. In English, Fratcher, *Trust*, and in French Béraudo, *Trusts*, are exceptions to the rule.

[9] S. Tondo, in 'Ambientazione del trust nel nostro ordinamento e controllo notarile sul trustee', in *Atti Milano*, chapter 15, discusses this question at length. He formulates interesting linguistic proposals, and asserts that the singular with the definite article (. . . *au trust* . . .) and the plural without the article (. . . to trusts . . .) are equally suited to satisfying the expression of an abstract term.

I would tend not to take great account of definition problems when considering an institution which has developed historically over the centuries and which has been subjected to what has been, all things considered, rather limited legislative interference. Above all, there are many who believe that the typology of trusts cannot be ascribed to any unifying theory, since there exist examples in which one can clearly identify a trust, but which equally clearly challenge any attempt to apply systematic consistency.[10] I believe that this belief is incorrect, and that it is possible to propose a notion – or, perhaps, a definition – of trusts which grasps the essence of the institution in its many forms, though these forms are so markedly different, both functionally and structurally, that the use of the word 'trust' in the singular may be allowed only when a systematic approach is attempted.

The word 'trusts' in the plural serves in the first place to underline the polymorphic nature of the institution, as appears from actual use, which is a long way from the classic purpose of protecting the assets of a family.[11] In the second place, use of the plural serves to bring to light the fact that no systematic dimension exists in common law, where what we shall call the 'English-law model' has been subjected to various modifications outside England which have not been accepted in the trust's land of origin, or, *vice versa*, where it has undergone developments in England which have not always been acknowledged in other jurisdictions.[12]

The laws of Australia, Canada, New Zealand and the United States will frequently be referred to,[13] even if only as a counterpoint to English law, in

---

[10] I am referring to the so-called 'anomalous trusts', of which more in chapter 3 §2.b.

[11] In *Target Holdings v. Redferns* (1995) the House of Lords, with reference to the rules concerning breach of trust, stated:

it is in any event wrong to lift wholesale the detailed rules developed in the context of traditional trusts and then seek to apply them to trusts of quite different a kind . . . it is important, if the trust is not to be rendered commercially useless, to distinguish between the basic principles of trust law and those specialist rules developed in relation to traditional trusts which are applicable only to such trusts and the rationale of which has no application to trusts of quite a different kind (362).

[12] In *Invercargill City Council v. Hamlin* (1996) the Privy Council confirmed the legitimacy of local developments in common law, even where they contrast with precedents of the House of Lords (the case dealt with a decision from New Zealand in the area of the responsibility of the public authorities for failure to supervise the construction of a building).

[13] There is not really an Australian, Canadian or American law in the area of trusts, because trusts fall within the competence of the individual states, and not of the federal government. Both in Australia and in Canada, state or provincial laws on trusts have been passed, while in the United States, the Restatements of Trusts and of Restitution, as well as the model laws adopted by most of the States, are almost always applied, as, for example, with the revocatory action which may be commenced against the creation of a trust which prejudices the rights of creditors.

the context of the basic model to which they all belong. English law will, however, be the principal subject of this book, and the implicit point of reference for every comparative illustration.[14]

In effect, plurality within common law has been complicated by the laws promulgated in recent years by many States, giving rise to a kind of 'rush for the trust' in which tax havens have played a noteworthy role. While the evolution of Australian, Canadian, New Zealand and United States law has been substantially in line with the traditional English model, the 'rush for the trust' is bringing about the creation of a model, which we shall call the 'international trust model', notably different from the English model, although inspired by the same fundamental principles.

The plural 'trusts' also serves to underline that the multiplicity of legislative experiences has taken on a new dimension as a result of the adoption of special laws in civil or mixed law jurisdictions. This may be due to the 'rush for the trust', or to already existing tendencies which had their origins in the perception that there was an opportunity to introduce new transactional instruments, and thereby compensate for certain limitations which were impeding the development of the traditional civil-law instruments. It may have been due, finally, to the persistence of old transactional forms, to which new functions are nowadays attributed. Civil-law legislation on trusts contains many elements which are common both to those legal systems and to the international trust model, to such an extent that it is unclear whether they should be traced back to this model, or whether, in fact, they permit the identification of a separate civil-law trust model.

It is a matter of regret that common law and comparative literature on trusts[15] should have dedicated so little attention to types of legislation which do not belong to the traditional model, above all because they are of significant technical value, and have been applied by judicial bodies at the highest professional level.[16] It is also to be regretted that civil-law scholars

[14] Whether the 'American' trust belongs to the English model is doubtful; see U. Mattei, *Il modello di common law*, Turin, 1996. The author not only submits that the American model is autonomous with respect to that of England, but states that 'today, the paradigmatic experience is American' (p. 196).

[15] A review of current literature in the area of trusts is found in D. W. M. Waters, 'The Role of the Trust Treatise in the 1990s', in 59 Missouri LR (1994) 121. It is interesting to compare this position with that of Hanbury, Equity (see above, footnote 6), who proposed a 'modern manual of equity' in the wake of the Law of Property Act and the Trustee Act of 1925.

[16] Despite its scarcity, I have paid particular attention in my research to the case law of States such as Barbados, Jersey and the Cayman Islands which adhere to the international trust model. A reading of the judgments reveals an unexpectedly high standard.

have rarely sought to describe in detail the solutions adopted by civil-law systems other than their own.

b The purpose of the individual chapters

The next chapter is dedicated to those types of trusts which are customarily considered by comparative literature to be of secondary importance, or which the literature completely ignores. I have chosen to begin my explanation of English law in this way because I am convinced that the 'heart of the trust' should be sought not in the classic area of expressly established trusts but in implied, constructive and resulting trusts, some of which have long histories, while others are called, for a variety of underlying motives of evaluation, 'new models' of trusts.[17] The fact that even in current writings in the English language they are categorized as 'secondary' has its origins in a cultural inertia which contents itself with explanatory models which are often more than a century old.

The developments on which we shall dwell have created a distance between English law and the laws of Australia, Canada, New Zealand and the United States, and, in general, that of those countries which borrowed the English law during the colonial period. It is not possible to forecast whether we are looking at an unbridgeable gap: what is certain is that English case law, while containing some exaggeratedly novel elements, has provided evidence of a conceptual clarity and a level of intellectual sophistication which, it seems, will not be easy to adopt, especially within the legal environment of the United States and the countries most closely tied to it.[18]

The legal remedies offered by equity are also described in chapter 2. Even though they are obviously a typically English product, and cannot, therefore, be exported, an understanding of them is essential if one is to be able to grasp the institutional context of trusts as a whole. I conclude the

---

[17] The expression is taken from Lord Denning's opinion in *Eves v. Eves* (1975), 771.

[18] I must warn the reader that there are authoritative opinions which contrast radically with the one I have expressed in the text. I cite as a general example the unusually violent opinion of Jacobs, *Trusts*, p. 279: 'The recent English judicial effusions on this topic might display greater attraction if it were possible to know what they meant. But to peruse the English cases concerned . . . is to observe a wilderness of single instances, productive of no principle and indicative only of decay in legal technique.'

Gambaro, in *Proprietà*, pp. 633–4, is more radical still: 'L'insipienza giuridica dei giudici inglesi e la loro ignoranza verso le fondamentali categorie romanistiche . . .'; '[I giudici inglesi] hanno sempre ragionato con rozze categorie economicistiche.' It is noteworthy that Gambaro carries out his entire review of trusts without citing a single English judgment, except on one occasion, and then in passing. I am aware of no writing in which he has given reasons for his opinion.

chapter by considering the equitable foundation of constructive trusts, which is clearly of central significance to my theory – which considers the 'heart of the trust' to lie here – and by submitting a hypothesis for constructive and resulting trusts upon which I shall then attempt to build a unified theory of trusts.

A consideration of the issues which the civil lawyer customarily believes to be the *only* subjects belonging to the field of trusts, *viz.* the classic topics relating to expressly established trusts, either *inter vivos* or by will, are found in chapter 3. In analysing these classic topics we shall see how it has been possible to use venerable institutions to satisfy the needs of modern economies and societies, and how English case law has followed this practice and strengthened it. In conclusion, I illustrate the notions of 'entrusting' and 'segregation' on which the theory of trusts hinges, and show the difference between this and the notion of 'fiduciary relationship' in civil law.

In recent years, a growing number of common-law systems has promulgated comprehensive laws of trusts. I have decided to dedicate an entire chapter (the fourth) to them, both because, as I have already indicated, they are seldom discussed, and because these laws are new. At the end of chapter 4 I discuss those elements which come from English law and those which are peculiar to these laws, and sketch the international trust model, comparing it with the traditional English model.

In chapter 5, I shall present a panorama of non-common-law systems. These are sometimes referred to as 'importers' of the trust. Rarely have I come across such a brutal falsification of legal reality, which perpetuates itself thanks to second-, third- and fourth-hand references. Even the report on which the Hague Conference based the studies which led to the Convention on the Law Applicable to Trusts and on their Recognition is guilty of grave imprecision and misinformation. Subjects examined in the fifth chapter include neither 'trust-like devices' nor 'analogous institutions', to follow the language of the report, but rather civil-law trusts, which I identify by starting with the determination of 'minimum data' for comparison and verifying the cases where they may be found in civil-law systems. In other words, I will propose a comparative notion of the trust (on this occasion using the term in the singular).

It is doubtful whether it is possible to identify a trust model in the civil-law environment; it is certain, however, that the conceptual difficulties which non-common-law legislators have had to overcome have often been the same. We will, therefore, illustrate certain constants in these laws, from which lessons may be learned if a decision is taken to write an Italian law on trusts (an event which I hope will not come to pass). The Scottish and South African laws of trusts are treated separately: they share both a notable interaction with the English model and a conceptual legacy from civil law (the latter more evident in South Africa). The combination of these two elements has produced institutions which are perfectly compatible with the English trust model, not, however, with the legislative enactments of the civil-law countries examined in the fifth chapter.

Chapter 6 is dedicated to the Hague Convention of 1 July 1985, and in particular to showing that it hinges on a notion of trust which has very little to do with the English (or, in the language of the Hague, Anglo-Saxon or 'Anglo-American') trust model, to the point that I speak of a 'shapeless trust', the consequences of which are pointed out. The 'trust' in the Hague Convention therefore corresponds neither to the 'trust' in the English model nor to a comparative notion of the trust: it must be seen as a specific product which finds its home only within the provisions of the Convention. I then illustrate how the system of the Convention leads to the recognition of trusts wherever and by whomever they are established, and consequently also in civil-law countries by citizens of those countries.

This latter aspect, on which the attention of the legal professions is currently being concentrated, forms the subject matter of chapter 7, in which I examine the profiles of the institution of 'internal' trusts, that is to say, of trusts which although regulated by foreign law are in every other aspect 'Italian'. I demonstrate the distinctive elements with relation to civil-law situations, and make some remarks on the tax aspect of trusts in Italy.[19]

I have entirely omitted including any texts in an appendix, because a complete collection of laws on trusts has recently been published:[20] the reader will find all the necessary sources there.

3. *Regulae,* knowledge of foreign law, comparisons

Never more than in the case of trusts has the principle that comparison can only be made at the level of *regulae* been truer. I use the term '*regula*' in the sense in which it was used in European common law of the High Middle Ages, and therefore as it is understood in modern common law ('rule'):[21]

---

[19] Only the first part of chapter seven has been translated.

[20] M. Lupoi, *Trust Laws of the World,* Rome, 1996. An updated edition has just been published.

[21] I have attempted to show that English common law is a continuation of European common law of the High Middle Ages in my book *The Origins of the European Legal Order,* Cambridge, 2000 (*Alle radici del mondo giuridico europeo,* Rome, 1994). This theory is inextricably linked with that which identifies a *caesura* in the eleventh and twelfth

that is, as a criterion of judgment which is unequivocally *suited to the determination of a real case*. It is not a principle, because it is not generic enough; it is not a decision in a case, because it is not specific enough; rather, it is a (difficult) balance between these two extremes. The defects and limitations of this definition will be obvious to everyone, but I am not able to propose any other.[22]

The second and third chapters are based on the *regulae*, and not, the reader should be warned, on cases. The difference affects the method of the exposition, principally in the relationship between the scholar and his sources; obviously, it affects the purpose of the exposition; and finally, it affects the reader, of whom I ask a dual effort. In addition, I shall deal somewhat off-handedly and implicitly with the comparative themes which arise constantly, and I ask the reader to note these on his own, following the exposition of the *regulae* with patience and not rushing in search of principles which will frequently not be found. In any event, the choice of terms employed to explain a *regula* of foreign law inevitably has a comparative undertone.

It is this undertone which requires the *regula* to be formulated in such a way as to be comprehensible to the civilian without appearing strange (or inaccurate) to the common-law reader. Second-rate comparative literature is instantly identifiable by the large number of foreign legal terms which it contains. This is not a question of taste, which it would be an indulgence to debate here, but, more simply, one of intellectual shortcomings. Of course, when writing for a non-English readership there are terms which cannot be translated (for example, 'equity', 'trust', 'trustee' – all terms to which this entire book is dedicated! – and 'common law'), and others where once the meaning has been explained it is more appropriate to continue using the original word (for example, 'mortgage', 'estate' and 'charitable trust'), but these are fairly infrequent cases, even in an area as technical and specific as trusts. In most cases, the failure to translate (in the etymological sense of the word) only sig-

centuries, when continental Europe began to take a new path. P. G. Monateri, *Il modello di civil law*, Turin, 1996, chapter 1, endorses this position, and offers appropriate clarifications; cf. G. Santini, 'Le radici della cultura giuridica europea', in [1996] Contr. e impr./ Europa 43.

[22] Principles are not the same thing as *principia*, of which I have written at length in *Origins* (see above, footnote 21); the former belong to an analytical or conceptual explanation of a group of *regulae* which have a similar purpose, while the latter address the most important aspects and concerns of society, and therefore cut across the boundaries of different subjects.

For more details on the relationship between *regulae* and *principia* the study of Puerto Rican law, which has been Americanized by force, is very interesting; see L. Fiol Matta, 'Civil Law and Common Law in the Legal Method of Puerto Rico', in 40 AJCL (1992) 783.

nifies lack of knowledge, and, therefore, a lack of ability to explain.[23]

The 'importation' or 'reception' of the trust, which is frequently referred to in non-technical contexts, is the result of inaccurate translation (in addition to being erroneously based on a unified notion of 'trust'). Any civilian – not to speak of comparative-law scholars – would entertain possibly insurmountable doubts if it were suggested that one legal system had adopted by legislation a foreign institution which had its origins in and was developed by case law, especially if the sources and basic structures of the foreign legal system found no counterpart in the system which was adopting the institution. The developments in case law reviewed in the second and third chapters will clearly show how difficult it would be to 'import' the trust into legal systems which had gained no experience of it by belonging to the world of common law. What would be imported would, therefore, be a hybrid creation. This would not make it unworthy of citizenship, of course, but its certificate of citizenship would have to provide the appropriate morphological data.

The *regulae* may not be expressed without direct contact with the sources of the law, specifically case law (whatever formal importance may be attached to it), legislative enactment and practice. With regard to the former, it is sufficient to review the index of cases at the beginning of this volume to understand how I have tailored my studies. I was able to satisfy the dominance of case law fully only in the second and third chapters (concerning trusts in the traditional English model), while in the fourth and fifth chapters (concerning the international trust model and trusts in non-common-law systems, respectively) the large number of States under consideration, the newness of most of their legislation and the scarcity of relevant decisions made it impossible to be equally exhaustive. The reader will note, however, that I have been able to use a certain number of local precedents.

The reader may ask why there is no historical introduction. The reasons are threefold: in the first place, I described the history of the trust in a book I published in 1971, to which I shall make frequent reference. The second reason (and the only one which is of any methodological significance) is that I do not believe in historical introductions; they are often (perhaps of necessity) a kind of superstructure which leaves the reader unmoved, if not actually irritated. Besides, either a writer knows the history of his subject or he does not; if he does not, he can write all the historical sections he wants and will create only confusion; if he does, he will guide the reader through history as the need arises, and will from time to time offer him such

---

[23] Cf. R. Sacco, *Introduzione al diritto comparato* (4th edition), Turin, 1990, pp. 27–44.

information and views as may be appropriate.[24] In addition – and this is the third reason – I have realized that it is not necessary to give a historical explanation of the *regulae* based on general precepts of equity. There will be a few exceptions relating to the structural aspects of legal relationships and entitlements, and therefore for the most part where I present my unitary theory of trusts,[25] I shall furnish a historical explanation, within the limits of my ability, of certain basic *regulae;* otherwise, most *regulae* transcend the historical context. The precepts of equity belong to the universal.[26] It is more important to observe the systematic framework in which they occur, and thereafter to compare this framework, if it is appropriate to do so, with that of other legal systems. Here, if possible, one must evaluate the ability of systems which do not have a formal system of equity to embrace those precepts of equity which, because they belong to the universal, are probably present in all legal systems, but which, equally probably, may have been suppressed or violated.[27]

Indeed, when a *regula* is bred out of a principle of equity, it necessarily comes into contact with *regulae* which have a totally different origin, because they have their roots (in England) in the common law, and therefore in a different system of values. It is here, as we shall see, that one can appreciate the 'meaning' of equity in the present, rather than in clichéd discussions on Chancery case law and the assonance (for it is no more than that) with praetorian Roman jurisprudence which have become so trite over time that they now lack any cognitive capacity.[28]

---

[24] On the need to know the history of English law and its methods and reasoning, see, most recently, M. Graziadei, 'Il patto e il dolo', in P. Cendon (ed.), *Scritti in onore di Rodolfo Sacco,* Milan, 1994, I, pp. 589ff., at pp. 589–93 and references; other angles may be found in L. Moccia, 'Prospetto storico delle origini e degli atteggiamenti del moderno diritto comparato. (Per una teoria dell'ordinamento giuridico "aperto")', in [1996] Riv. trim. dir. proc. civ. 181.   [25] Chapter 2 §5.c and chapter 3 §3.

[26] Cf. I. C. F. Spry, *The Principles of Equitable Remedies* (4th edition), Sidney, 1990, ch. 1.

[27] In the course of chapter 4, we shall consider a number of systems which, although they do not have a separate equity jurisdiction, apply principles derived from the case law of the English courts of equity (see, for example, the judgment from Jersey referred to in chapter 4 §1).

The Scottish experience, on the other hand, illustrates one aspect of the obstacles to the expansion of the *regulae* of equity, where they are rooted in technical notions and may not, therefore, easily be exported: see chapter 3 §3, with reference to the decision in *Sharp v. Thomson* (1995).

[28] As A. Watson, has clearly pointed out in 'Roman Law and English Law: Two Patterns of Development', in L. Moccia (ed.), *Il diritto privato europeo: problemi e prospettive,* Milan, 1993, 9ff., but see also G. Gorla, 'Studio storico–comparativo della "common law" e scienza del diritto (le forme di azione)', in [1962] Riv. trim. dir. proc. civ. 25, §8.

The positions of G. Pugliese, 'Ius honorarium a Roma ed equity nei sistemi di common law', in [1988] Riv. trim. dir. proc. civ. 1105 and P. Stein, 'I rapporti interni fra il diritto romano classico ed il common law inglese', in *Incontro con Giovanni Pugliese* (various authors), Milan, 1992, 59, are more traditional.

2 The heart of the trust

1. Introduction

a Systematic and structural data

The *voluntarily* created trust is a legal category invented by the authors of the Hague Convention and unknown in English law (we shall speak of it again in chapter 6). The *expressly established* trust, on the other hand, is a category of acts of disposition which belongs to the English law of trusts. When one thinks of the trust, especially in the civil-law context, the implicit reference is to the expressly established trust. It should not, however, be considered to be the classic form of trust, or, historically speaking, as the first type of trust.

The line between a trust and a vague suggestion communicated to an heir or legatee has been a fine one for centuries, as has that between the trust and the fiduciary element present in many relationships, from bailment to representation. The fiduciary element, as we shall see, has assumed independent relevance in recent times, and this has in many situations caused a person invested with fiduciary functions under a different legal name to be considered to be a trustee in the technical sense.[1]

The coming into being of a trust traditionally occurs without formality. Recent laws in several countries, which we shall examine in the fourth chapter, sometimes use the expression 'in any other manner' when listing the sources of the trust, after having indicated the express declaration, oral or written, and conduct by which a trust is implied. In reality, when speaking of express trusts one should think in terms of a class of acts of disposition which includes a wide variety of kinds of conduct, any of which may be adopted by the settlor to cause the trust to come into being. Express

[1] See generally Graziadei, *Diritti nell'interesse altrui*.

trusts are certainly voluntary trusts, provided that the voluntary nature of the settlor's conduct has the purpose of bringing about the coming into being of a trust. In civil-law terminology, as we shall better see below, it is a 'form-free *negotium*'.

The distinction between express trusts and other types of trusts (implied, constructive or resulting) lies in the fact that the latter are the consequence of the *legal evaluation* of a voluntary act or situation which is not expressly or sufficiently clearly aimed at the creation of a trust. This distinction is extremely relevant, and receives clear support in section 8 of the Statute of Frauds of 1677,[2] and in a *dictum* of Lord Nottingham in 1672, which contrasts expressly established trusts with all other types.[3]

This distinction should not lead one to believe that we have found a homogeneous category which stands in contrast to the express trust. In their modern configuration, implied trusts show the same structure as expressly established trusts, whereas the structure of constructive and resulting trusts differs, although at first sight they are united by the lack of a person who makes a transfer, or settlor, and therefore (and this phenomenon is more evident in *constructive* trusts, as we shall see) by one of the most problematic aspects of non-express trusts: the patrimony of an individual, the trustee, loses its unity, although there is no act to that end, and a portion of that patrimony is identified (later on I shall suggest that the term 'segregation' be used here) which is, and remains, tied to the attainment of the purpose of the (non-express) trust. The consequence of this is that the 'personal' creditors of the trustee may not assert any rights to that portion of his patrimony.

From here, as we shall see more clearly in section 5, we arrive at the essential genetic incompatibility between one category of trusts and another,[4] and the need to transfer our investigations to functional and performance profiles, and to move on from these two, in order to arrive at a unified theory of trusts. This is what we shall do at the end of this chapter

---

[2] There are no requirements as to form in these cases in which 'a trust or confidence shall or may arise or result by the implication or construction of law'; the use of the verb 'result' should be noted. On the origins of the Statute of Frauds see T. G. Youdan, 'Formalities for Trusts of Land, and the Doctrine in *Rochefoucauld v. Boustead*', in CLJ (1984) 306, but see better below, chapter 2 §4.d.

[3] *Cook v. Fountain* (1676) 3 Swans 585, at 591: 'All trusts are either, first, express trusts, which are raised and created by an act of the parties, or implied trusts, which are raised and created by act or construction of law.' 'Implied trusts' in the terminology of the time are today called 'constructive' or 'resulting' trusts.

[4] A similar theory has been proposed by A. W. Scott, 'Constructive Trusts', in 71 LQR (1955) 39, at 40–1, but for different reasons.

with non-express trusts, and at the end of the following chapter with express trusts and the trust in general.

Moreover, all types of trust share a structural element which, for the moment, I shall express by making an apparently contradictory assertion: the subject matter of the trust belongs to the trustee, but it is not mingled with the rest of his patrimony, *because it is not his.*

b Terminology

The Oxford doctoral thesis of a Nigerian jurist[5] had the merit of aggravating the terminological uncertainties and the defect of being excessively free in its interpretation and criticism of judicial precedents, and even of written laws. It proposed a conceptual framework which, in the name of choices which the author claims to be 'correct', is only marginally reflected in current English law. It does, however, offer a sense of the final frontier at which the law of trusts might arrive. We shall stop long before that stage, and shall limit ourselves to those *regulae* which emerge (almost) without debate from English equity case law.

The classification of the trusts which are subject to such *regulae* is, however, a matter of controversy. They are trusts *which have not been expressly established.* There are three categories which may be used in the abstract: trusts which are created voluntarily, but with no express declaration (*implied trusts*); trusts which come into being because they correspond to situations described by the rules of equity (*constructive trusts*); and returning or residual trusts (*resulting trusts*). By the mere description of these three categories I have already taken a position which, I submit, is legitimate for two reasons: firstly, because English authors cannot agree among themselves; and secondly, because the comparative lawyer must when he deems it expedient interpret foreign law in the way which seems to him to be most suitable, and must not be afraid to propose new definitions, for which, of course, he must be held responsible.

Implied trusts: some authors hold that this category does not exist, or rather, that it is the same as that of resulting trusts. The fact is that laws refer to it constantly, and that many modern laws expressly provide for a trust which is created by implication. Furthermore, the most recent developments in case law are difficult to explain without reference to the notion of the implied trust.[6]

---

[5] G. Elias, *Explaining Constructive Trusts*, Oxford, 1990.

[6] For examples of implied trusts, see the Canadian decision in *Shabinsky v. Horwitz* (1973): sums added to a hotel bill as a service charge, were held on trust by the hotel for the waiters; see also *Paul v. Constance* (1977): C, who was separated from his wife, was living

Constructive trusts:[7] the most heavily subscribed opinion would have it that constructive trusts are created by law (and therefore pursuant to rules of equity which have their origins in case law) *against* the will of the defendant;[8] hence the view of constructive trusts as the result of a judgment, and the conclusion that they may be included within the category of legal actions or remedies. While this latter point of view, which was probably incorrect until a few years ago notwithstanding the traditional remedial perspective of English law,[9] is not without foundation and may even have a brilliant future,[10] the former is certainly erroneous. In some cases, constructive trusts give effect to the will of the person who is its trustee (I have already noted that constructive trusts do not have a settlor); this occurs where this will has not been manifested in the form required to create a trust, but equity nonetheless holds that this need not render it ineffective. In other cases, the constructive trust is the means by which the requirements of equity are carried out, principal among which are the apportionment of property and the suppression of fraud. *Fraud* is that behaviour which negates *trust*: in this sense, as we shall see, the constructive trust safeguards the fiduciary relationship in the widest sense of that term.

Resulting trusts, or returning or residual trusts: the crisis experienced by the traditional view of resulting trusts, which is the accomplishment of the supposed will of the settlor – and here lies the presumed distinction from *constructive trusts* – emerged with the recent judicial proposal that there is a distinction between automatic resulting trusts and presumed resulting

with P. After some years, C was awarded personal injury damages. Both before receiving the money and after, when he deposited it in the bank in his name, he declared to P that they belonged to both of them. When C died, and P claimed her share, the Court of Appeal decided that C's declarations had made him a trustee of the funds for him and P in equal shares.

Recourse was had to the implied trust to establish a new form of trust, called the *Quistclose trust*: see below, p. 51.

7 From now on I shall employ the English terminology, because the terminology I proposed above ('trusts which come into being because they correspond to situations described by the rules of equity') is clumsy.

8 This is from the Preliminary Report of the Hague Convention, which here, as elsewhere, suffers from grave omissions and is very imprecise. English writing frequently refers to the irrelevance of the will of the defendant; see, for example, A. J. Oakley, 'Has the Constructive Trust Become a General Equitable Remedy?', in CLP (1973) 17; and H. Kötz, *Trust und Treuhand*, Göttingen, 1963, p. 76: 'unabhängig von einem ausdrücklich geäußerten oder stillschweigenden Parteiwillen'.

9 For application to the area of ownership, see A. Gambaro, 'La proprietà nel common law anglo-americano', in A. Candian, A. Gambaro and B. Pozzo, *Property – Propriété – Eigentum*, Padua, 1992, pp. 3ff., at pp. 40–9. Further details are provided below in chapter 2 §5.e.

10 See, chapter 2 §5.

trusts: the latter, but not the former, are subject to proof that the intentions of the settlor were different. Where this proof is not provided, it would seem more appropriate to return to the older concept of *implied trusts*. By the term *resulting trust* is meant – correctly – that complex variety of cases in which the outcome is the only common denominator: following a rule of equity, the settlor retains an equitable interest which he would not otherwise have in an asset which is, or becomes, the subject matter of the trust.[11]

The line between implied trusts (for those who admit that they have a separate existence), constructive trusts and resulting trusts is often a fine one; a trust is often interpreted to be constructive by one author and implied or resulting by another.[12] Even judges contradict each other and give differing interpretations to precedents,[13] or do not believe that it is necessary to provide a detailed analysis of whether the trust under consideration is implied or constructive,[14] and lawyers sometimes err in choosing one concept rather than the other.[15] It would therefore seem to be preferable to speak generally of trusts *ex lege*,[16] and in so doing to return to the unified vision of the phenomenon which prevailed at the time of the Statute of Frauds.[17]

The implicit reference would naturally not be to the written law, but to the case-law rules of equity. Here two problems emerge: the first is that certain *regulae* relating to constructive trusts have been codified in some statute; the second is that there are trusts, known as statutory trusts, which are born of legislative acts, as we shall now see. Discussion could, therefore, continue *ad infinitum*, in part because (however strange this may seem) according to the English system of legal sources, the legislative adoption of a rule of case law does not necessarily sever its links with its original case-law setting.

In conclusion, in setting out the *regulae*, I have attempted to avoid problems of classification, and to align myself with current concepts, even

---

[11] Cf. Hayton, *Trusts*, 16–17. In certain of these cases, the original equitable foundation of the trustee's obligations of conscience plays an essential part, as in the recent decision of the House of Lords in *Westdeutsche v. Islington* (1996), see chapter 2 §3.e.

[12] G. Elias illustrates this well on more than one occasion in *Constructive Trusts* (see above, footnote 5).

[13] See the criticism directed by the Australian judge Glass JA towards his English colleagues in *Allen v. Snyder* (1977) (p. 691).

[14] There are numerous examples of this. The recent decision of the Court of Appeal in *Neville v. Wilson* (1996) (on which see below, chapter 2 §2.n) will stand for all of them.

[15] *Drake v. Whipps* (1995) (see below, footnote 201 this chapter and relevant text).

[16] *Trusts implied by law* is the category adopted by Underhill, *Trusts*, chapters 5–7; also A. J. Oakley, *Constructive Trusts* (2nd edition), London, 1987, p. 1.

[17] See above, footnote 2 and relevant text.

to the point of eliminating the separate category of implied trusts, I nevertheless believe, and of which I shall illustrate numerous exam Those of my readers who are civilians will be interested in understand trusts, not in becoming embroiled in complexities of definition which are, apart from everything else, of little relevance even for common-law jurists. I have not, however, renounced the reorganization of the *regulae* in line with my concept of the trust, so that they do not always coincide with the treatment they are given in the current literature. This may be no bad thing, considering that English writers frequently disagree among themselves.

c Statutory trusts

Statutory solutions often require the coming into being of a trust. In addition to those cases where a trust is used in administrative law,[19] the following examples are of relevance to us.

a. *Intestate succession*
When a person dies without leaving a will, an *ex lege* trust comes into effect over his estate.[20] The trustee who is appointed by the court has the responsibility of dividing among the legitimate heirs what remains after the payment of debts.

b. *Co-ownership*
It is the *ex lege* trust which comes into being in cases which correspond to the civilian *communion*, and permits one to proceed to a division of property.[21]
Since 1925, community of rights in real property may only be established in England by a *trust for sale* (now called a *trust of land*), of which the joint owners are both trustees and beneficiaries. The entire relationship is, therefore, based on equity, and not on common law, as a result of the abolition of the majority of legal estates by the Law of Property Act 1925, and their survival only under the rules of equity. As joint beneficiaries (technically, equitable tenants-in-common or joint tenants), the 'joint owners' have the right to enjoy and exploit the property, but, since there

---

[18] The justification for implied trusts may be traced back at least to *Cook v. Fountain* (1676): 'These last are commonly called presumptive trusts; and it is when the Court, upon consideration of all circumstances, presumes there was a declaration, either by word or writing, though the plain and direct proof thereof be not extant.'

[19] For example, the Historic Buildings and Ancient Monuments Act 1953, s. 8.

[20] Administration of Estates Act 1925, s. 33; Intestates' Estates Act 1952; see the Trusts of Land and Appointment of Trustees Act 1996, schedules 2 and 5.

[21] Law of Property Act 1925, s. 34 to s. 36, amended by the Trusts of Land and Appointment of Trustees Act 1996, schedule 2, 3, 4. See also the Settled Land Act 1925, s. 36. Cf. Hanbury, *Equity*, 271–88; M. D. Panforti, 'Intervento legislativo e reazione giurisprudenziale nella vicenda inglese del *trust for sale*', in [1996] 2 Riv. dir. civ. 485.

:, they may also secure its sale, thus terminating the
)ating *pro quota* in the sale proceeds.[22]

)perty to minors
)e the owner of rights in real property. Where a transfer
; place, it does not attain its purpose. Accordingly, the
at the transferor becomes the trustee of the right in
nor until the latter reaches the age of majority, or that in
insfer to a minor and a person with capacity, the latter
acts as trustee for the former.[23]

d. *Mental illness*
A judge may create a trust to hold the property of a person who cannot attend to his affairs due to mental illness.[24]

e. *Bankruptcy*
A trustee in bankruptcy succeeds to the assets of a bankrupt person as trustee for the creditors.[25]

f. *Family obligations*
Agreements among family members by which income from real property is used to make payments of income or other periodic payments have the effect of subjecting the property to a trust for the attainment of that purpose.[26]

g. *Sums received by financial intermediaries, lawyers and insurance and estate agents* The law provides that sums which a client pays to a lawyer for him to hold, or to an intermediary for delivery to a party to a contract, are received on trust.[27] A similar concept is expressed in the Financial Services Act 1986, which clearly provides the manner in which client funds should be deposited, how the accounts should be named and what documentation must be provided by the financial intermediary.[28]

d The equitable notion of fraud

If this book had an expansive analytical index and the reader were to consult it under the heading *fraud*, he would find a remarkable variety of references, and would in all likelihood draw the conclusion that *fraud* is a

---

[22] Cf. below, chapter 3, footnote 361 and relevant text; specifically on the new notion of 'trust of land', see Trusts of Land and Appointment of Trustees Act 1996, ss. 1 to 5.

[23] Trusts of Land and Appointment of Trustees Act 1996, schedule 1, p. 1.

[24] Mental Health Act 1983, ss. 95–6. A full consideration may be found in Graziadei, *Diritti nell'interesse altrui*, p. 157, footnote 6.

[25] Insolvency Act 1986. In *Re Dennis* (1995), it was decided that the succession is retroactive to the moment of the first act of bankruptcy (in the lower court, in 1992, the moment was identified in the declaration of bankruptcy).

[26] Trusts of Land and Appointment of Trustees Act 1996, schedules 1, 3.

[27] Solicitors Act 1974, s. 32 to s. 33; Insurance Broker (Registration) Act 1977, s. 11; Estate Agents Act 1979, s. 12 to s. 15.

[28] For more detailed examination, see Graziadei, *Diritti nell'interesse altrui*, pp. 378–83.

central theme of the law of trusts. In fact, *fraud* is a central theme of equity itself; it was so in the early days of Chancery, and it remains so today.

What is meant by 'equitable fraud' no one can state with certainty;[29] one might instinctively compare it with *dolus* in Roman law, and, for once, one would probably not be mistaken. *Fraud* and *dolus* both have a strong ethical component, which makes a powerful appearance when one passes from the action to the exception, and so to the concepts of *unconscionability* and *exceptio doli generalis*. Equity does not recognize typified procedural remedies, and has not, therefore, developed a theory of actions, but Roman law concepts, which extend *dolus* to any phase of the legal relationship, and *exceptio* to any kind of injustice, seem to mirror the framework which equity has developed in the course of the centuries. It is interesting to note (and this might merit detailed research) that the Anglo-Norman law of Jersey, which does not embrace a concept of equitable fraud of its own, recently had recourse to Roman law, and then to common law, in order to formulate a definition which might properly be employed in the area of trusts.[30]

Fraud, as we shall see on many occasions, certainly involves a corrupt will, but it also includes taking advantage, surprise, imposition and abuse of position.[31] The word *unconscionable* describes any legal situation the continuation of which would be in contrast with the precepts which are at the root of society, as that word is understood in any particular moment of history.[32] Although these are precepts of conscience, to introduce a theme to which I shall return often in this chapter, this does not mean they are not 'legal', i.e. that they are not sanctioned by equity; on the contrary, they find their proper legal form in equity, and give rise to well-recognized rules and appropriate means of protection.[33]

Deus est procurator fatuorum: a judge will take care of those who cannot take care of themselves, or who were not able to do so at a given moment. It could be a structural situation,[34] but more often it is a specific case, which

---

[29] Fraud also exists in common law, but its connotations are considerably more limited, and are almost entirely absorbed within the concepts of deceit, and recently, fraudulent misrepresentation: cf. G. W. Keeton and L. A. Sheridan, *Equity* (3rd edition), London, pp. 251–2.   [30] See chapter 4 §1.

[31] A complete panorama may be found in the monograph by L. A. Sheridan, *Fraud in Equity*, London, 1957 (although the profiles of equitable fraud are in constant evolution).

[32] Cf. W. J. Jones, *The Elizabethan Court of Chancery*, Oxford, 1967, pp. 422–48.

[33] Cf. W. Barbour, 'Some Aspects of Fifteenth-Century Chancery', in 31 HarvardLR (1918) 834, at 838–40.

[34] English case law in the area of the party with greater bargaining power has preferred to proceed on a case-by-case basis, leaving the enunciation of general principles to Parliament: see *National Westminster Bank plc v. Morgan* (1985), at p. 708, *per* Lord Scarman, and cf. Keeton and Sheridan, *Equity* (see above, footnote 29), pp. 255–6 and 258–63.

equity resolves with an exquisite eye for detail. We cannot go any deeper into the question in these preliminary reflections, which are intended merely to draw attention to the assonance between *fraud* and *dolus*, and to predispose the reader towards a diligent review of the rules of equity and a clear understanding of the confines of what equity considers to be unconscionable.

2. Trusts arising out of rules of equity (constructive trusts)

a Improper benefits obtained from a fiduciary relationship

A person who finds himself performing activities of a fiduciary nature is the constructive trustee of every benefit which he has improperly obtained as a consequence of the performance of those activities.

This rule, which historically gave rise to the modern theory of constructive trusts,[35] was settled by a 1726 decision[36] regarding the trustee of a leasehold who, when the lease expired, obtained a renewal for his own benefit. It should be noted that the leasehold which thus became the object of a constructive trust was not renewable, and that in any event the owner of the property was not prepared to renew it in favour of the trustee acting in that capacity.[37]

Later case law has expanded the notion of 'improper benefits', and has progressively extended the application of the rule, both objectively, to cases other than leaseholds (for example to a trustee who entrusts stockbrokerage responsibilities to the firm of which he is an employee (thereby receiving a part of the commission)[38]), and subjectively to any fiduciary. An examination of fiduciary relationships under English law would be beyond the scope of this book; even though the size of the 'fiduciary' category may only be a development of significant provisions of equity,[39] the field is

---

[35] F. W. Maitland, *Equity. A Course of Lectures*, revised by J. Brunyate, Cambridge, 1936, pp. 80–1.

[36] *Keech v. Sandford* (1726); cf. Restatement, *Restitution*, §§190 and 195. For an application in Trinidad and Tobago, see *Persad v. Persad* (1979).

[37] Leasehold is the enjoyment of immovable property for a fixed period, similar to the Italian *locazione immobiliare* except for its being classified as an estate, and for the requirement that the right enjoyed must be in real property: in fact, the expression 'any land' in the Law of Property Act 1925 includes the leasehold; in the case cited, leasehold related to income from a market. For further details, see Megarry, *Real Property*, pp. 306–60; Lupoi, *Appunti*, pp. 36–7, 145 and Gambaro, 'La proprietà' [*supra*, footnote 9], pp. 75–8.   [38] *Williams v. Barton* (1927).

[39] See, for example, *Gartside v. Isherwood* (1788), at p. 560: 'if a confidence is reposed, and that confidence is abused, a court of equity shall give relief'. In *Re Goldcorp* (1995), the Privy Council stated that 'the essence of a fiduciary relationship is that it creates obligations of

evolving, and is not yet ripe for proper definitions.[40] We can be certain that the following fall within the category, and are therefore subject to the rules under review:

- Lawyers[41]
- Company managers and executives[42]

a different character from those deriving from the contract' (98). For a similar finding in what is clearly a different systematic reality, see G. Ferri Jr., 'Le deleghe interne', in B. Libonati (ed.), *Amministrazione e amministratori di società per azioni*, Milan, 1995, pp. 175ff., at pp. 190–5.

More details may be found in Underhill, *Trusts*, 347–65. Among the most recent applications are the Australian decisions in *United States Surgical Corporation v. Hospital Products* (1983–1984); for the US cf. Restatement, *Restitution*, §192. For Scotland, see Wilson and Duncan, pp. 98–103.

[40] In this sense, see L. S. Sealy, 'Fiduciary Relationships', in CLJ (1962) 69; P. D. Finn, *Fiduciary Obligations*, Sydney, 1977, pp. 1–5; J. L. McDougall, The Relationship of Confidence, in D. W. M. Waters (ed.), *Equity, Fiduciaries and Trusts*, Toronto, 1993, p. 157; J. C. Shepherd, *The Law of Fiduciaries*, Toronto, 1981; J. C. Shepherd, 'Towards a Unified Concept of Fiduciary Relationships', in 97 LQR (1981) 51 (which takes up one of the central theses of his monograph, and approaches the civil-law position of the 'power to abuse' of the fiduciary); Elias, *Constructive Trusts* (see above, footnote 5), §3.2.2; recently, A. Mason, 'The Place of Equity and Equitable Remedies in the Contemporary Common Law World', in 110 LQR (1994) 238, at 245–8.

A list of the fiduciary categories appears in Goff and Jones, *Restitution*, p. 85, footnote 74; see also Keeton and Sheridan, *Equity* (see above, footnote 29), pp. 262–76; for the US, Scott, *Trusts*, §2.5.

An interesting controversy in the United States is that which sees the federal government as trustee of the Indian tribes: see 'Note, Rethinking the Trust Doctrine in Federal Indian Law', in 98 HarvardLR (1984) 422.

[41] *Boardman v. Phipps* (1967) where the indisputable honesty of the defendant was of no relevance, and a strict interpretation of the rule was applied to the use of information obtained by virtue of his being the trustee's lawyer (see a full discussion of the decision in Underhill, *Trusts*, 357–61; 366–7) and in G. Jones, 'Unjust Enrichment and the Fiduciary's Duty of Loyalty', in 84 LQR (1968) 472, at 481–6; *Brown v. IRC* (1964) on interest which matures from sums deposited with a lawyer.

The most recent case law has perhaps leant towards distinguishing among the different kinds of fiduciary relationship between a lawyer and his client, and some of the less significant ones have been identified: see *Target Holdings v. Redferns* (1995) see below.

[42] *Industrial Development Consultants v. Cooley* (1972): the managing director of a company learnt from the company's counterpart in contractual negotiations that it did not intend to sign the contract with the company, but might agree to do so with the director in person. Since the contract was one which promised good profits, the director resigned, and obtained the benefit of the contract for himself: he was held to be a constructive trustee of all profits in favour of the company. This case belongs to the wider category of '*corporate opportunity*'; see Jones, 'Unjust Enrichment' (see above, footnote 41), at 487–97 and cf. F. H. Easterbrook and D. R. Fischel, *The Economic Structure of Corporate Law*, Cambridge, Mass., 1991, chapter 4; E. McKendrick (ed.), *Commercial Aspects of Trusts and Fiduciary Obligations*, Oxford, 1992, in particular the contributions by D. D. Prentice, P. L. Davies and R. Goode.

Directors of companies are a classic case of persons who are bound by fiduciary

- Principals and agents in commerce[43]
- Partners[44]
- Military personnel[45]
- Public servants[46]

The relationship between a bank and its clients, on the other hand, is not yet well defined.[47]

The trustees of a pension scheme have recently found themselves obliged to seek authorization from a judge before proceeding with the distribution of the fund, even though it had been approved by all the interested parties, simply because they too would have derived a benefit in their capacity as members of the pension scheme.[48]

obligations: see, for example, *Regal v. Gulliver* (1941); *Selangor United Rubber v. Cradock (No. 3)* (1968); *Karak Rubber v. Burden (No. 2)* (1972); *Belmont Finance v. Williams Furniture* (1980); *Rolled Steel Products v. British Steel* (1986). For Canadian law, see *Canadian Aero Service* (1973), which adopts the strict line taken by English case law; previously, the Canadian courts had adopted the practice of making distinctions, and, in substance, taken a less strict line (*Peso Silver Mines* (1965); commented in S. M. Beck, 'The Saga of Peso Silver Mines: Corporate Opportunity Reconsidered', in 49 CBR (1971) 80): see Shepherd, *The Law of Fiduciaries* (see above, footnote 40), pp. 733–49. Singapore follows the English example: *Cheong Kim Hock v. Lin Securities* (1992).

   In Italian law discussion of the fiduciary obligations of managers is still in its infancy: see U. Patroni Griffi, 'Fiduciary duties e gruppi di società', in [1994] 1 Giur. Comm. 886; F. Ghezzi, 'I "doveri fiduciari" degli amministratori nei "Principles of Corporate Governance"', in [1996] Riv. soc. 465.

[43] For the case of agents who purchase for themselves instead of for their principal, see for example *De Bussche v. Alt* (1878); *Andrews v. Ramsay* (1903); *Regier v. Campbell-Stuart* (1939). On the relationship between agency and constructive trust see Kötz, *Trust und Treuhand* (see above, footnote 8), pp. 84–8 and, more generally, between agency and trust in the context of fiduciary relationships, M. Graziadei, 'Agency e trust', in *Atti Milano*, ch. 35; P. G. Jaeger, *La separazione del patrimonio fiduciario nel fallimento*, Milan, 1968, pp. 196–204.

[44] See the Australian decision in *Chan v. Zacharia* (1984), which dealt with the lease of commercial property; a partnership which carried out a commercial activity was placed in receivership. The partners failed to reach agreement on the renewal of the lease of the partnership premises by the due date, and the lease terminated. Two months later, one of the partners signed a lease with the lessor in his own name: the High Court of Australia (which is the highest court) held that he was the constructive trustee of the lease in favour of the partnership. For English precedents going back to the last century, see *Featherstonaugh v. Fenwick* (1810) and (with reference to facts similar to those of *Keech v. Sandford*) *Randall v. Russell* (1817).

[45] The most singular application is probably that made by the House of Lords in *Reading v. A-G* (1951), where it was held that a staff-sergeant stationed in Cairo was constructive trustee in favour of the Crown of payments he received while not in service but in uniform, and where thanks to the uniform he permitted the lorries of traffickers in contraband to pass through civilian checkpoints unchallenged.

[46] *A-G for Hong Kong v. Reid* (1993), of which more presently.

[47] I shall limit myself to citing the decision in *National Westminster Bank v. Morgan* (1985), which excluded the obligation on the part of a bank employee to advise a client to seek legal advice before providing security to guarantee a bank loan. For a more recent and restrictive approach, see below, chapter 3, footnote 215.

[48] *Re Drexel Burnham* (1995); see below, chapter 3, footnote 243.

A strict application of the rule under review may be found in *Guinness plc v. Sanders*,[49] which merits a brief description.

Guinness made a public offer to acquire a competitor. The Board of Directors entrusted the operation to a sub-committee consisting of three directors. When the offer had been successfully concluded, one of the directors asked the sub-committee to pay a fee of 5.2 million pounds to a consultancy firm which he controlled. The committee, which had been informed of the connection, passed a resolution in favour of it, and Guinness paid the amount requested.

When the Board of Directors learned of the payment, Guinness sued the director. The Court of Appeal, on the basis that the communication of the conflict of interest did not satisfy the relevant rules on the subject (Companies Act, 1985, s. 317.1), decided that the director should be held to be a *constructive* trustee (in favour of Guinness) of the sum paid to the company which he controlled: 'The basis of the constructive trust was in the combination of three factors, namely a fiduciary relationship, a breach of a duty arising in respect of that fiduciary relationship, and the receipt, in breach of duty, of property belonging to the person to which such duty was owed.'[50]

One theoretical difficulty of the rule under review relates to those cases in which the benefit obtained by the fiduciary does not involve the property of the other party or does not arise out of the use of that property,[51] for example, commissions paid in secret – the classic case of the bribe[52] – and, generally, those cases where systematic consistency demands that the fiduciary be considered to be the trustee of information which he has come by in that capacity,[53] or, even more vaguely, to be the trustee of the legal interests of someone who relied on him.[54]

The Privy Council has recently handed down a decision on this last point:

---

[49] 1988. [50] At p. 870.

[51] See the principles enunciated by Oliver J in *Swain v. Law Society* (1981), 813–14, approved by the House of Lords (at p. 619), and, in the same case, by Fox LJ, 823–4. The topic has recently been re-examined in an essay by Allen, 'Bribes and Constructive Trusts: *A-G for Hong Kong v. Reid*', in 50 MLR (1995) 87.

[52] R. M. Goode, 'The Recovery of a Director's Improper Gains: Proprietary Remedies for Infringement of Non-Proprietary Rights', in McKendrick, *Commercial Aspects* (see above, footnote 42), p. 137. Cf. Oakley, *Constructive Trusts* (see above, footnote 16), ch. 3; Goff and Jones, *Restitution*, pp. 666–70; Shepherd, *Law of Fiduciaries* (see above, footnote 40), ch. 19. On this subject, see principally *Lister v. Stubbs* (1890), where the negative response to the theory of a constructive trust was motivated by the lack of a pre-existing 'property right' of the company in the sum paid to the bank official.

Successive case law did not follow *Lister v. Stubbs* (which was criticized in the literature), and so a situation was created of precedents which could not easily be reconciled: see the *excursus* carried out by Lord Templeman in *A-G for Hong Kong v. Reid* (1993).

[53] Cf. McDougall, 'Relationship of Confidence' (see above, footnote 40); Finn, *Fiduciary Obligations* (see above, footnote 40), pp. 130–68; F. Gurry, *Breach of Confidence*, Oxford, 1984, pp. 158–62.

[54] We shall see later the important place which the entrusting has in the theoretical construction of the trust.

The defendant, a colonial bureaucrat in Hong Kong, received bribes, which he used to acquire real property in New Zealand. Having secured a criminal conviction, the Administration obtained temporary seizure of the property. Confirmation of the seizure order was denied, on the grounds that the Administration had no rights to the property, but the Privy Council held that the defendant was the constructive trustee of the property on behalf of the Crown.[55]

b Transfer of trust property

Equitable interests are exceptionable with respect to the acquirer of an asset or of the right encumbered by them unless the acquirer has had no notice of interests and the acquisition is for value.[56] In all other cases, he is the constructive trustee of the right which has been transferred to him,[57] and is therefore obliged to cause it to pass to the beneficiary[58] or, alternatively, to satisfy the purpose of the trust. The beneficiary is protected, where necessary, by the equitable 'tracing' technique, as I shall illustrate below.

This rule applies to all gifts, and generally to all transfers not for value, with respect to which the person to whom the right is transferred is defined as a 'volunteer', and also to transfers for value, when the purchaser has had 'notice' of the trust.

In the complex relationship between common law and equity, the question of the position of the person to whom a right subject to equitable interests is transferred is of central importance. The transfer is usually governed by rules belonging to the common law set of rules,[59] as is the case with the purchase and sale of real property which is the subject matter of a trust. It is for this very reason that the transfer does not, in principle, serve to remove the equitable positions which attach to the property (and which,

---

[55] *A-G for Hong Kong v. Reid* (1993). The Privy Council held that although the defendant was the 'owner' of the assets, in equity he was a constructive trustee in favour of the Crown, which therefore had the right to secure delivery of them even if the value of the assets had greatly increased in the meantime with respect to the value of the bribes. See the comment by Allen, 'Bribes and Constructive Trusts' (see above, footnote 51), who agrees with the solution but not the reasoning; D. Crilley, 'A Case of Proprietary Overkill', in [1994] RLR 57, is more critical.

[56] The classic English term is 'bona fide purchaser without notice'. Cf. Restatement, *Trusts*, §284; Restatement, *Restitution*, §§172, 202.
    On the origins of this doctrine see D. E. C. Yale, *Lord Nottingham's Chancery Cases*, London, 1961 (S S no. 79), II, Introduction, pp. 150–79.

[57] Pettit, *Trusts*, p. 157, with further detail; Underhill, *Trusts*, pp. 411–18; cf. Elias, *Constructive Trusts* (see above, footnote 5), §3.2.3; C. Harpum, 'The Stranger as Constructive Trustee', in 102 LQR (1986) 114, at 116–18.

[58] This is a classic case of the bare trust, on which see below, chapter 3 §3.a.

[59] But not necessarily, because the subject matter of the trust may also be an equitable legal position.

what is more, are usually unknown;[60] hence the recent case law which imposes a high degree of diligence when checking the equitable rights which third parties may claim in the property).

English legal writers have recently drawn attention to the distinction between *equitable interests* and *mere equities*, this latter term having been adopted to describe a personal position protected by equity, but more tenuously than is the case with *equitable interests*. I will return to this fundamental question at the end of this chapter, but the reasoning behind the rule under review should be highlighted now, since similar reasoning will also apply to rules which will be discussed later on.

At this stage, I would propose a notion which will be clarified later: every right has an equitable side which follows its own rules. A disposition may be unsuited to capturing this side, which therefore finds an appropriate arrangement in equity, where forms of protection are found which have the purpose of re-establishing the unity which the disposition has destroyed. A person who acquires property, whether for value or not, to the detriment of the beneficiaries of a trust, and who falls within the rule described here, is considered to be a constructive trustee of that which he has acquired, because only in this way can unity be restored. The obligations of the trustee will now be transferred to the person acquiring the property. As is always the case in equity, it is not the transfer which is under discussion (regardless of whether it is under common law or not); the transfer is neither revoked, nor cancelled, nor declared to be ineffective. What happens is that the unsatisfied equitable side serves to redirect the right which has been transferred towards its original objective by the imposition of a constructive trust.[61]

[60] In England, as in other common-law countries, forms of registration have nonetheless been introduced, but they only affect the range of equitable positions marginally (see below, footnote 142); for a detailed discussion of the subject see S. R. Coveney and A. J. Pain, *Interests in Land. A practical guide to effective protection at the Land Registry* (2nd edition), London, 1995.

It is relevant to note that legislative provisions exist which in some cases protect the purchaser by the mechanism of overreaching, which transfers certain third party rights from the estate or the physical asset to the price received by the seller (see, briefly, Lupoi, *Appunti*, pp. 70–3; in detail, C. Harpum, 'Overreaching, Trustees' Powers and the Reform of the 1925 Legislation', in CLJ (1990) 277; see Megarry, *Real Property*, pp. 256–65). Overreaching operates against beneficiaries of a trust where the seller is the trustee of a trust for sale or the life tenant of a settlement.

It should be taken into consideration that the system of land registration, begun in 1897, was completed in England and Wales only in 1990.

[61] The position of R. M. Goode in 'The Right to Trace and Its Impact in Commercial Transactions – II', in 92 LQR (1976) 528, at 532–3 which bases this constructive trust on the fault of the recipient, runs contrary to the authorities, and is unacceptable. It may be appropriate to clarify that English case law has denied that the constructive trust can be the sanction for commission of a tort: see *Metall v. Donaldson* (1989).

What I have just termed the 'unsatisfied equitable value' stems from the requirement of equity that benefits be abandoned which it would be unconscionable for a person deemed unworthy of protection to retain.[62] In equity (and here we find clearly recognizable structures of canon law), it is the conscience of this person which marks the object and the extent of the protection. The primary importance of the requirement of notice in purchases for value is evident, because it is that notice which binds the conscience of the purchaser.

Recent decisions have sought to identify new criteria for establishing when a person has notice of a trust and, more generally, of an equitable interest. This is a complex issue, because it makes use of nuances aimed at suppressing wilful shutting of the eyes to the obvious, wilful lack of care or gross negligence on the part of the person to whom the right is transferred:[63] in all probability, the only way out of the tangle of new problems posed by new technologies in the financial sector and the breakup of old class structures is to place more emphazis on considerations of conscience and probity than on legal criteria of liability, as the most recent case law has done.[64]

New developments in case law have emerged over the course of the last fifteen years from lawsuits involving the operations of international financiers who dissipate funds which have been entrusted to them, high-speed electronic transfers of funds, and speculative operations based on collusion. Earlier precedents involving the transfer of real property are of little

---

[62] Thus J. B. Ames, 'Purchaser for Value Without Notice', in 1 HarvardLR (1887) 1, at 3.

[63] According to the traditional definitions, the notice may be actual, constructive or imputed. The position of Restatement, *Trusts*, §288, 296–7 is very simple. See also the following rule and Harpum, Stranger (see above, footnote 57), 267–87.

In the recent decision in *Halifax Mortgage Services v. Stepsky* (1995), it was held that the information which the mortgagor had communicated to the lawyer who represented both him and the mortgagee could not constitute constructive notice to the latter, because of the lawyer's duty of confidentiality (rather, it has been noted, the lawyer should have withdrawn from representation of the mortgagee because of his conflict of interest).

[64] In *Re Montagu's Settlements* (1983–1985) (published in 1987) Vice-Chancellor Megarry affirmed that 'in considering whether a constructive trust has arisen in a case of the knowing receipt of trust property, the basic question is whether the conscience of the recipient is sufficiently affected to justify the imposition of such a trust'; having declared that 'knowledge' was preferable to the classic 'notice', the judge concluded as follows: 'knowledge is not confined to actual knowledge, . . . but includes . . . actual knowledge that would have been acquired but for shutting one's eyes to the obvious, or wilfully and recklessly failing to make such inquiries as a reasonable and honest man would make; for in such cases there is a want of probity which justifies imposing a constructive trust.'

See also *Lipkin Gorman v. Karpnale* (1987) and *Cowan v. Eagle Trust* (1992). The position of case law in the nineteenth century was rather more restrictive: see *Coleman v. Bucks* (1897).

use,[65] but we must recognize that English case law has adapted itself rapidly by taking the old rules regarding notice as a point of departure and extending them to all financial situations, defining two new paradigms: 'knowing receipt' and 'knowing participation'.

c Participation in a breach by a trustee: 'knowing receipt' and 'knowing participation'

A person who knowingly makes possible, profits from, or takes part or co-operates in a breach of trust is considered to be a constructive trustee (or, perhaps more correctly, is subject to the obligations of a constructive trustee[66]). By the term 'breach of trust' is meant a breach of the obligations of a trustee (including, naturally, a constructive trustee) or another person who has fiduciary responsibilities.[67]

A 1983 decision,[68] rendered after one hundred and twenty days of hearing, signalled a new orientation in case law in this area which has been clarified (and amended) in the last few years.[69]

The traditional criterion of the honest and diligent individual is no

---

[65] S. Gardner, 'Knowing Assistance and Knowing Receipt: Taking Stock', in 112 LQR (1996) 56, at 60–4.

[66] This is of importance in the debate on the procedural or substantive nature of the rules on constructive trusts: see the final section of this chapter.

[67] Cf. Underhill, *Trusts*, pp. 418–27; Jacobs, *Trusts*, §§1332–9; Harpum, 'Stranger' (see above, footnote 57), 115–16, 141–62. In formulating the rule, I have united two situations – 'knowing receipt' and 'knowing assistance' – which are usually kept separate in the literature on the basis of a dictum of Lord Selborne LC in *Barnes v. Addy* (1874), but which are treated together in the most recent writings.

The rule in question does not presuppose a failure to perform in the technical sense of the trustee's obligations. It therefore also includes cases in which the trustee has been duped by the third party: *Eaves v. Hickson* (1861). For cases of illegality by a professional or other persons charged by the trustee with performing a service, see Pettit, *Trusts*, pp. 175–6.

The notion of 'participant in the breach' does not belong to Italian legal culture, although in the last thirty years a door has been opened as a result of research into the phenomenon of inducing a breach (F. Ziccardi, *L'induzione all'inadempimento*, Milan, 1975). In English law, the principle was first clearly set forth in *Lumley v. Gye* (1853), where the element of notice that an opera singer was under an exclusive contract to a theatre was sufficient to hold that the conduct of the impresario who had convinced her to sing for him was wrongful (see, *per* Crompton J, p. 224: 'a person who wrongfully and maliciously or, which is the same thing, with notice').

[68] *Baden and Others v. Société Générale* (1983); in the decision five criteria of imputability based on the subjective state of the defendant are indicated. Previously, *Selangor United Rubber Estates v. Cradock (No. 3)* (1968).

[69] Cf. P. J. Millett, 'Recovering the Proceeds of Fraud', in 107 LQR (1991) 71; P. D. Finn, 'The Liability of Third Parties for Knowing Receipt or Assistance', in D. W. M. Waters (ed.), *Equity* (see above, footnote 40), 195; Gardner, 'Knowing Assistance' (see above, footnote 65) and other writing which will be indicated below.

longer sufficient, due to the complexity of many international financial transactions;[70] the idea that a person 'should have known' or 'should have realized' – that is, the idea of constructive notice – now tends to prevail, especially where a relationship with a bank or a financial institution is based upon the presumption that particularly high standards of honesty must be observed.[71] The solution depends on a large number of frequently intangible facts,[72] yet there seems to be an irreversible tendency to extend equitable obligations to persons who, although not participants in the breach, knew of it and carried out a role which made it possible,[73] and who find, or have found, themselves in a direct relationship with the property with respect to which the fiduciary has not exercised the responsibilities incumbent upon him.[74] On the other hand, it is precisely the need to stay

---

[70] The 1983 precedent cited above related to the transfer of four million dollars belonging to an investment fund.

[71] See *Bartlett v. Barclays Bank* (1980); see, chapter 3, footnote 409.

[72] As, recently, in the New Zealand decision in *Springfield Acres v. Abacus* (1994), and in *Eagle Trust v. SBC Securities* (1993) (see, previously, *Belmont Finance v. Williams* (1980)).

[73] In *Agip (Africa) v. Jackson* (1990), one of the elements related to the responsibility of the managers of companies which Agip formed in the Isle of Man to carry out certain payments and then closed down. The managers were local professionals, who had become convinced that this system had been designed to evade Tunisian exchange controls. Even though there was no connection between this purpose and the fraud later committed by an employee of Agip, who altered payment orders for the benefit of third parties, Fox LJ expressed himself as follows (at p. 469): [the managers] 'knew that something was concealed. The fact that the concealing was labelled as a "circumvention" does not alter that: it suggests some sort of impropriety . . . If the known facts indicate a lack of frankness, the person assisting in effecting the transaction in question must take the risk in the absence of further explanation that it is fraudulent.' Recently, in *Brinks v. Abu-Saleh* (1996), Rimer J has nevertheless held that a person who participates in the carrying out of an act which makes the actor a constructive trustee does not himself become a constructive trustee if he does not know that the illegality stems from a breach of equitable obligations (in the case in point, a wife who accompanies her husband from England to Switzerland to deposit three million pounds in cash into a bank is not a constructive trustee if she believes the purpose is to evade taxes, and is not aware that her husband is the accomplice of the perpetrator of a robbery, and the sum of money is the proceeds).
Finn, 'Liability' (see above, footnote 69), 214–17, proposes that the criterion of knowledge should be 'know or have reason to know', according to the terminology of the American Restatement; the author observes that if this criterion were to be applied, lawyers and professional consultants in general would easily find themselves in a situation of 'knowing assistance'; cf. Millett, 'Recovering' (see above, footnote 69), 85.

[74] *Agip (Africa) v. Jackson* (1990): a bank is a constructive trustee if it follows instructions to transfer funds arriving from abroad in spite of the fact that the person giving the instructions had informed the bank that the transfer was fraudulent and had been arranged by a disloyal employee; *Finers v. Miro* (1991): a lawyer is a constructive trustee if he takes care of transfers on behalf of a client, and if he has reason to suspect that the funds are from illicit sources. See also Harpum, 'Stranger' (see above, footnote 57), 130–4; Harpum, 'Liability for Intermeddling with Trusts', in 50 MLR (1987) 217; Hanbury, *Equity*, pp. 301–8.

within the confines of the specific dispute which leads one towards a different opinion regarding setting aside the notion of notice (which I believe to be artificial) in favour of the factual notion of knowledge,[75] and regarding the creation of a presumption of dishonesty connected with a conduct of deliberate omission. In other words, a third party who argues that he did not know, or did not understand, or even that he did not ask (where an honest and reasonable person would have asked) would be deemed to have the knowledge which he would have acquired if he had asked.[76]

In many cases, it is not necessary to embrace complicated methods of investigation into the subjective state of a person when the events themselves demonstrate the profit which a person has derived from the breach of the fiduciary. Consider, as an example, the following decision from New Zealand:[77]

A ship broker received the proceeds from certain sales and deposited the funds into his own bank account, with the aim of reducing his debt with the bank. The bank was following the deposits into and withdrawals from the account with special attention, because of the broker's extremely poor financial condition. The bank was aware that most sales were made on behalf of third parties, and therefore that the amounts received belonged to the broker's clients, and that he was only entitled to a commission. When the broker went bankrupt, the bank (which took the balance remaining in the account to cover shortfalls) was held to be constructive trustee of the amounts due to the broker's clients.[78]

---

[75] *Re Montagu's Settlement Trusts* (1987) (cf. see above, footnote 64); *Polly Peck v. Nadir (No. 2)* (1992) (*per* Scott LJ, 242); cf. M. Bryan, 'The Meaning of Notice in Tracing Claims', in 109 LQR (1993) 368; Finn, 'Liability' (see above, footnote 69); Harpum, 'Stranger' (see above, footnote 57), 120–7. A different view is that in El Ajou v. *Dollar Land Holdings* (1993), at p. 739, which was overturned on appeal: see below, p. 33.

Doubts had previously been expressed regarding the excessive ease with which the requirement of notice had been found by the judges, with the result that there was the risk that financial dealings would be paralysed: see Megarry V-C in *Re Montagu's Settlement Trusts* (1987), at pp. 285–6, and Knox J in *Cowan de Groot v. Eagle Trust* (1992). Cf. P. Matthews, 'Constructive Trusteeship: Proprietary Claims, Personal Claims and the Hague Convention', in 1 T&T (1995) no. 7 25, at 28–9.

It is significant that s. 6(2) of the Law of Property (Miscellaneous Provisions) Act 1994 refers to 'actual knowledge' of a purchaser, so as to give him a right of action relating to obligations not disclosed to him by the seller; s. 9(2) of the Trusts of Land and Appointment of Trustees Act 1996 takes the same approach, with reference to the 'knowledge' of a purchaser of 'land' from the beneficiary authorized by the trustees. It is well known that in canon law knowledge of a state of affairs or of a right which prejudiced the agent meant that he could not avail himself of the protection offered by civil law: cf. J. Gordley and U. Mattei, 'Protecting Possession', in 44 AJCL (1966) 293, at 308.

[76] See, nevertheless, in Canada and New Zealand respectively, the decisions in *Gold v. Rosenberg* (1995), and *Cigna v. Westpac Securities* (1996).

[77] *Westpac Banking Corporation v. Savin* (1985).

[78] The New Zealand Court of Appeal held that this was a case of 'knowing receipt' and that

A recent decision of the Privy Council appears to me to follow this line of reasoning, but with increased severity, making it clear that blame for the conduct need not necessarily be ascribable to the trustee: it is sufficient that it should relate to the conduct of the third party.[79]

A company doing business as a travel agency had a contract obligation to Royal Brunei Airlines to keep all amounts received from the sale of tickets in a separate account, in trust for the airline. The defendant was managing director and principal shareholder of the company. He mixed receipts from ticket sales with other funds received by the company in a single bank account. The company became insolvent, and the airline sued the defendant, claiming that he should be deemed to be constructive trustee of all sums received by the company.

The fact that the defendant, although a third party with respect to the contract, had full knowledge of the contractual obligations of the company was not contested. The question was whether responsibility arose out of that knowledge alone, or whether the third party had to show particularly reprehensible behaviour. The Privy Council chose a third route, that of dishonesty ('honesty is an objective standard'[80]), which permitted the avoidance of the reefs formed of the various degrees of knowledge and the artificial distinctions which result.[81]

The type of constructive trust which we have described, taken with the expansion of the limits of the category of 'fiduciaries', the supervision provided by tracing[82] and the discretionary remedies of equity offer a level of protection in English law and in the legal systems which draw inspiration from it[83] which cannot easily be found in other systems. A further example will usefully conclude these observations.

constructive notice on the part of the bank was sufficient. This is one of the fact-patterns mentioned above regarding the difficulty with this theory, because it becomes hard to distinguish when the rule holds 'should have known' to be sufficient, and therefore concludes that 'it is as if it had been known' and when it sanctions a lack of attention on the part of a person who should have, but did not, make inquiries; for example, in *Cowan de Groot v. Eagle Trust* (1992), it was held that the conduct of a person who sees real property on sale at a price far below market price and omits to make inquiries as to the reason is not reprehensible.

[79] *Royal Brunei Airlines v. Tan* (1995), which held that the criteria enunciated in *Baden* (1983) were of little use. The decision found that where a third party had received no asset, but was only an indispensable participant in the breach, he could not be held to be a constructive trustee and therefore answer for the losses according to the usual rules. On the criteria for discovering the subjective state of the third party, see also the Canadian decision in *Re Air Canada* (1993) cited by Matthews in 'Constructive Trusteeship' (see above, footnote 75).   [80] At p. 74.

[81] I do not share the perplexity expressed by Gardner, 'Knowing Assistance' (see above, footnote 65), 73–6 or of A. Berg, 'Accessory Liability for Breach of Trust', in 59 MLR (1996) 443.   [82] See below, chapter 2 §4.b.

[83] It is for only two decades that English case law has asserted the duty of a bank to assist persons who could not otherwise obtain reparation of a wrong, even in breach of bank secrecy laws: *Bankers Trust v. Shapira* (1980). The Grand Court of the Cayman Islands, a State which maintains strict bank secrecy, applied this principle in *C Corp v. P* (1994),

A fund manager based in Geneva allowed himself to be convinced by a Canadian group to invest sums entrusted to him by numerous investors (among them the plaintiff) in a purchase and sale of shares which turned out to be fraudulent. The Canadians moved the proceeds among Swiss, Gibraltarian, Panamanian and back through Swiss banks through myriad companies, and finally invested them in a (legitimate) real-estate project in London managed by the defendant company. Later, the Canadians were bought out by the promoters and left the project.

The defendant company had been put in contact with the Canadians by two individuals, one of whom had first acted for the Canadians and had then become chairman of the company, although without any active role, and had resigned shortly before the Canadians had made their investment. Using this personal nexus as a lever, the plaintiff asked that the defendant company be declared to be constructive trustee of the sums deposited with it by the Canadians, or of the shares which they had acquired.

The claim was rejected in the lower court,[84] but was accepted on appeal,[85] because the Court held that the chairman of the defendant company was the directing mind behind the investment in the real-estate project. He knew the origin of the funds invested by the Canadians, and the fact that he had no executive powers from the company was sufficient to rule out the hypothesis that the facts of which he was aware could be ascribed to the company, but not to avoid the constructive trust, because it bound him as directing mind of the operation, and, through him, the company (even though the operation was completed after his resignation).[86]

A constructive trust is one thing, but the responsibility borne by an individual who participates in the breach of a fiduciary obligation – or, in the most recent variation, who has not behaved honestly with respect to an action which he could have prevented or made less easy to carry out – is another. English law has not created a tort here, although there is

which dealt with an action commenced by a Texan businessman against fiduciaries who had obtained sums of money from him and deposited them in banks in the Cayman Islands. Furthermore, the court held that the bank, although innocent of wrongdoing, had become a constructive trustee at the moment in which it had been informed by the plaintiff of his serious reasons for believing that it was holding the sums obtained from him.   84 *El Ajou v. Dollar Land Holdings* (1993).   85 *El Ajou v. Dollar Land Holdings* (1994).
86 Here is another distinction between trust and agency.

It may be of interest to add that when the case returned to the lower court, the plaintiff sued the bankruptcy trustee of Dutch companies which had been used by the Canadians to hold other sums deriving from the fraud. From the evidence used in the English case, it emerged that at least a part of these sums came from funds which the plaintiff had originally entrusted to the fund manager in Geneva. The bankruptcy trustee was therefore declared to be a constructive trustee, and was ordered to deliver the sums to the plaintiff.

A particular (and controversial) aspect of this case was that other savers had also been victims of the fraud, but the sums involved were small. They had not, therefore, commenced an action. The English judgment imposed a constructive trust in favour of one plaintiff alone for all the sums acquired by the bankruptcy (which were less than the plaintiff's damages), and held that he was not required to divide any amounts with the remaining victims: *El Ajou v. Dollar Land Holdings (No. 2)* (1995).

literature to support this notion,[87] and it therefore finds itself in a state of theoretical uncertainty from which it will need to emerge.[88]

The fundamental knot to be unravelled relates to two situations. On one hand, there is the class of persons who have received no property or right against which a plaintiff may assert a claim: as stated at the beginning of this section, they are subject to the obligations of constructive trustees, but they are not constructive trustees. On the other hand, there are the many procedural remedies in equity, which in this area mostly operate to provide restitution rather than compensation in the form of damages. These remedies may be superimposed on to the procedural remedies of common law (contractual or tort actions), which usually provide for damages to compensate for losses.

d *Trustee de son tort*

A person who behaves as a trustee without actually being one (*trustee de son tort*) must discharge all the obligations of a trustee, as if he really was one;[89] his level of responsibility is determined according to the criteria established for trustees.[90]

e A seller of land not yet transferred

It is well known that a contract for the sale of land does not transfer ownership of the asset; this result is obtained by the later delivery, or conveyance,[91] followed by registration.[92] In the meantime, the seller

---

[87] C. Harpum, 'Accessory Liability for Procuring or Assisting in a Breach of Trust', in 111 LQR (1995) 545; G. McCormack, 'Assisting in a Breach of Trust: Principles of Accessory Liability', in [1995] TLI 102.

[88] For the consequences in the area of private international law see Berg, 'Accessory Liability' (see above, footnote 81), 448–50.

[89] *Mara v. Browne* (1896); *Carl Zeiss Stiftung v. Herbert Smith (No. 2)* (1969). There is a detailed discussion in Harpum, 'Stranger' (see above, footnote 57), 127–30. This rule has nothing to do with the doctrine of the *negotiorum gestio*, which common law does not recognize (cf. J. P. Dawson, '*Negotiorum gestio*: The Altruistic Intermeddler', in 74 HarvardLR (1961) 817; L. W. Aitken, '*Negotiorum gestio* and the Common Law: A Jurisdictional Approach', in 11 SydneyLR (1988) 585): South African law differs: Honoré, *Trusts*, p. 172.

[90] For the similar notion of *executor de son tort* see IRC v. *Stype Investments (Jersey) Ltd* (1982) and, in the Cayman Islands, *Cook-Bodden v. Kirkconnell* (1994).

[91] Cf. J. T. Farrand, *Contract and Conveyance* (4th edition), London, 1983; more generally A. Guarneri, *Diritti reali e diritti di credito: valore attuale di una distinzione*, Padua, 1979, pp. 23–5.

This subject has recently been effectively brought to light by M. D. Panforti, *La vendita immobiliare nel sistema inglese*, Milan, 1992 (pp. 103–7. For the seller's constructive trust). Brilliant considerations, based on the notion of 'operative laws', are to be found in R. Sacco, 'Il sistema del diritto privato europeo: le premesse per un codice europeo', in L. Moccia (ed.), *Il diritto privato europeo: problemi e prospettive*, Milan, 1993, pp. 87ff., at pp. 91–4.

[92] Registration of a purchase now has constitutive effect in English law: the sale is cancelled if the ownership title is not presented for registration within two months: Megarry, *Real*

is the constructive trustee of the property in favour of the purchaser.[93]

One of the consequences of this rule, which is rooted in a fundamental principle of equity, is that if the seller dies before the conveyance, a testamentary disposition relating to the property is ineffective, because the seller has lost the right to it; even though at the time of his death he was technically the 'owner', it is the purchase price, and not the property, which will be included in his estate.[94] Another consequence of the rule may be seen where the seller becomes bankrupt: the property which has been sold is excluded from the bankruptcy assets, as is always the case when an asset of a bankrupt person is subject to a trust.[95]

The relationship between the seller–trustee and the purchaser–beneficiary is rendered more complex by the continuing personal interest of the seller in the subject matter of the trust. Should the purchaser not perform, the contract is cancelled, and the trust is terminated.[96]

The rule in question is of particular interest in comparative studies, because civil-law systems also take account of the need to offer means of protection for the purchaser, albeit within the different framework provided by the rules regarding registration. Scottish case law, in a recent decision of the First Division, has rejected the English rule on the ground that it can only be justified if one acknowledges that the purchaser acquires

---

Property, p. 98. On the form of acts of transfer, see below, footnote 142.

The English system of real-estate registration is based on a rigid formalism, in clear contrast with the traditional framework of equity, as we shall better see below. From this we have case law which seeks ways out of the legislative formalism, causing uncertainty in the area of assets: cf. G. Battersby, 'Informal Transactions in Land, Estoppel and Registration', in 58 MLR (1995) 637 and the appeal court judgment in *Midland Bank v. Green* (1980) (later reversed by the House of Lords). On the relationship between registration and unregistered trusts (where the registration of trusts is permitted) see in Singapore *Chong Poh Siew v. Chong Poh Heng* (1995) and, in the Cayman Islands, *Cook-Bodden v. Kirkconnell* (1994); recently, in England, see *Lloyds Bank v. Carrick* (1996).

The equitable position of the purchaser between the contract and registration corresponds to one of the few cases of equitable interests which may be registered: Land Charges Act 1972, s. 2(2).

[93] *Green v. Smith* (1738); *Shaw v. Foster* (1872); *Earl of Egmont v. Smith* (1877); *Freevale Ltd. v. Metrostore* (1984). Cf. Oakley, *Constructive Trusts* (see above, footnote 16), ch. 6; D. W. M. Waters, *The Constructive Trust*, London, 1964, ch. 2.

[94] This result is of great importance where, as in England prior to 1925, legitimate succession devolved in different ways depending on the interest each component of the heirs had in the real or personal property; in the case examined in the text, the succession related to a building (real property), but the rules relating to sums of money (personal property): cf. Lupoi, *Appunti*, pp. 134–7. The same is true if the testator disposes of his real property in favour of one person and of his personal property in favour of another: even if at the time of death the estate includes real property 'owned' by the testator, the heir to the real property has no rights to it: the purchase price goes to the heirs to the personal property.   [95] Specific application in *Freevale v. Metrostore* (1984).

[96] In general see Underhill, *Trusts*, pp. 402–5.

an equitable interest at the moment the contract is concluded. Scottish law, while recognizing trusts and some forms of constructive trust,[97] does not recognize equity, and the decision in question did not see fit to acknowledge that the purchaser had a status which provided a form of protection *erga omnes* before the formalities of registration had been completed.[98]

f *Donatio mortis causa*

The use of the Latin term is compulsory here, because we are discussing an ancient principle of medieval European common law, from which equity has derived the rule which asserts the validity of a gift made by a person who, in contemplation of death, delivers an asset to the donee with a condition *si premoriar*. Where this delivery is inadequate to transfer ownership, a constructive trust arises at the moment of death. The executor of the will therefore has the obligation to complete the formalities necessary to make the gift effective.[99]

This rule has always generally been considered an anomaly in English law, yet it has recently been applied for the first time to a gift of real property, made orally and by the delivery of the key to a safety deposit box in which the documents of title were kept.[100] The Court of Appeal commenced its opinion by citing the Institutes of Justinian,[101] finding therein two of the three elements which constitute the principle according to English precedents: contemplation of death and a condition of predecease.Nevertheless, the Court had to depart from the Institutes when it

---

[97] See below, chapter 5 §3. *Stevenson v. Wilson* (1904), which dealt with a sale of shares and the refusal of the directors to enter the purchaser's name in the share register, deals specifically with this *regula*. The opinion of all the judges in *Sharp v. Thomson* (1995) (see immediately below), was that this was a precedent which could not be applied, as it was based on the particular facts of the case.

[98] *Sharp v. Thomson* (1995): 'ownership belongs to a single person at any one time and is transferred at one single moment in its entirety' (at p. 867, *per* Lord Sutherland).
   The case concerned the sale of movable property; the seller was a company which had granted a floating charge in favour of a bank on all its assets; the sale would have prevailed over the charge if it had been registered, but the holder of the floating charge exercised his right before the registration could take place, and prevailed in the dispute with the purchaser, who proposed the theory of the constructive trust without success in either the higher or the lower court.

[99] Cf. Pettit, *Trusts*, pp. 109–15; Hanbury, *Equity*, pp. 139–43; Waters, *Trusts*, pp. 174–9; Snell, *Equity*, pp. 380–6.

[100] *Sen v. Headley* (1991). The case concerned real property which was not subject to registration rules (unregistered land).

[101] Inst. II.7: *Mortis causa donatio est, quae propter mortis fit suspicionem, cum quis ita donat, ut, si quid humanitus ei contigisset, heberet is qui accepit: sin autem supervixisset qui donavit, reciperet, vel si eum donationis paenituisset aut prior decesserit is cui donatum sit.*

turned to examine the third element: the transfer to the donee, even by means of delivery of the *indicia*, provided that it was carried out in such a way as to grant the *dominium* over the subject matter of the gift to the recipient. This third element was traditionally linked to personal property[102] and, according to an 1827 opinion of Lord Eldon, served to prevent the possibility of a valid *donatio mortis causa* of real property, or, more generally, of an estate,[103] with regard to which formal rules of transfer exist.[104]

The Court had no doubt that the delivery of the keys of the safety deposit box was equivalent to the transfer of the *dominium* over the documents of title kept therein,[105] but the transfer had to relate to the *dominium* over the property to which the documents referred. Although the conduct of the donor on his deathbed left no doubt as to this,[106] there remained one final difficulty: English law does not permit the alienation of real property by oral declaration. It is here that the constructive trust comes to our assistance: the donor remains the holder of the estate (or, in civil-law terms, the owner), but, at the moment of his death, a constructive trust is created in favour of the donee which is binding upon the deceased's estate.

The *donatio mortis causa* of personal property has been revisited in recent times from the point of view of the assignment of the *dominium*. It was held that the assignment was lacking in a case involving the delivery of bank-savings-books, where the donor did not deprive himself of every possible right to use the funds deposited,[107] while it was held to be present where the donee received the keys of his father's car from his father before a potentially fatal operation.[108]

g Benefits deriving from the commission of a crime

For historical reasons which need not be listed here, a constructive trust exists where personal property, sums of money or other rights other than

---

[102] See, for example, *Birch v. Treasury Solicitor* (1950), regarding the gift of a sum of money by delivery to the donee of savings books in the saver's name.

[103] *Duffield v. Elwes* (1827), which concerned a mortgage.

[104] See below, footnote 142.

[105] Which, stated the Court, 'has been a ready means of developing our property law in modern times' (647).

[106] For a more complete discussion, see P. Sparkes, 'Death-Bed Gifts of Land', in 43 NILQ (1992) 35.   [107] *Greenidge v. Bank of Nova Scotia* (1984).

[108] *Woodard v. Woodard* (1991). The Court of Appeal held that the log book did not have to be delivered, since it is not an ownership document. The judgment of the High Court of Barbados in *Neblett v. Bentham* (1984) differs because of the specific circumstances of the case.

real-property rights become part of an individual's estate as a result of the commission of a crime. This rule, which is common to all common-law systems, including the United States,[109] although generally ignored by the literature, is of great interest to us because it is an important key to the theoretical construction of constructive trusts.[110]

h Undue payment

A person who receives a payment in error, and who is in a position to be aware of the error, is a constructive trustee of the amount received in favour of the payer.

This is a recent development in English law, and has its origins in a 1979 decision[111] in which the judge, who had to apply New York law and could not find any English precedents, decided that New York law on the subject conformed with the principles of English equity and should be followed by the English Courts.[112]

Chase Manhattan Bank mistakenly credited two million dollars to the Israel–British Bank, which went into liquidation one month later. The question was whether the American bank was the holder of a credit, like any other creditor, or whether it had the right to a specific remedy involving the delivery of any assets acquired with the sums paid in error. In the latter case the American bank would have the right to receive that asset as if it were its own (and would not, therefore, be in competition with the other creditors). The court accepted this theory, and held that the Israel–British Bank was the constructive trustee of the amount credited in error.[113]

The undue payment is considered in American law to be ineffective to transfer the ownership of the asset or the sum of money to the recipient.

---

[109] See the Australian decisions in *Black v. Freedman* (1910), according to which a thief is trustee of the stolen money, and *Rasmanis v. Jurewitsch* (1970), regarding a murder from which the murderer profited as a result of an interest by survivorship in an asset held in joint tenancy with the victim; for English law, see *Re Crippen* (1911), and the general pronouncements of Fry LJ in *Cleaver v. Mutual Reserve* (1892); for American law see *Ellerson v. Westcott* (1896). Cf. Jacobs, *Trusts*, §1310; Scott, *Trusts*, §493.2; Underhill, *Trusts*, pp. 395–6.

[110] Lord Browne-Wilkinson, in *Westdeutsche v. Islington* (1996), opportunely clarified that it was a constructive and not a resulting trust (p. 998).

[111] *Chase Manhattan v. Israel-British Bank* (1979).

[112] This affirmation could probably not be sustained today, since we now have a deeper knowledge of the differences between American and English law in the area of constructive trusts. See below, chapter 2 §5.e.

[113] The practical effect of these pronouncements, which concerned sums of money which could not be identified and an insolvent debtor/trustee, will be explained below in the discussion on tracing.

More precisely, according to strict law only the title is transferred, while 'equitable ownership' remains with the payer. In this manner, a constructive trust comes into effect, of which the recipient of the payment is trustee in favour of the payer.[114]

The difficulty in English law lies in whether to acknowledge such a wide-ranging principle or to make it conditional upon the existence of a fiduciary relationship, whether pre-existing or subsequent to the undue payment.[115] Prevailing opinion seems to lean towards the second alternative,[116] and, in the most recent decision on point, it was indicated that the reason why the Israel–British Bank assumed the obligations of a constructive trustee was because it became aware at a certain point that the payment had been made in error.[117]

Attention should also be drawn to convincing positions of a more radical nature in the literature, which hold that the undue payment deprives the act of delivery of the sum of money of its full attributive effect.[118]

i Undue influence or awe

Anyone who acquires a right as a result of the undue influence which he has exerted over, or of the awe in which he was held by, the transferor, is the constructive trustee of that right in favour of the transferor.[119]

---

[114] This is an application of the principles illustrated just above on the subject of transfers of trust assets.

    Alternatively, one might think in terms analogous to Art. 2033 of the Italian Civil Code, but in this case the payer loses the benefit of the constructive trust and finds himself the holder of a simple credit: see the discussion of this alternative in Birks, *Restitution*, 377–81.

[115] Cf. the decision in the criminal case *R v. Shadrokh-Cigari* (1988).

[116] Cf. *Sinclair v. Brougham* (1914) (the subject of contrasting opinions in *Westdeutsche v. Islington* (1996), to be considered today as of little authority, even if it has not been formally overruled); *Re Diplock* (1948): this case concerned payments carried out by testamentary trustees in favour of a hospital following an erroneous interpretation of the will. The solution has an echo in Roman law: see D. 12.6.2–3 on an action by third parties prejudiced by erroneous payments made by the heir.

[117] Thus Lord Browne-Wilkinson, in *Westdeutsche v. Islington* (1996), at p. 997: in detail see above, chapter 2 §3e.

[118] G. McCormack, 'Mistaken Payments and Proprietary Claims', in [1996] Conv 86; cf. Goff and Jones, pp. 107–24.

[119] Underhill, *Trusts*, p. 396 *et seq.*; Shepherd, *Law of Fiduciaries* (see above, footnote 40), 221–35; on the same subject, but without systematic concerns, see also Hanbury, *Equity*, 814–21; and cf. Kötz, *Trust und Treuhand* (see above, footnote 8), pp. 93–6 and C. C. Langdell, 'A Brief Survey of Equity Jurisdiction', in 1 HarvardLR (1887) 55, 111, 355, at 67, who shows why the limitations of procedural remedies of common law have made the intervention of rules of equity necessary.

The analogy between this rule and the previous one is clear,[120] given that in both cases the payer is considered by equity to be the holder of a right with respect to the property or right transferred, and not to the other party to the transaction.[121] In this way the other party becomes the constructive trustee of the property or right. The explanation for this form of constructive trust is often found in a specific definition of the equitable notion of fraud (of which we shall shortly see further examples), and in particular in the lack of conformity to criteria of honest and loyal behaviour between the contracting parties.[122] Into this category fall cases which have become so characteristic over the course of time that they have given rise to rebuttable presumptions relating to awe, for example between fiancé and fiancée[123] and between lawyer and client.[124] The presumption may be rebutted where it is established that the transferor consulted independent third parties before carrying out the act.[125]

We are not discussing duress, which common law recognizes and resolves by restitution,[126] but rather weaker phenomena, which belong to categories which cannot easily be placed in a civil-law context.

The creation of a constructive trust, as in many of the cases already considered, produces two principal effects: the segregation of the asset from the patrimony of the constructive trustee, so that his creditors cannot assert claims to it, and the obligation of restitution of the asset to the person who was subjected to the undue influence. According to a recent decision of the Court of Appeal of Singapore, undue influence may also manifest itself within a Board of Directors, and a third party who contracts with the company whose Board has been subjected to (recognizable) undue

---

[120] Elias reached the same conclusion in *Constructive Trusts* (see above, footnote 5), and treated them together.

[121] Thus, speaking expressly of 'ownership in equity', Lord St Leonards in *Stump v. Gaby* (1852).

[122] Snell, *Equity*, pp. 551–8. For a very stimulating historical review of similar phenomena, see J. L. Barton, 'The Enforcement of Hard Bargains', in 103 LQR (1987) 118; among the oldest precedents, see *Bridgman v. Green* (1755).

[123] Cf. *Re Lloyds Bank* (1931); *Zamet v. Hyman* (1961) (in the latter case both the fiancé and his fiancée were over seventy).

[124] Cf. *Willis v. Barron* (1902); *Wright v. Carter* (1903). On the relationship between *fiduciante* and fiduciary see P. D. Finn, *Fiduciary Obligations* (see above, footnote 40), pp. 82–7.

[125] Especially if he has consulted a disinterested lawyer: *Inche v. Shaik* (1929) *per* Lord Hailsham, 135.

[126] On which, see J. Beatson, 'Duress as a Vitiating Factor in Contract', in CLJ (1973–4) 97, principally dedicated to moral violence; Birks, *Restitution*, pp. 173–218.

influence on the part of one of its members is the constructive trustee of the sums paid to him.[127]

j Influence over the will of a testator

An heir (legitimate or by will) or other recipient of a testamentary disposition who induces the testator not to make a bequest, or to destroy a will containing a particular bequest, and tells him that he will see to it that the wishes of the testator are respected, is constructive trustee in favour of the person whom the testator intended to benefit.[128]

The testator therefore allows himself to be convinced to entrust the carrying out of his wishes to a person who, if he takes no action, will come by assets which the testator wishes to allocate to others. Although the systematics of English treatises lump these examples together, usually in the area of fraud,[129] they are not secret or half-secret trusts, because the rule under review does not stem from the desire of the testator to conceal his true intent from third parties, but from the profit obtained by the person who induces a change in the expression of the testator's will.

k Mutual wills

When two persons execute their wills by common consent, thereby disposing of their property in accordance with their agreement, at the moment when the first person dies[130] a trust is created which many believe to be a constructive trust.[131] The subject matter of the trust is the property of the survivor, increased by whatever is inherited from the deceased; the purpose

---

[127] *Cheong Kim Hoch v. Lin Securities* (1992). The undue influence was apparent, in the Court's opinion, because the company had purchased real property at over twice the market price.

[128] *Tharp v. Tharp* (1916); *Stickland v. Aldridge* (1804), tersely summarized in the footnote in *Mucklestone v. Brown*: 'An undertaking, express or implied, by which the formal insertion of a provision in a will is prevented, raises a trust against the party who entered into such engagement.' Cf. Scott, *Trusts*, §498.2.

  See also the decision of the Supreme Court of British Guyana (*Nisa v. Khan* (1946)), in the case of a testator who had not modified his will because his daughter, established as his heir, had promised him that she would transfer one of the properties she inherited to her sister: this was held to be a secret trust; see below, chapter 3 §1.f.

[129] For example, Hanbury, *Equity*, 152–3.

[130] *Re Cleaver* (1981). See R. Edwards and N. Stockwell, *Trusts and Equity* (2nd edition), London, 1995, pp. 276–80; Oakley, *Constructive Trusts* (see above, footnote 16), ch. 5; J. D. B. Mitchell, 'Some Aspects of Mutual Wills', in 14 MLR (1951) 136.

[131] *Re Hagger* (1930); *Re Green* (1951). For a Canadian precedent see *Re Grisor* (1980); for an Australian precedent see *Birmingham v. Renfrew* (1937).

of the trust is to ensure that the testamentary dispositions originally agreed are respected.[132]

If the second person modifies the dispositions contained in his will after the death of the first, the modifications are ineffective in equity, and when probate is commenced, the executors must refer to the trust imposed upon the property on the death of the first person.[133]

The theoretical basis for this rule does not affect the freedom to make bequests:[134] what we have before us is a classic mechanism of the relationship between equity and common law. Individuals who are bound by a testamentary agreement are free to dispose of their property as they wish, and to modify their wills, provided that they do not breach their mutual obligations. The fact that under normal circumstances this makes it impossible to modify the mutual wills, and therefore that the freedom to make bequests is little more than an unrealizable plan matters little to equity. Equity has its own principles, fundamental among which is the suppression of fraud, as that term is understood in equity. In a 1769 precedent[135] relating to a joint will, it was held:

> He that dies first does by his death carry the agreement on his part into execution. If the other then refuses he is guilty of fraud . . . For no man shall deceive another to his prejudice.

English case law has recently returned to this original line of reasoning, and has clarified that it is not essential that each will should provide for benefit to the other testator, since the basis of the rule is a concept of fraud

---

[132] For the sake of clarity, I use the term 'executors' in place of the more correct 'personal representatives'.

[133] See the full discussion of the theoretical underpinnings of this rule in the judgment of the Australian High Court in *Birmingham v. Renfrew* (1937), which was criticized in *In re Dale* (1993), because it found the underpinning of the rule in the reciprocal benefits between the testators (see below, in the text).

In *Goodchild v. Goodchild* (1996), the judge held that the understanding between husband and wife not to modify their respective wills had not been considered binding by the parties, and that therefore the surviving husband (who had remarried) had legitimately modified his will. Moreover, in arriving at a conclusion which caused inevitable puzzlement, the judge stated that he would issue an order to enjoin the husband's heirs from enforcing the moral obligation he had undertaken. The technical means employed by the judge was based on the type of action proposed: the plaintiff was the son from the first marriage, who complained that he had not received enough from his mother's will, because she was convinced that her husband had also made provision in favour of the son, as agreed between the couple.

[134] The freedom to dispose by will presents connotations different from those of Italian law. See, for example, the decision of the House of Lords in *White v. Jones* (1993), which ordered a lawyer who had delayed drafting a client's will to pay damages suffered by the individuals whom the client (who had died in the meantime) had instructed him to name as heirs.   [135] *Dufour v. Pereira* (1769), at p. 321.

which is in no way connected with the existence of a benefit to the survivor (as a consequence of which his obligation to stand by the agreement would arise): the other party has performed his side of the agreement, and the survivor must perform his.[136] His obligation is not contractual (as is the case, for example, with agreements of inheritance in German law): the agreement is certainly the source of a constructive trust,[137] out of which the obligations of which the beneficiaries may demand performance arise.[138]

1 Agreements void because of a defect in form, regarding the benefits due to the transferor of real property

Verbal agreements preceding or contemporaneous with a transfer of real property, which are void and of no effect because of a defect in their form, by which the seller is entitled to a right of enjoyment over a part of the property, may give rise to a constructive trust in his favour.[139]

This is so because the conduct of a purchaser who reneges on a verbal agreement only because it is not reproduced in writing at the moment of signing the purchase and sale agreement is fraudulent:[140] equity does not permit a statute to be used as an instrument of fraud.[141] It should be considered that the defect of form relates both to the creation of a right within the area of real property (and thus in common law) and to the creation of a trust (and thus in equity).[142]

---

[136] *In re Dale* (1993) (on two identical wills made by husband and wife in favour of their children).

On the same lines, but with reference to the case of an oral agreement between a testator and an heir regarding the final disposition *mortis causa* of the latter, see *Re Gardner* (1920): The heir was obliged to make disposition in favour of the persons orally indicated to him by the *de cuius* solely by virtue of having agreed to this at the time (without his expression of assent, the *de cuius* would not have bequeathed in his favour).

[137] In this sense, see the New Zealand decision in *Re Newey* (1994).

[138] Mitchell, 'Some Aspects' (see above, footnote 130), 141. In English law, the beneficiary of a contract in favour of a third party has no action against the promisor [this is no longer true: see Contracts (Rights of Third Parties) Act, 1999. Editor's Note].

[139] *Bannister v. Bannister* (1948) (below, in the text relating to footnote 143); *Binions v. Evans* (1972), as interpreted in *Ashburn Anstalt v. Arnold* (1988). For American law see Restatement, *Restitution*, §§180–3.

[140] For example, in *Re Densham* (1975), Goff J declared that it would be immoral if a party could renege on his undertakings only because they lack the written form required by the law (at p. 732). Over a century earlier, Romilly MR had expressed a similar opinion in *Davies v. Otty* (1865).   [141] See below, chapter 2 §4.d.

[142] The Law of Property (Miscellaneous Provisions) Act 1989, ss. 2(1)–2(3), prescribes the written form for real-property transfers. Previously, the Law of Property Act 1925, s. 40 provided that there was no action unless the agreement or a memorandum were in writing: from here we have the mention of ineffectiveness to add to nullity in the text

The plaintiff was the owner of two small houses. He agreed to sell them to the defendant at a below-market price provided that he was allowed to live in one of them (which was identified) for his lifetime. The deed of transfer of the property was a standard form deed, which therefore contained no reference to the agreement in favour of the seller. The Court held that the purchaser was a constructive trustee in favour of the seller of the right to live in the house.[143]

The theoretical framework of this decision is rather dubious, and all its basic premises have been widely challenged.[144] The declaration by the purchaser regarding the benefit to be attributed to the seller could be considered to be an express trust,[145] but in that case it would be void for defect of form. Alternatively, it could be a personal grant, but if so it would be unenforceable against third parties.[146] So we arrive at another institution of equity, proprietary estoppel.[147]

above: the former refers to the repealed law, the latter to the current law; cf. Megarry, *Real Property*, pp. 116–21. I note in passing that the reference in this footnote to the notion of 'real property' is not entirely correct; it should be to 'land' which, in the English system, includes leasehold.

The Law of Property Act 1925, s. 53(1)(b), not modified in 1989, establishes written proof of the creation of trusts of real property ('manifested and proved by some writing').

As we shall see below, chapter 2 §4.d, implied, constructive and resulting trusts are excluded from any requirement as to form.   [143] *Bannister v. Bannister* (1948).

[144] On fears that equitable decisions of this kind might upset the rules regarding the form of acts see Elias, *Constructive Trusts* (see above, footnote 5), ch. 4. Cf. Goff and Jones, *Restitution*, ch. 19.

[145] Thus we come to the problem of contracts in favour of third parties, which is traditionally not recognized in common law; among new developments, it should be noted that two Australian States, Queensland and Western Australia, have abolished the traditional rule of common law, enunciating rules similar to Art. 1411, para. iii of the Italian Civil Code. As this book goes to press, the Contracts (Rights of Third Parties) Bill is before Parliament in the United Kingdom.

Recent English developments have sought to place the contract in favour of third parties within the area of trusts, in particular when the promisee–signer may be considered to be trustee of the promise of which the third party would be the beneficiary. From a theoretical point of view, this construction does not appear to present problems, because any right which is subject to transfer may be the subject matter of a trust in which, as is usually the case, the settlor and trustee are two different persons. It is, therefore, mostly a question of fact. See the discussion of these matters in Béraudo, *Trusts*, §58; Jacobs, *Trusts*, §§217–26; and cf. Restatement, *Trusts*, §14. From a comparative viewpoint there is no structural similarity between the promissory trust and the Italian contract in favour of third parties: see my entry 'Trusts, (II) diritto italiano', in *Enc. giur. Treccani* (1966), §3.1.2–§3.1.3; cf. Scott, *Trusts*, §14.

[146] On the basis of registration rules contained in the Land Charges Act 1972. Cf. G. Battersby, 'Contractual and Estoppel Licences as Proprietary Interests in Land', in [1991] Conv 36.

The decision of the House of Lords in *Street v. Mountford* (1985), which in some cases makes the granting of personal enjoyment equivalent to tenancy, and includes the latter among interests in land, should be noted (the subject is extremely technical, and I do not believe it necessary to go into further detail).

[147] See below, footnote 323 and relevant text. According to D. J. Hayton, 'Equitable Rights of

m Transfer to a purchaser of the obligations of a seller towards a third party, notwithstanding the lack of form

A purchaser who is aware of obligations assumed by the seller in favour of a third party relating to property which is the subject of a purchase and sale agreement, and who agrees to assume those obligations, becomes a constructive trustee of the property in favour of the third party even if the sale instrument makes no reference to the assumption and the assumption is therefore invalid because of a defect of form.

This is one of the most controversial developments in English law. It originates in a 1972 decision[148] which, despite being widely criticized, was followed in 1982:

The purchaser of a large plot of building land, who had been informed by the seller that the seller had previously accepted an obligation towards a third party to build him a house on one lot, and who had undertaken to carry out that obligation, is constructive trustee of the property in favour of the third party, even if the undertaking had not been expressed in the final agreement and was therefore ineffective pursuant to the law on the transfer of real property.[149]

The judgment ordered the purchaser to carry out the construction of the house, as had previously been agreed by the third party with the previous owner.[150] In the face of an obligation which has been expressly assumed, the formal reasoning, which would allow the purchaser of the land not to keep his promise, thereby damaging an innocent third party, loses its effect.

n Oral agreement with equitable effect

The two preceding *regulae* demonstrate how equity does not come to a halt when confronted with preclusions arising out of a failure to comply with rules relating to the form of transactions, and has thus upheld and expanded one of its fundamental principles.[151] A very recent decision permits

Cohabitees', in [1990] Conv 370, the borders lack consistency: there is a single remedy against 'unconscionable' conduct on the part of the owner.

[148] *Binions v. Evans* (1972).

[149] *Lyus v. Prowsa Developments* (1982). See also *Asburn Anstalt v. Arnold* (1988). In *Lyus v. Prowsa Developments* the judge did not, of course, ignore the argument that the exercise of a right cannot be considered to be unlawful; nonetheless, he held that the purchaser of the land knew of the rights of the promisee because mention had been made of them in a prior act signed by the purchaser; accordingly, the fact that this was not reproduced in the final purchase seemed to the judge to be an expedient for depriving the promisee of the rights which would otherwise have been due to him.

[150] This is the typical equitable instrument of specific performance, of which more below in chapter 2 §4.g.

[151] More generally see below, chapter 2 §4.d.

us to articulate a more extensive *regula* than the two we have just seen: an oral agreement among several parties, by which each party agrees to the division of an equitable interest in which each has a joint interest, makes each party a constructive trustee of the others.[152]

The basis of this *regula* appears to be somewhat technical. The transfer of an equitable interest, as we shall see,[153] requires a writing, while, as we know, no writing is required to create a constructive trust. Accordingly, an oral agreement for the transfer of an equitable interest is void, whereas an oral understanding to apportion an equitable interest is valid, and each party is in the same position as a seller who is in the course of effecting a transfer.[154]

o Rights in the family home

When the property in which a couple lives together is, or has been acquired, in the name of only one person, but the other takes responsibility for certain later expenses, or assists personally with the maintenance or modernization of the property, on the assumption that the property is owned in common, a constructive trust is created whereby the owner of the house is a trustee in favour of the other party in equal measure to the latter's contribution, in all cases where the former has declared or led the latter to understand, expressly or by his conduct, that the property should be considered to belong to both. This rule is somewhat controversial as regards both its theoretical foundation and, to some extent, the description of the fact-pattern.

---

[152] *Neville v. Wilson* (1996). Shareholders of company U, holders of the relevant shares as nominees of company J, declared that they wished to transfer the shares to company J and end the fiduciary relationship. Owing to lack of care, nothing was done, and company J was later placed in liquidation on the basis of an informal agreement between the shareholders to share all assets and debts among themselves *pro quota*. Under English law, all assets not distributed by a company in liquidation belong to the Crown. The question to be decided was to whom the shares of U belonged.

  The Court of Appeal held that company J had an equitable interest in the shares of U, and that the agreement among the shareholders regarding the liquidation of J had transferred that interest to the shareholders of J, and had made each of them constructive trustee of the others up until the moment of the division of the shares of U. The right to the shares did not, therefore, pass to the Crown.

  As is often the case with English judgments which take on complex theoretical issues, the conceptual explanation is not particularly clear.

[153] See below, chapter 3 §1.a.

[154] See above, chapter 2 §2.a. The Court of Appeal, in *Neville v. Wilson* (1996) took advantage of the doubts left by the decision of the House of Lords in *Oughtred v. IRC* (1966), which dealt with an oral agreement by which a son transferred his equitable interest as the final beneficiary of a trust to his mother for value.

The school of thought which favours the recognition of a constructive trust to protect a person who is not the registered owner of a property has recently found acceptance in Canada[155] and New Zealand,[156] in decisions which have aroused considerable interest throughout the Commonwealth. The situation in Australia does not yet appear to be completely clear,[157] and these developments in case law have contributed to bringing about a pause and re-evaluation in England.[158] This has provided an occasion to reconsider the topic, and, in the first instance, to trace the line between oral constructive trusts and resulting trusts, which we shall consider shortly, based on the financial contribution at the time of purchase.

Some authors, interpreting the most recent case-law developments, prefer to base the relationship between the two cohabitants, where one is obliged to acknowledge to the other the existence of a right in the conjugal home, either on a promise by one party upon which the other party has relied (but which does not give rise to obligations of a legal nature),[159] or on conduct importing reliance,[160] or on an implied agreement between the

---

[155] *Pettkus v. Becker* (1980); *Sorochan v. Sorochan* (1986) (but from the view of unjust enrichment, and so with reduced potential as regards the theory proposed in the text: from this point of view see better the final section of this chapter). Every aspect of the topic of the constructive trust in Canadian law has recently been analysed, with his customary depth, by D. W. M. Waters, 'The Nature of the Remedial Constructive Trust', in P. B. H. Birks (ed.), *The Frontiers of Liability*, Oxford, 1994, II, p. 165; for my reasons for dissenting from his analysis, see below, pp. 86ff.

[156] *Hayward v. Giordani* (1983). But see *Pasi v. Kamana* (1986).

[157] *Allen v. Snyder* (1977) disagrees, but *Thwaites v. Ryan* (1984), *Calverley v. Green* (1985), *Muschinski v. Dodds* (1985), *Baumgartner v. Baumgartner* (1987), and *David Securities v. Commonwealth Bank of Australia* (1992) are more open (in these decisions, however, the explanation leans towards unjust enrichment: see the final section of this chapter).

For Australian developments, see Mason, 'Place of Equity' (see above, footnote 40), pp. 249–53; Jacobs, *Trusts*, §§1343–50.

[158] To a great extent, following the retirement of Lord Denning, its principal (and sometimes extremist) supporter; cf. D. W. M. Waters, 'The Role of the Trust Treatise in the 1990s', in 59 MissouriLR (1994) 121, at 139–40.

[159] This is the foundation seen by Elias, *Constructive Trusts* (see above, footnote 5), §3.1.2. Cf. *Hammond v. Mitchell* (1991): the entrusting claimed by the woman was based on a phrase uttered by the man (after he had explained why the house would be in his name alone): 'Don't worry about the future because when we are married it will be half yours anyway and I'll always look after you and [the boy].'

[160] Previously on the basis of the decision in *Gissing v. Gissing* (1971). The position adopted by New Zealand case law is an interesting one: it has the constructive trust spring from social conventions, to which a woman may legitimately expect a man to conform: *Gillies v. Keogh* (1989). The 'entrusting conduct' may give rise to the different structure of 'proprietary estoppel', treated on the same level as the constructive trust in a dictum of Lord Bridge in the recent decision of the House of Lords in *Lloyds Bank v. Rosset* (1990). On proprietary estoppel see below, footnote 323.

parties, even if it is not manifested in any formal manner.[161] In each of these cases, a constructive trust would be created whereby the person in whose name the property is held is a trustee in favour of the cohabitant.

There is a clear reference, in the first two interpretations, to well-known principles of English equitable rules.[162] Far from strengthening these principles, however, they weaken them in the eyes of those who have taken a critical position towards the notable creativity shown by the case law of English equity in the past decades. Use of the constructive trust in cases where the person who is not the named owner of the property would otherwise suffer damage consequent upon the reliance which he has placed in a promise or the conduct of the other person was, in fact, the line which was taken in decisions after the beginning of the nineteen seventies, although it fluctuated among the implied trust, the constructive trust and the resulting trust.[163]

If, on the other hand, one takes as a starting-point a presumed common intent which has not been formally put into effect, one remains in the traditional area of constructive trusts,[164] but the intent must be demonstrated. The judicial basis for opting for the constructive trust solution would not, therefore, be so much the issue of trust, although it must be present,[165] as an understanding between the two

---

[161] *Gissing v. Gissing* (1970); *Grant v. Edwards* (1986); *Lloyds Bank v. Rosset* (1990) (House of Lords); *Hammond v. Mitchell* (1991); *Stokes v. Anderson* (1991); *Springette v. Defoe* (1992). Cf., in the West Indies, *Cupid v. Thomas* (1985), characterized by the fact that the cohabitant had had fifteen children by six different women and took advantage of this fact to dispute the fact that any implicit agreement to share ownership of the 'conjugal' home could be inferred.

[162] See the expression of Fox LJ in *Ashburn Anstalt v. Arnold* (1989), at p. 25: 'the Court will not impose a constructive trust unless it is satisfied that the conscience of the estate owner is affected'.

[163] *Pettitt v. Pettitt* (1970); *Gissing v. Gissing* (1971) (see the analysis of Oakley, 'Has the Constructive Trust?' (see above, footnote 8)); followed in *Burns v. Burns* (1984), *Grant v. Edwards* (1986), and *Midland Bank v. Dobson* (1986). An example of an Australian judgment on these lines is *Higgins v. Wingfield* (1987).

[164] Returning to the discussion on terminology, (see above, chapter 2 §1.b), these are certainly cases of a constructive trust which does not come into existence against the will of the settlor (the owner of the asset).

[165] Greater weight to the requirements of justice arising out of the entrusting had been attributed in the judgments influenced by Lord Denning, as, for example, in *Hussey v. Palmer* (1972) and *Eves v. Eves* (1975). The latter, with the later decisions in *Grant v. Edwards* (1986), and *Hammond v. Mitchell* (1992), concerned cases where the man refused to place the house in both names and provided reasons which had no legal basis: it is not easy to decide whether and to what extent such conduct may have influenced the decisions in favour of the woman. The vein of case law based on substantive requirements of justice has not been lost, and has contributed to the development of new tendencies regarding the constructive trust as a remedy, of which I shall speak in section 5 of this chapter.

parties,[166] which may be informal, which lacks any evidence of the share to which the party not named as owner would be entitled,[167] and even presumed as far as the share due to each cohabitant[168] is concerned. In this way it becomes difficult to distinguish an understanding which involves promises by one party to which the other merely assents from tender expressions of affection.[169]

A proposal to distinguish between automatic constructive trusts and discretionary constructive trusts, the former founded upon a common intent, the latter, on the other hand, considered to be a medium of protection in equity,[170] has recently been put forward. It is a notion which merits further attention, since it has the advantage of imposing order in an area which by virtue of embracing structures from the most varied of backgrounds, which are therefore difficult to ascribe to common principles, has become extremely crowded in recent years. We shall review it again in the final section of this chapter.

It should be added that the rule set out above applies to every kind of cohabitation arrangement,[171] as, for example, in the case of parents who contribute financially to the purchase of a house by a married son, on the

---

[166] Lord Bridge, in *Lloyds Bank v. Rosset* (1990), at pp. 132–3, distinguished cases where an agreement, albeit an informal one, was made by the parties before the purchase (or, in exceptional cases, after) by those persons in whom a common intent was to be found from conduct during cohabitation in the property; in the second hypothesis, stated Lord Bridge, it is difficult to find a constructive trust in the absence of a contribution by the non-owner to the purchase price. Cases such as *Huntingford v. Hobbs* (1993), where the court found a kind of joint venture between the cohabitants, are different.

[167] This latter clarification comes from the decision of the Court of Appeal in *Drake v. Whipps* (1995), which I believe merits approval.   [168] *Midland Bank v. Cooke* (1995).

[169] The observation is made by Waite J in *Hammond v. Mitchell* (1991): 'the tenderest exchanges of a common law courtship may assume an unforeseen significance many years later when they are brought under equity's microscope'. For analogous problems in Italian law, see M. Bernardini, *La convivenza fuori del matrimonio*, Padua, 1992, ch. 6.

[170] D. J. Hayton, 'Constructive Trusts of Homes – A Bold Approach', in 109 LQR (1993) 485; previously, Hayton, 'Equitable Rights' (see above, footnote 147), criticized by P. Fergusson, 'Constructive Trusts – A Note of Caution', in 109 LQR (1993) 114.

[171] Thus, in express terms, the Australian judge Glass JA in *Allen v. Snyder* (1977), 689. Among the English precedents there are many concerning live-in relationships between unmarried persons, in part because in cases of a marriage, s. 24 of the Matrimonial Causes Act 1973 (which gives the court wide powers to distribute the property of the spouses) and s. 37 of the Matrimonial Proceedings and Property Act 1970 (concerning the contribution by a spouse to running expenses or improvements to the marital home) will apply. For example, *Cooke v. Head* (1972), *Eves v. Eves* (1975); *Equity & Law Home Loans v. Prestidge* (1992) where the dispute concerned the conflict between the rights of the wife as beneficiary in equity of a house purchased together with the husband and the financial institution which held the mortgage in guarantee of the bank loan; on mortgages, see below, chapter 3 §2.g.

understanding that they will live there with the young couple. The couple separates after some time: case law holds that the house is the subject of a trust in favour of the parents, and that the personal affairs of the couple have no relevance to the position of the parents/beneficiaries.[172]

Further effects of constructive trusts which follow the rule under review relate to dispositions of real property. According to the principles set forth above, the rights of a beneficiary of a constructive trust are exceptionable with respect to a third party purchaser and, since there is no form of registration, a purchaser (or a lender who has taken a mortgage from the owner of property[173]) finds himself in the same perilous position that he would have been in before the introduction of the land registration system. As a result, the level of certainty in the circulation of real property assets and the granting of loans against real property suffers.[174]

3. Returning or residual trusts (resulting trusts)

a Lack of completeness or ineffectiveness of transfers

When property is transferred to a trustee without the terms of the trust being clearly expressed, or where the conditions established by the settlor do not exhaust his equitable interest, or do not affect the entire property or the entirety of the rights being transferred, or if the trust is void or ineffective, the rights of the settlor (or that portion which he has not transferred) become the object of a resulting or 'returning' trust for the settlor.[175] This rule applies to the equitable aspect of the transfer, and not to

---

[172] Decisions in this area are not rare; in Australia see *Malsbury v. Malsbury* (1982), to which the facts described in the text refer.

[173] *Williams & Glyn's v. Bowland* (1980); *Midland Bank v. Cooke* (1995).

[174] Cf. G. Battersby, 'Informal Transactions' (see above, footnote 92); S. Gardner, 'Fin de Siècle chez *Gissing v. Gissing*', in 112 LQR (1996) 378. On the security of the purchaser, see Megarry, *Real Property*, pp. 60–2; Hanbury, pp. 276–80. It is precisely with reference to these problems that Hayton, 'Equitable Rights' (see above, footnote 147), proposes the abandonment of the classic theory of the constructive trust in favour of a purely procedural view which would impose the appropriate protection as a result and from the moment of the judgment.
This solution, which would involve the theoretical revisions of which we shall speak in section 5 of this chapter, only concerns some of the situations which hinder certainty in real-estate transfers. Another, more serious, situation because of its greater frequency, concerns the trust for sale with a purpose, where it cannot be discovered if the purpose is still current or not, with the result that the creditors cannot forecast whether the real property may be freely sold: see *Re Citro* (1991); *Abbey National v. Moss* (1993); cf. F. M. B. Reynolds, 'Creditors and Collateral Purposes', in 111 LQR (1995) 72.

[175] Previously, J. B. Ames, *Lectures on Legal History*, Oxford, 1913, pp. 427 and 431–2, with reference to a transfer of real estate accompanied by an oral declaration of trust (the essay appeared for the first time in HarvardLR, 1907). The most complete modern

that relating to the trustee, since the ineffectiveness of the transfer to the trustee would prevent the trust from coming into existence, and would not, therefore, allow for the application of the rules on equitable interests.

Where the equitable dispositions suffer from the defects indicated in the description of the rule above, the resulting trust effectively completes the equitable transfer of the right: equity will not permit the trustee to hold assets which do not have a proper destination. Unless the desire of the settlor to strip himself wholly and completely of the property is unequivocal,[176] every lacuna is dealt with in favour of the settlor, and those equitable interests for which no beneficiary has been named will therefore result to him.

b Delivery of a sum for a specific purpose

Where a sum of money is transferred to a person for that person to use for a specific purpose, for his own benefit or that of third parties, it is considered to be held in trust, and if the attainment of the purpose becomes impossible, it becomes the object of a resulting trust in favour of the settlor.[177]

In stating this rule I follow a 1968 decision of the House of Lords, where it was combined with the rules relating to the effect of these trusts on third parties, as well as later judicial applications.[178] I shall describe it in detail because of its special comparative interest.

Rolls Razor had an overdraft at Barclays Bank and was in serious financial difficulty. Despite this, the controlling shareholder wished to distribute the dividend which had been approved by a shareholders' meeting to the

---

enunciation of this rule is in the decision of Megarry J in *Re Vandervell's Trusts (No. 2)*, 1974, 294. For American law, see Restatement, *Trusts*, §§430–9 (cases of non-exhaustive trusts).

Recently, for an application of the Reverter of Sites Act, 1987, s. 1, see *Marchant v. Onslow* (1994) (where the purpose of a trust dating from 1848 could not be realized).

For other applications of the rule enunciated in the text, see *Re the Trusts of the Abbot Fund* (1900); *Re Cochrane's Settlement Trusts* (1955); *Re Gillingham Bus Disaster Fund* (1958).

[176] In this case, the Crown intervenes: *Re West Sussex Constabulary's Widows* (1970).

[177] The presentation is different in Scottish law: the creation of a trust with a purpose for which the assets in trust could be too great brings about the automatic return of the excess assets without any act of retransfer on the part of the trustee (due to the 'radical right' of the settlor: this notion has feudal origins): Wilson and Duncan, p. 18.

[178] *Barclays Bank Ltd v. Quistclose Investments Ltd* (1968); a similar decision in *Re Kayford Ltd.* (1975); applied in *Carreras Rothmans v. Freeman* (1985); *Re EVTR Ltd* (1987); *Lord Napier v. Kershaw* (1993), and in the Australian decision in *Muschinski v. Dodds* (1985).

Cf. P. J. Millett, 'The Quistclose Trust: Who Can Enforce It?', in 101 LQR (1985) 269 and, in the general area of the trust as a guarantee instrument, M. Bridge, 'The Quistclose Trust in a World of Secured Transactions', in 12 OJLS (1992) 333; on the effect on the *par condicio creditorum* see C. E. F. Rickett, 'Trusts and Insolvency: The Nature and Place of the Quistclose Trust', in Waters (ed.), *Equity* (see above, footnote 40), 325; J. Maxton, 'The Quistclose Trust in New Zealand', in 13 NZULR (1989) 303.

shareholders. A company which he controlled lent the necessary amount to Rolls Razor, stipulating that it should be used exclusively to pay the dividend. Rolls Razor informed Barclays Bank of the operation and deposited the cheque issued by the lender, providing instructions to open a special dividend account and specifying how the amount should be allocated. Some days later, Rolls Razor decided to cease activity and to go into liquidation. The bank used the balance of the dividend account (no dividends had yet been paid) to cover the overdraft in the current account. The lender took action against Rolls Razor and the bank, and demanded restitution of the amount.

The decision of the House of Lords starts from the premise that the essence of operations of this kind is that the amount lent did not become the property of the borrower, and that a trust existed over it (in this particular case in favour of the shareholders, for the payment of the dividend). This did not exclude the possibility that it would remain a loan, and that once the amount had been applied to the anticipated purpose, the lender would be entitled to restitution. In any event, the 'flexible interplay of law and equity'[179] permits the fiduciary relationship which is the basis of the delivery of the amount to the borrower to develop into a resulting trust in favour of the lender if the purpose cannot be, or is not, realized. The bank was aware of the structure of and the reasons for the operation, and therefore that the amount was the subject of a trust.[180] As a result, the bank was bound on the basis of ordinary criteria applicable to whoever knowingly receives an asset which is subject to a trust, and should not, therefore, have used the dividend account to cover the overdrawn current accounts. Consequently, when the purpose of the trust became unattainable, the bank too was bound by a resulting trust in favour of the lender, to which it had to repay the amount.

The resulting trust we have just seen (also called the 'Quistclose Trust'[181]) falls within the general principle relating to trusts which are characterized by incompleteness or ineffectiveness, as in the first rule we considered on the subject of resulting trusts. It stands out (and therefore requires separate consideration), however, because the trust which is imposed on a sum which has a specific purpose does not stem from an established trust.[182]

---

[179] 582 (per Lord Wilberforce).

[180] See the reasoning in *Carreras Rothmans v. Freeman* (1985): 'The principle . . . is that equity fastens on the conscience of the person who receives from another property transferred for a specific purpose only . . . so that such person will not be permitted to treat the property as his own or to use it for other than the stated purpose.'

[181] With reference to the name of the defendant in *Barclays Bank Ltd v. Quistclose Investments Ltd* (1968), summarized above.

[182] In this way, a point of passage is created between debt and trust, which until then belonged one to common law and the other to equity (the observation is by the Australian judge Gummow J in *Re Australian Elizabethan Theatre Trust* (1991), 693); cf. Hanbury, *Equity*, pp. 50–3.

In fact, in one of the most recent applications of the rule under review, the case simply involved the loan of a sum of money (which was not deposited in a specific account) on condition that the borrower used it exclusively to acquire a certain piece of machinery. The Court of Appeal had no difficulty in finding a trust here,[183] so that, when the attainment of the purpose became impossible due to the insolvency of the borrower, the sum lent was burdened with a resulting trust in favour of the lender.[184]

c Making over assets in the name of third parties

When a person commits a sum of money for the purchase of any asset, but the contract is made in the name of a third party (or even by a third party), it is presumed until proved to the contrary that the asset is the subject of a resulting trust, and that the named owner is the trustee of that asset in favour of the person who paid the purchase price.[185]

This is a presumption which may be rebutted by proof that the contrary is true[186] or by a stronger presumption. A typical example of the latter is the presumption of advancement inherent in family relationships,[187] especially between father and son,[188] as in a recent decision of the European Court of Justice, which applied English substantive law.[189] It is interesting to note that the presumption of advancement operates when the named owner of an asset acquired by a husband is the wife,[190] but not *vice versa*,[191] or in the

---

[183] *Re EVTR Ltd* (1987). This seems to me to be an implied trust; see Dillon LJ 649: 'it was impliedly held by the company on a resulting trust', but 'impliedly' refers to the initial trust, and not to the resulting trust which followed on the impossibility of realizing it.

[184] More precisely, the mortgagee had paid the amount to the producer of the machine and, when insolvency followed, had taken it back with certain deductions. The question was whether the amount returned by the producer was due to the lender (the beneficiary of the trust on the money) or to the assets of the insolvency.

[185] The rule has its origins in 1788 with *Dyer v. Dyer*; see *Pettit v. Pettit* (1970), 814 *per* Lord Upjohn; Maitland, *Equity* (see above, footnote 35), pp. 78–80. For American law see *Restatement, Trusts*, §§440–60.
   In *Heseltine v. Heseltine* (1971), where the wife had contributed 80% of the purchase price of a house held in the name of the husband alone, it was preferred to speak of a constructive trust (as I have already observed, terminological uncertainty is frequent in this area).   [186] Pettit, *Trusts*, p. 128.

[187] In *Austin v. Austin* (1978), the High Court of Barbados excluded couples living together.

[188] And not between uncle and nephew, even where the uncle had no issue: *Drury v. Drury* (1675). For the case of illegitimate issue in another period of history, see the considerations of Lord Eldon in *Ex parte Pye* (1811).

[189] *Webb v. Webb* (1994). On the relevance to be attached to this pronouncement, see below, chapter 3 §3.f.   [190] *Re Eykyn's Trusts* (1877).

[191] *Re Curtis* (1885); *Mercier v. Mercier* (1903).
   The disparity between husband and wife for the purposes of the presumption of advancement has been legislatively abolished in Barbados: Law of Property Act, s. 192.2; previously, see *Griffith v. Griffith* (1981).

case of a purchase by a mother on behalf of her children,[192] or in the case of cohabitation.[193] It should be noted that the presumption of advancement in favour of a wife is losing its strength in the context of the new economic relationships between spouses.[194]

If the actual purchaser does not succeed in overcoming the presumption of advancement, the asset belongs completely to the named owner:

In the Canadian decision of B v. B,[195] a father acquired a ticket for the national lottery and registered it in the name of his twelve-year-old daughter. It was the winning ticket. The father could not overcome the presumption of advancement, and the entire winnings belonged to the little girl.

The rule under review goes together with the first rule stated in the area of resulting trusts, as in the case where a husband made his wife appear as the owner of certain assets which he had purchased, with the aim of dividing tax liabilities or preventing his creditors from executing judgments against the assets.[196] The presumption of advancement prevented the husband from claiming to be the beneficiary, and so he claimed that the trust was void for illegality (a fraud on the creditors), and asked to be recognized as the beneficiary of the resulting trust which arises in the event of the nullity of a trust. The English tendency[197] is to hold that the wife has acquired full rights to the asset.[198]

---

[192] This latter clarification, based on *Bennett v. Bennett* (1879), is not completely obvious. Canadian (*Cohen v. Cohen* (1985)) and Australian (*Nelson v. Nelson* (1995)) case law are against it. For American law see Restatement, *Trusts*, §453.

A discussion which takes in the entire panorama of the Commonwealth may be found in A. Dowling, 'The Presumption of Advancement Between Mother and Child', in [1996] Conv 274.

[193] Thus two West Indian decisions: *Mahadai v. Ragabir* (1967), and *Austin v. Austin* (1978).

[194] *Silver v. Silver* (1958), 525 (*per* Evershed MR). Cf. *Pettitt v. Pettitt* (1970).   [195] 1976

[196] In *Tinker v. Tinker* (1970) (see below, p. 118), the presumption of advancement led to denial of the claims of the husband to the marital home, which he had put in the name of his wife to avoid the risk of execution of judgments by creditors (he was a businessman) (see *Gascoigne v. Gascoigne* (1918)). In *Re Emery's Investment Trusts* (1959), registration in the name of the wife was for tax reasons, but the court did not allow this to prevail against the presumption of advancement: an application of a maxim of equity, according to which a plaintiff may not use his own fraudulent conduct to obtain a benefit (the 'clean hands' theory: cf. J. C. F. Spry, *The Principles of Equitable Remedies* (4th edition), Sydney, 1990, pp. 242–5); Z. Chafee Jr., 'Coming into Equity with Clean Hands', in 47 MichLR (1949) 877, which shows the topicality of this maxim: for the maxims of equity, see below, §4. For Australian law cf. Jacobs, *Trusts*, §§1212–15. See also Graziadei, *Diritti nell'interesse altrui*, pp. 274–85 in the sense of simulation as a category unknown to English law.

'Clean hands' has the semantic meaning 'pure', not the banal 'clean'. It may be that the expression was inspired by the Latin meaning of 'purus', as in 'Puras enim exigimus esse provincialibus iudicibus manus': Nov. 8.8.

[197] Differently in Australia (*Martin v. Martin* (1963)) and, it seems, in Canada (Waters, *Trusts*, pp. 295–301).

[198] On the position with respect to the creditors of the husband, see below, chapter 3 §1.i.

d Purchase of property in common

Where the funds for the purchase of property are furnished in part by one person and in part by another, but the property is purchased only in the name of one of them, a resulting trust comes into being, and the named owner is the trustee of that property in favour of the other person in proportion to the amount which the latter has paid.

This rule covers a different situation from that described in the context of constructive trusts[199] regarding the contribution by a spouse (or other cohabitant) towards the purchase or transformation of property, which may be in the form of work carried out by that person, and may follow the purchase (for example, payment of the mortgage[200]). The legal basis is different, too, because the rule which underlies the constructive trust is based on the equitable requirement that the named owner of the property must not profit unjustly from the legitimate expectations which the other spouse had formed as a result of the contribution he or she has made. When it is actually applied, however, the lines are less clearly defined, and as I have already mentioned, disputes have arisen on more than one occasion regarding the membership of a trust in one category or the other, especially when an understanding regarding the joint ownership of the property is added to the financial contribution, even though it may only be in the name of one of the couple.[201] The distinction between presumed and automatic resulting trusts, which has been proposed[202] and contested[203] by the courts, and which would place the trust under review (and that described in the previous rule) in the first category, does not assist the clarification process, because the constructive trust, whose borders with the resulting trust are in doubt, is, as we have already seen, also frequently based upon the presumed intent of the parties.

---

[199] See above, chapter 2 §2.0.

[200] *Re Gorman* (1990); *Re Pavlou* (1993), where the wife had remained in the marital home, and the benefits she had thus obtained had to be balanced against the mortgage payments which she had made. For the mortgage as part of the purchase price and contributions by the woman to the family expenses considered as a contribution to the purchase price because they allow the husband to make the mortgage payments, see Hayton, *Trusts*, pp. 171–2.

[201] In *Drake v. Whipps* (1995), the woman had contributed both to the purchase price and to the substantial improvement costs. Probably owing to an error, her lawyer couched the request in terms of a resulting trust, while the Court of Appeal found that there was a constructive trust based on the criterion of common intent (see above, chapter 2 §2.0.

[202] *Re Vandervell's Trusts (No. 2)*, 1974.

[203] Lord Browne-Wilkinson in *Westdeutsche v. Islington* (1996), at p. 991.

Special difficulties emerge when an element of illegality is added to this intent, as in a 1993 decision:[204]

Two partners used the proceeds from their joint business to buy a house in which they lived and worked together. The house was registered in the defendant's name alone so that the plaintiff could continue to appear to be indigent and take advantage of the relevant social benefits. When the relationship came to an end, the House of Lords held by a narrow majority that the unlawful purpose did not concern the title of purchase, and was therefore irrelevant.[205] The house was subject to a resulting trust in favour of the plaintiff. This is a presumptive resulting trust, but no reason was offered by the defendant to rebut the presumption.

e *Westdeutsche v. Islington* (1996)

A unanimous House of Lords has imposed a limitation on the movement in favour of the extension of the boundaries of resulting trusts. To the extent permitted a comparative lawyer, I would like to express my unconditional approval of the decision of the House of Lords.

A bank and a local authority executed an interest-rate swap agreement, pursuant to which the bank made a first payment to the local authority. A subsequent decision of the House of Lords held that such contracts were void if signed by local authorities, and the bank took action to have the amount reimbursed. The authority did not contest the action, and the dispute arose only around the issue of whether the authority had to pay the bank simple or compound interest.

It is clear that compound interest is due from a person who acts as a trustee;[206] hence the point to be decided was whether or not the authority should be considered to be trustee of the sum it had received pursuant to a void contract.

The theory proposed by the bank, which had been accepted by both lower courts, was a linear one: the payment pursuant to a void contract 'keeps' an equitable interest in the bank's property; thus there was a separation between legal and equitable ownership, and consequently a trust was created in favour of the bank. This theory was supported by legal writings, of which we shall speak in detail at the end of this chapter, which aspire to use the structure of non-express trusts to cover what appear to be gaps in ordinary restitutory remedies.

[204] *Tinsley v. Milligan* (1993).

[205] This was the point of dissent within the court: the minority adhered to the traditional line of precedents which was mainly rooted in the maxim '*in pari causa turpitudinis*'; the majority opted for a more modern approach, linked to the social perception of unlawfulness in the specific case.

[206] The action for restitution in common law gives rise to payment of the sum which has been unjustly obtained, plus simple interest (by statute: common law courts could not traditionally order payment of interest on sums owed). A second view of the case, which is of no interest here, concerned the exercise of the equitable power to add compound interest: the majority of the House of Lords was against this.

The contrary opinion of the House of Lords hinges on two concurrent reasons: the hypothetical trustee has no perception of the rationale which would create the trust (the nullity of the contract) and, at the moment that perception was formed, the alleged subject matter of the trust no longer formed part of the trustee's patrimony (the Council had, of course, spent the funds provided by the bank for its institutional purposes). In general, the House of Lords affirmed that payments pursuant to a void contract do not by themselves have the effect of submitting the subject matter of that transaction to a resulting trust.

4. The maxims and protection of equity

a Equity follows the law

The so-called 'maxims of equity'[207] sometimes seem to be more an enigma than a legal precept.

Let us consider the maxim 'Equity follows the law'. A jurist with only superficial knowledge of the history of English law might reflect that equity is the fruit of edicts of a special legal system, that of Chancery, which was born and evolved in contrast with common law and might, therefore, interpret the maxim to mean 'equity comes after the law', with an eye to natural law, thus dramatizing the contrast between equity and technical and feudal common law. This is not at all the case: in the maxim, 'law' undoubtedly means 'common law', with direct reference to the system with which it is in competition. The key to a correct interpretation therefore lies in the verb 'follows', which must be translated as 'imitates', and not 'comes after'.[208] Equity imitates common law because it models its rules on those of common law. It represents a very advanced structural approach for its time: A. W. Scott, the great American scholar in the field of trusts, saw this at the beginning of this century, although he erred in his detailed conclusions when he reasoned that equity constructs equitable interests as common law constructs legal estates in the same assets.[209] Scott confused the structure with the contents, but his underlying intuition regarding the interpretation of the maxim was correct.

The maxims of equity, in addition to being difficult to translate, cannot

---

[207] See the detailed analysis in Edwards and Stockwell, *Trusts and Equity* (see above, footnote 130), pp. 23–45; Hanbury, *Equity*, pp. 26–31; Snell, *Equity*, pp. 27–44; G. Criscuoli, *Introduzione allo studio del diritto inglese. Le fonti*, (2nd edition), Milan, 1994, pp. 222–30.

[208] Maitland, *Equity* (see above, footnote 35), pp. 106–16; Megarry, *Real Property*, p. 56; see also Hanbury, *Equity* (see above, footnote 21), 214–15.

[209] A. W. Scott, 'The Nature of the Rights of the Cestui que Trust', in 17 ColLR (1917) 269, p. 271.

be comprehended intuitively. One of the reasons for this lies in the fact that they were not formulated to be precepts or preceptive principles, but to act as guidelines for the Courts. The grammatical subject of the maxims is equity, and the legal reference is the system as equity wishes it to be expressed in a judgment; the natural target is, therefore, the judge. The maxims of equity are rules governing the production of rules by the sources of law, or rather, by the only source which equity recognizes, which is case law.

It is here, in my view, that we find the explanation for another singular aspect of English law, which is the legislative conservation of equity case law. Take the instance of the Statute of Limitations: a legislative rule sets forth the period within which a right of action must be exercised, as is the case in every legal system, but a special rule permits equity judges to hold that a right has been barred even before the term has expired. This is the legislative acknowledgment of the maxim of equity which states: 'delays prejudice equity', by which is meant that prolonged inaction on the part of the holder of a right renders him less deserving of judicial protection.[210] It must, of course, be a right which belongs to the sphere of equity (for example, the rights of a beneficiary of a trust). The English lawmakers (like those in the United States) have identified the differing origins of the enunciation of rigid limitation periods and the flexibility of the maxims of equity; they have, I would say, identified the underlying divergence which I pointed out above between rules addressed to judges and those intended for private persons. They have not found it possible to encroach upon the former, and have thereby recognized their superior status as a customary rule-making source.[211]

b Tracing

The correct interpretation of the maxim 'equity follows the law' which we have just discussed allows us to understand the nature and purpose of 'tracing'.

Tracing in common law (and here the term 'common law' is used in its technical sense to distinguish it from equity) is a procedure which has the purpose of following an asset. It relates to movable property, which it

---

[210] 'Delay defeats equity.' This is the equitable theory of '*laches*' (perhaps from the Latin '*laxus*') retained by many laws in the area of limitations, for example by Art. 36 (2) of the Limitation Act, 1980: 'nothing in this Act shall affect any equitable jurisdiction to refuse relief on the grounds of acquiescence or otherwise'. See Spry, *Principles* (see above, footnote 196), pp. 222–42; Hanbury, *Equity*, pp. 639–40, 701–3, 758–60; on special applications in Admiralty see U. R. Vass and X. Chen, 'The Admiralty Doctrine of Laches', in 53 TulLR (1992) 495.   [211] In a more complete context see below, chapter 2 §4.d.

follows (within certain limits) through its various transmutations right to the current owner, against whom appropriate restitutory action will be taken. In this sense it has often been said that it is more of a probative technique than an action[212] (those who consider it to be an action have rightly asserted that it does not belong to the category of actions *in rem*[213]).

This procedural aspect is frequently confused with that of the effects which common law connotes with the process which follows the favourable completion of a tracing. This process belongs to the category of recovery actions (of personal property, what is more), and allows the claimant to prevail over the creditors of the defendant, even in the event of his bankruptcy. The odd (for a civilian) outcome that the judgment leads to an award of damages (in an amount equal to the value of the asset) rather than to delivery of the asset derives from the historical peculiarities of actions of *detinue* and *trover*, which it is not appropriate to discuss in detail here.[214]

Common-law tracing experiences problems when its target is money or fungible assets which can no longer be identified.[215] Equity, as we shall see, is more at ease here, in part because it can impose a charge on all sums at the defendant's disposal. This is a peculiarity of equitable tracing, which

---

[212] Pettit, *Trusts*, p. 506; P. Millett, 'Recovering' (see above, footnote 69), 72 and, in a judicial context, in *Boscawen v. Bajwa* (1995), 776. This use seems to be clear: see P. B. H. Birks, 'Trusts in the Recovery of Misapplied Assets', in E. McKendrick, *Commercial Aspects* (see above, footnote 42), pp. 149ff., at p. 157: 'it is important that tracing should be understood as a process of identification and no more'.

[213] R. M. Goode, 'The Right to Trace and Its Impact in Commercial Transactions – I', in 92 LQR (1976) 360, at 369–70.

[214] See the original analysis made by P. Matthews, 'The Legal and Moral Limits of Common Law Tracing', in P. B. H. Birks (ed.), *Laundering and Tracing*, Oxford, 1995, ch. 2.

Common law did not historically recognize an action to claim personal property (except for *replevin*, which is of little use, because of its archaic connotations and because it was limited to disputes regarding acts of self-protection by the lord), since the possessor could always liberate himself by paying the value of the asset: Megarry, *Real Property*, p. 14. The situation was changed by the Common Law Procedure Act 1854, which gave judges the discretionary power to order the defendant to deliver the asset claimed.

[215] Against this argument see, Goode, 'Right to Trace' (see above, footnote 213), 378–81. For a case of common-law tracing regarding sums deposited in a bank together with others, see *Banque Belge v. Hambrouck* (1921); recently, *Lipkin Gorman v. Karpnale* (1991) decided the claim by a law firm against a Playboy Club to recover sums paid by a partner of the firm for gambling debts, using the firm's bank account. The House of Lords permitted the tracing, holding that the law firm was the holder of a *chose in action*, that is, a credit towards the bank, and that it could, therefore, 'follow' the right as it materialized, that is, the amount leaving the account, and so into the hands of whoever might come to know of it, that is, the Playboy Club.

On both decisions, see Matthews, 'Legal and Moral Limits' (see above, footnote 214), 53–66, who holds that both interpreted the precedents wrongly.

apart from this is modelled on common-law tracing. The other obvious peculiarity is that it applies to trusts and fiduciary situations, and generally to all relationships which are regulated by equity.[216] In the area of trusts, tracing also operates when the trustee has mixed trust assets with personal assets and it therefore becomes necessary to return to the appropriate condition of separation.[217] It follows that the peculiar nature of equitable tracing is a consequence of the nature of the interest protected, which is equitable and cannot, therefore, be protected at law.[218]

Tracing in equity is, in theory, different from common-law tracing, not only because of the conditions of the action and the subject matter (equitable interests and not rights *in rem*), but also because it does not lead to a declaration that an asset belongs to the plaintiff (as in common law), but rather to the imposition of a duty on the defendant, usually to deliver.[219] For example, in the case of a tracing action against a person to whom a trust asset has been improperly transferred, the judgment assigns the duties of a trustee to the defendant, and, therefore, the reallocation of the asset to the trust property (or directly to the plaintiff). Once an action of recovery has succeeded, judgment may be executed against any third party who is not protected by the equitable rule relating to a good-faith purchaser for value,[220] which we have already described, and is not affected by any transformation which the asset may have undergone in the meantime. This has two important consequences, both of which are transparently modelled on common-law procedure. The first is that in the event a trustee becomes bankrupt, a tracing action by the beneficiary leads to his not being in competition with the trustee's creditors, following the general rule relating to the segregation of trust assets from the trustee's property:[221] in

---

[216] This clarification has long been, and still remains, controversial (in the important decision in *Re Hallett* (1880), it was limited to fiduciary relationships; see the recent opinion of Millet J in *Agip v. Jackson* (1991)), but those who disagree with it state that equity is very liberal in finding the existence of fiduciary relationships (see above, chapter 2 §2.a): P. Oliver, 'The Extent of Equitable Tracing', in [1995] TLI 78. More restrictive are Goff and Jones, *Restitution*, pp. 83–6.

[217] For a historical introduction to these topics, see A. J. Oakley, 'The Prerequisites of an Equitable Tracing Claim', in 28 CLP (1975) 64.

[218] D. J. Hayton, in 'Developing the Law of Trusts for the Twenty-First Century', in 87 LQR (1990) 87, at 98, expresses the opinion that equitable tracing is probably developing in the direction of also being available to whoever may claim a 'legal base' (Oakley, 'Prerequisites' (see above, footnote 217) was more open on these lines, p. 82); Hayton, without stating it explicitly, refers to a person whose title in law does not have equitable limitations (on this concept see below, chapter 2 §5.c).

[219] For comparisons with Roman Law, see Johnston, *Roman Trusts*, pp. 227–33.

[220] See above, chapter 2 §2.b.

[221] See recently Rickett, 'Trusts and Insolvency' (see above, footnote 178); T. Oditah, 'Assets

any case, in equity the claimed asset 'belongs' to the plaintiff, who is, therefore, not a creditor like the others; he is demanding that which in equity is *his* (this terminology will be explained below). The second is that once the asset has been converted from one form to another (for example, money into the real property which it was used to purchase), the new asset is likewise considered to belong to the plaintiff 'in equity'. It is irrelevant that at the moment in which it is discovered by the plaintiff it may be worth considerably more than the asset (in this case the money) to which the plaintiff would otherwise have had a right. These two aspects are connected with a third: if an unfaithful fiduciary acquires property with funds which have been entrusted to him and, when pursued by the plaintiff, delivers the property to him, the transfer is not subject to revocation in bankruptcy proceedings.[222]

It may appear that these considerations have practical application where a dispute concerns assets which have been identified; on the contrary, they are most frequently applied in cases where the dispute involves sums of money, which is the classic example of an asset which can be dissipated or commingled, or property which has been identified but has been sold and converted into money (and then, perhaps, invested in real property).[223] Where the acquirer of an asset is safe from the beneficiary's tracing action because the circumstances of the acquisition do not render him subject to the two types of constructive trust which we discussed above,[224] or because the asset no longer exists,[225] the beneficiary's action lies against the trustee, and its objective is, therefore, the money which he has obtained. If, on the other hand, the acquirer of the asset is held to be a constructive trustee of it, the action will be against the money if the acquirer has transferred the asset to a third party who is not a constructive trustee.

Equity has developed complicated rules for tracing money, and for following the 'trail' into assets into which the money has been converted. When sums of money are being followed, the rules relating to the so-called mixed funds are observed. This is normal practice in cases where the trustee has deposited the sums together with his own money, and has then used them in unidentifiable ways.[226] By the use of presumptions, equity

---

and the Treatment of Claims in Insolvency', in 108 LQR (1992) 459; H. Anderson, 'The Treatment of Trust Assets in English Insolvency Law', in E. McKendrick, *Commercial Aspects* (see above, footnote 42), p. 167.   [222] *Taylor v. Plumer* (1815).

[223] On this and other general aspects, see P. G. Jaeger, *Separazione* (see above, footnote 43), pp. 210–22; Graziadei, *Diritti nell'interesse altrui*, pp. 453–62 (above all for procedural aspects).

[224] See above, chapter 2 §2.b–§2.c.

[225] *Re Diplock* (1948), at p. 521; see also *Borden v. Scottish Timber* (1981), at p. 46.

[226] Cf., though dated, R. H. Maudsley, 'Proprietary Remedies for the Recovery of Money', in

correlates the money which is the object of the tracing with investments or purchases subsequently made by the trustee (or by anyone who has improperly received sums from him, thus in turn becoming trustee of those sums).[227]

When the sums of money which are the subject of the tracing have been invested with other funds in a durable asset which already belonged to the defendant, the plaintiff enjoys a privileged position with respect to the asset (an 'equitable charge'), and may have the asset sold and obtain satisfaction from the proceeds.[228] Where, on the other hand, the sums have been spent in such a way that they cannot be recovered (in payment of debts, for example), the plaintiff has to content himself with the normal protection afforded to a creditor, unless he is in a position to be able to avail himself of the higher levels of protection available to the payer, whose place he takes.

75 LQR (1959) 234, especially at pp. 239–43. Among recent applications, one of the more complex is *Space Investments v. Canadian* (1986) (on which see below, chapter 3, footnote 376), the reasoning behind which gave rise to diverse positions in case law: see the New Zealand decision *Liggett v. Kensington* (1993), rejected in its entirety by the Privy Council (under the name *Re Goldcorp Exchange* (1995): see below, pp. 140–41).

[227] Please refer to the manuals: Pettit, *Trusts*, pp. 508–10; Underhill, *Trusts*, pp. 852–6; 860–3; Jacobs, *Trusts*, §§ 2714–17; Hanbury, *Equity*, pp. 646–68; also Birks, *Restitution*, pp. 363–70; Goff and Jones, *Restitution*, pp. 86–93; Keeton and Sheridan, *Equity* (see above, footnote 29), pp. 505–13. It should be pointed out, nevertheless, that the traditional rules in this area are nowadays seen as being in need of revision: see the New Zealand decision *Registered Securities* (1991), with reference to *Clayton's Case* of 1816, and the opinions of Woolf LJ and Leggatt LJ in *Barlow Clowes v. Vaughan* (1992).

The customary law of Ghana recognizes analogous rules: see S. K. B. Asante, 'Fiduciary Principles in Anglo-American Law and the Customary Law of Ghana – A Comparative Study', in 14 ICLQ (1965) 1144, at 1178–81.

[228] Goff and Jones, *Restitution*, pp. 83–6, correctly point out that the equitable tracing rules were developed with reference principally to trusts, so that courts' discretion must, in the case of complex tracing, identify the most appropriate action on a case-by-case basis.

Bishopgate v. Homan (1995), was one of the procedures connected with the death of the publisher Robert Maxwell and the collapse of his group: a pension fund which he controlled had deposited significant sums into an overdrawn account belonging to one of the companies of the group. The company was placed in liquidation, but now had substantial liquidity following the sale of a part of its assets, and was on the point of making a first distribution to its creditors. The trustees of the pension fund sought to block the distribution on the grounds that the company's assets were encumbered by an equitable charge in their favour. Their demand was rejected on the grounds that it was not possible for a tracing to have a non-existent asset, or, to be precise, a debt, as its purpose, such as that arising out of the relationship between the company (into whose overdrawn account the sums were deposited) and the bank. An equitable charge presupposes the possibility of a tracing and continuity, whether physical or consequent upon the transformation of a physical asset. Although it was handed down by the Court of Appeal, this judgment is unsatisfactory due to the excessive technicality which it inspires.

This decision is in line with the equally unsatisfactory judgment of the Privy Council *In re Goldcorp Exchange* (1995), on which see below, pp. 140–41.

It is pertinent to refer to a recent decision of the Court of Appeal on the subject:[229]

Mr. B agreed to sell some real property to an individual who was to finance the purchase by means of a bank loan secured by a mortgage on the property. The property, however, was subject to a charge in favour of third parties. The bank transferred the funds to the purchaser's lawyers so that they could take care of the repayment of the charge. They carried out their duties, but the sale was not concluded.

Creditors of Mr. B distrained the property, which was by now free of the charge, and secured a judicial sale. The bank asserted a claim to the proceeds of the sale, declaring that since the money had been spent by the lawyers in the context of a fiduciary relationship, it could be followed, and the bank could obtain every advantage consequent upon the manner in which it had been used.[230] Since the money was to be provided to Mr. B only when the sale had been concluded and the mortgage in favour of the bank had been recorded, the Court held that the bank substituted the third-party holder of the charge and was therefore privileged with respect to Mr. B's ordinary creditors. Accordingly, the proceeds of the sale belonged to the bank.

The relationship between tracing and the constructive trust is somewhat nebulous, although in theory the former is a probationary procedure, while the latter belongs to substantive law. In borderline cases, as we shall see in the next section, the constructive trust tends to be the subject matter of a judgment which, once entered, gives the beneficiary access to a tracing proceeding.

A tracing commenced against a volunteer in good faith[231] may in some cases give rise to the defence that the trust property was used in a manner which makes the plaintiff's claim seem inequitable: for example, where the volunteer has spent trust funds to improve certain of his property, his good faith saves him from the imposition of a charge on that property. This is not the case if the volunteer acts in bad faith[232] or, according to an alternative

---

[229] *Boscawen v. Bajwa* (1995).

[230] Tracing caused some problems, because the money had passed from the bank to the purchaser's lawyers, then to the lawyers of Mr. B, and then to the lawyers of the owner.

[231] As we have already seen, a volunteer is a person who does not provide consideration.

[232] Only recently have these rules (called 'change of position') been definitively accepted in England: *Lipkin Gorman v. Karpnale* (1991) (House of Lords), with the warning that they had to be developed on the basis of the cases; in this instance (see the facts above, footnote 215), the Playboy Club was ordered to return not the sums spent by the lawyer, but only his gambling losses. For earlier decisions, see *Re Diplock* (1948); *R v. Tower Hamlets* (1988); *Rover International Ltd v. Cannon* (1989); cf. Hanbury, *Equity*, pp. 668–71 and, for a complete review of the matter, P. Key, 'Change of Position', in 58 MLR (1995) 505.

In the different sense of unjust enrichment, see Birks, *Restitution*, pp. 410–15, and the critical comments of Matthews, 'The Legal and Moral Limits' (see above, footnote 214), pp. 57–8 and 66–70. For American law, see G. K. Scott, 'Restitution from an Innocent

reading of the precedents, if he was in a position to know that the sum received was not due him.[233]

Leaving aside other considerations, it is precisely this *fungibility of the object of the beneficiary's action* which places it outside the ambit of real actions. As has been well put recently,[234] equitable tracing may be explained by considering that the right of the beneficiary relates not to the *res* which is the object of the trust, but to its value, or the *quantum* of wealth which is within the *res*, or else, where there was a sum of money from the start, by imposing a charge on any funds into which that sum has been deposited (and, naturally, on any later transformations[235]).

Tracing serves the rights of the trust beneficiary. These rights therefore need to be identified, and we shall attempt to achieve this at the end of chapter 3. At the same time, we shall illustrate the means by which equity attacks an ownership right. Nevertheless, if we identify tracing on the basis of the notions available to us up to this point, it is easy to see that it is employed within the framework of a personal, not a real action, notwithstanding the fact that English writers often write of a 'proprietary remedy', of a 'real right available in equity',[236] or, more correctly, of an 'equitable obligation *in rem*'.[237] It should be remembered in this regard that since the earliest case law on trusts it has been the *conscience of the defendant* which is constrained by conduct which causes damage to the beneficiaries,[238] and, in the words of the maxim of equity which historically created the procedural remedy which is the injunction, 'equity acts *in personam*'.[239]

There are three further observations to be made on this subject. The first is that, as was noted a hundred years ago, the Court of Chancery did not have the power to issue judgments declaring or creating real rights.[240] The

Purchaser who is not a Purchaser for Value', in 62 HarvardLR (1949) 1002; Scott, *Trusts*, §480; Restatement, *Restitution*, §178.

[233] *Boscawen v. Bajwa* (1995), *per* Millett LJ at 779.

[234] B. Rudden, 'Things as Thing and Things as Wealth', in 14 OJLS (1994) 81.

[235] We saw an example of this in *El Ajou*, see above, p. 33.

[236] Goode, 'Right to Trace' (see above, footnote 213).

[237] Gardner, *Introduction*, ch. 13. Cf. D. W. M. Waters, 'The Common Law Trust in the Modern World', in *Forum Internationale*, 1984, 3, at 4–5; Hanbury, *Equity*, pp. 18–21.

[238] See the decision of 1471, in YB, Trin. II Edw. IV, fo. 8, recalled by F. W. Maitland, *Selected Essays*, H. D. Hazeltine, G. Lapsley, P. H. Winfield (eds.), Cambridge, 1936, p. 166, footnote 1: 'Si mon feoffee de trust etc. enfeoffa un autre que conust bien que le feoffor rien ad forsque a mon use subpoena girra vers ambideux: scil auxibien vers le feoffee come vers le feoffor . . . pur ceo que en conscience il purchase ma terre.' The same source of inspiration is followed in *Sinclair v. Brougham* (1914), on which see Oakley, 'Prerequisites' (see above, footnote 217), 74–80.   [239] See below, chapter 2 §4.f.

[240] Langdell, 'Brief Survey' (see above, footnote 119), 118.

second is that tracing does not necessarily lead to the identification of an asset to be transferred to the plaintiff, because one possible outcome of the tracing is the imposition of a charge, which has the effect of placing the plaintiff in a privileged position with respect to the other creditors. The third is a consequence of the extension of the action to all fiduciary circumstances and beyond: in many tracing situations, the plaintiff has never had a right, either in common law or in equity, to the asset which he is following in his action; we have seen an example of this in the constructive trust imposed on those who accept bribes or secret commissions.[241] Tracing therefore has the effect of transferring to the plaintiff ownership of an asset which has never been his, or of a second asset to which the 'trail' of the first has led, and which may belong to a person other than the one who originally had the fiduciary obligation. It is not, as we have just recalled, the *res* which is followed; nevertheless, what the plaintiff obtains is by definition segregated from the remainder of the defendant's property, and the defendant is subject to the customary obligations of a trustee.

c Fraud and legal requirements

The significance of the diversity between the written law and equity, which is where we left the subject 'equity follows the law', is perfectly recognized in the maxim 'equity does not allow a statute to be made an instrument of fraud',[242] of which we have already seen some examples in the area of constructive trusts, and in the peculiar equitable notion of 'fraud'.

The written law as formally passed by Parliament is affected by an intrinsic limitation each time it is called upon to operate in the world of equity. There is, in all probability, another influential fact: equity is a system based on conscience. Recent *dicta* have reaffirmed this, and have applied it in contexts which are far from those of the origins of equity:[243] the manner in which it is applied, although frequently leading to propositions which are very technical, and difficult for the civil-law jurist to understand, follows a process of development which is essentially different from that followed by codified (English) law.

In the light of these considerations, it is easy to understand why, in the preliminary remarks with which I began this book, I contested the traditional view of equity as a supplement to common law, and concluded that, in fact, it was a restrictive and outdated belief. Both common law and

---

[241] See above, p. 25.
[242] Sheridan, *Fraud in Equity* (see above, footnote 31), pp. 146–66.
[243] Recently, *Westdeutsche v. Islington* (1996) see above, chapter 2 §3.e.

statute law are frequently willing rivals of equity.[244] This rivalry was born out of the incurable diversity between equity and common and statute law (there is also rivalry between the latter two, as a consequence of the assertion that common law had earlier origins; it is manifested, for example, in claims of the inherent jurisdiction of judges[245] and in the survival of doctrines and rules of common law after centuries of obscurity[246] or after the enactment of laws on the same subject matter (except, naturally, where they are expressly repealed). Not only is equity not a 'supplement' (even though from the beginning it has shrewdly presented itself as such), but it is recognized by the legislature itself to be a combination of principles and rules which in general cannot be traced back to laws emanating from the legislature. On the contrary, the legislature often orders that formal recourse be had to the rules of equity, and blunts the rivalry by limiting its own powers in favour of equity. The opposite is never true.

The evolution of modern English law in the area of the form of the creation of a trust seems to me to offer solid support to this statement.

d Equity and the form of the trust instrument

When the Statute of Frauds was passed in 1677, the creation of trusts was shrouded in secrecy. 'Trust or Confidence' was a popular hendiadys with deep roots in legal terminology and, one might correctly say, in everyday language.[247] The secrecy evolved from the absence of rules relating to the form of the *negotium*, in contrast with the publicity which accompanied the

---

[244] This is the provocative theory of B. Rudden, 'Equity as Alibi', in S. Goldstein (ed.), *Equity and Contemporary Legal Developments*, Hebrew University of Jerusalem, 1992, p. 30; the result is that equity took for itself areas of law which the common law had refrained from claiming, and that the traditional common-law procedures did not take advantage of remedies of equitable origin, which have been available for over a century since the acclaimed fusion of the two jurisdictions.

The decision of the House of Lords in *Westdeutsche v. Islington* (1996), in which it refused to grant compound interest in an action for money had and received (see above, chapter 2 §3.e) seems to confirm the interpretation of Rudden.

[245] For its application in the area of the trust see H. H. Camp, 'The Variation of Trusts Act 1958: A Departure from Traditional Principles of Trust Law', in 34 TulLR (1959) 87.

[246] 'Loss of a common law remedy by desuetude would I think be a novelty in our law and I see no advantage in introducing such a principle'; 'I do not know of any doctrine of irrevocable desuetude in the doctrines of the common law': *per* Lord Reid and Lord Kilbrandon, respectively, in *McKendrick v. Sinclair* (1972). Cf. J. M. Thomson, 'Desuetude and the Common Law', in 89 LQR (1973) 27.

[247] See the report of a case from 1560, *Katharine, Duchess of Suffolk v. Herenden*, published by J. A. Baker, 'The Use upon a Use in Equity 1558–1625', in 93 LQR (1977) 33, at 37: 'tout ceo conveiance fuit sur truste et confidence'.

livery of seisin of transfers in common law (in the area of real property).

Voices of alarm were raised in several quarters, principally by supporters of the feudal prerogative. It had been possible to dispose of personal property by will for little more than a century (Statute of Wills (1540)), and the indiscriminate use of trusts further wore away the certainty of ownership and weakened the chains of feudal loyalty.[248] Lord Nottingham, who had an important role in the drafting of that part of the statute which concerned equity (even though several portions of his text were in the end radically revised), was of the opinion that any transfer of real property required a writing, and should otherwise be declared null and void.[249] A different conclusion, that the writing had a purely probative purpose, prevailed.[250] As far as the creation of trusts was concerned, the principle was codified in section 7 of the law of 1677,[251] and lasted in England, in this area and in contracts and other dispositive acts in land law, until 1989, when it was abolished only for the latter cases.[252] It is still in existence in many of the legal systems which were influenced by the English system.[253] Section 8, however, excludes those trusts which today we call constructive or resulting trusts.[254] Current English law still holds both to the rule and

---

[248] Cf. P. Hamburger, *The Conveyancing Purposes of the Statute of Frauds*, in 27 AmJLH (1983) 354.

[249] Youdan, 'Formalities for Trusts' (see above, footnote 2), 313.

[250] For a modern view of the Statute of Frauds, especially of s. 4, on the principle of written proof, see Spry, *Principles* (see above, footnote 196), pp. 245–84.

[251] 'All declaration or creations of trusts or confidences of any lands, tenements or hereditaments, shall be manifested and proved by some writing signed by the party who is by law entitled to declare such trust, or by his last will in writing . . .'

[252] Law of Property (Miscellaneous Provisions) Act 1989; cf. Megarry, *Real Property*, pp. 116–22.

[253] Law of Property Act 1925, s. 53(1)(b): 'A declaration of trust respecting any land or any interest therein must be manifested and proved by some writing signed by some person who is able to declare such trust or by his will.'

   No formality is required, on the other hand, for trusts of assets other than 'land'.

   Once a trust has been created the written form is required for any act of transfer, otherwise it is voidable (even, notwithstanding the evident contradiction, where the trust has as its subject matter assets or rights transferable without formality: cf. Pettit, *Trusts*, p. 86): 'A disposition of an equitable interest or trust subsisting at the time of the disposition, must be in writing signed by the person disposing of the same, or by his agent . . .'

   On the form of the transfer of immovable property to the trustee, see above, footnote 142.

[254] 'Provided always that where any conveyance shall be made of any lands or tenements, by which a trust or confidence shall or may arise or result by the implication or construction of law . . . such trust or confidence shall be of the like force and effect as the same would have been if this Statute had not been made.'

   See now the Law of Property Act 1925, s. 53(2): 'This section does not affect the creation or operation of resulting, implied or constructive trusts.'

the exception, so that trusts which are not expressly established are exempt from any requirements as to form.[255]

Equity has, nevertheless, prevailed over the provisions of the law in cases where it was faced with examples of express trusts created without the formal requirements being complied with; that is, where the settlor had observed the rules regarding the manner of transfer to the trustee,[256] but not those regarding the declaration of the trust.[257] The trustee had, therefore, acquired the property, and wished to keep it, while claiming that the trust had not been validly established. Conduct of this kind appeared to be fraud, and since 1897[258] it has been held that if the settlor could present witnesses to prove the creation of a trust[259] then this was not constructive or resulting, but express or presumptive.[260] Accordingly, the courts did not hide behind section 8 of the law,[261] but faced the rule on form (section 7) head on and defeated it in the name of the canons of equity, taking strength from the paradoxical argument that if they decided otherwise the

[255] The rules of the Statute of Frauds which we have illustrated were in force in England until 1925, when they were reformulated without substantial innovations (it should be nonetheless taken into consideration that the Law of Property Act 1925 followed the Law of Property Act 1922 and the Law of Property (Amendment) Act 1924; the laws of 1922 and 1924 are considered reforms, while that of 1925 is a consolidation). The consequences in the area of interpretation are important: see Megarry, *Real Property*, pp. 12–13.

In Canada, the original text of the Statute of Frauds is still in force in some provinces, while in others the language has been brought up to date; the same may be said of the United States: Waters, *Trusts*, pp. 188–9; Scott, *Trusts*, §40.1 and for Australia: Jacobs, *Trusts*, §§701–9.

[256] There would be no problem if the form of transfer were to be lacking, since there would not be any effective transfer.

[257] The first research on the subject, which compared the English and American solutions of the time, was carried out by J. B. Ames, 'Constructive Trusts Based Upon the Breach of an Express Oral Trust of Land', in *Lectures* (see above, footnote 175), 425ff.

[258] *Rochefoucauld v. Boustead* (1897) (Court of Appeal).

[259] Typical of this approach is the judgment of the High Court of Trinidad and Tobago, *Kunja v. Bruce* (1984), which dealt with a case like many others of oral agreements, with respect to which adherence to legal principles regarding the form of the documents would be in disharmony with common sentiment. The plaintiff wished to acquire land, but did not have the entire amount necessary; the defendant agreed to lend him the difference, had the plaintiff give him the money he had, and purchased the land in his name on the understanding that he would transfer it to the plaintiff when the loan had been repaid. The defendant was held to be trustee of the land for the plaintiff.

[260] The conceptual explanations of the prior judgments are less clear, although they reached the same result when they found for a trust: see, for example, *Davies v. Otty (No. 2)* (1865), and *Haigh v. Kaye* (1872). See, recently, *Neville v. Wilson* (1996) (see above, footnote 152).

[261] Now s. 53(2) of the Law of Property Act, 1925, which was not amended by the Law of Property (Miscellaneous Provisions) Act 1989.

trustee's fraud would prevail thanks to the very law (the Statute of Frauds) which had been passed to suppress fraud.

e 'Equity looks at that as done which ought to have been done'

This maxim has the effect of transporting the consequences of an action which a person has not yet carried out, but which he has the duty of carrying out, into the present. In other words, it considers an obligation which has not yet been performed as having already been carried out (even if the period within which it was to be performed has not yet expired).[262]

One of the most notable applications of this maxim gave rise to the theory of conversion, which is worth illustrating even though it has been repealed with effect from 1 January 1997.[263] Where the trust instrument provides that the trustee should sell real property, administer the proceeds so as to provide the income to the beneficiaries, and divide the proceeds among them after a certain period, the beneficiaries' interest is in a sum of money from the moment of the creation of the trust and, as a result, throughout the period required by the trustee to sell the property.[264] Accordingly, if a beneficiary dies before the property has been sold, leaving his real property to Tom, and his personal property to Dick, his interest in the trust passes to Dick.[265] This is an application of the principle of conversion, by which the legal category to which property belongs no longer depends on its type, but on that of the property into which it is to be transferred or converted, and equity converts the 'is to be' into 'is'. A trust which provides for an unconditional obligation on the part of the trustee to sell gives rise to a conversion.

This has numerous consequences.[266] For example, the constructive trust which we saw arising between the time of the execution of the purchase and sale agreement and the transfer of the rights of ownership is based on the conversion of the rights of the seller from the property to the purchase price, because the time required to perform an obligation sanctioned by

---

[262] Cf. Maitland, *Equity* (see above, footnote 35), Lecture 18.

[263] Trusts of Land and Appointment of Trustees Act 1996, s. 3.

[264] Cf. W. J. Swadling, 'Beneficial Co-Ownership Behind a Resulting Trust and the Problems of a Trust for Sale', in [1986] Conv 379.

[265] I have taken this example from Pettit, *Trusts*, p. 679. I have simplified the circumstances and omitted the distinction between real and personal property, on which see Lupoi, *Appunti*, pp. 32–5, 143–8; Gambaro, 'La proprietà' (see above, footnote 9), pp. 60–72.

[266] They were even more numerous in the system of succession prior to 1925, when there were different rules of hereditary devolution depending on whether it concerned real or personal property. For the identification of the moment and process of codification of the distinction, see B. Rudden, *The New River. A Legal History*, Oxford, 1985, pp. 213–20.

equity must not cause damage to the creditor.[267] The purchaser is, therefore, the owner in equity, even though the seller remains the owner under common law.[268] The constructive trust operates to impose a trust on the rights of the seller, and the purchaser is the beneficiary of that trust until the formalities of transfer have been completed.

Similarly, a constructive trust which has a bribe as its subject matter (and thereafter every asset which it is used to acquire) has been justified in terms of an application of the maxim 'equity looks at that as done which ought to have been done'. In fact, it has been reasoned that the fiduciary has the duty to deliver to his principal all sums he has received. In equity, they belong to the principal, and not to the fiduciary, from the moment they were paid. As a result, the constructive trust safeguards the legal position of the principal, as in every case where a fiduciary has appropriated an asset which has been entrusted to him.[269]

Given that the provisions of the laws often refer to the notion of 'owner', the application of the theory of conversion might lead to results which the legislators did not intend, so that they find themselves constrained to explain that conversion will not be taken into consideration with regard to certain rules. As we know, English law frequently confirms the *judge-made* rules of equity.[270]

f 'Equity acts *in personam*': the injunction

The injunction is a typical equitable procedural remedy, and remained beyond the power of the common-law courts until the mid-nineteenth century. There is a maxim of equity which states 'equity acts *in personam*', with reference both to the conscience of the defendant and to the procedural mechanism leading to the judicial edict which is the injunction.[271]

With regard to the former, the maxim considers the *persona* to be the yardstick for every rule of equity, which is considered to be a system based on conscience; with regard to the latter, it is in the *persona*, and not in the subject matter of the dispute, that the maxim identifies both the recipient of the edict and the mechanism for carrying it out.

The injunction may be issued at the conclusion of the action, while it is

[267] I use 'creditor' in the civilian sense of a person who has a right to demand performance.
[268] *Hillingdon Estates Co v. Stonefield Estates Ltd* (1952) (*per* Vaisey J, 631).
[269] Birks, *Restitution*, pp. 387–9 and R. M. Goode, 'Ownership and Obligation in Commercial Transactions', in 103 LQR (1987) 433, at 441–5, take a different position, but it precedes the recent case law on which I base the rule expressed. See above, chapter 2 §2.a.
[270] It should nevertheless be remembered that the Trusts of Land and Appointment of Trustees Act 1996, s. 3, has restricted conversion to testamentary trusts where the testator died before the law came into effect.
[271] Cf. Spry, *Principles* (see above, footnote 196), pp. 317–553.

in progress or before it has been commenced. Its contents may be positive or negative, its duration limited or permanent. As we shall see when we discuss specific performance, the dualism between common law and equity is revealed in the prohibition against the issuing of an injunction where an award of damages (which is a typical remedy of the common-law courts) proves to be appropriate to protect the plaintiff's interests. Consequently, case law in equity tends to grant an injunction in cases where the value of the right which has been damaged is not easy to quantify.

In the area of trusts, an injunction against a trustee usually has an inhibitory purpose, to protect beneficiaries who have reason to fear a breach of the obligations arising out of the trust.[272] The sanction which is applied in the event of non-compliance is contempt of court, a term which does not mean 'lack of respect for the court', but rather 'disobedience of an order of a judge'.[273] The contempt arises solely out of the non-compliance, without any significance being attached to the legitimacy of the order or the intention of the person committing it (these circumstances are, however, taken into account when imposing the punishment).[274] The sentence may be up to two years in prison.[275] The judge may limit himself to the imposition of a financial sanction or may use indirect means of coercion, such as sequestration of assets.[276] The whole field of injunctions has been in evolution over the past twenty years, and even today there remain uncertainties in several areas.[277] These are due in

---

[272] See, for example, *Express Newspapers v. Keys* (1980): threat of an illegal strike which would have prevented publication of a daily newspaper; in the area of strikes, see also *Hubbard v. Pitt* (1975).

[273] See recently, *Polly Peck v. Nadir* (1992) (order to a trustee not to dispose of an asset).

[274] Those who may be interested in seeking the origins of this expression and its meaning in European common law of the High Middle Ages may refer to my essay 'Il diritto comune europeo in Inghilterra: profili terminologici', in M. Lupoi, L. Moccia and P. Prosperetti (eds.) *Scintillae Iuris – Saggi in memoria di Gino Gorla*, Milan, 1994, 1965, II, §4.

[275] This subject matter is now partially regulated by a special law: Contempt of Court Act, 1981; see also the procedural rules in the Rules of Supreme Court, ord. 45, r. 5.

[276] It should be noted that in the United States the sentence for contempt of court may often be of indefinite duration, that is, until the judge's order has been obeyed (as was the case in England until passage of the special law of 1981).

For a review of civil contempt as an instrument to force the reluctant party to obey (and not as a punishment for disobedience), see L. S. Bares, 'Civil Contempt and the Rational Contemnor', in 69 IndLJ (1994) 723.

[277] For recent decisions on contempt of court see *In re R* (1994); *Villiers v. Villiers* (1994); *Burton v. Winters* (1993); *R v. Clerkenwell Metropolitan Stipendiary Magistrate* (1992); *Duo v. Osborne* (1992); *R v. Palmer* (1992); *Universal Thermosensors v. Hibben* (1992); *M v. Home Office* (1992).

As is usual in criminal matters, the directors of a company may be punished for violation of an injunction issued against the company (*Director General of Fair Trading v. Buckland* (1990)), and a third party who collaborates in the violation may also be punished (*Acro v. Rex Chainbelt* (1971)).

part to the essentially discretionary nature of the device,[278] which therefore does not lend itself to the enunciation of precise rules, and in part to the multiplicity of considerations which a judge must take into account before granting the injunction or issuing it subject to certain conditions. Among these considerations are the traditional maxims of equity, such as 'he who comes into equity must come with clean hands',[279] or 'he who seeks equity must do equity', or, of course, the one we have discussed above, 'delays prejudice equity'.

In the developments in case law to which I have referred two novel forms of protection are relevant: the 'Mareva Injunction' and 'Anton Piller Orders'.[280] Both – but above all the former – have attracted the attention of comparative lawyers throughout the world, in part because they represent the discovery of procedural techniques which are well known in civil law. They have been likened to the French *sequestre* and to the order to a party to show a document,[281] but the comparison is a false one, firstly because the *regulae* formulated by the case law regarding these two forms of protection interact with the maxims of equity; and secondly because the remedies are completely discretionary.

Let me make one final point (leaving it to books on the subject to deal with these complex subjects): in contempt-of-court proceedings, the judge adopts a strange position, as if he were the injured party, and he has the power (although it is exercised only rarely) to act on his own initiative against the offending party.

---

[278] One of the most discussed points concerns the 'prima facie case' of the plaintiff's claim. See, *inter alia*, J. T. Stratford v. Lindley (1964); American Cyanamid v. Ethicon (1975); Mothercare v. Robson Books (1979); De Falco v. Crawley (1980); Locobail v. Agroexport (1986); R v. Kensington Borough Council (1989). On injunctions in general, see A. Frignani, *L'injunction nella common law e l'inibitoria nel diritto italiano*, Milan, 1974, where the origins of the institution are described (pp. 38–65).
    The decision of the House of Lords in American Cyanamid v. Ethicon (1975), enunciated the principle whereby the burden of the claimant was limited to demonstrating that his claim was not without foundation. It was, as has been pointed out, an action to obtain an injunction to prevent actions being taken before the case on the merits was filed (the so-called *quia timet*) and it was therefore argued that a heavier burden falls upon the claimant where the request is for a final injunction or an injunction ordering the defendant to do some positive act. In this way, the principles enunciated earlier by the House of Lords in J. T. Stratford v. Lindley (1964) (cf. Hanbury, *Equity*, 740–52) and the classic theory of the prima facie case, comparable to the Italian *fumus boni iuris* are saved (see Locobail International v. Agroexport (1988)). The fact remains that English case law has shown notable generosity in the granting of injunctions in recent years.
[279] For the prevention of disclosure of confidential information, see Goff and Jones, *Restitution*, pp. 662–5.   [280] For an application of this, see above, footnote 196.
[281] On the latter in cases of breach of confidence see Gurry, *Breach of Confidence* (see above, footnote 53), pp. 417–27.

g 'Equity acts *in personam*': specific performance

Another typical form of protection in equity is specific performance, which belongs to the same systematic context as the injunction.[282] It has no special application in the field of trusts, its basic function being a general one, namely to provide protection when the purely compensatory remedies available under common law prove inadequate. There are recent developments in certain contractual areas, where, for example, a party is instructed not to avail himself of a right which in that particular case would lead to a result which would be unacceptable in equity.[283]

One point of contact between common law and equity occurs where a party undertakes to establish a trust relating to certain property. There is a clear rule that it is not possible to obtain an order for specific performance of a promise of, or a 'preliminary agreement' for, a trust in favour of a volunteer (a person who has not promised or supplied consideration). This is because, in the words of another maxim of equity, 'equity will not assist volunteers.' It should be noted that equity and common law take divergent positions in this area, too: in common law, a promise contained in a document bearing a seal is always binding, and the seal, it is often said, replaces the consideration required in every contract. In equity, on the other hand, one looks at the substance, and a seal does not change the fact that the promisee is a volunteer, and does not, therefore, merit protection.[284] In English law,[285] there is also the special case of a promise to create a trust of assets which the settlor has yet to acquire, either because they belong to third parties or because the assets are in the form of money which the settlor will obtain from the sale of property.[286]

h The receiver

A receiver may be nominated by a court to protect the integrity of trust assets or to ensure that the trust is properly administered. In the latter case,

---

[282] Among the most recent applications, see *Gidrxsleme v. Tantomartransportes* (1995); the issue of a Mareva injunction against a bank requires exceptional circumstances, see *Polly Peck v. Nadir (No. 2)* (1992).

[283] In general: E. Fry, *A Treatise on the Specific Performance of Contracts* (6th edition) by G. R. Northcote, London, 1985, and, with a more modern outlook, G. Jones and W. Goodhart, *Specific Performance*, London, 1986; Spry, *Principles* (see above, footnote 196), pp. 50–316.

[284] Among the most frequent cases are those which permit a party to recover the asset granted due to failure to pay an instalment: see M. Pawlowski, 'The Scope of Equity's Jurisdiction to Relieve against Forfeiture of Interests in Property other than Land', in JBL, 1994, 372. For the contiguous problem of sales on instalment see T. G. Youdan, 'Equitable Relief for Defaulting Purchasers of Land', in Waters, *Equity* (see above, footnote 40), p. 241.   [285] Hanbury, *Equity*, p. 686; Snell, *Equity*, pp. 120–1.

[286] Not in American law; see Scott, *Trusts*, §17.3.

the most common procedure is the substitution of one trustee by another. For instance,[287] a receiver was appointed by a decree to administer union funds because the trustees were about to transfer them abroad, thereby removing them from the grasp of an existing attachment order.

The difference between the appointment of a receiver and the substitution of one trustee by another lies in the fact that the receiver is an aide to the judge, and answers to the judge (and not to the beneficiaries).[288]

5. Equity and non-express trusts

a Express and non-express trusts: how they differ

Is it correct to assert that it is foolish to treat trusts generally, and in particular to place express trusts on the same footing as constructive and resulting trusts within a single *figura iuris* (*the* trust, as civil lawyers would use the term)?[289]

The response is cautiously in the affirmative. This caution may, however, be cast aside when writing for an audience of civilians, who still today need the kind of healthy but extravagant controversy which will abruptly transport them from the ambiguities to which out-of-date writings have enslaved them (and this is as true for Italians as it is for French, Spaniards or Germans).

If we think back to the cases of constructive or resulting trusts cited some pages back, we may easily identify six elements which from a structural viewpoint radically distinguish them from express trusts:

1. the beneficiary did not necessarily have any claim to the asset which is the subject of the constructive or resulting trust prior to its creation;
2. there is no individual who can be identified as the settlor and who carries out an act of transfer in favour of the trustee;[290] and, in fact,
3. the trust relates to property of the trustee which is in no way defined with respect to the other assets which make up his estate until the constructive or resulting trust is declared;
4. there are no requirements as to form;
5. there is always a beneficiary;
6. the obligations of the trustee are those of a bare trustee, and are, fundamentally, to deliver the subject matter of the constructive or resulting trust to the beneficiary (or to the original trustee).

[287] See the precedents and the opinions expressed in the literature discussed by R. P. Meagher and J. R. F. Lehane, 'Trusts of Voluntary Covenants', in 92 LQR (1976) 427.

[288] *Clarke v. Heathfield (No. 2)* (1985).

[289] Cf., for the analogous American position, Restatement, *Trusts*, §16A.

[290] Scott, *Constructive Trusts* (see above, footnote 4), p. 41: 'It is, it seems to me, a foolish thing to attempt to include in one definition these two things.'

For now, we shall leave aside the last three elements, and briefly study the first three, starting at the top. One might object that it is normal practice that the beneficiary has never had rights in the trust assets; it is the case even with express trusts. This is true, but the source of the beneficiary's right is different: in one case it is an act by the settlor, and in the other, since by definition there is no settlor (either in fact or in law[291]), it is an act of the law (the rules of equity). The consequences of this are significant for an explanation of the institution: on one hand, in the case of express trusts, there is an indirect transfer from the settlor to the beneficiary (through the trustee), while in the case of non-express trusts the transfer is immediate, and takes place between trustee and beneficiary; on the other hand, it is in this way that constructive trusts may be distinguished from certain resulting trusts, where the beneficiary is the owner of the right before it is transferred to the trustee, and the right 'returns' to him when the circumstances described above are present.[292]

Nevertheless, there is no settlor even in resulting trusts, or at least there is no settlor of the right which is the subject matter of the resulting trust. It is this lack of one of the parties to the relationship which allows constructive and resulting trusts to be placed together, in contrast to express trusts.

Another point of affinity between constructive and resulting trusts (and of contrast with express trusts) is in the third element listed above. Equity encumbers an asset of the trustee, where no encumbrance previously existed,[293] or where there had previously been a different kind;[294] while in the case of express trusts it is an asset of the settlor which is encumbered by the settlor himself.

Having highlighted the reasons why express trusts have relatively little in common with constructive and resulting trusts, we shall now seek to identify the legal data which unite them and which will, in the end, permit a single discussion of the trust which would be impossible without preliminary clarification of the reasons for the differences.

b Expressly and non-expressly established trusts: how they are alike

As we shall see in more detail at the end of chapter 3, the trust according to the English model is generally characterized by three elements: the entrusting, the segregation, and the equitable obligation of the trustee towards

---

[291] In trusts where a person makes himself trustee of his own property there is an act of disposition: the declaration of trust.

[292] That is, for the defect of the form required for the creation of the trust.

[293] See above, chapter 2 §§3.a–3.b.

[294] This is true of all constructive trusts and of those resulting trusts which concern placing assets in names different from those of the persons who paid the purchase price.

the purpose of the trust. It may be appropriate to state at this time that legal systems which follow the international trust model (see chapter 4) and civil-law systems (see chapter 5) do not recognize the third element, since it belongs to equity, but they substitute it with others, which we shall consider in due course.

In the case of the constructive trust, the entrusting of an asset or right to a trustee takes place by operation of law. As I have observed, it is singular that a person (the constructive trustee) should unexpectedly find himself suffering a change in the character of his title to a particular asset: that which belonged to him 'completely', or which seemed to belong to him completely, now belongs to him as a trustee.[295] The constructive trust makes a 'fiduciary' of a person who may have had no idea that he was one and who, more often than not, had no intention of being one.[296] In other words, we have a fiduciary by force, which is an apparent contradiction in terms, and, therefore, an 'unknown trust'.[297] Nonetheless, it is here that the strength of the constructive trust is found, and herein, as I shall explain further below, lies the distinction between this figure and the restitutory models into which American law has squeezed it. Once the existence of a constructive trust has been ascertained, the owner of the right is the trustee, just as if the entrusting had been the result of an act of transfer in his favour (the express trust). One can already see how little the notion of 'fiducia', as the term is understood in the civil-law context, has in common with the trust as an institution.

The situation with resulting trusts is analogous, but less dramatically evident. Here there is already either a trustee of an express trust or a trustee of a trust which the law presumes to exist until proved otherwise. What changes is the subject and the object of the juridical encumbrance. If the provisions of the trust deed cannot be fulfilled, or there is no provision in the trust instrument for the contingency which has come to pass, or it has become necessary to protect a person who is not the owner of the asset or interest in question, a trust is declared, and what was latent comes to light through a judicial decision. Here too, however, there is an entrusting of the asset to the trustee of the resulting trust: the new subject matter or the new

---

[295] This is true for other kinds of resulting trusts.

[296] This statement has nothing to do with the procedural view of constructive trusts as a remedy (on which details see above, chapter 2 §5.a). I would simply underline that the constructive trust is the outcome of an act of will aimed at creating a trust, even though, as we know, in some cases it gives effect to a will which was not sufficiently clearly manifested to bring an (express) trust into existence.

[297] Maitland, Equity (see above, footnote 35), p. 83.

object of the encumbrance, or the declaration of an encumbrance which already existed implicitly, change the 'ownership', exactly as we have just seen happen with the constructive trust.

In both cases, the segregation of the subject matter of the trust follows the entrusting. Since there is no voluntary act of settlement in favour of the trustee, the segregation only rarely manifests itself externally by means of the *indicia* which a diligent trustee must put into effect; on the contrary, more often than not one must combat an attempt by the trustee to commingle the trust assets with the remainder of his property, and, more often still, to claim segregation of the property against the trustee's creditors, frequently in bankruptcy proceedings. We have often seen in the pages dedicated to the *regulae* on constructive and resulting trusts how the prime interest of the beneficiary is to obtain segregation of the trust assets against other claimants who have the rights of a creditor over the trustee's estate in general, and cannot satisfy their claims over the assets which are the subject of the trust.

The legal position of a beneficiary is, in fact, the same as that of the beneficiary of an express trust. His equitable right allows him to take action against a trustee who dissipates the trust assets or who uses them in a manner not permitted by law (here, as we have seen, there is no initial trust instrument to which reference may be made), and against third parties who, as participants in the breach, or as recipients of the assets in breach of the legal requirements, find that they too are in the position of constructive trustees.

These, therefore, are the reasons why constructive and resulting trusts are, like express trusts, members of the general class of trusts.

c Theoretical basis of constructive and resulting trusts

Trusts which have not been expressly established cannot be understood if they are not placed in the uneven and complex context which brings equity into the foreground.

Over the centuries, equity has cherished the belief that there is an open category of interests which are protected by the Courts, which was later identified by the generic term 'mere equities'. They are different from equitable interests in that they are commonly held to be collateral and lacking in independent protection,[298] but both belong to the vague general category of 'equities'.

While the system of equitable interests with regard to third parties has

---

[298] The expression is Lord Browne-Wilkinson's in *Westdeutsche v. Islington* (1996), at p. 986.

already been described when dealing with transfers effected by the trustee and the failure of the trustee to perform his obligations under the trust (breach of trust), mere equities are more treacherous. They are often purely personal, and expire in the event of the transfer of the asset to which they refer. In other cases, they affect third parties in a devious way, because they can also apply to an equitable interest alone and, following the theory of presumed notice, bind a third party purchaser.[299] Here the question becomes yet more complicated, because the purpose of certain mere equities is to validate a request for a procedural remedy, for example the annulment of a contract for deceit, and it is nevertheless claimed that they can be the subject of an act of transfer, both *inter vivos* and *mortis causa*.[300]

It is not necessary to go into this any further, because this last reference to restitutory remedies suffices to introduce the subject which is of interest to us. A mistake of law does not permit an action for restitution.[301] Equity, however, overcomes this limitation and orders the recipient of the payment to transfer the funds to the person who has the right to them, as in the case where executors interpret a will incorrectly and deliver certain sums to charities instead of to the heirs.[302] The *regula* thus expressed may be justified if we consider that the funds belong to the heirs 'in equity': as a

---

[299] For a discussion of these concepts, see A. R. Everton, '"Equitable Interests" and "Equities" – In Search of a Pattern', in [1976] 40 Conv (1976) 209.   [300] See above, chapter 2 §2.c.

[301] The conceptual development in this area still needs much more detailed research. See, for example, Underhill, *Trusts*, p. 397, who, with reference to the actions mentioned in the text, speaks, without further explanation, of equitable interests without 'full incidents', that is, without all their usual characteristics; in any event, in *National Provincial Bank v. Ainsworth* (1965), Lord Upjohn expressly declined to define the concept of 'mere equity' with respect to that of 'equitable interest' (at p. 488). Cf. Ames, 'Purchaser for Value' (see above, footnote 62), p. 2: 'Every equity attaching to property is an equitable estate.' But see *Kleinwort Benson Ltd v. Lincoln City Council* (1998), 3 WLR 1095.

[302] Thus in Roman law: J. Hallebeck, 'Developments in Mediæval Roman Law', in E. J. H. Schrage (ed.), *Unjust Enrichment. The Comparative Legal History of the Law of Restitution*, Berlin, 1995, pp. 59ff., at pp. 67–8. South African law has recently accepted the opposite solution: *Willis Faber v. Receiver of Revenue* (1992). For a comparative view, see R. Zimmerman, 'Unjustified Enrichment: The Modern Civilian Approach', in 15 OJLS (1995) 403, at 410–12.

The insufficiency of the mistake of law as grounds for a restitutory action has been the subject of criticism: see the Consultative Paper n. 120 of the Law Commission, *Restitution of Payments Made Under a Mistake of Law* and, for Scottish law, R. Evans-Jones, 'Some Reflections on the *condictio indebiti* in a Mixed Legal System', in 111 SALJ (1994) 759. It is also true that there is a tendency to see a mistake of law in circumstances which Italian law would place in the area of '*indebito oggettivo*'; for example, in *Woolwich v. IRC (No. 2)* (1992), the basis for the right of the taxpayer to reimbursement of taxes paid as the result of an invalid rule was traced back to the Bill of Rights of 1688, but the taxpayer had also claimed that there was a mistake of law.

On payments vitiated by mistake of fact, see Goff and Jones, *Restitution*, pp. 107–23.

result, they may claim them from whoever has come into possession of them.[303]

If we compare this case to that of the fiduciary who obtains an improper benefit from his duties,[304] we may discern a rule which will serve to identify a theoretical basis for non-express trusts. In a payment made to Tom of an amount which should have been paid to Dick as a result of a mistake of law, equity sees a defect *ex parte solventis*, who has transferred an asset which in equity belongs to Dick, and Dick may claim it back from whoever received it.[305] In more precise terms, the act of transfer is not completely effective because equity discovers within it a defect in its transactional legitimacy[306] and, by once again following the maxim 'equity follows the law',[307] permits use of the same remedy which is available to an owner if a third party disposes of his property. The mechanism of equity is to 'retain' an equitable interest in favour of the payer, so that the title of the receiver, as I shall explain further below, cannot be considered to be complete in equity.[308] This theoretical explanation applies to cases of cancellation of a contract due to mistake or fraudulent misrepresentation, or for lack of consideration[309] where the

[303] *Re Diplock* (1948). See also the case before the higher court; the House of Lords, *Ministry of Health v. Simpson* (1951), where it was stated (at pp. 269–73) that equity makes no distinction between mistake of fact and mistake of law. It should be pointed out that this last statement concerns personal actions by an heir or a legatee against executors who have made undue payments, and not the tracing.

[304] This is the analysis proposed by Birks, *Restitution*, p. 143, with which I am in agreement.

[305] See above, chapter 2 §2.a.

[306] I interpret in this way one of the findings of *Re Diplock* (1948), 530, concerning the restitutory remedy assisted by tracing: 'Equity may operate on the conscience . . . provided that as a result of what has gone before some equitable proprietary interest has been created and attaches to the property.'

[307] This, for example, is how the case of *Chase Manhattan Bank v. Israel-British Bank* (1979), examined above should be interpreted: 'a person who pays money to another under a factual mistake retains an equitable property in it and the conscience of that other is subject to a fiduciary duty to respect his proprietary right': [1981] 1 ch. 105 at 119. The phrase 'retains an equitable property in it' is exactly what I mean when I speak of a defect in the act of transfer; it is equitably incomplete, and what is lacking 'belongs' to the payer: following the judgment in *Westdeutsche v. Islington* (1996), it should be clarified that the circumstances of the case must be such as to bind the conscience of the recipient.   [308] See above, chapter 2 §4.a.

[309] In *Lonrho v. Fayed* (1992), it was stated that the contract vitiated by mistake causes an equitable interest to be maintained in the patrimony of the damaged party, who, thanks to this, may claim cancellation of the contract and the subsequent restitutory protection. But it had already been decided in *Stump v. Gaby* (1852), that the transferor who had been subject to undue influence in giving consent retained an 'equitable ownership' in the transferred asset.

In *Liggett v. Kensington* (1993), the Court of Appeal of New Zealand held that customers of a company which had sold, but not delivered, precious metals, 'retained a beneficial

circumstances are such as to bind the conscience of the recipient.[310]

Where, on the other hand, a fiduciary improperly receives a sum of money or an asset, the defect is *ex parte accipientis*. Equity cannot grant a remedy modelled on restitutionary remedies in favour of the person on behalf of whom the fiduciary must perform his fiduciary obligations, because the sum of money or asset has never been his, and has never been intended for him (and herein lies the contrast with the case of a payment vitiated by a mistake of law). The relationship between a fiduciary and that which he has improperly acquired is not legally perfect in the eyes of equity. It therefore challenges the completeness of the acquisition and identifies the element which prevents that completeness from being achieved precisely in the equity due to the person who is to benefit from the fiduciary obligations.[311] It is equity which *attacks the title of acquisition* and draws it, by means of the constructive trust, into the legal domain of the beneficiary. This reasoning also explains the irrelevance of the subjective state of the fiduciary, which characterizes the rule we saw above,[312] and which is based not the existence of an illicit act, but on an equitable defect in the procedure of the transfer of the sum of money or the asset to the fiduciary.[313]

At this stage, we must reevaluate the *regula* relating to benefits stemming from the commission of a crime.[314] Historically, as we indicated when discussing tracing, common law had no restitutory action outside the area of real property. To find that a thief is a (constructive) trustee of stolen

interest' in the sums of money deposited for the purchase, and that it was privileged with respect to the other creditors of the company (the New Zealand decision was reversed by the Privy Council: In re *Goldcorp* (1995), because the contract between the parties did not justify such a conclusion: see better below, pp. 140–41).

[310] In the words of the Privy Council in In re *Goldcorp* (1995): 'so as to leave behind . . . a beneficial interest' (101). Cf. P. B. H. Birks, 'Restitution and Resulting Trusts', in S. Goldstein (ed.), *Equity* (see above, footnote 244), p. 335, criticized analytically by Lord Browne-Wilkinson in *Westdeutsche v. Islington* (1996), 991–2 (see also *per* Lord Goff, 973–4).

[311] Probably not only when the recipient knows the reason for the invalidity of the contrast and the asset transferred to him is still identifiable within his patrimony, even though the House of Lords expressed itself thus in *Westdeutsche v. Islington* (1996).

[312] An equity outlined in these terms becomes, in substance, a defect in the receipt by the recipient which, however, only equity can identify; the very recent case law in the area of bribes (see above, chapter 2 §2.a) thus finds its systematic classification. Cf. the difficulty in which Hanbury, *Equity*, pp. 649–50 finds himself when he follows a different view.

[313] In one of the first cases regarding company directors, Lord Russell expressed himself thus: 'The liability arises from the mere fact of a profit having, in the stated circumstances, been made.'

[314] The theory of Shepherd, 'Fiduciary Relationships' (see above, footnote 40), 75–8, may be placed in this class. The fiduciary wields a power which belongs to the 'settlor', to whom any benefit obtained by the fiduciary therefore belongs. In the civilian field, cf. E. Betti, *Teoria generale delle obbligazioni*, Milan, 1955, III, pp. 144–5.

property may appear to be a far-fetched conclusion, born from the desperation of jurists, but it is not. When an action was sought which would place the stolen property in a privileged position with respect to other creditors of the thief – in effect, a full action for recovery of personal property – no other solution was technically possible. The equity – or rather, the equitable ownership – which remains in the victim of the theft gives rise to a notion of 'ownership due', and the system sets out to implement this by means of a constructive trust. Ownership is 'due', but then it exists in equity, where what ought to be in the outside world is foreshadowed.[315] Once again, we notice a defect *ex parte accipientis*; it is therefore correct to consider the thief to be a constructive trustee.

A third type of situation is the equity which arises after a complete and undisputed acquisition following an event, voluntary or otherwise, which causes the completeness of title to fail and grants an equity to a third party. One instance of this may be found in the case of a seller where the sale is pending:[316] he is still the 'full owner' under common law, but the purchaser 'is already the owner' according to equity (the same mechanism applies in the example we have just considered of heirs with regard to a payment vitiated by a mistake of law), and in the event of a double sale he may take action against the second purchaser to obtain the transfer of the property. The same conceptual formulation underlies the first attempt at a theoretical explanation of the constructive trust in the marital home, made by the House of Lords: an equity arises in favour of a person who is not the registered owner of property as a result of certain kinds of conduct on the part of the registered owner.[317] It should be no surprise that such a radically equitable interpretation did not find favour in Scotland.[318]

To sum up: equity may find an original defect in the act of transfer on the part of either the transferor or the transferee (in both cases the title of ownership is weakened), or a defect in the title of the owner which occurs after the acquisition. These defects do not, of course, apply to title in the legal sense (that is, under common law), but rather in the equitable sense (that is, from the perspective of equity).

---

[315] See above, chapter 2 §2.g.

[316] The reasoning behind the judgment of 1471, referred to above, footnote 238 should be recalled: 'pur ceo que en conscience il purchase ma terre'. The notion of *due ownership* can claim ancient ancestors, since Grotius, referring to the position of the fedecommissary, speaks of *eigendoms verwacht*: see B. Beinart, 'Fideicommissum and *modus*', in [1968] ActaIur 157, at 172, footnote 116.   [317] See above, chapter 2 §2.e.

[318] *Lloyds Bank v. Rosset* (1991), *per* Lord Bridge at p. 115: from this moment on, the opinion continues, 'the claimant has some kind of inchoate right or "equity"', to bend the ear of the court of conscience to listen sympathetically to his tale': the vagueness of the conceptual structure should be noted.

The expression 'belongs in equity', which I have used frequently, thus reveals as much its nature as a tropology as its technical classification: it relates to the completeness or fullness of the title of purchase of a person (it does not matter whether the title is legal or equitable), against which another person may take action because *what is lacking in the former's title is his*. This is not, therefore, ownership in the sense of a position with reference to an asset, but is ownership of an equity which, like a wedge forced under a door, leads to the breakup of the title, and allows the property to which the title refers to enter. The term 'proprietary' does not describe a subjective position, but the *effects* (and not the purpose) *of the protection*, and in particular the *segregating effect* of the trust and the ensuing priority of the rights of the beneficiary with regard to certain property over the rights of the other creditors of the trustee.[319] The notion of 'ownership due' which I proposed above passes from a potentiality to effectiveness by means of a constructive or resulting trust and the eventual later transfer of the asset to the beneficiary.[320]

By carrying our discussion to the subject of equities we have been able to identify a powerful line of thought in case law. We have seen clear traces of it on other occasions, for example with reference to the position of a cohabitee to whom a promise has been made, or in whom an expectation has been created, that the house in which the couple lives, but which is in the name of the other cohabitant alone, will be shared.[321] While the reliance placed in the registered owner and the damages resulting therefrom constitute the fundamental reasoning behind the decisions, the technical key lies in emphasizing the creation of an equity which impairs the fullness of title of the registered owner.

Placing this situation on a level with that which gives rise to proprietary estoppel[322] would mean not only transferring it to the sphere of procedural remedies (to which proprietary estoppel belongs[323]), but also doing away

---

[319] *Sharp v. Thomson* (1995).

[320] Millett J in *El Ajou v. Dollar Land Holdings* (1993), 736: 'Equity's power to charge a mixed fund . . . enables the claimants to follow the money, not because it is theirs, but because it is derived from a fund which is treated as if it were subject to a charge in their favour.'

[321] This seems to me to be exactly what the House of Lords was trying to say in *Lloyds Bank v. Rosset* (1991): 'in jurisprudential terms, the equity is a right that can give the claimant access or provide him with a channel to some proprietary or personal advantage'. This last explanation ('personal advantage') concerns cases which are different from the one under review, in which, that is, legal protection has no real effects, but leads to an award of damages 'the right will not in all cases lead to some proprietary gain: the right therefore in analytical terms is no more than a right that provides access to an interest in land through the courts or for a conferment of a right to the enjoyment of property or to the payment of money' (115).   [322] See above, chapter 2 §2.0.

[323] Estoppel consists, in general, of a procedural preclusion (which originally belonged to common-law procedure) relating to a claim or a defence which a party may put forward,

with the logic behind the loss of fullness of title. There is no doubt, as we have observed, that the latter produces uncertainty in legal transactions: nevertheless, it seems to me that the attainment of primary values should not be impoverished on account of a few inconvenient practical consequences.[324]

but which is declared by the court to be without any effect as a result of prior incompatible declarations or conduct by the same party, in reliance on which the other party has acted, to his prejudice (on this last requirement, see *Greasley v. Cooke* (1980) and, recently, *Wayling v. Jones* (1995)): cf. Edwards and Stockwell, *Trusts and Equity* (see above, footnote 130), pp. 39–42; for the United States, see Restatement, *Trusts*, §50; for New Zealand case law, which is very open to innovations in this and similar equitable cases, see *Stratulatos v. Stratulatos* (1988); also *Gillies v. Keogh* (1989), where, 331, a unified view of the various types of estoppel was proposed. In this sense, see also Australian case law: *Walton Stores v. Maher* (1988), and the other precedents examined by L. J. Priestley, 'Estoppel: Liability or Remedy?', in Waters (ed.), *Equity* (see above, footnote 40), p. 273.

Estoppel developed in the area of equity as proprietary estoppel and in the various forms of promissory estoppel (in this footnote, I shall limit myself to some very brief points).

Proprietary estoppel shares the nature of all equitable remedies; it is, therefore, discretionary and may, for example, be precluded by the conduct of the claimant. For example, when his behaviour has been reprehensible, (applying, that is, the maxim 'he who seeks equity must do equity'): cf. Megarry, *Real Property*, pp. 434–7. When it is granted, it has the effect of making the request incontestable, since the other party cannot deny the facts which might block it. It may be useful to reconsider a passage from the decision in *Ramsden v. Dyson* (1866): 'If a stranger begins to build on my land supposing it to be his own, and I, perceiving his mistake, abstain from setting him right, and leave him to persevere in his error, a court of equity will not allow me afterwards to assert my title to the land on which he has expended money on the supposition that the land was his own' (*per* Lord Cranworth MR, 140).

The requirements of proprietary estoppel are still in evolution, and it is frequently used to sanction informal undertakings (see the following footnote); cf. P. Milne, 'Proprietary Estoppel in a Procustean Bed', in 58 MLR (1995) 412 and C. J. Davis, 'Proprietary Estoppel: Future Interests and Future Property, in [1996] Conv 193, but it is nonetheless certain that it prevails with respect to accounting books: cf. Battersby, 'Informal Transactions' (see above, footnote 92).

On the distinction between proprietary estoppel and constructive trust see the clear analysis in Pettit, *Trusts*, p. 190 and, with excellent arguments of legal politics, Fergusson, 'Constructive Trusts' (see above, footnote 170), 124–31. On the issue raised by 'acquiescence' see *Ramsden v. Dyson* (1866); *Inwards v. Baker* (1965); cf. Oakley, 'Has the Constructive' (see above, footnote 8), 37–8 and in general, Hanbury, *Equity*, pp. 880–90.

Promissory estoppel has enjoyed a notable development in the United States, in the Restatement of Contracts (2d), §90(1). It is the consequence either of the declaration of a fact or the indication of an intent, and gives rise to reliance damages (as opposed to expectation damages): cf. D. A. Farber and J. H. Matheson, 'Beyond Promissory Estoppel: Contract Law and the Invisible Handshake', in 52 UnChLR (1985) 903; E. Yorio and S. Thel, 'The Promissory Basis of Section 90', in 101 Yale LJ (1991) 111.

[324] In a recent decision by the Privy Council, *Lim Teng Huan v. Ang Swee Chuan* (1992), proprietary estoppel was successfully pleaded by a co-owner who had constructed a building on a part of the commonly owned land after obtaining the consent of the other owner to the construction (which had just commenced) and his agreement to transfer his share in exchange for other, unspecified, land. The Privy Council confirmed the

If this analysis is correct (and we shall immediately see numerous applications of it), it may be understood why continental European literature has erroneously placed the rights of the beneficiary in the context of ownership. It is sufficient to forget that we are dealing with equity and to start thinking in more familiar terms to be immediately attracted by lexical assonance and similarities. I shall deal with this issue later,[325] but I thought it appropriate to send a signal to the reader at this early stage.

d Applications and enhancements of the theory

I shall now illustrate the applications of this theory to all cases of constructive and resulting trusts, but will only refer to the headings of the relevant *regulae* as they were formulated above;[326] in the context of this section, the headings alone may prove to be unintelligible, and it may then be necessary to return to the *regulae* to understand the reasons for my choices case by case.

The defect *ex parte solventis* explains the rules regarding a transfer by a trustee in breach of the provisions of the trust, undue payment, undue influence or awe, agreements which are void for a defect of form, oral agreements with equitable effect and the transfer to a purchaser of the duties of the seller.

The defect *ex parte accipientis* explains the rules regarding improper benefits obtained by a fiduciary, participation in a breach by a trustee (when the participant has received trust assets), benefits from commission of a crime, influence over the will of a testator, delivery of a sum for a specific purpose, registration of property in favour of third parties and joint purchase of property.

The equity which arises after a perfected purchase explains the rules regarding the seller of real estate which has not yet been conveyed, *donationes mortis causa*, joint or mutual wills, rights in the family home and trusts containing incomplete or ineffective provisions.

judgment of the Court of Brunei, which had held that it would have been against conscience to permit the promisor to obtain the nullity of the undertaking he had assumed (for defect of form), given that in completing construction of the house the other party had relied on its performance. As a consequence, the judge ordered the promisor to transfer part of the common land (in return for the agreed consideration).

The case law of Trinidad and Tobago later took the same line: *Khan v. Khan* (1994); see also in Barbados, *Sealy v. Sealy* (1990).

[325] For a different opinion, see Hayton, 'Equitable Rights' (see above, footnote 147) and cf. the caution preached by Lord Browne-Wilkinson in *Westdeutsche v. Islington* (1996), 987: 'My Lords, wise judges have often warned against the wholesale importation into commercial law of equitable principles inconsistent with the certainty and speed which are essential requirements for the orderly conduct of business affairs.'

[326] See above, chapter 2 §§2 and 3.

The theory I have proposed also explains why constructive and resulting trusts have always been exempted from any requirements of form.[327] As we know, they do not originate with an act of transfer with the purpose of creating a trust but, according to my proposition, with the creation of an equity which follows an equitable defect in the title or the transfer: therefore, since a trust instrument is by definition lacking, it would not be possible to insist on formal requirements concerning the documents which create a trust. This is the explanation for the fourth of the points which distinguish constructive and resulting trusts from express trusts.[328]

Another issue, to which I attached some importance in my analysis in the previous pages, is also clarified: this is the power of equity judges not to apply written law where it has been used by a defendant as an instrument of fraud. These are cases where if the law were applied, it would have the effect of eliminating an equitable entitlement, or an equity, even though this was not its purpose. In other words, equities cannot be invalidated or weakened by legal requirements from other areas which are, by chance, exactly those on whose structure and effectiveness equity intercedes according to its own system of logic and rules.

The frequent references in case law and the literature to the conscience of a defendant and to a defendant's unconscionable behaviour relate to this system of logic and to these rules. Equity, being a system of conscience, bases every situation to which it affords protection, from an equitable interest to mere equities, on considerations which tend to elude legislative regulation. This concludes the discussion which began with our review of the maxims of equity.

It remains to be explained if the need to develop a general theory of non-express trusts really exists, given that English writing has not seen fit to undertake this task. Is this the usual civil-law vice (or habit) of making generalizations? As we shall see in the following pages, English authors are coming to the realization that an exclusively case-based approach to developing subjects is no longer sufficient;[329] the evolution of case law requires theoretical underpinning, and English writing can make use of the reflections of foreign jurists and comparative lawyers, if only to reject them. It is with this in mind that I will now apply the theory formulated above to explain decisions which awarded damages to plaintiffs who included in the list of claims accepted by the court demands for the compensation they intended to pay to those who attended to them during a hospital stay, whether contractually obliged to do so or not.

---

[327] See above, chapter 2 §2 and §3.
[328] See the Statute of Frauds of 1677, art. 8 and above, chapter 2 §4.d.
[329] See below, pp. 91–94.

The solutions offered by case law have been quite varied, and the House of Lords has recently indicated that the damaged party should be consider-ed the trustee of that portion of the sum paid to him which relates to services supplied by those who assisted him.[330] This amazed the English writers, who asserted that a trust of this kind does not fall within any known category.[331] This is hardly the point, however, because new catego-ries of trust (fortunately) emerge quite frequently, and there is no *numerus clausus* of trusts. It appears to me, following the line of reasoning suggested above, that the payment of damages to the victim falls within the typology of the equitable defect *ex parte accipientis*. Whether the victim had an obligation towards the third party who assisted him or not is irrelevant, because if he did not, it is the judgment which grants the right to the third party, and if he did, the judgment merely identifies the technical means for protecting a pre-existing right.

There seems to me to be no doubt that the conscience of the damaged party is affected by the legal position which a judgment of this kind creates, and that equity could not remain idle where he should redirect that portion of the damages set aside for those who assisted him elsewhere. In equity, this money 'does not belong to him' and it is therefore consistent that it should be removed from his general estate in favour of the damaged party's creditors.

e The constructive trust between substantive law and remedy; unjust enrichment

When American jurists involved in drafting the Restatements in the nine-teen thirties arrived at the question of trusts, they decided to tackle con-structive trusts in the Restatement of Restitution, and not in the Restate-ment of Trusts.[332] In particular, the constructive trust was treated as the subject of a judgment, aimed at striking a blow against unjust enrich-ment.[333] The attention of the foreign jurist cannot fail to be attracted by the fact that twenty years after the Restatement the major proponent of this systematic formulation wrote that it was not yet possible to define either

---

[330] In this sense, see Matthews, 'Legal and Moral Limits' (see above, footnote 214), 31.

[331] *Hunt v. Severs* (1994), with reference to *Cunningham v. Harrison* (1973), which had imposed the trust expressly.

[332] P. Matthews, 'Here a Trust, There a Trust, Everywhere a Trust, Trust . . .', in [1994] CJQ 302, 306, approved by Underhill, *Trusts*, p. 124, footnote 11.

[333] The two inspirations of this choice have given their reasons: W. A. Seavey and A. W. Scott, 'Restitution', in 54 LQR (1938) 29.

the concept of the constructive trust nor that of unjust enrichment.[334]

The fact is that unjust enrichment landed on the judicial scene in the United States without any serious theoretical preparation.[335] Enrichment without cause was one of the most problematic juridical categories of the Roman Law legacy to Western legal culture,[336] and it thus turned out to be nothing more than an assonance, a vague ideal of principle. In a system based on *regulae*, the fruits of the adoption of a principle cannot be foreseen and the principle of necessity becomes merely a catchphrase or publicity slogan.

Until a few years ago, the English legal community was united in rejecting the American form of unjust enrichment, and in affirming that it was not recognized in English law.[337] Recently, supporters of this theory have come forth, some enthusiastic,[338] others more cautious;[339] in any case, the winds from across the ocean seem to be about to reach England after having crossed the Great Lakes towards Canada and the Pacific Ocean towards Australia and New Zealand with ease.[340] If this is so, the lengthy

---

[334] Constructive trusts consequent upon the breach by the trustee of dispositions of a trust instrument or of an express trust are dealt with in the *Restatement of Trusts*.

[335] Scott, 'Constructive Trusts' (see above, footnote 4), 39–40. A re-examination of the technique of the Restatement is found in J. D. McCamus, 'Unjust Enrichment: Its Role and Limits', in D. W. M. Waters (ed.), *Equity* (see above, footnote 40), p. 129.

[336] Not even the essay by R. Pound, 'The Progress of Law', in 33 HarvardLR (1920) 420, where he states that the constructive trust is 'purely a remedial institution' (at 421) is one. In the choices of the drafters of the Restatements the backward state of American law compared with English law in the area of constructive trusts must also have had weight, as is shown, for example, by Ames, *Lectures* (see above, footnote 175).

[337] Cf. K. Zweigert and H. Kötz, *Introduzione al diritto comparato*, Milan, 1995, II, pp. 245–80; Zimmermann, 'Unjustified Enrichment' (see above, footnote 302), 291. The new Dutch Civil Code (*Burgerlijk Wetboek*) introduces the enrichment action in article 6:212; in South Africa, see *Blesbok v. Cantamessa* (1991), where van Zyl J objected to the traditional restrictive approach, which was hostile to recognition of a general action for unjust enrichment (see also D. H. van Zyl, 'The General Enrichment Action is Alive and Well', in [1992] ActaIur 115).

[338] See the *dictum* of Lord Porter in *Reading v. A-G* (1951), 523: 'the exact status of the law of unjust enrichment is not yet assured . . . I am content for the purposes of this case to accept the view that it forms no part of the law of England'; and Lord Diplock in *Orakpo v. Manson* (1978): 'there is no general doctrine of unjust enrichment recognized in English law' (at p. 104). In the same period, P. S. Atiyah, *The Rise and Fall of Freedom of Contract*, Oxford, 1979, p. 768 was completely negative.

   Although limited to the *restitutio in integrum* following termination of a contract for subsequent impossibility, Goff J affirmed that unjust enrichment 'is the basic principle of the English law of restitution' (*British Petroleum v. Hunt (No. 2)* (1982)).

[339] P. B. H. Birks, 'The Condition of the English Law of Unjust Enrichment', in [1992] ActaIur 1 and numerous other writings.

[340] J. Beatson, *The Use and Abuse of Unjust Enrichment*, London, 1991; Hayton, 'Developing the Law of Trusts' (see above, footnote 218), 97–103, holds that there is room 'to develop the

development of English law in the area of restitutory actions[341] would take a quantum leap into a new dimension.

English and Commonwealth authors are readying themselves with an admirable level of concentration. Writings on restitution, which were more or less non-existent until some decades ago, are common and detailed nowadays.[342] It appears that the long march of civil law towards a general auxiliary action on unjust enrichment is fast being duplicated in common law, unusually enough through the literature rather than case law.[343]

principle of unjust enrichment' in English law. In any case, the judgment of the House of Lords in *Lipkin Gorman v. Karpnale* (1991) (summarized above, footnote 215), is based on the unjust enrichment of the Playboy Club to the detriment of the law firm.

[341] In Canada the first sign was the dissenting opinion of Laskin J in *Murdoch v. Murdoch* (1974); final acceptance was in *Sorochan v. Sorochan* (1986), in the area of rights in the marital home (see, in more detail, Waters, 'Remedial Constructive Trust' (see above, footnote 155).

For New Zealand see *Avondale v. Haggie* (1979), *Gillies v. Keogh* (1989), *Powell v. Thompson* (1991), and *Re Newey* (1994) (cf. C. E. F. Rickett, 'Mutual Wills, Restitution, and Constructive Trusts – Again', in [1996] Conv 136).

On Australian law, see D. Ibbetson, 'Implied Contracts and Restitution: History in the High Court of Australia', in 8 OJLS (1988) 312; J. Beatson, 'Unjust Enrichment in the High Court of Australia', in 104 LQR 12 (1988): both discuss the judgment in *Pavey v. Paul* (1987), which had based the judgment against the contractor to pay the bidder the value of work it had performed on the basis of a bid which lacked the required written form for unjustified enrichment; see, in particular, 604: 'the concept of unjust enrichment . . . constitutes a unifying legal concept which explains why the law recognizes, in a variety of distinct categories of cases, an obligation to make fair and just restitution for a benefit derived at the expense of the plaintiff.' Subsequently, see *David Securities v. Commonwealth Bank* (1992).

[342] D. Ibbetson, 'Unjust Enrichment in England before 1600', in Schrage, *Unjust Enrichment* (see above, footnote 302), p. 121.

[343] The first work was by Goff and Jones, *Restitution*, in 1966; it nonetheless remained rather isolated, except for the numerous essays by G. H. Jones, among which are: 'Unjust Enrichment' (see above, footnote 41); 'Restitution of Benefits Obtained in Breach of Another's Confidence', in 86 LQR (1970) 463; 'Restitutionary Claims for Services Rendered', in 93 LQR (1977) 273. The first Canadian case law (*Pettkus v. Baker* (1980)) began the debate within the Commonwealth (see, for example, A. J. McClean, 'Constructive and Resulting Trusts – Unjust Enrichment in a Common Law Relationship', in 16 UBCLR (1982) 155); from here we have the monographs which set in motion the current research fever: G. H. L. Friedman and J. G. McLeod, *Restitution*, Toronto, 1982; P. B. H. Birks, *An Introduction to the Law of Restitution*, London, 1985, revised in 1989. There is also a special law journal, *The Restitution Law Review*.

See, more recently J. Beatson, *Benefit, Reliance and the Structure of Unjust Enrichment*, in CLP (1987), 71; Beatson, *Use and Abuse of Unjust Enrichment* (see above, footnote 340); A. S. Burrows, 'Free Acceptance and the Law of Restitution', in 104 LQR (1988) 576; E. McKendrick, 'The Battle of Forms and the Law of Restitution', in 8 OJLS (1988) 197, which discusses the relationship between contractual actions and restitutory actions in cases of contracts concluded using contrasting forms, which are regulated today by article 19 of the 1980 Vienna Sales Convention; the essays collected in A. S. Burrows (ed.), *Essays on the Law of Restitution*, London, 1991; Birks, *Condition* (see above, footnote 339); Birks,

This is not the place to go into detail on the general theme of enrichment and restitutory actions, which in English law on the one hand remains a prisoner of medieval conceptual schemes,[344] but on the other undoubtedly makes explicit the same equitable values which some continental writings had placed at the foundation of the action, but in a different cultural context.[345] It is precisely these equitable values which lead us once again to the constructive trust and to the debate on its attributes: in English law, as in that of other Commonwealth countries, it goes side by side with the debate on unjust enrichment, since unjust enrichment may have the effect of making a person a constructive trustee.[346] From the American point of view, in fact, the constructive trust is the procedural outcome of a state of unjust enrichment; in particular, it is the subject matter of a judgment of a restitutory nature.[347] These results are assured by making the party which

'Restitution and Resulting Trusts', (see above, footnotes 244 and 310), p. 335; A. S. Burrows, *The Law of Restitution*, London, 1993; A. Tettenborn, *The Law of Restitution*, London, 1993; Waters, 'Nature of the Remedial Constructive Trust' (see above, footnote 155); the fine collection of essays edited by Schrage, *Unjust Enrichment* (see above, footnote 302); K. Barker, 'Unjust Enrichment: Containing the Beast', in 15 OJLS (1995) 457, which holds, quite correctly, that the theoretical framework and the philosophical foundation of unjust enrichment must be studied more deeply.

[344] On the latter, see *Lipkin Gorman v. Karpnale* (1992), and *Woolwich v. IRC* (1992), both on restitution of sums of money; J. Beatson, 'Restitution of Taxes, Levies and Other Imposts: Defining the Extent of the Woolwich Principle', in 109 LQR (1993) 401; Evans-Jones, 'Some Reflections' (see above, footnote 302), with reference to Scottish law.

For a comparative study, see W. Lorenz, 'A Civil Lawyer Looks at Some Recent Developments of the English Law of Restitution', in M. Lupoi, L. Moccia and P. Prosperetti (eds.) *Scintillae iuris – Studi in memoria di Gino Gorla*, Milan, 1994, II, p. 1051; A. di Majo, Pagamento del debito altrui e arricchimento senza causa, in *Scintillae iuris*, III, p. 1865; B. Nicholas, 'Unjust enrichment and subsidiarity', in *Scintillae iuris*, III, p. 2037.

[345] For example, the action for money had and received, which is quite similar to the *condictio causa data causa non secuta* of classical Roman Law, and the action for *quantum meruit*, which has the purpose not of attacking the enrichment of one party but the loss suffered by the other (on *quantum meruit* see A. T. Denning, '*Quantum meruit*. The Case of *Craven Ellis v. Canons Ltd*', in 55 LQR (1939) 54, which contested its basis in *aequum et bonum*; J. L. Barton, 'Contract and *quantum meruit*: the Antecedents of *Cutter v. Powell*', in JlegH (1987), 48 (study of sixteenth and seventeenth century case law); Ibbetson, 'Implied Contracts' (see above, footnote 341), which establishes an historical context for the restitutory action for cases of works supplied without a valid contract, and therefore the relationship between *indebitatus assumpsit* and *quantum meruit* until the emergence of an obligation which has its basis in the law, and its sanction in the action for restitution (which here is consequent upon the unjust enrichment); Birks, 'Condition' (see above, footnote 339), 14–15.

[346] Cf. G. Dolezalek, 'The Moral Theologians' Doctrine of Restitution and its Justification in the Sixteenth and Seventeenth Centuries', in [1992] ActaIur 104; G. Andreoli, *L'ingiustificato arricchimento*, Milan, 1940, pp. 1–3; H. Coing, 'English Equity and the Denunciatio Evangelica of the Canon Law', in 71 LQR (1955) 223, at 234–6.

[347] Cf. Jones, 'Unjust Enrichment' (see above, footnote 41).

is under the obligation a constructive trustee, thus isolating the asset in question from the rest of his property, and so placing the beneficiary in a truly privileged position in relation to all other creditors.

The opinion which is gaining ground in England is syncretistic: it is accepted by many that there may be an action, side by side with the constructive trust as it is traditionally understood, which leads to the imposition of the structure of a constructive trust on an individual and on property.[348] The institutions of substantive law and remedial law would therefore co-exist.[349]

In the previous pages, we have seen many applications of equitable principles based upon the emergence of a fraud or inequitable or unconscionable conduct in constructive trusts, and I have drawn attention to their ancient origin and lasting interest.[350] These equitable values may too easily be linked to the area of remedies not to justify a call for caution,[351] given that the constructive trust, as we know, leads to redress *in re*, and permits the use of tracing where the constructive trustee has disposed of the asset and the third party is not protected from the tracing. There is general agreement that the evolution of English law (and the same may be

---

[348] On the American position, see: A. J. Oakley, 'Has the Constructive Trust?' (see above, footnote 8), 17–19; Elias, *Constructive Trusts* (see above, footnote 5), pp. 155–68; Waters, 'Nature of the Remedial Constructive Trust' (see above, footnote 155), 167–8.

[349] In this sense, among others, Hayton, *Trusts*, pp. 178–80; Hanbury, *Equity*, pp. 296–7. See also below, footnote 359, with reference to the more recent pronouncement of the House of Lords in *Westdeutsche v. Islington* (1996).

This double belonging of the constructive trust is also accepted in American writings, from which we have the division of the topic between Restatements of Restitution and of Trusts, which I have referred to above. Maudsley, 'Proprietary Remedies' (see above, footnote 226), 237, observes that in this case the remedial constructive trust should be called 'constructive quasi-trust'.

[350] Thus also in Canada: see *Lac Minerals v. International Corona* (1989), 48: 'The constructive trust does not lie at the heart of unjust enrichment. It is but one remedy, and will only be imposed in appropriate circumstances'; and at p. 50: 'it is not the case that a constructive trust should be reserved for situations where a right of property is recognized. That would limit the constructive trust to its institutional function, and deny to it the status of a remedy, its more important role.'

[351] Specifically on the constructive trust see again *McCormick v. Grogan* (1869), *per* Lord Westbury, 97: 'a Court of equity, proceeding on the ground of fraud, converts the party who committed it into a trustee for the party who is injured by that fraud'; in the United States, *Beatty v. Guggenheim* (1919), 386: 'When property has been acquired in such circumstances that the holder of the legal title may not in good conscience retain the beneficial interest, equity converts him into a trustee' (*per* Cardozo J); in Canada *Sorochan v. Sorochan* (1986), 7: 'The constructive trust constitutes one important judicial means of remedying unjust enrichment'; recently, in New Zealand, *Powell v. Thompson* (1991), 615: 'a constructive trust is one of the most productive concepts by which equity reverses the unconscionable' (*per* Thomas J).

said of other legal systems in the Commonwealth) should not arrive at the quantum leap which I described above, and should not, therefore, embrace generic equitable values, thus provoking a flood of the extremely burdensome consequences of the constructive trust.[352]

The first question which must be answered, therefore, is this: does the constructive trust belong to two categories (substantive and remedial)? It is clear that if the answer is in the affirmative, it would not be classified as an action, but rather as the subject matter of a judgment, because the action would be for unjust enrichment, as in American law. A second problem would therefore be that of the choice between the enrichment which would be eliminated by a standard award of damages or restitution, and that which would be 'restored' to the other party by the imposition of a constructive trust.[353]

Unjust enrichment, as has been explained in English legal writing, may produce numerous reactions under the law,[354] including those of a restitutory nature. The restitution may be either through the award of damages or *in specie*, sometimes, in the latter case, by the imposition of the duties of a constructive trustee on the person who has unjustly enriched himself. There is no point on this occasion in joining the debate on the notion of unjust enrichment in English law, which is still extremely open, both as regards the very admissibility of the category and, once it has been accepted, on its confines.[355] We should limit ourselves to bringing to light the fact that the constructive trust as a remedy against unjust enrichment seems to represent a conceptual short-cut,[356] which creates the risk of trivialization, and of forcing unjust sacrifices on one party alone each time the facts do not lend themselves to inclusion in the logic of a transfer to one individual

[352] Already explained in J. B. Ames, 'The Origin of Uses and Trusts', in 21 HarvardLR (1908) 261, at 262; and see the first point of Langdell, 'Brief Survey' (see above, footnote 119): 'Equity jurisdiction is a branch of the law of remedies.'

[353] Cf. R. A. Samek, 'Unjust Enrichment, Quasi-Contract and Restitution: A Study in Organizing Legal Rules', in 47 CBR (1969) 1; R. P. Austin, 'The Melting Pot of the Remedial Trust', in 11 UnNSWLJ (1986) 66, which holds that it is more appropriate to leave the area of trusts and enter that of the (new) equitable rights (he lists a number of examples, including secret trusts; for a different list, see Goff and Jones, *Restitution*, ch. 2).

[354] These are the terms on which Waters, 'Nature of the Remedial Constructive Trust' (see above, footnote 155), bases his essay.

[355] Birks, *Restitution*, considers unjust enrichment to be an 'event', giving rise to 'responses' of various kinds, which may not be restitutory.

[356] In *In re Goldcorp* (1995), the Privy Council treated the 'remedial restitutionary right' as a 'nascent doctrine', still 'in an early stage' (at p. 104). Birks, 'Condition' (see above, footnote 339), at p. 8, writes of a 'raw condition'. Cf. Hayton, *Trusts*, pp. 181–3 and recently Lord Browne-Wilkinson, 'Constructive Trusts and Unjust Enrichment', in 10 TLI (1996) 98.

of the entirety of a benefit which has been obtained from another,[357] or wherever the basic theoretical foundations and the *ratio* of non-express trusts are lacking. In fact, on the basis of this last observation, supporters of the remedial constructive trust are obliged to exalt the traditional characteristics of actions in equity and, in substance, to recognize that the judge has a dual discretion regarding first the granting of the remedy and second its structure in each case.[358] All this subversiveness does not seem to me to be necessary.[359] A judgment as to the worth of a legal claim and the comparison of conflicting interests occur when one finds, or fails to find, the circumstances which, as I suggested in the first pages of this section, allow an equity to exist in favour of a person, thus making him the beneficiary of a constructive trust. At the moment a fiduciary accepts a bribe, to return to one of the most recent applications of this rule, a constructive trust arises; and precisely because it arises at that moment, the beneficiary has priority over all creditors of the dishonest fiduciary as far as the amount of the bribe and the assets into which it has been converted are concerned, and the fiduciary is transformed by law into a

---

[357] It is no coincidence that the only clear affirmation on this subject was by Lord Denning MR in *Hussey v. Palmer* (1972), 1290: '*It is an equitable remedy.*'

[358] Cf. A. M. Haycroft and D. M. Waksman, 'Frustration and Rescission', in [1984] JBL, 207. English law makes a wrong distinction between restitutionary damages arising out of a wrong, which a breach of contract is held to be, and the restoration of the prior situation as the effect of subsequent impossibility or the nullity of the contract. Cf., on the former point, I. M. Jackman, 'Restitution for Wrongs', in CLJ (1989) 302; D. Friedman, 'Restitution of Benefits Obtained through the Appropriation of Property or the Commission of a Wrong', in 80 ColLR (1980) 504; on the latter, *Rover v. Cannon* (1989), and J. Beatson, 'Restitutionary Remedies for Void and Ineffective Contracts', in 105 LQR (1989) 179.

Regarding the historical reasons why the breach belongs to the general category of wrongs, cf. M. Graziadei, 'Il patto e il dolo', in P. Cendon (ed.), *Scritti in onore di Rodolfo Sacco*, Milan, 1994, I, pp. 589ff., at pp. 593–603.

For the comparative view, see D. P. Visser, 'Unjustified Enrichment: A Perspective of the Competition between Contractual and Enrichment Remedies', in [1992] ActaIur 203. In Italian law, the excess of the enrichment with respect to the impoverishment limits the judgment to the amount of the latter: P. d'Onofrio, 'Dell'Arrichimento senza causa', in Commentario Scialoja, *Branca*, Bologna and Rome, 1981, p. 589.

[359] Cf. Hayton, 'Equitable Rights' (see above, footnote 147); Allen, 'Bribes and Constructive Trusts' (see above, footnote 51), at pp. 92–4. Lord Browne-Wilkinson also seems to have accepted this position in *Westdeutsche v. Islington* (1996), at p. 999: 'the remedial constructive trust, if introduced into English law, may provide a more satisfactory road forward ... Since the remedy can be tailored to the circumstances of the particular case, innocent third parties would not be prejudiced ...' In a non-judicial context, see Browne-Wilkinson, 'Constructive Trusts' (see above, footnote 356), especially at p. 99.

Cf. Waters, 'Nature of the Remedial Constructive Trust' (see above, footnote 155), 179–85; at page 180, he takes the position that the concession of retroactivity of the constructive trust, or the lack thereof (and therefore the attribution of a substantive rather than a remedial nature to it) is at the discretion of the judge.

constructive trustee.[360] The same is true for an undue payment, where the sum paid in error does not belong to the recipient of the payment 'beneficially', that is, according to the canons of equity.[361] The strength of the affirmation that the bribe belongs to the other party to the fiduciary relationship 'in equity', or that the sum paid in error does not 'belong in equity' to the recipient of the payment cannot be weakened without placing fundamental structures of the English legal system at risk.[362]

It is doubtless simpler to return to a subjectivism which, although it has probably never been known to equity,[363] is often ascribed to its formative phases, or to embark upon a meta-sociological analysis which permits an appropriate solution to be moulded on a case-by-case basis.[364] The theoretical error which lurks within this formulation is not so much to hold that there are obligations for breaches of which the system provides no remedy (not even an equitable remedy – a contradiction of the history of equity) but to allow a battle relating to title to be fought in the arena of remedies.

In conclusion, the constructive trust always has what the literature calls a 'proprietary base', not, as I hope I have explained sufficiently clearly,

[360] It does not even seem necessary to English case law, nor, notwithstanding its adherence to the American model of constructive trust, to Canadian case law. On the latter, see *Lac Minerals v. International Corona* (1989): '*Restitution is a distinct body of law governed by its own developing system of rules*' (*per* La Forest J, 45).

One might, perhaps, have hoped for greater flexibility on the part of English case law in applying the customary equitable rules in actions belonging to common-law categories. For example, a judgment for payment of compound interest in an action for money had and received such as that in *Westdeutsche v. Islington* (1996) (see above, chapter 2 §3.a), would have reduced the distance between an equitable remedy and one of strict law and satisfied a requirement of justice which otherwise puts pressure on prior judicial notions, and leads to the inconveniences described in the text. The minority position of Lord Goff and Lord Woolf was theoretically explained as an equitable insertion 'in aid of common law remedies', and in this sense it merits the highest consideration beyond the specific case.

[361] For a different analysis, see Goode, 'Recovery' (see above, footnote 52), and R. Goode, 'Property and Unjust Enrichment', in Burrows, *Essays* (see above, footnote 343), 221–31.

[362] In *Chase Manhattan v. Israel-British Bank* (1981) (see above, chapter 2 §2.h) the question was whether the constructive trust should be considered an institution of substantive law. In this case, New York law was to be applied in an English court. The clear response was that it was 'a rule of substantive law'; as we noted, and as has been authoritatively confirmed (Lord Browne-Wilkinson in *Westdeutsche v. Islington* (1996), 997), it was a misunderstanding of New York law.

[363] Canadian case law notes this, although in a decision such as that in *Peter v. Beblow* (1993), which led to the pronouncement of a remedial constructive trust: 'There is a tendency on the part of some to view the action for unjust enrichment as a device for doing whatever may seem fair between the parties. In the rush to substantive justice, the principles are sometimes forgotten' (*per* McLachlin J, 643–4).

[364] Barbour, 'Some Aspects' (see above, footnote 33), especially 837–41 has denied this, employing excellent argumentation.

because it gives the beneficiary an entitlement belonging to the area of property or of *real* rights, but because it diminishes the entitlement of the constructive trustee without a necessary corresponding accrual of (property) rights in favour of another party.

3   The traditional English model

1. The creation of a trust

a The trust instrument and its form

The Convention of Rome on the law applicable to contractual obligations excludes trusts from its objects, but not the 'analogous institutions in continental law', because – as the *Giuliano–Lagarde Report* observes – they are 'usually of a contractual origin'.[1] This is a significant gesture of recognition at the international level: trusts and contracts belong to distinct legal worlds. The civil lawyer inevitably tends to pull trusts in the direction of contracts.[2] This causes irreparable damage if it is allowed to influence comparative analysis.

Express trusts would have been in a position to enter the area of contracts if fourteenth- and fifteenth-century common law had not been dominated by procedural forms which were still far from possessing a general 'contractual' action, and if consensualism had had independent significance in the area of real property.[3] Furthermore, there soon emerged certain types of trusts, in particular testamentary trusts and those where the settlor appoints himself as trustee, which would in any case have impeded trusts from entering the field of contracts.[4]

---

[1] M. Giuliano and P. Lagarde, 'Relazione', in *GUCE* C282 of 30 October 1980, 1.

[2] D. W. M. Waters, 'The Common Law Trust in the Modern World', in *Forum Internationale*, 1984, 3ff., at 19–20; C. Larroumet, '*La fiducie inspirée du trust*', in D [1990] Chron 119, correctly points out the incompatibility between contract and trust, as does M. Bianca, in her comment on article 1(2)(g) of the Convention of Rome, *Le leggi civili commentate* (1995), 931.

[3] On some of these points, see F. W. Maitland, *Equity. A Course of Lectures*, revised by J. Brunyate, Cambridge, 1936, pp. 107–11.

[4] There could have been contractual types of *trusts* and non-contractual types of *trusts*, as is occurring today (see below; this once again shows how necessary it is to speak of *trusts* in the plural).

The two latter types of trust should not be considered to be exceptions or anomalies; on the contrary, they clearly manifest the characteristic unilateral nature of the trust instrument. Express trusts have a unilateral act as their foundation, or, as I would put it, a unilateral legal *negotium*,[5] which is followed by one or more acts of disposition. The distinction between an institutional and a dispositive *negotium* is often of no practical relevance,[6] but it does have theoretical significance, because it illustrates the two levels – equity and common law respectively – and the different rules which apply to each. Even the testamentary trust, where it would seem that creation and disposition should coincide, and where the formal requirements of a will appear to preclude any different procedure for establishing the trust,[7] may present this distinction. It is also the case with secret and semi-secret trusts, of which we shall speak shortly. In any event, even in ordinary testamentary trusts, the will contains the act which creates the trust, while the transfer of the assets to the trustee is the duty of the personal representative.[8] Even in cases where the settlor appoints himself as trustee, where a separation between the two phases would seem to be unthinkable, it is possible, though unusual, that there may be one, such as when the declaration of trust concerns future conduct on the part of the settlor. We shall see examples of this in the next section.

The act of disposition, when the trustee and the settlor are not the same person and when it takes place *inter vivos*, consists in the transfer of a right. This transfer to the trustee is essential if the trust is to come into being.[9] If it does not take place, equity does not provide the beneficiary with any

---

[5] I shall go into further detail on this classification from the civilian point of view in chapter 7; for English law, see below, pp. 163–65.

    As further proof that in English law the legal *negotium* of creation is unilateral even when it occurs outside a disposition *mortis causa* and trusts in which the settlor is the trustee see precedents such as *Petty v. Petty* (1853), which have found a valid declaration of trust where a person deposited sums of money in a bank in the name of the uncle of his illegitimate son, declaring to the cashier that they were to be used for the upkeep of the baby.

[6] Hanbury, *Equity*, 482: 'In the case of an *inter vivos* trust, the trustees will ordinarily be parties to the deed in their official capacity, and the trust is constituted upon the conveyance of the trust property to them.'

[7] In England, as in many other common-law countries, the will requires the signature of the testator and two witnesses (Administration of Justice Act 1982, s. 17).

[8] In English law, the transfer from the testator to the trustee is not a result of the will, but of the later act of investiture to be carried out by the executor: see below, chapter 3 §1.h.

[9] *Milroy v. Lord* (1862). Cf. Scott, *Trusts*, §32.

    In a testamentary trust it is the executor who causes the transfer in favour of the trustee. For the special position of trustees of a settlement, see below, footnotes 361 and 449.

remedy, even though there is a valid act of creation,[10] because the beneficiary is considered to be a volunteer, and therefore not deserving of protection. Once again a maxim of equity is of assistance: 'equity will not perfect an imperfect gift.' Only a beneficiary of a trust who has provided consideration to the settlor may claim that a trust has been created under these circumstances (one traditional kind of consideration in this area would be marriage).[11]

Acceptance by the trustee (where he is not also the settlor) may take place at a later moment. English law does not provide for either formal acceptance or formal refusal (a 'disclaimer'), because both may be inferred. Nevertheless, refusal is usually expressed formally.[12] Acceptance may not take place, or it may become ineffective due to successive events, without any effect on the creation of the trust.[13]

The act which creates a trust *inter vivos* is not subject to any form because, as we already know, the formal requirements, from the Statute of Frauds of 1677 to modern legislation, relate exclusively to proof of the establishment of the trust,[14] and only apply to trusts of land; any other kind of property may become the subject of a trust pursuant to an oral declaration.[15] In the case of land, the proof, in contrast to what is meant in Italian law by a form *ad probationem*, does not concern the existence of a trust instrument, but the intention of the settlor. This distinction means that writings which post-date a mere oral declaration are sufficient to establish that a trust has been created, and that proof of the establishment of the trust may also be

[10] Except in particular cases, as, for example, by proprietary estoppel (see above, chapter 2, footnote 323).   [11] Cf. Underhill, *Trusts*, pp. 144–6; Scott, *Trusts*, §30.

[12] Cf. Underhill, *Trusts*, pp. 436–41; Scott, *Trusts*, §35. It should be noted that except with secret trusts, the obligation to accept the position of trustee or executor is not enforceable (except, I would assert, when it has been undertaken for consideration).

[13] Cf. Scott, *Trusts*, §§101–2. Equity provides procedures for substitution of a trustee who has died and for the appointment of another trustee where the one indicated by the settlor has not accepted the appointment: see below, chapter 3 §1.c and footnote 349.

[14] See above, chapter 2, footnote 254. For a view of the entire subject, see Gardner, *Introduction*, ch. 5. Waters, *Trusts*, p. 187 correctly entitles the relevant chapter 'Proving the Trust'.

[15] The creation of a trust of assets included in the notion of *personal property* requires no writing. Once again in recent times a trust of a significant shareholding has been recognized as valid which was created by an oral declaration by a person who had agreed with an executive of the company that he would transfer a number of shares to him, could not find a fiscally advantageous method of doing so and declared orally that he would hold the shares aside for so long as was necessary to find a solution: *Hunter v. Moss* (1994). One should note that the shares were described by quantity, but had not been individually identified (as in 'the shares represented by certificate no. 5'); we are in the area of trusts where the settlor appoints himself trustee and therefore cf. the precedent cited below, footnote 24.

obtained by taking the effect of several writings together, where none of them taken alone would be sufficient for the purpose.[16] On this subject, it should be remembered that equity generally looks with disfavour on defences which attempt to deny an obligation on the basis of a lack of required form. Rules which distinguish between expressions which create a trust and expressions of entrusting, desire or hope which do not produce the same effect are more complex.[17]

The act which transfers the subject matter of the trust to the trustee is, on the other hand, subject to the usual formal requirements pertaining to the transfer of that particular type of right.

Given that the act by which a transfer is effected and that by which a trust is created are subject to different formal rules, it is quite possible that of the two separate acts which exist within a single context or a single document, one may be valid and the other not. In such cases, it is normally the act by which the transfer is carried out which is vitiated (since it is subject to more restrictive formal requirements). The result is that the act by which the trust was created has no effect.

Once the trust has been established, writing becomes a requirement for the validity of any act of transfer of equitable entitlements which arise out of the trust: the liberal attitude which prevails in matters relating to establishment yields to the need for certainty.[18] Equity permits an easy passage from the world of common law into its own, but once this has been completed (and it was more desirable that it should be in the times when equitable case law was asserting itself in the area of trusts), it requires that formalities be complied with which are as restrictive as their equivalent in common law, if not more so. As a result, while a trust not pertaining to land may be created orally, the beneficiary may not effect a later transfer of his rights except in writing.[19]

---

[16] Pettit, *Trusts*, pp. 79–80.

[17] In this case, one speaks of *precatory trusts*, which are legally without effect. Many examples, given that it is a question of fact, and the evolution in case law may be found in Underhill, *Trusts*, pp. 111–16 and Waters, *Trusts*, pp. 109–17; Scott, *Trusts*, §25. For a historical review, see D. E. C. Yale, *Lord Nottingham's Chancery Cases*, London, 1957 (SS, no. 73), I, pp. 128–9; cf. Johnston, *Roman Trusts*, pp. 214–19.

[18] Despite this, *Neville v. Wilson* (1996), see above, chapter 2 §2.n.

[19] A complete review is in Underhill, *Trusts*, pp. 210–18.
    This peculiarity is in line with the equally curious situation which permits oral lease contracts (Law of Property Act 1925, s. 54(2), as amended by the Law of Property (Miscellaneous Provisions) Act 1989, s. 2(5)(a)), but imposes a writing where they are being assigned: see G. Battersby, 'Formalities for the Disposition of Equitable Interests under a Trust', in [1979] Conv 17.

b The settlor as trustee

The trust instrument appoints the settlor as trustee;[20] given the freedom of form in this area, there is nothing to prevent the declaration of trust from being substituted by conduct from which the declaration may be inferred. This is an implied trust, of which we have already spoken.[21]

With both express and implied trusts, cases where the settlor and the trustee are one and the same are fairly frequent. Many of the examples examined in the previous chapter belong to this category,[22] such as trust receipts, which make a purchaser of merchandise a trustee of the documents of title in favour of the bank which has advanced the payment; we shall see other examples when we discuss trusts in business operations. The declaration of trust must be manifested in some way[23] and someone, usually the beneficiary, must be made aware of it, so as to bring about a modification in the legal sphere which is functionally analogous to that produced by the transfer to a trustee.[24]

[20] For American law, see Restatement, *Trusts*, §17(a): 'A trust may be created by . . . a declaration by the owner of property that he holds it as trustee for another person.'

According to J. H. Langbein, 'The Contractarian Basis of the Law of Trusts', in 105 YaleLJ (1995) 625, at 672–5, a trust declaration which names the settlor as trustee is not a part of the 'modern' trust. As frequently happens in current US writing, every so often a scholar emerges who believes that he can revolutionize every commonly held belief on the basis of pure instinct, which is usually bereft of any serious conceptual backing or systematic connections (see also below, footnote 346). That trusts in which settlor and trustee are one and the same are perfectly 'modern' will appear absolutely clear when I describe trusts created for business purposes (see below, chapter 3 §2.h).

[21] See above, chapter 2, footnote 6 and relevant text; in particular on the application of the Quistclose trust see chapter 2 §3.b.

[22] For example, the seller awaiting the transfer (see chapter 2 §2.e), and certain of the precedents cited concerning a 'participant in a beach of trust' (see chapter 2 §2.c). See again *Re Kayford* (1975), in which a company in difficulty paid deposits from clients into a special bank account so as to be able to repay them if, once the bankruptcy had occurred, it was no longer able to carry out the contracts. For further detail see below, pp. 138–49.

[23] *Midland Bank v. Wyatt* (1994).

[24] In certain cases specification will suffice; as when a person declares that he is trustee of twenty cases of a certain wine, but has eighty cases in his cellar: *In re London Wine Shippers* (1975); cf., however, *Hunter v. Moss* (1994) (see above, footnote 15).

The principles of English law on the form of the creation of a trust when settlor and trustee are one were reviewed by Scarman LJ in *Paul v. Constance* (1977). The case concerned a current account in the name of a man who, having deposited into it sums received as damages for personal injury, had authorized his live-in partner to make withdrawals, and had on several occasions stated that the amount in the account belonged to both; the Court of Appeal found a trust in these statements.

This precedent is sometimes considered as an authority for the different rule that a person may make himself a trustee without any declaration, but by conduct alone. A dictum of Scarman LJ (198), follows this line, but the decision reached by the Court on this occasion was based on the expressions employed by the man.

To demonstrate the legal breadth of this category, it is appropriate to recall one of its first applications in case law:

Mr. Pye wished to help one of his natural daughters, who had married in France. He asked a friend to obtain a life annuity in favour of the woman, but in the name of Mr. Pye, since she was married. After some time, Mr. Pye gave the friend a power of attorney to transfer the annuity to the woman. The transfer took place, but in the meantime Mr. Pye had died. The Lord Chancellor found that it was not necessary to decide whether the exercise of the power of attorney by the friend was valid (under French law), because Mr. Pye, by his conduct, had made himself trustee of the annuity in favour of his daughter, so that on his death the annuity was hers.[25]

The theoretical attributes of trusts of this kind are rather interesting, especially in the light of what we have proposed as an explanation of constructive and resulting trusts: the holder of a right (whatever it may be, even if purely equitable[26]) deprives himself of a part of his interest and assigns it to another person (the beneficiary) or for the attainment of a purpose.[27] His interest is modified because an equity comes into being.[28] It is of no importance whether this purpose (we spoke of 'property which is owing') is achieved through a trustee or directly by means of an undertaking which the settlor assumes in person, because in both cases there is clear evidence of what we shall see is an essential structural element of the trust: the equitable obligation which falls on the trustee (whether he is a third party or the settlor himself) as a result of the lack of the equitable completeness of his title.[29]

c Powers to consent; powers of appointment

I place under a single heading two conceptually distinct phenomena which, it seems to me, can be unified on the view that in both cases there is an intervention in the workings of the trust by third parties.

Section 3 of the Trustee Act 1925 states that the power to invest in those securities identified in the law as acceptable investments

---

[25] *Ex parte Pye* (1811). This decision is also analysed by Graziadei, *Diritti nell'interesse altrui*, pp. 248–50.

[26] It should be recalled that a trust may have as its subject matter an equitable position, and not, as is commonly stated in the civilian area, only an entitlement recognized by common law (from here is born the claim of 'dual ownership': at common law for the trustee, and in equity for the beneficiary).

[27] See the expression of Jessel MR in *Richards v. Delbridge* (1874), 14: [the settlor must] 'so deal with the property as to deprive himself of its beneficial ownership'.

[28] Cf. above, chapter 2 §5.c.

[29] For the different explanations in Italian law, see N. Lipari, *Il negozio fiduciario*, Milan, 1964, pp. 153–4, 181–7, 390–4.

shall be exercised according to the discretion of the trustee, but subject to any consent or direction required by the instrument, if any, creating the trust or by statute with respect to the investment of the trust funds.

The trust instrument may, therefore, provide that a third party, who may be the settlor himself, may give instructions to the trustees regarding those investments, or that the consent of the third party must be sought. While it is unclear whether this is a beneficial power or a fiduciary power where the third party is also a beneficiary of the trust,[30] what is of interest is that the law expressly provides for a restriction in the usual powers of the trustee.[31] On the other hand, this limitation is nothing exceptional, because, as will become clear in the course of this chapter, it is the settlor who determines what powers the trustee will have, and what powers he will retain for himself or grant to third parties. While the totality of the rights and powers which would normally result from the transfer of the right to the trustee may be directed elsewhere by the settlor,[32] tax consequences may result when the trustee is not fully autonomous, and in certain instances the very validity of the trust may be placed in doubt.[33] We find here the theoretical basis for the protector, who is a typical component of the international trust model[34] and is not regulated by English law, even though the first mention of the protector in a statute dates back to 1833.[35] This gap in the English law has been partially filled by the recent Trusts of Land and Appointment of Trustees Act 1996, which contains numerous provisions which expand the class of cases where the exercise of a trustee's functions is subject to the consent of a third party.[36] Moreover, the necessary transactional formulae had already been developed by solicitors some time previously.[37]

The second phenomenon to be considered concerns the appointment of new trustees. While the traditional interpretation was that trustees should 'co-opt' other trustees to take the place of those who had died, the Trustee Act provides that this power may, in a series of circumstances, be exercised

---

[30] Underhill, *Trusts*, p. 586; in the first case, the third party may also exercise the power in his own interest, but in the second only in the interests of the beneficiary. The term 'power of appointment' is used in a different sense in the area of discretionary trusts, where the appointment is the distribution of an asset to a beneficiary.

[31] The tenant for life of a settlement has similar, but more generalized, powers. On this position, see below, footnote 361.   [32] Cf. Hayton, *Trusts*, pp. 126–7.

[33] All these arguments will be dealt with below.   [34] See chapter 4 §4.h.

[35] Fines and Recovery Act 1833 on entail.

[36] Trusts of Land and Appointment of Trustees Act 1996, ss. 8, 10, 14.

[37] J. Kessler, *Drafting Trusts and Will Trusts. A Modern Approach* (2nd edition), London, 1995, pp. 85–7.

by a third party.[38] Among these is that of the trustee who is absent from the United Kingdom for more than twelve months.[39] There is nothing exceptional here either, since trust instruments usually contained a clause which reserved the appointment of new trustees to the settlor or his successors, but the recognition on the part of the legislature of the granting of this power gives further strength to the modern figure of the protector.

The manner in which a power of appointment is exercised has recently provoked discussion, because in certain cases it was used to cause a trust to cease to be resident in the United Kingdom for tax purposes as a result of the fact that all the (new) trustees were foreign residents, while in other cases the appointment of new non-resident trustees had been requested of a court for the same purpose, where there was no one who could make the appointments. The tendency in case law is to find that a trust governed by English law may have (new) non-resident trustees only where objective circumstances justify it – for example, where the beneficiaries move abroad – but certainly not where the purpose is exclusively tax related.[40]

The power of appointment does not only apply to the nomination of trustees; on the contrary, its purpose is, technically speaking, the distribution of trust assets to one or more individuals. This power may be granted to the trustees (as is usual in discretionary trusts, of which we shall speak later), but also to a third party. In both cases, it may have different levels of

[38] S. 36(1)(a): 'person or persons nominated for the purpose of appointing new trustees'.

[39] It is customary that a trustee has the power to appoint his successor. In practice, nonetheless, there are usually two or more trustees (generally no more than four, and in many cases this is the limit established by the law); when one is lacking, the others co-opt the successor. S. 36 (1) of the Trustee Act 1925, permits the exercise of the power to appoint a new trustee by the person nominated by the settlor or by the other trustees even in the simple case where one of the trustees remains abroad for more than twelve months. The power of the court to appoint trustees is governed by s. 41 (1) of the Trustee Act 1925 which follows the maxim 'Equity does not want for a trustee.'

The appointment of a new trustee requires that the trust assets be conveyed to him, since he becomes their co-owner.

See Underhill, *Trusts*, pp. 733–9; Pettit, *Trusts*, pp. 318–25; Hanbury, *Equity*, pp. 483–6.

Unless there is a contrary disposition in the trust instrument, the final beneficiaries of a trust of land may now unanimously appoint and revoke appointment of trustees of the trust (Trusts of Land and Appointment of Trustees Act 1996, s. 19), see below, footnote 348.

[40] An emphatic decision was rendered by Lord Denning MR in *Re Weston's Settlements* (1968), where the proposed variations would have made the trust subject to Jersey law instead of English law (the beneficiaries were minors); the decisions in *Re Seale's Marriage Settlement* (1961), and *Re Chamberlain* (1976), however, were favourable: in both cases, the beneficiaries had no relationship with the United Kingdom (in one case they had moved to Canada, while in the other they were French).

On the change of the applicable law of a trust, see P. Matthews, *Changing the Proper Law of a Trust*, London, 1990.

binding effect, from a so-called 'mere power' to a legal obligation to exercise the power which has been granted.[41]

d Revocable trusts; 'grantor trusts'

Acknowledgment of the revocability of a trust may, in many instances, render it functionally comparable with a testamentary disposition. This is particularly true of dispositions in favour of beneficiaries which take effect on the death of the settlor (who is the beneficiary, or among the beneficiaries, for so long as he is alive).[42] Here rules of substantive law and tax rules intertwine; the former to bring about the nullity of the trust instrument if it does not comply with the structural requirements of a testamentary disposition, and the latter to forestall the evasion of inheritance tax.

The revocability of a trust does not in and of itself have anything abnormal about it, and it is clearly accepted by English law[43] within the framework of the theory of 'powers' (which may be comparable to the Italian '*potestà*'[44]) so long as it is provided for in the trust instrument.[45] When a trust is the result of a declaration by a settlor who has appointed himself as trustee, the revocation, following the conceptual interpretation proposed above, simply restores those equitable rights of which he had made himself the guardian to his personal estate. When, on the other hand, the trust has a third party trustee, the revocation also involves the elimination of the title which he comes by as a result of the transfer effected by the settlor in his favour, and the restoration to the settlor of the equitable interests of which the trustee was the guardian.

Revocable trusts were in frequent use in the United States until 1924, when the Revenue Act held that income from a revocable trust was to be attributed to the settlor ('grantor'), even if he was not a beneficiary of the trust.[46] As happens regularly in the United States, the creativity of tax consultants forced the tax authorities to keep sharpening their weapons, up until current sections 671–9 of the Internal Revenue code. The process began with trusts of short duration, and with those which gave the settlor ample powers of direction.[47] After the new tax statutes of 1946, which

---

[41] Cf. Waters, *Cours*, pp. 240–3. See also chapter 3 §2.d.

[42] This topic is discussed by Waters, *Trusts*, pp. 157–61.

[43] Differently in Canada: see Waters, *Trusts*, pp. 152–61.

[44] Cf. Hanbury, *Equity*, pp. 61–7, 172–5. A discussion of the concept *power*, illustrated in the previous section, follows in chapter 3 §2.d.

[45] A trust created by a court on the assets of a person suffering from mental illness is always revocable (this is an example of statutory trusts: see above, chapter 2 §1.c).

[46] Revenue Act 1924, §219(g).

[47] The Supreme Court gave a negative response in *Helvering v. Clifford* (1940).

concentrated on the notion of control and power retained by the grantor, came the fashion for trusts where the trustee was under the influence of the grantor. From this, in 1954, came the tax definition of the 'adverse party', that is, a person whose interest in the management of the trust was such that it could not be presumed that he exercised his powers according to indications from the grantor.[48]

Today, the rules on 'grantor trusts' are extremely complex.[49] When the creation of a trust contains dispositions which would cause it to fall within the classification of a 'grantor trust', the result is that the assets held on trust are considered still to be a part of the settlor's estate for all tax purposes.[50]

In the United States, so-called 'living trusts' are in wide use, principally because of the slowness and high cost of probate procedures in testate succession. They are trusts, usually revocable, to which the settlor progressively attributes his assets, so that at the time of his death little or nothing remains in his personal estate. The settlor is the beneficiary of the trust for as long as he lives, and at the moment of his death, the trustee turns over the trust assets to the designated beneficiaries without the need to pass through probate or management of the estate by the executor.[51]

e The notion of 'estate' and the duration of trusts

This area has distinct rules which are often erroneously grouped together under the heading of 'the rule against perpetuities'. They deal with issues which are among the most technical and difficult in the area of real property, and oblige us to provide a historical background in the hope of succeeding in describing the current law clearly.[52]

---

[48] The evolution of the rule is traced in B. I. Bittker and L. Lokken, *Federal Taxation of Income, Estates and Gifts* (2nd edition), Warren, Gorham & Lamont, 1991 with periodic supplements, §80.1.1.

[49] The American tax authorities regularly find a grantor trust where the settlor reserves to himself the power to remove the trustee and to substitute him with another. Following two contrary decisions of the tax court, the authorities took steps, and enunciated the principle that the power to substitute the trustee is not sufficient to justify a finding of a grantor trust: Revenue Ruling 95–8 (from *FT World Tax Report*, 1995, 169).

[50] The subject is dealt with in W. H. Newton, *International Tax and Estate Planning* (2nd edition), McGraw-Hill, 1993 with periodic supplements, §§6.05–6.26; R. E. Madden, *Tax Planning for Highly Compensated Individuals* (2nd edition), Warren, Gorham & Lamont, 1989 with periodic supplements, ch. 9; Bittker and Lokken, *Federal Taxation of Income* (see above, footnote 48), ch. 80.

[51] For a detailed review, see Waters, *Cours*, pp. 279–304; for tax aspects, see later, chapter 3 §2.k and §2.l.

[52] A common-law jurist might, perhaps, find some of the phrases I use somewhat extravagant; I have sought to choose my terms so as to be comprehensible to the civilian without

The formulaic procedure of common law, as we know, did not offer any protection to a third-party beneficiary of a use (later to be called trust) against the owner of the estate. The granting of a procedural remedy by the court of equity played on the obligation of conscience which the owner of the estate had undertaken when accepting the transfer of the estate with an agreement in favour of the settlor[53] or a third party. This was an obligation which, since there was no action before the common-law courts, found its enforcement in equity. This explains why estates in equity were the same as in common law, although preceded by the word 'equitable'. In this way, the estates recognized by equity, defined without distinction as 'estate' or 'interest' were added to those recognized by common law (legal estates): the latter belonged to the person whom today we call the trustee; the former to the beneficiary. Just as the legal estate defines the position of the trustee before common-law courts, so the equitable estate, or interest, defines the position of the beneficiary before equity courts. This parallelism, as we know, conforms with the maxim 'equity follows the law'.[54]

All legal estates other than freehold[55] and leasehold were eliminated between 1882 and 1925 (thus, if one wants to look for a legal system which imposes a *numerus clausus* of property rights, one will find it in England), and the plurality of estates was retained only in equity. From this we have the highly important consequence that today special forms of devolution, ownership or subject matter of a right, to which limited estates corresponded, are only possible in equity and, therefore, by means of a trust. To give an idea of the importance of this exclusive aspect of equity it is sufficient to note that both the life estate and any form of co-ownership (and English law recognizes two kinds, according to whether they provide for the right of accrual in favour of the survivor[56]) may occur only under the rules of equity and therefore, fundamentally, through a trust.[57]

We must now move on to two categories which were born in the area of real property, but which, for the reasons stated above, may today only be found in equity: remainder and reversion.

---

affecting the correctness of my explanation of the rules. The classic text is J. H. C. Morris, *The Rule against Perpetuities*, London, 1956, but it is sufficient to see Megarry, *Real Property*, pp. 174–214.

A precise account of the reasons for and evolution of the rule against perpetuities is found in J. C. Gray, *The Rule against Perpetuities*, Boston, 1942, §123–§200.1.

[53] The first trusts were probably in favour of the settlor; for an explanation of this statement, see later, chapter 3 §3.a.   [54] See chapter 2 §4.a.

[55] Technically: fee simple absolute in possession.

[56] Joint tenancy and tenancy in common respectively: see chapter 2 §1.c.

[57] In more detail, and in an historical context, Graziadei, *Diritti nell'interesse altrui*, pp. 182–95.

The remainder is the result of a disposition which grants an estate to a person from the moment when an estate ceases to exist, where that estate has been granted to another person at the same time (for example: 'to X for his life, remainder to Y in fee simple'). Reversion, on the other hand, describes the case of a grantor of an estate with reference to the moment in which the estate which he has granted to a third party ceases to exist. Both types show the importance of approaching English law from the viewpoint of the relationship between a person and an estate, rather than that between a person and the physical property. In both cases, in fact, the person who is entitled to the remainder or the reversion is the owner of an estate which is vested in him, just like the other person who is entitled to the estate of which he is awaiting the coming to an end.[58] Every estate is alienable, and in every case rights may be established in favour of third parties, even a mortgage;[59] this again demonstrates the importance of not thinking in terms of the physical property.[60] Until the sixteenth century, the distinction between the estate and the physical property was recognized, and so, therefore, was that between the rights which one or the other had as their subject matter. For this reason, the estate was defined as 'time in the land'.[61]

Remainder and reversion belong to a category called 'future interests',[62] but it should be noted that what is 'future' is not the estate, but the interest, which is seen here as the right to enter into a physical relationship with the asset. One speaks, therefore, of estates which are 'vested in inter-

---

[58] The traditional view is that the explanation provided in the text only applies to real property. B. Rudden, *The New River. A Legal History*, Oxford, 1985, dedicated his research to a systematic classification of the new forms of wealth, and thus brought to light the fact that shares of real-estate companies, and even public obligations, were long considered to be 'realty', to the point of referring to fee simple of shares and obligations.

[59] Commonly, but erroneously, translated into Italian as '*ipoteca*': see chapter 3 §2.g; our review illustrates that it is a burden on the estate, not the physical asset; cf. Gray, *Rule against Perpetuities* (see above, footnote 52), §562–§71.1.

[60] Cf. Graziadei, *Diritti nell'interesse altrui*, p. 171, footnote 33.

[61] 'The land itself is one thing and the estate in the land is another thing, for an estate in the land is a time in the land, or land for a time, and there are diversities of estates, which are no more than diversities of time': one of the lawyers in *Walshingham's Case*, 1579, at 555 (cited by A. J. McClean, 'The Common Law Life Estate and the Civil Law Usufruct: A Comparative Study', in 12 ICLQ (1963) 649, at 650, n. 1).

[62] A. Gambaro, 'La proprietà nel common law anglo-americano', in A. Candian, A. Gambaro and B. Pozzo, *Property – Propriété – Eigentum*, Padua, 1992, pp. 3ff., at pp. 80–6; cf. A. Chiodi, *Situazioni prodromiche* in *common law* e in diritto Italiano: uno sguardo comparativo su *reversion ruda proprietà e aspettativa reale*, in *Quadrimestre* (1992), §1 and §3 and A. Chiodi, entry titled 'Future interest', in Digesto (4th edition), Sez. Civ., vol. VIII, Turin, 1992.

est', in contrast with those estates which are 'vested in possession'. Estates may occur in an unlimited number of combinations (if it were not for the rule on duration which we shall describe shortly): even the remainder may be defined chronologically, for example, with reference to the life of its owner, so that the limitation proposed above could have been 'to X for his life, remainder to Z for his life, remainder to Y in fee simple'. In this way, three estates would have been created, all vested, the first 'in possession' and the other two 'in interest'.

Contingent estates belong to another category, and do not, strictly speaking, fall within the category of estates, because they are suspended subject to a contingency: nonetheless, once the contingency has been satisfied, the estate is vested.

When transferred into equity, these categories retain the same elements they had in common law, although, of course, with reference to equitable interests. The determination of who has the right of ownership of an estate or interest in possession has been of special importance since the Trusts of Land and Appointment of Trustees Act 1996 came into force on 1 January 1997, because owners of an (equitable) interest in possession in a trust of land have acquired a number of rights with respect to the trustee and there has emerged a legislative notion of beneficiaries who 'taken together are absolutely entitled to the property subject to the trust'.[63] This notion also carries common-law concepts over into equity and identifies both the ultimate beneficiaries of a trust, in favour of whom there will be vesting at common law when the trust terminates, and prior beneficiaries who are the holders of the equitable rights: when this chronological split is re-united, the result is a right which is complete and unlimited.[64]

This category is not the same as the group of persons (beneficiaries who are capable and of age) in favour of whom case law has recognized the right to obtain the early dissolution of a trust.[65] On the basis of the Variation of Trusts Act 1958, the courts are given wide discretion, and are responsible for protecting the rights of minor or unborn beneficiaries; in the latter case, the court is never bound by an agreement among the beneficiaries.

---

[63] Trusts of Land and Appointment of Trustees Act 1996, s. 19.

[64] As Romer J put it in *Re Smith* (1928), 919: 'you treat all the people together just as though they formed one person'.

[65] Underhill, *Trusts*, pp. 710–16; Hanbury, *Equity*, pp. 599–601; Gardner, *Introduction*, pp. 159–61; similarly in Scotland: Wilson and Duncan, pp. 178–9.

 The Trusts of Land and Appointment of Trustees Act 1996, granted many other rights to beneficiaries, such as that of being permitted to enter into possession of the trust property in the case of a trust of land: see better below, pp. 169–70.

The first, and oldest, rule,[66] developed three centuries ago and later adapted to the modern classifications of English law, concerns the period within which every estate must acquire certainty of ownership. This rule does not directly concern trusts, but relates generally to every transfer which involves the granting of rights in favour of persons other than those in whose favour the first transfer is made. In the case of a trust, the transfer is in favour of the trustee, but the trust instrument must indicate to whom the assets will eventually be transferred by the trustee. We are, it should be noted, speaking of rights governed by common law, not the equitable interests of beneficiaries during the life of the trust. Normally, at the moment of creation of the trust, the so-called future interests come into existence; for example, at the end of the trust period, the assets may be passed to the youngest of the settlor's children who has living offspring. If, at the time of creation of the trust, the settlor is still able to have children, it is evident that the youngest of the settlor's children alive at that date who has living offspring will be the owner of an interest, but it is not possible to know whether the assets will be his or whether they will belong to a child who is born later to the settlor. In any event, even a child who is born later will not have the certainty that he will receive the asset, unless he himself has a child (and in this event, there is a further uncertainty, which is that the offspring of the child must be alive at the time of death of the settlor if his parent is to be the beneficiary).

The rule under review as traditionally expressed[67] states that a trust is void if any interest vests (not necessarily in possession) after a period which is twenty-one years after the death of a person who was living (or had been conceived) at the moment of creation of the trust.[68] This is the so-called perpetuity period. In order to comply with the rule, it is necessary that the totality of the ownership be vested in one or more persons within this period of time.[69] The correct description of the rule is, therefore, 'against

---

[66] Cf. Lupoi, *Appunti*, p. 124ff.

[67] Codified in the Perpetuities and Accumulations Act 1964, s. 3.

[68] The rule had previously been that the nullity afflicted a trust where its distribution *could have* taken place after the set period. This was one of the most frequent cases of nullity, because the period was to be established at the moment of creation of the trust and the trust was null if its term could occur after the perpetuity period, considering even the most remote possibilities. The law of 1964 introduced the 'wait-and-see' criterion, which was also viewed with favour in the United States: L. W. Waggoner, 'Perpetuities: a Perspective on Wait-and-See', in 85 ColLR (1985) 1714.

[69] For example, a trust which sees A as the life tenant and B as his successor, within the prescribed period, is valid; A and B together exhaust the 'proprietary' rights to the property on trust; it is of no interest when A should die and B consolidate his position: B is, in fact, the holder of a vested interest.

remoteness of vesting'. The complexity of the subject led to criticism over the years, recently by the Law Commission.[70]

Furthermore, the Perpetuities and Accumulations Act 1964 permits an alternative system for calculating duration: a pre-determined period of no more than eighty years, within which vesting must take place.[71] As we shall see in chapter four, most recent legislation which follows the international trust model has abolished the rule against remoteness of vesting in its traditional form in favour of a period pre-determined by the settlor, which must be within the maximum term established by law. The systematic classification of this latter type of rule is, however, different; the rule sets forth the duration of the trust, and not the time within which vesting must take place.

The second rule, also known as the rule against perpetual trusts, voids a transfer which has the purpose of blocking the assets (or, more correctly, the income from the assets) beyond the perpetuity period described above. It is of no particular interest to us.[72]

The third rule, ratified by the Perpetuities and Accumulations Act 1964,[73] deals with the limitation of access to income from a trust, and establishes a

[70] Law Commission Consultation Paper no. 133, October 1993; cf. C. Emery, 'Do We Need a Rule against Perpetuities?', in 57 MLR (1994) 602 and J. Goldsworth, 'The Rule against Perpetuities', in 2 T&T (1995), n. 1, 13. The Consultation Paper, after a complete re-examination, concluded in favour of a new law. The Law Commission examined all aspects of the topic; it discussed, for example, whether an embryo preserved by cryonics was to be held to have been 'conceived': if the reply was in the affirmative, it would be classed as a 'living or conceived person' and would, therefore, be one of the parameters of the duration of the trust (see §5.79).

In fact, one of the problems raised by the Perpetuities and Accumulations Act 1964 concerned the definition of 'living persons' at the moment of the disposition. While the traditional rule imposed no limits on this concept, the law defined certain categories of person from which the person or persons whose lifetime acted as the term of reference had to be chosen. This made it possible that dispositions which were valid in common law would not be valid in statute law. For example: 'remainder to the first of my descendants who shakes X's hand' is valid in common law because the vesting will take place, if at all, during the life of X. It is not, however, valid under the law of 1964 if X does not belong to the class of persons who may be chosen (I have taken the example from Hanbury, *Equity*, p. 343, footnote 89).

On the 'lives' to be adopted as the parameter for the duration, the question has been asked in all seriousness whether they may refer to animals: see Meredith J in *Re Kelly* (1932), at pp. 260–1.   [71] S. 1.

[72] But see chapter 3 §2.b, on the duration of so-called anomalous trusts.

In general, for the history of legislation which tends to limit the ties which a settlement (this is the classic title of any legal operation which blocks the circulation of real property until all the conditions established by the settlor have been fulfilled), see the clear and concise explanation by M. Graziadei and B. Rudden, 'Il diritto inglese dei beni e il trust: dalle res al fund', in *Quadrimestre* (1992), 458, §§9–12.

[73] S. 13 (1), which adds other provisions to those of the Law of Property Act 1925, ss. 164–5.

series of alternative periods (accumulation periods), one of which must be identified by the settlor. The purpose of this rule has nothing to do with that of the preceding rules, which concern the identification of the person who owns rights to the trust assets. This rule allows a trust to generate income in favour of the beneficiaries without ignoring the legitimate wishes of the settlor to delay receipt of the income so as to increase the capital.[74] In any event, it is possible that the period of limitation of access to the income may be reduced at the request of a sole beneficiary[75] (or, if there is more than one, of all of them jointly).

The position of the beneficiary who asks to receive his share before it is due is different again:

A testamentary trust included all the shares of a company. The beneficiary of 46/80 asked to be relieved from the obligation of waiting for the end of the trust term, and for his portion of the shares to be delivered to him. The other beneficiaries opposed this, observing that he would obtain a majority share, which would be worth more than his percentage with respect to the shares on trust. They obtained the sale of all the shares, and the division of the proceeds according to the provisions of the trust.[76]

f The secret trust

There is a secret trust when a maker of a will communicates privately to Tom that he will transfer (or has transferred) certain property to him in his will, or that the property will come to him by intestate succession, but that Tom must use it for a certain purpose or in favour of certain beneficiaries. Tom's acceptance (or lack of objection)[77] binds his conscience,[78] even if he does not know exactly what the testamentary dispositions are,[79] and so a trust is created, conditional upon the event of the testamentary disposition or the death of the transferor without a will.[80]

---

[74] To the interested reader I would signal that the problem of common-law interests which we saw just above also affects the area of equitable interests. Beneficiaries who cannot take income are nonetheless holders of a vested equitable interest in possession.

[75] This rule goes back to *Saunders v. Vautier* (1841).   [76] *Lloyds Bank plc v. Duker* (1987).

[77] Thus two precedents from the nineteenth century, later followed on several occasions: *Tee v. Ferris* (1856), and *Moss v. Cooper* (1861); in the latter case, acceptance was also seen as 'acquiescence either by words of consent or silence' (*per* Page Wood V-C, 366).

[78] 'In these cases the Court has compelled discovery and performance of the promise, treating it as a trust binding the conscience of the donee, on the ground that otherwise a fraud would be committed': Kay J in *Re Boyes* (1884), at p. 535.

[79] The metaphor of Lord Wright in *Re Keen* (1937), 242 is a fine one: the heir or legatee to whom the testator communicates that the assets granted him are subject to a trust according to conditions contained in an envelope not to be opened until after his death is like the captain of a ship 'under sealed orders'.

[80] There is a full treatment of this subject, which is of topical interest, in Hanbury, *Equity*, pp. 152–68; Jacobs, *Trusts*, pp. 106–17; Waters, *Trusts*, pp. 215–38 (referring to secret and

According to English case law, there is no problem regarding form, because (and here we see once again the venerable but still vigorous dichotomy between common law and equity) the creation of a trust occurs outside the will, and at a different level: the will gives Tom the right of legal ownership of the assets (that is, according to common law), while equity imposes a trust on them.[81]

Here again we come across the problems we saw when we looked at the constructive trust: if the property in question is land, the creation of an express trust would require writing, which is usually absent in the case of secret trusts. Some of the literature classifies the secret trust as a special kind of constructive trust,[82] which is, as we know, exempt from requirements of form; other writers, on the other hand, prefer to consider it an express trust which may be enforced in spite of its lack of form, because otherwise the trustee would be allowed to act fraudulently (within the broad meaning which equity gives the word 'fraud'), sheltered by the statutory requirements as to form. In any event, these writers insist, the secret trust is on a different level from a testamentary trust, and so requirements of form which apply to a will are not applicable to the secret trust.

This is exactly the point. The peculiarity of the secret trust is that it does not involve the transfer of any assets to the trustee except following the death of the settlor. It can, like a testamentary transfer, be freely revoked: to achieve this not even an express declaration by the settlor is required; it is sufficient that in his new will he does not leave the asset in question to the secret trustee or, in the case of a trust in an intestate succession, that he draws up a will which produces different results.[83]

The recognition of secret trusts has its place in a long cultural tradition, in which three distinct entities (figures) co-exist. One is that found in the

---

half-secret trusts see the following paragraph). For Ireland see L. A. Sheridan, 'English and Irish Secret Trusts', in 53 LQR (1951) 314. See also the decision *Nisa v. Khan* (1946), of the Supreme Court of British Guyana.

[81] Also in the United States: see Scott, *Trusts*, §55.

The terms I have used in the text, although they conform to current terminology, are not correct. They adopt the erroneous view of a dichotomy between common law and equity in the area of trusts, while, since the very first pages of this book, I have reminded the reader that the subject matter of a trust may also be an equitable entitlement. The same is true in the area of succession. A secret trust may, therefore, have as its subject matter an equitable entitlement of the deceased, which the heir will receive bound in a (secret) trust.   [82] A special case because it is contractual in nature.

[83] The consequences of the death of the trustee prior to the death of the settlor are not clear. At that moment, as I have already pointed out, the transfer to the trustee cannot yet have taken place; from this one should infer that the trust, which is stuck in a preliminary phase, will lose its effect. See E. H. Scamell, 'Secret Trusts', in 16 Sol (1949) 224.

Roman testamentary heir (which should not be confused with the '*fideicom-missum*', because the heir or fiduciary legatee derives no benefit from the granting *mortis causa*[84]) and in certain examples of the *heredero de confianza* of Catalan law,[85] and is characterized by the very narrowly defined responsibilities of the fiduciary, who is a mere *nudus minister*. The second, which is typical of secret trusts, is characterized by the durability of the appointment and, therefore, of the purpose, so that the heir is obliged to use the assets of which he comes into possession for the benefit of the beneficiaries.[86] Both these entities are different from the third *fideicommissum* which came into being with the development in many parts of Europe of the medieval *fideicommissa*, and which has the peculiar attribute that the first beneficiary may use the asset for his benefit, as may later beneficiaries.

The legal sanctioning of secret trusts dates at least from 1560,[87] and it is hard not to associate it with the rehabilitation of the Roman *heres fiduciarius* accomplished by canonical and continental writers, who enunciated rules of substance and form identical to those which would later emerge in English equity.[88] What is more, in England the basis of the protection was

---

[84] For evolution in Roman Law, see Johnston, *Roman Trusts*, ch. 4.
   The distinction is blurred by the simplification which is typical of sources from the High Middle Ages, so that the term *fidecommissarius* is given to a person who in Roman law would have been an heir or a fiduciary legatee; see, for example, the following testamentary provision: *Commissarios meos volo esse Perum et Iohannem patruos meos, quorum fidei committo vendendi ac disponendi suo arbitrio quecumque voluerint de meis bonis* (published in A. Iglesia Ferreirós (ed.), *Actes del i simposi jurídic Principat d'Andorra / República de San Marino*, Andorra, 1994, I, p. 549).

[85] For a summary of this, see J. Garrigues, 'Law of Trusts', in 2 AJCL (1953) 25, at 29, footnote 10.

[86] It should be noted that particular forms of *fideicommissum* may be effected by means of secret trusts, In fact, it is permissible (*Re Gardner (no. 1)* (1920), *Ottaway v. Norman* (1972)) for a trust to impose the obligation on the trustee to make dispositions by will to a person previously identified by the testator. A disposition is also allowed which permits the trustee to use the subject matter of the trust (money) for his own requirements, and then to make disposition in favour of a previously identified person. In this latter case, which corresponds to the *fideicommissum residui* (Nov. 108), one speaks of a *floating trust*, on which see the Australian decision *Birmingham v. Renfrew* (1937), followed in England by *Re Cleaver* (1981). This term is also used with reference to agreed wills, see above, chapter 2 §2.k: *Re Goodchild* (1996).
   For Roman–Dutch common law, which obliges the first appointee to keep at least one quarter of the patrimony intact, see S. van Leeuwen's *Commentaries on Roman–Dutch Law* (2nd edition), London, 1921, I, pp. 380–1.

[87] This was an *inter vivos* trust: J. H. Baker, 'The Use Upon a Use in Equity (1558–1625)', in 93 LQR (1977) 33, at 35; on occasions, the purpose was to evade the laws on *mortmain* (*Strickland v. Aldridge* (1804)).

[88] See the passage by C. A. de Luca, *De confidentiali haeredis institutione et substitutione*, quoted by Graziadei, *Diritti nell'interesse altrui*, pp. 227–8, footnote 2: *haeres fiduciarius tenetur restituere haereditatem sibi relictam una cum fructibus at die mortis testatricis ita ut ex ea nullum*

identified in the prevention of fraud, but in the nineteenth century it came into conflict with the rules regarding the form of a will,[89] and there seemed to be only one road to follow: secret trusts do not belong to the law of succession, and cannot be considered to be the same as testamentary dispositions or codicils.[90] They are express trusts made *inter vivos*, in which the schism which we have already looked at between the act of creation and act of transfer is particularly evident. Among the many consequences of this is that which permits a person who acts as a witness to the document to be a beneficiary of the trust,[91] and that the death of the beneficiary before that of the settlor probably does not prejudice the effectiveness of the secret trust, since the rights of the beneficiary are transferred to his heirs.[92]

This brings the question of form to the foreground, with reference not to the law of succession, but more generally to the rules on the creation of trusts. The trustee may not hide behind the lack of a writing, because equity will not allow a statute to be invoked to permit the commission of a fraud;[93] it does not, therefore, seem necessary to convert the trustee into a constructive trustee.[94] If we apply the theory which I have proposed to explain constructive trusts,[95] the transfer in favour of the secret trustee, whether by will or by intestate succession, is, according to the terminology which I have suggested equitably defective *ex parte solventis* as a consequence of the declaration of trust. An equity is created in favour of the secret beneficiary which attacks the title of the trustee and limits it.[96]

It is of interest, I think, to show how the rule which establishes a resulting trust in favour of the settlor when the dispositions of a trust are

---

commodum consequatur, quia haeres fiduciarius non est vere, et proprie haeres sed reputatur tamquam minister, custos, et depositarius. See also below, footnote 472.

[89] Cf., for an analogous situation, the *donatio mortis causa*, on which see above, chapter 2 §2.f.

[90] See *Re Blackwell* (1929), 340 *per* Lord Sumner; *Re Young* (1951), 346 *per* Dankwerts J ('the whole theory of the formation of a secret trust is that the Wills Act has nothing to do with the matter'); *Re Snowden* (1979), 177, *per* Megarry V-C. For a recent Canadian application of a testamentary trust, see *Re Riffel* (1988).

[91] *Re Young* (1951). Cf. A. J. Oakley, *Constructive Trusts* (2nd edition), London, 1987, p. 120 and Gardner, *Introduction*, p. 82. Whoever is witness to a will cannot be the recipient of any of its dispositions (as is also provided in article 597 of the Italian Civil Code).

[92] *Re Gardner (no. 2)* (1923); against this, Hayton, *Trusts*, p. 49, on the basis that a trust of a *spes* cannot exist. According to English law of successions, a legatee who pre-deceases the testator does not transfer his right to his heirs.

[93] D. R. Hodge, 'Secret Trusts: the Fraud Theory Revisited', in [1980] Conv 341; see, although *obiter*, *McCormick v. Grogan* (1869). On the maxim of equity referred to in the text, see above, chapter 2 §4.c and §4.d.   [94] Cf. Hanbury, *Equity*, pp. 165–7.

[95] See above, chapter 2 §5.c.

[96] The *remedial* short-cuts provided by the constructive trust and described in §5 of the previous chapter are not, therefore, necessary.

ineffective works in this case.[97] If the settlor has put off communicating the identity of the beneficiaries to the secret trustee, and dies before he can do so, the secret trust is nonetheless effective, and becomes a resulting trust in favour of the settlor. Since he is dead, the estate, and in the final analysis the intestate heirs, become the beneficiary.

g The half-secret trust

A trust is half-secret when it is created openly in the text of the will, but the conditions which regulate it are not set forth and are usually known only to the testator and the trustee.

Contrary to what we have just seen with the secret trust, here we are squarely within the law of succession.[98] The heir or legatee is appointed as trustee in the will, which lacks final indications as to the trust purpose or the beneficiaries. The prevailing opinion is that the trustee must come to know these conditions and accept them before, or at the same time as, the will which establishes the trust is prepared and executed. The justification given for this, which is somewhat weak,[99] is that the testator cannot complete testamentary transfers without respecting the form of the will, and so a trust created in this way may not be given its content after it has been created in the will,[100] in which one finds phrases such as 'to X on trust for the beneficiaries I have mentioned to him' or even 'to X on trust for the purposes of which he is aware'.

It is true, as has often been mentioned, that the trustee may never profit personally from his appointment, as opposed to what may occur in a secret trust, and that where the choice of beneficiaries is lacking, ineffective or void, the estate will be the beneficiary by means of a resulting trust. Questions of validity would therefore appear to be on different levels in these two types of trust, because in the case of secret trusts, evidence is needed of the declaration of trust in its entirety, whereas with half-secret trusts, it only concerns the agreements which, although they do not have

---

[97] See above, chapter 2 §3.a.

[98] This opinion, contested by W. S. Holdsworth, 'Secret Trusts', in 53 LQR (1937) 501, is self-evident; cf. Sheridan, 'English and Irish Secret Trusts' (see above, footnote 80), but see also later in the text.

[99] Immediately opposed by Holdsworth, 'Secret Trusts' (see above, footnote 98). In any event, P. Matthews, 'The True Basis of the Half-Secret Trusts', in [1979] Conv 360, at 366, shows that acceptance by the half-secret trustee is not necessary.

[100] *Re Blackwell* (1929) (*per* Viscount Sumner, 339). See also *Re Keen* (1937); *Re Bateman* (1970); *Re Beatty* (1990); cf. Pettit, *Trusts*, pp. 116–17; Hanbury, *Equity*, p. 160; Waters, *Trusts*, pp. 225–7. For the United States, see Scott, *Trusts*, §55(8), who, in conformity with the US view, considers both secret and half-secret trusts to be testamentary trusts.

the form of a will, would serve to complete an appointment which is clearly and validly expressed in the testamentary document. Where the same questions are posed in the context of proof of testamentary intent, one would, as we have seen, turn in one case to the theory of fraud, and in the other to the theory of incorporation by reference,[101] so as to overcome objections based on the formal requirements of expressions of testamentary intent. In this way, however, one elects a highly technical solution for half-secret trusts which may not always be suitable for giving effect to the intent formulated by the settlor outside the will. On the other hand, it has been observed that a wider view of fraud would solve every question relating to proof easily,[102] especially taking into consideration the fact that the fundamental point of half-secret trusts is not the risk that the trustee might profit from them,[103] but the objective requirement that limitations should not be placed upon the implementation of an intent which has been formally expressed, albeit only partially.[104]

If this were the correct interpretation, the distinction between secret and half-secret trusts would tend to disappear, as it already has in Irish law.[105] Moving on from considerations of proof in testamentary issues, one would come to a revisitation of the juridical basis of the two types of trust and make them one and the same. This would, in my view, be an excessively drastic result.[106]

A comparison between the fiduciary heir as in article 627 of the Italian civil code, and the two types of trust examined above illustrates, first of all, a partial diversity of areas of application, given that secret trusts also apply to intestate succession.[107] Secondly, English law permits exactly what

---

[101] This last theory was proposed by Matthews, 'True Basis' (see above, footnote 99); *contra* Hodge, 'Secret Trusts' (see above, footnote 93), 349–50. For similar situations (with different outcomes) in Italian law, see N. Lipari, *Il negozio fiduciario* (see above, footnote 29), pp. 370–7.

[102] B. Perrins, 'Secret Trusts: Are they *Dehors*?', in [1985] Conv 248 holds that the discussion should be kept exclusively at the level of probative rules.

[103] This could never happen because, as pointed out just above, the trustee is described as such in the will, and so either the trust is valid, or its subject matter returns to the estate and follows the rules regarding the property of the deceased which is not subject to specific bequests. It should be noted that the legal action is often raised by the half-secret trustee who requests that the conditions under which he must act be judicially confirmed.   [104] Cf. Hodge, 'Secret Trusts' (see above, footnote 93), 341, especially at 341–3.

[105] Sheridan, 'English and Irish Secret Trusts' (see above, footnote 80), 323.

[106] D. Wilde, 'Secret and Semi-Secret Trusts: Justifying Distinctions Between the Two', in [1995] Conv 366.

[107] See, moreover, G. Mirabelli, 'La disposizione fiduciaria nell'art. 627 c.c. (Contributo allo studio dell'interposizione di persona)', in [1955, 1957] Riv. trim. dir. proc. civ. 1074; Lipari, *Il negozio fiduciario* (see above, footnote 29), pp. 182–4, 359–80.

article 627 forbids: an action to ascertain the fiduciary nature of the testamentary dispositions (secret trust) or the exact contents of the fiduciary dispositions (half-secret trust). Thirdly, English law permits an action of specific performance against a secret or semi-secret trustee, which is precluded by Italian law.

h Trustee and personal representative

In English law, the devolution of the estate does not occur directly to the chosen heirs. The very notion of being called to the estate is unknown. The estate (and here the word 'estate' does not refer to a specific asset, but to the entire estate of the deceased) is transferred by law to personal representatives (who usually number at least two) appointed by the court or by the testator (and confirmed by the court[108]), whose role is to pay debts, collect credits, settle all other pending matters, and after no less than one year divide the net amount remaining according to the dispositions of the will or the laws of intestate succession.[109] Of course, it may happen that the estate has been placed in trust by the testator, and therefore the transfer to the trustee will take place, just as in the case of any other person, at the end of the administration period.[110] During the administration period, the beneficiaries of the testamentary dispositions have no rights in the assets, not even equitable rights, even when identified assets are bequeathed to legatees.[111]

---

[108] Technically, he is called an executor if appointed by the testator, and an administrator if appointed by a court. On the entire subject, see Snell, *Equity*, pp. 309–79.

[109] C. Sawyer, *Succession, Wills & Probate*, London, 1995, ch. 12–13; C. V. Margrave-Jones, *Mellows: The Law of Succession* (5th edition), London, 1993; Lupoi, *Appunti*, pp. 134–7; in detail A. Miranda, *Il testamento nel diritto inglese. Fondamento e sistema*, Padua, 1995, pp. 87–99, 407–44; E. Calò, *Dal Probate al family trust*, Milan, 1996, ch. 1. With special reference to intestate succession: C. H. Sherrin and R. C. Bonehill, *The Law and Practice of Succession*, London, 1994.

[110] Where immovable property is involved, a writing is required; this is also the case if the trustees and personal representatives are the same persons (as often happens).

[111] This was not certain until recently: cf. V. Latham, 'The Right of the Beneficiary to Specific Items of the Trust Fund', in 32 CBR (1954) 520, at 521–2 and 527–31; Underhill, *Trusts*, pp. 13–14.

The key decision on this subject is from the Privy Council (on appeal from an Australian court, *Commissioners of Stamp Duties v. Livingston* (1965)): the testator's widow was the sole heir. The inheritance included immovable property in Queensland, but the widow had her domicile in New South Wales. When the widow died during the period of administration of the husband's estate, the question arose as to whether inheritance duties were due on the immovable property in Queensland. The Privy Council decided that they were not, because the widow could not be considered to be their owner.

Moreover, a disposition which states 'all shares in my name and every other right which I may have' also has the effect of transferring rights of the testator to property of which he is the heir, even if it is still in administration: *Re Leigh's Will Trust* (1970).

The personal representative has his origins in ecclesiastical courts rather than in those of equity, and is not a trustee, both because heirs and legatees are not in any equitable relation to him, and because his obligations are due to the estate, and, finally, because he occupies his position virtually without any time-limit; in fact, when the administration period ends and the funds have been distributed, any supervening debt or credit will serve to reactivate the personal representative's functions.

Among the many other differences which may be identified between the two positions, there is also the fact that each personal representative may act individually with regard to personal property, whereas trustees must act jointly. On the other hand, the obligations which fall upon the personal representatives are of a fiduciary nature, at least insofar as they may not derive any personal benefit from their role,[112] and the law frequently treats them like trustees.[113]

i The *actio pauliana*

The Fraudulent Conveyances Act was passed during the reign of Elizabeth I,[114] and remained the law in England until 1925, and is still the law, with some modifications, in much of the Commonwealth.[115] Transfers made with intent to defraud the creditors of the transferor are void, unless the person receiving the asset has supplied good consideration and had no notice of the transferor's intent.

This is an *actio pauliana* in the true sense of the word: it is raised by a creditor, and has the effect of restoring the debtor's estate to its prior condition. The action granted by the Elizabethan statute passed into s. 172 of the Law of Property Act 1925, and then into ss. 423–5 of the Insolvency Act 1986, and has maintained its character as an action in favour of all

---

[112] In this sense it has been held that the guardian is a trustee: *Duke of Beaufort v. Berty* (1721), 704–5.

[113] Hanbury, *Equity*, pp. 55–61; cf. Béraudo, *Trusts*, §46. Recently, see Trusts of Land and Appointment of Trustees Act 1996, s. 18.

[114] 13 Eliz ch 5 (1571), followed by 18 Eliz. I c. 4 (1576). Legislation in this area had begun nearly a century earlier with 3 H. VIII c. 4 (1487).

[115] For example, in Australia until the Bankruptcy Act of 1924. These rules also remained in force for a long period in the United States, where to date no uniformity among the States has yet been achieved. Some, in fact, have remained with the Elizabethan law, while others have adopted the Uniform Fraudulent Conveyance Act of 1918, and others still the Uniform Fraudulent Transfer Act of 1984 (to which I shall refer below with the acronym UFTA). In general, see chapters 2 and 3 of D. E. Osborne (ed.), *Asset Protection: Domestic and International Law and Tactics*, Clark Boardman Callaghan, 1995.

Bankruptcy is a federal matter, and has been codified in the Bankruptcy Code (US Code, title 11), which has recently been amended by the Bankruptcy Reform Act 1994.

creditors.[116] Nonetheless, its borders are well defined: from an objective point of view, the transfer must be free or for inadequate consideration ('undervalue'), and the intent to obtain an advantage to the detriment of the creditors must be established.[117]

Proof of the intent of the transferor is often objective. The current view is that the transfer of all assets into a trust, when a person is, generally speaking, subject to liability for the conduct of his affairs, whether they be commercial or professional, is sufficient to bring it within the provisions of the statute.[118] Other values direct the courts' reasoning when the transfer of the assets into a trust contains elements of a sham, and where the settlor subsequently seeks to recover the assets from the trustee because the grounds which had induced him to create the trust no longer exist. English case law does not easily allow the trust to be done away with.

An individual was about to acquire a garage, with the intention of starting a business. In the same period, he purchased the house where he was to live with his wife, and put it in his wife's name. He later requested in a legal action that the recording in his wife's name be recognized as giving rise to a resulting trust. Lord Denning refused, using a simple argument: 'As against his wife he wants to say that it [i.e. the house] belongs to him. As against his creditors that it belongs to her. That simply will not be.'[119]

The action of revocation in a bankruptcy, introduced by the Bankruptcy Act 1914, may now be found in the Insolvency Act 1986.[120] It affects trusts established by the bankrupt person without consideration or for insufficient consideration during the two years prior to the filing of the bankruptcy petition, or five years if the settlor was already insolvent or became insolvent as a result of the creation of the

[116] S. 423(2)(a): a judge has the power to issue appropriate orders with the purpose of *'restoring the position to what it would have been if the transaction had not been entered into'*.

[117] The Insolvency Act 1986, s. 423 (3): 'In the case of a person entering into such a transaction, an order shall only be made if the court is satisfied that it was entered into by him for the purpose: a) of putting assets beyond the reach of a person who is making, or may at some time make, a claim against him, or b) of otherwise prejudicing the interests of such a person in relation to the claim which he is making or may make.'

[118] *Re Butterworth* (1882); see Underhill, *Trusts*, p. 266. P. Matthews, 'The Asset Protection Trust: Holy Grail, or Wholly Useless?', in 6 OTPR (1996) 57, at 72, observes acutely that the choice of applicable law for a trust to which assets are transferred which is different from that which would normally have regulated the trust, and is more favourable to the settlor could be an indication of an intent to evade taxes being put into action.

In the United States, s. 4 (a)(1) of the Bankruptcy Code provides for the case of a person who, at the moment of the disposition, 'was engaged or was about to engage in a business or a transaction for which the remaining assets of the debtor were unreasonably small in relation to the business or transaction'.   [119] *Tinker v. Tinker* (1970) (542).

[120] Ss. 339, 341 and 342. See H. Anderson, 'The Treatment of Trust Assets in English Insolvency Law', in E. McKendrick (ed.), *Commercial Aspects of Trusts and Fiduciary Obligations*, Oxford, 1992, p. 167.

trust.[121] The notion of 'insolvency' is broad, and includes the case where the remaining estate of the settlor is insufficient to satisfy prospective obligations.[122] Courts have a wide range of orders at their disposal, the most direct of which is an order to the trustee to transfer the assets placed in trust (or those resulting from their transformation or conversion) to the receiver.

The subject of creditor protection has acquired greater importance in the United States, where professionals, who are exposed to costly actions based on their professional responsibility, are moving towards placing all their assets in trust rather than take out ever more burdensome insurance policies.[123] This is the subject matter of the so-called 'asset-protection trust', of which we shall speak later.

j Reasons for nullity

Invalidity of a trust is not an exceptional event, because this is an extremely technical area which has few general principles and many specific rules, not always reducible to a cohesive system.[124]

In the first place, the declaration of trust must be reviewed, whether it relates to the settlor himself or a third party. The so-called 'precatory trust', of which we have already spoken, belongs to the area of ethics, not law; it frequently comes up in the context of semi-secret trusts,[125] because in these cases the testamentary disposition does not, from a technical standpoint,

---

[121] The law also deals with other cases, among which are trusts established for the benefit of a creditor: Insolvency Act, 1986, s. 340.

  The recent decision *In re Kumar* (1993) is interesting: the husband, in the context of a rearrangement of his dealings with his wife, transferred the entire ownership of the family home, which had until then been owned jointly, to her. The wife thereby became responsible for the mortgage. The couple divorced shortly thereafter, and the judge refused to recognize any property right in the husband's assets in favour of the wife, holding that she had already received enough. After three months, the husband became bankrupt, and the bankruptcy court revoked the transfer to the wife because the amount of the mortgage which she had assumed was lower than the value of the right she had acquired. On the effects of bankruptcy on the equitable relationship of co-ownership (joint tenancy) see *In re Dennis* (1992) and (1995).

[122] The law speaks of 'contingent or prospective liabilities'; the former are conditional obligations, while the latter do not correspond to any legal category, and, in the absence of a precise definition from case law, one must conclude that the legislators wished to strike at those who intend to 'make themselves safe' against the possibility that certain economic situations might develop which might damage them.

[123] Cf. D. E. Osborne, 'Asset Protection for United States Clients', in [1995] JIntPl 12.

[124] Traditional teachings, according to which the creation of a trust must satisfy three certainties (certainty of words, certainty of subject matter and certainty of object), are of little use. They had their origin in the first half of the nineteenth century: *Wright v. Atkyns* (1832); *Knight v. Knight* (1840).

  It should be pointed out that in all cases of nullity, the trust is converted into a resulting trust in favour of the settlor, or, if he is deceased, in favour of his estate.

[125] See above, chapter 3 §1.g.

always create the relationship which the testator intended; indeed, it is often made in non-technical language which refers to private entrustings or understandings between the testator and the trustee.[126]

As I have stated above, the creation of a trust requires the transfer of an entitlement to the trustee (if he is not the settlor). As a result, a declaration of trust which does not identify a trustee is void. In the case of a testamentary disposition, however, the court has the power to appoint a trustee and so give effect to the disposition. There is a theoretical explanation for this apparent anomaly which is based on the peculiar system of inheritance under English law: the estate passes to the personal representative in all cases, and he must, among other duties, ensure that effect be given to the trust by means of the transfer of the assets to the trustee at the end of the administration period.[127] In the case of trusts among living persons, on the other hand, the transfer cannot take place if no person in whose favour the transfer is to be made (i.e. the trustee) has been appointed, and it is for this reason that the creation of the trust is null and void.

A trust is also null and void if it does not observe the requirements regarding the duration or maximum term during which the income may be accumulated.[128]

Trusts are also declared null and void where the grant of the benefit is conditional upon conduct which is judged to be contrary to public policy[129] or family or matrimonial morals.[130] In these cases, there is often an important distinction between a condition subsequent and a determinable interest: the latter, whose limits are frequently hard to define in English law, does not lend itself to a simple comparison with civilian classifications, since it appears to be a final term of the transaction which may or may not occur, and may therefore be confused with a condition

---

[126] The distinction is made between *executed* and *executory* trusts. One uses the term *executory trusts* each time the settlor indicates the fundamental elements of the trust in the required form, but where he has not foreseen a series of events which in the absence of a special law a judge will have to regulate by seeking to reconstruct the presumed wishes of the settlor (for a fairly detailed discussion, see Béraudo, *Trusts*, §80). The language of *executed trusts*, on the other hand, which may be recognized by their professional appearance, is interpreted by a court with regard being given to its literal meaning. For a recent application of the distinction between *executed* and *executory* trusts, see *Davis v. Richards & Wallington* (1990).   [127] See above, chapter 3 §1.h.

[128] The so-called *rule against perpetuities*, see chapter 3 §1.e.

[129] For example, in *Thrupp v. Collett* (1858): a testamentary trust for payment of fines issued to poachers. On beneficial dispositions which discriminate on grounds of race or gender, see Hanbury, *Equity*, pp. 332–3.

[130] See the Canadian judgment *Re McBride* (1980), regarding a testamentary trust which the court held to have induced the son of the settlor to obtain a divorce. The English decisions in *Re Johnson* (1967), and *Re Caborne* (1943) reach the same conclusion.

subsequent.[131] As is often the case in this area, the distinction has its roots in technicalities relating to deeds of transfer of real property, so that 'to X for so long as he remains unmarried' creates a determinable interest, whereas 'to X on condition that he does not marry' is a condition subsequent.[132] The consequences of this distinction are significant: an illicit or immoral condition subsequent is treated as if it had not been imposed, while a determinable interest connected to an immoral or illicit event is void from its creation.[133]

There is also a nullity where the provision creating the trust is insufficiently certain regarding the purpose of the trust or its beneficiaries, or where the beneficiaries defined in such broad terms as to make control of the acts of the trustee by the courts impossible,[134] or where they are so vague that the satisfaction of the conditions upon which the loss of a beneficiary's rights is dependent cannot easily be verified.[135]

Leaving aside categories of trusts which have no beneficiaries,[136] the last case of nullity concerns the lack of required formalities. We have referred to them on more than one occasion, and have shown how they may often be overcome by recourse to the constructive trust. In any event, it is worth recalling three types of attribution *mortis causa*, to establish how little significance form has in English law. I am referring to the *donatio mortis causa*, the revocable trust and the secret trust. In each of these cases one sees the structure of the testamentary disposition (freely revocable, effective at the settlor's death), but not the form, and in each of these cases the *regula*

---

[131] Cf. A. di Majo, 'Termine (dir. civ.)', in *Enc. Dir.*, XLIV, Milan, 1992, pp. 189–90, pp. 195–6. It was not by chance that this question led M. Allara, *Le nozioni fondamentali del diritto civile*, Turin, n.d., p. 620 to write of 'proprietà temporanea', given that the idea of temporary 'real rights' is typical of the English legal system.

[132] Cf. Megarry, *Real Property*, pp. 197–9; Hanbury, *Equity*, pp. 190–1, 334–5; Snell, *Equity*, p. 136.

The notion of determinable interest may perhaps be better understood if one brings to mind the concept of *escheat* (see Lupoi, *Appunti*, pp. 8, 19): the escheat of an estate does not involve re-entry by the lord (which would be a reversion, and therefore an estate in its own right), but the extinction, death or loss of an estate. In English real property it is not possible for property to belong to no one, even for an instant, and so there is always a superior lord who finds himself in the same position as that of the grantor of the vacant estate prior to the grant (it could be the same lord or a different one, according to events which had occurred in the meantime): cf. F. W. Hardman, 'The Law of Escheat', in 4 LQR (1888) 318, at 322–4. Escheat is, therefore, an incident of tenure, and not a mechanism of succession or transfer, or, for that matter, a limit on the duration of an estate.

[133] This distinction also has consequences for the rules against remoteness of vesting: see chapter 3 §1.e and the regulation of protective trusts: see chapter 3 §2.e.

[134] *Re Hay's Settlement Trusts* (1981); *R v. District Auditor* (1986). But see *Re Denley's Trust Deed* (1969), and below, the conclusion of chapter 3 §2.b.

[135] Cf. Hanbury, *Equity*, pp. 335–7.   [136] See below, chapter 3 §2.b and §2.c.

which disciplines it pre-dated legislation on the form of wills. This is a typical device of the English legal system, which tends to leave (judge-made) *regulae* in place unless they are clearly and specifically repealed by statute.

2. Typology of trusts

a Business trusts

The business trust is an American, and to a lesser extent Canadian, institution, and is now of very limited significance. I mention it here only because on occasions the term 'business trust' is used as if it belonged to a general category of trusts relating to business matters; in fact, the latter now corresponds to purpose trusts, which will be dealt with in the following section.

The business trust[137] was a regular trust used for business purposes. A document was usually issued which certified the extent of the rights over the profits due to each beneficiary. The beneficiary was at the outset the person who had contributed capital to the trust. The structure was, therefore, comparable to a type of company: the trustees (board of directors) were elected by the beneficiaries (shareholders). The *raison d'être* of this structure was the backwardness of corporate legislation in the United States in the nineteenth century. From a tax standpoint, it still has advantages today.[138]

The business trust was highly criticized when it first emerged as a 'new monster'.[139] One of its first applications was in the so-called Massachusetts Trust, which was a primitive form of holding company in use at a time

---

[137] Cf. D. T. Trautman, 'Study on business trusts and charitable trusts', in Actes, p. 111; D. W. M. Waters, 'Comments on business and charitable trusts in Canada', in Actes, p. 118.

[138] Fundamentally, the lack of taxability of the trustee and the direct imputation of taxes on profits to the beneficiaries. In the case of the *Massachusetts trust* these advantages were eliminated in 1935, when the Supreme Court decided that the rules on direct taxation of joint-stock companies were to be applied. Other forms which developed later in the United States have enjoyed varying degrees of success. In many cases, the tax purpose was a different one: to take advantage of the depreciation of assets acquired by the trust. Briefly, the mechanism was to create a trust with initial funds sufficient to pay a part of the purchase price of an asset with a short depreciation period. The remainder of the purchase price was obtained by means of a loan secured by the asset. Income from the asset (a classic case dealt with rail wagons) was just sufficient to repay the loan, but the beneficiaries of the trust took the benefit of the depreciation allowances, which were calculated on a capital value (the entire purchase price of the asset) which was significantly greater than the amount they had paid into the trust.

For English law, with reference to trusts which carry out business activities (*trading trusts*), see Hayton, *Trusts*, pp. 61–2; D. J. Hayton, 'Trading Trusts', in Glasson, B5.

[139] F. M. Stimson, 'Trusts', in 1 HarvardLR (1887) 132.

when one company in the United States could not own shares in another. Statutory enactments, which are nowadays known as 'antitrust' laws aimed at suppressing the financial and industrial power of these business trusts. This explains the origins of the assonance between the words 'antitrust' and 'trust', which still causes confusion in the minds of laymen.

The term 'business trust' is also currently used in another sense, to designate that type of trust which does not pertain to the settlor's family, emotional or personal interests.[140] This led users of the term to commit an error of perspective, and to consider this type of trust as being in some way spurious or of secondary importance. On the contrary, it represents a field of ever-increasing importance (as much in the area of legal analysis as in economics), and the developments corroborate the belief which I expressed at the beginning of this book that one must always use the word 'trusts' only in the plural.

b Purpose trusts

It is often held that trusts which have no beneficiaries are null and void: in other words, a trust may not consist of property directed towards the fulfillment of a purpose. So-called purpose trusts have no place in English law, because there is no person (the beneficiary) who can insist on the trustee's performance.[141]

The charitable trust, to which we shall dedicate the next section, is an exception to this principle, but it is such a noteworthy one that it casts doubts on the very foundation of the principle.

There are also anomalous trusts which do not conform, either to the above principle or with respect to one another. For example, trusts for the construction and maintenance of tombs, for saying masses, for the upkeep of a specific animal, in favour of associations and for the promotion of fox-hunting are valid.[142] They are subject to the general rules of duration

---

[140] Thus, for example, Waters, *Trusts*, pp. 438–53.

[141] 'A trust may be created for the benefit of persons but not for a purpose or object . . . For a purpose or object cannot sue': *Leahy v. A-G for New South Wales* (1959), at p. 478 *per* Viscount Simonds; 'There must be somebody in whose favour the court can decree performance.': *Morice v. Bishop of Durham* (1804), at p. 405 *per* Sir William Grant MR (where, in any event, the reference was more to the vagueness of the powers granted to the trustee than to the absence of specific beneficiaries). For the United States, see Scott, *Trusts*, §124.

[142] It is self-evident that these are rules whose existence is due to judicial oversight and which must, therefore, be applied restrictively: see Harman LJ in *Re Endacott* (1959). For trusts for the upkeep of dogs in particular, see J. C. Gray, 'Gifts for a "Non-Charitable Purpose"', in 15 HarvardLR (1901) 509. On the entire question of anomalous trusts, see P. Matthews, 'The New Trust: Obligations without Rights?', in A. J. Oakley (ed.), *Trends in Contemporary Trust Law*, Oxford, 1996, which examines the reasoning behind each

explained above, with particular regard to the second rule concerning perpetual trusts,[143] and it has often been held that the trustee may not be coerced into performing any obligation (hence the traditional term 'trusts of imperfect obligations'). Furthermore, in the case of testamentary trusts, a court may oblige the trustee to accept the obligation to act required by the settlor for the attainment of a purpose, thus permitting the heir to take action if the trustee does not perform.[144]

A third exception, noteworthy because it is a recent development which has caused writers to revisit the basis of the principle which nullifies trusts without beneficiaries is a trust which has a certain number of persons who derive benefit from it, although there is some doubt as to whether they can be defined as beneficiaries in the technical sense.

A piece of land was transferred by a settlor to a trustee for a pre-determined period, to be used as a sports centre for employees of a company.

If this arrangement is identified as a trust for purposes, it is null and void (and it cannot be salvaged as a charitable trust, because its purpose is not included in the list of purposes of charitable trusts). On the other hand, it does not identify any specific beneficiaries in the usual sense of holders of an equitable interest, and therefore risks being null and void for lack of beneficiaries or, in any event, for lack of certainty. The court, however, declared it valid. Apparently there is distinction between the cases where the beneficiaries' interests are indirect and imprecise and those where the terms employed by the settlor identify those, or the category of those who have a right to take action against the trustee to ensure performance of the trust.[145]

It is evident that the beneficiaries we are talking about are not the usual type of beneficiaries, which are individuals to whom a proprietary interest in the trust assets is traditionally, albeit erroneously, attri-

---

individual rule; Pettit, *Trusts*, pp. 52–7; Underhill, *Trusts*, pp. 97–102 and pp. 102–8 on the complex rules regarding trusts in favour of unincorporated associations, on which I shall not dwell.

In Ireland a testamentary trust which requires the trustee to use the trust assets to the 'best spiritual advantage' of the settlor is valid: *Re Gibbons* (1917).

[143] See above, chapter 3 §1.e. In particular on the duration of trusts for the upkeep of a tomb, see Pettit, *Trusts*, p. 223.

[144] I have used the word *heir* for the sake of simplicity. The technical notion is that of the *residuary legatee*.

[145] *Re Denley's Trust Deed* (1968); cf. *Re Lipinski* (1976) ('when, then, the trust, though expressed as a purpose, is directly or indirectly for the benefit of an individual or individuals, it seems to me that it is in general outside the mischief of the beneficiary principle', at p. 382), and the limitations expressed by Vinelott J in *Re Grant's Will Trust* (1980). We shall see a possible different reading of the terms of the problem at the end of this chapter.

buted.[146] It is not sufficient, therefore, to point out that case law, at least since the beginning of the twentieth century, has taken a more liberal position than in the past, and has held trusts to be valid which, if the traditional theory had been applied, would undoubtedly have been void.[147] In my opinion, this evolution in English law re-instates the correct view of the beneficiary's position – upset for over a century by the concept of equitable ownership. It restores to the procedural level (who can sue a trustee?) a subject improperly transferred to substantive law.[148]

Those who, quite appropriately, contest the inclusion of the category of trusts we are discussing within the category of purpose trusts[149] are nonetheless held back by the view that in any trust structure other than charitable trusts there must be a person who can demand that the assets of a trust be made over to him. But this is not true even of classic trusts; there is nothing to prevent the subject matter of a trust from consisting of revenues deriving from a chose in action or the use of a building. The beneficiaries, whether identified by name or as members of a class, can only 'enjoy' the right or the asset which produces revenue or profit; they cannot make it their own. This should not, however, hide the fact that they make the subject matter of the trust (not the trust assets) their own, and are therefore beneficiaries in the technical sense. In other words, even if the trusts assets are unattainable, the beneficiaries of these trusts can certainly take action against the trustee to secure performance of the provisions of the trust instrument. Only an unrefined view of the trust phenomenon with no appreciation of anything other than its economic aspects, a view to which I do not subscribe, could lead to the conclusion that a beneficiary is a person who has the right to demand the early dissolution of the trust and the delivery of the trust assets to him; this would mean exacerbating the contrast between charitable trusts, where this person obviously does not exist, and ordinary trusts. On the contrary, these two classes of trust both have individuals who can take action against the trustee for the perform-ance of the trust; nullity derives from a lack of these individuals and therefore has an exclusively procedural explanation. In substantive law, on the other hand, there need not be a person who compensates for the

---

[146] Hanbury, *Equity*, p. 354 notes this, for example.

[147] *Re Trusts of the Abbott Fund* (1900): an amount was collected for the upkeep of two elderly deaf-mute ladies. The judge held that they were not beneficiaries in the technical sense, but that the trust was nonetheless valid. On the death of the two ladies, since there was no beneficiary, a resulting trust would come into being, and the amounts in the fund at that time would be divided among those who had established it.

[148] See the *dicta* at the beginning of this section.

[149] Matthews, 'New Trust' (see above, footnote 142).

equitable defect in the title of the trustee of a purpose trust by owning what the trustee lacks. This is one of the keys to the unified theory of trusts[150] to which I will come later in this book.

c Charitable trusts

The term 'charities' describes both charitable trusts and corporations which have a charitable purpose. The latter belong to the category of non-profit-making entities, but are not its only members.[151] The rationale for the existence of this category is a favourable tax regime, which in some jurisdictions is the same for all non-profit entities. For this reason, particularly in the United States,[152] we see anti-avoidance laws passed to combat the numerous entities which are formed exclusively to obtain tax advantages.[153]

In England, charitable uses emerged in the sixteenth century, with the encouragement of the Church. The Elizabethan statute of 1601[154] was passed to suppress abuses which were evident even then,[155] and listed in its preamble a series of purposes for which these trusts could be established.[156] This list was certainly not intended to define what is intended by charitable uses (or today by charitable trusts); no statutory enactment has filled the gap.[157] For centuries, case law continued along the path of interpretation,

---

[150] See below, chapter 3 §3.d.

[151] Cf. L. Gandullia, 'La regolamentazione fiscale degli enti "non profit"', in R. Artoni (ed.), *Gli enti non profit. Aspetti tributari*, Padua, 1996 (Antologia, n. 5), 3, where a full comparative analysis may be found.

[152] Also recently developed in England with the Charities Acts of 1992 and 1993.

[153] It is in the United States that tax planning by means of charitable trusts has been most widely applied. It has also employed techniques which recognize tax credits consequent upon donations in favour of charities, and which exempt the charities from the imposition of taxes on gains from assets received as gifts.

[154] Eliz. I c. 4 (Charitable Uses Act).

[155] In fact, it complains that assets destined for charitable uses 'have not been employed according to the charitable intent of the givers and founders thereof, by reason of frauds, breaches of trust, and negligence in those who should pay, deliver and employ the same.'

[156] The first category identified by the Elizabethan law concerns trusts created 'for relief of aged, impotent and poor people'. The term 'impotent' is an indication from European common law, since it transfers into English the semantic significance of *impotentes* which, in late Roman law, and later in High Medieval law, meant the opposite of *potentes*. It is different from *divites/pauperes* as a coupling, because it is a political, and not a class, matter: the *impotentes* are those who enjoy no access to the protection which the law provides in the abstract, and who are subject to abuses from the *potentes*. For a more detailed discussion, see my book *On the Origins of the European Legal Order*, Cambridge, 2000, pp. 264–8 (*Alle radici del mondo giuridico europeo*, Rome, 1994).

[157] Not even the Charities Act 1993, which must be considered to be a reworking of the whole subject, attempts any kind of definition. The term 'charitable purposes', which is central to the legislative discipline implicitly refers to rules of case law. For the similar situation in the United States, see Scott, *Trusts*, §348–§403.

and so did not achieve very clear results. In an opinion of Lord Macnaghten in a decision from 1891,[158] four categories of purpose were listed: relief of poverty, advancement of education, advancement of religion and other purposes beneficial to the community. Although it is often cited in literature and case law as the authoritative definition in the area of charitable trusts, it is clear that this opinion did not represent a major step forward from the Elizabethan statements.[159]

The structural characteristic of the charitable trust is that the trustee must use the trust property for a charitable purpose. From a comparative standpoint, it would not be proper to state that a purpose is charitable if it is for the public good or in the public interest (for these notions have different meanings in the various systems of law), or that the satisfaction of this requirement is sufficient to give a trust the character of a charitable trust, thereby saving it from the nullity usually imposed upon purpose trusts. In fact, only those purposes are charitable which are found to be so by the courts on the basis of the Elizabethan statements and other pronouncements made over the centuries.[160] Even expert jurists may err, and draft a trust instrument which is completely null and void.[161]

For example, trusts in favour of the poor are always held to be charitable, apparently even if the poor people are to be selected from among the settlor's relatives,[162] but they are not so when the purpose of the trust is extended to the welfare or general protection of the health or well-being of the public; these are notions which have been held to exceed the recog-

---

[158] *Commissioners for Special Purposes v. Pemsel* (1891), 11.

[159] See, in fact, the restrictive comments of Lord Wilberforce in *Scottish Burial v. Glasgow* (1968), at p. 154. Cf. G. Iudica, 'I trusts di pubblico interesse', in *Atti Milano*, ch. 33.

[160] A legislative definition has never been attempted. For example, s. 96(1) of the Charities Act 1993 limits itself to the statement that '*charity*' indicates 'any institution, corporate or not, which is established for charitable purposes'.

[161] Two examples, important in that in both cases the trust instruments had been prepared by first-class solicitors, are the trust established by Lord Astor, the press baron, to promote harmony among nations and the independence of the press, and the will of George Bernard Shaw, which left certain property for the development of a forty-character alphabet and the transliteration of his work *Androcles and the Lion* into that alphabet. Both were declared null: see, respectively, *Re Astor's Settlement Trusts* (1952), and *Re Shaw* (1957).

The Charity Commissioners have drafted a model instrument, which provides for numerous variations, for the creation of charitable trusts which are not especially complicated.

[162] Hayton, *Trusts*, p. 108; this is an old line of English precedents which were re-examined by the House of Lords in *Oppenheim v. Tobacco Securities* (1951) (although the inspiration must also be old, since it may also be found in article 902 of the Italian Civil Code of 1865). On the notion of 'poverty' for the purposes of charitable trusts see Waters, *Trusts*, pp. 551–62.

In Canada a trust has been held to be charitable which provided for the school education of the testator's male descendants: *Re Doering* (1949).

nized limits.[163] The magnitude of the category of beneficiaries cannot be judged by its numerical size alone, in part because when determining whether a trust qualifies, the size issue is considered together with the verification of whether the purpose is among those permitted for charitable trusts. The two aspects tend to become confused, as in the case of decisions on charitable trusts with a religious purpose: a trust in favour of a small contemplative monastic community has been held not to be charitable, whereas one in favour of members (equally limited in number) of a synagogue has been held to be charitable,[164] the reasoning being that the members of the synagogue lived within society, whereas the monastic community did not.[165]

Placement within one or another of the four categories of Lord Macnaghten may also frequently be contested. While it had always been held that a trust for the promotion of sporting activities could not be charitable,[166] a Canadian decision has drawn attention to the conditions of our modern, sedentary, lifestyle, and to the benefits which the public in general derives from the encouragement of sporting activities.[167] The House of Lords has held a trust for the promotion of sport among students to be charitable, although the decision was based on different considerations: sport completes a school education.[168]

One sure limitation is that a trust with a political purpose ('political purpose' must be taken with a very wide meaning) is never charitable,[169] nor are trusts dedicated to the reform of existing statutes or the introduction of new ones. Charitable status has been denied to Amnesty International,[170] as it has been to the Anti-Vivisection Society.[171] The case law on

---

[163] *A-G of the Bahamas v. Royal Trust* (1986), and *D'Aguiar v. IRC* (1970). See also *Hadaway v. Hadaway* (1955), which held that a trust for the establishment of a bank which would offer low interest rates to farmers on the island of St Vincent was not valid.

[164] I refer, respectively, to *Gilmour v. Coats* (1949), and *Neville Estates v. Madden* (1962). Cf. Gardner, *Introduction*, pp. 93–5, 103, 106.

See also *Re Hetherington* (1989), where a trust for the holding of masses was held to be charitable where the public was admitted to the service. Recently, see *Re Le Cren Clarke* (1996): a trust which sustains the activity of healing by the laying on of hands (in a Christian religious context) is valid.

[165] The latter, said the judge, 'live in this world and mix with their fellow-citizens' (at p. 853).

[166] *Re Nottage* (1895).   [167] *Re Laidlaw* (1985).

[168] *IRC v. McMullen* (1980). A charitable trust for the preparation and upkeep of playing-fields for children from the borough has been discussed in *Oldham Borough Council v. A-G* (1993).

[169] *Re Koeppler's Will Trusts* (1984), which declared the nullity of a trust established to promote international co-operation in the West (the trust was salvaged by placing it within the class of those with an educational purpose).

[170] *McGovern v. A-G* (1981). Amnesty International has created a trust to promote, *inter alia*, the abolition of laws permitting torture or inhuman or degrading punishment.

[171] *National Anti-Vivisection Society v. IRC* (1948).

this subject is extensive,[172] and may well be considered to be a mirror of the values of English society (or, more precisely, the social class to which judges belong).

English law has made up for the lack of a person who can demand performance of a trustee's obligations by recognizing that the Crown, as *parens patriae*, may exercise rights which in ordinary trusts belong to the beneficiaries. From this we obtain the methods of public control over charitable trusts, from compulsory registration,[173] to the institution known as the Charity Commissioners,[174] to the right granted the Attorney General to take action both against the trustees of charitable trusts and against whoever has appropriated assets belonging to a charitable trust.[175]

The special attributes of a charitable trust do not end here. They are exempt from the rules regarding duration and against perpetuity[176] and

[172] I refer the reader to H. Picarda, *The Law and Practice Relating to Charities* (2nd edition), London, 1995; G. W. Keeton and L. A. Sheridan *The Modern Law of Charities* (4th edition), by L. A. Sheridan, Chichester, 1992; Tudor, *On Charities* (7th edition), by D. G. Maurice and D. B. Parker, London, 1984; Hanbury, *Equity*, p. 388–430; Jacobs, *Trusts*, §§1017–51; Pettit, *Trusts*, pp. 226–61; Waters, *Trusts*, pp. 551–601; Béraudo, *Trusts*, §§242–81 (and §§325–45 for American law). For private-international views, see V. T. H. Delaney, 'Charitable Trusts and the Conflict of Laws', in 10 ICLQ (1961) 385.

There is a journal which specializes in this subject: *Charity Law and Practice Review*.

[173] Charitable trusts with a low value and some very old ones (such as the Universities and the schools of Eton and Winchester), charities connected with religious worship and certain institutions of national importance are excluded. There are about 180,000 registered charitable trusts. In 1989, it was estimated that the total of tax exemptions and other forms of support of charities exceeded £2.5 billion.

Compulsory registration was imposed by the Charities Act 1960 and is today regulated by s. 3 of the Charities Act 1993. An automatic consequence of registration is the application of the favourable tax rules.

[174] The Charity Commissioners were founded in 1853. They carry out auxiliary duties to those of the trustees of the charitable trusts, but also inspect and impose sanctions (ss. 16–18 of the Charities Act 1993) and authorize the trustees to carry out actions which are necessary (but probably not in conformity with the trust instrument: s. 26). In general see Picarda, *Law and Practice* (see above, footnote 172), pp. 540–646.

[175] In some cases, local authorities can also act: Charities Act 1993, ss. 76–9.

The question regarding universities, which are (as stated above) exempt from harmonization and registration procedures, is completely different. Until the Education Reform Act 1988 many of these entities (for example, the colleges of Oxford and Cambridge) were subject to the local law of their founders, applied by means of special representatives, known as *visitors*, who exercised complete and exclusive jurisdiction (without the possibility of appeal to the regular courts); see Picarda, *Law and Practice* (see above, footnote 172), pp. 513–39; Pettit, *Trusts*, pp. 277–83. This is another institution of European Common Law, the medieval foundation (in the continental European sense of the word).

[176] The rule 'against remoteness of vesting' (cf. see above, chapter 3 §1.e) applies only if the beneficiary is not a charitable trust (*Christ's Hospital v. Grainger* (1848)). The rule against perpetual trusts is, on the other hand, never applicable to charitable trusts (see, for the sake of curiosity, the decision in *A-G v. Webster* (1875) concerning a charitable trust

may, therefore, last for ever; uncertainties regarding purpose which might lead to the nullity of an ordinary trust may be resolved by a court. Here the theory known in old French legal language as *cy-près* is applied (we may note an interesting application of this theory in South Africa[177]): when the purpose indicated by the settlor may not be attained, the court will identify the most similar purpose possible and modify the trust instrument accordingly. The court's intervention is permitted both at the moment of creation of the trust and successively, to take account of circumstances which may arise later.[178]

The borders between an ordinary trust and a purpose trust (charitable or otherwise) are not always easy to discern; a large number of possible beneficiaries sometimes points in the direction of a purpose trust, but this is a conceptually unacceptable shortcut (in the same way as we have just seen that a small number of beneficiaries does not exclude the possibility of a charitable trust).

d Discretionary trusts

As an alternative to the settlor's pre-determining the beneficiaries and the equitable position to be attributed to each of them, the trust instrument may leave these decisions to the trustee (or to the protector[179]). The trustee

---

created in 1585).

[177] *President of Conference of the Methodist Church* (1993): a testamentary trust was created in 1899 for the construction and upkeep of a home for needy white children. The trustee turned to the court in 1993, explaining that the home had always housed around 120 children, but that in the last few years there had been a dearth of needy white children, and that this situation would worsen in the future, while (the trustee emphasized) there were many needy non-white children. When the new South African law on trusts came into force (see chapter 5 §3.b), the judge modified the trust instrument, and removed the adjective 'white'.

[178] Charities Act 1993, s. 13(1). Cf. Picarda, *Law and Practice* (see above, footnote 172), pp. 279–309; Pettit, *Trusts*, pp. 294–307. For a recent controversial decision, see H. A. Delany, 'Charitable Status and Cy-Près Jurisdiction: An Examination of Some of the Issues Raised in *In Re Worth Library*', in 45 NILQ (1994) 364. For an old application, see *A-G v. Peacock* (1676).

[179] All the powers indicated below are usually tied to the consent of the protector of the trust, when one has been provided for. It should be kept in mind that the protector does not (or never should) have a positive role in deliberations on the administration of the trust and the distribution of income and capital, because otherwise he would be a trustee. The protector may give advice and, from the strictest legal view, withhold his consent from the carrying out of an activity which may not be carried out without his consent. This does not mean that there may be an *impasse* in the relationship between protector and trustee, because the protector usually has the power to revoke and substitute the trustees. On the protector, rare in traditional English practice, but very common internationally, see below in detail, chapter 4 §4.h and also article 629 of the Italian Civil Code.

may also be left responsibility for the decision whether to distribute the entire income or only a part of it to the beneficiaries, or indeed nothing to anyone,[180] at least within the period during which the law permits the income from a trust to be accumulated.[181] In a discretionary trust, one or more of the beneficiaries may be ignored by the trustee on distribution of either income or capital. Those trusts which identify one or more beneficiaries as holder of an (equitable) right to receive income or capital are known as fixed trusts.[182]

The beneficiaries of a discretionary trust are distinguished by membership of a category (for example, the descendants of the settlor[183]), or by simply being included in a list drawn up by the settlor, and completed by him or a person to whom he has granted the necessary power. In the case of a category, one should bear in mind the rule illustrated above which voids a trust without certain beneficiaries.[184] In the case of discretionary trusts, the content of the trust instrument must be such that it may be determined with certainty whether any one person belongs to the category or not; this is not the same as saying that all the members of the category must be known.[185]

There are, therefore, many types of discretionary trust. What they have in common is a lack of beneficiaries having any right other than that to be taken into consideration by the trustee as possible recipients of a distribution of income (or capital, usually, but not necessarily, at the termination of the trust[186]). The discretion of the trustee may not be challenged,[187] and

---

[180] *McPhail v. Doulton* (1970). On the position of the trustee, see P. D. Finn, *Fiduciary Obligations*, Sydney, 1977, pp. 34–76.   [181] See above, chapter 3 §1.e.

[182] Gardner, *Introduction*, ch. 8; Hanbury, *Equity*, p. 100.

[183] Here, too, the criterion of nullity of a trust for lack of certainty is applied; these criteria have been definitively laid down by the House of Lords in *McPhail v. Doulton* (1970), but there is still cause for perplexity (see, in fact, Megaw LJ in a successive phase of the same case, 1973, 24).   [184] See above, chapter 3 §1.j.

[185] On this issue, see Hanbury, *Equity*, pp. 103–10.

[186] Cf. *Gartside v. IRC* (1968); *Re Weir's Settlement* (1969); *Sainsbury v. IRC* (1970); *Quinn v. Executive Director* (1981): the first three are tax disputes. On the tax treatment of discretionary trusts, see below, chapter 3 §2.k.

[187] Whence a limitation on the ordinary powers of beneficiaries to be informed of reasons for decisions of the trustee, because the principle by which a trustee is never required to explain how he has exercised his discretion comes into effect (for example: in distributing income to one beneficiary rather than to another). The minutes of meetings among trustees during which it is discussed to whom benefits will be distributed, are subject to the beneficiaries' power of inspection: *Re Londonderry's Settlement* (1965): 'the trustees are given a confidential role and cannot properly exercise that confidential role if at any moment there is likely to be an investigation for the purpose of seeing whether they have exercised their discretion in the best possible manner' (936, *per* Danckwerts LJ).

On the other hand, the trustees of a discretionary trust cannot preclude the exercise of their powers either by agreement among themselves or by means of agreements with

the beneficiary may not ask a court to exercise it in the trustee's place.[188] Given that the status of the beneficiaries lacks substantive content,[189] the trustee in bankruptcy of a beneficiary has no rights against the trustee.

Nevertheless, if the beneficiaries belong to a closed category (that is, one which may not incorporate any new members) or to a list which may not be expanded either by the settlor or his nominee, the general rule is that they may act together against the trustee to obtain an early termination of the trust from the court, they themselves determine how to divide the assets.

Discretionary trusts may be distinguished from the granting of a power.[190] While the former oblige a trustee to carry out the intent of the settlor, albeit in the manner determined by the trustee in his discretion, a power does not oblige the person on whom it has been conferred to do anything. In both cases there are trustees, but the position of the beneficiaries differs, because the beneficiaries of a power (in particular of a power of appointment, that is, to identify the beneficiary of a trust) have no equitable interest. Beneficiaries of a discretionary trust, on the other hand, do have an equitable interest, as, in the case of a trust with a power of appointment, do those who have been named in case the power is not exercised in favour of anyone.[191]

The lines between the two are not always clearly drawn, in part because case law takes the position that, like the trustee, the holder of a power is subject to fiduciary duties (protected by the 'fraud on a power' doctrine[192]) and that trustees cannot unreasonably defer the exercise of their discretion.[193] In effect, powers in the broad and narrow sense share both teleological elements and the ability to influence the legal position of others directly,[194] and tend to be confused one with the other in non-technical or

third parties, even if they are the beneficiaries: cf. Finn, *Fiduciary Obligations* (see above, footnote 180), pp. 25–33.

[188] In *Re Lockers* (1977), the trustees had negligently remained inactive for a long period. When they were reminded by a beneficiary, they had the intention of giving effect to the distributions not effected in previous years, but in the meantime the class of beneficiaries had changed. The request by the trustees that the division be decided by a judge was rejected; the discretionary power belongs to the trustees, and it must be they who exercise it.   [189] Cf. Waters, *Cours*, pp. 233–40 and 286–9.

[190] In general, see D. M. Maclean, *Trusts and Powers*, London, 1989.

[191] In general, see Hanbury, *Equity*, pp. 169–88.

[192] Maclean, *Trusts and Powers* (see above, footnote 190), ch. 3.

[193] *Re Gulbenkian's Settlements* (1970). Among the knots which have not yet been unravelled in the writings is the distinction between powers and those types of discretionary trusts in which the trustee may decide not to distribute any income to any beneficiary. See also the analysis by Megarry V-C in *Re Hay's Settlement Trusts* (1981).

[194] For these reasons it does not seem to me to be wrong to compare it with the Italian notion of *potestà*.

business language. One school of thought suggests that uncertainties regarding the validity of purpose trusts be resolved by recourse to powers, so that the transfer is effected not in favour of the trustee but to the person who would otherwise be the ultimate beneficiary of the trust,[195] granting a third party (who would otherwise be the trustee) a power which substantially gives the authority to determine the destination of the trust property.[196]

e Protective trusts

The beneficiary of a trust is, as we know, the holder of an equitable interest which may be transferred or mortgaged, but may also be attacked by creditors. In most of the United States, if the intention is to protect the beneficiary of a trust from third-party claims, usually from creditors whose rights are the result of his excessive lifestyle or bad eye for business, the settlor may provide the beneficiary of a trust (normally a beneficiary for life) with an interest which may not be transferred either voluntarily or by statute. Accordingly, not only may he not dispose of his interest in any way, but his creditors may not appropriate it either:[197] this is what is known as a 'spendthrift trust', a reference to the wasteful ways of the beneficiary. His position is protected because it may not be modified.

In English law, which does not permit a beneficial interest to be defined in such a way that it may not be attacked by creditors, the same purpose is attained by other means. The protective trust was codified in 1925,[198] by enacting that the equitable position granted to the beneficiary terminates, and the trust becomes discretionary (if it was not so already) when any event occurs which has the result that sums which would otherwise have been the beneficiary's can no longer be received by him.[199] The protective trust has the further consequence that the protected beneficiary cannot transfer his equitable right; the penalty for such an act is the loss of the right and the transfer of the benefit to the

---

[195] We have observed in the appropriate section that trusts of purposes, where valid, are nonetheless subject to the rules on duration of trusts. There must, therefore, be a person to whom the subject matter of the trust is transferred when the termination date of the trust arrives.   [196] Hanbury, *Equity*, pp. 377–9.   [197] Cf. Béraudo, *Trusts*, §§296–300.
[198] Trustee Act 1925, s. 33.
[199] An unusual decision was that in *Re Gourju's Will Trusts* (1942): owing to the war, the beneficiary moved to Nice, which was occupied by the Germans. The English laws provided that all income due to persons domiciled in territories occupied by the enemy was acquired by a special government office (Custodian of Enemy Property); since the trust in question was a protective trust, the result provided by the Trustee Act 1925 was applicable, and the beneficiary lost the benefit, which was distributed to the successive appointees.

subsequent beneficiaries (usually the spouse and children[200]).

The beneficiaries of a discretionary trust into which a protective trust has been converted are the original beneficiary, his spouse and his descendants, or, if there are none, his legitimate heirs or whoever else has been named by the settlor. Of course, it is possible, within the time limits prescribed for trusts, to create a number of subsequent beneficiaries, each of whom is protected in the manner just described.

The result of an event such as the bankruptcy of a beneficiary is, therefore, that the trustee will provide for the needs of the beneficiary's family and his own personal needs, since rights so conferred may not be attacked by creditors (for example, by allowing him to remain on trust property or by acquiring personal property and allowing him to use it). The wording of the trust instrument of a protective trust may simply refer to legal provisions, thus leaving regulation of the trust to the law, or, since the relevant statutory provisions may be waived, may regulate the matter at the settlor's discretion. It is nonetheless fundamental that the events which must take place for the equitable position of the beneficiary to be transformed should not be in the form of a condition subsequent, which would be null and void and therefore not considered to form part of the trust instrument.[201] The equitable position of the beneficiary needs to correspond to a determinable interest.[202] It should be noted that nothing prevents the trust instrument from providing that if the beneficiary's interest terminates and the trust becomes discretionary, the original arrangement will come back into force after a certain lapse of time.[203]

---

[200] *Gibbon v. Mitchell* (1990).

[201] Any condition subsequent is null if it is triggered by a transfer by the beneficiary, his bankruptcy or the execution of an attachment by his creditors: see Underhill, *Trusts*, pp. 183–4, 189.

A condition subsequent which causes an equitable interest to fail has always been viewed with disfavour in English law if it limits the freedom to make transfers; if the equitable interest is *absolute* – that is, not subject to successive interests (for example: 'to X in trust for Y') – it is also forbidden to place conditions which provide for legal devolution in the case of intestate succession: for example, the provision 'to X in trust for Y, but, if Y predeceases X without a will, for W' is null with respect to the part which provides for the transfer in favour of W.

[202] S. 33 of the Trustee Act 1925 defines the interest of the beneficiary 'until he . . . does or attempts to do or suffers any act or thing', which results in the loss of the income which is due him.

[203] Cf. *Re Richardson's Will Trusts* (1958). For a singular example of trustees in dispute with a beneficiary who cannot avoid incurring debts, see D. Boleat, 'Who would be a Professional Trustee?', in 2 T&T (1996), n. 4, 12.

f Asset-protection trusts

One of the ends sought by means of *inter vivos* trusts is that of bringing about the removal from the settlor's estate of assets which might otherwise be attacked by his creditors, such as suppliers or other business contacts, dissatisfied clients who sue a consultant for damages, spouses during divorce proceedings and so on.

The term 'asset-protection trust' is originally American, but in international practice its use rapidly came to be extended to a number of situations, more or less based on the trust, but all sharing the above purpose.[204] They are, naturally, subject to two kinds of limitation: the *actio pauliana*, where the conditions for one exist,[205] and tax rules relating to grantor trusts.[206] The latter also provide for criminal sanctions against the consultants of a person who has recourse to one of these structures with the aim of prejudicing the rights of his creditors (a fraudulent conveyance[207]).

The theoretical feature of the asset-protection trust may be seen in cases where the structure employed is at the outer limits of the standard configuration or crosses over the line and becomes a sham. Except under an action for revocation, no criticism may be levelled at a person who places his estate on trust by transferring it to a trustee who actually administers it in favour of beneficiaries (among whom may be the settlor himself). Divestiture of all the settlor's personal assets (and, therefore, the loss of any rights on the part of his creditors to a general charge against his estate) is a natural result of this situation, and is a typical element of a trust. This is not the same as the case of a person who wishes to *prevent an effective transfer to the trustee* by keeping substantial powers to manage, and possibly even dispose of, the asset by means of a series of transactions and connected entities which, in the end, leave the settlor in the same position of control as before.

This is a very complex problem; it is too easy to make generalizations and snap judgments such as 'nothing has changed'. On the other hand, those legal systems which have dealt with trusts for centuries are perfectly well equipped to use technical notions to distinguish among the various

---

[204] A complete view of these structures from the United States viewpoint, is found in Osborne (ed.), *Asset Protection* (see above, footnote 115).

[205] See above, chapter 3 §1.i; for international-model trusts, see below, chapter 5 §4.e.

[206] See above, chapter 3 §1.d. These are the least relevant: in fact, American practice is to structure trusts for asset protection as grantor trusts, in that the settlor wishes as a rule to be one of the beneficiaries. This means that from a tax point of view the trust has no effect; the purpose of becoming a person without property for the creditors becomes important again.

[207] Matthews, 'Asset Protection Trust' (see above, footnote 118), pp. 84–5.

structures. Let us consider the case of a settlor who, after creating a trust for investment purposes, later decides to dispose of a part of the capital to acquire goods, such as an aeroplane. There is nothing to prevent the trustee, or a company controlled by the trustee, from purchasing the aeroplane and leasing it to the settlor at market rates.[208] Take also the simple situation of the holder of a controlling interest in a company of which he himself is managing director who transfers that interest into a trust: he stays on as managing director, but loses ownership; he earns a salary but no longer receives dividends (unless he is a beneficiary). It seems to me that no objections may be raised to a trust of this kind; it may be the settlor's wish to remain as managing director, but in all probability it will also represent the only way to avoid damaging the interests of the company. What counts is that the controlling interest is no longer his, and that as a result the trustee may appoint new managers if circumstances require him to do so. It is evident that a different conclusion would be reached if the trustee is a trust company owned by the settlor.[209]

Certain effects derive naturally from a trust. If the settlor wishes to benefit from the advantages of a trust but wishes to do away with some of the inconveniences, then he may well find himself creating something which no longer corresponds with the typical trust structure – in fact, it may not be a trust at all.

g The mortgage and the *pactum commissorium*

We shall shortly see a number of financial and commercial applications for trusts, so the time is right to make some observations on the mortgage, which is the functional equivalent of the civil-law *hypothèque*.

By a mortgage, a creation of the medieval European *ius commune* which, like so many other creations, survived into common law,[210] a mortgagor

---

[208] This structure is described by H. Rosen, 'Having the Cake and Eating It', in 2 T&T (1996), n. 3, 12. The writer correctly emphasizes that it is a legitimate, remunerative investment for the trust.

[209] In fact, one of the most recent techniques, used in the context of trusts belonging to the international model (see chapter 4), is the incorporation of a company which has as its purpose the management of trusts and is used to manage the trust created by the same person who controls the company.

[210] This is one of the central themes of my book *Origins* (see above, footnote 156). With reference to Lombard law, see G. Diurni 'Fiducia'. *Tecniche e principi negoziali nell'alto medioevo*, Turin, 1992, where many sources are examined, some of which would be subject to a different review in a comparative light and from the viewpoint which I propose; see, for example, the expression *tivi in affiduciato dedi et tradavi* in a manuscript from 776 (p. 128), which shows the *infiduciatio* as the equivalent of an estate, of which the *traditio* or conveyance is made, because it is an estate in possession. The provision of Liut.

transferred ownership in property (or, more correctly, an estate) to a mortgagee, thereby guaranteeing a loan. When the amount had been punctually repaid, the mortgagee had to re-transfer the property to the mortgagor (instead of interest payments the creditor received the yield of the property[211]). There is an evident structural analogy to trusts, and in fact English equity immediately decided that the mortgagor, although stripped of the right of ownership, remained the holder of an equitable right (the equitable estate) to 'redeem' the property from the mortgagee when he had repaid the loan with interest (redemption). This juxtaposition between common law and equity would, nonetheless, be eliminated in the contrary case, where repayment was not made: the mortgagee combined the positions of strict law and equity (foreclosure), and the asset became completely his.[212]

In the course of time, both equity and, later, specific statutes intervened to prevent the mortgagee from unjustly enriching himself by appropriating property which was worth more than the capital amount of the loan, and provided for various sales procedures subject to judicial control.[213] The theoretical mechanism was not modified, however, in part because English law does not recognize the covenant of forfeiture as a *legal* prohibition; however, an *equitable* obligation is imposed on the creditor,[214] and the

---

58 *cuicumque dederit aut infiduciaverit* is the same effect.

[211] In general, see Fisher and Lightwood's *Law of Mortgage* (10th edition) by E. L. G. Tyler, London, 1988; Snell, *Equity*, pp. 299–452; A. Chiodi, 'Mortgage', in *Digesto, Sez. Priv.*, XI, Turin, 1994, 465.
    One of the first cases was *Porter v. Hubert* (1672–3) where the interest rate due from the borrower also had to be determined.

[212] Lupoi, *Appunti*, p. 108 *et seq.*

[213] Cf. Waters, *Constructive Trust*, ch. 3; G. Elias, *Explaining Constructive Trusts*, Oxford, 1990, §3.2.2. and footnote 104 for the position of the creditor as constructive trustee of the debtor with regard to sums obtained from the sale in excess of his credit. Legislative provisions regarding the sale of the mortgaged property are found in s. 101 of the Law of Property Act 1925.

[214] In recent years, there have been interesting developments in case law regarding the relationship between a creditor and a person who owns an equitable right in property subject to a mortgage. On this subject, the decision should be noted in *Barclays Bank v. O'Brien* (1992), where the Court of Appeal held that the lending bank has the duty to check that the terms of the mortgage are clearly comprehensible to the third party providing the mortgage where he is liable to be under the influence of the debtor. As a result, since the husband was the debtor, and the wife, who had granted the mortgage, complained that she had understood from her husband that the mortgage guaranteed a debt lower than the actual one, the mortgage was effective only for the lower sum. This decision placed the duty on the bank to deal directly with the grantor of the mortgage. The Court probably adhered to a recent school of thought, firmly rooted in the essential foundations of equity, which holds that the performance of a contract must not be permitted where it would be against the precepts of conscience not to intervene; cf.

nullity of agreements which hinder the exercise of the debtor's right of redemption has been sanctioned since 1683.[215] The legislative amendments of 1925 affected the form of the relationship, but not the substance.[216] For example, the right of the creditor to obtain possession[217] and the distinction between mortgages of a legal estate and those of an equitable interest (equally feasible) remain, as, above all, does the fundamental distinction from the civilian functional equivalents, since the subject matter of a mortgage is an estate or other entitlement, not an asset.

h Trusts for business activities

The devices I have just described, which are usually employed within the scope of a trust, are the same as those which allow a large number of guarantee-type transactions which in civil law are either too complex, impossible or pointlessly costly. It is normal practice, especially in the United States, to place whole companies or branches of companies in trust, so that the trustee (the financial lender or the lead bank in the loan transaction) is given the same powers to dispose of the assets as the entrepreneur had, and which the trustee will use in case of need.

An analogous situation exists where the purpose of the transaction is to provide a guarantee to creditors: the trust may benefit both the creditors existing at the moment of its creation and those who come after: thec

above, chapter 2 §4.g: specifically, see D. W. M. Waters, 'Banks, Fiduciary Obligations and Unconscionable Transactions', in 65 CBR (1986) 37. Recently, see D. Hayton, 'Constructive Trusts of Homes – A Bold Approach', in 109 LQR (1993) 485, at 488–9.

For those readers who may not be familiar with the English system of justice, let me point out that a decision of the Court of Appeal has great authority and binds all judges of equal or lower level. For a picture of the organization of English justice, see L. Moccia, *Il sistema di giustizia inglese. Profili storici and organizzativi*, Rimini, 1984; G. Criscuoli, *Introduzione allo studio del diritto inglese. Le fonti* (2nd edition), Milan, 1994, pp. 283–318; E. Vianello, 'Appunti sulle recenti riforme processuali in Inghilterra', in [1993] Riv. trim. dir. proc. civ. 893.

[215] *Howard v. Harris* (1683). The creditor becomes trustee of the right which is the subject matter of the mortgage when the debtor has lost the right to reacquire it (redemption): Trusts of Land and Appointment of Trustees Act 1996, Schedule 2.1 (previously, see Law of Property Act 1925, s. 31).

[216] The reforms of 1922–5, which were united in their impulse to create a system of registration of real property, led the mortgage system nearer to the *hypothèque*. Alongside the methods which, although modernized, are still tied to the old real-property structures, we see the mortgage established by means of a simple transcription. It is worth recalling that the structure of the continental *hypothèque*, although rejected in common law, had been accepted by Admiralty case law.

[217] On the manners and forms of exercise of this right, see P. Brimelow and N. Clayton, *Mortgage, Possession, Actions*, London, 1994, pp. 39–88.

THE TRADITIONAL ENGLISH MODEL

company or branch is managed by the trustee, who can approve further financing or activate the guarantee, depending on the state of the company.[218] These devices assume a special relevance where the purpose is to guarantee the desired outcome of a sale agreement. The aim in one case may be to protect a supplier of materials, or in another a purchaser who has paid a deposit; the structures to be used will be very different.[219]

In the first case, both a sale with a security interest[220] and payments based on a pledge are very problematical from a theoretical point of view.[221] Although it may be technically possible to create a trust to which the finished product belongs, so that proceeds from its sale flow to the trust and the trustee divides them among the entrepreneur and the various suppliers involved, the path which is usually followed in England is to oblige the entrepreneur to deposit all the proceeds into a special bank account; this is not usually a trust in the strict sense of the word, but rather an equitable charge (subject to compulsory registration[222]).

[218] Cf. A. Gambaro, 'Problemi in materia di riconoscimento degli effetti dei trusts nei Paesi di civil law', in [1984] 1 Riv. dir. civ. 93 at 102–3; on the functionally analogous mechanism of the floating charge, which is, however, based on different legal presuppositions, see J. Weisman, 'Floating Charges: Recent Developments under Israeli Law', in CLP (1988) 197; S. Worthington, 'Floating Charges – An Alternative Theory', in [1994] CLJ 81; E. Gabrielli and G. A. Danese, 'Le garanzie sui beni dell'impresa: profili della floating charge nel diritto inglese', in Banca, Borsa (1995) 663. For a case concerning a floating charge, see immediately below in the text.

[219] For banking operations, see V. Visconti, 'Le operazioni trustee', in Comm. intern. (1992) 137.

[220] On which see the important decision of the House of Lords in a Scottish case Armour v. Thyssen (1990) (which is in the line of cases following after Aluminium Industries v. Romalpa (1976)), where there was a retention of title clause to guarantee the payment of any debt of the seller in favour of the purchaser. The House of Lords distinguished between transfer of possession and the dominium; this is a distinction which is not unknown to English law, even if it appears to have continental antecedents: see, for example, Dixon v. Olmius (1795), where the delivery to a married woman of debentures which were the subject of a testamentary disposition in her favour was judged to have transferred the dominium and therefore to preclude any interference by the husband ('gave her dominion over them'), and see, donatio mortis causa above, chapter 2 §2.f.

On the effect of title-retention clauses in English law and proposals for modification of current regulation, see the report of the Crowther Committee, Report of the Committee on Consumer Credit, London, 1971 (Cmnd 4596); for Scottish law, which maintains the civil-law requirement of dispossession, see Wilson and Duncan, pp. 59–67.

[221] See, in general, C. Angelici, 'Consegna' e 'proprietà' nella vendita internazionale, Milan, 1979; specifically E. Gabrielli, Il pegno 'anomalo', Padua, 1990, pp. 103–17; E. Gabrielli, 'Le garanzie rotative', in various authors, 'I contratti del commercio, dell'industria e del mercato finanziario', in Trattato F. Galgano (ed.), Turin, 1994, I, 853; A. Gommellini, 'Il pegno e le gestioni patrimoniali', in [1994] 1 Riv. dir. comm. 181ff., especially at 195–206; F. Leduc, 'Le gage translatif de propriété: mythe ou réalité?', in [1995] RTDC 307.

[222] Companies Act 1985, s. 395; cf. Hayton, Trusts, p. 63; M. Bridge, 'The Quistclose Trust in a

The reason why recourse is not had to a trust is that the finished product is, by definition, the sum of a series of elements and not the simple transformation of raw materials. A contractual provision pursuant to which the finished product belongs to the supplier of the raw materials for so long as payment for the materials is not made which is customary in civil-law jurisdictions (such as Germany), is considered to represent the equivalent of the creation of a guarantee, and therefore of an equitable charge.[223] The case of a sum of money delivered to the entrepreneur on trust is different: here the asset which is subsequently purchased with the money represents a simple conversion, so that the trust over the money is transferred to the asset purchased.[224]

A similar case concerns the entrepreneur who purchases assets which he keeps in his bulk deposit on behalf of the third parties who provided the funds for the purchase and to whom the assets belong. There is nothing to prevent the use of a trust, but the technical aspects to be considered are numerous and complex, as in the following example.[225]

Goldcorp proposed to the general public investments in gold and other precious metals. The investor indicated what he wanted to purchase with the funds he made available, and had the immediate right to take delivery of the metals; if he did not, they remained in custody of the company. The company found itself in financial difficulty, and borrowed from a bank, providing a floating charge over its assets. The company failed, and a dispute arose between the bank and the investors who had not taken delivery of their precious metals, of which there was not, in any event, a enough for all of them. The Privy Council, reversing the decision of the New Zealand High Court, decided in favour of the bank.

The only means by which the investors could have prevailed would have been by claiming a proprietary interest, on the grounds that the existing metals should be considered to be theirs (although only in equity); even a constructive trust would have been enough.[226] The Privy Council rejected the numerous suggestions of a proprietary interest in favour of the investors, fundamentally because the assets were not identified.[227] The decision would have been completely different if the metals due to each investor had been identified, or if the investors had

World of Secured Transactions', in 12 OJLS (1992) 333. For Scotland, on the conflict between the owner of a charge and a third-party purchaser of a corporate asset, see *Sharp v. Thomson* (1995).

In the United States, article 9 of the Uniform Commercial Code regulates secured transactions, which are subject to registration.

[223] *Re Peachdart* (1984); see also *Borden v. Scottish Timber Products* (1981).

[224] In the absence of agreement, there would be a constructive or resulting trust, depending on the circumstances.   [225] *Re Goldcorp Exchange* (1995).

[226] In chapter 2 we saw a number of cases where the effect of a constructive trust was to exclude the relevant property from the bankruptcy.

[227] Thus, later, Lord Browne-Wilkinson in *Westdeutsche v. Islington* (1996), 990.

provided the company with sums which had to be applied for the acquisition of the metals.[228]

A trust in the technical sense also arises in certain cases of down-payments or other sums received by an agent: a typical case is that of travel agents dealing with airlines,[229] although care should be taken here that the agreement should not lend itself to being judicially construed as establishing an equitable charge, with the consequent danger that it will be ineffective because its formalities are lacking. It is probable that the obligation of the agent to keep all receipts segregated in a special bank account and the attention which the principal pays to ensuring that this obligation is respected nullify this danger.[230]

A purchaser who has paid a sum on account may be easily protected by a trust, whether it arises by agreement between the parties or as the result of an initiative of the seller. The theoretical difference between the two is nonetheless important. The result of an agreement between the parties is that the deposit paid by the purchaser does not become a part of the seller's property: the trust funds are supplied by the purchaser, who deposits the amount directly into the hands of the trustee (who may also be the seller). The result of the seller's initiative, on the other hand, is, apparently, that he earmarks a company asset (the deposit) in favour of one of his creditors. This was the case in *Re Kayford*:[231]

An entrepreneur with business problems deposited sums provided to him by a client for the purchase of assets in production into a special bank account (called the 'Customers' Trust Deposit Account'). The court held that there had been a trust over the assets which the entrepreneur had simply underlined, so that the funds had never been at his complete disposal and were not, therefore, available to his creditors.

A similar case to the types just examined is the trust relating to distribu-

---

[228] The New Zealand court, on the other hand, considered these payments to be the subject matter of a trust, with the result that, since the precious metal which should have been purchased with them was not available, the investor–beneficiaries had the right to follow the amounts into any property into which they had been transformed (*tracing*, see above, chapter 2 §4.b), and therefore into the corporate assets. The final effect was these assets were held to 'belong in equity' to the investors, and the bank could not satisfy its credits from them.

With reference to decisions such as that of the Privy Council, the observation of C. K. Allen, *Law in the Making* (7th edition), Oxford, 1964, p. 416 is correct: 'it is a matter of regret that in certain respects our system of equity, springing from such liberal principles, should have developed on lines which sometimes seem to be the opposite of natural justice'.

In contrast, see the opinion of P. Birks, 'Proprietary Restitution: an Intelligible Approach', in [1995] TLI 43.   [229] *Stephens Travel Service v. Qantas* (1988).
[230] Cf. *Re ILG Travel* (1995).   [231] 1975.

tion, on occasions through the involvement of companies which finance the distributor's purchases. Ownership passes to the ultimate purchaser when the price is paid into a 'trust account'; as seen above, the price does not become a part of the distributor's estate, and therefore passes exclusively for the benefit of the manufacturer or the company which has financed the distributor.[232]

The effect of segregation, which is typical of trusts, is to permit regulation of the 'withholding guarantee' in procurement contracts. Companies which are active in the international field often have bad experiences when it comes to requesting the release of withheld funds at completion of a project, either because final certification has to be issued by persons allied with the contractor, or because, in any case, the sums to be collected are in the hands of the contractor. I think it would be useful to refer to a recent judgment involving an Italian company:[233]

The construction contract for an oil pipeline called a 5% retention. The contractor was an Iraqi government body which, at the same time that it made progress payments of 95%, deposited the remaining 5% in an account at the Banca Commerciale Italiana in London in the name of the Iraqi Rafidain Bank. Other sums to be credited to the contracting firm (Saipem) were deposited by a third party.

The sums in the account were held on trust for the contracting firm, and Rafidain Bank was the trustee. The trust instrument provided that the amounts deposited into the trust account from time to time would be transferred to the contracting firm at the end of the project, provided that the contracting firm produced certain Iraqi certifications.

The pipeline was built, but was seriously damaged in the war between Iraq and Kuwait. Saipem requested the release of the certification, without success. It therefore sued both the contractor and the trustee (the contract provided that all disputes would be subject to English law).

The Court of Appeal held that Saipem could not prevail in an action on contract, but that its claim should be founded upon its position as beneficiary of a trust. From this point of view, the trustee could legitimately refuse delivery of the sums in the account only where equitable reasons allowed; if, the Court reasoned, the procedures provided in the trust instrument (the production of certificates) could not work, the judge had the power to substitute others: the trust could not remain 'in limbo'. Turning to the merits of the case, the Court pointed out that the lack of certificates did not affect Saipem's claim, because no one had ever claimed that the job had not been completed. It therefore instructed the trustee to deliver the sums held in the trust account to Saipem.

There exists another, completely different, function of the trust, to ensure the survival of a company (usually a partnership or a small company) after the death of a partner, by 'paying off' his heirs. This is what in Italy has

---

[232] Indications in Waters, *Cours*, pp. 331–2.   [233] *Saipem Spa v. Rafidain Bank* (1994).

come to be known as a 'consolidation clause' which has been the subject of court decisions which have contested its validity in the by-laws of companies.[234] The technique followed in common law is often the creation of a trust, the trustee of which takes out an insurance policy on the life of each of the partners for the benefit of the trust (with a principal amount determined to be sufficient to re-acquire the shares of each), and each partner undertakes to provide the trustee over time with the amounts necessary to pay the annual premiums.[235] When a partner dies, the trustee delivers the insurance proceeds to his heirs and transfers the deceased's interest to the surviving partners.

The function of trusts created without any particular formalities by lawyers, notaries or estate agents who find themselves holding funds or ownership interests belonging to third parties is different again. This type of trust works to segregate the asset which has been 'deposited' from problems which might affect the recipient, but its role is above all to provide a guarantee to a third party who has an interest in the asset so deposited or to whom the asset must, under certain circumstances, be delivered.[236] The settlor, in fact, loses any rights to the trust fund, which has left his estate and which is not therefore susceptible to attack by his creditors.

Other cases covered by trusts are those where a right must be divided among a number of persons, but where it is necessary nonetheless to maintain unity in relations with the outside world. One of the first applications was found in the area of rights arising out of petroleum exploration concessions in the United States. The first recipient of a concession often found it practical to transfer his rights to a specialist company in exchange for a payment (in the form of a royalty) based on the results of extraction of the crude, and then subsequently, depending on how the business went, to 're-sell' his right to the royalty, thereby capitalizing his position. The subject matter of this 're-sale' were the shares into which his right was sub-divided for the purpose of the re-sale and the purchasers of the shares were obliged to act as a single person in their relations with the oil

---

[234] And which held that they become a (prohibited) testamentary contract.

[235] It is, of course, possible that a shareholder may omit to supply the trustee with the sums necessary for this end. Trust instruments propose a number of solutions in this case.

[236] In American terminology it is called 'escrow' and is used with great frequency. In many of the States of the Union – for example in California – real-property acquisitions take place by depositing the entire purchase price with the escrow agent at the time of signing of the contract (which, as already noted, does not transfer ownership): it is the agent, who has the power to receive transfer of the property, who delivers the purchase price to the seller, at which time, once the title search has been concluded, the transfer takes place. For this and other forms, see U. Morello, 'Fiducia e trust: due esperienze a confronto', in *Fiducia, Trust, Mandato e Agency*, Milan, 1991, 17ff. at pp. 66–74; G. Provaggi, 'Agency escrow', (*ibid.*) 291.

company. The solution was the creation of a trust, to which all the shares belonged. In this way, the right was re-created as a single entity, and the trustee had the duty of maintaining the relationship with the oil company, checking accounts, and so on. In time a market for the beneficiaries' rights emerged which still exists today.[237]

This last observation draws attention to one of the peculiarities of trusts which address the interests of several persons who have interests in a single business transaction. These interests fall within the category of beneficial rights (since the ownership rights are reserved to the trustee), and thereby acquire their own dynamic. This helps us to understand the application of trusts to the regulation of those phenomena which civilian legislations identify by a variety of terms, such as the Italian 'multiproprietà', which translated literally means 'multiple ownership'.

If we take note of the fact that the English term for 'multiple ownership' is 'time-sharing', the limitations of the Italian approach may be more easily understood; while the latter concentrates on the static moment and the ownership of the right, the former looks to the dynamic moment and the exercise of the right. It will come as no surprise, therefore, that the trust makes an appearance in almost all forms of time-sharing. It is easy to understand how this happens: the trustee has ownership of the property, and the beneficiaries have enjoyment of it either directly or because they receive income from it. The enjoyment is, of course, for the period of the year which has been agreed with each beneficiary.[238] It is an equitable right which, precisely because it is equitable, is also negotiable. According to the model accepted in many countries, the beneficiaries are often brought together as members of a club, which issues them with certificates which confirm the period to which each is entitled and the manner in which it may be used.[239]

---

[237] Indications in Waters, *Trusts*, pp. 447–8.
[238] The American configuration is different: see G. Alpa, 'Aspetti della multiproprietà nell'esperienza nord-americana recente', in [1983] 1 Riv. dir. civ. 69; E. Calò, 'Multiproprietà e consumer protection negli Stati Uniti d'America', in *Quadrimestre* (1985), 496; for France, see E. Calò, 'La nuova legge francese sulla multiproprietà', in [1985] Vita not. 1938; A. Negri, 'La multiproprietà nel sistema francese', in [1989] Cont. e impr. 615; G. Alpa, 'I modelli delle esperienze straniere', in G. Alpa and M. Iasiello (ed.), *La multiproprietà*, Padua, 1993, pp. 43–56.
[239] For a complete analysis, see U. Morello, 'Multiproprietà', in *Digesto Sez. Priv./Civ.* IV; G. Alpa and I. Cavanna, 'Trust e multiproprietà', in *Atti Milano*, ch. 14; basic points in G. Caselli, *La multiproprietà* (3rd edition), Milan, 1995.

i Trusts for financial operations

Trusts have numerous functions in the field of finance. I shall indicate just a few of them.

Trusts were used internationally in the area of bond issues, guaranteed by assets which the issuing company segregated from its own and transferred to trustees who either had full ownership rights or a pledge interest;[240] this is a technique which is still in use today.[241]

The best-known financial function of trusts is in the area of pension funds.[242] In their usual configuration, both in England and in the United States, pension funds are provided with contributions from an employer and the employees on a voluntary or compulsory basis.[243] Each enterprise tends to have its own pension fund, which is exempt from taxes on income and capital gains.[244] Pension fund trustees rarely manage the

---

[240] This is one of the oldest uses, even in Japan and Mexico, and among the most frequent today. See V. E. Cappa, 'The Corporate Debenture Holders of South American Countries', in 43 YaleLJ (1934) 571; cf., also for other international uses of the trust, C. Amato, Commento all'art (11th edition), in A. Gambaro, A. Giardina and G. Ponzanelli (eds.), 'Convenzione relativa alla legge sui trusts e al loro riconoscimento', in [1993] *Leggi civ. comm.* 1267, §5; F. C. Rich, 'International Debt Obligations of Enterprises in Civil Law Countries: The Problem of Bondholder Representation', in 21 VaJIL (1981) 269.

The case of the so-called 'Young Loan', frequently quoted in the literature, is different, because the Bank for International Settlements carried out the functions of a trustee only for the purposes of paying the sums which the debtor (the German Government) periodically remitted to the bank.

[241] Indications in H. Kötz, *Trust und Treuhand*, Gottingen, 1963, p. 124. For Eurobonds, Luxembourg has passed a law which comes close to the trust mechanism.

[242] Recently, G. Moffat, 'Pension Funds: Fragmentation of Trust Law' in 56 MLR (1993) 471 and, for decisions which show how complex the subject is, *Davies v. Richards & Wallington* (1990); *Imperial Group Pension Trust v. Imperial Tobacco* (1990); *Re Drexel Burnham* (1995). The latter decision shows the limits of the English notion of the fiduciary obligation: the trustees of a company pension fund were also employees of the company. The company was placed in liquidation, and the trustees developed a scheme for the distribution of the fund which at the same time satisfied retired, dismissed and current employees. Everyone was in agreement, but the trustees did not feel they should proceed because they were also beneficiaries. Only after much hesitation did the judge recognize that a situation had developed which allowed the trustees to seek judicial directions and, therefore, in substance, authorization (which he granted).

The legislative experiment which introduced pension funds into Italy (d.lgs. 21 aprile 1993 n.124) has not to date produced many results.

The total of pension funds in England was estimated in 1992 to be £500 billion.

[243] In this latter case, as in England with the PAYE (Pay As You Earn) system, the employer performs functions which have been delegated to him by the government.

[244] For more detail, see L. Gandullia, 'Brevi note sul regime fiscale dei fondi pensione complementari in Italia e all'estero', in Artoni (ed.), *Gli enti non profit* (see above, footnote 152), pp. 291ff., at pp. 305–9.

funds in person;[245] management is generally centralized in large investment organizations or insurance companies. Major problems arise, especially in England and Canada, when the enterprise ceases operations and the fund has more assets than the employees have a right to,[246] or in the event of a merger.[247]

There are also those trusts in the field of labour relations which distribute shares of a company to its employees.[248] The basis of the trust is sums of money deposited periodically by the company into the hands of the trustees used to purchase shares of the company which they then distribute to those employees who satisfy certain requirements. The duties of trustees of these trusts are delicate, for example when the company finds itself the target of a hostile takeover bid and the trustees have to decide what stance to adopt.

A large number of beneficiaries can be found in a type of trust which has recently been developed in the United States, and which is created in connection with a lawsuit commenced on behalf of consumers using the procedural technique known as the 'class action'. It usually happens that two facts coincide: a large number of claimants, who are often not identifiable individually, and the small sum of money due to each. It therefore seemed more convenient to oblige the defendant manufacturer to deposit the damages into a specially created public interest trust for the benefit of the particular category of consumers.[249]

Investment for a large number of beneficiaries is normally carried out by

---

[245] When they do, they must have as their purpose the greatest possible income, even if this involves investment in a rival company; see *Cowan v. Scargill* (1985). The numerous limitations placed by English law on the freedom of pension fund trustees to act have now been removed by the Pensions Act 1995.

[246] *Mettoy Pension Trustees v. Evans* (1990). For an analysis on the contrast between contract and trust see Waters, *Cours*, pp. 320–4.

[247] European jurists will also find the *Report of the Pension Law Review Committee*, chaired by Professor Roy Goode, HMSO, 1993 (CM 2342), of great interest, because it takes account of the observations of the numerous organisms which have interests in pension funds and of the experience of decades of activity.

[248] These trusts are known as ESOP (Employee Share Ownership Plans); see G. Meruzzi, 'Back to Back Loans', in [1995] Cont. e impr. 841ff., at 855–9. For Jersey law, see Matthews and Sowden, §§12.11–12.16; for Scotland, see Wilson and Duncan, pp. 97–8. Cf. G. Tamburi and C. Salvato, *Azionariato dei dipendenti e stock option*, Milan, 1996, which also contains statistical revelations on the best results obtained by companies with employee shareholders.

[249] K. Barnett, 'Equitable Trusts: An Effective Remedy in Consumer Class Actions', in 96 YaleLJ (1987) 1591, cites *State v. Levi Strauss & Co.* (1986): the well-known producer of jeans had to pay thirty cents to millions of consumers (the programme for management of the damages alone, which involved sending letters to the entire population of California (!) cost over two million dollars).

'investment trusts' or 'unit trusts'.[250] The structure of unit trusts is recognized the world over. They are created by an entity which intends to carry out an investment activity with sums collected from the public; the trustee is a company which specializes in financial investments (often controlled by the promoter himself); the initial beneficiary is the promoter, who subdivides his equitable interest into units (hence the name 'unit trust'), which he makes available to the public through a distribution network.[251] The amount deposited by a purchaser of a unit becomes the property of the trustee, and so the trust fund grows. The investments are made by the trust, and the income therefore belongs to the beneficiaries (the owners of the units[252]). Shares acquired by the trust are deposited with a bank, which frequently also acts as a trustee (in the guise of a custodian trustee, as opposed to a managing trustee[253]). One limitation of unit trusts, though not a particularly significant one, is that they are subject to the same rules regarding duration as ordinary trusts.

Still in the area of shares, we find voting trusts.[254] Voting trusts may have a short duration (one shareholders' meeting), or a long one, and every decision on the use of the vote and other rights attaching to the shareholder's status as a shareholder may be completely assigned to trustees, or the trustees' decisions may be conditional upon the wishes of the settlors (who are also the beneficiaries) or their nominees. In the case of a trust which lasts for only one shareholders' meeting, the purpose of the settlors is to ensure that none of them changes his mind, and, at the same time, that no third party may intervene in the resolution process, for example by subjecting the shares of one person to attachment. In this type of temporary trust, the trustee usually has no discretion.[255] In all cases of voting

---

[250] The former term is used in the United States to mean a quoted company which has investment in shares as its purpose; in England, the latter indicates a phenomenon which is similar to the Italian 'fondi di investimento aperti'.

[251] Many aspects are regulated by the Financial Services Act, 1986; see R. Lener, 'La circolazione del modello del "trust" nel diritto continentale del mercato mobiliare', in [1989] Riv. soc. 1050, at 1058–9; Graziadei, *Diritti nell'interesse altrui*, pp. 361–70. Many unit trusts have their base in Jersey: see Matthews and Sowden, §§12.17–12.20.

[252] The distinction between the position of a shareholder and the owner of a unit has been discussed in detail in the Australian decision *Charles v. Federal Commissioner of Taxation* (1954) (609).

[253] In the last century, these types of trust were called management trusts. A detailed review of recent case law on the subject of custodian trustees may be found in M. Timms, 'Global Custody – an Overview', in 1 T&T (1995), n. 9, 6.

[254] The essays by T. Joyce, 'Shareholders Agreements: a US Perspective', and L. Simonetti, 'Gli Shareholders Agreements in Inghilterra', in various authors, *Sindacati di voto e sindacati di blocco*, Milan, 1993, p. 353 and p. 432 respectively.

[255] As in *Booth v. Ellard* (1980), concerning a 'bare' trustee.

trusts, ownership of the shares is transferred to the trustee, otherwise it would fall outside the scope of trusts.[256]

When financing an industrial project, where it is projected that repayment will be made with the proceeds, a bank is appointed as trustee of income from all sales, and it supervises collection of the income and its division between the entrepreneur (to guarantee cash flow) and the lenders.[257]

In syndication operations, one bank usually occupies the role of trustee in favour of the others; the latter confer the amounts for which they have accepted responsibility upon the former on trust, and the trustee bank is responsible for delivering them to the borrower company as the project proceeds. In general, in all financial operations in which more than one party is involved, it is convenient to enable one of them (the trustee) to act in the interests of all, even though their positions may not be at all the same. The trust ensures that sums collected and distributed by the trustee cannot be touched, and guarantees a satisfactory framework for the fiduciary obligations which fall upon the trustee bank.[258]

There is no doubt that this type of trust touches upon the rules governing guarantees. So each time new financial resources reach a company, their economic effects are not accompanied by the ordinary legal consequences of enhancing the company's assets for the benefit of all its creditors, because the purpose for which the resources are granted imposes a trust, of which the financing party itself is the beneficiary.[259]

A trust often intervenes in cases where new financial means are secured for a company, for example, where the use of these resources is conditional upon authorizations being obtained, or on other external factors. During the intervening period (after funds have been obtained, but before the condition has occurred or it has been determined that it cannot be satisfied), the financial resources which the company has obtained are subject to a trust, whose beneficiaries are the subscribers, and they do not, therefore, technically belong to the company.[260]

---

[256] Thus, correctly, Kötz, *Trust und Treuhand* (see above, footnote 241), pp. 124–5.

[257] U. Draetta, 'Il "project financing" nella prassi del commercio internazionale', in [1994] Dir. del comm. int. 495; G. Dossena, *Project financing e asset securitization*, Milan, 1996; W. Ternau (ed.), *Project financing. Aspetti economici, giuridici, finanziari; fiscali e contrattuali*, Milan, 1996; G. Imperatori, *Il project financing*, Milan, 1995.

[258] S. Carbone, 'Il trust ed il suo impiego nelle operazioni del commercio internazionale', in *Atti Milano*, ch. 18.

[259] This is the case with operations modelled on the *Quistclose* trust (see above, chapter 2 §3.b), which have been analysed from a security point of view by Bridge, 'Quistclose Trust' (see above, footnote 222), who reached the conclusion that they do not pose any threat to creditors.

[260] Thus in *Re Nanwa* (1955), where the entrepreneur became bankrupt, and the sums

Still in the field of financial operations we find the system of securitiz-ation of credits, where the receivables of a company are acquired *en masse* by a party which employs financial resources provided by investors, who receive shares or other securities issued by that party in exchange.[261]

j Family-interest trusts

I have left family trusts until last, although historically they were the first, because they are too often considered to be the only kind of trust. Modern society no longer looks with favour upon a pre-determination of succession for several generations, and social conditions no longer favour stability or, from the economic point of view, income. We must, therefore, take another look at this kind of trusts: it appears to me that this should be done in chapter seven, which is dedicated to trusts in Italy.[262]

Finally, I should add that the overview of the use of trusts in these pages is far from being exhaustive. It is obvious,[263] but no exaggeration,[264] to say that trusts lend themselves to unlimited uses.

k Applicable law and non-resident trusts

The first two pages which Ernst Rabel dedicated to trusts in private interna-tional law, in line with the opinion of the other writers he quoted, demon-strated the high degree of uncertainty regarding the rules of conflict in the

received were not added to the bankruptcy assets, and were returned to the subscribers.

261 These schemes can be very complex: see A. Frignani, 'La "securitization" come strumento di smobilizzo dei crediti di massa (profili di diritto comparato europeo)', in [1995] 5 Foro it. 294, who finds that it is possible to set up such schemes in Italy by means of a trust; in Argentinian law, after the law of 1955 on *propiedad fiduciaria* (see later, chapter 5), see S. V. Lisoprawski and C. M. Kiper, *Fideicomiso. Dominio fiduciario. Secur-itización*, Buenos Aires, 1995.

262 See, nonetheless, the interesting perspectives of Waters, *Cours* (see above, footnote 41), pp. 279–304, where numerous modern forms of family trusts are indicated, and see also below, chapter 3 §3.j for Italian law aspects. The reader should note that chapter seven has not been translated into English in its entirety, and that the part relating to family trusts has been omitted.

263 'What can a trust be used for?' asked P. Lepaulle, *Traité théorique et pratique des trusts*, Paris, 1932, p. 12, answering: 'For everything.' For a discussion on the uses of trusts, see Waters, *Cours* (see above, footnote 41), ch. 4; Fratcher, *Trusts*, paragraphs 39–68; with special reference to offshore trusts (those I place in the international trust model: see below, chapter 4) see R. Miller, 'Offshore Trusts – Trends towards 2000', in 1 T&T (1995), n. 2, 7.

264 Examples of the uses of trusts in public international law are provided in Béraudo, *Trusts*, §12; cf., for other public international issues, J. Gold, 'Trust Funds in International Law: The Contribution of the International Monetary Fund to a Code of Principles', in 72 AmJIL (1978) 856. The most recent case of a trust in the international sphere is probably the Trust Fund to Assist States in the Settlement of Disputes, created in 1989 by the Secretary-General of the United Nations: see P. H. F. Bekker, 'International Legal Aid in Practice: The ICJ Trust Fund', in 87 AmJIL (1993) 659.

area of trusts, the lack of reliable precedents, and the profoundly unsatisfactory nature of judicial attempts to impose a system in this area.[265] In
England, Graveson affirmed that the rules of conflict on trusts are to a large
extent uncertain and incomplete,[266] and Morris, in 1980, expressed the
opinion that it would be premature to attempt to create a classification.[267]
In Canada, Waters had no hesitation in writing of 'rudimentary patterns'.[268] In Australia, Jacobs pointed out the absence of detailed discussion,
and Forsyth has recently written of underdevelopment.[269] A volume from
1987 which looked at Australian, English and American law drew attention
to uncertainties and conflicts in almost every area of private international
law.[270]

I could continue with the citations,[271] but I do not believe any more are
required to demonstrate the backwardness of common-law systems in the
area of private international law; in any event, the deep uncertainty which
prevails in this area will now be highlighted in a rapid overview of the
picture provided by the individual legal systems. The problems in arriving
at general rules are perfectly clear, and apply to the whole area of trusts: it

---

[265] E. Rabel, *The Conflict of Laws*, Ann Arbor, MI, 1958, IV, pp. 445–6.

[266] R. H. Graveson, *Conflict of Laws* (7th edition), London, 1974, p. 530.

[267] J. H. C. Morris, *Conflict of Laws* (2nd edition), London, 1980, p. 367; cf. Dicey and Morris,
Conflict of Laws (10th edition), London, 1980, p. 674.

[268] Waters, *Trusts*, p. 1123, writes of 'rudimentary patterns' in case law, and continues: 'The
author in this field can only set out the framework within which the law appears to be
developing, and suggest the conclusions which appear so far to have emerged from the
few authorities that exist.'

[269] Jacobs, *Trusts*, §2901 commences thus: 'There has been in England and Australia little
academic or judicial exegesis of the trust in the conflict of laws.' C. F. Forsyth, *Private
International Law* (2nd edition), Cape Town, 1990, p. 310: 'The law relating to the conflict
of law aspects of trusts is underdeveloped to say the least.'

[270] A. Wallace, 'Choice of Law for Trusts in Australia and in the United Kingdom', in 36 ICLQ
(1987) 455.

[271] Even P. Lepaulle, 'Trusts and the Civil Law', in 15 JCompL (1933) 18, at 29, declared before
the law faculty of London: 'One knows that English and American courts have rendered
very confused decisions on the point of determining the law which must pass on the
validity of an *inter vivos* trust.' The situation did not change in the following years, as we
have seen.

See also G. W. Keeton, Trusts in the *Conflict of Laws*, in 4 CLP (1951) 107: 'it is somewhat
unexpected to find that decisions upon questions of conflict of laws are extremely rare';
See V. Latham, 'The Creation and Administration of a Trust in the Conflict of Laws', in 6
CLP (1953) 176: 'It is surprising that there has been so little written on this subject.' P. M.
North and J. J. Fawcett, *Private International Law* (12th edition), London, 1992, p. 880 recall
Keeton's statement, and add that the case law remained scarce, with only episodic
analysis, 'and uncertainty as to the relevant rules in a number of areas'. Recently, A.
Dyer, 'International Recognition of the Trust Concept', in 2 T&T (1996), n. 3, 5 at p. 10:
'Even in the common law countries the precedents for determining the applicable law
for a trust are generally few and inconclusive.'

is sufficient to consider the diverse profiles of testamentary trusts in international law when compared with *inter vivos* trusts, or of the family trust or others with an altruistic purpose, compared with those with a commercial or financial purpose, or of purpose trusts compared with discretionary trusts, and it will be many decades before complete case-law solutions will be found.[272] In addition to this, we should keep in mind that there are differences in the substantive law of common-law jurisdictions, with the result that trusts which are valid in one system may not be so in another.[273]

It is of fundamental importance to take account of this backwardness and these problems, because this is the only way to appreciate that one of the aims of the Hague Convention was finally to lay down certain, uniform rules, which common-law practitioners (but certainly not civil-law practitioners) felt to be absolutely necessary. The final report takes note of this almost unwillingly,[274] and the representatives of civil-law jurisdictions present at the Conference had not noticed it.[275] However, texts published since the Convention came into effect have expressed relief that an untenable situation had finally been resolved.[276]

Let us put aside for a moment issues of public policy, which seem to make their appearance every time factual or legal elements involved in a private international problem come from civil law, with the result that the conflict, in the absence of a mechanism for providing uniformity, quickly ends

---

[272] Rabel, *Conflict of Laws* (see above, footnote 265), p. 451 observes that insufficient attention has been paid to the typology of trusts, and that the rules enunciated so far are modelled on the family trust.

[273] For example, in *Jewish National Fund v. Royal Trust Company* (1965), the trust would have been charitable and valid under New York law, but void for uncertainty of purpose under British Columbia law. For other examples, see below, footnote 293.

[274] Explanatory report no. 14: 'Cependant, il est apparu que, même dans les rapports entre eux, les Etats de common law trouvaient utiles les règles de conflit de la Convention, étant donné que leurs systèmes nationaux de droit international privé diffèrent en la matière.'   [275] Gambaro, *Proprietà*, p. 637, footnote 64, declared, in fact, that he had not.

[276] After the Convention came into force, the treatment in the manuals of rules of conflict relating to trusts was much simplified, and credit for this was given to the Convention: see J. H. C. Morris, *The Conflict of Laws* (4th edition) by D. McClean, London, 1993, p. 376: in common law there was 'a dearth of authority', but 'the position was transformed by the enactment of the Recognition of Trusts Act 1987 [the law which ratified the Hague Convention]'; Dicey and Morris *On the Conflict of Laws* (12th edition) under the general editorship of L. Collins, London, 1993, p. 1088: 'Until the enactment of the Recognition of Trusts Act 1987 there was considerable uncertainty as to what law governed trust, case law and literature being equally sparse'; J.-G. Castel, *Canadian Conflict of Laws* (3rd edition), Toronto and Vancouver, 1994, pp. 512–16. (It is singular to note that this author affirms that the Hague Convention 'was prepared primarily to aid civil law countries facing trust law issues', but that, in the self-same sentence, he states that in the Canadian provinces which have not ratified the Convention, until ratification takes place, 'uncertainty and unpredictability will prevail'.)

up with the non-application of the foreign law. A good example is the rule on 'forced heirship': the international trust model, of which we shall speak in the next chapter, tends to declare the law of the settlor incompetent, or not to apply it, when it leads to the nullity or ineffectiveness of the transfer of assets to the trustee. It is evident that a court from the settlor's jurisdiction will reach completely the opposite solution, but it is less well known that New York case law has already refused to apply foreign law in the area of the law of forced heirship.[277] Here we do not see civil-law systems which are protecting themselves from an invasion of trusts, but common-law systems which are protecting the validity of their own trusts when they conflict with foreign laws.[278] If we recall the fundamental distinction between the creation of the trust and the grant to the trustee,[279] we see three principal topics: the creation of the trust, the transfer to the trustee, and the exercise of the trustee's functions. When one speaks of the 'law governing the trust', one is thinking of the first and the last topic as if they were one.

i. The creation of the trust

With trusts of personal property, the determination of the applicable law of the trust, which decides questions relating to the validity of the act whereby a trust is formed, appears to be left in principle to the will of the settlor,[280] and, in its absence, to the 'proper law', which is that of the legal system with which the trust has its closest contact.[281] The American Restatement, nevertheless, conditions the effectiveness of the settlor's choice upon the existence of a 'substantial relation to the trust'.[282]

---

[277] *Matter of Renard* (1982); cf. Scott, *Trusts*, §593.

[278] The only author who has dealt with this subject is Rabel, *Conflict of Laws* (see above, footnote 265), pp. 461–4, but see A. Duckworth, 'Forced Heirship and the Trust', in Glasson, B1, who refers to English (p. B1–35) and Florida (p. B1–59) precedents which applied foreign laws (Greek and Venezuelan, respectively) relating to institutions unknown in English law (the dowry and the rights of legatees). Only in the second case, however, was a trust involved, and it was, furthermore, in that ambiguous form known as the *Totten trust*.   [279] See above, chapter 3 §1.a.

[280] English writing sustains this: Graveson, *Conflict of Laws* (see above footnote 266), p. 531, as does Australian: Jacobs, *Trusts*, §2802–93, but there are not sufficient authorities in the common-law systems to state this principle with certainty: cf. Forsyth, *Private International Law* (see above, footnote 269), p. 312.

[281] For applications, see *Re Lord Cable (deceased)* (1976); for Australia see *Augustus v. Permanent Trustee* (1971); for Canada see *Middleton v. Middleton* (1980) (a pension fund). Cf., prior to these decisions, P. E. N. Croucher, 'Trusts of Movables in Private International Law', in 4 MLR (1940) 111.

[282] Restatement *Trusts, Conflict of Laws (Second)*, §269(b)(i) (testamentary trusts), §270(a) (*inter vivos* trusts).

Where the settlor has not indicated the applicable law of the trust, the solution proposed by the Restatement varies according to whether it is a testamentary or a living trust. In the former case, the law of the State in which the testator has his domicile is applied, because it is held that the testamentary trust is attracted by the law which governs the succession.[283] In the latter case, recourse is had to the criterion of the 'most significant relationship'. Furthermore, the implementation of the settlor's choice is conditional on the fact that the testator's domicile or the most significant relationship do not run contrary to the 'strong public policy' of the State.

The settlor's freedom of choice is, on the other hand, unlimited under Canadian law,[284] in which it would appear that a sure solution for *inter vivos* trusts is lacking.

In the case of trusts of immovable assets, recourse is generally had to the law identified by the rules of conflict of the State where the asset is located,[285] but there are exceptions if the trust is linked to a matrimonial agreement.[286] In any event, the inevitable prevalence of the immovable character of the trust property, which is such as to lead to a connecting link different from that used for trusts of personal assets, is the subject of controversy.[287]

As far as the capacity of the settlor is concerned, there are no sure criteria, and two tendencies prevail: one looks to the law applicable to the trust,[288] and the other to the personal law of the settlor.[289]

Literature in the area of *inter vivos* trusts, especially in Australia and South Africa,[290] tends to make use of criteria developed in contract law, and makes the point that, in the common case of a trust instrument prepared bilaterally between the settlor and the trustee, there is no reason to seek alternative solutions.[291]

---

[283] Rabel, *Conflict of Laws* (see above, footnote 265), pp. 449–50; thus also in South Africa: Honoré, *Trusts*, pp. 574–7.

[284] Castel, *Canadian Conflict of Laws* (see above, footnote 276), §384.

[285] Restatement *Trusts, Conflict of Laws*, §278; J.-G. Castel, *Canadian Conflict of Laws* (see above, footnote 276), §389; Forsyth, *Private International Law* (see above, footnote 269), p. 311.

[286] Cf. Graveson, *Conflict of Laws* (see above, footnote 266), p. 532.

[287] Honoré, *Trusts*, pp. 563–8; Graveson, *Conflict of Laws* (see above, footnote 266), p. 533.

[288] P. E. Nygh, *Conflict of Laws in Australia* (3rd edition), Sydney, 1976, pp. 438–41.

[289] Or, to use common-law terminology, to the *lex domicilii*: cf. Jacobs, *Trusts*, §2803; Honoré, *Trusts*, p. 577, who adds the law of the place where the creation of the trust takes place.

[290] But this is, of course, influenced by the connotations of the trust in South African law, on which see below, chapter 5 §3.b.

[291] The use of contractual criteria for determining the applicable law of *inter vivos* trusts has been confirmed by the High Court of Australia in *Augustus v. Permanent Trustee* (1971).

ii. The transfer to the trustee

The transaction by which transfer to a trustee is effected is an act of transfer which is subject to normal rules of conflict, but two important matters must be clarified.

In the first place, the specific principles of the trust may interact with those normally used to determine, for example, if the act of transfer relates to personal or real property.[292]

In the second place, the act of creation and the transfer may be carried out in a single document (as is usually the case with testamentary trusts), but they remain subject to different conflict rules. As a result, the transfer to the trustee may be in contrast with the imperative rules of the law applicable to the trust, or with those of the law applicable to the transfer to the trustee.[293]

iii. The exercise of the trustee's functions

According to some theories, the law of the administration of the trust is held to be the same as the one governing the trust.[294] Other theories hold it to be that of the law of the place where all or most of the assets are located.[295] According to others it is held to be that of the place where the trustees reside or operate;[296] and according to yet others, in the case of testamentary trusts, to be that of the testator's domicile.[297] In general,

---

[292] This distinction does not correspond to that of national law: the beneficiary of a trust for sale of immovable property is, as we know, the owner of personal property, because the equitable theory of conversion considers that the sale has already taken place (see above, chapter 2 §2.e); in private international law, on the other hand, it is held that the right of the beneficiary is in immovable property: *Re Berchtold* (1923). In more detail see Latham, 'Rights of the Beneficiaries', 522–7.

[293] For example, an Englishman drafts a will valid under English law which creates a trust of property in Scotland, regulated by Scottish law, which allows a duration which is in contrast with the unwaivable English rules on perpetuity (see above, chapter 3 §1.e): the trust would, therefore, be void. English and Australian case law has, however, decided that it is valid: *Fordyce v. Bridges* (1848); *Re Mitchner* (1922). It would seem that the situation with *inter vivos* trusts is different: *Augustus v. Permanent Trustee* (1971).

[294] Cf. Graveson, *Conflict of Laws* (see above, footnote 266), p. 538.

[295] Latham, 'The Creation and Administration' (see above, footnote 271), 185.

[296] This is probably the solution most frequently advanced, at least when the trust subject matter is not immovable property. See for all Jacobs, *Trusts*, §2809, with the important clarification that one must not look at the residence of the trustees, but at the place where they carry out their administrative duties concerning the trust property. It should be borne in mind, however, that it is now common practice that there is not only more than one trustee, but also that they reside and work in different places, while still being bound by the rule that trustees must always act together.

[297] Castel, *Canadian Conflict of Laws* (see above, footnote 276), §387; Forsyth, *Private International Law* (see above, footnote 269), p. 313.

furthermore, there is a tendency to allow the settlor to choose the law of administration of the trust, at least for trusts of personal property.

There is an unsolved problem of regulating the borders between the law applicable to the trust itself and that of the management of the trust: is an act of transfer, set in motion by a beneficiary relating to his interest in the trust, regulated by the law of the administration of the trust?[298] Do the rules on duration of the trust belong to validity or administration?[299] And what of the rules which permit the trustee or the beneficiaries to change the law relating to administration of the trust?[300]

The resulting trust which arises when an expressly created trust fails is almost without precedent in all of common law;[301] there is absolutely no precedent relating to constructive trusts.

iv. The domicile of the trust

Discussion of identification of the domicile of the trust is related to these last three issues, because it is normally held that a non-resident trust is taxable in a State only with regard to income earned there, and then according to criteria applicable to non-residents.[302] The domicile of the trust is also relevant to issues of jurisdiction, because article 5(6) of the Brussels Convention of 1968,[303] in its list of *special jurisdictional grounds*,

---

[298] The Restatement distinguishes between cases regarding movable or immovable property, and only in the former case is the law of the administration of the trust called upon (§273); Waters, *Trusts*, pp. 1125–6 and L. G. Hoar, 'Some Aspects of Trusts in the Conflict of Laws', in 26 CBR (1948) 1415, at 1416 are of a different opinion.

[299] For other opinions, see the precedents cited by Jacobs, *Trusts*, §2803, footnote 8.

[300] It may happen that the substitution of the trustees leads to the identification of a different law governing the administration of the trust: and that one must therefore decide whether the effectiveness of the substitution depends on the law regulating the validity of the trust or that of the administration at the moment of the substitution.

[301] On this, see above, chapter 2 §3.a. On the rule of conflict, see the differing opinions of Scott, *Trusts*, §583 and Jacobs, *Trusts*, §2803.

[302] 'Residence' of the trust is the object of rather complex rules in England: see Taxation of Chargeable Gains Act 1992, §§69(1) and 87; cf. C. Masters, 'Non-Resident Settlements – UK Reporting Requirements', in 1 T&T (1995), n. 2, 20. In English law, trusts which, although entrusted to English professional trustees, have been created by foreigners and have their patrimony abroad, are considered to be non-resident: J. F. Avery Jones *et al.*, 'The Treatment of Trusts under the OECD Model Convention', in [1989] Dir. prat. trib. 1510, footnote 7; see 1522–7 for the US position, and also, in more detail, Newton, *International Tax* (see above, footnote 50). On treaties against double taxation, see the conclusion of chapter 3 §3.a.

[303] Added upon the accession of Denmark, Ireland and the United Kingdom (Convention signed in Luxembourg on 9 October 1978).

The report by P. Schlosser to the Convention of Accession, no. 114 (also in R. Clerici, F. Mosconi and F. Pocar, *Codice del diritto internazionale privato della Comunità Europea*, Milan, 1992, §10), makes it clear that it was inspired by the notion that for trusts *there exists a*

includes one whereby the settlor, the trustee and the beneficiaries of a trust may be summoned to appear, in their relevant capacities, before the judges of the contracting State in whose territory the trust is domiciled. One notes with a certain annoyance that English jurists have not missed the chance to make the point that when discussing domicile, civil-law jurists show their lack of understanding of trusts.[304] This opinion, expressed in a more courteous manner, will be a recurring theme in the preparatory works of the Hague Convention.

In the United States, one speaks of the 'residence' of a trust, and the subject is disciplined by the Small Business Job Protection Act 1996. A trust is considered 'resident' when an American court can exercise jurisdiction over the administration of the trust, and the decision-making powers are effectively in the hands of trustees residing in the USA.[305]

3. The notion of trust

a The bare trustee and double-taxation treaties

Frequent among the first trusts were those which, in civilian language, would be held to be cases of *interpositio*. In the codicil to his 1399 will, John of Gaunt began by recalling that he had purchased *and had caused to be purchased for his own use* lordships, castles and land, and went on to give instructions to those holding 'title' to these assets to dispose of them in favour of certain beneficiaries.[306] The expression used by the testator, '*a mon eops*' corresponds to the Latin '*ad opus meum*', and defines what would soon come to be called '*use*': the purchaser of the asset (or rather, usually the purchasers in the form of a joint tenancy, to avoid the risk of succession on the death of one of them[307]) is just a straw man, a mere holder with no

centre, which may carry out functions similar to those of the head office of companies without legal personality. The 'domicile', pursuant to article 53.2, is determined by the judge according to the private international law rules of the forum.

[304] J. H. C. Morris and P. M. North, *Cases and Materials on Private International Law*, London, 1984, p. 96: 'Of course it is artificial and novel to speak of the domicile of a trust at all. But continental lawyers seem to think that a trust is some kind of unincorporated association; and it seemed best to go along with them when it did no obvious harm.'

[305] It should be noted that both criteria make reference to factual situations rather than to criteria of legal classification.

[306] 'jeo Johan . . . ay puchacez et fait purchacer a mon eops diverses seigneuries, manoirs, terres . . .' from F. W. Maitland, *Selected Essays*, H. D. Hazeltine, G. Lapsley, P. H. Winfield (eds.), Cambridge, 1936, p. 160. Note the expression 'at mon eops', to which I shall return immediately in the text. For the irrelevance of the *use* in common law see below, chapter 3 §3.e.

[307] In feudal real property one naturally used the term *tenancy* rather than *ownership* (Lupoi, *Appunti*, pp. 5–8). Joint tenancy involves the right of accretion (*ibid.*, pp. 48–9) and appears to be an application of *Gesamthandschaft*.

autonomy of action, subject to the orders of his principal, a *nudus minister*.

In 1535, when the Statute of Uses declared that all uses were 'executed', that is, that the estate which was the subject of the use was granted by law to the beneficiary of the use, the express objective of the legislature was not uses in general, but was limited to passive uses.[308] It was only the mere *interpositio*, often in favour of religious orders to avoid the laws on mortmain, and always to the detriment of the feudal lords, which felt the consequences of the law, which would surely not have been passed with that objective if the phenomenon of passive trusts had not already been quite widespread.

The bare trust is the successor to the primitive trust. From a systematic point of view, a trust is 'bare' when the trustee is not faced with a group of successive beneficiaries, or when the trustee is not called upon to carry out any activity other than maintaining ownership of the asset or performing merely administrative tasks.

These two profiles may emerge separately. The lack of a group of later beneficiaries means that the existing beneficiaries are the final ones on whom the assets must be conferred at the end of the trust term. As we know, this group of beneficiaries may effect an early termination of the trust, and it is logical to expect that they may also give the trustee binding instructions regarding trust management. On the other hand, a trust may be bare for the simple reason that the settlor wanted it that way,[309] and that he has made other arrangements for the execution of administrative duties, or has relieved the trustee of the full range of duties which he would normally have.[310] To be more precise, one should speak of a nominee

---

[308] In technical terms, the 'holder' was a *feoffee*, because *enfeoffment*, that is, the delivery of the estate, had taken place in his favour; he was, however, a *feoffee to uses*. The Statute of Uses had the effect of *executing* the use, that is, of eliminating the *feoffee*, and transferring the estate *ex lege* to the beneficiaries; the explanation for this showed that this had been decided in order to favour the beneficiaries against abuses by the *feoffees*. In *Dillon v. Freine* (1589–95), 132a, a judge declared as follows: 'the statute hath advanced uses, and hath now established safety and assurance for *cestuy que use* against his *feoffees*; for before the statute, the *feoffees* were the owners of the land, and now the statute hath made the *cestuy que use* owner of the land'; the law, he goes on, operates 'by divesting the whole estate out of the *feoffees* . . . and vesting it in the *cestuy que use*'.

[309] Graziadei, *Diritti nell'interesse altrui*, pp. 213–16, with particular regard to immovables.

[310] The recent decision in *Ingram v. IRC* (1995), is of notable interest, and is also useful for an understanding of certain English tax techniques, together with the type of trust declared by the owner of a right (see above, chapter 3 §1.b): Lady Ingram transferred immovable property to her lawyer, who on the same day declared in a writing that he was the trustee of it on behalf of his client. The following day, the lawyer entered into a rent agreement with Lady Ingram, and immediately thereafter transferred the property, with the lease, to her children and grandchildren. They drafted a declaration by which they proclaimed themselves to be trustees of the property in favour of certain beneficiaries (indicated by Lady Ingram). A dispute arose with the tax authorities, which

agreement, and here we leave the area of trusts and enter that of agency or the *Romanistic fiducia*, which may normally be revoked by the principal (while trusts are usually irrevocable). Furthermore, while a nominee agreement can never become a trust – not even a bare trust – an active trust may become passive or bare for a subsequent lack of the initial beneficiaries or where the duties of the trustee are later simplified.

The current terminology does not distinguish these aspects well,[311] probably as a result of tax dispositions which treat them equally, either directly or indirectly, by imputing income from the trust to the beneficiaries.[312] They are not distinguished even in international/professional practice, which, as we shall see in the next section, tends to move away from active trusts in favour of passive, or bare, trusts.

The Statute of Uses was repealed in England in 1925, but remained in force in other common-law jurisdictions, for example in New York and, in the case of trusts of real property alone, in Florida; here, a bare trust in the pure sense of a merely passive holding has no effect, because the right which is the subject of the trust passes to the beneficiary *ex lege*.

The distinction between active trusts and bare trusts is relevant both because of the different treatment of the trustee's liability,[313] and because

claimed that the complex operation was to be considered to be the creation of a trust by Lady Ingram, who had nonetheless retained an interest (the lease). The judgment handed down in the Chancery Division was in favour of the taxpayer, for reasons which do not interest us here, but stated that the position of the lawyer was that of a nominee, and that a nominee may not contract with his principal, so that the lease was void. [Since the publication of the original Italian version of this book, the decision was reversed in the Court of Appeal ([1997] 4 All ER 395) and again in the House of Lords ([1999] 1 All ER 297). Editor's note.]

A legislative example of the bare trustee seems to me to be that provided by the Law of Property (Miscellaneous Provisions) Act 1994, s. 14 (1). The property of a person who dies intestate is transferred ('vested') in the Public Trustee until a judge appoints an administrator, but this transfer to the Public Trustee 'does not confer on him any beneficial interest in, or impose on him any duty, obligation or liability in respect of, the property'.

The Public Trustee is, fundamentally, a public entity ('corporation sole'), which has the duty to accept the appointment as trustee of all private trusts (except charitable and business trusts). It was created in 1906, and has recently been given new duties, such as those relating to the property of persons afflicted by mental illness. For more detail, see Underhill, *Trusts*, pp. 767–80.

[311] Hanbury, *Equity*, pp. 72–3, deals with them together; Glasson, §A1.148 uses the term 'bare trust or nomineeship'. For a detailed analysis, see W. D. Goodman, 'The Character of the Bare Trust in Canadian Tax Legislation', in D. W. M. Waters (ed.), *Equity* (see above, footnote 39), pp. 219ff., at pp. 219–22.

[312] Indirectly in England, directly in the American federal system: see above, chapter 3 §2.k and §2.l.

[313] See the decision of the House of Lords in *Target Holdings v. Redferns* (1995): technical violations of the trust which may be imputed to an ordinary trustee cannot be imputed

of the application of double-taxation treaties. Numerous treaties signed by the United Kingdom, including that with Italy,[314] exclude the possibility that income from a trust may belong to the category of 'other income'. It is, therefore, taxed in the country where it is produced (and may enjoy the benefit of any tax relief allowed by other treaty provisions, of which we shall speak shortly) and not, as is the rule with 'other income', in the State where the recipient of the income is resident. Arrangements of this nature may be found in less recent treaties which do not provide for the exclusion described above.

In American-style double-taxation treaties,[315] the definition of 'person' includes trusts,[316] and the definition of 'Resident of a Contracting State' includes trusts wherever the trustee is liable for tax on their income in that State 'either in its hands or in the hands of its . . . beneficiaries'.[317]

Where reference is made to double-taxation treaties, one must first determine whether the trust into which certain income flows is a trust or a nominee agreement (this latter situation is similar to that of the so-called 'conduit companies'[318]). I am in no doubt that legal relationships properly belonging to the field of trusts are excluded from the treaty provisions which deal with this category and from those treaties which, following the OECD model, might include it in the notion of 'person'.[319]

---

to a bare trustee; for the facts of the third case, see below, p. 176.

[314] Ratified by Law 5 November 1990 No. 239, article 22.1, on 'other income': those portions of the income of a resident of a contracting State not dealt with in the preceding articles are taxable only in the State of residence, as long as the income is derived from a trust.

The treaty with the United Kingdom follows the most recent British diplomatic practice. It may be found in identical or nearly identical form in treaties signed by the United Kingdom with Sweden, Norway and Belgium: cf. F. Sonneveldt, 'Trusts and Tax Consequences in the United Kingdom', in F. Sonneveldt and H. L. van Mens (eds.), *The Trust. Bridge or Abyss Between Common and Civil Law Jurisdictions?*, Deventer, 1992, p. 31.

[315] Published in 1981. It may be found in the Appendix to D. E. Osborne (ed.), *Asset Protection* (see above, footnote 115), 3–1.   [316] Article 3.1.a.

[317] Article 4.1.b; 'its hands' probably refers either to the resident trustee or to income taxed at source.

The rule on capital income deriving from the sale of real property is extended to the transfer of a beneficial interest in a trust which is the owner of real property: article 13.2.

[318] The subject of the report entitled *Double Taxation Conventions and the Use of Conduit Companies*, published with three other reports under the title *International Tax Avoidance and Evasion – Four Related Studies in Issues of International Taxation*, no. 1 (OECD, Paris, 1987).

The commentary on article 1 of the OECD Model Convention of 1992 (nos. 11–26) discusses conduit companies at length: see S. Mayr, *Il nuovo modello OECD*, in File, 1993, 89; on the use of this type of company for business activities outside Italy, see V. Uckmar, 'I trattati internazionali in materia tributaria', in A. Amatucci (ed.), *Trattato di diritto tributario*, Padua, I.ii, 1994, pp. 754–60.

[319] OECD Model Convention 1992, article 3.1. The trust is expressly included in the notion of *person* in the USA–Canada treaty of 1980, article 3(1)(e).

Remaining in the area to which trusts strictly belong, I am not convinced by the literature which holds trusts to be 'persons', because a trust would be a 'body of persons' (and the definition in the OECD model includes 'body of persons'), and because the trustee would certainly be a 'person' in any event.[320] A charitable trust with significant assets is probably a 'person',[321] but this does not mean that every trust will be. In my opinion, in the case of charitable trusts the trust assets, its long-term purposes and the lack of beneficiaries create an objective element which prevails over the personal element of the trustees, whereas the same cannot be said for non-charitable trusts. It seems to me that an initial distinction must be introduced here: charitable trusts, according to the OECD model definition, are 'persons' if they have significant assets, where other trusts may not be, and when they are not, one must look to the trustees as 'persons', not to the trust.

It is on this basis that one should approach the problem of residence, which is usually resolved by applying the concept of the place of management. The notion of place of management is extraneous to those charitable trusts where the objective element of the assets of the trust referred to above prevails, and requires one important clarification when it is applied to other trusts: the place of management to be taken account of is not where the trustee conducts his business but where he conducts the business of the trust.[322] We are, therefore, within the provisions of Article 4.3 of the OECD model, which does not concern individuals, and which, in order to resolve the problem of double residence, provides that the location where the place of management is located will prevail. Each time the trust carries out a commercial or financial activity, or has significant invested capital at its disposal,[323] the residence of the trustees is, in principle, irrelevant and it will be to the trust, and not to the trustees, that one must first look to identify the residence and, therefore, the application or lack thereof of a particular double-taxation treaty.[324]

The second distinction, therefore, is between the various types of trusts and trustees. To affirm that bare trusts are completely transparent for the purposes of the treaties, and therefore that the tax relationship is established between the source State and the beneficiaries, is without doubt an

---

[320] P. Baker, *Double Taxation Conventions and International Tax Law* (2nd edition), London, 1994, p. 85.

[321] OECD Model Convention, Comment on article 3, no. 2, with reference to foundations.

[322] In this way, tax rules approach the private–international rules on the administration of a trust, connected to the place where the trustee carries out his duties (see above, chapter 3 §2.m).

[323] Avery Jones *et al.*, *Treatment of Trusts* (see above, footnote 302) pp. 1527–8.

[324] *Ibid.*, pp. 1546–7.

exaggeration in principle, but it may be correct on a case-by-case basis.[325] One must nonetheless take care not to confuse bare trusts with fixed trusts. Fixed trusts, as we know, are those where the income is attributed to one or more beneficiaries in a pre-determined measure, but this does not necessarily mean that the trustee's role is passive or purely administrative.[326] While the bare trust is always fixed, the contrary is not, therefore, always true.

Thus we arrive at the rules of the OECD model which, in order to grant certain advantages, impose the condition that the person receiving the income must be its beneficial owner.[327] There is no doubt, as I see it (and I am surprised that this observation has never been made), that trusts which lack beneficiaries (such as charitable trusts, although the same is true for purpose trusts, wherever they are permitted) are the beneficial owners of all the income they receive. With other types of trusts, the problem must be considered bearing in mind the reasons why the limitation regarding beneficial owners was introduced in the 1977 version of the OECD model. It was desired to exclude income received by intermediaries and nominees, and later by conduit companies, which have only a formal existence[328] and which are normally incorporated in one State rather than another with the sole purpose of taking advantage of the double-taxation treaties of which that State is a signatory (in addition to other tax advantages provided for in its laws[329]). It is difficult to attribute the same motives to a trust. Whoever uses a conduit company also has the means to control it (in fact, control is an absolute requirement), and the same is true of inter-

---

[325] This, it seems to me, is also the opinion of Baker, *Double Taxation* (see above, footnote 321), p. 85.

[326] In the application of the double taxation treaty of 28 July 1967 (and successive modifications) between France and the United States, France adhered to the American technique of considering those trusts to be transparent where the beneficiaries have a right to receive matured income (see the Note of 25 March 1981 of the Direction Générale des Impôts, in *Bull. Off. Dir. Gén. Imp.*, 25.3.1981 para. 59).

[327] Articles 10, 11 and 12 on dividends, interest and royalties: 'if the recipient is the beneficial owner of the dividends' (article 10; similarly articles 11 and 12). Avery Jones *et al.*, *Treatment of Trusts* (see above, footnote 302), pp. 1548–50 correctly state that here 'beneficial owner' does not have the technical meaning given to it by English law, but rather a wider sense (see below in the text).

The Italian translation in its double-taxation treaties is 'beneficiario effettivo' (in the 1984 treaty with the United States) or 'proprietà effettiva' (in the 1957 treaty with the Netherlands). As we shall see below, no account may be taken of these translations.

[328] Cf. Baker, *Double Taxation* (see above, footnote 321), p. 229.

[329] As is well known, the reaction against so-called 'treaty shopping' is very vigorous nowadays. Recently, the United States have included a treaty-shopping clause in double-taxation treaties with France (1994) and the Netherlands (1995), while the treaty with Switzerland has been blocked due to Swiss opposition to a clause of this type.

mediaries and nominees. The other element which conduit companies, intermediaries and nominees have in common is the lack of autonomy of the person who receives the income: he is essentially an inanimate tool[330] in the hands of his principal.[331]

May these characteristics be found in trusts, in the relationship between trustee and beneficiaries? It does not seem so to me. The choice of trustee is too important to be conditioned by tax considerations, since assets over which he exercizes the rights of an owner are placed irrevocably in his hands. The trustee has (or rather, must have) will and autonomy. His obligations are not towards the settlor who created the trust, but towards the beneficiaries. Generally speaking, therefore, the limitation which applies to the beneficial owner does not apply to trusts or the purpose of the trust,[332] and there is no reason to distinguish between the taxation of fixed trusts, on one hand, and discretionary or accumulation trusts on the other.

Tax issues relating to bare trusts are more complex, because it would appear that the motives behind the introduction of the concept of the beneficial owner find their target where the settlor and beneficiary of a trust are one and the same and the trust is a bare trust, or – and this is the same thing for the purposes of our discussion – a revocable trust, and the role of the trustee is merely passive or administrative. In this case, the functional analogy with conduit companies and the reduction of the trustee to the role of a nominee may not be easily refuted. The result is that treaty provisions will be applied or ignored by having regard not to the residence of the trustee, but to that of the settlor/beneficiary.[333]

b The legal position of the settlor: the emerging contractual element

When we looked back over the history of trusts, we saw that the first examples were frequently cases of nominees (*interpositio*), and were, there-

---

[330] This is an old common law definition of 'agent'.

[331] International tax practice has trivialized the figure of the nominee, who has performed extremely important functions in the defence of religious or ethnic minorities over the centuries; see the discussion on the law of Andorra by L. Puig I Ferriol, 'El prestanoms en el Dret Andorrà', in Iglesia Ferreirós (ed.), *Actes* (see above, footnote 85), p. 699; and for South Africa Honoré, pp. 141–3.

[332] Thus, although using different reasoning, Baker, *Double Taxation* (see above, footnote 321), pp. 86–7, also with reference to the regulation of capital gains.

[333] The Ministerial Resolution of 7 May 1987 n. 12/431, in [1987] Bollett. tribut. di informazioni 1386 is to be approved: Italian shares were held by an English bank as nominee of an American bank, the manager of a pension fund: the double-taxation treaty with the United States, and not that with the United Kingdom, was rightly applied.

The decision of the Board of Review of Hong Kong, reported in WTR (1995) 214, where the nominee acted in the purchase and re-sale of land, is along the same lines.

THE TRADITIONAL ENGLISH MODEL

fore, in an area which today we define as contractual. When John of Gaunt asked his trusted friends to acquire land in their name but '*ad usum*' of John himself (and with money which he provided), we were obviously in the area of undisclosed agency, buttressed by a strong fiduciary element. John could obtain the transfer of the *land* to himself at any time, but – and this is more significant – could provide that ownership by his friends should proceed '*ad usum*' no longer of John but of persons indicated by him (as in fact happened in his will).

There was an identical mechanism by which a person transferred an asset which was already his to his friends, as in the classic case of a departure for the Crusades or on a dangerous journey, where instructions were given in the event he did not return, but provision was made to take back the property if the story ended happily.[334] Contrary to what one might expect, legal structures of this kind have nothing to do with English law as it developed after the Norman Conquest in 1066, but can be traced back to the Anglo-Saxon period and to early medieval continental Europe.[335]

There exists, therefore, a contractual dynamic in the area of trusts, and every theoretical approach must take account of this fact; not, let it be clear, merely out of historical interest, but because, as always happens with strong structures, no successive conceptual (or even legislative) stratification has succeeded in eliminating it; it will be recalled that we explained the validity of the secret testamentary trust exactly by reference to this *reading of historical events*.[336] The modern bare trust established by the settlor for himself belongs to the same context, and it is for this reason that when we spoke of double-taxation treaties above we placed it on a footing with nominee agreements.

This context has, nonetheless, receded in the course of the history of equity, and we shall speak of it in the final pages of this chapter. It is sufficient at this stage to remind ourselves that the classic English family settlement of the seventeenth and eighteenth centuries[337] was characterized by the entrusting of an estate to trustees with no residual aspect of

---

[334] The secret trust reported by Baker, 'Use Upon a Use' (see above, footnote 87) was of this kind; it concerned a transfer without consideration by an exiled nobleman to a faithful retainer while the former was leaving for exile; but, as the legal document declared, 'tout ceo conveiance fut sur trust et confidence a sa use que H [the retainer] et ces heirs refefferont', and so they would have returned the property to the nobleman if he returned from exile.

[335] I have cited the sources in my essay 'Il diritto comune europeo in Inghilterra: profili terminologici', in M. Lupoi, L. Moccia and P. Prosperetti (eds.), *Scintillae iuris. Studi in memoria di Gino Gorla*, Milan, 1994, II, 1065, §9.   [336] See above, chapter 3 §1.f.

[337] Lupoi, *Appunti*, pp. 58–61. The settlement has definitively disappeared since the Trusts of Land and Appointment of Trustees Act 1996.

control in favour of the settlor. The fact that equitable estates were modelled on those of common law meant that situations arose in favour of the beneficiaries which were similar to those which developed when an estate was transferred into the name of a number of later owners; from this we have the theory which saw beneficiaries as 'owners in equity', on which we shall dwell later. For the moment, we are only interested in drawing attention to the fact that the trust in its classic configuration, which began in the eighteenth century, saw the settlor divest himself of the assets at the moment of transfer to the trustees. Contractual connotations had disappeared because the transfer of an estate is a unilateral transaction and the creation of rights to it in favour of third parties, whether in common law or equity, is the transferor's business. It is up to him, by using the words of purchase or the words of limitation, to define the estate which he is transferring and any other estates which he may lawfully create at that moment.[338]

The origins of the unilateral nature of the institution of the trust therefore lie in the unilateral nature of every transfer of an estate (and here too we may see a mark of that European unity which was broken by the so-called legal renaissance in Bologna): the 'loss of control' by the settlor is a modern phrase which has no historic value, but is nonetheless expressive, and serves to help understand, in the words of the old maxim of French common law, that '*donner et retenir ne vaut rien*'.[339] This does not mean that the settlor may not retain influence, or, to put it more correctly, powers.[340] This withholding of powers (for example, to substitute the trustee or to

---

[338] Cf. Lupoi, *Appunti*, pp. 16–17.

[339] The reference is to the decision of the Royal Court of Jersey in *Rahman v. Chase Bank* (1991) (see below, footnote 344). For an application of the maxim in the interpretation of article 771 of the Italian Civil Code, see P. Perlingieri, 'Sulla costituzione di fondo patrimoniale su "beni futuri"', in [1977] Dir. fam. 265, at 272–4.

[340] The notion of *power* is explained above, chapter 3 §1.c.

Modern practice has developed a series of mechanisms which correctly reduce the absolute separation between the settlor and the trust; some have been described in the preceding pages. In the first place, the trust may be revocable; secondly, the settlor may, in the trust instrument, grant himself the right to appoint new trustees where the original trustees are lacking; thirdly, the settlor may himself be the trustee or one of the trustees; finally, the settlor may indicate himself as the beneficiary or one of the beneficiaries, and may in any event reserve the right to add other beneficiaries to those named in the trust instrument. Where the trust has as its subject matter shares of a company controlled and managed by the settlor, he naturally retains control, because his position as manager is not affected; in theory, he may not be re-elected at the end of his term, but this is a marginal theory (with respect to which there are preventative techniques, but see below, footnote 408). An indirect means of control, especially in systems other than the English system, is obtained by the appointment of a protector, or by delivering a letter of wishes to the trustee: we shall speak of this in the next chapter.

name other beneficiaries) falls within the logical parameters of every uni-lateral method of disposition. Its limitation, obviously, lies in the effective-ness of the grant and consequently the exercise of the powers of adminis-tration and, where relevant, of transfer which result naturally in favour of the trustee and which the settlor may not appropriate for himself:[341] even in a case of genuine doubt as to how to act, the trustee must turn to a court and not to the person who created the trust. If this limitation is not complied with, the grant becomes ineffective and so, therefore, does the trust.

This aspect of trusts is difficult for those living under civil-law systems to understand (we shall speak of it when we discuss the relationship between the trust and the *fiducia*), but above all it is hard for those who, whatever kind of system they live under, turn to trusts for tax reasons. The more a trust is motivated by these reasons the less the classic configuration of the trust corresponds to the will of the settlor. The tax authorities of many States have noticed this, and have passed laws which lead to the non-recognition of a trust as such if certain elements, such as the loss of control of the trust assets on the part of the settlor, are lacking.[342] Fiscal ineffective-ness and nullity do not always go hand in hand; the latter entails the former, but not *vice versa*. It is a fact that creators of trusts, especially if they are of personal property, are less and less prepared to hand over manage-ment entirely to the trustee. The rapid rise of discretionary trusts has introduced a further new element: the need to guide the trustee in the exercise of his discretion, which is often little more than a fiscal expedi-ency, so as to give life to the intentions of the settlor as they may be varied in the course of time, without the settlor appearing to be the *dominus* of choices seemingly made by the trustee.

It is not hard to see that such arrangements belong in the realm of simulations, to which the usual rules of protection of third parties, includ-ing the forced heirs and creditors of the settlor, apply.[343]

The proliferation of trust companies, which are dedicated to the assist-

---

[341] See the analysis by Graziadei, *Diritti nell'interesse altrui*, pp. 242–7.

[342] American and British tax statutes have dealt with this matter repeatedly.

[343] To say that a trust in which the management duties are in reality carried out by the settlor, and not by the trustee, is a 'sham' a 'popular and pejorative word', in the words of Diplock LJ in *Snook v. London & West Riding* (1967), 802, means, more correctly, to affirm that the trust is a simulation. The word 'sham' came into use internationally after the decision of the Court of Jersey in *Rahman v. Chase Bank* (1991): the wives and children omitted by the settlor (who was Muslim) obtained a declaration of nullity of the trust, by showing that the trustee had no administrative autonomy, and regularly followed the instructions given to him by the settlor.

ance of their clients in creating and later managing trusts, has kept step with the spread of trusts in legal systems which did not previously recognize them, or which now regulate them more liberally in order to attract foreign clients, and with the discovery by these clients (including those from common-law countries) of the advantages offered by these new regimes.[344] In such cases there is no doubt that the client *contracts* with the trust company or with law firms which provide similar services. Not even in this case, however, is the *juridical* nature of the trust affected, and the natural role of the trustee as the person in charge of protection of the interests of the beneficiaries – not, of course, of the settlor–client – is unchanged. What is affected is of much greater significance: it is the essence of the relationship between settlor and trustee, and not its reconstruction in legal terms.

An emerging contractual element may, therefore, be noted. No one, fortunately, has claimed that it may nobly be justified as a return to the origins of trusts. It is, in truth, a distortion of the fundamentals of the institution as they have been defined over the last three centuries, and an ill-concealed step towards the field of contracts. Furthermore, contractual instruments are already perfectly well delineated, and there is no need to infect both trusts and contracts at the same time.[345]

---

[344] They belong to what I define as 'the international trust model', which is dealt with in the next chapter.

[345] Langbein, 'Contractarian Basis of the Law of Trusts' (see above, footnote 20), has recently sustained that the trust is a 'deal' and that its characteristic aspect is not the legal event which precedes it, but the (contractual) definition of the powers and responsibilities of the trustee. This pronouncement is subject to limits which the author himself applies: trusts where the settlor and trustee are one, charitable trusts (because they relate to 'quasi-public institutions'), and constructive trusts (because they are a kind of 'equitable remedy') are excluded. As for the other types, the author declares that the testamentary trust is contractual (he terms it 'contractarian': this is probably the same thing, since he refers to the 'law of contract') because the trustee accepts his duties voluntarily. This theory leaves one dumbfounded.

Its strong point is its historical analysis: the trust begins as an agreement. This position is correct, and I have explained the reasons for it and its limitations above. Langbein passes, however, from the fourteenth century to today without pausing for breath, and asks himself why we do not follow the original source of inspiration. To respond, it is sufficient to require that his analysis be extended to the three categories of trusts which he has decided to omit, or to claim that justification be given for statements such as that the ownership by the trustee 'is a mere historical convention, a way of speaking', which is the opposite of what is held by hundreds of decisions from the entire world of common law. It would be enough to ask for a minimum amount of conceptual consistency, and to remind the author that it does not seem to be possible, with reference to testamentary trusts, to speak of 'party autonomy over the terms'. Finally, one should remind the author of an element which he completely ignores: the existence of the system of equity. I shall not refer to comparative considerations put forward by

c The office of trustee

Whether the trustee be the settlor himself or a person chosen by the settlor or by the person to whom the settlor has granted this power, by an earlier trustee, by a court,[346] or, following recent legislative innovation, by the beneficiaries,[347] his obligations are always exclusively either to the beneficiaries (among whom, let it not be forgotten, the settlor may appear, alone or as the equal of the others), or to the purpose of the trust. With respect to the beneficiaries, who may often find themselves in conflict, the trustee must behave in an absolutely neutral manner. It is sufficient to consider the case where there is a beneficiary of the income from the trust and another, subsequent, beneficiary of the capital: certain risky, high-income investments exist which are generally of more interest to the former, but which place the interests of the latter in peril. Other investments, for example in real estate, are attractive to the latter, but may produce a low income for the former.[348]

The neutrality of the trustee extends to disputes concerning the validity of the trust or whether it may be contested by creditors of the settlor. He has no obligation whatsoever to take a position; on the contrary, according to the latest case law he is expressly required not to take sides.[349]

The duties of the trustee are performed without charge: it is, neverthe-

the author, which are based almost exclusively on the Preliminary Report of the Hague Convention, and which end with the following statement: 'In Europe, contract does the work of trust.'

[346] For the particular case in which the Public Trustee found itself appointed to be the sole trustee of a trust which required two, see *Re Duxbury's Settlement* (1995).

[347] Trusts of Land and Appointment of Trustees Act 1996, s. 19: where the trust instrument does not provide for any person to have the power to appoint new trustees, and the beneficiaries have reached the age of majority, and have capacity, and could, as a group, obtain the termination of the trust, the beneficiaries may unanimously demand that a trustee resign (that is, they may revoke his appointment), and may, in any case, appoint new trustees.

This provision applies to any trust with beneficiaries, and may be waived by the settlor in the trust instrument. See also above, chapter 3 §1.c.

[348] *Learoyd v. Whiteley* (1887): 'the business of the trustee . . . is the business of investing money for the benefit of persons who are to enjoy it at some future, time, and not for the sole benefit of the person entitled to the present income. The duty of a trustee is not to take such care only as a prudent man would take if he had only himself to consider; the duty rather is to take such care as an ordinary prudent man would take if he were minded to make an investment for the benefit of other people for whom he felt morally bound to provide.' Recently, see *Nestlé v. National Westminster Bank* (1993) (1279–80 *per* Staughton LJ).

[349] *Alsop Wilkinson v. Neary* (1995), which disapproves *Ideal Bedding v. Holland* (1907). In both cases, a revocatory action had been commenced by the settlor's creditors.

Cayman Islands law is different: *In the matter of Lemos* (1993), see below, chapter 4, footnote 255.

less, customary for the settlor to provide for compensation. If he does not, or if it appears to be insufficient, a court may make provision for payment, or increase the amount, as the case may be.[350]

The trustee, as we saw in our discussion of constructive trusts, must not derive any profit from his position (apart from his compensation[351]) or, as it is put in Scottish law, he must not make himself *auctor in rem suam*;[352] moreover, he must not place himself in a position where it may be thought that he is deriving profit. For example, if he acquires a trust asset, the contract is voidable at the request of any beneficiary without the need to establish loss;[353] the trust assets, in other words, are not accessible to the trustee, even where, in fact, this absolute bar is unjustified,[354] such as when he acquires them at a public auction.[355] It is a true incapacity,[356] which does not even cease pursuant to termination of a trustee's appointment.[357] There is an obvious case of conflict of interest when the trustee is also one of the beneficiaries of the trust; in this case he must seek independent advice, and, in special cases, turn to a statute to obtain direction.[358] There are numerous cases where the trustees and the beneficiaries are the same, such as in co-ownership (for example, of the matrimonial home) which, as we shall see, may come into effect only by means of a trust for sale of which the co-owners are at the same time trustees and beneficiaries. In general, the English judiciary does not take the place of the trustees willingly, and is

---

[350] The principle that there will be no charge is, however, hard to overcome: see *Barret v. Hartley* (1866), and *Re Gates* (1933).

[351] No fiduciary may place himself in competition with the persons to whom he owes a duty. For the case of the executor of a will, see *Re Thomson* (1930).

[352] Wilson and Duncan, ch. 26.

[353] See an important dictum of the nineteenth century: 'And it is a rule of universal application, that no one, having such duties to discharge, shall be allowed to enter into engagements in which he has or can have a personal interest conflicting with the interests of those whom he is bound to protect' (*Aberdeen Railway v. Blaikie Brothers* (1854), 471 *per* Lord Cranworth LC).

[354] This observation was made in the precedent from 1726 which established the rule on improper benefits obtained by the trustee (see above, chapter 2 §2.e): 'it might seem hard that the trustee is the only person of all mankind who might not have the lease; but it is very proper that rule should be strictly observed, and not in the least relaxed.'

[355] *Campbell v. Walker* (1800). The situation is the same in Barbados: *Re Cox* (1948–57).

[356] This concept of 'disability', is expressed by Megarry V-C in *Tito v. Waddell (no. 2)* (1977).

[357] Cf. Pettit, *Trusts*, p. 426.

[358] For a case where the compensation due a trustee had to be determined, see *Re Duke of Norfolk's Settlement* (1982).

A recent pronouncement of the Privy Council considered the frequent case where the trustee is also a bank employee, and has made it clear that the obligations arising out of the trust prevail over those arising out of the employment relationship: *Kuwait Asia Bank v. National Mutual Life Nominees Ltd.* (1990).

reluctant to give directions where it believes that the trustees should take the decision alone or where it suspects that it does not have before it a complete version of the facts and elements to take into account before arriving at the issuance of an order, especially in the case of discretionary trusts.[359]

On this subject, one should recall the position in which the trustee of a settlement finds himself: here, the life tenant, who is not by definition the final beneficiary, has all the powers of an owner, including those to enjoy the assets directly and to transfer them, and is subject to the single obligation to cause the sale proceeds to be placed in the hands of the trustees. In this way, the subject matter of the trust is transferred from the asset to the amount received from its sale.[360] The successive beneficiaries will therefore enjoy the income from a sum of money or from the personal property in which it has been invested by the trustees.

In the new category of the trust of land, the holders of an interest in possession[361] have the right to occupy the property if the trust instrument provides for it or if the property is available.[362]

[359] Cf. *Re Drexel Burnham* (1995) (on which see above, footnote 242); but see the concluding statement of Vinelott J in *British Steel Coal Corporation v. British Steel Coal Staff* (1993): 'Common sense dictates that no man should be asked to exercise a discretion as to the application of a fund amongst a class of which he is a member.'

On the general subject, see the detailed reasoning of Lord Oliver in the decision of the Privy Council in *Marley v. Mutual Security* (1991).

[360] At the moment in which he transfers, the life tenant is trustee in favour of the later beneficiaries, and is therefore subject to the rules on conflict of interest.

Apart from the trust for sale, 'settled land' after 1925 means (Lupoi, *Appunti*, pp. 60–1, 116–17 and, more fully, Graziadei, *Diritti nell'interesse altrui*, pp. 195–210) the granting of a benefit for the lifetime of the beneficiary ('life estate'), with one or more successive beneficiaries; since 1882, the holder of a life estate, called a life tenant, acquired the right to transfer the legal estate, so the trust automatically transferred to the proceeds. As a result of having the right to transfer the legal estate, the life tenant had the rights of an owner, although the trustees of the settlement are also owners. This contradiction was resolved by registering the acquisition by the life tenant consequent upon the creation of a trust, without making mention of the trust, and instead registering a 'restriction', pursuant to which no transfer could take place unless the purchase price was delivered to Tom and Dick (who were the trustees of the settlement): see also below, footnote 449. A similar procedure is followed with the trust for sale (a comparison between the two institutions may be found in Graziadei, *Diritti*, pp. 210–13). For the special elements of this discipline, see S. Coveney and A. Pain, *Interests in Land* (2nd edition), London, 1995, pp. 184–90, 205–8.

This area has been revolutionized by the Trusts of Land and Appointment of Trustees Act 1996, pursuant to which the rules of the Settled Land Act 1925 ceased to be effective for trusts created after the new law came into force, on 1 January 1997.

[361] See above, chapter 3 §1.e.

[362] Trusts of Land and Appointment of Trustees Act 1996, s. 12. Section 13 deals with the case where there is more than one beneficiary, and with the powers of the trustees, with the

The beneficiaries have the right to inspect trust documents when they wish, including correspondence among the trustees,[363] and to obtain periodic accounting;[364] in some cases, they have the right to be consulted.[365] In reality, a good trustee remains in constant contact with the beneficiaries of a trust; after all, he manages it in their interest and, within the limits of the requirements of the trust instrument, he has no reason to ignore their wishes.[366]

The new provisions introduced by the Trusts of Land and Appointment of Trustees Act 1996 strengthen the position of the final beneficiaries of a trust of land when they are holders of an interest in possession. The trustee must consult them, and, subject to the interests of the trust, must give effect to their wishes.[367] This is, however, a requirement which the settlor may waive in the trust instrument. When the trustee sells the property at the request of the beneficiaries, however, the trust is transferred to the proceeds of the sale, and is therefore no longer a trust of land. As a result, the obligation of the trustee to consult the beneficiaries and give effect to their wishes lapses.

The powers of the trustee, seen from the point of view of equity, are those necessary to achieve the purpose of the trust, and no more. It is therefore impossible to discuss them comprehensively except to make the fundamental observation that the assets or rights on trust belong to the trustee and accordingly that it is legitimate to carry out any act available to an owner.

English statutes,[368] which deal with this matter in great detail, state very few rules of truly general application. Except in particular cases, they do

aim of maintaining equal treatment among the beneficiaries (including the imposition of payment of a sum by the beneficiary in possession in favour of the others).

[363] Except in the case of discretionary trusts.

[364] The beneficiaries may, of course, ask the court to issue orders to the trustee to act or refrain from acting in a certain manner.

[365] Law of Property Act, 1925, s. 26 (3), as modified in 1926.

[366] Cf. Finn, *Fiduciary Obligations* (see above, footnote 180), pp. 21–2.

[367] Trusts of Land and Appointment of Trustees Act 1996, s. 11. In the case of dissent among the beneficiaries, the trustee must accede to the wishes of the majority (calculated according to the value of the interests of each in the trust). [The reader should refer to the joint report of the Law Commission and Scottish Law Commission Trustees' Powers and Duties 1999, published since the Italian original of this book.]

[368] Principally the Trustee Act 1925 and the Trustee Investment Act 1961.

As I write, the repeal of this law is under proposal. The British Government has published a preliminary document (*Investment Powers of Trustees, a Consultation Document* by HM Treasury, May 1996) in which it is held that the Trustee Investment Act 1961 imposes unnecessary limitations on the powers of investment of trustees, and proposes, *inter alia*, the elimination of the traditional list of permitted investments, emphasizing that the trustee has the duty to consult experts each time he must take a decision which he does not have the necessary competence to take alone.

not prevail over the provisions of the trust instrument, and are limited to a complementary purpose. The concern of the legislature has always been not to paralyse the activities of the trustee, which would block the circulation of the assets. The development of legislative rules has therefore been along two lines: on the one hand, to give the trustees powers, especially powers of sale, within a series of typical circumstances; and on the other, to prescribe which management acts or which types of investment are certain to fall into the category of trustee powers.[369] The most recent legislation in this area took a dramatic step when it established that in the case of trusts of land the trustees are provided with all the powers of an absolute owner.[370]

On this subject, one must bear in mind that in trust instruments the sections concerning the powers of the trustees tend to be rather complex, and become even more complex in the practical working of a trust because of the rules which state that trustees of a trust must always act together[371] and personally.[372] This latter requirement, which has been held to have been surpassed by modern society,[373] has been mitigated by legislation.[374]

---

[369] On the types of investment, the laws enunciate with great precision the categories of securities in which the investment is safe (cf. W. Goodhart, 'Trust Law for the Twenty-First Century', in 10 TLI (1996) 38, at 38–40). Questions concerning investments in movables have become considerably more complex in recent decades, due to the high degree of specialization which they require. Even giving the responsibility to specialist companies is not always the right solution, because their standards do not necessarily correspond to those required of trustees. In the United States, many States (including California, Delaware, Illinois and New York) have adopted the text formulated by the American Law Institute: Restatement Third of Trusts: Prudent Investor Rule (1992) and have passed a Prudent Investor Act after the model of the Uniform Prudent Investor Act of 1994, following the indications for exemption of the trustees' responsibility.

[370] Trusts of Land and Appointment of Trustees Act 1996, s. 6(1): 'For the purpose of exercising their functions as trustees, the trustees of land have in relation to the land subject to the trust all the powers of an absolute owner.'

[371] Cf. Hanbury, *Equity*, pp. 475–6. The similarity to article 7002 of the Italian Civil Code should be noted, but I cannot explain it.

[372] The principle of equity is that a trustee may never delegate his powers, except to carry out menial tasks, and when he does, he is responsible for the agent's actions. For the United States, see Scott, *Trusts*, §171.

The Trusts of Land and Appointment of Trustees Act 1996, s. 9, generally permits trustees to delegate their functions to the final beneficiaries of a trust by means of a power of attorney, and not to be liable for actions of those beneficiaries unless the trustees have been insufficiently prudent in appointing them.

[373] Cf. Pettit, *Trusts*, pp. 428–38.

[374] The Trustee Act 1925, s. 23, and the Powers of Attorney Act 1971, s. 9, allow trustees of a trust to delegate their duties, so that management activities involving investments are very often conferred by the trustees upon specialist companies or professionals. The trustee is, however, liable for *culpa in eligendo*; cf. Hanbury, *Equity*, pp. 549–55. A co-trustee may delegate his powers, but only from year to year, and not to another trustee of the

It is natural that the trustee must, in the first place, preserve the trust assets and not commingle them with his own:[375] violation of this requirement, which is often held to be a peculiar element of the trust, and its distinctive feature,[376] and at times is punished by the law,[377] led case law in the last century to affirm that the total amount which arose out of the commingling belonged to the beneficiaries.[378] Today, it is preferred to grant the beneficiaries a privileged position with respect to the property and, where necessary, to apply tracing rules to the mixed funds.[379] Furthermore, contrary to what a civil-law mentality may lead one to think, the existence of a trust does not require any publicity; on the contrary, the law expressly forbids mention in a share register that shares are owned by a person as

same trust: Trustee Act 1925, s. 25.

This restriction does not resolve the cases of the trust for sale described in the text, since where husband and wife are co-owners of a home, one may not charge the other with the responsibility of selling it. The problem was solved by a law from 1935 (Enduring Powers of Attorney Act), which contained provisions which many people found too broad: it provided, for example, that the later mental incapacity of the principal had no effect on the power of attorney he had granted, and that the power of attorney could also have as its purpose acts relating to the functions of a trustee as such (and not just the performance of certain management acts). Furthermore, the delegating trustee must observe very specific formalities, such as the communication of the granting of the power of attorney to a series of parties.

While many common-law countries permit the use of powers of attorney for single acts, none permits such wide-ranging ones: Law Commission, *The Law of Trusts. Delegation by Individual Trustees*, 1991 (Consultation Paper No. 118), p. 5. See also Law Reform Committee, *Powers and Duties of Trustees*, 1982 (Cmnd 8733). [Since the Italian edition of this book, the Trustee Delegation Act 1999 has been enacted. Editor's note.]

[375] On the accounting which a trustee must keep, see P. M. B. Rowland, *Trust Accounts* (3rd edition), London, 1994.

The duty to keep trust assets separate from personal assets raises two special issues where the trustee is the bank in which the trust account has been opened. Firstly, the sums belonging to the trusts are, of course, mixed with all the other sums deposited by clients of the bank. Secondly, the bank uses the sums, as it does others, for its own ordinary activities. It cannot be sustained that there is a breach of trust where the trust instrument allows the bank-trustee to deposit the trust amounts with itself. The question arose before the courts of the Bahamas, and was finally decided by the Privy Council (*Space Investments Ltd v. Canadian Imperial Bank* (1986)) against the beneficiary of the trust (the bank had become insolvent in the meantime, and it was necessary to determine whether the beneficiary could commence a tracing action, and, since this was not possible, obtain a charge or privileged position with respect to the bank's assets): 'There is no justification for the intervention of equity. The settlor has allowed trust money to be treated as if it were customer's money'; the decision would have been different if the bank-trustee had acted in breach of trust. See *Bank of Credit* (1994) (a decision of the courts of the Isle of Man).

[376] *Henry v. Hammond* (1913), 521, *per* Channell J; cf., in Singapore, *Lee Hiok Woon v. Lee Hiok Ping* (1993).   [377] See above, chapter 2 §1.c.   [378] *Lupton v. White* (1808).

[379] See above, chapter 2 §4.b.

trustee,[380] and, with some exceptions, the situation is the same in the area of real property.[381] Not even the practice of having bank accounts in the name of the trust or the trustee is universal.[382]

There are numerous reasons for this apparently strange state of affairs. Firstly, it is normal for there to be several trustees, and, as we have just observed, trustees must always act together. Secondly, English law has always favoured the free circulation of assets. Thirdly, the rights and obligations arising out of a trust belong to the realm of equity, while land registries and other forms of disclosure belong to common law.[383] To the civil lawyer, these explanations will seem somewhat incomplete and limited: he will ask, for example, what prevents a person who is being hounded by creditors or has filed for bankruptcy[384] from declaring that certain personal property in his possession is subject to a trust in favour of a third party and, with the agreement of that third party (the so-called beneficiary), segregating it from the justified claims of the creditors. There is only one answer to questions of this nature: centuries of English case law

---

[380] Companies Act 1985, s. 360.

[381] Law of Property Act 1925, s. 74: 'Subject to the provisions of this Act as to settled land, neither the registrar nor any person dealing with a registered estate or charge shall be affected with notice of a trust express implied or constructive, and references to trusts shall, so far as possible, be excluded from the register.'

[382] A trustee who wishes to (or who is obliged to by the terms of the trust instrument) may open bank accounts in his name as trustee, or directly in the name of the trust. See, however, below in the text.

[383] The Law Society of England and Wales was extremely surprised to see that the Hague Convention was contemplating introducing a rule on the registration of trusts (it was to be included in article 12 of the Convention). It is useful to report the observations sent to the Conference in their entirety:

We find the existence of this article surprising and do not understand its purpose. It is a fundamental principle of English law that trusts are 'veiled'. The existence of a trust and the fact that the trustee is not the true owner of the assets are irrelevant to the world at large and are not disclosed publicly by registration or on documents of title. A trust concerns only trustee and beneficiary (and the tax authorities).

In fact, it is regarded as desirable or even necessary for the protection of persons dealing with the trustee that they should not be concerned whether he is a trustee or the true owner of assets. For example, a buyer of assets which are in fact held by a trustee on trust must be able to enter into a transaction without regard to whether the trustee is the absolute owner or not. If a purchaser were to be obliged to enquire about true ownership and whether a trustee has authority to sell, this would often constitute a serious inconvenience. It would make trust assets less readily marketable than their non-trust equivalents, which would inevitably be reflected in a reduction in their value. (Actes, p. 160)

[384] On the regulation of assets held on trust where the trustee becomes bankrupt, see P. G. Jaeger, *La separazione del patrimonio fiduciario nel fallimento*, Milan, 1968, pp. 189–93.

furnish no examples of this having occurred. One should seek to understand the reasons for this, but this would mean moving to a different comparative law level, that of *principia*, and this is not the appropriate place to do so.[385]

Many rules have evolved in case law concerning the exercise of a trustee's powers.[386] They were formulated in times of orderly economic development and low inflation, and doubts have recently been expressed as to whether they will always be appropriate,[387] while other uncertainties have been created by the emergence of interests to which it was thought in the past that trustees should pay no heed.[388] In case of doubt, the trustee may (or

---

[385] I have conducted research among a large number of professional trustees and lawyers who specialize in trusts, both in England and in other common-law countries. I have thus learnt of a situation which I had not imagined existed. Many of them open the accounts into which the liquid assets of the trust are deposited in their own name to avoid the bank requesting a copy of the trust instrument and thereby learning the names of the beneficiaries of the trust. Others follow the same procedure because, on the basis of recent case law on the responsibility of banks as a result of irregular movements of funds by a trustee (see above, chapter 2 §2.c), the bank where the account has been opened may request proof that a particular movement of funds is within the powers of the trustee. Finally, yet others believe it is sufficient to assign a letter of the alphabet to identify accounts connected with trusts which they administer (such as: 'John Smith, account A'). This is enough, in their opinion, to demonstrate that the funds belong to a trust in case of a dispute.

Only one of my correspondents' replies gave an example which is not far from that described in the text. It described a trust company (and so the least likely to affirm that funds which are its own actually belong to a trust), which does not have bank accounts of its own, but which uses an accounting firm to collect its compensation, pay salaries and so on. In this way, my correspondent maintains, any account in the trust company's name must be a trust account.

[386] For example, that wasting assets, or assets which will lose value over time must be transformed into money unless the settlor wishes otherwise: *Howe v. Earl of Dartmouth* (1802).

[387] See *Nestlé v. National Westminster Bank* (1993), at p. 126 *per* Dillon LJ: 'Trustees should not be reckless with trust money but what the prudent man should do at any time depends on the economic and financial conditions at that time, not on what judges of the past, however eminent, held to be the prudent course in the conditions of fifty or one hundred years before.'

[388] Consider the emerging phenomenon, of United States origin, which leads to every economic activity being judged from the point of view of its political correctness. In the area of trusts, the question has been raised by the Bishop of Oxford as to whether the trustees of a trust with religious purposes could invest in shares of companies with purposes such as the production and sale of arms, or which practised forms of racial discrimination. See *Harries v. Church Commissioners* (1992) (which contains a good description of the regime of the trust created for the upkeep of the Church of England); P. Luxton, 'Ethical Investment in Hard Times', in 55 MLR (1992) 587.

rather, must) turn to a court to obtain an order[389] and, if necessary, ask it to modify the provisions of the trust instrument.[390]

The rules regarding the responsibility of the trustee, partially codified in the Trustee Act of 1925, have always been extremely rigid, first of all because they do not take account of any subjective requirement: the good faith of the trustee and the ends he was seeking to achieve are of no relevance whatsoever.[391] The responsibility arises out of the objective fact that he has not acted in compliance with the conditions which regulate the specific trust or with the duties of a trustee in general.[392] Liability for damages, to which judicial dismissal of the trustee may be added, always contains a restitutory element,[393] and the notion of restitution includes the return to the trust both of the assets or rights of which the trust has been deprived and of the profit which the trust would have received if the trustee had not failed to perform his obligations.[394] A trustee who is responsible for the loss of a trust asset[395] must pay a sum equal to the maximum value which the asset would have attained between the date of the breach of the conditions of the trust and the date of the judgment,[396] except that the fact

---

[389] It is curious that the question whether a trustee may appeal against the decision of a court has been raised. The prevailing opinion is that he may only in exceptional cases. The recent case of *Oldham Borough Council v. A-G* (1993), was appealed, but the appeal concerned the refusal of the judge in the lower court to give instructions to the trustees. This is, in all probability, an application of the same principle of neutrality which, as we have just seen, obliges the trustee not to take a position in cases where the validity or the exceptionability of a trust is challenged in court.

[390] For the modification of a settlement of 1705, see *Hambro v. Duke of Marlborough* (1994). The alert reader will notice that the duration of this trust exceeded all limits imposed by the rule against perpetuities; this was possible because the trust was created by Parliament in recognition of the achievements of the Duke of Marlborough.

[391] In general, see Hanbury, *Equity*, pp. 499–542; Underhill, *Trusts*, pp. 825–80; Béraudo, *Trusts*, §§210–27; Graziadei, *Diritti nell'interesse altrui*, pp. 438–43.

[392] *Royal Brunei Airlines v. Tan* (1995), referred to above, at the end of chapter 2 §2.c.

[393] Cf. Gardner, *Introduction*, pp. 214–18.

[394] Compound interest is always added to the sums to be reimbursed by the trustees. This is another difference between common law and equity: the legal remedies of the former did not traditionally permit a judgment for the payment of any form of interest. In modern law, a restitutory action against a person who is not a trustee or a fiduciary includes the payment of simple interest: *Westdeutsche v. Islington* (1996) (a detailed analysis of this case may be found above, chapter 2 §3.e).

[395] For example, real property mortgaged by the trustee in breach of the conditions of the trust and later sold by the mortgage-holder at a public auction: *Jaffray v. Marshall* (1993). It is possible to insure against the responsibility of the trustee: see C. Baxter, 'Trustees' Personal Liability and the Role of Liability Insurance', in [1996] Conv 12.

[396] Provided that there has been, or could be, the opportunity to transfer it: *Jaffray v. Marshall* (1993); disapproved by the House of Lords in *Target Holdings v. Redferns* (1995), at p. 366 (see immediately below in the text).

that the loss would have occurred anyway is a mitigating factor.[397] On the subject of this last rule a recent decision merits mention:[398]

A law firm received instructions from a finance company to register a mortgage on real property to guarantee a loan in favour of the purchaser. The purchaser instructed the same law firm to follow the matter. On the basis of appraisals provided by the purchaser, both the finance company and the law firm believed that the purchase price was 2 million pounds. The agreed loan was 1.5 million pounds.

The finance company delivered the sum to the law firm so that it could deliver it to the borrower at the moment of the purchase and registration of the mortgage. The law firm delivered the sum before these events took place, and, furthermore, informed the company that the guarantee had been perfected. When the truth was discovered, the mortgage having, in the meantime, been recorded, the property was sold by the finance company for 500,000 pounds. An action ensued against the law firm, which worked out that the finance company would have incurred the loss in any event, because the value of the property was not that which had been claimed by the borrower and accepted by the finance company as correct, and the Court of Appeal, in a majority decision, held that the repayment obligation of the trustee arose at the moment of the breach, and that other facts which brought about the loss were of no relevance. The House of Lords, on the other hand, pointed out that although the breach by the trustee was incontestable, there was no causal connection between the breach and the damage: it would have occurred even if the law firm had followed the instructions of the finance company to the letter. In reaching this conclusion, the House of Lords held the law firm to be a bare trustee.[399]

The responsibility which falls on trustees is so strict that a trustee does not usually carry out a management act or a transfer unless he is certain that the act falls within the scope of his powers.[400] Furthermore, he risks being held responsible even if he is excessively prudent and interprets the extent of his powers erroneously, in the sense that he underestimates them.[401] The statutory rules in this area also aim to simplify the preparation of trust instruments,[402] but radical revisions have been called for to liberalize the

---

[397] See the different approaches followed in *Bristol & West Building Society v. May May & Merrimans (a firm)* (1996), and *Bristol & West Building Society v. Mothew (t/a Stapley & Co.)* (1996) (Court of Appeal), commented by P. Matthews, 'Breach of Trust and the Use of Hindsight', in 2 T&T (1996), n. 9, 13.

[398] *Target Holdings v. Redferns* (1994) (Court of Appeal) (1995) (House of Lords).

[399] For this notion, see above, chapter 3 §3.a.

[400] For a recent case regarding the sale of a piece of land which was the subject matter of a trust to buy another, see *Oldham Borough Council v. A-G* (1993).

[401] *Nestlé v. National Westminster Bank* (1994).

[402] For example, by listing in detail the movable investments which a trustee may make without authorization. In Australia, see the Trustee Act 1925 of New South Wales, s. 14; the Trustee Act 1958 of Victoria, s. 4; the Trusts Act 1973 of Queensland, s. 21; the Trustee

system, with the additional aim of making English trusts more competitive with those of other countries.[403]

It is, of course, possible that one breach might bring about a benefit to a trust (for example, an investment which is not authorized by the trust instrument, but which nonetheless turns out to produce a high return) and that a successive breach produces a loss: the rule is that the trustee may not compensate one result with the other.[404]

Where there is more than one trustee, each is responsible,[405] and each must act as soon as he comes to know of a breach which has been committed by another trustee, and generally speaking each must keep himself up to date on how the other trustees are performing their duties. When more than one trustee commits a breach, their responsibility to the beneficiaries is joint and several; as far as their internal relationship is concerned, the level of responsibility is assessed according to general principles.[406]

The only defence for a trustee is that offered him by s. 61 of the Trustee Act of 1925: 'to have acted honestly and reasonably'. This is, obviously, a vague criterion, and above all one which is applied in a rather limited fashion in case law, which on some occasions adopts the criterion of *diligentia quam in suis*, and on others that of a prudent businessman. Furthermore, it must always be borne in mind that the trustee's obligation is of a fiduciary nature, and is towards the beneficiaries. Accordingly, a trustee is held responsible where, in his capacity as controlling shareholder of a company managed by some of the beneficiaries he is content to accept reports presented by the Board of Directors to the meetings of the shareholders.[407]

Act 1936 of South Australia, s. 5; the Trustees Act 1962 of Western Australia, s. 16; the Trustee Act 1898 of Tasmania, s. 5. Most of these Acts have undergone numerous subsequent amendments.

[403] D. J. Hayton, 'Developing the Law of Trusts for the Twenty-First Century', in 106 LQR (1990) 87.

[404] Underhill, *Trusts*, pp. 849–50. See, nonetheless, *Bartlett v. Barclays Bank* (1980), below, footnote 407, for the case where the loss and the profit occur as the result of two operations attributable to a single breach of trust.

[405] Trustee Act, 1925, s. 30 (1). See, on the other hand, article 709.3 of the Italian civil code, for executors of wills.

[406] Now codified in the Civil Liability (Contribution) Act 1978.

[407] *Bartlett v. Barclays Bank* (1980). The judge held that a professional trustee such as Barclays Bank in a position of control of a company is held to a higher level of diligence than simply listening to reports in a shareholders' meeting. Section 61 of the Trustee Act 1925 exonerates a trustee who acts 'honestly and reasonably'; in the case in point, the judge stated, the first was present, but not the second.

The allocation of blame in evaluation models connected with the personal and professional characteristics of the agent has benefited in Italian law from the compara-

It is doubtful whether provisions which relieve the trustee of responsibility are valid, at least where they include a breach of trust arising out of conduct which goes beyond ordinary negligence.[408]

With regard to third parties with whom he contracts, the trustee responds with all his property to the obligations which he assumes:[409] the third parties have nothing to do with the trust; on the contrary, as we noted above with regard to title to assets of a trust, it is sometimes the trustee himself who does not hold himself out as being a trustee. This personal liability has become particularly weighty since the passing of the Law of Property (Miscellaneous Provisions) Act of 1994, because a trustee who effects a sale may even find himself obliged to provide guarantees to the purchaser with reference to possible defects of title of which he has no knowledge.[410]

The Statute of Limitations *never* operates in favour of a trustee when he has acted fraudulently or where he has appropriated a trust asset;[411] in other cases the limitations period is six years.[412]

It should be noted that English law does not make distinctions among different types of trust in the area of responsibility: a constructive trustee is subject to the same rules as those provided for an express trust.

d The trustee

Having arrived at this point in our treatment of trusts according to the English model, we have the elements necessary to enter the territory of conceptual definitions and systematic classifications. We shall begin with

tive work carried out by M. Bussani, *La colpa soggettiva*, Padua, 1991 (for the case of the specialist professional, see pp. 293–7).

[408] Cf. Hanbury, *Equity*, pp. 473–4; Graziadei, *Diritti nell'interesse altrui*, pp. 443–6. A restatement of English law on this subject is supplied by P. Matthews, 'The Efficacy of Trustee Exemption Clauses in English Law', in [1989] Conv 42, who distinguishes between exemption clauses in the real sense and clauses which limit the obligations which fall upon a trustee. For the former category, see the recent pronouncement from Jersey in the *Federated Pension Services* case, on which see below, p. 231.

[409] The trustee has the right to make good his losses from the trust assets (the *right of indemnity*). The right may be exercised on his behalf by the trustee's creditors.
    The right of indemnity is coupled with an equitable charge over the trust assets.

[410] The trustee may certainly make good his losses from the trust assets, but this is not always significant (as in the case where the sole trust asset is real property which the trustee must sell: see the comments of J. Goldsworth, 'An Unhappy Lot?', in 1 T&T (1995), n. 10, 2).

[411] In this case, a crime may also have been committed under the Theft Act 1968. It is interesting that the case of a trustee who uses possession or other advantages from a piece of real property for his own benefit falls within the notion of theft: Theft Act 1968, s. 4 (1) (a).

[412] Limitation Act 1980, s. 21. The same is true of an action by the Attorney General for the protection of rights arising out of a charitable trust.

the trustee, since he is the *only essential person* in a trust: it may lack a settlor, as in the case of constructive and resulting trusts, it may lack beneficiaries, as with charitable and purpose trusts and new forms of trusts, but it can never lack a trustee.[413] Any attempt to understand trusts (and to ascertain whether a notion of trusts exists) must, therefore, begin with the trustee.

The multiplicity of types of trust is reflected in the many kinds of trustee: from a bare trustee, to a person who finds himself a trustee against his will, to a trustee appointed by law, to a trustee who is also a beneficiary, to a trustee who is also a settlor. From a functional point of view, then, there are numerous kinds of trustee, which have very little to do one with the other. It is a serious error for the civil lawyer to speak of *the* trustee; this derives from another error, which by now the reader will consider to be sheer foolishness, which is to speak of *the* trust. On the other hand, common-law literature is often misleading and imprecise in its juridical analysis (as we shall see in general terms when we discuss the beneficiary), because it pays little attention to comparative issues, and is over-eager to dress up as a Pandectist without understanding how to put his clothes on properly. This is the reason for the scarcity of citations in the following pages from legal writings.

The trustee, as I have just pointed out, is the only essential person. He is the holder of a right, not (as one of the most frequent misinterpretations would have it) of a right recognized by common law,[414] but of a right of some sort, or some sort of entitlement.

This entitlement (i.e., the subject matter of the trust) may have been granted him without consideration, by a deed *inter vivos*, or for value; it may have been acquired by him in a non-trust context, to be subjected to a trust at a later stage; it may have been transferred to him by a court, for him to carry out a *munus*; it may have been acquired by him with the simultaneous creation of a trust because the law does not allow certain ownership scenarios to develop outside the field of trusts. The source of the entitlement belonging to the trustee is subject to the same variations which oblige us to refer to trusts and trustees in the plural.

The *title* of the trustee, or, more generally, of belonging, is considered by equity to be incomplete.[415]

It is not in any way a requirement that what is lacking to render the title held by the trustee equitably complete should belong to a third party. It may well not

---

[413] As we know, 'Equity does not want for a trustee': see above, footnote 39.

[414] Among the few people who have not fallen into this trap is C. Reymond, 'Le trust et le droit suisse', in ZfsR, 1954, 118, at 129: 'On lit souvent dans les auteurs continentaux que seuls les droit reconnus par le Droit commun peuvent etre constitués en trust. Il n'en est rien.'

[415] This is the theory I expounded above, chapter 2 §5.c.

belong to anyone, and the equitable defect of title of the trustee remains just that, but persons may or may not exist who have the right to avail themselves of that defect. In most cases, these persons exist: one example would be a government body or private person who has the right to take action to enforce the performance of a trust instrument establishing a charitable trust; another would be those who, while perhaps not technically defined as beneficiaries, may nonetheless claim performance of trusts which bring them benefit.[416] Such persons do not, on the other hand, exist in so-called anomalous trusts.

The *quantum* which is lacking for equitable fullness of title imposes limitations on the way the entitlement of the trustee is exercised, or on its transfer at the end of the trust period, or both. The *quantum* may reach different values. Its highest level is certainly that which grants the entitlement of the trustee to a third party, namely to the final beneficiary of a trust, who is entitled to receive the subject matter of the trust. Therefore he joins his position with that of the trustee bringing about an equitably complete title, upon termination of the trust. The lowest level is of a merely procedural nature, as with the beneficiaries of an entirely discretionary trust, who may only expect that the trustee will not omit to determine whether or not to exercise his discretion in their favour.

Facing the unvarying element which the lack of equitable fullness represents, there exists a number of very diverse situations. They range from the (equitable) obligation claimed by the person who owns a corresponding (equitable) right, to unenforceable or imperfect (equitable) obligations; they range from the existence of an (equitable) creditor to the existence of a person who may assert a claim for performance relating to his own or else to a general interest, to the lack of existence of any person who may sanction the obligations of the trustee.

This element of *quantum* which is lacking for equitable fullness of title does not, therefore, necessarily (or at least usually) give rise to a balanced structure. It is also susceptible to variation with the passage of time, and may, therefore, provoke a re-evaluation of the positions of the trustee and of those third parties who may have some kind of interest in the subject matter of the trust, or who may demand that the trustee should not appropriate for himself the *quantum* which he lacks in equity. If, as has just been indicated, this *quantum* imposes limitations on the manner in which the trustee may exercise his rights over the subject matter of the trust, or over its transfer on termination of the trust, or both, the variations it

---

[416] The reference is to trusts of the type discussed above, at the end of chapter 3 §2.b.

undergoes with the passage of time transfer the trustee from one category to another, so that an active trustee may become a passive or bare trustee.

The lack of equitable fullness of title has its relevance in the world of equity. I am not envisaging here the world of equity as being antithetical to that of common law, given that the right of the trustee may well itself be equitable, but it illustrates the consequences of the lack of equitable fullness which, by definition, may only be understood and recognized by equity by the application of its characteristic methods. The equitable limitations which afflict a trustee as a result of the lack of equitable fullness of his title of belonging never limit the validity or effectiveness of his actions. Whereas, as we shall see in chapter 5, it may be that in a civil-law context an act of transfer by a trustee can be attacked by means of an *actio pauliana* or an action for nullity, equity follows different paths: the transfer of the equitable defect of title into the title of those who derive their title from that of the trustee; exposure of the property with which the trustee had enriched himself to the same lack of fullness of title which already characterized his position; the maintenance of an equitable interest in a person so as to render the title of whoever has received something from him incomplete, so that he becomes trustee of that interest; and so on, as in the various cases which we have seen in the course of this chapter and the one which precedes it. The difference with respect to the possible civil-law context to which we have alluded demonstrates the uniqueness of the English solutions, which are rooted in the notion of being bound in conscience, which is an obligation in the true sense of the word, sanctioned by law, or, if one prefers, the foundation of a legal (i.e. equitable) obligation.

The equitable defect in the title of the trustee *does not affect the extent of his right*, but limits its use or places constraints on its final destination. The subject of the right, which may be a physical asset, a chose in action, an expectation or an equitable position (or even the equitable position of beneficiary under a trust), is not the subject matter of the trust – the subject matter of the trust is the right of the trustee, or, more precisely, his entitlement to it.

This entitlement forms part of the trustee's estate, like any other active legal position which he has. When the trustee assumes a responsibility as a result of a breach of the trust rules, he responds with all of his property under English law. The reverse is not true, however: a responsibility from another source does not affect the right which is the subject matter of the trust. This right, as we shall better see below, is segregated and is unaffected by the consequences of actions and deeds which do not involve the trustee in his role as trustee.

It is precisely because the subject matter of the right of the trustee is not the subject matter of the trust that, except in the case of express provisions (where they exist) of the trust instrument (where one exists), the trustee may change it freely, and any conversion or transformation is subject to exactly the same lack of equitable fullness of title, which, from this point of view, never changes. To the extent that it is a part of his estate, the trustee may use the right in the customary form and with the customary methods, and is not even obliged to describe himself as a trustee in his dealings with third parties.

It may be the trustee's responsibility to ensure that the economic substance, or the *quantum* of wealth, of the trust does not undergo any changes, even though its *objective elements* may have altered as a result of the trustee's acts,[417] or, in other cases, strenuously to defend the original subject matter of the right and to act exclusively to improve its potential to provide income, but it does not seem necessary at this point to repeat in different words the review of the typology of trusts which we carried out in the previous pages. One single unchanging fact presents itself here, which should be added to the lack of equitable fullness just mentioned: the entitlement of the trustee is the subject matter of the trust because it is *entrusted* to the trustee. As with the notion of segregation, we must postpone our discussion of the notion of entrusting for a few pages, and simply make the point that the trustee's equitable obligations arise out of an entrusting.

The equitable obligations of the trustee contain one element which requires an omission and one which requires action: the former is not to act with contempt for that portion of the equitable position which does not belong to him (even if, as we have seen, it may well not belong to others, either); the latter consists in acting in such a manner that the entrusting attains its goal. This may presuppose the impingement on third party interests, the exercise of powers, or, as we have seen, the transformation of the subject matter of the right into a trust. In these senses, the position of the trustee is a mixture of obligations and powers; the latter are, naturally, to be used to accomplish the entrusting,[418] so that the obligatory aspects

---

[417] Cf. B. Rudden, 'Things as Things and Things as Wealth', in 12 OJLS (1994) 81; Graziadei, *Diritti nell'interesse altrui*, pp. 216–19; see Maitland, *Equity* (see above, footnote 3), p. 218: 'We get the idea of a trust fund . . . that is dressed up in one costume or another, but which remains the same beneath all these changes of apparel'; and D. W. M. Waters, 'Analogues of the Trust and its Constituents in French Law, Approached from the Standpoint of Scots and English Law', in W. A. Wilson (ed.), *Trusts and Trust-like Devices*, London, 1981, pp. 117ff., at pp. 123–4 and 131.

[418] C. Reymond, 'Réflexions de droit comparé sur la Convention de la Haye sur le trust', in RDICD (1991), 7, at 21: 'la propriété du trustee est pour lui un moyen d'action'.

take precedence, and determine the legal position of the trustee.

If the equitable obligations of the trustee form the nucleus of his legal position, and if the trustee is the only necessary person in the trust, *the equitable obligations of the trustee are*, as an inevitable consequence, *the nucleus of all trusts*.[419] This topic may be concluded by returning to the lack of equitable fullness of the trustee's title: it is the proprietary element of the entrusting – that is, the imprint which the entrusting leaves on the title of ownership which causes it to be born without, or stripped of, a quantity which only equity can appreciate and value. The obligations of the trustee are predisposed to attain the entrusting, and are enforced, wherever possible, by drawing on the lack of fullness of title; hence we have the forms of equitable protection, which follow the right on trust, prior to and apart from the trustee and his normal duty to provide indemnification, and which take no account of any modifications, subjective or objective, which the right may have undergone.

The distinction between trusts and other similar legal structures derives from the points I have already made: in the similar structures the equitable defect in the title of ownership is not to be found, and so every development relates to the title and its cause and origins, and occurs normally in the areas of property, contract or unjust enrichment.

e The beneficiary

Beneficiaries are, to use the language of consumerism, an option in trusts. They are not, therefore, of any value in the identification of the structure of a trust.

In the earliest trusts we saw the use of 'contractual' language which, in a different legal context, would have made trusts into completely different creatures from those they became, and might have led in the direction of special forms of mandate or, as happened in South Africa, for example,[420] of legal structures modelled on the contract in favour of a third party. Secret trusts, and to some extent half-secret trusts, are survivors of the contractual tendency, and it is essential to take into account that in both cases the

---

[419] J. B. Ames, 'Purchaser for Value without Notice', in 1 HarvardLR (1887) 1, at 9 had already seen this: 'The trustee is the owner of the land and of course two persons with adverse interests cannot be owners of the same thing. What the *cestui que* trust really owns is the obligation of the trustee; for an obligation is as truly the subject matter of property as any physical *res*.'

It is interesting to note, I believe, that the definition of a trust as obligation of a trustee characterized the Indian Trust Act of 1882 and the Trust Ordinance of Ceylon (1917), which was modelled after it: see L. J. M. Cooray, *The Reception in Ceylon of the English Trust*, n.p., 1971; on the system of Ceylon (now Sri Lanka) in general, see I. Jennings and H. W. Tambiah, *The Dominion of Ceylon*, London, 1952.   [420] See below, chapter 5 §3.b.

transaction which created the trust precedes the transfer, and the latter is left to the lasting wishes of the settlor until the final moment, when he puts it into effect by means of a unilateral transaction *mortis causa*.[421]

The tendency which prevailed, and which characterized express trusts was, in fact, in favour of unilateral structures. This, as we have already seen, is in line with the unilaterality which is present in all transfers in the area of real property, where the description of the estate to be transferred, its limits and the purpose of the transfer is the transferor's affair. Expressly created trusts took root in this terrain, which left an indelible mark on them, even where the transaction no longer concerned real property.

In this early period, the beneficiary could be the settlor, so that the structure of the *interpositio* which characterized the first trusts and the substantially passive role of the trustee came to the forefront, or else one or more beneficiaries could be appointed by the settlor. In the latter case,[422] the obligations of the trustee varied from the simple protection of the enjoyment of the beneficiaries to taking possession of the asset and setting aside the profit intended for the beneficiaries. As we have just seen, the variability of a trustee's obligations within a wide spectrum is a normal aspect of trusts.

The obligation of the trustee was one of *conscience*, because, as already stated above, the common law did not include an action to protect the beneficiaries.[423] Until the fifteenth century even equity did not concern itself with trusts; this was left to the ecclesiastical courts and to the religious authorities in general. The *denunciatio evangelica*, that fertile mother of modern law, was for centuries delegated to fill the void in civil laws.[424] The ecclesiastical courts which flowered in England as elsewhere in Europe in the twelfth century, adopted the same techniques for the resolution of disputes in a more formal manner. Their links with the Holy See were as close as they could be,[425] so we are justified in thinking that the

---

[421] By making a will, or, as the case may be, omitting to make a will or to modify an existing will.

[422] I use the singular to identify the trustee as a concept; as I have pointed out on more than one occasion, the rule is that there must be more than one trustee.

[423] *Abbot of Bury v. Bokenham* (1535), 12a, *per* Fitzherbert J: 'the use is nothing in law, but is a confidence; . . . the common law doth never favour the use; for a use is not a right, nor is any action given in law, if a man be deforced of it'.

　　Dillon v. Freine (1589–95), referring to a prior opinion: 'uses were but imaginations, and nothing in the consideration of the law, or for which the law hath given any remedy; and that the *cestuy que use* had nothing in the land, for if he came upon the land, he was, by the law of the land, a trespasser to the *feoffees*'.

　　Cook v. Fountain (1676): 'uses at Common Law were nothing but secret confidences'.

[424] H. Coing, English Equity and the Denunciatio Evangelica of the Canon Law, in 71 LQR (1955) 223.

[425] Almost half the decrees of Alexander III (1159–81) had their origins in English disputes:

Roman–Canonical classifications were used regularly, as occurred – and occurred for centuries – in the so-called English civilian jurisdictions.

Usus, as we know, is a Roman-law category, a real right *in re aliena*; common law, on the other hand, however much it loved to break up estates, did not accept the plurality of real rights in the same way that Roman–Canonical law did. Estates, as we have already observed, attributed the right *to the property* to one person at a time; the English jurist naturally accepted 'real' relationships analogous to easements, and even the notions of dominant and servient tenements, but remained a long way from including them in the class of estates, and when it was suggested that the owner of a use should be considered to be on the same level as the owner of an estate, no less an authority than Fitzherbert asserted that it was 'an inconvenience and an impossibility'.[426]

It is not necessary to believe that the first transfers to trustees accompanied by an indication of a use in favour of a person other than the transferor mirrored the Romano–Canonical *usus*. Some, such as the noted concessions for the benefit of the Franciscan friars (from 1225), certainly were of this type. As we know, the friars could not own anything, and, according to the strictest interpretation, could not own any right, on pain of violating their vow of poverty. In fact, when called to account, they denied having any right in the property granted them, and used technical terms such as 'tenants at sufferance', or 'occupants at the will of the owner of the land', to describe their position. The sources, however, speak of *usus*, and, more significantly still, of *ususfructus*;[427] it would therefore seem impossible to avoid reaching the conclusion that the use which was debated in canonical courts was anything other than *usus*, if not actually *ususfructus*.

A discussion of this kind is accompanied by insuperable nominalistic ambiguities.[428] The English 'use' did not necessarily grant possession of the asset ('possession' is used here in a non-technical sense, to give it its greatest semantic weight, which is direct enjoyment), and this was sufficient to place it in an area radically different from the one in which the

A. Padoa Schioppa, 'I limiti all'appello nelle decretali di Alessandro III', in various authors, *L'educazione giuridica, VI – Modelli storici di procedura continentale*, Naples, 1994, II, pp. 35ff., at p. 37.

[426] *Abbot of Bury v. Bokenham* (1535), at p. 12a: 'for it is an inconvenience and an impossibility in law, that two men severally should have several rights and fee-simples in one and the same land simul and semel'.

This essential aspect had already been well grasped by M. Buonincontro, *Trust and Civil Law*, in [1959] 2 Riv. dir. civ. 680.

[427] A collection of sources and opinions expressed by historians may be found in S. W. DeWine, 'The Franciscan Friars, the Feoffment to Uses, and Canonical Theories of Property Enjoyment before 1535', in JlegH (1989) 1.

[428] Cf. A. Gambaro, 'I trusts e l'evoluzione del diritto di proprietà', in *Atti Milano*, ch. 6.

Roman–Canonical categories were found, and, at the same time, radically outside the 'ownership' concepts of common law. This led to a series of consequences.

The first of these was that ecclesiastical systems, from the *visitatio* to the truly *territorial* courts[429] tended to operate, as would have been their sole task in any event, without contesting relationships which arose in the civil law – *non enim intendimus judicare de feudo . . . sed decernere de peccato*[430] – a trait which the court of equity would make its own.

The second was that, when stripped of its unnecessary real aspects, use was an obligation (which was, for reasons we have already seen, one of conscience) which fell to the trustee. It was not because the *fides* was involved that it fell within the religious sphere: the trustee did not give the *fides* because the transaction by which he became a trustee was a unilateral act by the settlor; nor did the language employed by the settlor, unlike in the case of the first Roman *fideicommissum*,[431] call the *fides* into question. The reason why it belonged in the religious sphere is much more profound, and pre-dates that concept of fraud which we have seen to be such an important part of equity ancient and modern: profiting from an entrusting by hiding behind the formal requirements (in this case, the lack of a properly worded form of action): hence an unjust enrichment,[432] which was graver still when, as in the case of the Franciscans, the trustees were selected because they were *amici spirituales* of the beneficiaries.

The third consequence was that, when the court of equity came into the picture, it found it had the same kind of needs that the religious courts had: while the latter required regulation of the borders with the Royal Court, the former sought regulation of the borders with common law. Neither had the power to impinge directly on to matters involving land, or thereby to grant forms of protection or impose obligations which would have any direct effect on estates on land.

---

[429] Proceedings on uses before the ecclesiastical courts have been discovered by R. H. Helmholz, 'The Early Enforcement of Uses', in 79 ColLR (1979) 1503, in the registers of the diocesan courts of Canterbury and Rochester between the end of the fourteenth and the middle of the fifteenth centuries.

[430] Innocent III, Papal Decree 'Novit', reported by Coing, 'English Equity' (see above, footnote 425), 227. On the late Roman origins of this rule see G. Vismara, *La giurisdizione civile dei vescovi*, Milan, 1995, pp. 32, 45–6, 127.

[431] For which the *verba dispositiva* were *Fidei tuae committo*; see for example, D. 30.123; cf. Johnston, *Roman Trusts*, pp. 9–14.

[432] Here I disagree with Coing, who is thinking of the contract for the benefit of third parties and the promise of a trustee in favour of the beneficiary. Helmholz, on the other hand, is thinking of an oath and ecclesiastical jurisdiction in the area of succession. On the jurisdiction of the English ecclesiastical courts over matters regarding the violation of an oath, see R. H. Helmholz, '*Assumpsit* and *Fidei Laesio*', in 91 LQR (1975) 406, where the author also supplies quantitative data on the noteworthy frequency of these cases.

Equity, which was feeling its way forward after having lost, first, the sure hand of canonical law as a guide and then its contacts with Rome, used expressions such as 'owner in equity', which were purely linguistic terms, which might lend themselves, as in fact they did, to misinterpretation. In this way a minority but nonetheless vigorous position developed in the literature which saw the beneficiary of a trust as the owner of a right *in rem* in the property which was the subject matter of the trust. (As will appear from the enunciation of this theory, it is from a sphere which is quite different from the one in which I placed trusts in my discussion of the trustee in the previous pages.) In the last decades of the nineteenth century and the first of the twentieth, a controversy arose which Maitland sought to bring to an end with sensible and sensibly expounded reasoning.[433] Although he had an unequalled knowledge of English history, he committed the error of crossing over into the terrain of his adversaries, that of tracing, and of arming himself with concepts and terminology which were foreign to the tradition of English law.[434] It is there that the battle was fought, and even today common-law writings, though they take refuge in conciliatory positions between the opposing theories, have not recovered from a clash which took place on unsuitable terrain and which, therefore, could produce neither victors nor losers of the war.[435]

I believe that the theory which I have proposed in this volume permits me to keep discussion of this subject quite brief, because anyone wishing to reach different conclusions must necessarily begin by contesting the features which I have attributed to the trustee and, therefore, to the trust. Nevertheless, out of respect for those who came before me, I shall make a few observations. In doing so, I shall remain faithful to the current, inappropriate, English terminology, since because the problem is a false one, as is the basis on which it is formulated, there is absolutely no point in establishing a comparative framework.

A conceptual clarification must nonetheless be offered so as not to fall victim to the misunderstandings which have produced the current *impasse.* When one speaks of a right *in rem*, one sometimes transposes the notion of equitable ownership, which belongs in the domain of equity, to legal ownership. As we noted above, this produces little more than a linguistic term which cannot have legal existence because it contradicts the structure

---

[433] Maitland, *Equity* (see above, footnote 3), pp. 23–9, 106–22.

[434] This observation, with which I find myself in total agreement, is by D. W. M. Waters, 'The Nature of the Trust Beneficiary's Interest', in 45 CBR (1967) 217, at 223–6. Still from Canadian writings, with reference to decisions in the area of taxes, see E. J. Mockler, 'Note', in 40 CBR (1962) 270.

[435] Cf. Graziadei, *Diritti nell'interesse altrui*, pp. 417–22.

of equitable rules and remedies, unless the trust is subversively transformed into something akin to the *bewind* in Roman–Dutch law.[436] It is a conceptual error to which Scottish jurists did not fall victim.[437] Others have thought that the beneficiary has the right to *attain* the purpose of the trust. This, as we know and as we shall see again presently, is not the case. On yet other occasions, the beneficiary has been suggested as the 'true' owner, since the trustee is a temporary owner, a transient and fungible figure.[438] In this case there is a stronger link with the legal framework, but the solution must be supplied by the notion which I proposed some pages back[439] of 'due' ownership, which by the very terms which describe it belongs to the realm of obligations[440] and illustrates the original tensions of the obligations of conscience surfacing at the legal level.[441]

I believe that one of the deepest roots of the misunderstandings which prevail in this area lies in the concept of ownership, and in its lack of association with the concept of real property; to use the weaponry of the latter to deal with the former cannot lead, and has not led, anywhere. In English law, following early medieval meanings not unknown in civilian legal terminology, terms relating to ownership are being used in the area of obligations (civil lawyers too, and not only in recent times, use the phrase 'ownership of credits').[442] In any event, when no less an authority than A. W. Scott affirms that the creditor is the owner of a right *in personam* in relation to the debtor, but also of a right *in rem* in relation to the rest of the world which must not interfere with the relationship between creditor and debtor,[443] the conceptual confusion reaches its apex.

---

[436] See below, chapter 5 §3.b with reference to South Africa; it is peculiar that this tactic was attempted in order to make the trust acceptable for the civilian culture of Louisiana: R. A. Pascal, 'The Trust Concept and Substitution', in 19 LouisianaLR (1959) 273.

[437] The famous definition of Stair, which was hailed by all, states: 'the property of the thing intrusted . . . is in the person of the intrusted, else it is not a proper trust'; cf. T. B. Smith, *Studies Critical and Comparative*, Edinburgh, 1962, p. 200. See today *Sharp v. Thomson* (1995) (on which more see below, chapter 5 §3.a).

[438] This is, substantially, the position of Salmond *On Jurisprudence* (12th edition), London, 1966, pp. 256–62 (forgetting that the beneficiary is only an optional element of the trust).

[439] See above, chapter 2 §5.c.

[440] Millett J in *El Ajou v. Dollar Land Holdings* (1993), 736 has recently reaffirmed this principle, but employed unusual language: 'Equity's power to charge a mixed fund . . . enables the claimants to follow the money, not because it is theirs, but because it is derived from a fund which is treated as if it were subject to a charge in their favour.' It will not escape the reader's attention that this position is perfectly consistent with that which I proposed when I explained the unitary notion of constructive and resulting trusts (see chapter 2 §5.c); see also the Privy Council decision reported below in footnote 454.

[441] Cf. Johnston, *Roman Trusts*, pp. 225–38 and p. 239 footnote 47.

[442] Cf. B. Cassandro Sulpasso, 'La "réification de la créance" in diritto francese', in [1995] 2 Riv. dir. civ. 533.

[443] A. W. Scott, 'The Nature of the Rights of the *Cestui Que Trust*', in 17 ColLR (1917) 269, at 274.

Not to continue to use *in rem* and *in personam*, as has been proposed,[444] would probably be a wise decision.[445] In the few observations which follow, therefore, I shall limit myself to examining whether and in what cases the beneficiary may obtain the asset held on trust (a right *in rem*: not even this term has any equivalent in English law) or exercise any of the powers over that asset which are available to an owner.

To begin with the usual topic, we have already seen that tracing does not lead to the transfer of an asset or right to the beneficiary of a trust, but to the imposition of a new trust on the asset (or to a reimposition of the original trust). It might even be a bare trust, but it will always be a trust nonetheless, and its subject matter will always remain the same right which attached to the trustee, even where the subject matter of the right has been changed in the meantime.

What is more, the beneficiary of a trust does not even have the right to obtain the asset where the highest level of equitable entitlement, that of the beneficiary of a bare trust, is present.[446] The reason for this is that in order to obtain the subject matter of the trust, *he must terminate the trust*. At that moment, however, he is no longer the beneficiary of the trust, but rather the person who has been appointed to receive the subject matter of the trust as a successor to the trustee.[447] *The equitable fullness of title is re-established* in favour of the beneficiary *because the trust is no longer in existence*.

There is an even more extreme fact-pattern, which is that of the life tenant of a settlement, who has the right to possess the asset, to put it in his name, and to transfer it. The life tenant who transfers the trust property is subject to the obligations of the trustee, and is himself a trustee, in favour of the beneficiaries who have been designated to succeed him: he cannot touch the proceeds of the sale, which must be received by the trustees of the settlement.[448]

Among essays contemporary with Scott's, attention should be paid to W. G. Hart, 'The Place of Trust in Jurisprudence', in 28 LQR (1912) 290 and, in contrast to Scott, H. F. Stone, 'The Nature of the Rights of the *Cestui Que Trust*', in 17 ColLR (1917) 467.

[444] Waters, 'Nature of the Trust Beneficiary's Interest' (see above, footnote 435).

[445] Cf. the position of A. Guarneri, *Diritti reali e diritti di credito: valore attuale di una distinzione*, Padua, 1979, and, on our subject, Graziadei, *Diritti nell'interesse altrui*, pp. 424–5.

[446] See above, chapter 3 §3.a.

[447] This situation should be compared with that of the principal who insists on the transfer of the asset acquired by the agent; he does not terminate the mandate, but insists on performance.

[448] This fact, which has already been pointed out (see footnote 361), may appear to put in doubt the fundamental theory which sees the trustee as the full owner of the subject matter of the trust. Here, the trustee has no direct contact with the asset, and cannot carry out any act of transfer; one might say that he holds nothing: his only function is to be available at the moment of transfer to receive the proceeds ('only on sale do they come

Having looked at the highest level of entitlement, let us now review the lowest, which is that enjoyed by a beneficiary of a totally discretionary trust. We know that a beneficiary only has procedural equitable rights: to this one absolutely cannot, in total contradiction of the structure of discretionary trusts, add a 'real right' in the trust assets (whatever the definition of 'real right' may be). This observation leads us to recall that the concept of the equitable owner is child of the settlement of land, which was fundamentally unchanged until the reforms of the end of the nineteenth century. Today, on the other hand, the subject matter of the right of the trustee, as we tried to emphasize when we examined the legal position of the trustee, is constantly changing, and must, by definition, be able to circulate with the greatest possible ease:[449] it seems to be obvious that there can be no 'owners' other than the trustee.

Our mention of the contents and subject of the 'real right' demonstrate that none of the powers of the owner of a real right attach to the various types of beneficiary of a trust, and that no asset may be taken or directly used by them; on the contrary, the hypothetical asset which would be the subject matter of the right of the beneficiary may be transformed by a third party (the trustee), even in the course of performance of obligations arising out of the trust.[450]

forward, hands outstretched for the price': Bernard Rudden in a letter to this author).

This line of reasoning confuses the legal sense and the material sense of 'to hold' and forgets that the subject matter of a trust is the entitlement to an asset and not the asset itself, or, from an economic point of view, the value of the asset to which the entitlement relates.

The trustees of a settlement are the owners of the estate even if they cannot dispose of it and the power of disposition is granted exclusively to the life tenant. The granting of the exercise of a right to a third party does not affect the ownership of the right. And the rule that the sale price must be paid to the trustees, who are the only persons entitled to provide a receipt for it, supports the conclusion that the estate (seen as a value) belongs to the trustees. When that value is transformed into money, the trustees resume their role, because the reasons which historically led (through the Settled Lands Acts) to the partial equivalence of life tenant and 'full owner' are no longer present. (I hope I will be excused the civilian 'contamination', but I believe it explains the contrast more effectively.) The structure after the Trusts of Land and Appointment of Trustees Act 1996 is no different.   [449] Cf. Graziadei, *Diritti nell'interesse altrui*, pp. 499–502.

[450] A. M. Honoré, 'Rights of Exclusion and Immunities against Divesting', in 34 TulLR (1959–60) 453, at 464–5, identifies the 'real rights or interests in property' where 'the right over the property, or the right to do something or have something done in relation to the property is not liable to be divested' (for a recent review in Italian writing, see Gambaro, *Proprietà*, pp. 201–31).

In the cases under discussion, the right of the beneficiary is, by definition, *liable to be divested*. As we shall see later in the text, it is the standpoint from which the position of the beneficiary is viewed which is wrong and which leads to no result. The classic theories of analytical jurisprudence, according to which, what is more, the right of the

These considerations become even more relevant when one examines trusts which have as their subject matter a chose in action or a guarantee (which are extremely frequent in contemporary use). Equity has no difficulty whatsoever in pointing up the lack of equitable fullness in the trustee's title, so that the obligations of the trustee are no different from

the classic case of the estate of real property;[451] the theory of the 'division of property', on the other hand, is experiencing clear and serious difficulties, on which I do not think it necessary to dwell.

Allow me to make one final observation of a systematic nature. It is clear that any analysis of the ownership status of a beneficiary must be included within the framework of common law and not of equity, so that the right of the beneficiary, when taken together with that of the trustee, leads to complete ownership. This, one might say, is somewhat similar to the relationship between a usufructuary and a bare owner,[452] but it is precisely this affinity which has no place in the history of English real-property law, which was (as we have pointed out on several previous occasions) based upon estates and not relationships with physical property. It is this superficial affinity which shows that this construction is untenable in relation to trusts which have no beneficiaries: how could a trustee in such a case be the holder of the same ownership position which he would have where there are beneficiaries, given that there would be no one to whom the real right due to the beneficiaries could be granted? Notwithstanding this, the rights and obligations of the trustee are defined in the same way, whether or not there are beneficiaries. The superficial affinity which we are disputing here is equally untenable when there are beneficiaries but, as very often happens, they are not the final beneficiaries, that is, those to whom the subject matter of the trust is destined when the trust is finally terminated. This category of beneficiary will never have a direct relationship with the subject matter, which is, by definition, intended for others: how could they be included in any 'ownership' context?

---

beneficiary of a trust seems to belong to the class of the *jus in personam ad ius in rem acquirendam*, are, therefore, of little use: J. Austin, *Lectures on Jurisprudence* (5th edition), London, 1885, lecture xiv.

[451] Yet again, the reasoning depends on the fact that in the case of a trust of immovables, the estate, and not the physical asset, is the subject matter of the trust.

[452] A comparison between the life tenant and usufruct has been carried out by McClean, 'Common Law Life Estate' (see above, footnote 61), without, however, the due attention being given to the position of the equitable life tenant, which is the only one permitted by English law today. The position of H. Battifol, 'The Trust Problem as Seen by a French Lawyer', in 33 JcompL (1951) III 18, at 22, is different.

The negative response to all these questions leaves a bitter aftertaste, as it seems that too many changes need to be made to the current view, and that the beneficiary (when there is one) is placed in a subordinate position. This is not the case, however. One only has to modify the legal basis and it will be seen that the beneficiary's position is strengthened, but in equity, where it belongs.

We should recall once more that beneficiaries are not a fundamental element of the trust, and we can do perfectly well without them; it is not correct, therefore, to approach the trust by using the beneficiaries as a point of departure, or to define the position of the trustee differently according to whether there is a beneficiary or not, or according to the type of beneficiary who may be identified from the class of trust. It would, in fact, be difficult to sustain the theory that the trustee is in some cases the complete owner and in others a limited owner, so that in the former cases the limits to his rights would belong to the realm of obligations, and in the latter cases to the realm of real rights.[453]

When the legal basis for consideration is the lack of equitable fullness of the trustee's title, then the beneficiary can be correctly identified: he is the person whose own equitable interest corresponds to the trustee's lack of complete title. He is thus entitled to use this lack of completeness to pursue his own interest (while in the case of the charitable trust as we have seen, a person entitled to take action against the trustee does so in the public interest, not his own). The interest may be that of preserving something of economic value to which he will be entitled one day (this is the concept of 'due ownership' explained above[454]). It may be that of preserving an enjoyment in which he has the right to participate now or in the future.[455] Finally, his interest may be the restoration of his position to ensure the fulfilment of either of the last two points. In the majority of constructive trusts where the beneficiary's interest is immediate, then the constructive trustee must bring the trust to an end and transfer its subject matter to the beneficiary.

---

[453] Similar, that is, to the *fideicommissum*. The Privy Council had the opportunity to compare the trust and the *fideicommissum* in *Sitty Kadija v. De Saram* (1946), on appeal from the Supreme Court of Ceylon, and traced the clear border between the two structures, taking account, *inter alia*, of the position of the beneficiary: 'In the trust, the interest of the beneficiary, though described as an equitable ownership, is properly *jus neque in re neque ad rem*, against the bona fide alienee of the legal estate it is paralysed and ineffectual; in the *fideicommissum* the *fidei* commissary, once his interest has vested, has a right which he can make good against all the world, a right which the fiduciary cannot destroy or burden by alienation or by charge.'

[454] See chapter 2 §5.c.

[455] The new types of trusts for purposes are captured thus (see above, chapter 3 §2.b).

In this wide range of cases, the subject matter of a beneficiary's claim, when protected, *relates to the right of the trustee*, and, in particular, his ownership interest in that right. *There is a pre-eminent ownership profile, but it relates to the trustee, and not the beneficiary.* The beneficiary will prevail *in specie* against other creditors of the trustee because he holds the key to the reconstruction of complete ownership of that particular right, and completes this reconstruction in his own interest. It is in order to protect that interest that the title of the trustee is not equitably complete. The peculiarity of equity lies entirely in this mechanism, which may be described, but not reproduced, in civil-law terms.

The beneficiary of today is precisely what he was five centuries ago. The modern development of trusts, express or otherwise, has served to strengthen the winning structures: in the case of the former, they are those which have their roots in unilaterality; in the case of the latter, they are those with their roots in the rules of equity. Both have embedded themselves even more firmly in obligations of conscience which continue to be the preferred terrain for equity.[456]

f *Webb v. Webb*

The judgment rendered by the Court of Justice of the European Union on 17 May 1994[457] is of crucial importance to our discussions.

The case involved a resulting trust arising out of a registration made by a father in the name of his son at the moment of acquisition of real property in Antibes. The relationship between father and son broke down, and the father took legal action in England to have a resulting trust declared, and so to obtain the transfer of the property into his name. The son claimed that the action should have been filed in France, since article 16 of the Brussels Convention of 1968 states that the courts of

---

[456] The recent passage of the Trusts of Land and Appointment of Trustees Act 1996 confirms the position I have proposed.

As we have seen on more than one occasion in the previous pages, the new law strengthens the position of the beneficiaries (of the final beneficiaries) with regard to the trustees, and it would, therefore, have been quite simple to provide rules which had this reinforcement derive from a view of the beneficiaries as 'effective owners' (if I may, for once, use a term which is as current in civilian writing as it is unacceptable). Instead, the law, which obliges trustees to consult the beneficiaries, and even to give effect to their wishes, makes an exception of 'the general interest of the trust' (s. 11(1)(b)), which is the responsibility of the trustees. It should be noted that we are discussing beneficiaries who have the right under the new law to appoint and dismiss trustees if the trust instrument is silent (s. 19), and even to enter into possession of real property on trust (s. 12). In spite of this, their personal position is solely within the sphere of Equity. S. 6(1) of the law puts an end to all debate: trustees of a trust of land have 'all the powers of an absolute owner'.

[457] Procedure C-294/92, *Webb c. Webb*.

the contracting state where the property is situated 'shall have exclusive jurisdiction . . . in proceedings which have as their object rights *in rem* in, or tenancies of, immovable property'.

The point of the lawsuit was whether the right claimed by the father belonged to the category of 'rights *in rem*' and not if his action was a real action. It is essential to understand this distinction, because otherwise one thinks in terms of the action,[458] and makes reference to the principle (correct and evident, but of no relevance) according to which the distinction between real property and personal actions 'has little in common with the distinction between real and personal rights'.[459]

Both the European Community judges and the judge *a quo* had, furthermore, properly expressed the terms of the matter to be decided, and one of the important aspects of the two decisions from a comparative point of view lies in the use by the English judge of terminology which belongs, as he points out, 'to concepts of the civil-law systems of the original member states. It does not readily fit in with the system of legal and equitable interests in property obtaining in England and Wales and in both parts of Ireland.'[460] The action commenced by the father against his son, observed the English judge, was based on a fiduciary relationship, which is ensured protection by an order *in personam*. The plaintiff did not request a declaration of ownership or a change in his son's title, or even a declaration that he was the owner of the property. This reading of the decision *a quo* concludes with the observation that the judgment requested 'does not seek to disturb the title of the defendant'[461] and that the object of the judgment was not rights *in rem*.

Before the Court of Justice, the British Government supported the position of the plaintiff and asserted that the action did not concern a real right.[462] The Commission, on the other hand, took the defendant's side, and classified the action as a *reivindicatio* and the *petitum* as a real right.[463] With this, we see a classic outline of the problems discussed in the preceding pages.

The Court of Justice decided that for the exclusive competence provided for in article 16 of the Brussels Convention to apply, 'the action

[458] As in G. Contaldi, 'La Convenzione di Bruxelles and il "trust": brevi note sull'interpretazione dell'articolo 16.1 conv.', in [1996] 1 Giust. civ. 1531.

[459] Gambaro, *Proprietà*, p. 629, footnote 50; S. Carbone, *Lo spazio giudiziario europeo*, Turin, 1995, p. 67 on the other hand, takes the correct position.   [460] *Webb v. Webb* 1416.

[461] 1419. I do not know the source of Gambaro's conviction that 'trattandosi di una questione relativa al titolo . . .'.

[462] From the conclusions of the Attorney General (in Recueil, 1994, I-1717), no. 24.

[463] *Ibid.*, no. 26.

must be founded upon a real right' (and not that it must be a 'real action') and, as the English judge had found, a claim by a beneficiary based on a trust against the trustee for the transfer of the trust assets by the trustee is not a real right, and must therefore be sought by means of a personal action.[464]

From a procedural point of view, therefore, the decision of the Court of Justice consecrates the lack of involvement of the beneficiary in any questions of 'ownership' and the absence of any real rights which he may assert against the trustee.

g Trust, entrusting and segregation

The historical principle of every *fiducia* lies outside systems of law. We have clear evidence of this from the Roman *fideicommissum*,[465] and we have just seen it in the original trusts. That the entrance of the concept of *fiducia* into a legal system would spell its demise, because a 'legal' *fiducia* would be a contradiction in terms, is a theory on which there is no point in wasting words;[466] and in any event, a trust, if it is *fiducia*, is legal *fiducia*.

In our current (civilian) legal terminology, the fiduciary is a part of a relationship with a principal.[467] There may be third-party beneficiaries, but, as in the case of the trust, they are incidental. The fiduciary relationship, therefore, is created and develops essentially between the two persons who gave life to it. This observation is sufficient to exclude the trust from the definition, because we know that the settlor ceases to have any role the moment he transfers the right which is the subject matter of the trust to the trustee. The settlor may retain various kinds of powers, but this is an incidental matter which does not affect the structure of the relationship and which, in any event, includes a limit beyond which the trust is void or a sham. Accordingly, to speak of a trustee as one would of

---

[464] Cf. C. MacMillan, 'The European Court of Justice agrees with Maitland: Trusts and the Brussels Convention', in [1996] Conv 125.

[465] Inst. II.23.1: *et ideo fideicommissa appellata sunt, quia nullo vinculo iuris, sed tantum pudore eorum qui rogabantur continebantur.*

[466] Cf. Lipari, *Negozio fiduciario* (see above, footnote 29), pp. 82–4, 87–8; I would only add that, from a comparative viewpoint, the *legal fiducia* may spell the death of the *fiducia* in those systems where the *principia* do not lend themselves to the structural openness which characterizes the trust. For example, strong principles such as 'la carta canta', with the result that form prevails over substance, is in conflict with the *fiducia* and reduce it to the level of a workaday management type of *negotium*. See a more detailed explanation in section 1 of chapter 7.

[467] In fact, the duty to re-transfer the asset to the *fiduciante* is a characteristic element of the fiduciary relationship from the modern viewpoint: see Gambaro, *Proprietà*, p. 611.

a (civilian) fiduciary is a serious error, which has been contested to no effect for sixty years.[468] The key element in a trust is the 'entrusting', not in the sense of the trust which someone places in the fiduciary, which is as much a truism in civil law as it is in English law, but in the entrusting of the right to the trustee. The entrusting is an inherent element in the genetic unilaterality of the trust. The fiduciary who enters into an obligation with me to attain a certain result (whether in the form of a contract or an agreement is of no importance) is one case, and the person to whom I transfer a right or, more correctly, *entrust* a right, and who assumes obligations simply by virtue of not having objected to receiving the entrusting is another. The fiduciary of the original Roman *fideicommissum* is, from this point of view, a trustee,[469] and the entrusting is the natural and necessary consequence of the *commendatio*.[470] The semantic similarity between the Italian terms '*affido*' and '*confido*', which has remained unchanged over the centuries,[471] illustrates the area of *fiducia* with which we are dealing; it is the same area which, with typical redundancy, the Spanish language calls '*comisiones de confianza*' and which in English is classified by the hendiadis '*trust and confidence*', which was employed by equity in its first era of creativity.

The so-called power of abuse, which has been studied at length in civilian literature, has nothing to do with the trust, which if it is *fiducia* is legal *fiducia*, as we have already stated; the system knows how to react to the abuse, which is an illegal act like so many others. The entrusting in the trust is the fiduciary vesting of a right in the trustee, for the trustee to attain certain interests or purposes, either through or as a result of ownership of that right. There are analogous instances of entrusting in civil law, for example the issuance of a general power of attorney *ad negotia*, but they are only partial (in that they do not involve a substantive transfer to the trustee) and purely functional.

We know that the limit of the entrusting lies within the title of owner-

---

[468] F. Weiser, *Trusts on the Continent of Europe*, London, 1936, p. 45, where he affirms that the German *Treuhänder* does not merit any higher title than *quasi trustee*. The essential lack of contact between the trustee and the *Treuhänder* of German law is a theme of Kötz, *Trust und Treuhand* (see above, footnote 241); for Swiss law, see the similar position of P. P. Supino, *Rechtsgestaltung mit Trust aus Schweizer Sicht*, St Gallen, 1994, pp. 84–93 and *passim*.

[469] This is the basis of the theory of Johnston, *Roman Trusts*. For developments in South Africa, see B. Beinart, 'Trusts in Roman and Roman–Dutch Law', in Wilson (ed.), *Trusts and Trust-like Devices* (see above, footnote 418), pp. 167ff., at pp. 174–9.

[470] Cf. Johnston, *Roman Trusts*, pp. 22–4.

[471] See the *Theatrum veritatis* of Cardinal de Luca, IX, *De testamentis*, disc. XLVI, no. 8: '*ut in testamento contineantur verba talia quae fiduciam praecise importent . . . del quale mi confido, e sò, che esequirà la mia mente*'.

ship, and that it is significant only in equity. We also know that this limit cannot affect the title in its 'real' dimension or in the area of ownership, which must be complete.[472] Finally, we are also aware of the protection which equity offers the entrusting. On the basis of these elements, therefore, we can state that *the entrusting of the right to the trustee is symmetrical with the loss of all entitlement by the settlor* (but, and I hope I may be excused for repeating this, not necessarily with the acquisition of any entitlement by a third-party beneficiary). The settlor may retain precisely those rights which the trustee lacks, and in this case we would be closer to the *fiducia* as *fiducia* is understood in the civilian tradition; this was the situation with older trusts of the nominee type or in any event those in favour of the settlor himself, and is apt to be the case with more modern trusts where, as we have seen above, a contractual element is added. We are, however, conscious of the technical and conceptual limitation: if there is no entrusting in favour of the trustee, there is no trust. In trusts which are not expressly created, on the other hand, the entrusting of the right to the trustee is the work of equity, and an equitable entitlement comes into being in favour of a beneficiary at the same time.

In the case of express trusts, the entrusting is the specific *vestitura* of the transfer of the right by the settlor to the trustee; it is the entrusting which explains the limitations in the exercise of the trustee's right and which supplies the teleological dimension to the evaluation of his conduct. One of the consequences of the entrusting, as the term is intended here, is a further demonstration of the distance from the civilian concept of the *fiducia*: a trustee who is in doubt as to how to conduct himself turns neither to the settlor nor to the beneficiaries, but to a court.[473] If he looks to the former, he will not obtain any guarantee of the legitimacy of the actions which the settlor authorizes him to take, except in the case of the bare trust, where the 'bareness' of the trust signifies, using the suggested terminology, that the title of the trustee lacks any equitable content and that this content belongs entirely to the beneficiaries. There is also entrusting in the case of the bare trust, but it is reduced to the minimum.

'Entrusting' also has a second meaning, however, which is equally relevant to our topic, even if it only relates to trusts with beneficiaries: the beneficiaries have the right to rely on the trustee. This second meaning of 'entrusting' (the same double meaning is found in the French term 'con-

---

[472] For the *Treuhand*, on the other hand, Kötz, *Trust und Treuhand* (see above, footnote 241), pp. 125–7.

[473] Unless, in the case of trusts of land, he can turn to the final beneficiaries, pursuant to the Trusts of Land and Appointment of Trustees Act, 1996.

fiance') is connected with the equitable limitation of the trustee's title of ownership; while the former explains the limitation, the latter gives it preceptive content. The former concerns the birth of the trust, the latter the dynamic moment. The beneficiary has no reason to place 'trust' in the trustee, but has the right to expect that he will work towards the attainment of the goal which the settlor (or the law) has given him to reach. This is precisely the sense in which the term 'entrusting' characterizes the relationship between the *fiduciante* and the fiduciary in the civilian tradition.[474]

It should be noted that entrusting occurs in all types of trust. In those where the settlor appoints himself trustee, and identifies a right which is from that moment the subject matter of the trust, he removes the fullness of title which he previously had, and becomes the trustee of the interests which the trust was created to realize. To say that in constructive or resulting trusts the entrusting is an act of the law is not a play on words: if equity could decree that a certain right belonged to a beneficiary, there would be no room for entrusting, because the beneficiary would acquire his right by judicial ruling. We know, however, that equity can only appoint a defendant to be trustee in favour of a plaintiff. This is no small degree of protection, but nevertheless, the plaintiff does not immediately achieve the purpose for which he commenced the legal action. The right remains in the defendant, but in the form of an entrusting, so that he must use it, according to the circumstances, as the trustee of an express trust would have, or terminate the trust and transfer or re-transfer the right to the beneficiary.

To conclude the topic of *fiducia*, it does not seem to me, as far as express trusts are concerned, that we can speak of *fiducia* in the momentary relationship between settlor and trustee, because this relationship is much more meaningful, and translates into the entrusting of the right; nor can we do so with regard to the relationship between trustee and beneficiaries, because it is much less significant, and translates into the faith of the beneficiaries (who can in any event do nothing else) that the trustee will perform his duties correctly. As far as trusts which have not been expressly created are concerned, the former relationship is lacking and the latter is no different from the case of express trusts.

These conclusions may seem clearer if one speaks of 'fiduciary ownership'. The trust is fiduciary ownership. It is not a special, novel real right, but a general category present in numerous legal systems. If we pass from

---

[474] G. Criscuoli, *Fiducia e fiducie in diritto privato: dai negozi fiduciari ai contratti uberrimae fidei*, in [1983] 1 Riv. dir. civ. 136 at 140.

trust *in* the fiduciary to the entrusting of the right *to* the fiduciary, in the two senses illustrated above of the removal of residual entitlements of the *settlor* and the purposes imposed by equity, then fiduciary ownership is created, which is the specific *status* of the fiduciary owner. This is not necessarily a trust in the sense of the traditional English model, with which we have been occupied until now, and which, with all its complexities and historical stratification, would appear to be difficult to export, but in the sense of structures which share certain essential elements with the trust which are also adequate from a comparative point of view. I shall discuss certain applications in civil-law systems in chapter 5.

The right entrusted to the trustee is segregated from the rest of his property. *Segregation* is a necessary consequence of entrusting on two grounds, one systematic, and one functional.[475] With regard to the systematic grounds, the right which has been entrusted cannot be mixed with the trustee's property because the title of ownership is not equitably complete. It is not, therefore, homogeneous with other properties which make up the trustee's estate, and this lack of homogeneity extends to the relationship with other rights relating to other trusts which may have been granted to the trustee. Both the subrogation and the passage of the segregated right from a trustee to his successor (a phenomenon to which the literature has not to date devoted sufficient attention) justify the segregation. The succession to the segregated right or group of rights of one trustee in place of another is a real transfer[476] which takes place without the successor trustee being prejudiced by any personal situation of the predecessor. As far as the functional grounds are concerned, the entrusting cannot take place if the entrusted right could be affected by acts and deeds which are not relevant to the exercise of that right, such as, for example, if it were to be included in the estate of the trustee, or if it were susceptible to attack by the trustee's creditors. One consequence is the protection of the beneficiary or the purpose of the trust each time that equity works to transfer the lack of fullness of title from the original right to a different right of the trustee or his successors. This different right is also segregated, and the two circumstances indicated above will apply.

Segregation has an especially disruptive effect in these last cases, sometimes as a result of a tracing action, sometimes as a result of the declaration of a constructive trust unconnected with tracing, because assets which until that moment made up the general security of the creditors of the trustee (who may not even have realized that he was one) become

[475] See chapter 7 §1.c.
[476] This in fact requires compliance with the form required for the vesting of a right.

surrounded by a protective barrier which segregates them from the remaining elements of the trustee's property and locks them in a trust. The protection of the beneficiaries, as we see, is much more powerful in this context than it would be with a right *in rem* or *ad rem* from which consequences of this kind could ensue only with great difficulty, or to a limited extent.[477]

[477] See chapter 5 §4.g, on the revocatory action in civil law systems.

4   The international trust model

1. Introduction

From a comparative point of view, the international trust model has a number of significant characteristics: it came into being over about ten years; its foundation is exclusively legislative; a large number of legal systems (around twenty) has embraced it; and none of them can be seen to be the moving force behind it – on the contrary, all have collaborated in its evolution.[1]

Not all these legal systems belong to the common-law 'family'.[2] One is plainly a civil-law jurisdiction (Malta), another (the Seychelles) no longer is, but has maintained close conceptual ties to the Napoleonic code, a third (Mauritius) mostly is, since the Napoleonic code is in use there alongside laws of evidently English inspiration, especially in the commercial field; two (Guernsey and Jersey) have a unique history due to the lasting influence of Norman law, European common law[3] and French law prior to codification.[4] We shall see that Malta, the Seychelles and Mauritius show some terminological intractability, but no more than that, while Jersey has had to amend its law of trusts because there was the risk that a principle of Norman law would lead to the nullity of many trusts created locally.

From the point of view of the theory of sources, the international trust

---

[1] The laws cited in this chapter have been published in M. Lupoi, *Trust Laws of the World*, Rome, 1996.

[2] To speak of 'families' or of '*grandi sistemi*', the second of which has actually been included in the title of university courses, is, in my opinion, of little use, even solely from a practical point of view.

[3] Not the *ius commune*, but High Medieval common law and its continuation in local custom. For this position, see my book *The Origins of the European Legal Order*, Cambridge University Press, 2000 (*Alle radici del mondo giuridico europeo*, Rome, 1994).

[4] From here we have the authority which is recognized in the *opinio doctorum*. Every judgment in Jersey contains a list of the writings cited in the reasoning.

model has a connotation which is typical of European common law: that of being open. Some of the legislative systems which we shall examine declare as such expressly on occasion,[5] but more often than not, in the case of those legal systems which have at some time in their history formally adopted English law, such a declaration is unnecessary. In English law, the notion that an Act of Parliament may completely discipline any subject matter is, by definition, unknown.[6] As a result of their adoption of English law (in some cases, this took place some time ago), the development of these systems has been indelibly marked; whether or not they passed legislation similar to English laws (and I am referring in particular to the Trustee Acts of 1893 and 1925 and to the Trustee Investments Act of 1961) before attaching themselves to the international trust model, or whether they limited themselves to the application of case law, the channels of communication have never been interrupted.[7] On the contrary, they have become multi-directional, due to the fact that, as happens in mature common-law legal systems (for example those of Australia, Canada and New Zealand), judicial precedents from, let us say, Bermuda or Jersey are treated with great respect everywhere, but above all as expressions of common principles from which it is appropriate that common *regulae* should be drawn. This is why in chapters 2 and 3 we have deviated from the practice commonly followed by English writers and reviewed, and made frequent reference to, case law from countries other than England.

The laws of the international trust model do not, therefore, have an undefined common substratum, but rather a common system of reference, and all of them draw from the world of equity. Here we must understand each other clearly. None of these systems has a separate equitable jurisdiction, but all of them accept the vision of equity as the expression of

---

[5] Trusts (Jersey) Law 1984, article 1(5): 'This Law shall not be construed as a codification of laws regarding trusts, trustees and persons interested under trusts'; adopted in the Turks and Caicos, Trust Ordinance 1990, s. 2(2).

[6] It will be recalled that we have come across cases where case-law precedents prior to the passing of a law have been held to be binding on the court. Even in cases where a matter which has been regulated by case law becomes the subject of legislative provisions, all the prior case-law principles are held to be saved (except, of course, where they expressly contrast with the law). There are, on the other hand, legislative provisions (some of which we shall meet in this chapter) which repeal a 'doctrine' of case law.

[7] Both the term 'communication' and the notion of 'open' systems are tied to the teachings of Gino Gorla. See, in particular G. Gorla, *Il diritto comparato in Italia e nel 'mondo occidentale' e una introduzione al 'dialogo civil law – common law'*, Milan, 1983, which is a development of the paper presented to the Congress of Taormina of 1981 on 'Cinquanta anni di esperienza giuridica in Italia'.

obligations of conscience at the juridical level. Hence we have a second, different, reason for the model being open.

Equitable principles are present in varying degrees in all these legal systems. The difference from equity in its traditional sense therefore relates to the way they operate, and more precisely, whether or not they prevail over antagonistic principles. In the field of trusts, but also in other areas traditionally regulated by common law alone, we have had many opportunities to observe the capacity of equity to expand, and the means by which it ceaselessly closes gaps, breaks down barriers or creates new methods for regulating social tensions. It is a structure of the English legal system which certainly cannot be exported in its entirety, but this does not mean that this end cannot be achieved in another way, through the determination of disputes on a case-by-case basis. In effect, the decision of the Royal Court of Jersey on a central topic of equity, that of fraud (which as we have seen crosses over many equitable *regulae*) demonstrates the prevalence of (typically English) equitable standards over antagonistic principles.[8]

The exclusion clause in a trust instrument, which made the trustee responsible only if he had acted fraudulently, was clearly void because it was in conflict with the Trusts (Jersey) Law 1984, article 26(9), as amended in 1989:
'Nothing in the terms of a trust shall relieve, release or exonerate a trustee from liability for breach of trust arising from his own fraud, wilful misconduct or gross negligence.'

There was also an exception to the limitations period to sort out. As in English law, an action against a trustee is exempt from the Statute only if he is guilty of fraud. It was necessary, therefore, to define the concept of fraud. The Jersey judge [at page 308] had no hesitation in accepting the widest and most discretionary notion proposed in English law by Lord Evershed: *'conduct which, having regard to some special relationship between the two parties concerned, is an unconscionable thing for one to do to the other.'* (*Kitchen v. RAF Association* (1958) per Lord Evershed, at page 249).

The Court concluded that the definition of *dolus* given by Labeo, and that of Pothier of *dol* come together in the same conceptual area (to sustain this theory it could have cited a *dictum* of 1751: *'fraud, which is dolus malus'* Lord Harwicke in *Earl of Chesterfield v. Janssen*, at page 155). In the face of objections in the literature, the same judge, in the later case of *Midland Bank v. Federated Pension Services* (1994) [of which more below, page 231], stated as follows [at page 25]: 'We have been interpreted as extending that concept beyond criminal fraud to a concept of equitable fraud purely in the English sense. That was not our prime intention and perhaps we may take this opportunity to make ourselves clear. We were expressing the view that the time-honoured concept of '*dol*' within this jurisdiction was so surprisingly similar to the English concept of equitable fraud that we were able to extend the doctrine in that way.'

---

[8] *West v. Lazard Brothers* (1993).

The opening up of the model in the ways just described means that it cannot be comprehended without looking at both the juridical experience of English equity, by which the model is clearly apt to be influenced,[9] and the application of that experience in the legislative context which is currently the exclusive source of the model, but which will later be clarified in appropriate judicial decisions which will establish new elements which are liable to become common assets of the international model. These elements do not stand out unequivocally in legislative pronouncements, which therefore need to be brought to bear on specific factual issues if they are to be transformed into operative rules, above all where they deviate from the traditional English trust model.[10]

The international trust model does not describe a trust which is different from that identified in the traditional English model. Its specificity lies, in the first place, in the fact that it has codified equitable solutions, thus rendering them more generally applicable and more easily available. Secondly, it has disciplined aspects of the regulation of trusts which are still uncertain in English law. Thirdly, it has removed roadblocks to development which the English law of trusts sometimes suffers from as a result of legal precedents which may be overturned only by the passage of a law. Fourthly, it has developed new rules to satisfy needs which did not exist or were not foreseen in the formative period of the English law of trusts (and which English case law is also attempting to satisfy, but with the limitations inherent in the tools at its disposal). Fifthly, it has taken a position on theoretical questions of great moment, with respect to which case-law sources (in general, but specifically in common law) tend to declare themselves incompetent. Finally, it has promulgated rules of private international law aimed at securing the exclusive competence of local law.

These theoretical elements are matched by the tax exemptions which seek to supplement the practical significance of the model, and which usually accompany every aspect of the existence of trusts following the international model; they play on the *economic* foreignness of these trusts in relation to the system whose laws regulate them. In this context, some

---

[9] *West v. Lazard Brothers* (1993), at p. 248: 'There is an equitable jurisdiction in Jersey. It stems from the concept of fairness. This court is not bound to follow slavishly every rule of the English Chancery courts. It looks to decisions and principles in those courts for guidance . . . It does not "pick and choose" but once it has properly adopted an English concept, it can build on it, amend it or supplement it, provided it does so consistently.'

[10] A useful and reasoned collection of precedents is found in G. Kodilinye, *The Law of Trusts in the West Indies. Cases and Commentary*, Barbados, 1991 (some unpublished decisions are included).

speak of *offshore trusts*, on which extensive literature has developed, most of which is of interest to professionals.[11]

2. Overview of legal systems

1. Anguilla

The British colony of Anguilla[12] wanted to shake off its unenviable reputation as a tax paradise good for any purpose,[13] and in 1992 began to pass laws which were in line with international standards.[14] Among the most recent laws are the Trusts Ordinance and Fraudulent Dispositions Ordinance, both of 1994, which borrow provisions from similar laws of other Caribbean countries, singling out those most favourable to foreign clients. Anguilla has elected to pass legislation which does not distinguish between 'domestic' and 'international' trusts. It has mainly followed the law of Belize, with minimal, but judicious, modifications, and therefore certain formulations of the law of Guernsey and, earlier still, of Jersey. One can also see borrowings from the laws of the Cayman Islands. The Trusts Ordinance 1994 is a form of codification which, except for regulation of revocatory actions, which was left to the Fraudulent Dispositions Ordinance 1994, unites all the law on trusts in a single text.

The law of Anguilla is peculiar in that it is the only one which accepted the rule which appeared for the first time in the Trust Ordinance 1990 of the Turks and Caicos Islands which gives the settlor the right to prescribe any duration for the trust he might wish, including an indefinite term.[15]

---

[11] Among the most recent works are: N. Harris & Partners, *Use of Offshore Jurisdictions*, London 1995; Withers Solicitors, *International Trust Precedents*, London, 1996; D. E. Osborne (ed.), *Asset Protection: Domestic and International Law and Tactics*, Clark Boardman Callaghan, 1995.

    The lines between the legal profession, the promotion of the tax attractions of a State and pure marketing of fiduciary services have become very fine. It is enough to consider the *Offshore Exhibition* held periodically in London – a trade show pure and simple.

[12] This is a rare case of a country launched towards independence which decided instead to retain its status as a British Dependent Territory. Anguilla has nine thousand inhabitants.

[13] In 1990, the British Government carried out an inspection of all banks operating in Anguilla. Thirty-one out of forty-four had their licences revoked, and still more licences were revoked subsequently.

[14] For example, using as a basis the state law of Wyoming (which was the pioneer of this kind of legislation) it introduced Limited Liability Companies, which are the latest rage in the United States. For an explanation of the principles of LLCs in Italian, see M. Gardenal and J. C. Nardi, 'Società Usa: un altro modo di dire "limited"', *Comm. int.* (1995) 880.

[15] Trusts Ordinance 1994, s. 6(1).

2. Antigua and Barbuda

Among the last to appear on the scene of trusts aimed at an international clientele, the law of Antigua, which is not yet in force, continues the tendency which we have already seen in nearby Anguilla towards the adoption of laws which borrow provisions from similar laws of neighbouring countries.

The life of Antiguan trusts will be particularly long (120 years); their secrecy will be protected by the same laws which have been passed to ensure bank secrecy.

Antigua is among the very few countries in the world which effectively call for no form of imposition of income tax, except for a tax on corporate income, and it does not recognize any estate duty or gift tax. For some time, it followed a policy of granting 'easy passports', but the disrepute into which the country fell in the eyes of international opinion forced it to repeal the laws which facilitated the attainment of citizenship.

3. The Bahamas

The English Trustee Act of 1893 was adopted in the Bahamas the same year, and remained the main legislative source for nearly a century.[16] No modifications followed independence in 1973, until the Bahamas joined the 'race for the trust', which led to the passing of the Trust (Choice of Governing Law) Act of 1989, the Fraudulent Dispositions Act of 1991,[17] and more recently the Perpetuities Act 1995 and of the Trustee Act 1998.[18]

Because of the fragmentary nature of the legislation (which is being sorted out by means of a single law currently in debate in Parliament[19]), the legislative foundation has remained English, with its origins in case law. Moreover, it is interesting to note that here the new figure of the protector, which has been specifically regulated by many States in their new laws, is based on a provision of the Trustee Act 1893.[20]

---

[16] As is well known, the Bahamas were the first landfall of Christopher Columbus. They became a British colony in the second half of the seventeenth century, and obtained their independence in 1973. The highest court is the Privy Council.

[17] A global revision of the law on trusts is being carried out. It has led to the drafting of a Trustee Bill, which has yet to be debated in Parliament.

[18] It should be noted that the Bahamas, like many of the other States we are looking at, has taken restrictive measures to combat the recycling of funds: Money Laundering (Proceeds of Crime) Act 1995.

[19] Since first writing the Italian version of this book, the Trusts (Choice of Governing Law) (Amendment) Act 1996 has been enacted, although the law referred to here is still being debated.

[20] Trustee Act 1893, s. 3: 'Every power conferred by the preceding sections shall be exercised according to the discretion of the trustee, but subject to any consent required by the

4. Barbados

Barbados differs from other Caribbean States in the care which it has taken to negotiate double-taxation treaties and treaties for the protection of investments.[21] The usefulness of these treaties is debatable, except in marginal cases, but they certainly place Barbados in an advantageous position compared with other countries which take part in the 'race for the trust'.[22] The Barbados law of trusts dated from 1979, and substantially followed the English Trustee Act of 1925.[23] International clients required something different, and so the International Trusts Act of 1995 was passed, which is reserved for 'international' trusts. The drafters of the law did not adopt other countries' solutions, sight unseen, but examined them one by one. For the definition of the term 'trust', they took that found in article 2 of the Hague Convention, but, unlike other countries, they changed it, (correctly) omitting the phrase '*inter vivos* or on death'. Furthermore, they wisely kept alive almost all of the law of 1979, so that the punctilious description of the rules regarding the activity of trustees, typical of the English law of 1925 and the laws which took it as their inspiration, was not lost.

5. Belize

The Trusts Act 1992 of the Central American State of Belize[24] (drafted by English jurists) is one of the laws which has been most imitated.[25] It belongs to the school developed in Jersey and Guernsey, but also took into account all the other legislative options, and reconsidered every phrase so as to arrive, where possible, at a technically more precise formulation, or at one which adhered more closely to the subjects developed in English case law.[26]

instrument, if any, creating the trust with respect to the investment of the trust funds.' In England, this rule was transfused into the current Trustee Act 1925, s. 3, on which see above, chapter 3 §1.c.   [21] Negotiations for a treaty with Italy are under way.

[22] Double-taxation treaties are in force with Canada, Finland, Norway, the United States, Sweden and Venezuela.

[23] Barbados was a British colony from 1627 to 1966. The highest court is the Privy Council.

[24] Formerly British Honduras, the only British colony in Central America. It became independent in 1981, after over three-hundred years of colonial status. The highest court is the Privy Council.

[25] The Trusts Act is a general law on trusts. Unlike others, therefore, it is not aimed at trusts with an international character. The subject was previously covered by the Trusts Act of 1923.

[26] Let me give an example. In English law, as we know, the requirements of knowledge which render a person jointly responsible for the breach of a trustee, and therefore make him a constructive trustee, are a matter of debate (see above, chapter 2 §2.c). While the Guernsey law exonerates a person who acted 'without notice of the breach of trust' (Trusts (Guernsey) Law 1989, s. 38(1)) the Belize law uses the words: 'without any actual, constructive or implied notice' (Trusts Act 1992, s. 51(1)).

Among the original aspects of the Belize law we note: the provisions of the so-called 'variant types of trust', that is, those, like the Muslim *waqf*, which belong to foreign legal systems; the broadening of the notion of charitable trusts with the clarification (in contrast with English case law) that a charitable trust may carry out its activities exclusively abroad; the legislative regulation of the letter of wishes; and a complete definition of trusts for purposes (which are not permitted in English law).

Belize trusts, which were the first to break the barrier of one-hundred years of duration,[27] have found great favour with international clients, especially Americans, in competition with the Cook Islands, culminating with the latest creation from the imaginative minds of tax consultants (but not only those working in Belize): to appoint a local company controlled by the settlor as trustee.[28]

6. Bermuda

Bermuda is among the most active centres of offshore activity, especially in the areas of insurance and investment funds,[29] and voted to retain its colonial status.[30] It is one of the oldest British colonies, and belongs to that group of countries (some of which are still colonies, and others independent States), such as the Bahamas, Barbados, Belize, the British Virgin Islands and the Cayman Islands, which have found it necessary to introduce radical innovations to the laws of trusts which they received *by legislation* during the colonial era.[31] By two 1989 laws[32] and one of 1990,[33] the field of trusts has, therefore, been widely re-visited. The main contributions of

---

[27] Apart from the laws which provide for an indefinite duration, the longest period provided for today is 150 years: Cayman Islands, Perpetuities Law 1995.

[28] I have already indicated, see chapter 3 §3.a, that structures of this kind do not belong to the area of trusts. They are, in fact, also generally discouraged by local professionals, who, if anything, lean towards structures such as those which will be described below when we discuss the Cook Islands.

[29] There are around 1,400 insurance companies, most of which are 'captive', with income from premiums of 18 billion dollars. There are almost 600 investment funds, which have the benefit of legislative incentives, above all fiscal in nature. Bermuda is in second place after Luxembourg as the international centre for these funds.
   Another frequent use of the trust in Bermuda is in the area of the pension funds of multi-national groups.   [30] Referendum of August, 1995.

[31] The Trustee Act of 1975 was modelled on the English Trustee Act of 1925. Technically, Bermuda adopted current English law on 11 July 1612. Prior precedents have, however, always been very persuasive. The highest court is the Privy Council.

[32] Trusts (Special Provisions) Act (amended in 1998) and Perpetuities and Accumulations Act 1989. The Trust Companies Act 1991, regulates the establishment and activities of companies which look after the creation and management of trusts.

[33] Conveyancing Amendment Act.

Bermuda to the international trust model are in the requirements of the revocatory action (maintained, however, along English lines), the reproduction of certain provisions of the Hague Convention (from the definition of a trust to the criteria for identification of the applicable law of the trust[34]), and provisions relating to the capacity to create a trust, the limits of application of foreign law as set forth in the local norms of private international law, and the new definition of purpose trusts, which are freely permitted.

The law of Bermuda includes an attachment in which the powers of the trustee are listed, which the settlor may incorporate by reference in the trust instrument. Other States later followed suit.

7. The British Virgin Islands

A British colony since the end of the seventeenth century,[35] the British Virgin Islands attracted international attention when they 'invented' International Business Companies in 1984 in a law which, although imitated by many States in the Caribbean and elsewhere, has maintained the most favour in the financial world.[36] There were frequent abuses, especially in the early years, and the government, in agreement with those of Britain and the United States, has recently passed laws against money-laundering and for international co-operation on criminal matters.

The Trust Ordinance of 1961[37] has been amended and extended by the Trustee (Amendment) Act of 1993, in which (and this is the only example of this) the rule whereby the trustees reach decisions by a majority was ratified, and the office of the 'managing trustee' is provided for.[38]

The Hague Convention is in effect as a result of its having been ratified by the United Kingdom.

8. The Cayman Islands

The Cayman Islands were deserted when Columbus landed there during his final voyage to the Indies, and remained so for centuries. They depended for

---

[34] The law also applies to implied and constructive trusts, and the trustee includes the personal representative: these are two significant departures from the standard of the Hague Convention. Both in this field and in others, the relationship between the ratification of the Hague Convention (which took place as a result of British ratification) and the special law of Bermuda is unclear.   [35] The highest court is the Privy Council.

[36] There are currently over 150.000 companies incorporated in the British Virgin Islands (around thirty thousand in each of the last three years).

[37] The new law, in addition to modifying certain existing rules, has inserted the articles from no. 80 on into the law of 1961.

[38] British Virgin Islands, Trustee (Amendment) Act 1993, s. 85 and s. 97.

administrative purposes on Jamaica, which was conquered by the British in 1755, and did so until 1962, when Jamaica chose independence and the Cayman Islands wanted to remain as a British colony.[39]

Here, too, in addition to the adoption of English law in 1727 when the colony was established, the legislation conformed to the English legal system, and was kept up to date as time passed. Since 1987, the Cayman Islands have been a very active participant in the 'race for the trust', passing five laws which, especially as regards the rules on conflict of laws and revocatory actions, have received wide assent. Expeditious legislative intervention has taken account of the evolution of English law, which has been changed where a contrast with the requirements of financial activities was identified. The most recent example concerns cases where a bank is both a trustee and an (irregular) depository of a sum of money.[40]

This legislative presence has manifested itself in many other sectors, for example with limited-life companies and limited-duration companies, structured for American clients, and has enjoyed a very positive institutional response at all levels of financial business.[41]

9. Cyprus

Cyprus, where the English law on trusts in force in 1960 is applied, dedicated a special law to international trusts in 1992.[42] It would be more accurate to use the term 'foreign' trusts, since the law deals with cases where neither the settlor nor the beneficiaries are resident in Cyprus, and the assets on trust do not include any property located in Cyprus. As with

---

[39] Confirmed in 1990. The highest court is the Privy Council.
   In the course of this brief overview, I have decided not to go into details on British colonial law, but it may be worth noting that there are various 'grades' of colonization. For example, the British Virgin Islands are a *self-governing* colony, where the Governor is the representative of the Queen, while the Cayman Islands are a colony in the strict sense of the word, and the Governor represents the British Government. For the various categories in British colonial law, see K. Roberts-Wray, *Commonwealth and Colonial Law*, London, 1966, ch. I.
   For specific constitutional matters regarding the Cayman Islands see E. W. Davies, *The Legal System of the Cayman Islands*, Oxford, 1989, pp. 9–33.

[40] We have discussed this above, chapter 3, footnote 375. The Property (Miscellaneous Provisions) Law 1994 'repealed' the prior English case law with the following provision: 'A trust may be validly created of an existing debt notwithstanding that the debtor is the trustee of the trust, and the effect of so doing is that he has an equitable obligation to the beneficiaries on the same terms as the debt to make payment into the trust fund.'

[41] It is estimated that 900 investment funds have their base in the Cayman Islands, and that forty-seven of the fifty leading banks in the world have operations there.

[42] International Trust Law 69(I)/92. The trust is nothing new to Cyprus, where a special law was passed in 1955: Trustees Law (ch. 193). It is relevant to point out that Cyprus is bound to observe English precedents (including those of equity) on trusts, unless dispensed by a specific law (Cyprus Court of Justice Law, 1960, s. 29).

many laws of this kind, at least one trustee must be resident in Cyprus.[43] It should be noted that the requirements regarding the settlor and the beneficiaries are respected where one or the other, or both, are Cypriot companies with offshore company status.

Cypriot law is distinguished by the linearity of its content, which is made possible thanks to the lasting vigour of the previous legislation and English case law on trusts, so that the legislator only had to make provision for those elements which distinguish the 'international' trusts from ordinary trusts.[44]

In contrast with most States which participate in the 'race for the trust', Cyprus, which is a member of the Council of Europe, is actively involved in the area of international treaties, both against double taxation[45] and for international co-operation on criminal matters.

10. Cook Islands

The Cook Islands were never a British colony. Their geographical position, in the middle of the South Pacific, at an enormous distance from any other country, did not make them an object of interest.[46] They were first a British protectorate, and then part of New Zealand in 1901. They became independent in 1965.[47]

The production of laws on trusts in the Cook Islands was originally influenced by the legislation of New Zealand, and, thereby, of England,[48] and was characterized by the abundance of laws (one may count five between 1948 and 1991 and subsequent amendments) to favour the creation of trusts by foreign clients.[49] The laws of the Cook Islands have supplied the basis for numerous laws of other States, for example on the

---

[43] This would normally be a Cypriot offshore company, because physical persons resident in Cyprus must have authorization from the Central Bank to acquire assets abroad.

[44] In general, see C. Mavrocordatos, 'Cyprus' International Trusts', in *Atti Milano*, ch. 37.

[45] Twenty-six treaties are in force, including one with Italy. Six of these are with former communist countries. On the relationship between trusts under Cypriot law and the double-taxation treaties, see the three articles in 2 T&T (1996) no. 7.

[46] The Cook Islands are 1,200 km. from Tahiti, 3,000 from New Zealand, and 4,700 from Hawaii.

[47] The highest court is the Privy Council. On the constitutional relationship between the Cook Islands and New Zealand, see D. Bourke, 'The Constitutional Relationship of the Cook Islands with New Zealand', in OI (Nov. 1996) 31.

[48] The local judges are often retired New Zealand judges. The introduction of the common law into the Cook Islands has followed an unusual path through New Zealand, which extended to them the law in force on 14 January 1840 (this, obviously, was English law).

[49] The Cook Islands began to encourage foreign investments in 1977. They had the idea of International Business Companies before the British Virgin Islands, but the laws of the latter were more respectful of business needs and technically more correct; hence their success. The Cook Islands have amended their law seven times since 1981 to catch up.

definition of what is intended by a charitable purpose, on revocatory actions, and on the definition of the term protector.[50] They are among the firmest of all laws on the subject of the exclusive competence of local law for all questions of capacity, the validity of the trust instrument and the transfer of assets to the trustee. Nonetheless, they exaggerate when they classify as trusts acts which, as we shall see, lack any of the trust's distinguishing elements.[51]

The Cook Islands are particularly fashionable in the United States for the establishment of protective trusts in favour of professionals and business-people; the former, strangled by the high cost of malpractice insurance, often find it convenient to transfer their assets into a trust created in a country which, like the Cook Islands, offers protection against potential dissatisfied clients.[52]

11. Gibraltar

The trust law of Gibraltar is almost identical to current English law be-cause, as in many colonies,[53] English laws in existence prior to the establish-ment of the colony took effect automatically, and successive laws were adopted by imperial, and later local, legislation. Gibraltar, like Hong Kong, has adopted the rules of the Hague Convention as a consequence of its ratification by the United Kingdom. The technique is, however, particular to these two legal systems, which provide for the passing of a domestic law which reproduces the Convention, with later modifications pursuant to reservations or other reasons.[54]

In 1984 a consolidation (in the English sense of an ordered reproduction of a multitude of preceding provisions) was issued.[55] Later, tax exemptions for foreign trusts were introduced, and rules on revocation in the event

---

[50] The most active disciples have been Mauritius and Nevis.

[51] A complete revision of the laws is under way.

[52] The most frequently followed technique consists of placing the assets in a partnership, the capital of which is divided into two units, one of 99% and the other of 1% both owned by the settlor. All the management responsibilities are given to the holder of the 1% unit. The settlor keeps the 1%, and places the 99% unit on trust.

More recently, the preferred method has been to incorporate a company with different classes of shares. Those which give rise to rights to the profits go to the trust, while those which carry voting rights go to the settlor.

[53] Gibraltar has been a British colony since 1704. It belongs to the European Union (pursu-ant to article 227 no. 4 of the Treaty of Rome; for an up-to-date picture, see J. Chincotta, 'Gibraltar – Status in the European Union', in OI (April 1996) 16). The highest court is the Privy Council.   [54] For precise indications, see above, chapter 1, footnote 7.

[55] Trustees Ordinance 1984. See also the Registered Trusts Ordinance, 1999.

of bankruptcy were passed which are less severe than their English equivalents.[56]

12. Guernsey

Guernsey, like Jersey, is not part of the United Kingdom, and is not a colony. Technically, it belongs to the English monarchy[57] as it did in 1204, when the King of England lost all his possessions in Normandy except the Channel Islands (Jersey, Guernsey, Alderney and Sark).

English law has never been adopted in these islands; nor have the English judicial authorities ever had jurisdiction.[58] Although the Parliament in Westminster has the power to legislate for the Channel Islands, a constitutional practice has developed by which no law regarding them may be passed without the prior consent of the local legislative institutions, more accurately by the legislative organs of each island, because 'Channel Islands' is a purely geographical expression of no legal significance whatsoever.[59]

The law of Guernsey, as is the case with the other islands, developed almost exclusively from case law, on the basis of Norman custom. Given the proximity to the French coast,[60] and a population which was, until the last century, predominantly of French origin, medieval French legal writing and custom were mirrored precisely in the islands. Even today, the French writers of the sixteenth to the eighteenth centuries treatises (that is, prior to the civil code) and the *coutumiers* are an authoritative written source of law.

The English influence, especially in the last century, has been strong both at the legislative and case-law level, but it should not be overestimated. Since there has been no codification, and legislative production is scarce, rules from European common law, or specifically from Norman common law, may be applied at any moment, and may give rise to unpredictable results.[61] As far as trusts are concerned, Guernsey, although not without

---

[56] The Bankruptcy (Amendment) Ordinance 1990; the revocatory action may be attempted only where the debtor has had notice of the third-party claim, and the value of the estate after the transfer is less than the total of the debts.

[57] It is more correct, since 1701, to say that it belongs to the Crown.

[58] The highest court is the Privy Council. This is not a contradiction, since constitutionally the Privy Council is neither an English nor a British court.

[59] Jersey and Guernsey are part of the customs union of the European Union, but are not subject to Community regulations except in the areas of customs and tariffs: Protocol no. 3 to the treaty of accession signed by the United Kingdom on 22nd January 1972.

[60] Guernsey is 48 km. from the Normandy coast; Jersey is only 20 km. away.

[61] I shall return to this argument in a few pages when I deal with Jersey.

specific legislative and case-law experience,[62] was obliged to yield to the initiative of Jersey, which made the first move in 1984, and introduced the first amendments in 1989. This delay turned into an advantage, however, because Guernsey, although using the laws of Jersey as its inspiration, and often reproducing them to the letter, did not miss the chance to refine their composition.[63] The result was that some States which took the law of Jersey as their model nonetheless preferred in many cases to follow the more precise expression of the laws of Guernsey.

The Hague Convention is in effect in Guernsey due to its ratification by the United Kingdom.

13. Hong Kong

In general, the same applies to Hong Kong as to Gibraltar, including acceptance of the Hague Convention.[64]

The creation of trusts in Hong Kong has for some time been influenced by the uncertainties about the future of the colony. Trusts tend, therefore, to be subject to a foreign law, and the seat of the trust tends to be abroad, while the actual administration remains in Hong Kong. In many trusts created earlier, the trustees have been substituted by others resident abroad.[65]

---

[62] See the interesting essay by St-J. A. Robilliard, 'Foundations of Guernsey as a Trust Jurisdiction', in 2 T&T (1996) no. 8, 6.

[63] I shall give two examples. On the constructive trust: Trusts (Jersey) Law 1984, article 29: '(1): Subject to paragraph (2) where a person (in this article referred to as a constructive trustee) makes or receives any profit, gain, or advantage from a breach of trust he shall be deemed to be a trustee of that profit, gain, or advantage. (2) Paragraph (1) shall not apply to a bona fide purchaser of property for value and without notice of the breach of trust.'

Trusts (Guernsey) Law 1989, s. 38(1): 'A person who derives a profit from a breach of trust, or who obtains property in breach of trust, shall be deemed to be a trustee of the profit or property, unless he derives or obtains it in good faith and without notice of the breach of trust.'

On the definition of trust: Trusts (Jersey) Law 1984, article 2: 'A trust exists where a person (known as a trustee) holds or has vested in him or is deemed to hold or have vested in him property (of which he is not the owner in his own right): (a) for the benefit of any person (known as a beneficiary) whether or not yet ascertained or in existence; or (b) for any purpose which is not for the benefit only of the trustee; or (c) for such benefit as is mentioned in sub-paragraph (a) and also for any such purpose as is mentioned in sub-paragraph (b).'

Trusts (Guernsey) Law 1989, s. 1: 'A trust exists where a person (*a trustee*) holds or has vested in him, or is deemed to hold or have vested in him, property which does not form, or which has ceased to form, part of his own estate: (a) for the benefit of any person (*a beneficiary*) whether or not yet ascertained or in existence; or (b) for any valid charitable or non-charitable purpose which is not for the benefit only of the trustee.'

[64] Apart from membership of the European Union, of course.

[65] On the legal system of Hong Kong see P. Wesley-Smith, *The Sources of Hong Kong Law*, Hong

14. The Isle of Man

The constitutional position of the Isle of Man is similar to that of the Channel Islands.[66] The King of England purchased it in 1765 from the Earl of Derby, and for this reason the island is, at least in theory, a personal domain of the Crown, and is not part of the United Kingdom. The parliamentary tradition of the Isle of Man, as is well known, is second in age only to that of Iceland, and the British Parliament does not legislate for it. The constitutional convention which has come into being provides for an informal agreement being reached, and approval of an identical text by Parliament in London for the United Kingdom, and by the local parliament for the island.

Trust law in the Isle of Man was regulated by the Trustee Act of 1961 (on the English model of the Trustee Act of 1925 and the Trustee Investment Act of 1961) and successive laws, parallel to English laws, including the Perpetuities and Accumulations Act, until the recent Trusts Act 1995,[67] which sets forth private international norms, and follows the modern tendency to reject the application of foreign laws which prejudice the validity of trusts governed by local law. The Isle of Man has accepted the Hague Convention in the same manner as Gibraltar and Hong Kong.

One significant difference from English law may be found in the protection of the creditors of the settlor; local law has remained that of Elizabethan legislation and the later Fraudulent Assignments Act of 1736.[68]

15. Jersey

Since 1984, Jersey has had four trust laws,[69] a clear demonstration not only of the interest, but also of the determination with which the local government has confronted the subject. The first law deals with many aspects of trusts, with the warning that it does not constitute[70] a codification, and is therefore intended to be neither exhaustive nor conclusive. The two laws which followed introduced modifications of limited interest, except for one, which has been widely imitated: in determining the validity and

---

Kong, 1994.

    More generally, also with reference to the future of the Colony after its return to China: P. Wesley-Smith and A. H. Y Chen (eds.), *The Basic Law and Hong Kong's Future*, Hong Kong, 1988.

[66] And its position with respect to the European Union is identical. The highest court is the Privy Council.   [67] In force since 17 January 1996.

[68] An exhaustive analysis may be found in P. H. Hobson, The Statute of Elizabeth, in 2 T&T (1996) no. 4, 22.

[69] Trusts (Jersey) Law 1984; Trusts (Amendment) (Jersey) Law 1989; Trusts (Amendment No. 2) (Jersey) Law 1991; Trusts (Amendment No. 3) (Jersey) Law 1996.   [70] Article 1(5).

effectiveness of a transfer of trust assets, the provisions of the settlor's national law in the area of succession (or of the law which regulates his succession) are of no relevance. The most recent law (Trusts (Amendment No. 3) (Jersey) Law 1996) permits the creation of trusts for purposes, in accordance with the rules which had in the meantime evolved in the international trust model, as we shall see presently.

In regulating the source of the trust, Jersey law is agnostic – 'a trust may come into existence in any manner' – and goes on to place an express declaration of a settlor, which may also be oral, and his conduct, or that of a third party, on the same level. Within this same framework are embraced the statutory rules for constructive trusts, which do not exclude the possibility that there may be other cases, in addition to those listed, where a constructive trust arises.

Considering the extreme complexity of the tasks they undertook, the Jersey legislators completed them with great success.[71] The insertion of trusts into a body of law based on custom and heavily characterized by concepts of European common law, and, of course, lacking any traditions of equity, could have distorted the institution.[72] To the merits of the legislators, backed up by interesting writings,[73] we should add worthy case law which has regularly found against local banks (operating as trustees) and significant pension funds precisely on questions involving the conceptual structure of trusts and the obligations of the trustee.[74]

---

[71] We shall see in the course of this chapter that Jersey has inspired many other laws of the international model. See the summary in Matthews and Sowden, §§xx–xxiii. Cf. in general C. Davies, 'Trusts in the Island of Jersey', in *Atti Milano*, ch. 38.

[72] As I shall have the chance to make clear in the course of my review of Jersey and Guernsey in §2, I am referring to European common law as I defined it in *Origins* (see above, footnote 3). With particular reference to Jersey institutions which belong to that world, see the survival of the *centenarius* (pp. 384–5) and the execution of contracts for the sale of real property before a judge sitting in open court (pp. 279–82). I would add now, although the cultural reference is to a later historical period, the rule of custom by which a person may prohibit another from carrying out a legal act which he believes to be prejudicial to his own interests by going up to him in public, bare-headed and before witnesses, and pronouncing on bended knee '*haro, haro, haro, à l'aide mon prince, on me fait tort*' (R. Morris, 'Trustee's Liabilities Explored', in 1 T&T (1995) no. 10, 6; for a correct and more detailed overview, see C. S. le Gros, *Traité du droit coutumier de l'Île de Jersey*, Jersey, 1943, pp. 28–35). In general on the legal system of Jersey see R. Lemasurier, *Le droit de l'Île de Jersey*, Paris, 1956.   [73] Matthews and Sowden.

[74] *West v. Lazard Brothers* (1993), cited above, footnote 8; *Rahman v. Chase Bank* (1991) (see above, chapter 3, footnote 345); recently, *Federated Pension Services v. Midland Bank* (1995), see below, p. 231.

While discussion of the case which gave rise to the judgment in *Rahman v. Chase Bank* (1991), was still raging, the Trusts (Amendment) (Jersey) Law 1989 was passed, which, inserting s. 8A into the law of 1984, stated: 'Nothing in the terms of a trust shall cause a transfer or disposition of property to a trust to be invalidated by application of the rule "*donner et retenir ne vaut*".'

The Hague Convention is in effect in Jersey as a result of British ratification.

16. Malta

Structurally, Malta belongs to the world of civil law. The influx of English law has been evident in many areas of business law, but it has not affected trusts.

The Maltese law of 1988 was, therefore, aimed solely at foreign trusts (called 'offshore' trusts): the settlor and the beneficiaries must be non-resident, and real property located in Malta may not be included in the trust assets. The law sets out a wide-ranging discipline, in which one notes the example of Jersey and an intention to conform with the provisions of the Hague Convention, to which was recently added a programme to shed Malta's most evident connotations as a tax paradise and to become a member of the European Community. Hence we have the Recognition of Trusts Act of 1994, which acknowledges the Hague Convention,[75] generalizes the discipline of trusts (no longer 'offshore'), and adapts itself to legislative elements – for example, the protector – which had in the meantime been introduced into other systems.

A particular aspect of the Maltese law is the provision for nominee companies, which are professional companies to which are entrusted responsibilities towards the Government and in the area of ensuring that foreign persons respect Maltese law. If there is only one trustee, it must be a nominee company; if there is more than one, one of them must be a nominee company.[76] This provision, which is accompanied by the compulsory registration of trusts, gives rise to a problem, because Maltese trusts, although they have lost the 'offshore' denomination, may not own shares in Maltese companies.[77] This limitation is of some significance, since Malta likes to propose itself as an international financial centre.[78]

Another peculiarity, taken, what is more, from the law of Western Samoa, lies in the registration of trusts through a *unilateral declaration* by the trustee. He may refrain from declaring the name of the settlor, provided that he certifies that he has personally ascertained that the settlor is a 'qualified person'.[79] Registration of foreign trusts is also permitted,

---

[75] According to the English technique, which we have already seen in Gibraltar. The text of the Convention is attached to the act of adoption, but with certain amendments: for example, article 13 is excluded, and article 15 is not applied to movables.

[76] Offshore Trusts Act 1988, s. 18.

[77] M. Ganado and J. M. Ganado, 'Malta Trusts: New Law Revives Interest', in 1 T&T (1995) no. 9, 20.

[78] Cf. O. Grech, 'The Law of Trusts of Malta', in *Atti Milano*, ch. 39.

[79] Malta, Trusts Act 1988, s. 7(2) and s. 7(3); similarly Nevis International Exempt Trust Ordinance 1994, s. 37.

provided that they have a Maltese trustee (i.e. an authorized nominee company).[80]

17. Mauritius

Mauritius, too, belongs to the world of civil law, and the French *code civil* has remained in force, although there is strong English influence in many areas of the law.[81]

The international good fortune of Mauritius has been its double-taxation treaty with India, which has made it the base for numerous investments.[82] In the meantime, it has signed other treaties on the same subject,[83] has reviewed its company laws, and has passed two laws on trusts, one for its citizens (which we shall deal with in the next chapter), and one for the foreign market.[84] We shall examine the latter law in this chapter because it belongs to the international trust model, and develops the innovation promoted by Western Samoa regarding the non-compulsory disclosure of the name of the settlor in the request for registration of an international trust.[85]

The law takes the Guernsey law as its inspiration, but, like Malta, sets out the conditions of 'foreignness' required for a trust to be considered 'international' and to enjoy, *inter alia*, the relevant tax exemptions.

18. Nauru

Nauru was a German protectorate until 1920, and was then granted by the League of Nations to Australia, which brought it to independence in 1968. English law was incorporated by statute in its entirety in 1922. This was confirmed in 1971, but it was also made clear that it was necessary to adapt it to local requirements.[86]

In that year, a period of independent legislation began which included the Foreign Trusts, Estates and Wills Act of 1972.[87] This law, which remained unknown to most people, contains two innovative provisions

---

[80] Malta, Trusts Act 1988, s. 43A, added to by the Recognition of Trusts Act 1994.

[81] Mauritius became a British colony in 1810, and became independent in 1968. The highest court is the Privy Council.

[82] The treaty between Mauritius and India reduces Indian tax withholding on dividends to 5%.   [83] Including Italy.   [84] Offshore Trusts Act 1992.

[85] Offshore Business Activities Act 1992, s. 30.

[86] Customs and Adopted Laws Act 1971, amended in 1972 and again in 1976, article 4(4) and article 5. Attached to the law there is a list of areas to which the adoption does not apply. The total population of the State is approximately 6,000.

[87] In the same year, the Nauru Trustee Corporation Act was passed, which creates a trust company which is appropriate to act as trustee of local trusts and as executor of estates which include assets located within the State.

which were later introduced in varying degrees in other countries involved in the 'race for the trust': the legislative abolition of the rule against perpetuities, and the unlimited recognition of trusts for purposes.

The law of Nauru, although the first of its kind, did not attract international attention, because it was not followed by a complete reform of the field, which remained in all other aspects faithful to the traditional rules of the English model.

19. Nevis

The federation of St Christopher and Nevis in the Eastern Caribbean allows each of the two islands to have its own legislation.[88] The law passed by Nevis in 1994 does not, therefore, apply to the other member of the federation.

Since, like the other colonies of which we have spoken, Nevis adopted English law, it, too, had a trust law, as a result of the English Trustee Investments Act of 1961.[89]

The Nevis law of 1994 is clearly influenced by the 1992 Belize law, but it is also clear that the target of the law is an American clientele, especially professionals,[90] which explains the adherence to the Cook Islands model in the area of revocatory actions against the settlor by his creditors, with the addition of the provision of a guarantee as a condition of having the right to proceed with an action.

The law of Nevis, unlike that of Belize, only covers international trusts, which are, as usual, characterized by the non-residence in the country of settlor and beneficiaries, the residence of the trustee, and the absence of rights in real property located in the country.

20. Niue

The law which was passed in Niue in 1994 (the Trust Act) also follows the Belize model without any particular variations, except for the broadening of the purposes permitted in charitable trusts.

It is, like the law of Belize, a general trust law, and is not limited to international trusts. At the same time, trust companies are regulated, with particular attention being paid to those incorporated by foreigners with the purpose of managing one or more specific trusts.[91]

---

[88] Independence dates from 1983.   [89] Trustee Ordinance 1961.

[90] This can also be seen from the terminology. The protective trust is defined as a 'spendthrift trust', as in the United States (Belize had used the term 'protective or spendthrift trust').   [91] Trustee Companies Act 1994 and Trustee Companies Regulations 1994.

21. Saint Vincent

Saint Vincent and the Grenadines, independent since 1979,[92] have chosen a completely independent path in the area of trusts. At the suggestion of a group of Swiss professionals, a special law was passed in 1976, which has been amended on a number of occasions in the meantime, and which does not regulate trusts (which are covered by rules adopted during the colonial period), but rather the 'Saint Vincent and the Grenadines Trust Authority'.[93]

This Authority acts as an intermediary between persons establishing trusts and the government, and in particular the Trusts Registry. The registration of an 'international'[94] trust is compulsory, but the government preferred to create an intermediary to carry out all the preparatory work, including the receipt of registration rights. In addition, the Authority may act as trustee.

One final singular aspect is the web of joint interests with the Swiss professionals which emerges from the creation of a joint venture between the Swiss and the government, called the St Vincent Trust Service A.G., headquartered in Zurich, but managed from Vaduz, with one of the Swiss professionals being a member of the Authority.[95]

22. Seychelles

As in the case of Mauritius, we must divide our discussion of the Seychelles between this chapter and the next, because the Seychelles has a civil-law form of trust and another which follows the international model.

The latter was introduced in 1994,[96] taking the Mauritius law, and, therefore, the Guernsey model, as its major inspiration. Among the particular aspects to be noted is the manner of completion of the transfer, borrowed through the Mauritius law, which protects the confidentiality of trusts. The law, in fact, expressly prohibits mention of the names of the settlor and the beneficiaries in the declaration of registration (which is compulsory).[97]

The Seychelles legislature, in common with many in other States, has undertaken to improve the wording of the laws, which has often been taken unchanged from foreign laws.[98]

---

[92] The highest court is the Privy Council.
[93] Saint Vincent and the Grenadines Trust Authority Act 1976; amended in 1980, 1982 and 1990.
[94] As usual, at least one trustee is required to be resident in the State. Unlike other laws, the settlor may also be resident, provided that the beneficiaries are not.
[95] I have taken this information from the article published in OI (October 1994) 33.
[96] International Trusts Act, subsequently the International Trust Act in 1996.   [97] S. 76.
[98] See, for example, article 27(a), where, after having set forth the common principle that

23. Turks and Caicos

Like the Cayman Islands, the Turks and Caicos were long governed by Jamaica,[99] and opted to maintain colonial status when Jamaica became independent.[100]

Unlike other Caribbean territories which we have considered briefly, the Turks and Caicos are of no importance from the standpoint of international finance. Their small population[101] and history as a base for drug operations during the 1980s have kept banks away, and have led to the signing of collaboration agreements with the United States and adhesion to multilateral treaties on criminal issues. Also controversial was the policy of attracting rich foreigners by offering them citizenship, which was radically reviewed in 1994.

In the past few years, the government of the colony has followed a policy which has the purpose of creating favourable conditions for access to international capital markets, and the Trust Ordinance of 1990[102] is in line with that policy. It is closely modelled on the Jersey law, with a noteworthy command of technical and technological issues. Among the original aspects of the law of the Turks and Caicos are, for example, provisions regarding revocatory actions and the abolition of the rule against perpetuities in all its forms.[103]

United Kingdom ratification of the Hague Convention also extends to the Turks and Caicos.

24. Vanuatu

After being joint property of England and France as the New Hebrides, Vanuatu became independent in 1980.[104]

As we have seen with other tax havens, Vanuatu relaxed controls of the

---

the trust assets must be transferred to the trustee, it provides for the case where the assets are in the name of a *nominee* of the trustee, and, following the terminology of article 2 of the Hague Convention, where they are *under the control* of the trustee.

[99] They were initially under the Governor of the Bahamas.

[100] The highest court is the Privy Council.   [101] In 1990 the islands had 12,350 inhabitants.

[102] Followed by the Trustee (Licensing) Ordinance 1992 to regulate the activities of trust companies. A simple commentary on the Trust Ordinance is found in P. Kenny, *Kenny's Guide to Company and Trust Law in the Turks and Caicos Islands*, London, 1993, pp. 39–76.

[103] Although the Turks and Caicos law has often been used by States which followed the model of Jersey, Guernsey and Belize, the first of the two provisions cited here has not been adopted by any State, and the second only by Anguilla. In 1998 the Voluntary Disposition Ordinance was issued.

[104] Legislation on business matters following independence has an English imprint: see the Companies Act 1986 and the International Companies Act 1993. The latter falls within the well-trodden path of International Business Companies. The Trust Companies Regulation, on the other hand, dates from 1971, prior to independence.

flow of funds for some time, and then, like other tax havens, realized that in the long term it was better to conform to international standards.[105] It therefore took part in international efforts against organized crime, and among other actions it passed a special law, the Serious Offences (Confiscation of Proceeds) Act 1989, which has recently shown excellent results.[106]

Two proposals for a trust law, both drafted by Australian jurists, are currently awaiting approval by the local parliament:[107] one consolidates the general trust law, while the other covers international trusts. The former closely follows the English Trustee Act and Australian State laws, principally that of New South Wales, whereas the latter contains numerous innovative provisions, for example in the areas of applicable law and charitable trusts. Since several years have passed since the draft law, it is not possible to say whether it will be approved. I shall not, therefore, take further account of it in this chapter.[108]

25. Western Samoa

The International Trusts Act of 1987[109] is an example of the first wave of international trusts, where more emphasis was placed on tax and confidentiality aspects than on the legal issues which came to the fore following the Hague Convention and the debates in the literature which followed it.

It was the requirement of confidentiality which motivated the provision that the trust instrument, the registration of which was optional, can omit mention of the names of both the settlor and the beneficiaries, and only needs to include the names of the trust and the local trustee, who declares that the prerequisites exist for the trust to be considered international.[110] All the other elements are contained in separate deeds, publication of which is subject to criminal sanctions.[111] Confidentiality is further guaranteed by the requirement that any civil

---

[105] Twenty banks were closed by the government of Vanuatu in 1994.
[106] In 1994, the US police tracked down a former drug trafficker who had 'retired', investing his capital in Australia, and later, having liquidated it, in a Vanuatu trust. The Vanuatu trust company was notified by the US authorities that the sums belonging to the trust were to be considered to be the proceeds of crime, and asked the local courts for authorization to block all trust operations. Later, the Attorney General of Vanuatu obtained a confiscation order (from 1 T&T (1995) no. 7, 5).
[107] For now, English law is being followed, but the protector (here called the *appointor*), has emerged in practice.
[108] In the current laws, there is a Trust Companies Act 1971, but not a law on trusts.
[109] Amendments were made later, but they are of no great importance. See, however, the 1997 International Trusts Regulations and International Trusts Bill.
[110] S. 11. We shall see in chapter 5 that a form of registration without the names of the settlor and the beneficiaries is provided for in Liechtenstein.   [111] S. 19.

procedure involving trusts must be carried out in closed proceedings.[112]

As to the rest, the basic rules are once again English (they have been expressly adopted[113]). They have been modified according to the original Cook Islands law, and therefore mainly in the area of purpose trusts, but contain no innovations in the area of applicable law, the significance of the national law of the settlor, or revocatory actions brought by a creditor of the settlor.[114]

3. Structural elements of the model: consolidation of English *regulae*

In this section, I shall set out a series of *regulae* which English law has developed by legislation or case law, and which are codified today in many of the laws following the international trust model, which have often taken the opportunity to introduce clarifications and refinements. On matters of more general importance, we shall see that some of the countries which had already issued a law modelled on the English Trustee Act are excluded, because they did not see the need to place under examination issues which they held to be principally theoretical.

a Acceptance of the trustee

In English law, the acceptance of the trustee is presumed: it is the duty of a trustee who has been appointed to declare his non-acceptance, but acceptance is also implied from decisive conduct.[115] The provision first enunciated in the Jersey law is based on these case-law *regulae*:

No person shall be obliged to accept appointment as trustee, but a person who knowingly does any act or thing in relation to the trust property consistent with the status of trustee of that property shall be deemed to have accepted appointment as a trustee.[116]

The term 'appointment' underlines the unilateral nature of the trust

---

[112] S. 19(2). This provision is also found in other laws.

[113] Which has as its subject matter 'English common law and equity': s. 4(3)(b).

[114] It is worth pointing out that Western Samoa may be distinguished from the general picture of young Pacific States because of its high literacy rate of 98%.
The rules of Western Samoa on the recognition of foreign judgments are set forth by M. R. Drake, 'Western Samoa – The Recognition and Enforcement of Foreign Judgments', in OI (April 1996) 29.   [115] See above, chapter 3 §1.a.

[116] Trusts (Jersey) Law 1984, article 14, adopted in Malta, Trusts Act 1988, s. 19(1); similarly Trusts (Guernsey) Law 1989, s. 15(2): 'A person appointed as trustee need not accept the appointment, but he shall be deemed to have done so if he knowingly intermeddles with the trust or its affairs'; adopted in Mauritius, Offshore Trusts Act 1992, s. 25(1); in Seychelles, International Trusts Act 1994, s. 24(1); and in Anguilla, Trusts Ordinance 1994, s. 21.

instrument, which, as we have already seen, is an essential element of the English trust. What we called the 'emergent contractuality' is seen in other provisions, and in particular in international practice; in only one case, as we shall see, does it appear on the scene in a crude fashion.

b The juridical position of the trustee

Since the Hague Convention described the legal position of the trustee in non-technical terms, it did not *define* the trustee.[117]

The laws adhering to the international model, which were generally conceived to follow the conceptual provisions of the Convention therefore found themselves faced with two possibilities: to take a clear position and place the trustee within the English system, or to adapt to the vagueness of the Convention. The numerous laws which have defined the trustee have all chosen the first path, including those which followed the Jersey law:

> Subject to this Act and to the terms of the trust, a trustee shall in relation to the trust property have all the same powers as a natural person acting as the beneficial owner of such property.[118]

If the desire were to adapt to the vagueness of the Convention and the emerging contractual nature of trusts, it would be easy to speak of the trustee as if he were a fiduciary or administrator, or, in any case, a person with limited powers and rights. The definition quoted above, on the other hand, is squarely within the orthodox English model tradition, and emphasizes an aspect of the relationship between the trustee and third parties which we have already seen in the English model: the trustee acts towards the outside world as a '*beneficial owner*', that is, as a person acting on his own behalf.

c The juridical position of the beneficiary

At the end of the previous chapter we saw the terms of the false problem of so-called equitable ownership and the division of the property right between the trustee and the beneficiaries, and we concluded that in English law, the beneficiary has no right *over* the property in trust, and that there is no overlap of ownership positions.

The new laws also take a position on this evidently central issue, and,

---

[117] We shall discuss this in chapter 6.
[118] Trusts (Jersey) Law 1984, article 20, adopted in Malta, Trusts Act 1988, s. 24(1) and in Turks and Caicos, Trust Ordinance 1990, s. 23(1); similarly Trusts (Guernsey) Law 1989, s. 26: 'Subject to the provisions of this Law and to the terms of the trust, a trustee has, in relation to the trust property, all the powers of a beneficial owner', adopted in Mauritius, Offshore Trusts Act 1992, s. 35(1) and in Seychelles, International Trusts Act 1994, s. 34(1).

following on this occasion mostly in the wake of Guernsey, define the juridical position of the beneficiary as belonging to personal or movable property:

The interest of a beneficiary is personal property and, subject to the terms of the trust, may be dealt with or charged accordingly.[119]

In this case, too, it would have been easy, and certainly more favourable for a clear understanding of the institution by civil-law clients in the area of international trusts, to have used different language. There are probably two reasons why this did not happen: the first is inherent in common law, and lies in the need, partly for tax reasons, for the beneficiary to lack rights in the trust property; the second is the desire to make the legal distinction between a trust and a transaction in favour of a third party clear. From the point of view of both the legal status of the beneficiary and the distinction between *fiducia* and the trust, these laws confirm the situation with respect to the English trust model which I proposed at the end of the previous chapter.

Personal property, in fact, is historically a category of rights to which real remedies do not belong:[120] to define the legal position of the beneficiary of a trust as being within the realm of personal property or even to define it as movable property makes it legally impossible that the ownership right of the trustee be limited by any real right of the beneficiary. It could not be otherwise, once the conceptual position of the trustee, as we have just shown, is construed as the full and unlimited owner of the right in trust.

d Obligations of trustees

The criteria which apply to the performance of a trustee's obligations have been developed by centuries of English case law. The new laws have, in

---

[119] Trusts (Guernsey) Law 1989, s. 10; less correct is the Trusts (Jersey) Law 1984, article 9(10): 'The interest of a beneficiary shall constitute movable property', which together with the second part of the Guernsey rule, passed in to the law of Malta, Trusts Act 1988, s. 9(6): 'The interest of a beneficiary under a trust shall constitute movable property, even if the trust property includes immovable property'; (7): 'Subject to the terms of the trust, a beneficiary may, by instrument in writing, sell, charge, transfer or otherwise deal with his interest in any manner' (on this point, the analysis of Matthews and Sowden, §§8.4–8.5 is not satisfactory).

The Guernsey definition has been adopted by other States: see Turks and Caicos, Trust Ordinance 1990, s. 11, which completes the second part: 'Subject to the terms of the trust, may be sold, pledged, charged, or otherwise dealt with in any manner applicable to such property.'

Mauritius, Offshore Trusts Act 1992, s. 20, adopts the completed rule and adds *transferred* (already in the Maltese text); also in Belize, Trusts Act 1992, s. 11, Anguilla, Trusts Ordinance 1994, s. 11, Seychelles, International Trusts Act 1994, s. 19 (which, however, returns to *movable*), and Niue, Trusts Act 1994, s. 12.

[120] Cf. Megarry, *Real Property*, pp. 13–15.

some cases, sought to codify the level and type of diligence required of the trustee, as, for example, in Belize which says a trustee must:

a) act with due diligence; and b) observe the utmost good faith; and c) act to the best of his skills and abilities; and d) exercise the standard of care of a reasonable and prudent man of business.[121]

Other laws, however, have affected civil-law notions which show the influence of conceptual data foreign to trusts: Guernsey cites the diligence of a *'bon père de famille'*,[122] while Malta cites that of the *'bonus paterfamilias'*,[123] both notions unknown in English law. All legal provisions have in common the requirement of the *'utmost good faith'*, an especially high standard of conduct which clearly shows the fiduciary nature of the relationship, and the direction of the trustee's obligations towards the beneficiaries or the realization of the purpose of the trust, and absolutely not towards the settlor.[124] One of the most recent statements, in the law of Mauritius, is worthy of note:

(1) A trustee shall in the exercise of his functions observe the utmost good faith and act: (i) with due diligence; (ii) with care and prudence; (iii) to the best of his ability and skill.
(2) Subject to this Act, a trustee shall execute and administer the trust and exercise his functions (a) in accordance with the terms of the trust; (b) only in the interest of the beneficiaries or in the fulfilment of the purpose of the trust.[125]

Provisions regarding the prohibition against carrying out operations which

---

[121] Belize, Trusts Act 1992, s. 27(1), inspired by the Trusts (Jersey) Law 1984, article 17(1): '(a) act (i) with due diligence; (ii) as would a prudent person; (iii) to the best of his ability and skill; and (b) observe the utmost good faith'. The Belize rule is repeated *verbatim* in Mauritius, Offshore Trusts Act 1992, s. 27(1) and in Anguilla, Trusts Ordinance 1994, s. 27(1).

[122] Trusts (Guernsey) Law 1989, s. 18(1): 'A trustee shall, in the exercise of his functions, observe the utmost good faith and act *en bon père de famille*.'

[123] Malta, Trusts Act 1988, s. 21: 'Trustees shall in the execution of their duties and the exercise of their powers and discretions act with the prudence, diligence and attention of a *bonus paterfamilias* and observe the utmost good faith.'

[124] Trusts (Jersey) Law 1984, article 20(2): 'A trustee shall exercise his powers only in the interest of the beneficiaries and in accordance with the terms of the trust'; adopted in Malta, Trusts Act 1988, s. 21(a)(2) and in Trusts (Guernsey) Law 1989, s. 18(2), which adds 'charitable purposes' to the beneficiaries.
Belize, Trusts Act 1992, s. 27(3) is on the same track: 'A trustee shall owe a fiduciary duty to the beneficiaries of the trust, the members of a class for whose benefit the trust was established, or the purpose for which the trust was established'; adopted in Anguilla, Trusts Ordinance 1994, s. 27(3).

[125] Mauritius, Offshore Trusts Act 1992, s. 35(2), which improves the Guernsey text. The International Trusts Act 1994, s. 26 of the Seychelles is almost identical to the Mauritius law.

are in conflict of interest[126] and the obligation of impartiality,[127] even where they conform to English law, appear to be purely secondary and superfluous.

Once again, it is the same group of countries which lacked any prior rules on trusts (except for Belize, which nonetheless elected to legislate the entire subject matter) which felt the need to set forth other rules which in English law are obvious; for example, that the trustee must hold the trust property in his name, or must, in any event, control it,[128] even if through the use of nominees,[129] that the trust property must be held separate from the trustee's other property and be identifiable as such (and not, it should be noted, identified as such),[130] and so on. The Maltese provision which charges the trustee with the responsibility of checking that the trust is not used to carry out illicit activities, and to report to the authorities if this happens,[131] is of special note.

As always, only case law can give us precise indications of what constitutes a breach of trust: issues relating to the level of diligence to which the trustee is held are not, in and of themselves, conclusive, because 'utmost good faith' has nothing to do with diligence. On this subject, the Court of Appeal of Jersey has rendered a decision of fundamental importance, of which we shall speak a few pages further on.[132]

---

[126] Trusts (Jersey) Law 1984, article 17(4)(b); Malta, Trusts Act 1988, s. 21(3); Trusts (Guernsey) Law 1989, s. 20 adopted in Mauritius, Offshore Trusts Act 1992, s. 29, adopted in Seychelles, International Trusts Act 1994, s. 28; Belize, Trusts Act 1992, s. 27(6) adopted in Anguilla, Trusts Ordinance 1994, s. 27(6).

[127] Trusts (Jersey) Law 1984, article 19; Malta, Trusts Act 1988, s. 23; Trusts (Guernsey) Law 1989, s. 25(1), adopted in Mauritius, Offshore Trusts Act 1992, s. 34, and in Seychelles, International Trusts Act 1994, s. 33; Turks and Caicos, Trust Ordinance 1990, s. 22; Belize, Trusts Act 1992, s. 30; Anguilla, Trusts Ordinance 1994, s. 30.

[128] Trusts (Jersey) Law 1984, article 17(3)(b); the Trusts (Guernsey) Law 1989, s. 19(a) improves on it: the trustee must '(a) ensure that the trust property is held by or vested in him or is otherwise under his control', adopted in Belize, Trusts Act 1992, s. 27(5) and in Anguilla, Trusts Ordinance 1994, s. 27(5).

[129] This explanation appears in the Seychelles, International Trusts Act 1994, s. 27; on the notion of the nominee see above, chapter 3 §3.a.

[130] Trusts (Jersey) Law 1984, article 17(6): 'A trustee shall keep trust property separate from his personal property and separately identifiable from any other property of which he is a trustee. Adopted in Trusts (Guernsey) Law 1989, s. 23; in Mauritius, Offshore Trusts Act 1992, s. 31; in Belize, Trusts Act 1992, s. 27(8); in Seychelles, International Trusts Act 1994, s. 30; and in Anguilla, Trusts Ordinance 1994, s. 27(8).

The civilian idea of the separate estate is echoed in Malta, Trusts Act 1988, s. 3(2): 'The trust property shall be held by the trustee as a separate fund, distinct and separate from that of the trustee.'

[131] Malta, Trusts Act 1988, s. 42.   [132] See below, p. 231.

e Unanimity among trustees

The obligation of trustees always to act together, which comes from English law, was included in the Jersey law and recognized by numerous other States,[133] although, as in English law, they permit the trust instrument to provide that the trustees may adopt majority decisions.[134] The law of the British Virgin Islands, which enacts the principle of majority decisions, is an exception.[135]

f Delegation of trustee powers

As we know, this is a thorny problem in English law, in which the fundamental criterion of personal action by the trustee is eroded, in the case of trusts containing funds to be invested, by the modern necessity of relying on specialists. The laws repeat the general prohibition of the delegation of the trustee's powers,[136] but also recognize the advisability of the trustees' delegating responsibilities of a managerial nature.[137]

The nature of the responsibility which follows on the act of delegation is not well defined in English law, and oscillates between hostility on principle to activities not carried out by the trustee in person and criteria close to those of *culpa in eligendo* and *culpa in vigilando*. The laws of the international model adopt these latter criteria, as is the case of the law of Belize, according to which the trustee is not responsible for the acts of the delegate:

[133] Trusts (Jersey) Law 1984, article 18(1)(2), adopted in Trusts (Guernsey) Law 1989, s. 24(1); in Turks and Caicos, Trust Ordinance 1990, s. 21(1); in Mauritius, Offshore Trusts Act 1992, s. 33(1); in Belize, Trusts Act 1992, s. 29(1); in Anguilla, Trusts Ordinance 1994, s. 29(1); and, for the most part, in Malta, Trusts Act 1988, s. 22.

[134] Trusts (Jersey) Law 1984, article 18(3), adopted in Trusts (Guernsey) Law 1989, s. 28(3)(4); in Turks and Caicos, Trust Ordinance 1990, s. 21(3); in Seychelles, International Trusts Act 1994, s. 32; mostly in Belize, Trusts Act 1992, ss. 29(3) and (5), which establishes the rules of a majority in charitable trusts; the Belize rule is adopted in Anguilla, Trusts Ordinance 1994, ss. 29(3) and (5).

[135] British Virgin Islands, Trustee (Amendment) Act 1993, s. 85; this law treats trustees as a type of board of directors and provides (in s. 87) that a managing trustee may be appointed.

[136] Barbados, Trustee Act 1979, s. 27; Trusts (Jersey) Law 1984, article 21. The Jersey provision was adopted in Malta, Trusts Act 1988, s. 25(1); Turks and Caicos, Trust Ordinance 1990, s. 24(1); Mauritius, Offshore Trusts Act 1992, s. 38(1); Belize, Trusts Act 1992, s. 43(1), adopted in Anguilla, Trusts Ordinance 1994, s. 34(1).

[137] If permitted by the law or the trust instrument: Trusts (Jersey) Law 1984, article 21(2), adopted in Malta, Trusts Act 1988, s. 25(2); in Turks and Caicos, Trust Ordinance 1990, s. 24(2); in Belize, Trusts Act 1992, s. 34(2); in Anguilla, Trusts Ordinance 1994, s. 34(2); in Mauritius, Offshore Trusts Act 1992, s. 38(2), which provides particular forms where the mandate lasts more than twelve months (adopted and extended in Seychelles, International Trusts Act 1994, s. 38). Barbados, Trustee Act 1979, s. 29(1) allows a mandate without limit of time where a trustee must be abroad for over a month; see also Bermuda, Trustee Act 1975, ss. 15 and 17.

provided that the trustee exercised the standard of care of a reasonable and prudent man of business in: (a) the selection of the delegate or appointee; and (b) the supervision of the activities of the delegate or appointee.[138]

g Responsibilities of the trustee

We know that in English law a trustee answers with all his property to third parties and to the beneficiaries (or to whoever may take action to obtain the performance of charitable trusts) with respect to all of obligations contracted for, even if he has declared that he is a trustee. One of the reasons for this, in the area of the relationship between a trustee and third parties, lies in the fact that a trustee is not obliged to introduce himself as such, and that in England the trust property is, by custom or by law, often not specifically identified to third parties.

The severity of this rule goes together with the imprescriptibility of actions against a trustee who is guilty of fraud (within the wide definition which this term has in English equity), and with the prohibition against compensating for losses with profits.

These latter two requirements have been retained in the international trust model, but the nullity of certain clauses of waiver of responsibility has been added, and the force of the former has been weakened, since it would have caused no small problems in the realm of professional trustees.

To begin with this last point, the rule in the Jersey statute is that a third party may look to recover his losses from the trust property alone where

in any transaction or matter affecting a trust a trustee informs another party to the transaction or matter that he is acting as trustee;[139]

otherwise, the trustee responds with all his property. If the obligation is not the result of a breach of trust, he may seek compensation from the trust property.

The imprescriptibility of an action in cases of fraud by the trustee or by a

---

[138] Belize, Trusts Act 1992, s. 34(3), adopted in Anguilla, Trusts Ordinance 1994, s. 34(3).

For other formulations, see Trusts (Jersey) Law 1984, article 28(3): the trustee is not responsible if he has acted 'in good faith and without neglect', adopted in Turks and Caicos, Trust Ordinance 1990, s. 24(3).

Barbados, Trustee Act 1979, s. 29(1) is perhaps closer to English law when it states that the trustee is usually responsible, provided that he has selected the proxy 'in good faith and supervised with a reasonable degree of care'; s. 29(2), on the other hand, calls for responsibility on the part of the trustee wherever the reason for the proxy was the absence of the trustee from the State.

[139] Trusts (Amendment) (Jersey) Law 1984, article 28, as amended in 1989; similarly Malta, Trusts Act 1988, s. 32; Trusts (Guernsey) Law 1989, s. 37; Mauritius, Offshore Trusts Act 1992, s. 48, adopted in Belize, Trusts Act 1992, s. 26(1)(2), and in Anguilla, Trusts Ordinance 1994, ss. 26(1) and (2).

third party with the trustee's assistance, and in cases of an action to re-obtain trust property, is a constant in all the systems under review.[140]

The prohibition against compensating for losses with profits has likewise been generally recognized. The wording most often followed is that of Guernsey:

A trustee may not set off a profit accruing from one breach of trust against a loss or depreciation in value resulting from another.[141]

A trustee is, therefore, protected from claims by third parties provided that he introduces himself as a trustee when he assumes an obligation, but he is not protected from those of beneficiaries. With a view to making the latter duty hard to escape, the Jersey law has sanctioned the nullity of clauses which exonerate or limit the responsibility of a trustee with the following provision, which has been taken up in the laws of other countries:

Nothing in the terms of a trust shall relieve, release or exonerate a trustee from liability for breach of trust arising from his own fraud, wilful misconduct or gross negligence.[142]

The importance of this rule lies, in the first instance, in the use of the notion of fraud, which, as we saw at the beginning of this chapter, has the same range of application as it does in English equity, and, in the second place, in the recourse to 'gross negligence'. This category, which does not appear in the traditional arsenal of common law,[143] has recently been

---

[140] Limiting ourselves to the new laws (because in all the other States it derives from the prior application of English law), see Trusts (Jersey) Law 1984, article 53, adopted in Trusts (Guernsey) Law 1989, s. 71(1); in Turks and Caicos, Trust Ordinance 1990, s. 58(1); in Belize, Trusts Act 1992, s. 56(1); in Nevis, International Exempt Trust Ordinance 1994, s. 20(1); in Anguilla, Trusts Ordinance 1994, s. 56; in Seychelles, International Trusts Act 1994, s. 79; in Niue, Trusts Act 1994, s. 57(1).

Malta, Trusts Act 1988, s. 41(1), did not go as far as sanctioning an imprescribable action, but came very close, providing for a term of thirty years.

On the notion of fraud in Jersey law, see the precedent cited above, footnote 8.

[141] Trusts (Guernsey) Law 1989, s. 34(2), adopted in Mauritius, Offshore Trusts Act 1992, s. 44(2); in Belize, Trusts Act 1992, s. 50(2); in Nevis, International Exempt Trust Ordinance 1994, s.14(2); in Seychelles, International Trusts Act 1994, s. 43(2); in Turks and Caicos, Trust Ordinance 1990, s. 29(2) (clarifying that compensation is allowed where the profit and loss relate to the same unauthorized operation or activity; the same rule may be found in Louisiana, Trust Code, §2203).

The rule in the Trusts (Jersey) Law 1984, article 26(2), substantially adopted in Malta, Trusts Act 1988, s. 30(2), is similar to that of Guernsey.

[142] Trusts (Jersey) Law 1984, article 26(9), added in 1989.

[143] This is another demonstration of how the authorities of European common law have leaked into the Jersey law. The identical provision of the Turks and Caicos, Trust Ordinance 1990, s. 28(10), in fact, omits the word 'gross'.

It is not by chance that none of the four laws which have adopted the Jersey rule *verbatim* are common-law jurisdictions: Trusts (Guernsey) Law 1989, s. 34(7); Mauritius, Offshore Trusts Act 1992, s. 44(4); Malta, Trusts Act 1988, s. 30 added to by the Recogni-

characterized as 'a serious or flagrant degree of negligence'; it does not, however, involve 'any question of intentional or reckless fault'.[144]

FPS was a non-profit English organization which managed a number of pension funds. The government of Jersey entrusted to it the pension fund of employees of a hospital. After some years had passed, the government decided to transfer management of the fund to a local bank, and informed FPS that the passage would take place on December 31, 1988.

It was precisely during this period that the Financial Services Act, which obliged pension funds to enter into contracts containing certain specific clauses with employers, came into force in England. With the transfer of the fund assets imminent, the directors of FPS decided that the Jersey pension fund fell within the ambit of the law, and began preparing the contract. On December 31, they liquidated the fund and deposited the proceeds in an interest-bearing bank account. The preparation of the contract took some time, and was concluded in January, 1989. At the beginning of February, the directors of FPS requested a legal opinion regarding the need for the contract. The opinion was in the negative. They immediately transferred the fund property to the new manager.

The employer and the new trustee of the pension fund commenced an action, claiming that the delay in the delivery of the fund property was a breach of trust, and seeking damages.[145]

The legal problem was a linear one: the instrument establishing the trust (pension fund) exonerated the trustee from responsibility except for 'a breach of trust knowingly and wilfully committed'. For the plaintiffs to prevail, FPS would have had to have committed a breach of trust knowingly and wilfully. No one doubted the good faith of the directors of FPS. The lower court rejected the claim, but the Court of Appeal accepted it for two reasons: in the first place, 'knowingly and wilfully' refers to the conduct from an objective point of view, and not to the knowledge, or lack thereof, that a breach of trust was being committed; in the second place, and in any event, the conduct of the directors of FPS fell within the definition of gross negligence, with regard to which the exoneration clauses were not effective. The gross negligence lay in the fact that the directors did not request a legal opinion on the applicability of the Financial Services Act to a Jersey pension fund immediately.

There is also case law from the Cayman Islands on the question of wilful

tion of Trusts Act 1994; Seychelles, International Trusts Act 1994, s. 43(4).

In Scotland, respecting the civil-law tradition, it is held that the exoneration clause does not cover the *culpa lata*: Wilson and Duncan, p. 460.

I believe that the first use of the term 'gross negligence' in English judicial terminology was in *Pass v. Dundas* (1880) (at p. 666).

[144] *Midland Bank v. Federated Pension Services* (1995) (1994 in the lower court). It is significant that the Jersey court took its position from Scottish precedents, that is, from a system with strong civil law antecedents (on Scotland, see below, chapter 5 §3.a). Cf. R. Nobles, 'Trustees' Exclusion Clauses in Jersey and England', in 10 TLI (1996) 66.

[145] If the funds had been invested on the Stock Exchange, it would have enjoyed a substantially greater increase in value than that provided by interest received from the bank where they had been deposited while awaiting transfer to the new manager.

default which substantially adheres to the civil law notion which equates *dolus* with '*culpa lata*'. The wilful default was seen in the reckless lack of care towards the interests of the beneficiaries, and in particular the mainte- nance of the property which was the subject of the trust.[146] As with the Jersey precedent, any enquiry into the aims of the trustee or, more than ever, into his awareness of being in breach, is of no importance.[147]

h Third parties contracting with a trustee; participants in a trustee's breach

Third parties who contract with a trustee are exposed to responsibility, to the extent of being held to be constructive trustees if the trustee is breach- ing the provisions of the trust and they know of this. The requirement of knowledge, as we know, has been the subject of partially contrasting pronouncements in England.

These are two issues which have common borders, but which are distinct cases. On the one hand, there is the person who contracts with a breaching trustee without deriving any specific advantage from the transaction, but who objectively speaking makes himself an instrument of the breach. On the other hand, there is the person who actually profits from the breach.

The Jersey law treats the first hypothesis as follows:

A bona fide purchaser for value without actual notice of any breach of trust: (a) may deal with a trustee in relation to trust property as if the trustee was the beneficial owner of the trust property; and (b) shall not be affected by the trusts on which such property is held.[148]

It does not, however, go into detail on the notion of 'notice', which is central to the determination of the responsibility of persons contracting with a trustee. The Turks and Caicos law takes advantage of developments in English case law, and deals with this issue, but it does not have any imitators.[149]

---

[146] *Beesham Ramdin's Estate* (1994).

[147] For a similar position in Italian law, see G. Ferri Jr, 'Le deleghe interne', in B. Libonati (ed.), *Amministrazione e amministratori di società per azioni*, Milan, 1995, pp. 175ff., para- graph 4.

[148] Trusts (Jersey) Law 1984, article 51(1), adopted in Malta, Trusts Act 1988, s. 40, in Trusts (Guernsey) Law 1989, s. 69, in Turks and Caicos, Trust Ordinance 1990, s. 56, in Mauritius, Offshore Trusts Act 1992, s. 76.

[149] Turks and Caicos, Trust Ordinance 1990, s. 56(3) 'A person who deals with a trustee shall not be personally liable in respect of any breach of trust on the part of the trustee, unless, in respect of that dealing, that person: (a) has actual knowledge of the breach of trust; or (b) wilfully disregards circumstances which would cause an honest and reason- able person to conclude, on a balance of probabilities, that a breach of trust exists; or (c) would have actual knowledge of the breach of trust if he made the enquiries which would be made in the circumstances by an honest and reasonable man.'

As regards the second issue, there are two series of provisions, one based on Jersey law and the other on Guernsey law: the latter has been further revised by the law of Belize, which, in conformity with English law, states that notice may be 'actual, constructive, implied'.[150]

i Constructive trusts and the form of the trust instrument

Maltese law is the only one which, after the provisions described above, makes no other statement on the matter. The omission is understandable, because the constructive trust, since it is the 'heart' of the trust, does not lend itself to being included in a reality which is distant from those values which formed the basis of the history of equity.

Jersey and Guernsey must be given credit, therefore, (and others have, perhaps unnecessarily followed them) for having taken the courageous step of declaring that the list of constructive trusts is still open:

This section does not exclude any other circumstances in which a constructive trust may arise.[151]

There is a link between this opening of the category and the rules on the form of the trust instrument.

First, Jersey:

(1) [except for unit trusts] a trust may come into existence in any manner; (2) a trust may come into existence by oral declaration, or by an instrument in writing (including a will or codicil) or arise by conduct.[152]

But later, and above all, Guernsey:

---

[150] Trusts (Jersey) Law 1984, article 29(1): 'where a person (in this article referred to as a constructive trustee) makes or receives any profit, gain, or advantage from a breach of trust he shall be deemed to be a trustee of that profit, gain, or advantage' provided that he is (2) 'a bona fide purchaser of property for value and without notice of the breach of trust'; adopted in Malta, Trusts Act 1988, s. 33(1), where it was clarified who might hold himself to be beneficiary of the constructive trust, and where 'onerous title' is used instead of 'for value'; the first part of the Jersey rule was also adopted in Turks and Caicos, Trust Ordinance 1990, s. 32(1); the second part was used in a reformulated version.
      Trusts (Guernsey) Law 1989, s. 38(1): 'A person who derives a profit from a breach of trust, or who obtains property in breach of trust, shall be deemed to be a trustee of the profit or property, unless he derives or obtains it in good faith and without notice of the breach of trust'; adopted in Mauritius, Offshore Trusts Act 1992, s. 49(1); in Seychelles, International Trusts Act 1994, s. 48(1) adopted in Belize, Trusts Act 1992, s. 51(1), which adds: 'without any actual, constructive or implied notice', and in Nevis, International Exempt Trust Ordinance 1994, s. 15(4), and in Anguilla, Trusts Ordinance 1994, s. 51(1).

[151] Trusts (Guernsey) Law 1989, s. 38(3); adopted in Mauritius, Offshore Trusts Act 1992, s. 49(3), in Belize, Trusts Act 1992, s. 5(3), in Nevis, International Exempt Trust Ordinance 1994, s. 15(3), in Anguilla, Trusts Ordinance 1994, s. 51(3). Similarly Trusts (Jersey) Law 1984, article 29(4).

[152] Trusts (Jersey) Law 1984, article 7(1); adopted in Turks and Caicos, Trust Ordinance 1990, s. 7(2).

A trust other than a unit trust may be created by oral declaration, or by an instrument in writing (including a will or codicil), by conduct, by operation of law, or in any other manner whatsoever.[153]

This lays down the essential conditions of the trust as an open institution. Jersey had already taken a major step when it referred to 'conduct', even though it was more suited to identifying implied trusts than constructive trusts. Guernsey completed the move by adding 'by operation of law'. In any event, both clearly indicate that the list is not closed, since they include, either at the beginning or the end 'in any manner'.[154]

To sweep away any remaining doubt, the law of Belize states as follows with regard to express trusts:

No formalities or technical expressions are required for the creation of a trust provided that the intention of the settlor to create a trust is clearly manifested.[155]

Here too, Malta has paid for its civil heritage. When it stated that a trust may be created only by will or other written deed,[156] it made evident the limits of its attachment to the international trust model, just as it did when, while recognizing constructive trusts in typical hypothetical situations, it did not admit that the list was still open. Mauritius takes a half-way stance, often, and not by coincidence, in the company of Malta and the Seychelles. Mauritius, like the other two, adopted the rules on constructive trusts completely, but then was unable to accept that a trust might arise 'by conduct', or even 'in any manner'. It accepted an oral form of trust, but insisted on registration in every case.[157]

There are three poles: the open list of constructive trusts, freedom of form and the fiduciary obligations of the trustee. None of them enjoys an existence completely independent of the other two, and one or two of them alone are not sufficient to identify either the structure of the English trust

---

[153] Trusts (Guernsey) Law 1989, s. 6; adopted in Belize, Trusts Act 1992, s. 5(1), in Nevis, International Exempt Trust Ordinance 1994, s. 44(1), and in Anguilla, Trusts Ordinance 1994, s. 5(1).

[154] It may be that the new laws have overdone the anti-formalism. Barbados realized this, and now requires a writing for international trusts: International Trusts Act 1995, s. 5; a writing is also required in Belize where the subject matter of the trust is real property located within the State: Trusts Act 1992, s. 5(4): 'A trust (other than a trust by operation of law) respecting land situated in Belize shall be unenforceable unless evidenced in writing'; adopted in Anguilla, Trusts Ordinance 1994, s. 5(4) and in Niue, Trusts Act 1994, s. 6(3).

[155] Belize, Trusts Act 1992, s. 5(3), which adopts, and improves, Trusts (Guernsey) Law 1989, s. 6(3). The Belize rule is adopted in Nevis, International Exempt Trust Ordinance 1994, s. 44(2), and Trusts Ordinance 1994, s. 5(3).

[156] Malta, Trusts Act 1988, s. 7(1): 'will or other instrument'.

[157] Mauritius, Offshore Trusts Act 1992, s. 16: 'An offshore trust (a) may be created by an oral declaration, or by an instrument in writing, a will or codicil' and must be registered; adopted in Seychelles, International Trusts Act 1994, s. 15.

model or, from this fundamental point of view, the international model in its closest configuration to the system of equity.

j Tracing

Those same legal systems which have adopted the constructive trust by legislation or which, where adoption is not necessary, have seen fit to include it among the provisions of their new laws, have also undertaken to provide a legislative formulation of the principles of equitable tracing. Tracing, as we know, is not an action, but a probative technique which leads to the identification of an asset, or the asset into which a prior asset has been transformed, in the hands of the person who will, as a result, be considered a constructive trustee.[158] From a practical legal viewpoint, however, tracing appears to be an autonomous procedural remedy, and it is this view which emerges from the Guernsey law, which improved upon the wording of the earlier Jersey law, and has therefore been held as the model to be reproduced:

Without prejudice to the personal liability of a trustee, trust property which has been charged or dealt with in breach of trust, or any property into which it has been converted, may be followed and recovered unless (a) it is no longer identifiable; or (b) it is in the hands of a bona fide purchaser for value without actual, constructive or implied notice of the breach of trust or a person (other then the trustee) who derived title through such a purchaser.[159]

k *Cy-près* in charitable trusts

The theory of *cy-près* is of fundamental relevance in the regulation of charitable trusts in all cases where the purpose desired by the settlor is, or later becomes, partly or entirely unrealizable. The rules which have evolved in England are rather complex, and are in need of rationalization. The Turks and Caicos legislature has seen to this, extending the rules to all trusts for purposes, and other countries have drawn inspiration from its example.[160]

---

[158] See above, chapter 2 §4.b.

[159] Trusts (Guernsey) Law 1989, s. 67; adopted in Malta, Trusts Act 1988, s. 40(A)(1) supplemented by the Recognition of Trusts Act 1994 (but without letter (a) and with 'alienated' instead of 'charged'); and in Belize, Trusts Act 1992, s. 52(1) (but without the final words). The Belize rule has been adopted in Nevis, International Exempt Trust Ordinance 1994, s. 16, and in Anguilla, Trusts Ordinance 1994, s. 52(1). The Guernsey law has also been adopted in Mauritius, Offshore Trusts Act 1992, s. 74, which defines the various hypotheses more effectively. This has in turn been adopted in the Seychelles, International Trusts Act 1994, s. 72.

See also, similarly, Trusts (Jersey) Law 1984, article 50(3).

[160] Turks and Caicos, Trust Ordinance 1990, s. 42; adopted in Mauritius, Offshore Trusts Act 1992, s. 65; mostly adopted in Belize, Trusts Act 1992, s. 45(1), which in turn has been

l Protective trusts

Before the English Trustee Act of 1925, the protective trust required special professional skills of the drafter of the trust instrument; after 1925 it was sufficient to refer to the law. This is also the case in countries which passed comprehensive trust laws after 1925.[161]

Protective trusts are a type of trust of noteworthy importance in the area of trusts of a family nature; the category has, therefore, been expressly provided for in the new laws.[162] In English law, a protective trust cannot be in favour of the settlor; this limitation has been removed by Belize, whose initiative has enjoyed a certain following.[163]

m Resulting trusts

The most common case of resulting trust arises when the provisions of the trust instrument cannot be carried out. The trustee, to whom the right was in any case transferred (the distinction between the act of creation and the act of transfer must be recalled here), does not lose his status, but the trust results to the benefit of the settlor, who may obtain its immediate termination.[164]

This extremely technical rule of English law may be found in the new laws, starting from that of Jersey, but with a singular difference: each of the six States which have taken it up has modified it in some way.[165]

adopted in Nevis, International Exempt Trust Ordinance 1994, s. 11(1); in brief also in Malta, Trusts Act 1988, s. 16(2).

The legislators of Barbados, International Trusts Act 1995, s. 14(1), do an effective job, but have the benefit of a Trustee Act of 1979 modelled after the English Trustee Act of 1925: 'Where a trust is created for a non-charitable purpose, the terms of the trust may provide that the doctrine of *cy-près* is, *mutatis mutandis*, applicable thereto.'

[161] Cyprus, Trustee Law, 1955; British Virgin Islands, Trustee Ordinance 1961, s. 32; Cayman Islands, Trust Law 1967, s. 31; Bermuda, Trustee Act 1975, s. 25; Barbados, Trustee Act 1979, s. 37. Not in the Bahamas, however, where the law dates from 1893.

[162] Trusts (Jersey) Law 1984, article 31; adopted in Turks and Caicos, Trust Ordinance 1990, s. 34; adopted (but simplified) in Malta, Trusts Act 1988, s. 13, taken from the Recognition of Trusts Act 1994. Cook Islands, International Trusts Amendment Act 1989, s. 13F, modified by the International Trusts Amendment (No. 2) Act 1989. Trusts (Guernsey) Law 1989, s. 40, adopted in Mauritius, Offshore Trusts Act 1992, s. 51, and in Seychelles, International Trusts Act 1994, s. 50.

[163] Belize, Trusts Act 1992, s. 12; adopted in Anguilla, Trusts Ordinance 1994, s. 12; partially adopted in Nevis, International Exempt Trust Ordinance 1994, s. 6.

[164] See above, chapter 2 §3.a.

[165] Trusts (Jersey) Law 1984, article 10(6): the assets will be 'held by the trustee in trust for the settlor absolutely or if he is dead for his personal representative', but the article deals only with certain cases of nullity; in other cases, the owner of the asset is not considered a trustee (see also s. 45 for the case of a foreign trust which cannot be recognized); Malta, Trusts Act 1988, s. 16(1); Trusts (Guernsey) Law 1989, s. 11(5); Belize, Trusts Act 1992, s. 7(5), adopted in Nevis International Exempt Trust Ordinance 1994, s. 23(4).

Malta, Trusts Act 1988, s. 15(2), extends this to the case of revocation of a trust.

n Bringing forward the date of termination of a trust

Here too English law is clear: if all the beneficiaries have legal capacity and wish to bring a trust to an early end, the trustee may not oppose their wishes.

The rule was first formulated in the Turks and Caicos law, and later followed by others:

Notwithstanding the terms of the trust, where all the beneficiaries are in existence and have been ascertained and none are minors or persons other than minors who under the law of the Islands or of their domicile do not have legal capacity, they may require the trustee to terminate the trust and distribute the trust property among them.[166]

The Cook Islands law of 1994 takes the opposite position, and so favours the settlor: if he has decided that the trust income should be accumulated and not distributed for a certain period, the wishes of the beneficiaries are of no effect.[167] This difference derives from the extremely unusual legislative practice of this country, of which we shall soon find other examples.

o Definition of trust

I have left the definition of the trust until last: it leads us to the second part of this discussion, where we shall see solutions which show originality when compared to those of English law.

The definition of the trust is *in between*, because, like all definitions in common law – and perhaps not only in common law – it has a modicum of regulatory contents. In the specific arena of trusts, furthermore, we have seen how although analyses may be made and conceptual reconstruction attempted, definitions may be proposed only with great difficulty and much caution.

There are two specific problems that make a definition of the international trust model difficult. Firstly, one is attempting to define a concept for people who are not familiar with the concept of 'trusts' in general. Secondly, the existence of the Hague Convention – the initial engine of the 'race for the trust' – also complicates such a definition.

The Convention defines or describes the trust in article 2,[168] and in

---

[166] Turks and Caicos, Trust Ordinance 1990, s. 43(3); adopted for the most part in Belize, Trusts Act 1992, s. 47, but with a new requirement: the beneficiary of a protective trust may not bring about the early termination of the trust. The Belize rule has been adopted in Nevis, International Exempt Trust Ordinance 1994, s. 31, in Anguilla, Trusts Ordinance 1994, s. 47 and in Niue, Trusts Act 1994, s. 48.

A different formulation of this rule was to be found in Malta, Trusts Act 1988, s. 13, which was repealed by the Recognition of Trusts Act 1994 and inserted in shorter form into s. 17(3).   [167] Cook Islands, International Trusts Act 1984, s. 10.

[168] See below, chapter 6 §1.d.

chapter 6 we shall show why it does not refer to the English trust model, but to an amorphous trust which is a creation of the Convention itself. I shall provide only two facts at this early stage: first, that article 2 finds a trust even where the act of transfer to the trustee is lacking, it being sufficient for the Convention that the trust property be placed 'under the control' of the trustee;[169] and second, that the Convention makes no provision for constructive or resulting trusts, because, although it meant to make reference to them, it identifies a completely different category, which is that of trusts created pursuant to a judgment.[170]

The definitions in the new laws are all influenced by article 2, albeit to differing degrees.

At one extreme we find Bermuda, which repeats article 2 of the Convention *verbatim*,[171] and Barbados, which (very reasonably, it must be recognized) elects to omit the phrase 'by deed *inter vivos* or on death' from a text which in all other respects repeats that of the Convention word for word.[172] By adhering to the definition in the Convention, which is very far from the English model, Bermuda and Barbados have either revolutionized their trust law or carried out a purely cosmetic operation. In support of the latter it must be considered that the Barbados law only concerns international trusts, while domestic trusts are still regulated by the prior law of 1979, which is modelled on English law.

The British Virgin Islands take an intermediate position. Having repeated the Convention rule, and evidently come to the realization that their trust law was about to be revolutionized, they understood that they needed to add the rider that by 'trust' was also meant implied, constructive and resulting trusts.[173]

The dominant position, however, is the one which passed from Jersey to Malta, Guernsey, Turks and Caicos, Belize, Mauritius, Nevis, the Seychelles and Anguilla. According to the Guernsey format:

A trust exists where a person (a 'trustee') holds or has vested in him, or is deemed to hold or have vested in him, property which does not form, or which has ceased to form, part of his own estate: (a) for the benefit of any person ('a beneficiary')

---

[169] The reader may recall that I believe that trusts have as their subject matter the rights of the trustee, and not the assets which are the object of these rights. In the text, I am following the terminology of the Convention.

[170] If my readers will recall the discussion at the end of chapter 2 on the US position, which sees the constructive trust as a remedy to unjust enrichment, they will understand the origins of the provision of the Convention.

[171] Bermuda, Trusts (Special Provisions) Act 1989, s. 2(1) and s. 2(2).

[172] Barbados, International Trusts Act 1995, s. 3.

[173] British Virgin Islands, Trustee (Amendment) Act 1993, s. 2(2)–s. 2(5).

whether or not yet ascertainable or in existence; or (b) for any valid charitable or non-charitable purpose which is not for the benefit only of the trustee.[174]

For the sake of convenience I shall quote the first part of article 2 of the Hague Convention from the official English text:

the term 'trust' refers to the legal relationship created *inter vivos* or on death by a person, the settlor, when assets have been placed under the control of a trustee for the benefit of a beneficiary or for a specified purpose.

A comparison of the two definitions leads to a number of considerations:

(a) Guernsey does not mention the settlor; this is the only way it could correctly include constructive and resulting trusts, which, as we know, do not require a settlor, in the definition;

(b) as a result, Guernsey mentions neither a transfer nor the assumption of control, but rather, with technical precision, the vesting in the trustee, that is, the mechanism which we saw as typical in the acquisition of an estate;

(c) following the wording of article 2 to the letter, Guernsey then uses 'estate' in the other sense of the term, that of 'property', and states that the property does not form part of the trustee's 'own estate'; it therefore becomes part of the trustee's estate – because otherwise the law would have read 'does not form part of his estate' – but under special circumstances: this shows the segregation of the subject matter of the trust.

4. Structural elements of the model: new *regulae*

Up until now, we have seen the similarities between the international model and the English model. I shall now try to identify the rules of the international model which differ from those of the English model. On occasions, they will contradict the corresponding English rule, on others they will be improvements, and on yet others, they will be innovations, such as the compulsory registration of trusts.[175] In each case, however, there is a common thread: the diverse social features of the recipients of the rules and the diverse objectives of the legislators. We shall see the emerg-

---

[174] Trusts (Guernsey) Law 1989, s. 1. The Jersey formulation, which is only slightly different, was adopted in Malta, Trusts Act 1988, s. 3(1), which added 'in the name or under the control' of the trustee to be in conformity with the text of the Convention.

The Guernsey definition has been adopted with formal modifications of no significance by Turks and Caicos, Trust Ordinance 1990, s. 3; Belize, Trusts Act 1992, s. 2; Nevis, International Exempt Trust Ordinance 1994, s. 53; Anguilla, Trusts Ordinance 1994, s. 3. With more substantial modifications it has been adopted by Mauritius, Offshore Trusts Act 1992, s. 4; and by Seychelles, International Trusts Act 1994, s. 2 (in the definitions).

[175] Provided for in Barbados, the Cayman Islands, the Cook Islands, Malta, Mauritius, Nevis, Niue, the Seychelles and Western Samoa; it is optional in Anguilla.

ence of a cohesive design and of an institution which may be looked at from more than one point of view: for example, as an adaptation of the English traditional trust to the needs of the international business community, as a reaction against the restrictions of civil-law systems in the area of family and succession, or as a functional alternative to traditional instruments, which the increased awareness of national tax legislation has brought to a crisis point.

Each of these interpretations may be maintained.

a Applicable law of the trust

Under article 6 of the Hague Convention, the applicable law of a trust is that intended by the settlor. This intention may be made explicit in the trust instrument; if it is not, it must be deduced by interpreting the instrument, and, if necessary, from the circumstances of the case.

If the intention of the settlor, as determined at the conclusion of this procedure, indicates a legal system which does not recognize the trust or the particular type of trust in question, article 7 states that the trust will be regulated by the law with which it has the closest ties. To this end, the elements to be taken into consideration are left to the court, but the Convention lists four to which the court must pay special attention: the place where the settlor has indicated the trust should be administered, the place where the trust property is located, the place of residence or the domicile of the trustee, and the purpose of the trust and the place where it is to be carried out.

Private international law of common-law States remains, as we know, far from making such clear statements;[176] it is understandable, therefore, that no less than thirteen States rushed to make them their own. Some adopted the text to the letter, either that of article 6 (thus retaining more freedom in evaluating the 'circumstances of the case' where the wishes of the settlor are neither express nor implicit),[177] or that of both articles 6

---

[176] See above, chapter 3 §2.m.

[177] Cayman Islands, Trusts (Foreign Element) Law 1987, s. 4: 'In determining the governing law of an international trust regard shall first be had to the terms of the trust and to any evidence therein as to the intention of the parties [note the plural]; and the other circumstances of an international trust may be taken into account only if the terms of the trust fail to provide such evidence'; adopted in Cook Islands, International Trusts Amendment Act 1989, s. 13G; in Bahamas, Trusts (Choice of Governing Law) Act 1989, s. 6; and in Anguilla, Trusts Ordinance 1994, s. 61(1).

Equally limited to the rule in article 6 are Trusts (Jersey) Law 1984, article 4 (supplemented in 1991: cf. Matthews and Sowden, §§4.5–4.12): 'The proper law of the trust shall be the law of the jurisdiction (a) expressed by the terms of the trust as the proper law; or failing that (b) intended by the settlor as the proper law; or failing either (c) with which

and 7.[178] Others have adapted the rules stated in the articles, and have tried to improve on their wording[179] or to revise them so as to favour local law.[180] Others have passed a law which limits itself to reproducing the text of the Convention, but with certain significant omissions (which do not, however, concern the choice of applicable law).[181]

With respect to the possibility that certain aspects of a trust might be regulated by a different law (article 9), and that the applicable law may be changed (article 10), there is general compliance. Furthermore, modification of the applicable law touches a nerve which is especially sensitive for many of the States involved in the 'race for the trust': the so-called 'flee clause', which is also used in corporate by-laws for cases where the political situation in a State of which a company is a national makes it advisable for the shareholders to move elsewhere. The rule contained in the text of the Convention was immediately accepted by the new laws, which have followed in the wake of the Cayman Islands law of 1987 and frequently made it explicit that 'migration' is acceptable only where it does not lead to the invalidity of clauses of the trust instrument or regarding the rights of the beneficiaries, or, more generally, where the new law recognizes the validity of the trust in question.[182] The Cayman Islands have recently returned to

---

the trust at the time it was created had the closest connection'; and Trusts (Guernsey) Law 1989, s. 3, adopted in Mauritius, Offshore Trusts Act 1992, s. 7. Jersey later amended the law to add the criteria in article 7 of the Convention: see the following footnote.

[178] Bermuda, Trusts (Special Provisions) Act 1989, ss. 5 and 6; Turks and Caicos, Trust Ordinance 1990, s. 4(1) and (2); Trusts (Amendment No. 2) (Jersey) Law 1991 s. 1(3); Barbados, International Trusts Act 1995, s. 8(1); Mauritius, Offshore Trusts Act 1992, s. 7; Belize, Trusts Act 1992, s. 4(1) and 4(2); British Virgin Islands, Trustee (Amendment) Act 1993, s. 80(1); Nevis, International Exempt Trust Ordinance 1994, s. 4; Seychelles, International Trusts Act 1994, s. 6.

Malta, Trusts Act 1988, s. 5(2), supplemented by the Recognition of Trusts Act 1994, refers directly to the Convention.

See, in any event, the following footnotes.

[179] Turks and Caicos, Trust Ordinance 1990, s. 4 omits the paragraph from article 6 of the Convention, so that the criteria of article 7 of the Convention become a specification of the 'circumstances of the case' with which the first sub-paragraph of article 6 concludes.

[180] Belize, Trusts Act 1992, s. 4 (1)(c): if the law so defined 'does not provide for trusts or the category of trusts involved, then the proper law of the trust shall be the law of Belize', adopted in Nevis, International Exempt Trust Ordinance 1994, s. 4.

Barbados, International Trusts Act 1995, s. 8(1), puts the third criterion of article 7 of the Convention (residence or domicile of the trustee) first.

[181] This is the case in Hong Kong, Recognition of Trusts Ordinance 1989, which is the statutory instrument enforcing the Convention, less, *inter alia*, article 13.

[182] The change of the applicable law is generally permitted by the Trusts (Jersey) Law 1984, article 37, adopted in Trusts (Guernsey) Law 1989, s. 46e, and in Mauritius, Offshore Trusts Act 1992, s.7(3); only a change to a foreign jurisdiction is permitted by the Turks and Caicos, Trust Ordinance 1990, s. 40 provided that '(a) the change cannot invalidate

the problem to permit the expatriation of a trust even if the new applicable law permits a trust period which is shorter than that provided for by Cayman Islands law.[183]

To conclude, as far as determination of the applicable law is concerned, the international trust model conforms to the methods provided for by articles 6, 7, 9 and 10 of the Hague Convention.

b The applicable law of the creation of the trust

The applicable law of a trust determines its validity (article 8 of the Convention). Given that, as we shall see in more detail below, questions relating to the validity of wills or other juridical acts on the basis of which certain property is transferred to a trustee are not part of the Convention (article 4), the term 'validity of a trust' must mean the validity of the act by which the trust is created.

The capacity of a settlor to establish a trust is not dealt with separately by the Convention, probably because it was felt that it should be submitted to the same law which regulates the validity of the trust (we shall discuss this at the appropriate time).

The law of the Cook Islands was the first to confront this issue, and was also the most radical:

A trust registered under this Act shall be a valid trust notwithstanding that it may be invalid according to the law of the settlor's domicile or residence or place of current incorporation.[184]

any other terms of the trust, any purpose of the trust and any interest of a beneficiary; and (b) the change is consistent with the intention of the settlor'; this is also permitted by the Bermuda, Trusts (Special Provisions) Act 1989, s. 6(2), provided that the foreign law recognizes the validity of the trust; a change in either direction, with the exception of clauses which might conflict with the new law, is permitted by Belize, Trusts Act 1992, s. 4(5) and (6), adopted in Nevis International Exempt Trust Ordinance 1994, s. 4(5) and (6) and in Niue, Trusts Act 1994, s. 5(5) and (6); it is allowed provided that the jurisdiction from which the trust comes permits it (where it is coming into the State) or where the new jurisdiction permits it and recognizes the interests of the beneficiaries (where it is leaving the State) in: Cayman Islands, Trusts (Foreign Element) Law 1987, s. 4(4), adopted in Bahamas, Trusts (Choice of Governing Law) Act 1989, s. 5, in Cyprus, International Trusts Law 1992, s. 9, British Virgin Islands, Trustee (Amendment) Act 1993, s. 81, Anguilla, Trusts Ordinance 1994, s. 61(4), Seychelles, International Trusts Act 1994, s. 6(3) and (4), Isle of Man, Trusts Act 1995, s. 3, and Barbados, International Trusts Act 1995, s. 8(2) and (3).

[183] Cayman Islands, Perpetuities Law 1995, s. 14. This provision was necessary because, as we shall see below, the law of the Cayman Islands allows a longer duration than any other law (except those which permit perpetual trusts).

[184] Cook Islands, International Trusts Act 1984 s. 5(2), adopted in Nevis, International Exempt Trust Ordinance 1994, s. 3(1).
   The law continues with s. 5(3): 'In determining the existence and validity of a trust

Two solutions presented themselves. States, like Bermuda, introduced a general rule about the capacity to establish a trust. This laid emphasis on the law of the settlor in testamentary trusts.[185] The majority of States, however, considered only those trusts regulated by their own law and made it govern questions regarding the capacity of the settlor as well: they selected differing criteria to regulate private-international aspects of the *act of transfer*, which we shall discuss in the next section.

The Cook Islands abandoned its extremist position in the area of establishment of the trust, and in 1989 aligned itself with the generally accepted position.[186] Bermuda, in spite of its general rules on capacity to establish a trust, provided that questions relating to the capacity of the settlor of a Bermuda trust should be determined on the basis of local law.[187] Guernsey, followed by Mauritius and the Seychelles, adopted a more liberal system, and provided for the use of either the local law (which regulates the trust), or that of the domicile or nationality of the settlor, or the law which regulates the transfer: accordingly, a trust is validly established if the settlor has the capacity to establish it in the eyes of one of these laws.[188]

For the international trust model, the capacity to *establish* a trust is regulated by the same law as that which regulates the trust.

c The applicable law of the transfer to the trustee

The most complex issues emerge when one looks at the act of transfer, with regard to which, as we have seen, the Hague Convention offers no guidance.

The Guernsey rule which we have just cited on the subject of the capacity to establish a trust also deals with capacity to effect the transfer, which is subject to one of the four laws described in the rule, among which is that of the settlor's domicile. Jersey has adopted only the last of these.[189]

registered under this Act the Court shall apply: (a) the provisions of this Act; and (b) any other law of the Cook Islands; and (c) any other law, which would be applied; if to do so would validate the trust.'

[185] Bermuda, Trusts (Special Provisions) Act 1989, s. 10(1): Bermuda law is applied in the case of a trust *inter vivos* of movables; the law of the testator's domicile is applied in the case of a testamentary trust of movables; and the *lex rei sitae* is applied in the case of a testamentary trust of immovables; adopted in Barbados, International Trusts Act 1995, s. 15 and partially in Isle of Man, Trusts Act 1995, s. 1. See also Belize, Trusts Act 1992, s. 7 (2)(b)(iv) and 9(1): capacity is regulated by the law of Belize; adopted in Niue, Trusts Act 1994, s. 8(2)(b)(iv).

[186] Cook Islands, International Trusts Amendment Act 1989, s. 13H.

[187] Bermuda, Trusts (Special Provisions) Act 1989, s. 10(2), again followed by Barbados.

[188] Trusts (Guernsey) (Amendment) Law 1990, s. 11A(1)(b); Mauritius, Offshore Trusts Act 1992, s. 11(2)(b), adopted in Seychelles, International Trusts Act 1994, s. 10(2)(b).

[189] Trusts (Amendment) (Jersey) Law 1989, s. 8A(2)(a): the capacity to transfer to a trust is regulated by the law of the domicile of the settlor if he is not domiciled in Jersey;

The solution applied by the majority is more detailed. In principle, issues of both capacity and validity of the transfer are subject to the law which governs the trust, but as far as the latter are concerned, the foreign law indicated by specific connecting criteria will prevail.

This system was adopted by the law of the Cayman Islands:

> All questions arising in regard to a trust which is for the time being governed by the laws of the Islands or in regard to any disposition of property upon the trusts thereof, including, without prejudice to the generality of the foregoing, questions as to: (i) the capacity of any settlor; (ii) any aspects of the validity of the trust or disposition or the interpretation or effects thereof; (. . .) are to be determined according to the laws of the Islands, without reference to the laws of any other jurisdictions with which the trust or disposition may be connected, provided only that . . .

and the specific link with the jurisdiction, which I shall now discuss, follow.[190]

The local law, which is the applicable law of the trust, is, therefore, competent in principle to regulate every aspect both of the trust and of the disposition, but recognizes exceptions to this basic principle. These are: title of the settlor to the right transferred; the capacity of a transferring company (by capacity in this context it is intended that the doctrine of *ultra vires* be applied, *viz.* compliance with the corporate purpose) which is left to the law of the place of incorporation of the company; the form of the transfer; the validity of the deed of transfer of real property, which is left to the *lex rei sitae*; and the validity of a will or a testamentary disposition, which is left to the law of the testator's domicile.[191]

Both the general rules and the exceptions are, however, subject to such different intentions as may be expressed by the settlor.

This set of rules has been very widely applied.[192]

It seems to me that we may conclude that the international trust model

adopted in British Virgin Islands, Trustee (Amendment) Act 1993, s. 83(1) and, although not *verbatim*, in Cyprus, International Trusts Law 1992, s. 3(1); it should be noted that the domestic law of Cyprus recognizes the rights of the heirs, so that the final part of s. 3 (i) reads: 'The law relating to inheritance or succession in force in the Republic or in any other country shall not affect in any way the transfer or disposition referred to above or the validity of the International Trust.'

[190] Cayman Islands, Trusts (Foreign Element) Law 1987, s. 5, first part.
[191] Cayman Islands, Trusts (Foreign Element) Law 1987, s. 5, second part.
[192] Bahamas, Trusts (Choice of Governing Law) Act 1989, s. 7; Cook Islands, International Trusts Amendment Act 1989, s. 13H; Bermuda, Trusts (Special Provisions) Act 1989, s. 10(2); Turks and Caicos, Trust Ordinance 1990, s. 13(1); Anguilla, Trusts Ordinance 1994, s. 62(1); Barbados, International Trusts Act 1995, ss. 16 and 17; Isle of Man, Trusts Act 1995, s. 4.

leaves to foreign law substantial and formal questions of validity of the transfer of a right to a trust by a foreign settlor (or a settlor who is subject to a foreign law), while the solution regarding issues of capacity is less certain. As we shall immediately see, unanimity is retrieved when it comes to ratifying limits to the application of a foreign law.

d Limits of application of foreign laws or judgments

Jersey, although attaching capacity to the law of the domicile, made no reference to the law applicable to the transfer to the trustee, and so the usual rules of private international law remained in force. In many cases, they led to the same result as the specific requirements of the Cayman Islands law just referred to: the application of a foreign law to the act of transfer or some of its aspects.

In the years immediately following the signing of the Hague Convention and the emergence of the new laws, the serious difficulties which the application of foreign laws involved came to light: on the one hand, the limits which many jurisdictions, both civil and religious, placed on the freedom to dispose of assets gratuitously, *inter vivos* and by will; on the other, property rights which are recognized with increasing frequency in favour of a spouse; and, finally, creditor-protection laws.

There is no doubt that the private international principles of the international trust model which we have seen up until now lead, or may lead, to the application of a foreign law in the areas which we have described above. This result was unacceptable for everyone, and so the only answer was to declare that foreign law was inapplicable in the above areas, even if it was prescribed by the rules of conflict of laws.

The Jersey law of 1989, which has had only one imitator, deals exclusively with foreign laws on hereditary succession;[193] that of Guernsey, which has two imitators, adds a provision which crosses over specific areas, and deals with a nullity which may be imposed by a foreign law which does not recognize the trust as an institution.[194] This is not a novelty, since it was

---

[193] Trusts (Amendment) (Jersey) Law 1989, s. 8A(2)(b): 'no rule relating to inheritance or succession (including, but without prejudice to the generality of the foregoing, forced heirship, *légitime* or similar rights) of the law of his [the reference is to a settlor who is not resident in Jersey] domicile or any other system of law shall affect any such transfer or disposition or otherwise affect the validity of such trust'; adopted in British Virgin Islands, Trustee (Amendment) Act 1993, s. 8 3(1), but in simplified form.

[194] Trusts (Guernsey) (Amendment) Law 1990, s. 11A(1): neither the creation of the trust nor the act of transfer 'is invalidated by any foreign rule of forced heirship or by reason of the fact that the concept of trusts is unknown to or not admitted by the law of a jurisdiction other than Guernsey'; adopted in Mauritius, Offshore Trusts Act 1992, s. 11(2)(a), and in Seychelles, International Trusts Act 1994, s. 10(2)(a).

already present in the Cayman Islands law of 1987 which has once again established the typical formulation regarding the inapplicability of foreign law:

It is expressly declared that no trust governed by the laws of the Islands and no disposition of property to be held upon the trusts thereof is void, voidable, liable to be set aside or defective in any fashion, nor is the capacity of any settlor to be questioned by reason that: (a) the laws of any foreign jurisdiction prohibit or do not recognize the concept of a trust; or (b) the trust or disposition avoids or defeats rights, claims or interests conferred by foreign law upon any person by reason of a personal relationship to the settlor or by way of heirship rights, or contravenes any rule of foreign law or any foreign judicial or administrative orders intended to recognize, protect, enforce or give effect to any such rights, claims or interests.[195]

As may be seen, this prohibition, which has been adopted *verbatim* by many other laws, is a complete one.[196]

The Bermuda law formulates the problem differently. In substance, the difference lies in the fact that it concerns only foreign laws, and not foreign judgments as well, omits the hypothesis that the nullity is sanctioned by foreign law which does not recognize the trust as an institution, includes protection of creditors among issues reserved to the local law, and, finally, adds an arrangement – which is a pure facade – which permits the application of rules of a foreign law when they correspond to those of the local law:

Where a trust is validly created under the laws of Bermuda the Court shall not vary it or set it aside pursuant to the law of another jurisdiction in respect of (a) the personal and proprietary effects of marriage; (b) succession rights, testate and intestate, especially the indefeasible shares of spouses and relatives; (c) the protection of creditors in matters of insolvency,[197] unless the law of Bermuda has corresponding laws or public policy rules.[198]

---

[195] Cayman Islands, Trusts (Foreign Element) Law 1987, s. 6.

[196] The Cayman Islands rule has been adopted in the Bahamas, Trusts (Choice of Governing Law) Act 1989, s. 8; in Turks and Caicos, Trust Ordinance 1990, s. 13(2); in Anguilla, Trusts Ordinance 1994, s. 63; in Nevis, International Exempt Trust Ordinance 1994, s. 29, s. 48; in Isle of Man, Trusts Act 1995, s. 5; in Cook Islands, International Trusts Amendment Act 1989, s. 13 I, which in (b) omits 'by reason' and adds 'or (c) the laws of the Cook Islands or the provisions of this Act are inconsistent with any foreign law'; the omitted part appears in s. 13E.

It should be noted that the term 'personal relationship' is given a very broad definition in the law, so as to include parent and child, husband and wife and cohabitation relationships.

[197] By 'insolvency', as in English law, is meant not bankruptcy, but the inability of a person to perform payment of his obligations due to the insufficiency of his estate.

[198] Bermuda, Trusts (Special Provisions) Act 1989, s. 11. In *Garner v. Bermuda Trust Company* (1992) the Court of Appeal decided that this rule was also to be applied to trusts created before it came into force, because it was a common-law concept.

This formulation was taken up by Belize in 1992, without the final 'unless', and with the reintroduction of the reference to foreign judgments and the addition of tax issues,[199] and was adopted by some of the laws which came later.[200]

The fact that Bermuda, unlike the Cook Islands, does not declare that it does not recognize foreign judgments is of little significance, but shows greater prudence on the part of the legislature. In fact, it is quite possible for a foreign court to rule on a family, succession or matrimonial matter by applying the law of Bermuda relating to trust issues, and there would be no justification for not recognizing such a judgment. For this reason, the laws of the Cayman Islands (which have recently been strengthened[201]), Belize and their numerous followers,[202] seem excessive, and may violate obliga-

[199] Belize, Trusts Act 1992, s. 7(6): 'Where a trust is created under the law of Belize, the Court shall not vary it or set it aside or recognize the validity of any claim against the trust property pursuant to the law of another jurisdiction or the order of a court of another jurisdiction in respect of (a) the personal and proprietary consequences of marriage or the termination of a marriage; (b) succession rights (whether testate or intestate) including the fixed shares of spouses or relatives; (c) the claims of creditors in an insolvency; (d) the imposition of any foreign tax or duty.'

[200] Anguilla, Trusts Ordinance 1994, s. 7(6); Niue, Trusts Act 1994, s. 8(6); Barbados, International Trusts Act 1995, s. 18. Note that Anguilla has recognized both the Bermuda and the Cayman Islands rules.

[201] Cayman Islands, Trusts (Foreign Element) (Amendment) Law 1995, s. 5, amends Cayman Islands, Trusts (Foreign Element) Law 1987, s. 6, adding that foreign law may not even be applied to the rights and duties of the trustee and the beneficiaries. The reason for this may be found in the fact that certain foreign persons had obtained foreign judgments which, while they were on the subject of the validity of the trust, had the effect of securing judgments against the beneficiaries and in favour of heirs (for example). The new wording of s. 6 prevents judgments of this type from being recognized in the Cayman Islands (as expressly stated in the new s. 6B, which was introduced in the law which effected the amendments).

The same law inserted another new provision after s. 6 of the Trusts (Foreign Element) Law 1987, in the form of s. 6A: it states that the rights of foreign heirs are not to be considered as affecting the assets of their predecessor (in substance, that they may not give rise to real actions against these assets, as is permitted in some jurisdictions), and that obligations towards heirs are not included among those which permitted the damaged party to commence a revocatory action.

[202] See Cook Islands, International Trusts Amendment Act 1989, s. 13D: foreign judgments against the settlor, a beneficiary, a protector or a person appointed to act for a trust or an asset of a trust, either by the trustee or by the beneficiaries, will not be recognized, notwithstanding the provisions of any treaty or statute, if 'that judgment is based upon the application of any law inconsistent with the provisions of this Act', or if 'that judgment relates to a matter or particular aspect that is governed by the law of the Cook Islands'; adopted in Nevis, International Exempt Trust Ordinance 1994, s. 28.

The Belize, Trusts Act 1992, s. 7(7) is less categorical, but has a similar effect: s. 7(6), which I have transcribed above, prevails over the Reciprocal Enforcement of Judgments Act; adopted in Anguilla, Trusts Ordinance 1994, s. 7(7) and in Niue, Trusts Act 1994, s. 8(7).

tions assumed at the international level by means of bilateral or multi-lateral treaties on the recognition of foreign judgments, which cannot be waived by a domestic law.[203]

The international trust model excludes the application of foreign laws in the area of succession, property rights between spouses and the protection of creditors with respect to acts of transfer against their interest. This last subject, however, although in a private international context it is included only in those laws which take Bermuda as their inspiration, is a constant in the model, as we shall now see in our discussion of revocatory actions (*actio pauliana*).

e The revocatory action

The Turks and Caicos law limits itself to making the principles of English law (discussed above) only slightly less severe towards the debtor, by requiring the creditor to demonstrate that the settlor became insolvent as a result of the transfer.[204] This solution characterizes the international trust model.[205]

The more widely accepted requirement comes from the Cayman Islands law, however:

Every disposition of property made with an intent to defraud and at an under-value shall be voidable at the instance of a creditor thereby prejudiced.[206]

The 'intent to defraud' is defined thus:

---

[203] Belize and Anguilla are bound by the Reciprocal Enforcement of Foreign Judgments Act. The Cook Islands, on the other hand, have complete freedom in this area (except for a treaty with New Zealand), since they have not even ratified the Hague Convention of 1970 on the Taking of Evidence Abroad.

On the ties in this area within the Commonwealth see K. W. Patchett, *Recognition of Commercial Judgments and Awards in the Commonwealth*, London, 1984.

[204] Turks and Caicos, Trust Ordinance 1990, s. 61. An examination of offshore legislation on the field of the revocatory action has been carried out by P. Matthews, 'The Asset Protection Trust: Holy Grail, or Wholly Useless?', in 6 OTPR (1996) 57, at 69–72 and by B. Engel, 'Asset Protection Trust and Legislation Specificity', in 2 T&T (1996) no. 3, 23 (Engel was a pioneer in the area of asset protection trusts for a US professional clientele). I would also mention D. Osborne, *Asset Protection: Domestic and International Law Tactics*, Clark, Boardman Callaghan, 1995.

[205] As was already the case in Western Samoa, International Trusts Act 1987, s. 5(2). Mauritius, Offshore Trusts Act 1992, s. 10(3), follows the same line: 'The Court may declare an offshore trust void or voidable, where it is proved beyond reasonable doubt that the offshore trust was made with the intent to defraud persons who were creditors of the settlor at the time when the trust property was vested in the trustee'; adopted in Seychelles, International Trusts Act 1994, s. 9(3). A rule which also follows this line, although tepidly, may be found in the Bankruptcy (Amendment) Ordinances 1990 of Gibraltar.   [206] Cayman Islands, Fraudulent Dispositions Law, 1989, s. 4(1).

'Intent to defraud' means an intention of a transferor wilfully to defeat an obligation owed a creditor.[207]

There is a notable change here with respect to English law, because the revocatory action may only be commenced by a creditor who was already a creditor at the moment in which the transfer to the trust took place.[208]

The importance of the Bermuda law is less direct; in place of 'intent to defraud', it uses the term 'requisite intention':

A disposition the dominant purpose of which is to put the property . . . beyond the reach of a person or class of persons who is making, or may at some time make, a claim against him.[209]

This rule seems to extend to foreseeable creditors, provided that they have already been identified.

As far as the burden of proof, which clearly falls upon the creditor, is concerned, the Bermuda law adopts an unusual criterion which obliges the court to weigh the evidence regarding the 'requisite intention' 'on a balance of probabilities', and not in the usual way.

Where these partially differing laws come together is in their determination of the consequence of a successful application of the revocatory action. The transfer to the trust is revoked, but the current owner of the property and each of his predecessors (the trustee and whoever has received it from him in any manner, except in bad faith – and here we see the distinction with the English rule of the 'bona fide purchaser for value') obtain a charge, that is an obligation *in rem* to guarantee the reimbursement of any consideration which may be deposited and all legal costs incurred in their defence. Finally, every distribution carried out in favour of a beneficiary is safe, unless it was in bad faith.[210]

---

[207] Cayman Islands, Fraudulent Dispositions Law, 1989, s. 2. The limitations period is six years.

 The Cayman Islands provisions have been adopted in Bahamas, Fraudulent Dispositions Act 1991; in Anguilla, Fraudulent Dispositions Ordinance 1994, s. 4 (but in both cases the limitations period is two years); and in Barbados, International Trusts Act 1995, ss. 19 and 20 (but the limitations period is three years, and 'and at undervalue' is amended to read 'or at undervalue': this is a substantial difference).

[208] Cyprus, International Trusts Law 1992, s. 3(2) arrives at the same result: 'intent to defraud the creditors of the settlor at the time of the transfer of his assets into the trust.'

[209] Bermuda, Conveyancing Amendment Act 1994, s. 36A.

[210] Cayman Islands, Fraudulent Dispositions Law, 1989, s. 5 (a)(i): 'the transferee shall have a first and paramount charge over the property, the subject of the disposition, of an amount equal to the entire costs properly incurred by the transferee' when he defends his interests in court; and furthermore, (ii) 'the relevant disposition shall be set aside subject to the proper fees, costs, pre-existing rights, claims and interests of the transferee (and of any predecessor transferee who has not acted in bad faith)'; and also, (b) any distribution received by the beneficiary will remain in effect 'if the court is satisfied that the beneficiary of a trust has not acted in bad faith'; adopted in Bahamas, Fraudulent

There remains the Cook Islands law, which has been modified on two occasions. Although it does not include the provisions we have just seen in the event of a successful revocatory action, it takes its inspiration from the Cayman Islands system, but it is distinguished from it by certain specific rules:[211]

(1) With regard to proof, the standard is that of a criminal trial: 'where it is proven beyond reasonable doubt by a creditor that an international trust settled or established or property disposed to an international trust . . .';

(2) It must be demonstrated that the disposition: (a) took place 'with principal intent to defraud that creditor of the settlor' and (b) rendered the settlor incapable of satisfying that creditor's claims from his property;

(3) The intent to defraud is excluded if the property remaining to the settlor immediately following the transfer which is being challenged was sufficient to satisfy that creditor (s.13B(2));

(4) An intent to defraud does not arise merely out of the fact that the settlor retained powers in the trust or is a beneficiary of it (s.13B(5));

(5) The trust instrument is not cancelled, but the trust must satisfy the creditor who has taken the action;

(6) If the trust does not have sufficient assets because it has made a transfer in favour of a person who is not a bona fide purchaser for value, the transfer is void (s.13B(6));

(7) An action may not be commenced if the act took place more than two years after the creditor's right arose – s.13B(3);

(8) Or if the claim arose later – s.13B(4);

(9) The limitations period is one year.

A recent appeals court decision from the Cook Islands merits comment.[212]

Between 1988 and 1989 the apartments in a condominium built in California by some of the defendants were sold.[213] In 1992, some of the purchasers commenced

---

Dispositions Act 1991, s. 5(1), in Antigua, Fraudulent Dispositions Ordinance 1994, s. 5, and in Bermuda, Conveyancing Amendment Act 1994, s. 36D, where the test of good faith on the part of the third-party purchaser is re-applied (this is closer to English law, as with all dispositions in the area of the revocatory action), but no condition is imposed to block the distributions to beneficiaries; also in Barbados, International Trusts Act 1995, s. 21.

[211] Cook Islands, International Trusts Amendment Act 1989, s. 13B(1), later amended by the International Trusts Amendment (No. 2) Act 1989 and the International Trusts Amendment Act 1991; adopted in Nevis, International Exempt Trust Ordinance 1994, s. 24 (which obliges the creditor to pay a deposit of EC$25,000: s. 55), and, only as to the first part, in Mauritius, Offshore Trusts Act 1992, s. 10(3).

[212] *South Orange Grove Owners Association v. Orange Grove Partners* (1995). See the succinct comments of B. Engel, 'Cook Islands Considers International Trust Act', in 2 T&T (1996) no. 3, 30; mine are based on the complete text of the judgment.

[213] A construction company and its controlling shareholders. The other defendants were the trustees of the trusts described here.

an action against the builder, claiming defects of various kinds. In April 1994, the California court ordered the defendants to pay damages of over 6 million dollars.

The plaintiffs sought unsuccessfully to execute the judgment, and discovered that the losing parties had disposed of all their property by transferring it to shelf companies and thereafter to trusts created in the Cook Islands. In December 1994 the plaintiffs commenced a legal action before a judge of the lower court of Ratoronga (the capital) pursuant to s.13B of the law and, asserting their credit following the California judgment, requested an interim Mareva injunction to attach the trust assets.[214] The request was rejected by the lower court, because the judge found that the period of limitations to commence the action had already expired in December 1994: the question was, therefore, to identify the moment when the period began to run.

The specific provision of the local law would appear to leave no room for interpretation, since it states: 'in the case of an action upon a judgment, the date of the cause of action accruing shall be the date of that act or omission . . . which gave rise to the judgment itself'.[215] It would seem, therefore, that the legislature intended to erect a formidable barrier: if the period on the basis of which an action could be taken before a foreign judge began to run at the moment the *claim* arose, it was clear that in normal cases the period would have run completely before the foreign judgment was rendered; there would, therefore, be no possibility of an action in the Cook Islands based on a foreign judgment.

On appeal, the Cook Islands judge formulated an incredible interpretation of the law, which was made possible by Californian civil procedure, where a judgment is rendered by a judge pursuant to the verdict of a jury. The act which gave rise to the Californian judgment, the Cook Islands judge affirmed, was neither the plaintiffs' claim, nor, earlier still, the purchase of the defective apartments, but the jury's verdict. The period within which to take action in the Cook Islands commenced on the date of the verdict,[216] and therefore the action was commenced in a timely manner.[217]

Along with the technical/interpretive aspects, perhaps the judge's statement at the end of the judgment is of greater significance: 'We would be loath to interpret the International Trusts Act as a statute which was extended to give succour to cheats and fraudsters by totally excluding the legitimate claims of overseas creditors.'[218]

---

[214] On the Mareva injunction see above, chapter 2 §4.f.   [215] S. 13B(8)(b).

[216] In this case, the date of the verdict and the date of the judgment were the same.

[217] At 25.

[218] At 27. The judgment is dated 6 November 1995. The following 5 December, the parties appeared before the same judge to discuss the question (which had been postponed) of whether or not judgment would be published (because s. 23(2) of the International Trusts Act 1984 states that all proceedings relating to trusts are to be heard *in camera*, and details of the proceedings are not to be published without leave of the court).

The judge authorized publication, and rejected the argument that 'confidentiality and secrecy are the cornerstone' of financial activities in the Cook Islands.

Before concluding, I believe it would be of interest to examine a Cayman Islands rule, which has been adopted by other States, and which, as formulated, would appear to state an obvious principle:

Nothing in this law shall validate any disposition of property which is neither owned by the transferor nor the subject of a power in that behalf vested in the transferor and nor does this Law affect the recognition of foreign laws in determining whether the transferor is the owner of such property or the holder of such power.[219]

Nonetheless, the term 'owned' has a semantic force which may not easily be compressed. This force recently came to light in a case in which the defendant was a member of the Kuwaiti Royal Family who was accused of misappropriating 450 million dollars during the period when he was responsible for his country's foreign investments. This amount, it was claimed in an action commenced in order to have the transfers which he later carried out in favour of trusts established in offshore States declared ineffective, was not 'owned' by the defendant because his title was defective as a result of the misappropriation of the funds.[220]

All those States which have not declared the inapplicability of foreign laws in the area of protection of creditors either follow the system of the Cayman Islands or the Cook Islands, or, like the Turks and Caicos, have passed an autonomous law.[221] It seems to me, therefore, that one might conclude that the international trust model has limited the range of the English type of revocatory action with regard to subjective and objective profiles, and to conditions for bringing a claim. There is no doubt that the international model leans towards placing substantial obstacles in the path of a settlor's creditors.

f Trusts for purposes, charitable or otherwise

In English law, trusts for purposes other than charitable trusts are not recognized,[222] and charitable trusts suffer from the problem of an antiquated description of the area which makes up 'charity'. Charitable trusts are trusts for purposes, but they are characterized by a special purpose which permits a wide range of tax breaks and subjects them to forms of public vigilance. The unsatisfactory state of English law, which too often

---

[219] Cayman Islands, Fraudulent Dispositions Law, 1989, s. 7; adopted in Bahamas, Fraudulent Dispositions Act 1991, s. 7, and in Barbados, International Trusts Act 1995, s. 23.

[220] *Grupo Torras v. Sheik Fahad* (1995). The action is still going on in England, while the Bahamas court has issued a Mareva injunction (see above, chapter 2 §4.f), and has blocked the trust funds.

[221] Only Jersey, Guernsey, British Virgin Islands and Mauritius have not.

[222] This is the traditional enunciation of the principle. For the modern interpretation to be applied to this subject, however, see above, chapter 3 §2.b.

excludes purposes which are commonly regarded as being worthy and altruistic from the class of purposes for which charitable trusts may be established, has been noted by the new laws, which have laid down definitions which are closer to a modern mentality. First, the Cook Islands identified the following purposes:

(a) for the relief of poverty; (b) for the advancement of education; (c) for the advancement of religion; (d) for other purposes beneficial to the community,[223]

to which Belize added human rights and protection of the environment[224] and, most recently, Niue has added the promotion of amateur sports.[225] Charitable trusts, as we know, are exempt from limitations of term, and require a public body which will ensure performance by the trustees. The new laws retain both these rules of English law, adapting the latter to their own system, and permitting the settlor himself to designate who may enforce observance of the trust instrument (and it may be the settlor himself or his descendants). Finally, it is a frequent requirement that at least one trustee be local and, to make possible any checks which may be permitted, that he keep documentation regarding the activities of the trust within the State.[226]

It is clear that, at this point, the distinction between the two basic kinds of purpose trust, charitable and otherwise, tends to disappear if the formulation laid down by Nauru since 1972 is followed:

Any person may create in Nauru a trust in perpetuity or for any lesser duration for a purpose or purposes, whether charitable or not[227]

and that the identity of the structure – that is, the lack of beneficiaries – prevails.[228]

This is why certain laws treat all trusts for purposes alike, and require

[223] Cook Islands, International Trusts Act 1984, s. 12(1), adopted in Western Samoa, International Trusts Act 1987, s. 6, in Mauritius, Offshore Trusts Act 1992, s. 14(1), in Cyprus, International Trusts Law 1992, s. 7, and in Seychelles, International Trusts Act 1994, s. 13.
[224] Belize, Trusts Act 1992, s. 14(1), while s. 14(3) clarifies that a charitable trust may only operate abroad (which is not permitted in English law); adopted in Anguilla, Trusts Ordinance 1994, s. 14(1) and (3).   [225] Niue, Trusts Act 1994, s. 15 (1)(f).
[226] On the obligation of a person appointed as protector or the equivalent, and the consequent power of the courts to appoint one where a trust for purposes finds itself without, see Nauru, Foreign Trusts, Estates and Wills Act 1972, s. 6; Cook Islands, International Trusts Act 1984, s. 12(2), adopted in Mauritius, Offshore Trusts Act 1992, s. 15(4) and in Cyprus, International Trusts Law 1992, s. 7(3); Bermuda, Trusts (Special Provisions) Act 1989, s. 13(1)(e): 'a person to enforce the trust'; British Virgin Islands, Trustee (Amendment) Act 1993, s. 84(2)(d) and (5); Belize, Trusts Act 1992, s. 15(2), adopted in Anguilla, Trusts Ordinance 1994, s. 1 5(2), and in Barbados, International Trusts Act 1995, s. 10(1)(c) and 12(1).   [227] Nauru, Foreign Trusts, Estates and Wills Act 1972, s. 6(1).
[228] Thus, expressly, in Mauritius, Offshore Trusts Act 1992, s. 15, adopted in Seychelles, International Trusts Act 1994, s. 14.

them to have a protector or another person (an 'enforcer' or a 'designated person') qualified to act against the trustees, permit them to be discretionary, and specify that the trust instrument must contain a disposition which determines the final destination of the trust property.[229] Non-charitable purpose trusts (first proposed in the Bermuda law) have begun to be generally accepted, subject only to their legality, and to the possibility and specificity of their purpose.[230]

This kind of trust for purposes is assuming great importance in international finance, where an operation requires a control centre which is not a profit centre. In fact, the lack of beneficiaries signifies that the trustee may dedicate himself exclusively to duties which are completely different from those of the classic trustee: he does not produce income, but rather supervises the status which has been entrusted to him in such a way that the operation which he is in a position to direct as a consequence of that status attains its intended goal. The trustee must, therefore, be given the necessary power to pursue the purpose profitably, such as ownership of a controlling block of shares together with the relevant right to vote them (but not the right to collect dividends). From here we have the new classes of voting trusts, blocking syndicates and shareholders agreements to resist hostile takeover bids.

Other profiles emerge when we look at the applications of trusts in financial or commercial operations, and we come to the realization that the trust often has a 'segregation' function, with regard not to the trustee's remaining property, but to persons who are involved in the operation under various guises. One or more of these persons also takes on the role of beneficiaries of the trust, but they are beneficiaries who only appear at the

---

[229] Recently, Jersey, Trusts (Amendment No. 3) (Jersey) Law 1996, which introduced articles 10A, 10B and 10C and places charitable trusts on a par with trusts for purposes in general.

[230] Bermuda, Trusts (Special Provisions) Act 1989, s. 13, sets forth provisions which are common to all trusts for purposes: 'for a purpose or purposes (whether charitable or not)' provided that they are 'specific, reasonable and possible' and lawful, and created 'by deed or by will'; adopted in British Virgin Islands, Trustee (Amendment) Act 1993, s. 8 4(2), in Mauritius, Offshore Trusts Act 1992, s. 15, and in Seychelles, International Trusts Act 1994, s. 14.

Similarly in Cook Islands, International Trusts Act 1984, s. 12(2), adopted in Mauritius, Offshore Trusts Act 1992, s. 14, and in Cyprus, International Trusts Law 1992, s. 7.

See also Belize, Trusts Act 1992, s. 15(1) on trusts 'for a purpose which is non-charitable' (which requires that the purpose be 'specific, reasonable and capable of fulfilment'), adopted in Nevis, International Exempt Trust Ordinance 1994, s. 8(1) and (3), in Niue, Trusts Act 1994, s. 16, and in Anguilla, Trusts Ordinance 1994, s. 15: trusts 'for a commercial or other purpose which is non-charitable'.

As we shall immediately see, the exemption from limits as to duration also tends to be extended from charitable trusts to all trusts for purposes.

time of termination of the trust, that is, at the conclusion of the operation for which the trust was established. It seems more opportune, therefore, to have recourse to a trust for purposes, in which these persons will be the ones to whom the trust property will be granted when the trust purpose is attained, without their being able to claim any right to it in the meantime. The result is that third party creditors cannot interfere in the activities of the trustee, as they might have been able to do if the beneficiaries of a distribution under a trust for purposes had been the beneficiaries of an ordinary trust: in this case, their rights would be subject to attack by creditors, and therefore to being enforced by these creditors or by judicial custodians.

A further issue which arises from the lack of beneficiaries in trusts for purposes is that of secrecy: there is no risk that it will be violated to comply with the requirements of communication which the law imposes on a trustee in favour of beneficiaries.

Finally, a trust for purposes permits the carrying out of an activity without the need to 'consolidate' it in financial statements, as opposed to what would happen if the same activity were entrusted to a controlled company. It also permits presence in a foreign State without the risk that this presence might constitute a permanent establishment.

In the international trust model, charitable purpose trusts are free from the restrictions of English law regarding their purpose, and are permitted for any altruistic purpose. Non-charitable purpose trusts, where they differ from the former, are permitted without limitations, except for requirements of legality, possibility, identification of the purpose and the existence of a person who may demand their performance.

g Duration of the trust

Non-charitable purpose trusts are usually limited as to duration to that established for non-purpose trusts. The increasing proximity to charitable trusts has, however, had the effect in many cases of making exemption from limits of duration common to all trusts for purposes.[231]

The final term of a trust is, as we know, a serious problem in English law, where it is seen more specifically as the period within which the vesting of the right transferred to the trustee must take place in favour of the final beneficiaries.[232] This is typical of 'family' trusts, where the settlor wishes

---

[231] The possibility that a trust for purposes may be perpetual is sanctioned by Mauritius, Offshore Trusts Act 1992, s. 12(2); Cyprus, International Trusts Law 1992, s. 7(3); British Virgin Islands, Trustee (Amendment) Act 1993, s. 84(3); Nauru, Foreign Trusts, Estates and Wills Act 1972, s. 6; Barbados, International Trusts Act 1995, s. 7(2).

[232] See above, pp. 104–10.

the trust to terminate only when certain circumstances have come to pass and not simply after the lapse of a certain period of time, which might be insufficient or excessive with respect to his intentions. This is why the so-called 'rule against perpetuities', although opposed by many, has not been repealed.

The rule against perpetuities was a part of most of the systems which we are examining, because at a certain moment in their development they had adopted English law. Almost all of them have repealed it either by setting forth clear rules[233] or without any replacement,[234] and have promulgated rules which technically have a different purpose from the English rule: the final date of the trust.

With the exception of Nauru, the Turks and Caicos and Anguilla, whose laws permit trusts of all kinds to have perpetual duration,[235] the settlor must, therefore, determine the duration of the trust within the maximum time limits allowed by the relevant law,[236] it being understood, however, that he may also identify events whose occurrence will result in the early termination of the trust. Even in the rare cases where the rule against perpetuities has remained in force, the settlor may impose a final deadline for the trust: apart from the great length of the period, which is almost

---

[233] Turks and Caicos, Trust Ordinance 1990, s. 14, adopted in Anguilla, Trusts Ordinance 1994, s. 6. Cook Islands, International Trusts Act 1984, ss. 8 and 9, which does not repeal the rule against perpetuities, but rather those against double possibilities and accumulation, is an exception. The rule against double possibilities relates to cases (I do not understand why they should have been of such interest to the Cook Islands legislature) where, in the series of estates arising out of a real-property settlement, there is provision for a life estate in favour of a person as yet unborn and, after him, another estate in favour of an unborn person or the descendant of an unborn person. The Cayman Islands has legislated in a similar manner, Perpetuities Law 1995, s. 15.

[234] Belize, Trusts Act 1992, s. 6(3); Nevis International Exempt Trust Ordinance 1994, s. 5(3); Barbados, International Trusts Act 1995, s. 7(3).

[235] Nauru, Foreign Trusts, Estates and Wills Act 1972, ss. 4 and 5; Turks and Caicos, Trust Ordinance 1990, s. 14(1), adopted in Anguilla, Trusts Ordinance 1994, s. 6(1).

[236] The periods are as follows:

150 years: Cayman Islands, Perpetuities Law 1995, s. 4(1)
120 years: Belize, Trusts Act 1992, s. 6(1); Niue, Trusts Act 1994, s. 7
100 years: Trusts (Jersey) Law 1984, article 11; Cook Islands, International Trusts Act 1984, s. 6(1); Malta, Trusts Act 1988, s. 12; Trusts (Guernsey) Law 1989, s. 12; Bermuda, Perpetuities and Accumulations Act 1989, s. 3(1); Mauritius, Offshore Trusts Act 1992, s. 12(1); Cyprus, International Trusts Law 1992, s. 5(1); British Virgin Islands, Trustee (Amendment) Act 1993, s. 68; Nevis, International Exempt Trust Ordinance 1994, s. 5(1); Seychelles, International Trusts Act 1994, s. 11; Barbados, International Trusts Act 1995, s. 7(1).
80 years: Bahamas, Perpetuities Act 1995, s. 6.

always longer than the eighty years provided for in English law, in these latter legal systems the situation is the same as in England after the reform of 1968, and in fact one finds the 'wait and see' principle,[237] which we explained in chapter 3. These States, too, have abandoned the limits of the 'rule against accumulations': income may commonly be retained in the trust, without any distribution, for the entire duration of the trust.[238]

In conclusion, the international trust model requires that non-purpose trusts should have a predetermined duration, and that they may accumulate the income for all of that period; non-charitable purpose trusts have the same unspecified duration which is typical of charitable trusts.

h Protector

The first definition of the protector may be found in the law of the Cook Islands:

'Protector' in relation to an international trust means a person who is the holder of a power which when invoked is capable of directing a trustee in matters relating to the trust and in respect of which matters the trustee has a discretion and includes a person who is the holder of a power of appointment or dismissal of trustees.[239]

This is, technically speaking, a very accurate definition. It draws attention to the notion of power which clearly identifies the legal position of the protector. From this point of view, it is correct to affirm that the trust instrument may provide for 'the office of protector'.[240]

The figure which emerged in 1993 from the law of the British Virgin Islands is different:

---

[237] Cook Islands, International Trusts Act 1984, s. 7; Bermuda, Perpetuities and Accumulations Act 1989, s. 5; British Virgin Islands, Trustee (Amendment) Act 1993, s. 70; Cayman Islands, Perpetuities Law 1995, s. 3(2); Bahamas, Perpetuities Act 1995, s. 6.

[238] Bermuda, Perpetuities and Accumulations Act 1989, s. 15; Mauritius, Offshore Trusts Act 1992, s. 54(1); Cyprus, International Trusts Law 1992, s. 6; Belize, Trusts Act 1992, s. 6(4); British Virgin Islands, Trustee (Amendment) Act 1993, s. 78; Niue, Trusts Act 1994, s. 7(4); Seychelles, International Trusts Act 1994, s. 12; Nevis, International Exempt Trust Ordinance 1994, s. 5(4); Anguilla, Trusts Ordinance 1994, s. 6(4): this provision is not repeated in the Turks and Caicos law, from which Anguilla took its rule on the perpetual duration of trusts; Barbados, International Trusts Act 1995, s. 7(4).

[239] Cook Islands, International Trusts Amendment Act 1989, s. 3; adopted in Nevis, International Exempt Trust Ordinance 1994, s. 2.

[240] Belize, Trusts Act 1992, s. 16(1), adopted in Malta, Trusts Act 1988, s. 24A(1) added to by the Recognition of Trusts Act 1994; in Nevis, International Exempt Trust Ordinance 1994, s. 9(1); in Niue, Trusts Act 1994, s. 17(1); and in Anguilla, Trusts Ordinance 1994, s. 16(1). Cf. F. di Maio, 'Il protector e la sua funzione', in *Atti Milano*, ch. 34.

An instrument creating a trust may contain provisions by virtue of which the exercise by the trustees of any of their powers and discretion shall be subject to the previous consent of the settlor or some other person, whether named protector, nominator, committee or any other name; and if so provided in the instrument creating the trust the trustees shall not be liable for any loss caused by their actions if the previous consent was given.[241]

This person 'is not liable to the beneficiaries for the *bona fide* exercise of the power'.[242]

The relationship between protector and trustees is different here: in the first place, the settlor is identified as a potential protector; this solution, although a minority one, is not new, since the law of Belize already provided for it,[243] but it is the relationship between protector and trustees which is influenced by a context which has no equivalent in other laws. The assent of the protector has the effect of making the trustees not responsible for their actions. This turns the figure of the trustee upside down, and makes him in substance an agent. We shall discuss this again at the end of this chapter.

The customary view of the protector, on the other hand, is the one described in the law of the Cook Islands, as reported above: it is also present by implication in earlier laws, drafted before the protector phenomenon assumed the dimensions it has today: 'The terms of the trust may require a trustee to obtain the consent of some person before exercising a power or discretion.'[244] As described in these terms and in those of the Cook Islands, the protector is nothing extraordinary; in fact, the laws of the last century already permitted the mechanism, as the holder of powers which influenced the sphere of activity of the trustee.[245] An analogous structure may be found in the last paragraph of article 629 of the Italian civil code, which permits a testator to designate a person 'to supervise the performance of

[241] British Virgin Islands, Trustee (Amendment) Act 1993, which introduces s. 86(1).

[242] *Ibid.*, s. 86(3).

[243] Belize, Trusts Act 1992, s. 16(3), adopted in Nevis, International Exempt Trust Ordinance 1994, s. 9(3); in Niue, Trusts Act 1994, s. 17(3); and in Anguilla, Trusts Ordinance 1994, s. 16(3).

[244] Trusts (Jersey) Law 1984, article 20(3), adopted in Malta, Trusts Act 1988, s. 24(3), in Trusts (Guernsey) Law 1989, s. 28(2), which adds 'consult or', in Turks and Caicos, Trust Ordinance 1990, s. 23(3), for the most part in Anguilla, Trusts Ordinance 1994, s. 31(5) (although this law expressly regulates the protector along the lines of the Belize law).

[245] See, staying within the systems under review, Bahamas, Trustee Act 1893, s. 3: 'Every power conferred by the preceding sections shall be exercised according to the discretion of the trustee, but subject to any consent required by the instrument, if any, creating the trust with respect to the investment of the trust funds.'

the disposition' of a religious nature, even if the obligation to perform it falls upon the heir or the legatee.

What is extraordinary is the development of the protector in recent years, to the point of its being made compulsory in purpose trusts and becoming an almost unavoidable presence in ordinary trusts following the international model, possibly because the trustee is often a company with which the settlor has little contact and so tends to place in the protector that total and mutual confidence which is the traditional basis of a relationship with a trustee.[246]

The law of Belize describes the position of the protector succinctly: 'In the exercise of his office a protector shall owe a fiduciary duty to the beneficiaries of the trust or to the purpose for which the trust is created.'[247] It thereby places him within the category of fiduciaries, with all the extremely grave consequences which this entails in common law (prohibition against profiting, conflicts of interest, etc.; hence, among others, the rule that a protector may never appoint himself as trustee). It may seem rash to assert, as does the Belize law, that the protector is subject to fiduciary obligations towards the purpose of the trust (in the case of a trust for purposes); if we look carefully, however, the expression is a felicitous one, because it lays down that the protector participates in, but does not share responsibility for, the happy outcome of the entrusting. He is not a trustee, either at law or in fact, but he has the responsibility of collaborating or exercising vigilance, so that the entrusting is concluded positively.

One typical form of collaboration is in the area of discretionary trusts and in all cases where the trustee has the power to select or make evaluations of individuals; very often, the trustee would not be capable of taking appropriate decisions, except after long consultation, possibly with professionals. It is much more productive and, at the same time, more in line with the interests of the beneficiaries, if a person who is familiar with all issues relating to the beneficiaries lends support to the trustee, who will have no reason not to follow the suggestions the protector gives him unless he fears fraud on the part of the protector.

It is here that we can see the reason why, on the one hand, the fiduciary obligations of the protector are towards the beneficiaries or the trust

---

[246] Thus P. J. Hobson, 'Trust Deeds and Protectors', in 2 T&T (1996) no. 9 6, and the opinion of P. W. Smith QC, acting as a Chancery judge in *Steele v. Paz Limited*, from the Isle of Man, 1996, cited by P. Baker in 'The Reluctant Protector', in OI (May 1996) 33, where there is an interesting review of a number of systems.

[247] Belize, Trusts Act 1992, s. 16(5), adopted in Anguilla, Trusts Ordinance 1994, s. 16(5), in Niue, Trusts Act 1994, s. 17(5), and in Nevis, International Exempt Trust Ordinance 1994, s. 9(5).

purpose and not towards the settlor, and, on the other, why the protector cannot exonerate the trustee from his customary responsibilities. If the protector's obligations were to the settlor (as the British Virgin Islands law would seem to lead one to think), the entrusting principle would be under attack, and we would be on the road towards a fiduciary relationship of a contractual nature. If the protector could exonerate the trustee from responsibility, the very notion of entrusting would fail, and the trustee would become a kind of manager, operating jointly with the protector. The sphere of responsibility of the protector exists, but it is not to be confused with that of the trustee, nor is it superimposed on to it. He must fulfill his own fiduciary obligations even if they are in contrast with the valuation which the trustees give of their own (and *vice versa*[248]). Since the protector does not, and cannot, have any interest in management, not even that interest – which is prevalently moral in nature – which consists of defend-

---

[248] I would like to relate a tricky case decided by the Royal Court of Jersey (*Sociedad Financiera Sofimeca v. Kleinwort Benson* (1992)).

The case concerned control of an important Venezuelan bank, which was maintained by means of a trust of a short duration. The protectors of the trust, who had appointed the managers of the holding company the shares of which belonged to the trust, were attacked by some of the beneficiaries: the bank was the subject of a takeover bid, and the protectors were accused of favouring a certain faction. Furthermore, the termination date of the trust was approaching, so that unless distribution of the trust property were blocked, the protectors could ensure victory for the faction they were promoting.

Actions were also under way in Venezuela, but they would not have been decided before the date of termination of the trust arrived. The Jersey court, faced with facts of notable complexity, above all relating to foreign law, and an impressive quantity of documents (including a dozen opinions of eminent Venezuelan jurists: 'We have before us what we can only describe as a barrage and counter-barrage of affidavits', observed the judge) issued a decision in less than four months in which it showed complete command of the case and reaffirmed some principles of noteworthy importance.

The first is that a party requesting an injunction has the duty not to conceal any relevant facts, even if they are unfavourable to its case. In this case, the plaintiffs were reticent, and so, to use the old term, are in mercy before the Court: ('We feel that Mr Ramos de la Rosa did not probe and dig with sufficient effort to bring an unbiased and complete picture to the Court. At this point the plaintiffs are in mercy before the Court').

The second is that it is not necessary that the judge should instruct the trustees not to let themselves be influenced by the protectors. The trustees had always been absent from the scene, and had left the protectors to appoint the administrators of the holding company. This was an error. They had to start ensuring that no event could take place which would irreparably prejudice the interests of a party.

The third is that the rights of the beneficiaries of a trust do not extend to obtaining all documentation relating to the trust (on this point, see also the Grand Cayman precedent, below, footnote 255), especially if they are attempting to use the law of Jersey to obtain documents for use in a foreign lawsuit.

On the loss of confidentiality of a document produced in court, see *Continental Trust Company* (1991).

ing his earlier decisions (and including protection of his professional reputation), he prevails against the trustee. In a case where the trustee had challenged the protector's decision to revoke his powers, Bermuda case law has recently underlined the inability of the trustee to question the protector's conduct, unless he can demonstrate fraud.[249]

A protector who inserts himself actively in management of the trust, either by choice or because the trust instrument indicates accordingly, risks being considered a trustee. For him, the consequences of this are the assumption of a trustee's responsibilities,[250] but for the trust they could be a change of domicile, and therefore of the applicable tax law. Frequently, in fact, the protector is resident in the same State as the settlor, one with high or normal tax rates, we may suppose, while the trustees reside in a State with low tax rates. The trust income may become taxable in the former State where the protector's activism in management affairs leads to the conclusion that the centre of management of the trust lies there.

The laws indicate certain minimum powers, among which those to remove and appoint trustees[251] and to be kept informed on the progress of the trust[252] are more or less a constant, but the effective powers of the protector are those which the trust instrument grants him. There is often more than one protector; unlike with trustees, they make deliberations by a majority vote, and a dissenting protector has the right to make his dissent known in writing.[253]

The international trust model sees the protector as a participant in the fulfillment of the trustee's duties who also has his own duties and responsi-

---

[249] *Von Knieriem v. Bermuda Trust Company* (1994).   [250] See above, chapter 2 §2.d.

[251] It should be noted that this power does not contradict what I said in the text regarding entrustment. This is so firstly because there are no beneficiaries in trusts for purposes who may complain about the trustee's performance of his duties, so that the intervention of a protector serves to bring an entrustment which is held to be unsatisfactory to an end, and secondly because the removal of the trustee only signifies the transfer of the entrustment to another person (the new trustee). As I have explained in this book, what is of fundamental importance for the theory of entrustment is that for so long as he fills the role, the trustee is completely and directly responsible for the duties rising out of the trust instrument.

[252] *Per* various formulations, see Belize, Trusts Act 1992, s. 16(2); Nevis, International Exempt Trust Ordinance 1994, s. 9(2); Malta, Trusts Act 1988, s. 24A(2) added to by the Recognition of Trusts Act 1994; Niue, Trusts Act 1994, s. 17(2); Anguilla, Trusts Ordinance 1994, s. 16(2); Barbados, International Trusts Act 1995, s. 16(2); British Virgin Islands, Trustee (Amendment) Act 1993, s. 86(2).

[253] See Belize, Trusts Act 1992, ss. 16(6) and 16(7); adopted in Anguilla, Trusts Ordinance 1994, ss. 16(6) and 16(7); in Nevis, International Exempt Trust Ordinance 1994, ss. 9(6) and 9(7); in Niue, Trusts Act 1994, ss. 17(6) and 17(7); and in Barbados, International Trusts Act 1995, ss. 26(4) and 26(5).

bilities as a fiduciary for the protection of the beneficiaries or the trust purpose. This is why he has regularly been held to have the right to act or to intervene in proceedings relating to the administration of the trust.[254]

i Letter of wishes

Especially in the case of discretionary and purpose trusts, the settlor will see the need to communicate to the trustee criteria for identification of the beneficiaries or the specific means whereby the purpose will be attained, both of which can be specified in black and white in the trust instrument only rarely, as they are often extremely personal or confidential consider- ations, or at the very least indications which can be better formulated in everyday or business language rather than by using technical legal terms.

The letter of wishes has always existed in England, and is connected with the fiduciary element which is at the base of the trust. Its codification in Belize has led to a review of the applicable rules, as we have just seen in the case of the protector. The letter of wishes has been generalized, because even a trustee may prepare it and deliver it to the settlor so as to be sure that he has understood its purposes, and a beneficiary may send a letter of wishes to a trustee expressing how he would like the trustee's discretion to be exercised. These variations on a theme do not hide the fact that the letter of wishes to which the laws of the international model refer is the one prepared by the settlor. It leads to a great danger, however: the possible nullity of the trust.

The Belize rules, which strangely enough have no formal followers ex- cept for Anguilla and Niue, have nonetheless been accepted in interna- tional practice as appropriate, and are followed by one and all:

(a) the trustee may have regard to that letter or memorandum of wishes in exercising any functions conferred upon him by the terms of the trust; but (b) the trustee shall not be bound to have regard to that letter or memorandum and shall not be accountable in any way for his refusal to have regard to that letter or memorandum.

No fiduciary duty or obligation shall be imposed on a trustee merely by the giving to him of a letter of wishes or the preparation by him of a memorandum of wishes.[255]

If this rule is applied as written, no risk to the validity of the trust emerges, but the letter of wishes can certainly imperil the *entrusting* if it goes beyond its permitted limits. The letter of wishes is nothing more than the transpo-

---

[254] Cf. P. Matthews, 'Protectors: Two Cases, Twenty Questions', in 9 TLI (1995) 108.
[255] Belize, Trusts Act 1992, s. 13(4) and (5); adopted in Anguilla, Trusts Ordinance 1994, s. 13 (4) and (5); and in Niue, Trusts Act 1994, s. 14(4) and (5).

sition in ordinary language of the requirements which the settlor could, at greater expense and with greater effort, easily have put into the trust instrument. Let us not forget that the unilateral nature of the relationship means that the settlor is the architect of the formulation of the entrusting. The problem is not, therefore, one of restricting the entrusting in the trustee to an excessive degree, because at the worst one would end up with a 'bare' trust, but of causing it to fail by imposing an obligation on the trustee to *follow instructions* which the settlor or a third party give him *little by little*, thereby directing the type of relationship towards that of a fiduciary contract, and, therefore, towards the complete antithesis of the trust.[256]

[256] The courts of the Cayman Islands have heard a series of cases on the estate of the Greek shipping magnate Pandelis Christos Lemos, who had placed extremely large sums on trust. The trust was discretionary, and the beneficiaries were the children of his first and second marriage and those of his second wife. In his letter of wishes, the settlor had substantially disinherited the two children of his first marriage, indicating to the trustees that they should receive nothing if they contested the validity of the trust, and generally displaying a certain aversion towards them.

When Lemos died, the two children of the first marriage took action before the Greek courts, alleging that they had been deprived of their rights as heirs. They had the problem, however, of demonstrating what their father had transferred to the trustees, how the trustees had distributed the trust income and how they were about to divide the capital. The children than commenced an action in the Cayman Islands, and immediately obtained an order whereby the trustees were prohibited from transferring the trust property until the conclusion of the lawsuit (*Lemos v. Coutts* (1992)). They had problems with proceeding with the collection of the documents they needed for the Greek lawsuit: a simple *actio ad exhibendum* was not admissible, and so they added the bad faith of the trustees, on the grounds that they had taken the side of the widow and the children of the second marriage. The question was not a simple one, and it became more complicated when the trustees asked the court for permission to take the costs of the lawsuits in Greece and the Cayman Islands from the trust funds. The decision in this matter went in favour of the trustees, because it was held that they had the duty to defend the validity of the trust (*In the matter of Lemos* (1993)): on this last point, see Underhill, *Trusts*, pp. 563–4.

The underlying issue was faced by the Court of Appeal (*Lemos v. Coutts* (1993)), which confirmed that the trustees had the right to be reimbursed the costs of the actions, but not those relating to baseless counterclaims they had made (on the same subject, again in the Cayman Islands, see *Ojjeh Trust* (1994)). The plaintiffs could not be constrained to decide between the Greek and Cayman Islands actions (as the trustees claimed they could). The beneficiaries of the trust had the right to inspect trust documents, but this is not an absolute right ('it was by no means an absolute right') and the situation must be evaluated on a case-by-case basis. In the light of the serious allegations against the trustees, they had to provide an accounting to the plaintiffs on condition that the latter undertook to use it solely in the context of the action in the Cayman Islands for breach of trust, and not in the action pending in Greece.

The Onassis estate, part of which was in a trust, was also the subject of lawsuits, and it appears that a certain weight was given to a letter written by the daughter of the shipowner to the trustees of a trust she had created with a part of her inheritance asking them not to allow any intrusion by her husband.

The letter of wishes must, therefore, be exactly what its name suggests. The Belize law, fearing that the validity of trusts established locally by foreigners might be contested, confirms this in clear terms: the trustee is not obliged to follow the letter of wishes, and if the settlor wants certain of his instructions to be binding on the trustee, he must include them in the trust instrument.

In practice, we can be sure that letters of wishes will be scrupulously abided by. A professional trustee or trust company acting any differently would immediately find himself or itself with no clients, and would, in any event, be removed by the protector and substituted. This voluntary compliance is of no significance in terms of the legal reconstruction of the relationship which arises out of the delivery of a letter of wishes, except that professional trustees are often confused as to what their role is, until a court sees to it, at great expense, that they are redirected on to the correct path.

In the international trust model, therefore, the letter of wishes is a non-binding instruction to a trustee with which he will tend to comply.

j The emerging contractual element

A rule of the Cook Islands law states that a trust is valid even where the settlor

(a) Retains possesses or acquires a power to revoke the trust or instrument; (b) retains possesses or acquires a power of disposition over property of the trust or the subject of the instrument; (c) retains possesses or acquires a power to amend the trust or instrument; (d) retains possesses or acquires a benefit interest or property from the trust or any disposition or pursuant to the instrument; (e) retains possesses or acquires a power to remove or appoint a trustee or protector; (f) retains possesses or acquires a power to direct a trustee or protector in any manner; (g) is a beneficiary of the trust either solely or together with others.[257]

Here we are in the land of nominalism beyond the good or the bad. What is described in this rule is not a trust at all, but the exact opposite; rather, it is nothing at all. The trustee is an inanimate instrument with no free will, and every asset which is apparently placed in his name belongs entirely to the settlor. Here there is no reason for equity to take any interest; no conscience is involved save that of the drafters of the law. We are not even in the domain of agency, as has been suggested;[258] this is a simulation provoked by the *nomen iuris* which has been used. We are, clearly, in an area of contract, although it is hard to understand which one. In any case, a trust

---

[257] Cook Islands, International Trusts Amendment Act 1989, s. 13C.
[258] C. A. Cain, 'Which Domicile? A Crucial Question for APTs', in 1 T&T (1995) no. 10, 6, at 8.

of this kind cannot be recognized under the Hague Convention, because it does not even comply with the minimum standards laid down in article 2.

If it is true that what we have before us is a sensational example of abasement, the lack of clarity which lurks within the British Virgin Islands law, which we referred to above in the context of the protector, and which will probably be looked on with favour by many clients of local trust companies, is even more dangerous. A trust in which the trustee answers to the settlor and is relieved of responsibility if he follows his instructions, and in which the protector is not held to any fiduciary obligations towards the beneficiaries or the trust purpose, is the opposite of a trust (above all, where the local law permits one of the trustees to assume the role of delegated trustee). While it is my belief that a trust of this kind would not be recognized as such by English law, I am afraid that recognition would be compulsory pursuant to the Hague Convention. This illustrates only one of the misunderstandings which abound in the Convention, but does nothing to diminish the criticism which should be levelled at the British Virgin Islands legislature.

I also look on the Jersey law with disfavour. It reads: Nothing in the terms of a trust shall cause a transfer or disposition of property to a trust to be invalidated by application of the rule '*donner et retenir ne vaut*'.[259] When this law was passed in 1989, no one had a clear understanding of the regulatory significance of the Norman custom '*donner et retenir ne vaut*', of which we have spoken above. The *Rahman v. Chase Bank* decision was yet to be published, although the case had already been discussed and the direction the Court was taking had, perhaps, already been leaked.[260] The Court's reasoning concentrated on gifts without *traditio*, and was therefore applied to trusts in which control over the right was not effectively passed to the trustee: that is, without an entrusting, to use the terminology I suggested when I described the structure of a trust at the end of the previous chapter. If the 1989 Jersey legislature had intended to make trusts valid without an entrusting, it would have acted unreasonably, and would have betrayed the seriousness with which it had passed legislation in 1984.

These are all signs of a creeping contractual element which is emerging in international practice. Other signs may be found, such as in the law of the Cayman Islands, which, in deciding the applicable law of the trust, makes reference not to the wishes of the settlor, but to the 'intention of the parties', as if the transaction which gives rise to the trust were bilateral. On the other hand, model trust instruments are frequently drafted for contem-

---

[259] Trusts (Amendment) (Jersey) Law 1989, which added article 8A to the law of 1984; cf. Matthews and Sowden, §§10.27–10.30.   [260] See above, chapter 3, footnote 344.

poraneous execution by the trustee: this would have no relevance if taken alone, because it is evident that the modern trust is usually created in the presence of the trustee, but it takes on a different significance when it is placed within the general context. Anyone who has experience of international trusts can see that outward appearances do not always correspond to substance, and that professional practice drunkenly carries on with near-forgeries, but those who follow the case law from courts of the States involved in the 'race for the trust' will observe with satisfaction that the courts are perfectly sober.

5   Trusts in civil-law or mixed legal systems

1. Comparative data[1]

a Early misunderstandings

Maitland did his best to explain to von Gierke what a trust was, but the great German jurist confessed that he had understood nothing. Maitland probably emerged from this with pride, and with his belief that the trust was England's greatest contribution to the history of law strengthened. Civil lawyers developed two theories:[2] that the trust was a creature which was so closely tied to particularities of English law that a 'translation' was in the realm of impossibility;[3] and that in any case its characteristics were such that its insertion into civil-law countries (a term which, in truth, did not even exist in those times: one spoke of Roman law systems) would be impossible. No one, therefore, even tried to approach the trust, and no attention whatsoever was paid to the project presented by Limantour in Mexico in 1905.

In the decades which followed, these two theories were reinforced by the

---

[1] In this section, I return to some of the issues which I raised in different sections under the heading *Trusts* in the *Enciclopedia giuridica Treccani* (1995), and consider them in more detail.

[2] P. G. Jaeger, *La separazione del patrimonio fiduciario nel fallimento*, Milan, 1968, pp. 176–85.

[3] As examples: for Swiss law: C. Reymond, 'Le trust et le droit suisse', in ZfsR (1954) 199, at 188–212; P. P. Supino, *Rechtsgestaltung mit Trust aus Schweizer Sicht*, St Gallen, 1994, pp. 81–132; for Spanish law: J. Garrigues, 'Law of Trusts', in 2 AJCL (1953) 25; for Belgian law: J. L. Jeghers, 'La difficile intégration du trust anglo-saxon en droit civil belge', in RevNotB (1991) 311; for French law: J. Motulsky, 'De l'impossibilité juridique de constituer un trust anglo-saxon sous l'empire de la loi française', in RevCrit (1948) 451; for a different view, H. Battifol, 'The Trust Problem as Seen by a French Lawyer', in 33 JcompL (1951) III 18. In general, with criticisms of some aspects which are typically misunderstood by civilians, V. Bolgár, 'Why No Trusts in the Civil Law?', in 2 AJCL (1953) 204.

   Only rarely has case law followed the literature and found problems which are incapable of resolution: see below, chapter 6 footnote 93.

same scholars in France[4] – and later in Italy[5] – who attempted a detailed study of trusts. Not only did they lack comparative weapons, which the times, not being ready for comparative law, could not supply, but they did not even have sufficient experience either of the English legal system as a whole or of the enormous phenomenology of trusts.[6] As a result, they looked for similarities with civil-law categories, and so in France, in 1927, arrived at a concept of the trust as a patrimony by appropriation,[7] and in Italy, in 1935, as a dual-ownership structure within the context of a fiduciary transaction.[8] The debate between Franceschelli and Grassetti on the subject of this latter formulation sufficiently demonstrates how both writers were prisoners of the nominalism and conceptuality of their own legal system.[9]

---

[4] P. Lepaulle, whose final work was *Traité théorique et pratique des trusts en droit interne, en droit fiscal et en droit international*, Paris, 1932.

[5] R. Franceschelli, *Il trust nel diritto inglese*, Padua, 1935.

[6] A. Nussbaum, 'Sociological and Comparative Aspects of the Trust', in 38 ColLR (1938) 408, at 420, holds that Lepaulle developed a great partiality for trusts which 'proved detrimental to his discerning judgment'.

[7] In Lepaulle's article 'De la nature du trust' in *Journal de droit international*, followed by the monograph cited in footnote 4, where, at p. 355, he likens the trust to the *peculium* of Roman slaves.

The segregation typical in English-model trusts does not lead to the identification of a *patrimoine d'affectation*, which is a discredited notion, and one which cannot in any case be proposed to readers who have acquired familiarity with the phenomenology of trusts. In fact, it led writers (who have no following today) to compare trusts with the foundation. The position of Lepaulle and those who refer to him, in the direction of foundations, has been dealt with very briefly in international literature: see K. W. Ryan, 'The Reception of the Trust', in 10 ICLQ (1961) 265, at 271; Reymond, *Trust et le droit suisse* (see above, footnote 3), at 127; Nussbaum, 'Sociological and Comparative Aspects' (see above, footnote 6), at 419–29; Jaeger, *La separazione* (see above, footnote 2), pp. 184–5; F. Weiser, *Trusts on the Continent of Europe*, London, 1936, pp. 59–60; Battifol, 'Trust Problem' (see above, footnote 3), at p.25.

For a recent comparison between trusts and foundations, see A. Zoppini, 'Fondazioni e trusts (spunti per un confronto)', in *Atti Milano*, ch. 13.

[8] At the Semaine Internationale du Droit of 1937 in Paris, R. Franceschelli, in *Travaux de la semaine international de droit, V – La fiducie en droit moderne*, Paris, 1937, held that in order to introduce the *fiducia* in Italian law 'il s'agit d'introduire un nouveau droit réel'.

[9] R. Franceschelli, 'La garanzia reale delle obbligazioni nel diritto romano classico e nel diritto inglese (fiducia cum creditore e mortgage)', in *Studi in memoria di Aldo Albertoni*, Padua (1938), III, 517; C. Grassetti, 'Trust anglosassone, proprietà fiduciaria e negozio fiduciario', in [1936] 1 Riv. dir. comm. 548. Italian civilian literature was an evident victim of this: see, in fact, how the trust is presented in N. Lipari, *Il negozio fiduciario*, Milan, 1964, at pp. 84–7, and so on up to the essays published at the beginning of the 1990s with the coming into force of the Hague Convention (they could, in truth, have taken advantage of specialist writing and Jaeger, *Separazione* (see above, footnote 2), pp. 176–230).

b The *fideicomiso* in Latin America

Lepaulle's theory had success in Latin America because it coincided with a legislative reform movement promoted by the United States, which in 1921 had commissioned a study on the inefficiency of the Latin-American banking systems (the Kemmerer Report), and had obtained the response that one of the reasons for this was the lack of the trust. Panama took immediate action, with a 1925 law on the *fideicomiso*,[10] and the resistance of other countries (Creel's Mexican project dates from 1924, but passed into law only in 1932[11]) folded when they discovered in Lepaulle's theory a key to understanding the concept.[12] The original defect is still in existence, however; some writers still deny that the *fiduciario* receives ownership of the property entrusted to him from the *fideicomitente*.[13] The Mexican *fideicomiso* has displayed no incisive ability to make its presence felt, and has remained confined to very limited spheres.[14] Not even the enthusiastic encouragement of R. Goldschmidt, a jurist with a solid comparative foundation within the civil-law world, had any immediate effect outside Venezuela. Nonetheless, it was probably the Venezuelan law of 1956 which provided the impulse for a re-examination of the topic, and between 1971 and 1995, several States passed new laws which relinquish the limitations of the *fideicomiso* of the twenties and thirties with greater or lesser clarity: these States are Argentina, Colombia, Ecuador, Panama and Peru, and we shall discuss their laws in this chapter.[15]

c Basic comparative data

The States named above represent only a few of those from the 'family' of civil-law or 'mixed' legal systems which have introduced trusts into their

---

[10] Which was adopted almost in its entirety by the Puerto Rican law of 1928, which simultaneously promulgated a law on fiduciary companies; see L. S. Sánchez Vilella, 'The Problems of Trust Legislation in Civil Law Jurisdictions: The Law of Trusts in Puerto Rico', in 19 TulLR (1945) 374, where (at 383–9) the possibility of using the *fideicomiso*, which Alfaro had proposed but then put into doubt again, is re-examined.

[11] A law with a more limited purpose had been passed in 1926.

[12] Cf. Ryan, 'Reception of the Trust' (see above, footnote 7), 272; R. J. Alfaro, 'The Trust and the Civil Law with Special Reference to Panama', in 33 JcompL (1951) III 25. More details may be found in Jaeger, *Separazione* (see above, footnote 2), pp. 236–45.

[13] J. A. Domínguez Martínez, *Dos aspectos de la esencia del fideicomiso mexicano*, Mexico, 1994, ch. 3.

[14] As results from the research conducted by A. Stempel París, *Trust y Fideicomiso*, Caracas, 1955.

[15] I shall also speak of Mexico, since it is representative of the previous system; for other Latin-American countries although it is second-hand information, see, Fratcher, *Trusts*, notes 119–22.

The laws cited in this chapter are published in M. Lupoi, *Trust Laws of the World*, Rome, 1996.

legislation (I do not much believe in the term 'family'; it is little more than an expression). We have seen other States from the same 'family' in the preceding chapter, which was dedicated to the international trust model: there were four 'mixed' systems (Cyprus, Malta, Mauritius and the Seychelles) in which it was quite a simple matter to ensure that the common-law component prevails over civil law. Two of these countries (Mauritius and the Seychelles), furthermore, have created two separate institutions: one aimed principally at foreigners, and another, closer to a civil-law structure (which will therefore be examined in this chapter), for domestic use.

There are diverse reasons for legislating in the area of trusts: the direct influence of a common-law system (Quebec and Louisiana, and also, I would say, the Philippines, Venezuela, Israel, Panama, Mauritius and Argentina), the introduction of a strong ethnic component (South Africa), the decision to introduce a transactional device which is more suited to regulating financial operations than the local one is (Colombia, Ecuador, Japan, Peru and Russia), a cultural affiliation during a period of comparative development and the desire not to let a promising financial instrument get away (Liechtenstein), or the preferences of the comparative-law expert who drafted the code (Ethiopia and the Seychelles). In every case, however, there has been a growing awareness that the trust brings with it 'universal winning values':[16] this, as we shall better see in chapter 7, is the 'challenge' of trusts in civil-law systems.

The variety of reasons, together with the differences which exist among the systems in question, has not, however, led to normative rules which are radically different, except in the case of the Philippines, which adopted the rules in their entirety and which are probably destined to remain almost entirely theoretical.

In approaching the subject of trusts, two distinct comparative aspects intersect. The first is 'translation'; the second is 'comparison' in the true sense of the word. It was the limits of the former which led to the damaging consequences outlined above, but clearly one cannot proceed towards comparison in the true sense if a correct 'translation' is lacking. I have sought to provide one for the English trust model in chapters 2 and 3 of this volume, and for the international model in Chapter 4.

---

[16] R. Sacco, 'La circolazione del modello giuridico francese', in [1995] Riv. dir. civ. 515, at 520; more generally on the circulation of the models, see R. Sacco, *Introduzione al diritto comparato* (5th edition), Turin, 1922, pp. 132–68.

R. Savatier, in *Travaux* (see above, footnote 8), p. 149, states that French law is at a disadvantage because it has not developed the *fiducia*: 'en France la fiducie, à l'heure actuelle, est bien désirée par la pratique mais paralysée par le droit'.

If we are to speak of trusts as an element of a civil-law system, we must provide a preliminary definition of the basic invariable elements which characterize the legal structure to which the name 'trust' is given. A definition of this type, it should be noted, has a comparative goal, and therefore depends upon the heuristic approach of the comparative lawyer. One should avoid the 'shapeless trust' of the Hague Convention[17] and identify the following elements or basic comparative data by means of the topics discussed in the area of the traditional trust model of English law:

1. The transfer of a right to the trustee or a unilateral declaration of trust;
2. Lack of confusion between the right transferred to the trustee and other elements of his estate (segregation);
3. The loss by the settlor of any power over the trust assets as a natural consequence of their transfer to the trustee (entrusting);
4. The existence of beneficiaries or a purpose, and the resulting functionalism of the exercise of the right transferred to the trustee;
5. The imposition of a fiduciary component upon the exercise of the right, with principal reference to conflicts of interest.

One should evaluate whether further elements should be introduced – for example, the lack of relevance of modifications of the trust purpose, and the validity of a trust of which the settlor himself is trustee, and, in any event, whether they explain the chosen elements. One may observe that I have not said that the trust is not a legal person, but such a statement would be pointless, because it is an inevitable result of the second element listed above: if the subject matter of the trust is separated from the remainder of the trustee's estate, it is self-evident that it belongs to a person whose estate does not consist entirely of the trust. This person may well be a legal entity, but it was either pre-existing or, if it were created to hold the subject matter of the trust, it might in the future own other rights which would be separated from it; in neither case therefore, is there an 'institutionalization' of trusts. Finally, it is clear that the more examples are added to the basic elements listed above, the less comparative value the structure we have described will have; I have chosen a middle path which seems to me to be sufficiently discriminative.[18]

The only other attempt to identify the essential characteristics of the trust from a comparative viewpoint is that made by Professor Waters in a

---

[17] The subject of the next chapter.

[18] For other formulations, see the collection of articles in W. A. Wilson (ed.), *Trusts and Trust-like Devices*, London, 1981; in particular, 117ff., the article in this collection by D. W. M. Waters, 'Analogues of the Trust and Its Constituents in French Law, Approached From the Standpoint of Scots and English Law', who (at pp. 127–8) suggests data for identification which appear to me to be insufficient (but see immediately below in the text).

course held at the Hague.[19] It moves along lines which are substantially similar to mine, with two important distinctions, and with terminological nuances which merit more detailed discussion, because they serve further to clarify the sense of my approach.

Compared with the 'transfer of a right to the trustee' (the first of my 'basic comparative data'), he states that 'the property holder is a fiduciary who must have full title to the property under administration as opposed to some lesser right such as possession, detention or factual control'.[20] As to the first part of this sentence, I have preferred to attribute a fiduciary connotation to the use of the right transferred to the trustee, and to make it into a separate characteristic (see my fifth basic datum). I think it is correct to stick to this system, because the title 'fiduciary' receives no special attention in Waters' analysis, which concentrates on the notion of 'full title',[21] whereas it seems to me that for comparative purposes this serves to introduce potential schism with respect to civil-law notions. As to the second part of Waters' sentence, it does not seem to me to be correct to insist on 'full title', for, contrary to Waters' position, the trustee may well be the trustee of a 'lesser right' such as possession, detention and even factual control. As stressed in chapter 3, any legal entitlement may be the subject matter of a trust. The point is that such entitlement must be completely transferred to the trustee:[22] *it is the entitlement which is fully transferred; it is not the entitlement which must be full.*

The second characteristic mentioned by Waters corresponds substantially to my second 'basic datum',[23] while the third identifies an essential characteristic of the trust in a tracing action in favour of the beneficiaries, and Waters observes that no civil-law system permits beneficiaries under a management situation to have this kind of protection, except in cases where they are defined as owners.[24] Here, I must reluctantly dissent on both fronts. I do so with regard to the first because it comes from a 'proprietary' view of the position of the beneficiaries with which, for reasons already illustrated, I disagree.[25] As far as the second is concerned, I disagree because it is not true that civil-law systems do not possess systems of protection

---

[19] Waters, *Cours*, pp. 427–35. Waters' work was published at the same time as my entry entitled 'Trusts (I) Profili generali e diritto straniero' in the *Enciclopedia giuridica Treccani* (1995), in which I proposed comparative elements which, with certain modifications, I have set forth above in the text.   [20] Waters, *Cours*, p. 428.   [21] *Ibid.*, pp. 428–31.

[22] I have already shown at the appropriate point that the key is the existence of an act of transfer, including the cases where the settlor appoints himself as trustee (*fiducia statica*).

[23] 'The trust property . . . is free from the claims of the trustee's personal creditors' in Waters, *Cours*, pp. 431–2.   [24] *Ibid.*, pp. 432–4.   [25] See above, chapter 3 §3.e.

comparable to that provided by tracing.[26] It should be noted in passing that Italian law has no problem giving significance to 'notice',[27] and in situations comparable with those which allow tracing, it uses the far wider and more penetrating notion of 'good faith'.

The fourth and fifth characteristics proposed by Waters highlight, in more detail than my third 'basic datum', the independence of the trustee with regard to the settlor and the beneficiaries.[28] This greater detail comes from the specific significance which is given to the beneficiaries, whom I, on the other hand, consider to be an option in trusts. To concentrate the concept of trusts on the beneficiaries seems to me to be improvident in the comparative context for two reasons: first, because it points the civil lawyer in the direction of structures which should on principle be kept separate from trusts (from the contract in favour of third parties to the *fideicommissum*), and secondly because it underestimates the importance of the enormous expansion of trusts for purposes, charitable or otherwise. I attach great importance to these latter trusts, not only because they have become extremely frequent in the international trust model, but also because it is thanks to them that English law is turning its attention to a reconsideration of the very notion of the beneficiary.[29] If case law takes this to its ultimate level, it will demonstrate definitively that the classic beneficiary is not essential to the structure of the trust.[30]

2. Overview of legal systems

1. Argentina

Argentinian law no. 24441 of 9 January 1995, introduced the notion of 'propiedad fiduciaria', which was already implicit in the terminology of its civil code,[31] as it was in the civil codes of Chile and

---

[26] I would repeat that tracing is not, in my opinion, a remedy but a procedural technique: see above, chapter 2 §4.b.

[27] See, on the other hand, Waters, *Cours*, pp. 432: 'Registration often conceals a civil law jurisdiction's discomfort with giving too much rein to the notice doctrine.'

[28] 'The freedom of the trustee from counter instructions by the settlor or the beneficiary after the taking effect of the trust': *ibid.*, pp. 434–5.

[29] See above chapter 3 §2.b (the final part of trusts for purposes in chapter 3).

[30] The reader should be warned that the position I have taken on this last issue is (at least for the moment) an isolated one.

[31] Article 2662: *dominio fiduciario*; article 2841: *el propietario fiduciario*. See in general C. M. Kiper, *Régimen jurídico del dominio fiduciario*, Buenos Aires, 1989. Article 2662 was amended as follows by law 2441: 'Dominio fiduciario es el que se adquiere en razón de un fideicomiso constituido por contrato o por testamento, y está sometido a durar solamente hasta la extinción del fideicomiso, para el efecto de entregar la cosa a quien corresponda según el contrato, el testamento o la ley.'

Colombia.[32] It represents the most dramatic example of abandonment of the uncertainties surrounding the *fideicomiso*, and is the legislative confirmation of the positions of the most progressive writers which were, however, prohibited by various legislative terms. From 'destina', which leads to the 'dedicated property', to 'entrega', which shows a transfer, Argentinean law arrives at 'tramita', and identifies in the 'propiedad fiduciaria' the subject matter of the transfer.

The Argentinean *fideicomiso* is created by contract or by will. In contrast to the provisions of other South-American laws which we shall review, anyone may be a fiduciary.[33] Special laws have been passed for financial operations using the *fideicomiso* when they give rise to the issuance of valuables (*valori mobiliari*). For the moment, there is no specific tax legislation.[34]

Property in *fideicomiso* no longer belongs to the *fiduciante*, who loses all rights to it. They belong to the fiduciary, but may not be attacked by his creditors. As for the beneficiaries, the law distinguishes between those who are such during the life of the *fideicomiso* and those, who may be different, to whom the property must be delivered when it expires.

We shall see the individual provisions in section 4 of this chapter.[35]

2. Colombia

Colombia participated in the legislation of the twenties and thirties on the *fideicomiso*, but then the Commercial code of 1971 regulated 'de la fiducia',

---

[32] The Chilean code of 1855 (adopted almost in its entirety by the Colombian code, which was in force in Panama until 1916) regulates the *fideicommissum* under the name 'propiedad fiduciaria' (articles 732–63) with the following definition: 'Se llama propiedad fiduciaria la que está sujeta al gravamen de pasar a otra persona, por el hecho de verificarse una condición. La constitución de la propiedad fiduciaria se llama fideicomiso' (article 733).

[33] Provided that the fiduciary operates professionally as such with the public: (article 5).

[34] In the case of a *fideicomiso* regulated by Argentinean law with a local fiduciary, the *fideicomiso* appears to be a taxable entity (as is expressly established in other South-American laws), which must file an annual tax declaration. If the subject matter of the *fideicomiso* is foreign shares, the transfer to the fiduciary is not taxable, although the income may be. If it is, it is due from the *fideicomiso*, and therefore is not added to the personal income of the fiduciary. The treatment of income which is transferred from the *fideicomiso* to a foreign beneficiary is also uncertain. In Argentina, there is an annual tax on personal property (the Impuesto a los Bienes Personales) at a rate of 0.50%, as recently amended by decree no. 780 of 1995: it is doubtful whether the *fideicomiso* is a *persona* subject to the tax, or, alternatively, whether one must consider the beneficiary as such.

[35] For a first impression, see I. Beneventi, '"Trust" e "propiedad fiduciaria": la legge argentina', in [1996] Cont. e imp. 87. For a complete commentary, article by article, see E. I. Highton, J. M. Iturraspe, M. E. Paolantonio and J. C. Rivera, *Reformas al derecho privado. Ley 24.441*, Santa Fe and Buenos Aires, 1995, pp. 13–58; S. V. Lisoprawski and C. M. Kiper, *Fideicomiso. Dominio fiduciario. Securitización*, Buenos Aires, 1995; see also articles by L. Moisset de Espanés, 'Contrato de fideicomiso', and J. Giralt Font, 'Fideicomiso', both in [1995] RevNot 61 and 95 respectively.

taking its inspiration from the Venezuelan law of 1956, and finally, in 1993, a decree was issued to regulate the activities of financial companies carrying out fiduciary responsibilities.

As with other South-American laws, the phenomenon which interests the legislature is the *fiducia mercantil*. Acceptance of the responsibilities of a fiduciary is a commercial act, and is reserved to banks and authorized financial companies. This is the conceptual framework in which the 'fondos comunes de inversión' operate. It is a significant step, because when a manager qualifies as a fiduciary, he is subject to the obligations which arise out of the *fiducia*, and finds himself in a particular environment which is distinguished by such elements as the prohibition against relinquishing the appointment after he has accepted it[36] and the obligation to keep the property in *fideicomiso* separate from his own.[37]

The Colombian law is the only one which prohibits secret fiduciary relationships[38] and excludes the possibility that additional beneficiaries might be added later.[39] Adherence to the vision inspired by Lepaulle is revealed by the terminology which is used: 'patrimonio autónomo afecto a la finalidad contemplada en el acto constitutivo', but as we shall see in section 4, this adherence is a mere illusion.

3. Ecuador

Sections 410 ff. of the Ley de Mercado de Valores of 6 May 1993, which amended the Commercial code of 1857, introduced the *fideicomiso mercantil* into Ecuador. The legislative provisions must, however, be read together with the regulations of 26 August 1993,[40] which severely limit the field of application of the institution by stating that only banks, authorized financial companies and investment fund management companies can be fiduciaries.[41]

The Ecuador law takes advantage of debates in the literature on trusts, but it is certainly inspired by the Anglo-Saxon vision, although transposed into civil-law terms. On this subject, I would mention the following provisions: the conditions which regulate the *fideicomiso mercantil* may be secret (unlike, as we have just seen, the case in Colombia);[42] it is

---

[36] Código de Comercio, article 1232.   [37] Código de Comercio, article 1234 no. 2.
[38] Código de Comercio, article 1230 no. 1.   [39] Código de Comercio, article 1230 no. 2.
[40] Published in supplement 262 of the Registro Oficial.   [41] Article 41.3.
[42] Article 410 2nd paragraph, Commercial code (1857): 'El fideicomiso . . . se establece por instrumento abierto o cerrado'; article 10 of the rule: confidential provisions (which may be all or only some of those which regulate the relationship between transferor and fiduciary) can only be made known by order of a court. It should be noted that these provisions are confidential only for the period indicated by the transferor, and the fiduciary must come to know of them within the time limit established by the transferor.

irrevocable[43] and may have the attainment of a purpose as its intent;[44] and the fiduciary may not transfer his functions.[45]

The assets of the *fideicomiso* (and here we see a return to the typical South-American structure) represent an estate, separate from those of the settlor, the trustee and the beneficiaries,[46] to which is attributed a separate tax position.[47]

4. Ethiopia

The Ethiopian civil code of 1960, as a result of the impetus of René David, who drew up the preliminary project and marked it with civil-law categories, places regulation of trusts in its first book. Here we find a three-way division among physical persons, legal persons and dedicated property ('patrimoines d'affectation'). The trust, badly translated as 'fidéicommis' in the French version, belongs to the last category (as we have just seen with Ecuador), together with foundations.

The law was clearly written with a copy of the English rules before the drafters, because there are so many specific rules which are the same. For example, we find the limitation of the number of fiduciaries to four, which is the general limitation under English law, and the resulting provision, taken literally from the Trustee Act of 1925, which states that if more than four are appointed, the duties will be performed by the first four named; the prohibition against the fiduciary mingling the assets of the *fidéicommis* with his own; the power of the courts to vary the terms of the *fidéicommis*; the automatic inclusion of property acquired with sums obtained from the sale of other assets of the *fidéicommis*; the provision for a third party nominated by the settlor with the power to act to secure the withdrawal of the fiduciary and to nominate his successor; the exoneration of the fiduciary from responsibility if he has acted honestly and reasonably (this, too, comes directly from the Trustee Act); even a kind of protective trust;[48] and so on.[49] The fiduciary has 'the powers of an owner'[50] over the trust property, but his personal creditors cannot claim any right to the property,[51] which forms a body of property aimed at carrying out the instructions of the settlor.[52] There is a noteworthy attempt to establish a conceptual framework, and the language used is dry and technically praiseworthy.

[43] Article 412 of the Law.   [44] Article 7 of the Regulation.   [45] *Ibid.*
[46] Regulation, article 10.   [47] Regulation, article 9.   [48] Article 540.
[49] On the trust in Ethiopian law, see N. C. Vosikis, *Le trust dans le code civil Ethiopien*, Genève, 1975. See also, among other aspects, the revocatory actions by the creditors of the settlor (pp. 215–18) and the classification of tracing as a voiding brought by the beneficiary against *ultra vires* acts by the *fedecommissario* (p. 235).   [50] Article 527 no. 1.
[51] Article 536.   [52] Article 516.

5. The Philippines

The civil code of the Philippines of 1949 placed the trust among contracts. There are only a few provisions[53] which, untypically, concentrate not on express trusts but on a trust which the law calls 'implied'. This includes a number of cases, described in a list which has no pretensions to being all-inclusive, which correspond to some of the fact-patterns examined in the second chapter of this book as *case-law* creations of English law. Resulting and constructive trusts therefore appear in the Philippines law in codified form. There is also the mortgage, in its primitive sense of the transfer of an estate as a guarantee, which is evidently suited to local requirements.[54]

The 'general law of trusts' is, moreover, expressly included among the sources of the rules.[55] This is not a reference to a Philippines law of trusts, but to English and American case law. In this sense, one may speak of an adoption of the Anglo-Saxon trust by Philippines law, but it is one which is clearly dominated by shadows over the certainty of the law, since there are numerous points of contrast between English and American law in the area of trusts.[56] The Philippines legislature probably intended to refer to general principles of trusts, leaving applied solutions in specific cases to local case-law sources.

It is of interest to observe that the rules on trusts are placed in the volume on obligations, after general provisions for contracts, natural obligations and estoppel, and before purchase and sale.[57]

6. Japan

The 1896 civil code was strictly in the civil-law tradition, and when a need for trusts with investment purposes was later identified, it was preferred not to have renewed recourse to foreign jurists (as had been the case with the code). The scholar who had the responsibility of 'translating' an institution which had little connection with the Japanese tradition for property granted in trust for religious purposes arrived at a text which shows an evident intention not to deviate far from the English

---

[53] Articles 1440–57.

[54] Article 1454: 'If an absolute conveyance of property is made in order to secure the performance of an obligation of the grantor toward the grantee, a trust by virtue of law is established. If the fulfillment of the obligation is offered by the grantor when it becomes due, he may demand the reconveyance of the property to him.'   [55] Article 1442.

[56] 'American law', as I have already noted, does not even exist, because the trust is not an area in which federal law applies.

[57] I shall not take account of Philippines law in §4 because, as we have seen in the text, it is not autonomous. Perhaps one might reach a different conclusion from case law and from contractual sources, but I have not been able to do so.

model.[58] Contrast with the civil code system was inevitable, but it remained mostly at a theoretical level, since trusts in Japan have never had any impact on daily life. There are no family trusts, and absolute priority is given to investment purposes and, therefore, in general, to brief duration. Trustees are mostly financial managers, or managers of an industrial project, and settlor and beneficiary tend to be one and the same.

Six banks are authorized to carry out the functions of a trustee pursuant to the special laws of 1922, which have the purpose of regulating the fiduciary investment operations market, which had developed without controls after the first applications of the trust ('shintaku') to the area of building companies.[59]

The two laws of 1922, one on trusts and the other on companies which act as trustees, have been amended several times, and a law was passed in 1952 to regulate investments in debentures by investors through the issuance of 'certificates of benefit' in the name of the owner or to bearer.[60] Since 1972, it has been possible to use the trust to encourage savings by employees. Banking activities have recently been directed towards trusts of real property, especially where the property is also the subject of a financial operation.[61]

I shall limit myself to the 1922 trust law, which permits the creation of a trust by a deed *inter vivos* or by will,[62] and provides for forms of publication so as to ensure that the trust may be enforced against third parties (for example, the registration in share registers of trusts of shares).[63] The law sees as the basis of a trust a transfer which has no contractual elements as between settlor and trustee.[64] Acceptance by the trustee is a commercial act;[65] the transfer of the property to the trustee is the basis of the trust,[66]

---

[58] The task was given to a Japanese jurist, Torafiro Ikada, who had studied trusts in Tokyo under English and American teachers; see K. Takayanagi, in *Travaux* (see above, footnote 8), p. 71.

I have not found confirmation of the statement of M. Arai, 'Japan', in Glasson, I, ch. 21, A21.9, to the effect that Indian law was an important influence.

[59] At the beginning of the twentieth century, trusts connected with the issuance of bonds were used everywhere, even where there was no local law: Japan, however, passed specific regulations in 1905.

[60] I am quoting from English texts in the EHS Law Bulletin Series: *Trust Law*, 1922, amended in 1947; *Trust Business Law*, 1922, amended eight times; *Loan Trust Law*, 1952, amended in 1971.

[61] Special law of 1985. This type of operation is difficult to export, because it requires a bank, acting as trustee, to undertake a residential development, or in any case to carry out an enormous construction project.   [62] Articles 1 and 2.   [63] Article 3.

[64] Article 1 (I remind my readers that I am using an English translation). The Loan Trust Law of 1952, article 2 of which speaks of the 'contract of trust', is different.

[65] Article 6.   [66] Articles 15 and 22.

and the trust property does not become part of the trustee's estate; the trustee answers for the obligations he has assumed as trustee, within the limits of the trust property.[67]

With regard to the functions of the trustees, Japanese law lays down two principles which seem to be a constant in all systems which regulate fiduciary relationships: fiduciary duties cannot be delegated, and, if there is more than one trustee, they must act together.[68]

In the area of protection of a beneficiary against a third party who acquires trust property from the trustee in breach of the conditions of the trust, the Japanese solution demands some attention. Given the requirements of form which I have stated above, one would expect that the beneficiary would be able to take action only if the trust has been made public. The law, instead, revives a typical notion of English law, and permits the beneficiary to act against a third party who knew of the trust, or did not know of its existence due to his gross negligence.[69]

7. Israel

Israel had discovered the trust during British mandate (Charitable Trusts Ordinance, 1924), and had then used it to regulate joint investment funds (Joint Investment Trust Law, 1961). Later, normal practice adopted it, and many trust companies were formed, although there was no law to legitimize them.

It was only in 1979 that the trust came into general use, thanks to the Trust code.[70] Although the trust is an imported structure, the Israeli law first sought to define it: the trust is a relationship with property, as a result of which the trustee is obliged to act in the interests of a beneficiary or for the attainment of a specific purpose.[71] The basis of this relationship is identified in the law, in the contract with the trustee or in other acts of endowment;[72] the latter include *inter vivos* deeds and testamentary dispositions. The requirement that there should be a transfer of property to the trustee was included in the first draft of the law, but was abandoned in the final text. Both the reference to a contract with the trustee and the omission of the requirement of a transfer to the trustee represented a distancing from the English vision of the trust,[73] but supplied a precedent which turned out to be quite close to article 2 of the Hague Convention.

---

[67] Article 19.
[68] Articles 24 and 26. Articles 43 and 46 provide that a trustee may not resign except for very serious cause.   [69] Article 31.   [70] In force since 3 February 1980.
[71] Article 1.   [72] Article 2.
[73] Cf. J. Weissman, 'Shortcomings in the Trust Law', 1979, in 15 IsrLR (1980) 372, at 376–80.

The specific rules of the English model of the express trust are, however, closely followed, to the extent of requiring that a non-professional trustee should not as a rule have the right to be compensated, that in the case of multiple trustees unanimity is obligatory, and that in no case may the trustee acquire trust property.[74] Constructive and resulting trusts are also included in the law, either through the codification of the fact-patterns from these categories (for example, a trustee who derives an unjust profit from the trust, or a third party who receives trust assets knowing that the trustee is in breach of the trust provisions[75]), or as a result of wide-ranging pronouncements which may lead to the recognition of a trust in the absence of an express trust instrument.[76]

Israel recognizes land registration, and the law provides that a trustee may record information regarding the existence of the trust; the same also applies to company registers.[77] It is clear that as a result many questions regarding the position of a third party who contracts with the trustee lose their relevance.

8. Liechtenstein

In 1926, the Principality of Liechtenstein passed the Personen- und Gesellschaftsrecht which, in articles 897–932, regulated the *Treuhänderschaft* based on the English Trustee Act of 1925.[78] Two years later, article 932a on *Treuunternehmen*,[79] consisting of 170 articles, was added. This law was revised in 1980, and only seems to have been used in any significant fashion in recent times, since previously activity was orientated towards the domestic institutions known as *Anstalt* and *Stiftung*.[80]

The Liechtenstein law on the *Treuhänderschaft* has been studied very little, but is of great interest, because before the Maltese law and the French

---

[74] Articles 8 (a), 9 (a) (1) and 13 (a) respectively.

[75] Articles 5 and 14. Cf. J. Weissman, 'Shortcomings' (see above, footnote 73), 391. On protection of beneficiaries with respect to his creditors, see article 20.

[76] For example, article 17 (c): 'Where any property is de facto an endowment but no instrument of endowment exists in respect thereof . . .'.   [77] Article 4.

[78] According to the preparatory work, the decision was principally motivated by reasons of international competitiveness: Ryan, 'Reception of the Trust' (see above, footnote 7), 267.

[79] Also called *Geschäftstreuhand*.

[80] Regulated by articles 534–51; 552–70 respectively of the law.

For a comparison between the *Stiftung* and the trust see A. Schnitzer, 'Trust und Stiftung', in SJZ (1965) 197; K. Biedermann, *Die Treuhänderschaft des liechtensteinischen Rechts dargestellt an ihrem Vorbild dem Trust des Common Law*, Berne, 1981; S. N. Frommel, 'Trust anglosassone e Stiftung del Liechtenstein', in *Forum Internationale* (1993), no. 2, 20; with reference to the Swiss family foundation, see also H. H. Meyer, 'Trusts and Swiss Law', in 1 ICLQ (1952) 378.

fiducie project, it was the only example of the introduction of the trust into a European civil-law system.[81] It is characterized by considerable conceptual consistency, starting from its definition of a trustee (and not of the trust – a sound decision), which it equates, significantly, with the *Salmann*, recognized by certain of the old Germanic laws.[82] Furthermore, employing the relevant techniques of systematic arrangement, it transported all of the aspects of the trust into civil-law notions, without making them banal and without simplification. For example, it clarifies the non-contractual nature of the relationship between settlor and trustee,[83] establishes the powers of the trustee and the remedies available to the beneficiaries, and codifies a fact-pattern for the constructive trust,[84] and so on. It is innovative in its provision for certificates of benefit,[85] which are clearly inspired by other fiduciary institutions from the local legal system, and, perhaps, by the American business trust. Finally, with certain limitations, it recognizes trusts established abroad.[86]

Notwithstanding the fact that the law follows many English rules and principles, the needs of the local situation make their presence felt, in particular with regard to the aspects of the legal position of the settlor (who, as in other civil-law systems, has the right to receive reports[87]) and the requirement that the trust instrument be recorded.[88]

9. Louisiana

The State of Louisiana, which was governed by a *code civil* which was closely connected to the Napoleonic code,[89] saw the opportunity to introduce some

---

[81] F. Weiser, *Trusts on the Continent of Europe* (see above, footnote 7), pp. 53–4 also expresses his approval.   [82] Article 898.   [83] Article 903.   [84] Article 898.   [85] Article 928.

[86] Article 931.   [87] Article 923.

[88] There are two forms of registration, between which the settlor may choose freely. Either he deposits a declaration at the Registrar's Office that the trust (the name of which he must supply) has been created on a certain date, for a certain duration and with certain trustees (it should be noted that the names of the settlor and the beneficiaries are not required to be given), or he deposits the trust instrument. In the former case, the information on the register may be inspected by the public, and in the latter they are confidential.

[89] In the beginning (that is, from 1712), the *Coutume de Paris* was applied in Louisiana. Spain, which succeeded France in 1763, repealed all the laws and customs previously in effect (except the law of 1724 on slavery), and declared its own laws to be in effect. This involved indiscriminate adoption of Spanish laws, from the Theodosian code to the *Siete Partidas* of 1265 to (then) modern laws.

In 1801, Spain re-transferred the region to France, which immediately (1803) delivered it to the new American federation without having introduced any innovations in the area of sources of law. This created a difficult situation: the majority of the population remained French, but it was ruled by Spanish law within a federation dominated by English culture. It therefore became necessary to pass a modern civil code. After an

forms of trust at an early stage.[90] It was only in 1964, however, that a special law covering all aspects of the subject was passed.[91]

The law, which was inserted into the civil code, and has been modified on several occasions,[92] is extremely wide-ranging. It deals with customary issues by transposing the classic rules, but also tackles transactional structures which are typical of Louisiana or which have been particularly highly developed there, such as class trusts, and, naturally, confronts the issues which all civil-law systems must take on if they wish to pass laws which are as close as possible to those of the legal systems which gave rise to the trust.[93]

The trust in Louisiana has its origins in a contract or a will, and in the former case it must be in the form of a notarial deed.[94] The legal definition identifies 'the relationship resulting from the transfer of title to property to a person to be administered by him as a fiduciary for the benefit of another'.[95] This allows an heir's share of an estate to be placed in trust so that the heir receives only the income.[96] A similar system was adopted by the law of Venezuela, as we shall see, but only under certain circumstances. It should be noted in this regard that the provisions of the Louisiana civil code are extremely rigid in the area of forced heirship, and that as orig-

---

experimental law of 1808 (*Digest of the Civil Laws in Force in the Territory of Orleans*), this took place in 1825, and closely followed the Napoleonic civil code.

   On all these matters, see J. H. Wigmore, 'Louisiana: The Story of its Legal System', in 1 TulLR (1916) 1 (at the time the journal was called the Southern Law Quarterly).

[90] On trust law in Louisiana prior to legislation on the subject, see J. M. Wisdom, 'A Trust Code for the Civil Law, Based on the Restatement and Uniform Acts: The Louisiana Trust Estates Act', in 13 TulLR (1938) 79; F. F. Stone, 'Trusts in Louisiana', in 1 ICLQ (1952), 368; R. A. Pascal, 'Some ABCs About Trusts and Us', in 13 LouisianaLR (1953) 555. The first law, of 1882, only dealt with public interests trusts, thus permitting the endowment of Tulane University by Paul Tulane; other laws followed in 1902, 1914, 1920 and 1938 (Louisiana Estates Act). See also L. Oppenheim, 'Limitation and Uses of Louisiana Trusts', in 27 TulLR (1952) 41; Fratcher, *Trusts*, no. 115.

[91] The criteria followed by the drafters are illustrated in L. Oppenheim, 'The Drafting of a Trust Code in a Civil Law Jurisdiction', in W. A. Wilson (ed.), *Trusts and Trust-Like Devices* (see above, footnote 18), p. 137.

[92] It takes up articles 1721–2252 of the Revised Statutes, 1994 edition, from which I quote using the name 'Louisiana Trust Code', in accordance with local practice. The following articles deal with charitable trusts.

[93] Cf. Waters, *Cours* (see above, footnote 19), pp. 371–6.

[94] A complete set of forms may be found in A. B. Rubin, G. le Van and L. P. Hood, *Louisiana Wills and Trusts*, n.p., 1995.

[95] §1731. The trustee is defined (in §1781) as the person to whom an asset is transferred so that he may manage it as a fiduciary. On these classifications, see the decision of the Supreme Court of Louisiana in *Reynolds v. Reynolds* (1980); cf. D. W. Gruning, Reception of the Trust in Louisiana: the Case of *Reynolds v. Reynolds*, in 57 TulLR (1982) 89.

[96] §1841.

inally formulated they actually forbade deeds of gift exceeding a certain proportion of the donor's estate.[97]

10. Luxembourg

A Grand Ducal decree of 19 July 1983 introduced the *contrat fiduciaire* into Luxembourg law. I shall consider it briefly in section 4, because the conciseness of the normative provisions and their limitation to banking relationships prevent them from being given any more weight, at least for the moment.

11. Mauritius

As indicated in the previous chapter, Mauritius gave itself two laws on trusts in the space of three years: one for 'domestic' trusts, and the other for offshore or foreign trusts. We have already discussed the latter, which belong to the international trust model, and we shall consider the former in this chapter.[98]

It is a law of extraordinary importance:[99] the Napoleonic code is still in force in Mauritius, and Courts of equity do not exist. English-style legislation is placed alongside civil laws and the Islamic personal law of a very large part of the population; the Sharia *waqf*, which assign property for religious purposes, have been excluded from the area of application of the Mauritius law on trusts, since they are regulated by a special law.[100]

The greatest difficulty must have arisen in the definition of 'trust', which excludes both 'relationship' and 'contract' in favour of 'device'.[101] By means of this device, the settlor transfers property to a trustee so that he can use it in favour of a beneficiary or for an identified purpose.[102] This definition is less obvious than it might appear to be, since it places emphasis on the obligations of the trustee, and not on the objectives of the transfer to the trustee or of his rights in the trust assets.

---

[97] §1493–4; it was pronounced unconstitutional, and amended in 1981, 1989 and 1990.

[98] Trusts Act 1989, somewhat amended in 1990.

[99] Waters' judgment is equally positive, *Cours*, pp. 364–7.

[100] On the treatment of *waqf* in Somalian legislation, balanced between excluding them from the law and not permitting the loss of governmental control over huge estates, see M. Guadagni, *Xeerka beeraha. Diritto fondiario somalo*, Milan, 1981, p. 280–1; R. Sacco, *Le grandi linee del sistema giuridico somalo*, Milan, 1985, p. 191; cf. Fratcher, *Trusts*, no. 113, with reference to Sri Lanka; more generally, see S. Jahel, 'L'adéquation du droit musulman classique aux procédés modernes de financement et de garantie', in RTDComm (1985) 507.

[101] I think we should draw attention here to the influence of the terminology adopted by Fratcher, *Trusts*, which regularly refers to trusts as a 'device'.

[102] Trusts Act 1989, s. 2.

The Mauritius lawmakers have resolved many problems in an original fashion: for example, they decided to forestall any problems in the area of forced heirship by forbidding a 'stranger', that is, a person who does not belong to the category of legitimate heirs, to obtain benefits from a trust in a proportion greater than 25 per cent;[103] the tracing remedy available to the beneficiary is described, in the context of a revocatory-type action, by following traditional English rules relating to the position of a third party in good faith, sometimes by means of circumlocutions which it will not be easy to interpret in judicial practice. The Mauritius legislators are the only ones to have considered the problem of whether a trust may have the right of a beneficiary of another trust as its subject matter, and responded in the negative.[104]

On many occasions, the Mauritius law adopts rules from the English Trustee Act, as in the cases of the beneficiary who induces the trustee to commit a breach of trust, or the protective trust,[105] or, with certain refinements of detail, the maximum number of trustees and the consequences of indicating a higher number.[106]

This law, being different from both the Latin-American laws which impose an institutional fiduciary and from the laws of the 'race for the trust', which are aimed at an international clientele merits closer examination.[107]

12. Mexico

Mexican laws on the *fideicomiso* were finally defined in the *Ley General de Titulos y Operaciones de Crédito* of 1932; the subject which interests us may be found in articles 346–59 under the heading *Del fideicomiso*.

In the Mexican legislative view the *fideicomiso* comes into being, by an *inter vivos* deed or by will,[108] upon the transfer of rights or the ownership of property to an *institución fiduciaria* for a predetermined legal purpose, usually indicating one or more beneficiaries.[109] The rules regarding the recording of transfers must be complied with.

The fiduciary may not, therefore, be any person, but only an authorized *institución fiduciaria*, to which the right which is the subject of the *fideicomiso* is transferred. Mexican literature and case law agree that this transfer does not produce all the ordinary effects of transfers, and some have held that

---

[103] Trusts Act 1989, s. 4 (8).   [104] Mauritius, Trusts Act 1989, s. 4 (2).
[105] Trusts Act 1989, s. 86.   [106] Trusts Act 1989, s. 12.
[107] Mauritius case law had already considered trusts in *Austin v. Bailey* (1962) (my thanks to Paul Matthews for providing me with this precedent), and, instead of following the French path of assimilating them to profiles recognized by domestic law, it chose not to make any comparisons, but to evaluate if, and to what extent, the trust under review breached imperative provisions of Mauritius law.   [108] Article 352.   [109] Articles 346–7.

the law has introduced a new real right into the legal system, while others suggest that one should use the term *titularidad*.[110] The lack of a legal definition of the *fideicomiso* certainly carries weight in these discussions, since the law only describes the effects, and places the limitations of purpose imposed on the subject matter of the *fideicomiso* in the foreground.[111] The theory has recently been re-proposed that the affixing of the ties of a *fideicomiso* to an asset is a unilateral act which is connected with, but distinct from, the relationship with a fiduciary, which is contractual in nature.[112]

It should be noted that the *fideicomiso* is regulated by a law which forms part of the commercial law; as a result, the gaps must be filled by having recourse to other laws in the commercial field, to banking and commercial use and custom and, finally, to the civil code for the federal district.[113]

The *fideicomiso* is in wide use only in financial operations,[114] and in some cases in real-estate matters, but the recent privatization of the banking sector has favoured the injection of capital from the United States, and with this capital has arrived a wider view of possible uses of the *fideicomiso*. The tax laws consider the phenomenon fully.[115]

13. Panama

The US influence may clearly be seen in the new Panamanian trust law,[116] which differs from other Latin-American laws in the attention it pays to detailed regulation of situations which the others neglect, such as naming of beneficiaries left to a third party,[117] beneficiaries as a category,[118] and the

---

[110] V. R. Batiza, *Principios básicos del fideicomiso y de la administración fiduciaria* (2nd edition), Mexico, 1985, pp. 35–9; J. Barrera Graf, 'Naturaleza juridica del fideicomiso', in his *Estudios de derecho mercantil*, Mexico, 1958, p. 353; specifically, J. A. Domínguez Martínez, *Dos aspectos* (see above, footnote 13), ch. 3, who rejects the idea that the settlor transfers the property to the fiduciary; by the same author, see also *El fideicomiso* (5th edition), Mexico, 1995.   [111] Batiza, *Principios* (see above, footnote 110), pp. 33–5.

[112] Domínguez Martínez, *Dos aspectos* (see above, footnote 110), ch. 2.

[113] Cf. R. Mantilla Molina, *Derecho mercantil*, Mexico, 1950, p. 53.

[114] Which here too, as in many other States, saw the first applications, without a legislative basis, at the end of the nineteenth and beginning of the twentieth centuries (issuance of bonds for the construction of major railway lines). For a more up-to-date discussion, see R. M. Pasquel, *The Mexican Fideicomiso: The Reception Evolution and Present Status of the Common Law Trust in a Civil Law Country*, in 8 CJTL (1969) 8.

[115] Batiza, *Principios* (see above, footnote 13), pp. 108–24.

[116] Law of January 1984, no. 1. The prior Panamanian law of 1923 was much more limiting. It had been drafted principally by Ricardo J. Alfaro, later to become President of the Republic, whose degree thesis (published in 1920 under the title 'El fideicomiso') was on the trust; see Alfaro, 'Trust and the Civil Law' (see above, footnote 12); Ryan, 'The Reception of the Trust' (see above, footnote 7), at pp. 273–5.   [117] Article 16.   [118] Article 18.

transfer of the trust abroad and the change of applicable law.[119]

It is the American influence which led to clarification in article 1 that the settlor himself may be a beneficiary of the trust (although Venezuelan law had already provided for this in 1956), to the possibility of more assets being added to the trust property,[120] to the revocability of trusts,[121] and to the testamentary trust.[122] It is of singular interest, however, that the Panamanian law contains no provisions for the protection of beneficiaries.

On the other hand, the civil-law atmosphere in which the law developed is in strong evidence in the requirements as to form,[123] in the content of the trust instrument,[124] in the express exclusion of any type of oral, implicit or constructive trust,[125] and in the obligation to record a trust of land in the name of the trustee, so that it may not be attacked by third parties.[126] The Panamanian law was passed while the Hague Convention was already in preparation, and pre-dates its provision regarding the change in the applicable law of the *fideicomiso*.[127]

It goes without saying that Panamanian trusts are exempt from all taxes if they relate to immovable property located abroad, or movable property belonging to foreigners.[128]

14. Peru

The new banking law of 1993[129] still sees the *fideicomiso* as a special class of '*comisión de confianza*', and therefore as a commercial act, and reserves the role of the fiduciary to banks.[130]

The *fideicomiso* is seen as a contract, which must be a deed, and which is subject to being recorded if it involves real property,[131] but its source may also be a will. The contractual aspect of the relationship extends – uniquely – to the beneficiary, who may participate in the trust instrument and so make the benefit in his favour irrevocable.[132]

The Peruvian law permits the *fideicomiso* to have a philanthropic or cultural purpose, and in these cases it may have unlimited duration. The '*vitalicio' fideicomiso* for identified beneficiaries born or conceived at the date

---

[119] Article 38.   [120] Article 2.   [121] Article 7.   [122] Article 10.

[123] Article 4: a writing is required, but (*per* article 11) a public deed is required if the subject matter of the trust is real property located within the State.   [124] Article 9.

[125] Article 4.   [126] Articles 13 and 14.   [127] Article 38 2nd paragraph.

[128] Article 35 (which I have simplified).

[129] Ley General de Instituciones Bancarias, Financieras y de Seguros (legislative decree no. 770 of 30 October 1993); it may be found, together with an introduction and many other normative materials, in H. G. Salvattecci, *Ley general de instituciones bancarias, financieras y de seguros*, Trujillo, 1994. I shall use the abbreviated citation 'Ley general de bancos'.   [130] Article 315.   [131] Article 319.   [132] Article 321.

of establishment of the trust lasts until their death; in other cases, the term may not be more than twenty years.[133]

Protection of heirs ('*herederos forzosos*') is ensured by means of the prohibition against placing the property set aside for them into the *fideicomiso*, and they are also assisted by having a recovery action.[134] Furthermore, there is a rule similar to article 692 of the Italian civil code on substitution in the *fedecommesso* where the beneficiary of a trust is of unsound mind, but it extends to minor beneficiaries during the period of their minority.[135]

Among the characteristics of the Peruvian law are the provision for a committee which represents the beneficiaries in dealings with the fiduciary where they number more than five,[136] the requirement that in the banking area every *fideicomiso* must have a functionary with responsibility ('*factor fiduciario*'),[137] and the acknowledgment that beneficiaries are preferred creditors if the bank is placed in liquidation, thus giving them priority over the bank's account holders.[138] In this way, the position of a beneficiary of a trust pursuant to the English model is reproduced.

15. Quebec

Quebec's new civil code, which has been in effect since 1994, has only partially settled a debate in the literature which began in the nineteen seventies, when a commission worked at length on the rules existing in the code with the aim of extending their provisions to the area of '*fiducie*'.[139] These rules had been introduced in 1888, when the special law of 1879 was added to the third book of the 1866 code, in particular into the chapter on gifts.[140] In the course of this debate, some proposed, without success, both offering a courageous welcome to the concept of fiduciary ownership, which emerged instead in the Argentinean law of 1995, as we have seen, and giving the trust legal personality.[141]

There have always been public purpose trusts, such as McGill University,

---

[133] Article 325; a *fideicomiso* which manages funds for the economic development of the country can last for up to forty years.

[134] Article 317.   [135] *Ibid.*   [136] Article 340.   [137] Article 346.   [138] Article 331.

[139] Bibliography in Waters, *Trusts*, p. 1091, footnote 10.

[140] Articles 981a–981n. Quebec private law had remained the French common law in force in 1663 (in particular, as in Louisiana, the *Coutume de Paris* and the Royal Ordinances which preceded that date). Unlike what occurred in Louisiana on the passage to Spain, in this case, the transfer to England brought about no change in the private law of the region (called, at that time, 'Lower Canada').

On the laws of 1879, which have been repealed, see, in addition to the authors cited in the following footnotes, P.-B. Mignault, 'La fiducie dans la Province de Québec', in *Travaux* (see above, footnote 8), p. 35.

[141] Y. Caron, 'The Trust in Quebec', in 25 McGillLJ (1980) 421.

in Quebec, but the functional analogy with foundations was there to help their recognition.[142] The *fiducie* of the code was dealt with in just a few articles, and was a long way from offering a satisfactory normative framework for the requirements of the subject, private or commercial, especially when one considers that until a few years ago, a majority of the population of Quebec, especially in the capital, was of English or Anglophone descent.[143]

The rules of the new civil code placed the *fiducie* after the foundation, and considered the fiduciary property to be a '*patrimoine d'affectation*' distinct from that of the settlor, the fiduciary and the beneficiaries.[144] Both the conceptual suggestions of common law and the tendency which favoured the recognition of legal personality (the foundation model) were rejected, and it was decided to remain as close as possible to orthodoxy and to Lepaulle's position. The fiduciary is, therefore, fundamentally an administrator of dedicated property; the settlor disposes of it, but the fiduciary does not acquire it.

16. Russia

Among the latest entrants into the world of trusts is the Russian Federation. Decree no. 2296 of 24 December 1993, which was followed by regulations dated 1 February 1994, links the trust to the ongoing privatization process. It is not clearly connected with the work on the drafting of the new civil code, which has become law in the meantime,[145] and, probably to avoid pre-determining situations which would conflict with provisions of the code, it has for now been limited to shares of companies born out of privatization.[146]

The decree was inspired by the English and American law firms which are extremely active in the legislative field in Russia and in other Eastern European States, and begins with an extraordinary precept: 'The institu-

---

[142] See R. H. Mankiewicz, 'La fiducie québecoise et le trust de common law', in 12 RBQ (1952) 18.

[143] The last ten years have seen a decisive 'francophonization' in Quebec, and the emergence of a desire for independence from the Canadian federation. The referendum of 1995 nevertheless approved, albeit by a small majority, the preservation of federal ties.

[144] Article 1261. For a pungent criticism of the terminology used in the civil code, see M. Tancelin, 'Les faiblesses logiques du code civil du Québec', in M. Lupoi, L. Moccia and P. Prosperetti (eds.), *Scintillae Iuris – Studi in memoria di Gino Gorla*, Milan, 1994, I, 951.

[145] The second part of the civil code came into force on 1 March 1996. Chapter 53 is dedicated to the fiduciary administration of property. According to the first, and most authoritative, commentaries, the provisions of the code have the effect of repealing the decree reviewed in these pages (my gratitude to Gabriele Crespi Reghizzi for this information).   [146] Article 21.

tion of fiduciary ownership is introduced into the civil law of the Russian Federation', and, in fact, goes on to describe the creation and effects of a trust as the transfer of a property right to a trustee, who undertakes the obligation to use it only for the benefit of the beneficiary.[147] Apart from the fact that the drafters have forgotten that the trustee might die, and have not provided any mechanism for the appointment of a new trustee, this is an interesting exercise, but it is not possible to predict what fortune it will have.[148]

17. The Seychelles

The Seychelles adopted the Napoleonic code in 1808. They were transferred to England in 1814, but kept their code in force until 1976, when the new code became law.[149]

In the meantime, civil procedure had been substituted by the English model,[150] and English-type laws had been passed, especially in the commercial field. However, the new civil code did not break with French tradition,[151] to the point of retaining the division of the code into three books. It effects a considerable innovation, however, where it introduces an English-style trust for sale into the context of co-heirship in succession, and then of all forms of joint ownership: the right of co-ownership of immovable property is compulsorily converted into a right to receive a corresponding share of the sale price (this is optional in the case of movable property). The right of ownership therefore passes to a fiduciary (who may be one of the joint owners),[152] who will take care of the sale.

From here to the generalization of the structure was but a short step, and article 824 introduced the notion of the fiduciary: anyone may transfer movable property to a fiduciary for the attainment of a purpose. It was not necessary to break up the notion of ownership: the relationship between the fiduciary and his principal is regulated by the laws on agency, the passage of the property ensures that the purpose is attained, and the

---

[147] Article 3. It is a contract, in the form of a public deed (article 17).

[148] See above, footnote 145.

[149] On which see A. G. Chloros, *Codification in a Mixed Jurisdiction*, Amsterdam, 1977.

[150] This is characteristic of the British colonial system: not to interfere radically in substantive law, but to introduce the British justice system.

[151] Civil code of Seychelles Ordinance 1975, s. 5 (2): 'Nothing in this Ordinance shall invalidate any principles of the jurisprudence of civil law or inhibit the application thereof in Seychelles except to the extent that it is inconsistent with the civil code of Seychelles.'

On the methodology observed in the drafting of the code, see A. G. Chloros, 'The Projected Reform of the Civil Code of the Seychelles: An Experiment in Franco/British Codification', in 48 TulLR (1974) 815.   [152] Articles 815–23.

fiduciary's creditors have no action against the assets which make up the 'fiduciary fund'.

18. St Lucia

It is not widely known that the Quebec civil code was adopted by the English Caribbean colony of St Lucia in 1879. This was due to an historical accident (the transfer of a colonial jurist from Quebec to St Lucia). The two systems then had no further contact, which caused enormous problems of interpretation of the St Lucia code until they rediscovered each other and established a system of consultation.[153]

St Lucia was a French colony for a good part of the eighteenth century, but passed to England in 1804 with a promise that French law would be maintained (this is analogous to the situation in Quebec, also with regard to the sources of law). The St Lucia civil code of 1879 was revised in 1957, but it maintained the structural and conceptual aspects of the code civil, including the fundamental division into three parts. In any event, a fourth part, dedicated to trustees, was added in 1957. It mirrors the Trustee Act of 1925 with local adaptations (for example, a power of attorney granted by a trustee who absents himself from the colony must be in the form of a notarial deed[154]).

This fourth part is clearly uncoordinated with the remainder of the code; it is sufficient to observe that article 695 (which is the same as article 893 of the Napoleonic code) states that property may be transferred without consideration only by will or by gift, and that article 361 translates article 544 of the Napoleonic code on the definition of property rights verbatim. As a result, since there are no direct sources on the application of the fourth part of the code in the colony, I shall not include an examination of it in this chapter.

In any event, it is interesting to note that, as with all the civil law legal systems we are examining, that of St Lucia requires that the trustee appear as such in the land registry.[155]

19. Venezuela

The Venezuelan law of 1956[156] represented the first serious attempt in South America (influenced, but not bound, by other Latin-American experiences) to introduce a notion of trust with no restrictions as to its range of

[153] J. N. O. Liverpool, 'The History of the St. Lucia Civil Code', in *Essays on the Civil Codes of Québec and St. Lucia*, Montreal, 1985.   [154] Article 2165 (4).
[155] Land Registration Act 1984, article 81.
[156] The 23 July 1956, published in the Gaceta Oficial of the 17 August 1956, no. 496. It was later incorporated in the banking law of 1961.

applications into a country with a full civil-law tradition.[157]

The seriousness of approach is apparent from the definition, which concentrates on the obligations of the trustee: the *fideicomiso* is a legal relationship which sees the fiduciary obliged to use the property to the advantage of the beneficiary, who may also be the settlor.[158] The *fideicomiso* is created by a notarial deed[159] or by will,[160] and must be recorded in the land registry.[161] The duration is unlimited where subsequent beneficiaries are named, provided that they were alive when the disposition in favour of the first beneficiary was made.[162]

Among the most interesting provisions of the law are those regarding forced heirship: the settlor may, as an exception to the norms of the civil code, place the share of his property set aside for an heir in *fideicomiso* where the heir is spendthrift or insolvent, so that 'there is a serious threat to acquisitions of property' (in other words that they will finish in the hands of creditors).[163] The legal position of the beneficiary includes the right to claim *fideicomiso* property which has been appropriated by the fiduciary or has been improperly transferred by him,[164] and to assign his interest; in this case, however, the lack of a requirement of publication of these transactions creates difficulties with respect to the beneficiaries' creditors.[165]

The duties of a fiduciary may only be performed by banks, insurance companies and authorized financial companies. Venezuelan regulations, which are drafted better than their Mexican equivalents, have allowed the *fideicomiso* to expand in a way unknown in Mexico. Special laws regulate the activity of insurance companies and banks as trustees: the law of 1975 on severance payments to employees requires that a *fideicomiso* be established for each of them, and that the sum deposited in it be invested by the fiduciary 'en inversiones seguras, rentables y de alta liquidez';[166] the property of minors may be safeguarded by the creation of a *fideicomiso*; the performance of alimony obligations in favour of a spouse or children may be guaranteed by means of a *fideicomiso*

---

[157] The inspiration behind the law, and the editor of the report, was R. Goldschmidt, by whom see 'El fideicomiso en la reciente legislación venezolana', in 12 RevFDer, 89. He used the first legislative developments in Louisiana, in the area of trusts and the rights of heirs, for example. Goldschmidt had vast comparative experience. He graduated in Berlin in 1932 and in Florence in 1934, and was an assistant at the Università Cattolica of Milan, and a professor at San Gallo, Uruguay, Argentina and finally in Venezuela. See also N. Vegas Rolando, *El fideicomiso en Venezuela*, 291 (where the report on the Venezuelan law on the *fideicomiso* is reprinted).   [158] Article 1.   [159] Article 3.   [160] Article 4.
[161] Article 5. [162] Article 8. [163] Article 10. [164] Article 18 and article 24 no. 2. [165] Article 25.
[166] Labour Law, article 41.1. Cf. Louisiana Trust Code, §1921. The labour law was completely revised in the Ley orgánica del trabajo of the 20 December 1990 which, in article 108, regulates the *fideicomiso laboral*.

established pursuant to a judgment;[167] and financial companies are the object of rules regarding the assets they manage in the *fideicomiso*.[168]

3. Two special cases

a Scotland

Scottish law has based the trust on a typical medieval structure: the unconditional transfer of property, accompanied by a document (called a 'back bond'), in which the manner in which the property can return to the settlor is established.[169]

Scotland remained an independent kingdom until the beginning of the eighteenth century.[170] It had notable contacts with European law and European *ius commune* literature (principally through Dutch writers[171]) had a marked influence on it, especially in its formative period, establishing, *inter alia*, the system of sources, and giving predominant weight to *auctoritas doctorum*.[172] Still today, all legal texts regularly quote Scottish writers from the sixteenth to the beginning of the nineteenth centuries (the so-called 'institutional writers').

Of course, the proximity of England could not be ignored, even before formal union.[173] The Scottish legal system has also meticulously retained its own terminology and authorities:[174] in the specific area of trusts, the

---

[167] Law of 22 December 1961, article 2.

[168] Article 7.03 of the Venezuelan law of 1978 on *fideicomiso* operations by 'ahorro y prestamo' companies provides that they must 'contabilizar separadamente las operaciones relativas a cada fideicomiso e incluirlas en rubro aparte del balance'; the Venezuelan law does not need to clarify that assets in *fideicomiso* are not a part of the fiduciary's property, because this is the natural effect of the *fideicomiso*.

[169] It will be recalled that the mortgage also belongs to this tradition.

[170] The union between the Scottish and English kingdoms dates from 1603, but the political union only took place in 1707. The legal history of Scotland may be found in D. M. Walker, *A Legal History of Scotland*, Edinburgh, 1988–95 (3 volumes).

[171] The nineteenth century, on the other hand, saw frequent cultural contacts with German Law faculties: A. Rodger, 'Scottish Advocates in the Nineteenth Century: The German Connection', in 110 LQR (1994) 563.

[172] Cf. W. M. Gordon, 'Roman Law in Scotland', in R. Evans-Jones (ed.), *The Civil Law Tradition in Scotland*, Edinburgh, 1995, which includes a complete bibliography.

[173] R. Burgess, 'Thoughts on the Origins of the Trust in Scots Law', [1974] JR 196. On the indirect means by which English law has progressively pulled Scottish law closer to it, see R. Evans-Jones, 'Civil Law in the Scottish Legal Tradition', in his *Civil Law Tradition* (see above, footnote 172), p. 13; the author sees Scotland returning to its civil-law roots, thanks to the European Union and to university student-exchange programmes; from a different viewpoint, see P. B. H. Birks, 'The Foundation of Legal Rationality in Scotland', in Evans-Jones, *Civil Law Tradition*, p. 81.

[174] Cf. W. A. Wilson, *Introductory Essay on Scots Law* (2nd edition), Edinburgh, 1984, pp. 10–20 (I

settlor is called 'truster', thus drawing attention to the original sense of the institution, which I have tried to render by focusing on the entrusting. The truster is precisely the 'entruster', since the property which he transfers to the trustee 'can hardly be recovered from him, but by his faithfulness in following that, which he knows to be the true design of the Truster'.[175]

In Scotland, too, therefore, trusts were born outside the legal system, usually by means of oral declarations of fiduciary entrusting made contemporaneously with the transfer of the property;[176] in any event, the situation of persons having ownership of (movable) property and fiduciary duties was not unknown to the Scottish legal system, since it corresponded to that of the executor of a will in ecclesiastical law.[177] Important laws were passed during the seventeenth century, with the objective of foreseeing the abuses to which trusts lent themselves.[178] The typical features of trusts remained nebulous for a long period, however, since the Court of Session decided in 1891 that the trust could be attacked by the trustee's creditors.[179] It was the intervention of the House of Lords in this case, as in others, which, while

recommend this book as a simple presentation of the bases of the Scottish legal system, and especially of private law).

For example, the plaintiff is the 'pursuer'; the act by which a contractual proposal is made is a 'missive'; the owner of an estate is 'infeft' (in English, 'enfeoffed'); the Bar is the Faculty of Advocates; the injunction is the 'interdict'; 'induciae' the period within which to make an appearance; and the owner of a 'feu' (that is, an estate) is a 'fiar'.

There are other archaic expressions which defy translation, such as 'allenarly', which no one can explain, but which must be used when an asset is transferred to X for his life and then to his children, born or unborn.

There are glossaries, such as J. A. Beaton, *Scots Law Terms and Expressions*, Edinburgh, 1982; or A. G. M. Duncan, *Green's Glossary of Scottish Legal Terms* (3rd edition), Edinburgh, 1992.

[175] The quotation is from Stair, *Institutions of the Law of Scotland* (5th edition), Edinburgh, 1832, IV. vi. §2 (the first edition is from 1681).

[176] As in England, testamentary trusts came much later (this observation puts an end to Germanic theories, by which the trustee is a derivation of the Salman).

[177] On this and other historical aspects of Scottish trusts, see A. E. Anton, 'Medieval Scottish Executors and the Courts Spiritual', in 67 IurRev (1955) 129.

[178] I am referring to the laws of 1617 (on executors of wills), of 1621 (revocation) and of 1696 (proof of the creation of a trust); see T. B. Smith, 'Trusts and Fiduciary Relationship in the Law of Scotland', in his *Studies Critical and Comparative*, Edinburgh, 1962, pp. 198ff., at pp. 201–7.

[179] *Heritable Reversionary Co. v. Millar* (1891).

The Court of Session, which has its only seat in Edinburgh, has two levels in civil matters (Outer and Inner House). The House of Lords hears appeals from the Court of Session; in these cases, the court has a special configuration, so as to ensure the presence of judges familiar with Scottish law. Cf. M. C. Meston, W. H. D. Sellar and Lord Cooper, *The Scottish Legal Tradition*, Edinburgh, 1991, pp. 3–8.

English law is considered in Scotland as if it were a foreign law (it must, therefore, be proved before the court).

remaining within the tracks of Scottish law, permitted the enunciation of rules which were the functional equivalent of those of English law.[180]

In this way, the structures of the indigenous institution were eroded. The separate agreement which accompanied the transfer (the 'back bond') was first considered to be the equivalent of a *pactum de retrovendendo*, and in any event as the basis of an obligation of the trustee towards the settlor, or truster. No right of the settlor arose out of it, therefore, as against third parties purchasing from the trustee.[181] Using civil-law notions, Scottish writing initially considered the trust to be a combination of a deposit (of the trust property) and an agency relationship (*mandatum*),[182] but progressively came to understand that the area of contracts was limiting, and that the trust involved fiduciary obligations, the sources and the effects of which lay outside contract.[183] The problem which had to be resolved without the assistance of equity was the one which equity had solved without difficulty by using the concept of the equitable defect in the trustee's title. At first, Scottish case law adopted a line which was clearly inspired by the continental *fiducia*: the relationship was of a fiduciary nature, and the settlor had to bear the consequences of having wanted the trustee to appear to be the owner of the asset. The trustee was only apparently the owner, but mere appearance was sufficient to allow him to dispose of the asset. There would, therefore, be competing rights to the same asset: that of the settlor, the 'true' owner, and that of the trustee, the owner in the eyes of third parties. The beneficiaries would receive no protection, unless they were considered to be the equivalent of the beneficiary of a contract in favour of third parties.[184]

Positions which differed from the one just described manifested themselves, and the opinions of Bell, who was an author of considerable influence in the second half of the nineteenth century, gained increasing recognition, in particular the theory according to which the trust purposes 'operate as qualifications of the estate in the trustee, and as burdens on it preferable to all who may claim through him'.[185] It is fiduciary ownership: it is not a relationship between a principal and a fiduciary, and not the assumption of personal obligations by the latter, but a lack of completeness of a right, even if it follows upon the contract or agreement

---

[180] A succinct explanation of trust law in Scotland may be found in W. A. Wilson, 'The Trust in Scots Law', in Wilson (ed.), *Trusts and Trust-like Devices* (see above, footnote 18), p. 237.

[181] Cf. Wilson and Duncan, pp. 4–12.

[182] *Cunningham v. Montgomerie* (1879), 1337, *per* Lord President Inglis.

[183] *Allen v. McCrombie's Trustees* (1909), 720, *per* Lord Kinnear.

[184] Wilson and Duncan, pp. 15–18.

[185] G. J. Bell, *Principles of the Law of Scotland* (10th edition), Edinburgh, 1899, §1991.

between settlor and trustee.[186] An authoritative work expresses it thus:

A trust then is a legal relationship in which property is vested in one person, the trustee, who is under a fiduciary obligation to apply the property to some extent for the benefit of another person, the beneficiary, the obligation being a qualification of the trustee's proprietary right and preferable to all claims of the trustee or his creditors.[187]

The beneficiary, as in English law, is not the owner of any right in the trust property. As has recently been clarified, in Scottish law the phenomenon of the duplication (or splitting) of the ownership position does not exist, and there are no conflicting rights to the same asset.[188]

These systematic foundations from outside the world of equity make it hard to introduce rules which are analogous – at least from a functional point of view – to those of English law into Scotland. For example, it was asserted in 1971 that a trust of which the settlor appointed himself trustee would be a 'novelty', although it would be acceptable as a modern development.[189] Secret trusts are not valid, and it was only in 1995, with the Requirements of Writing (Scotland) Act, that the form of the trust instrument was legislated upon; among other elements, rules were introduced which were inspired by those applied by equity to situations where the declaration of trust does not have the required form but the beneficiary has relied upon it.[190]

Where adoption of English equitable rules is extremely difficult, and sometimes impossible, is in the area of constructive trusts, as has been clearly shown by the First Division of the Court of Session, which refused to allow the purchaser of an asset to be the beneficiary of a constructive trust during the period between the signing of the contract and the completion of registration formalities.[191]

---

[186] The analysis of Waters, *Cours*, pp. 351–3, is different.   [187] Wilson and Duncan, p. 20.

[188] *Sharp v. Thomson* (1995), 851, *per* Lord President Hope: 'It is not part of the law of Scotland that there exist *in the trustee and beneficiary concurrent rights of ownership in the property which is the subject of the trust.*' Previously Lord President Normand in *Inland Revenue v. Clark's Trustees* (1939): the beneficiary is the owner of 'nothing more than a personal right to sue the trustees and to compel them to administer the trust in accordance with the directions which it contains'. In detail, see Wilson and Duncan, pp. 144–55; on the same lines Smith, 'Trusts and Fiduciary Relationship' (see above, footnote 178), at pp. 221–3; D. M. Walker, *Principles of Scottish Private Law* (4th edition), Oxford, 1989, IV, pp. 56–7.

[189] *Allan's Trustees v. Inland Revenue* (1971), 63, *per* Lord Reid.

[190] Requirements of Writing (Scotland) Act, ss. 1 (3) and (4).

[191] *Sharp v. Thomson* (1995). In my opinion, the decision was partly influenced by the fact that the matter involved giving effect to a floating charge, which is held to be a foreign (that is, English) institution. The decision was in favour of the holder of the floating charge, but did not leave the judges satisfied. One of them noted, rather maliciously, that the legislative introduction of the floating charge did not leave the possibility of deciding

In many cases, on the other hand, Scottish law has found the means to arrive at suitable results within its own conceptual framework, as, for example, in the area of a trustee's conflict of interest, which has been couched in the terms of the civil-law principle of *auctor in rem suam*, or in developments of the *nobile officium*. The concept of the *nobile officium* consists fundamentally of the jurisdiction of the Court of Session, as a result of which the court may intervene, if asked to do so, to modify or add to the provisions of a public-interest trust. In Scotland, the concept of the charitable trust does not exist, because the law from the reign of Elizabeth I, to which we have already referred,[192] was passed when Scotland was still an independent kingdom. Accordingly, the distinction is between private and public-interest trusts; in addition to the Lord Advocate, any interested party may act to secure the performance of the latter.[193]

In contrast to the situation in English law, the trustee must make the trust public, in a land registry or a share register, for example. As we have just seen, and as we shall see in more detail below, this is a constant in non-common-law systems. Again in contrast to English law, proof of the existence of a trust obtained from witnesses was always inadmissible in Scottish law, and when problems emerged in this area, the Blank Bond and Trusts Act of 1696 was passed. It remained in force until 1995, and made a formal trust instrument (back bond) obligatory; if there was none, only an oath was accepted.[194]

We cannot go into further detail on Scottish trusts.[195] I wanted to point out the fundamental technical–systematic aspect of fiduciary ownership in a legal system with civil-law foundations which does not recognize equity, but it is equally important to have shown, albeit briefly, how some common-law rules have been adopted without any alterations to their conceptual framework, while in other cases the legal system has discovered the necessary implements, and in yet others the contrast with the English system has hindered the development of excessively technical rules.

---

otherwise open: 'The result is unsatisfactory, but it is the consequence of the introduction by Parliament of a concept which is alien to Scots law with a view to its commercial advantages but without sufficient regard to the protection which may be needed to avoid hardship to the purchaser' (Lord Hope, at 854).   [192] See above, chapter 3 §1.i.

[193] Wilson and Duncan, ch. 15; see specifically various authors, *Charity Law in Scotland*, Edinburgh, 1996.

[194] '*It is a sacred principle of the law of Scotland that trust cannot be proved parole,*' *Scott v. Miller* (1832), 29 *per* Lord Gillies.

[195] For tax issues, see M. H. Jones and S. A. MacKintosh, *Revenue Law in Scotland*, London, 1986, pp. 70–129.

b South Africa

The literature holds the South African trust to be in the civil-law tradition, and considers it to be a natural and original development of Roman–Dutch common law, and therefore a product of civil law.[196] A comparison with the Scottish experience shows that this is not an exaggerated claim.

The British arrived in South Africa (or rather, in the Cape Colony) in 1805, and progressively conquered the entire country, in which the dominant culture was Dutch.[197] Within less than two years the first trusts had appeared, but they existed side by side with Dutch institutions, principally the *donatio cum modo*[198] and the foundation ('Stigting'), which had had similar purposes since the previous century. Although there was no local system of equity, the English trust model was regularly applied by the new colonies, while the Dutch followed the traditions of their homeland, particularly with the appointment of a *bewindhebber*, that is, an asset administrator, as well as with the *fideicommissum* of European common law.[199]

The *bewindhebber* belongs to the *genus* of guardians and tutors: he is the holder of an office. The trustee is recognized as belonging to the same category, and the personal disinterest which characterizes his position is underlined. This first act of harmonization renders a second one more simple: to bring the trust and the *bewind* together under the common

---

[196] Honoré, *Trusts*, pp. 15–18.

    A clear explanation of the distinctive aspects of Roman–Dutch law may be found in R. Zimmermann, 'Römisch–Holländisches Recht – ein Überblick', in R. Feenstra and R. Zimmermann, *Das Römisch–Holländisches Recht. Fortschritte des Zivilrechts in 17. und 18. Jahrhundert*, Berlin, 1992, p. 9. It has recently been demonstrated that Roman law was also directly applied in South Africa, as a formal source of law, in matters relating to slavery: D. Visser, 'The Role of Roman Law in the Punishment of Slaves at the Cape of Good Hope under Dutch Rule', in *Mélanges Felix Wubbe*, Fribourg, 1993, 525.

[197] The first Dutch settlement was established in 1652. In that period of history, there was no unified law of the continental Dutch Territories, and so Dutch common law was mostly applied (Holland was one of the Seven Provinces).

    Situated on the route to the Indies, the Cape was for 150 years governed by the Dutch West Indies Company. When the British took over power, the Dutch population beyond the Orange River remained independent (Orange Free State) and in 1853 created a federation which took the name of the Republic of South Africa. The federation, together with Transvaal, fought the Boer War between 1899 and 1902, and, after the British victory, joined the Union which obtained independence in 1913.

[198] If enforceable, a gift which provides for the re-transfer to a third party is, in reality, a *fideicommissum*.

[199] For a treatment of the trust and connected issues in Roman–Dutch law, see L. I. Coertze, *Die Trust in die Romeins–Hollandse Reg*, Stellenbosch, 1948 and C. P. Joubert, *Die Stigting in die Romeins–Hollandse Reg en die Suid-Afrikaanse Reg*, The Hague, 1951 (which I have not had the opportunity to consult).

denominator of supervision of property not for personal benefit.[200] The *bewindhebber* manages property which belongs to the beneficiary; the trustee manages property which is his. This distinction was adjudged to be of secondary importance, and the law of 1988, which lay down general rules in the area of trusts for the first time, defines the trust as an 'arrangement' (which, as in Scotland, must be in writing), pursuant to which property is transferred either to a trustee so that he can manage it for the benefit of the beneficiary or for a purpose, or to a beneficiary (although placed under the control of a third party who must manage it for the benefit of the beneficiary or a purpose[201]).

A person cannot, therefore, name himself as trustee, as was also the case in Scotland until some decades ago.

The trustee (and from here on I shall not distinguish between the two sub-types of South African trust), is, in his capacity as trustee, the holder of an office, and is subject to judicial control from the moment of his appointment, which must be recorded, and may be required to provide security.[202] The placing of the trustee within the category of office-holders naturally involves the segregation of the trust property. A trust of real property must be recorded in the name of the trust or the trustee, whose status must be specified.[203]

We are, as will have been seen, in a completely civil-law environment. The interesting aspects of the South African solutions, on which we shall dwell for some time, lie in the great strength of the Roman–Dutch tradition which (unlike in Scotland) still permeates its legal system.[204] It has been

---

[200] This, for South African scholars, is the fact which characterizes the trust: H. R. Hahlo, 'The Trust in South African Law', in 78 SALJ (1961) 195, at 195–6.

[201] Trust Property Control Act 1988, s. 1.

[202] On the registration procedure and its function, see *Simplex v. van der Merwe* (1996).

[203] With regard to shares, the law (Companies Act 1973, s. 104) appears to leave each company free to recognize or not to recognize the trust. In practice, companies – or at least, companies quoted on the Stock Exchange – refuse to enter trustees in the share register *qua* trustees. The entry is therefore made in the name of the trustee without further specification: B. Wunsch, Book Review (Honoré's *South African Law of Trusts*), in 100 SALJ (1993) 549, at 554.

[204] It is not unusual for Grotius, Voet, Domat or Pothier to be cited in decisions in traditional areas in addition to the *Corpus Iuris*. On the influence of Grotius on Roman–Dutch property law, see A. J. van der Walt, 'Des Eigentumsbegriff', in R. Feenstra and R. Zimmermann, *Das römisch–holländische Recht* (see above, footnote 196), p. 485 (all the contributions in this volume demonstrate the lasting importance of the authors of common law).

For a detailed commentary on the role of Roman–Dutch law in South Africa, see R. Zimmermann, 'Roman Law in a Mixed Jurisdiction', in Evans-Jones (ed.), *Civil Law Tradition* (see above, footnote 172), p. 41, with updated statistics on citations of civil-law sources in South African decisions; M. Kaser, 'Das römische Recht in Südafrika', in 81

obliged to find a *modus vivendi* with the legal traditions of the English colonists, but it has not ceded its systematic consistency.

When in 1915 it became necessary to decide on a testamentary trust, the court took note of the fact that it was faced with a foreign institution. It observed nonetheless that the *fideicommissum* of the Roman–Dutch tradition did not necessarily require that the person to whom the property is granted should have the right to make any use of it. For example, it was common practice to transfer assets to a fiduciary in pre-marital agreements and in the case of the issuance of debentures guaranteed by real property.[205] The testamentary trust is, therefore, a *fideicommissum* of this type,[206] but it is by means of recourse to the theory of the classical *fideicommissum* that the trustee can exchange the trust asset for another of equal value even though he has been granted no specific power to do so.

Trusts *inter vivos*, on the other hand, were placed in a contractual context: the trustee was considered to be either a *donatarius gravatus* according to the structure of a *donatio sub modo*, or the promisor in a contract in favour of a third party.[207] Acceptance by the beneficiaries, which has no relevance in English law, has the same effect as acceptance by a third party in a *stipulatio alteri* (in the sense that it makes the designation of the beneficiaries irrevocable).[208] A trust usually has several beneficiaries, however, some of whom may not yet have been born. Since the South African trust is essentially revocable, only acceptance by the beneficiaries (or an express provision in the trust instrument) can make it irrevocable in favour of the accepting parties. In this regard, case law has applied the rules on the *fideicommissum*

ZSS, Rom. (1964) 1, which contains precise references to the rules of Roman law in force in South Africa, and to English influence on the structures of the legal system (for example, judicial precedent) as much as in the singular areas, but which attributes its conceptual framework to the Romanistic tradition.

[205] *Kemp, Estate v. MacDonald's Trustee* (1915). For a critique of the correctness of the interpretation of Roman law upon which the judgment was founded, see B. Beinart, 'Trusts in Roman and Roman–Dutch Law', in Wilson (ed.), *Trusts and Trust-like Devices* (see above, footnote 18), pp. 167ff., at pp. 176–9.

[206] Civilians have avoided the false analogy with the *sostituzione fidecommissaria*. As may easily be seen, the trustee operates on behalf of third parties, whereas the first appointee in a *fideicommissum* has enjoyment of the property on his own account, and the beneficiary of a trust has no rights in the trust property, while the fideicommissary and a successive appointee do. This distinction has an important practical effect, since replacement in a *fideicommissum*, unlike in a trust, is limited to the private sphere, and the fiduciary does not assume an office.

[207] Cf. Hahlo, 'Trust in South African Law' (see above, footnote 200), 202–5; Beinart, 'Trusts'(see above, footnote 205), p. 185.

[208] This is an old rule of Roman–Dutch law: see R. W. Lee, *An Introduction to Roman–Dutch Law* (5th edition), Oxford, 1953, p. 375 footnote 5.

in favorem familiae, with respect to which acceptance by the first beneficiary extends to all later ones.

The literature has correctly made clear that the fact that the office of the trustee is a matter of public record means that legal aspects of the institution of the trust must be separated from those relating to management. The former are contractual (or testamentary), while rules of public law apply to the latter, as, for example, in the case of the appointment or substitution of a trustee.[209] The trustee is answerable to third parties with the trust property, and not, as in the case of English law, with all his property.

The trust in South African law is, therefore, a centre of interests, like the *haereditas giacens*, and not a legal person, although in some cases it is considered to be a taxable person.[210] It, and not the English trust model, corresponds to the unfortunate vision of Lepaulle of dedicated property; in fact, a comparison has been suggested with the *universitas bonorum* of the Roman *pia causa*.

An action by a beneficiary against a trustee for breach of duties arising out of the trust arises in tort, not in contract, because the voluntary elements of the trust instrument are held to be subordinate to the public-law aspects of the institution.[211] With respect to third parties to whom the trustee has transferred trust assets, the beneficiary has no protection, except where negligent or fraudulent conduct may be imputed to the third party (giving rise to an action for damages against him) or, according to other experts, where an *actio pauliana* may be commenced because the transfer may be held to be a fraud on the creditors (in this context the beneficiary is considered to be a creditor of the trustee).[212] From a practical point of view, protection of the beneficiary is ensured by the obligation of the trustee to post a bond.[213]

As far as resulting and constructive trusts are concerned, South African law essentially counters with an action for unjust enrichment, and it is here that the weakness in the protection offered the beneficiary appears. Outside equity, certain situations lack protection or, more correctly, legal relevance. For example, the purchase of property in the name of T, using D's

---

[209] Honoré, *Trusts*, p. 26, makes the observation that a judge may not substitute a contracting party, but may substitute a trustee.

[210] The Income Tax Act of 1962 includes trusts within the definition of '*person*'. Tax issues relating to trusts in South Africa are described in Honoré, *Trusts*, pp. 361–412.

[211] The action is therefore subject to the usual limitation period. Cf. Beinart, 'Trusts in Roman and Roman–Dutch Law' (see above, footnote 205), pp. 192–8.

[212] B. Wunsh, in Glasson, I, A22.84.

[213] Already required pursuant to the Trust Moneys Protection Act 1934, and now by s. 6 of the Trust Property Control Act 1988.

money, can only be considered to be a gift or a *mandatum*, as would be the case in most civilian systems. Generally speaking, there is no mechanism which permits beneficiaries to prevail as a class over other creditors of a faithless trustee.

The protective trust is covered either by utilizing drafting techniques taken from the *fideicommissum*, where a condition subsequent brings about the passage to a subsequent beneficiary, or by granting the trustee discretion regarding the payment of income to the beneficiaries, so that the rights of the beneficiaries cannot be subject to a judgment obtained by their creditors.[214]

While English law, which does not recognize the *negotiorum gestio*, has been obliged to develop the *trustee de son tort*, South African law has remained on the path of Roman law, and grants the beneficiary an *actio negotiorum gestorum directa* against anyone who carries out the functions of a trustee without being appointed.

South African law, as will have been noted, is much more influenced by the civil-law tradition than is Scottish law. As a result, it has suffered the effects of the English trust model to a lesser degree, and its evolution is taking it along new paths.[215]

4. Comparative considerations

a Limits of these considerations and the exportation of the trust

None of the legal systems examined in section 2 (and from now on we shall consider only these systems) has legislated on pre-existing legal institutions. Even those countries, such as Japan and Mauritius, which had experience of the allocation of property for purposes connected with religion or worship, took a different route: to borrow as much as could be borrowed from the English trust model. This is the first limitation of the considerations which we are about to examine, and it is shared by every legislative instrument which puts down roots in a foreign culture rather than in its own, and, by chance, in systems with respect to which the paucity of common elements, either relating to the sources of law, or to their operating methods, or, finally, to the specific *regulae* and the *principia* which support them, is often significant. In the case of Japan, we have already seen that the letter of the law of 1922 has nothing in common with the manner in which trusts developed in Japan; they ignored areas of operation which the 1922 law had ruled upon, and spread into sectors of financial activity which the drafters of the 1922 law had not even taken into consideration.

[214] Honoré, *Trusts*, pp. 126 and 263.
[215] V. H. Sher, 'Trusts in South Africa', in 2 T&T (1996), no. 7, 12.

A second limitation is imposed by the consistency between legislative enactments on trusts and other precepts of the relevant legal systems. While in the previous chapter we had before us a fundamental similarity among common-law systems, and the means to comprehend cases of dissimilarity (Guernsey, Jersey and Malta), dissimilarity is now the rule. I have no grounds to believe that the principles regarding the revocatory action, succession or the diligence of a fiduciary are the same in Venezuela and Quebec, not to mention in Israel or Japan. The danger of nominalism lurks, and will probably become reality on more than one occasion.

A third limitation is language, because four of the laws which we shall review (Ethiopian, Japanese, Israeli and Russian) are known to me only in translation. This means that another source of misunderstanding must be added to those just noted, one which combines with them and increases exponentially the inevitable nominalistic side-effects of research of the kind we are conducting.

To conclude: what we are about to undertake is not a comparison, but a simple *drawing together of legislative expressions*, sometimes in translation. Despite this limitation, the exercise is nonetheless a useful one, because it illustrates tendencies and approaches to solutions which are too consistent to be simply the fruit of nominalistic errors. At the same time, it illustrates specific rules which are also too consistent for there not to be a high degree of probability that they mean what they appear to mean.

It may be worthwhile to spend a little more time on this last point. The trust which I described at the end of chapter 3 cannot be exported beyond the borders of the world of common law, because the notion of lack of equitable fullness of ownership on the part of the trustee, with all its consequences, is understood, and can survive, only in that world and within those legal systems which, being open-ended (like Jersey and Guernsey), may adopt an open equitable structure (as they have already demonstrated in their case law). The 'analogous institutions' of which the authors of the Hague Convention and others before them presumed to write do not, and cannot, exist,[216] and neither can a 'functional' analogy, to follow the latest fashion in comparative law proposed by those theoreticians who see in trusts only one or two aspects suited to the functional analogies, label them as *the* trust, and close the subject.

---

[216] Once again, we find P. Lepaulle, 'Civil Law Substitutes for Trusts', in 36 YaleLJ (1927) 1126 behind this tendency, which created the concept of 'trustlike', which is as current as it is vague and intellectually unjustifiable. The correct position is taken by Battifol, 'Trust Problem' (see above, footnote 3), who demonstrates that it is wrong to think in terms of structures analogous to the trust.

Civil-law systems, as we shall see at the end of this chapter, may reclaim *principia* which existed in their history and in some measure still exist: among these are the *fiducia* as an entrusting, freedom of form, the (pre-eminent) value of the promise, objective good faith, and the link between precepts of conscience and strictly legal principles and the resolution of the inherent conflict between them in favour of the former. The question is not, therefore, whether the express trust *inter vivos* must become a contract in a civil-law system, because an affirmative response is inevitable; it is not even whether it is legitimate to separate a patrimony notwithstanding the fact that it has, and will continue to have, an owner, since in this case too, the answer must be in the affirmative (as we saw in Italy with the introduction of articles 167–71 to regulate the *fondo patrimoniale*.[217] It is whether, having striven to understand trusts, one then wants to undertake a patient and unassuming evaluation of whether they might offer us an important opportunity to liberate our civil-law systems.

b The transfer to the fiduciary

The first 'basic datum' for comparative purposes, as I have indicated above,[218] is the transfer of the right to the trustee, and I shall now examine it in connection with the fourth (beneficiaries or a purpose). As we know this is typical of the so-called Romanistic *fiducia*, which must be distinguished from two contiguous institutions: the creation of a separate patrimony, which is a centre of interests, and the grant to the fiduciary of certain rights and powers in another person's property (that of the principal) which are sufficient to permit the fiduciary to carry out administrative acts and, in some cases, acts of disposition.

This classification is not of interest to us, and is not present in any of the legal systems under consideration. It characterizes the first generation of *fideicommissum*, especially in those countries, such as Mexico, where there are still doubts as to whether the fiduciary acquires a real position, with the equivalent loss of that same position by the settlor.

If one stops at the definition stage, the risk arises that the distinctions based on the transfer to the trustee will be evanescent, because of the effects on it of the second and third 'basic datum' described above (the lack of confusion between the right transferred to the fiduciary and the remainder of his patrimony, and the loss of all the settlor's rights as a natural result of the transfer), which frequently do not appear in the definitions and which, on the other hand, may, when taken alone, lead to misunder-

---

[217] See in more detail below, chapter 7 §1.c.   [218] See p. 271.

standings. Nonetheless, I prefer to follow an analytical process and, as we proceed from one 'basic datum' to the next, to allow this process to clarify the position of the institution in each legal system.

The transfer of the right from the *settlor* to the fiduciary is a condition *sine qua non* if a civil-law concept is to approach the trust. In the typical case of property subject to registration, for this condition to occur there must be a transfer which is no different as regards form and disclosure requirements from a normal alienation.

The law of Liechtenstein, which was passed at a time when the only precedents were early *fideicomisos* and the Japanese law of 1922, states as follows:

Treuhänder (Trustee oder Salmann) im Sinne dieses Gesetzes ist diejenige Einzel-person, Firma oder Verbandsperson, welcher ein anderer (der Treugeber) beweg-liches oder unbewegliches Vermogen oder ein Recht (als Treugut), welcher Art auch immer, mit der Verpflichtung zuwendet, dieses als Treugut im eigenen Namen als selbständiger Rechtsträger zu Gunsten eines oder mehrer Dritter (Begünstigter) mit Wirkung gegen jedermann zu verwalten oder zu verwenden.[219]

This is the definition of a relationship: the fiduciary receives an asset or a right (in this respect the law of Liechtenstein is extremely shrewd termino-logically; the other laws, with few exceptions, refer only to assets); this asset or right belongs completely to the fiduciary, and his ownership right is enforceable against all third parties; nonetheless, the fiduciary has the obligation to manage or dispose of the asset to the beneficiary's benefit. The trustee becomes the owner of the right to all effects and before all third parties,[220] including the settlor.[221]

The brief definition contained in the Venezuelan law follows the same lines:

El Fideicomiso es una relación jurídica por la cual una persona llamada fi-deicomitente transfiere uno o más bienes a otra persona llamada fiduciario, quien se obliga a utilizarlo en favor de aquél o de un tercero llamado benefici-ario[222]

as does that of the Luxembourg fiduciary contract:

Un contrat fiduciaire au sens du présent règlement est un contrat par lequel une personne, le fiduciant, convient avec un établissement de crédit, le fiduciaire, que le fiduciaire sera rendu titulaire de droits patrimoniaux, l'actif fiduciaire, mais

---

[219] Liechtenstein, Personen- und Gesellschaftsrecht, article 897.
[220] This is underscored in Ecuador, in the regulation dated 26 August 1993, article 41.5: the transfer to the fiduciary is 'en propiedad con caracter irrevocable'.
[221] For the exact formulation of this clarification, see Liechtenstein, Personen- und Gesel-lschaftsrecht, article 919, 2nd paragraph.   [222] Venezuela, Ley de fideicomisos, article 1.

que l'exercise de ces droits patrimoniaux sera limité par des obligations, le passif fiduciaire, déterminées par le contrat fiduciaire.[223]

The transfer of the right to the trustee and the assumption of the obligation by him are, therefore, the two structural elements of the act of creation of relationships which, where the other 'basic data' are present, are homologous to the trust.

The legal notion, which identifies both these elements and which is explained by them, was expressed for the first time in the Argentinean law of 1995:

Habrá fedeicomiso cuando una persona (*fiduciante*) transmita la propiedad fiduciaria de bienes determinados a otra (*fiduciario*), quien se obliga a ejercerla en beneficio de quien se designe en al contrato (*beneficiario*), y a transmitirlo al cumplimiento de un plazo o condición al fiduciante, al beneficiario o al fideicomisario.[224]

Sobra los bienes fideicomitidos se constituye una propiedad fiduciaria.[225]

It will have been noted that here, alongside a beneficiary, appears a reference to a purpose, upon the attainment of which the *fideicomiso* terminates. I shall discuss the purpose later.

Mauritius, although influenced by the desire to remain close to the terminology used by the Hague Convention, nonetheless describes the *negotium* in the same way:

Trust means a device whereby one person (*the settlor*) transfers property to another person (*the trustee*), to be held and dealt with by him for the benefit of a third person (*the beneficiary*), or for a charitable purpose or for any other purpose permitted by law.[226]

The structure of the *negotium* in the Louisiana law seems to me to be identical:

A trust . . . is the relationship resulting from the transfer of title to property to a person to be administered by him as a fiduciary for the benefit of another.[227]

because it describes the 'transfer of title' as a *negotium* whose purpose is the performance of the fiduciary obligations.[228]

The *propiedad fiduciaria* is the effect of the *fiducia*. We therefore see the

---

[223] Luxembourg, Granducal Decree of 19 July 1983, article 2.
[224] Argentina, Ley 24.441, article 1.   [225] Argentina, Ley 24.441, article 11.
[226] Mauritius, Trusts Act 1989, s. 2.   [227] Louisiana Trust Code, §1731.
[228] Thus also in the case of the only legislative formulation which defines the relationship without indicating its source: Israel, Trust Law (in the English translation), s. 1: 'A trust is a relationship to any property by virtue of which a trustee is bound to hold the same, or to act in respect thereof, in the interest of a beneficiary or for some other purpose.' This is the technique to be followed later by the Hague Convention.

systematic similarity with the trust, provided that the trust is understood within the framework I proposed at the end of chapter 3; that is, not as a relationship between trustee or fiduciary and 'settlor', but as a charter of the fiduciary owner; hence, one can look at the legal connection between trustee and the right transferred to him as fiduciary ownership.[229]

The transfer must be accompanied by the forms of registration provided for in the laws relating to each kind of property. In general, civil-law systems do not distinguish between the act of creation and the act of transfer, as is the case in English law. Although the laws often permit other assets to be added to those initially transferred,[230] a 'bare' act of creation, that is, one without a contemporaneous transfer, is not usually provided for.[231] From this we have the rules which subordinate the effectiveness of the *negotium* with regard to third parties, and thereby its enforceability, to the completion of the registration formalities regarding the transfer. Those systems which have rules on assets which circulate freely (for example, debentures or other bearer instruments), or which have no land registries

---

[229] Colombia, Código de Comercio, article 1226: 'La fiducia mercantil es un negocio juridico en virtud del cual una persona, llamada fiduciante o fideicomitente, transfiere uno o más bienes especificados a otra, llamada fiduciario, quien se obliga a administrarlos o enajenarlos para cumplir una finalidad determinada por el constituyente, en provecho de este o de un tercero llamado beneficiario o fideicomisario.'

Panama, Law no. 1 of 1984, article 1: 'El fideicomiso es un acto jurídico en virtud del cual una persona llamada fideicomitente transfiere bienes a una persona llamada fiduciario para que los administre o disponga de ellos en favor de un fideicomisario o beneficiario, que puede ser el propio fideicomitente.'

Ecuador, Código de Comercio, article 410, paragraph 1: 'Se denomina fideicomiso mercantil el acto en virdud del cual una o más personas llamadas constituyente transfieren dineros u otros bienes a otra llamada fiduciario, quien se obliga a administrarlos por un plazo o para cumplir una finalidad específica.'

Peru, Ley general de bancos, article 316, paragraph 1: 'El fiduciario adquiere la propriedad de los bienes y la titularidad de los derechos que constituyen el patrimonio fideicometido, sujeto al cargo de atender con ellos al cumplimiento de las finalidades señaladas en el instrumento constitutivo' (article 314 repeats the Venezuelan definition *verbatim*, see above in the text).

Similarly, Japan, Trust Law 1922 (in the English translation), article 1: 'A trust within the meaning of this law shall signify to transfer or otherwise dispose of a property right and cause another person to administer or dispose of the property in accordance with a specific purpose' and Russia, Decree of 24 December 1993, article 3 and 9, paragraph 1

The requirement of the Seychelles, civil code, articles 818, 824 and 825 is also extremely clear: the fiduciary is the owner of the assets; the provisional rules require that he alone should appear in the land registry (Chloros, *Codification* (see above, footnote 149)), p. 78.

[230] See, for example: Venezuela, Ley de fideicomisos, article 2: 'Los bienes transferidos y los que sustituyan a éstos . . .'; Panama, Law no. 1 of 1984, article 2; Mauritius, Trusts Act 1989, s. 4 (amended in 1990) for charitable trusts; Québec, code civil, article 1293; Russia, Decree of 24 December 1993, article 8; Argentina, Ley 24.441, article 4 b.

[231] Only Panama, as far as I have been able to discern, regulates the fact-pattern which in Italian is called the *fiducia statica*.

(for example, Mauritius), have provided for recording in a trust registry, sometimes as an alternative to the former.

The Venezuelan requirement is typical of the most widespread tendency:

La transferencia al fiduciario . . . solamente surtirá efecto contra terceros desde la fecha en que se haga la protocolización del documento constitutivo en la Oficina[232]

and is expressed in more general terms in the law of Peru:

Para oponer el fideicomiso a terceros se requiere que la transmisión al fiduciario de los bienes y derechos inscribibles sea anotada en el registro público correspondiente y que la de otra clase de bienes y derechos se perfeccione con la tradición, el endoso u otro requisito exigido por la ley.[233]

Another tendency is followed by the laws of Liechtenstein and Mauritius,[234] and by that of Israel, which, following the English tradition, also attaches relevance to the effective knowledge of persons contracting with the fiduciary.[235] We shall note below that civil-law systems, when confronting the subject of protection against wrongful transfers by the fiduciary, do not shrink from having recourse to the same concepts.

The transfer to the fiduciary, which has been one of the constants of the legal systems I have reviewed, does not appear in the laws of Ethiopia or Quebec. We should quote from both of them, so that the contrast between

---

[232] Venezuela, Ley de fideicomisos, article 5, for real rights in land. The requirement is the same in Panama: no. 1 of 1984, article 13: 'El fideicomiso constituido sobre bienes inmuebles situados en la República de Panamá sólo afectará a terceros, en cuanto a dichos bienes, desde la fecha de inscripción de la Escritura de fideicomiso en el Registro Público' (in all other cases, the effects date from the date of the notarial deed prepared by a Panamanian Notary); and in Argentina, Ley 24.441, article 13: 'Cuando se trate de bienes registrables, los registros correspondientes deberán tomar razón de la transferencia fiduciaria de la propiedad a nombre del fiduciario.'

[233] Peru, Ley general de bancos, article 319, paragraph 2. Thus also in Argentina, Ley 24.441, article 12: 'El carácter fiduciario del dominio tendrá efecto frente a terceros desde el momento en que se cumplan las formalidades exigibles de acuerdo a la naturaleza de los bienes respectivos', and earlier in Japan, Trust Law 1922 (in the English translation), article 3: 'With regard to property rights which are to be registered or recorded, a trust cannot be set up against third persons unless it is registered or recorded.'

[234] Liechtenstein, Personen- und Gesellschaftsrecht, article 912: there is a general publicity requirement for assets listed 'zur Wirkung der Treuhand gegenüber Dritten'; article 901: there is a duty to have trusts noted in the public registry (article 900): 'Ist Gegenstand einer Treuhänderschaft Vermögen, das in anderen öffentlichen Registern, wie Grundbuch, Patentregister und dergleichen, eingetragen ist und wird das Treuhandverhältnis in diese öffentlichen Register eingetragen' [one can omit it]. The requirement of annotation in the registry is shared with Mauritius (Trusts Act 1989, s. 7), and in both cases the purpose of the trust is not disclosed. Note that in Liechtenstein, the annotation may be omitted if the trust is registered (article 902).

[235] Israel, Trust Law (in the English translation), s. 5: 'A trust has effect vis-à-vis any person who knows or ought to know about it, and where a note has been entered under section 4 [which concerns forms of publicity] vis-à-vis the whole world.'

situations homologous to the trust and those which belong to the family of foundations is immediately evident:

Le fidéicommis est l'institution en vertu de laquelle un ou plusieurs biens sont constitués en une masse autonome, pour être administrée par une personne, le fidéicommissaire, selon les instructions données par le constituant du fidéicommis.[236]

La fiducie résulte d'un acte par lequel une personne, le constituant, transfère de son patrimoine à un autre patrimoine qu'il constitue, des biens qu'il affecte à une fin particulière, et que le fiduciaire s'oblige, par le fait de son acceptation, à détenir et à administrer.[237]

There is a clear contrast: here an autonomous patrimony or dedicated property is created and a purpose attributed to it, and it is entrusted to an administrator. The first of the 'basic data' for comparison which I described above – the transfer of the right to the trustee – is not, therefore, to be found in these two laws.

c The segregation of the trust assets

In the previous pages we have seen a wide-ranging phenomenology, and I have had the opportunity to illustrate what I mean by segregation, covered by the second 'basic datum': it derives from entitlements which *belong to a person* (the trustee), but which are not affected by his general obligations and therefore do not form part of the patrimony which constitutes the security available to his creditors (and they do not devolve on his death according to the rules of succession, and are not affected by his marriage, and so on), with the sole, and evident, exception of liabilities which derive from acts or facts relating to the segregated entitlement.[238]

The property set aside to attain the purposes of the Ethiopian *fidéicommis* and the Quebecois *fiducie* is not segregated, because, as in the case of foundations, it does not belong to the person who has the power to administer it and, in certain cases, to dispose of it. Obviously, the law of Québec makes the following provision:

Le patrimoine fiduciaire . . . constitue un patrimoine d'affectation autonome et distinct de celui du constituant, du fiduciaire ou du bénéficiaire, sur lequel aucun d'entre eux n'a de droit réel.[239]

The final words are rather significant. The Québec civil code was preceded

---

[236] Ethiopia, civil code (French edition), article 516. It should be noted that by the term *fidéicommissaire* is meant the fiduciary, and not, as with the *fidecomisario* of Spanish-language laws, the beneficiary.   [237] Quebec, code civil, article 1260.

[238] See in more detail below, chapter 7 §1.c.   [239] Quebec, code civil, article 1261.

by a lengthy controversy in the literature regarding the classification of the *fiducie*, and in particular the position of the beneficiary; here the law sides with the dedicated property, and no doubts linger regarding its autonomy. The requirements identified for the civil-law institutions which are homologous with the trust are different; segregation from the fiduciary's remaining assets is essential if homogeneity is to be achieved, because only by means of segregation may the relationship acquire that connotation of reality which allows us to speak of fiduciary ownership.

The Colombian Commercial code uses terms identical to those one could employ in Italian law:

Los bienes objeto de la fiducia no forman parte de la garantía general de los acreedores del fiduciario y sólo garantizan las obligaciones contraidas en el cumplimiento de la finalidad perseguida.[240]

The law of Liechtenstein, which had already defined assets in Treuhand as assets belonging to the fiduciary, makes a similar provision:

[in actions against the fiduciary regarding his personal debts] ist das Treuhandvermögen als Fremdvermögen zu betrachten und es haben daher die Gläubiger des Treuhänders hierauf keinen Anspruch.[241]

And so on with all the laws which belong to this model, on some occasions making specific provisions for the creditors of the fiduciary, and on others also for the creditors of the settlor or the beneficiary, on more than a few occasions using the expression 'separate property'.[242]

The segregation is sometimes evident to third parties because the

---

[240] Colombia, Código de Comercio, article 1227. See also Seychelles, civil code, article 832: '*Neither shall such properties or assets be seized by any creditor of the fiduciary in satisfaction of any claim that he may have against such fiduciary*' and Luxembourg, Granducal Decree of 19 July 1983, article 3(1).

[241] Liechtenstein, Personen- und Gesellschaftsrecht, article 915.

[242] Venezuela, Ley de fideicomisos, article 2: 'Los bienes transferidos y los que los sustuyan a éstos no perteneccen a la prenda común de los acreedores del fiduciario'; Argentina, Ley 24.441, article 14: 'Los bienes fideicomitidos constituyen un patrimonio separado del patrimonio del fiduciario y del fiduciante'; article 15: 'Los bienes fideicomitidos quedarán exentos de la acción singular o colectiva de los acreedores del fiduciario'; Russia, Decree of 24 December 1993, article 14; Panama, Law no. 1 of 1984, article 15: 'Los bienes del fideicomiso constituirán un patrimonio separado de los bienes personales del fiduciario para todos los efectos legales'; Ecuador, Regulation of 26 August 1993, article 41.6: 'El patrimonio constitutivo del fideicomiso es uno separado y independiente de aquel o aquellos del constituyente, fiduciario o beneficiario y por lo tanto, no puede ser objeto de medidas o providencias preventivas ni embargo por deudas o obligaciones de aquellos'; Colombia, Código de Comercio, article 1233: 'los bienes fideicomitidos . . . forman un patrimonio autónomo afecto a la finalidad contemplada en el acto constitutivo'; finally, with concise wording, Japan, Trust Law 1922 (in the English translation), article 15: 'The trust property shall not appertain to the trustee's estate of inheritance.'

transfer to the fiduciary of the assets under discussion has been subject to registration; on other occasions this registration is not possible, as when the assets are in the form of sums of money. At this point, so as to avoid any confusion, the duty to hold the assets on 'trust' separate from those of the trustee is imposed. This duty is omitted from laws which permit only banks and financial institutions to carry out fiduciary functions, because it would be of no relevance,[243] whereas it is customary in laws with a more general purpose, such as that of Japan:

The trust property shall be administered set apart from the trustee's own property and other trust properties, provided, however, that with regard to moneys that are trust property, it shall be sufficient to keep separate account of them;[244]

or that of Ethiopia:

[Duties of the fiduciary] (2) Il évite la confusion des biens qui font l'objet du fidéicommis et de ses biens propres. (3) Il est tenu de prendre, à cette fin, toutes mésures appropriées.[245]

Assets transferred to the fiduciary are, therefore, segregated *de iure*, but must also be segregated *de facto*.[246]

d Entrusting and powers retained by the settlor

We shall not look at the third of the 'basic data':[247] the loss of every right of the settlor as the natural result of the *negotium*; as we have seen with the trust, the settlor may retain certain powers or rights, and the limits of this retention are shown by the reduction of the ownership position of the trustee to the point that he becomes a simple agent or fiduciary nominee. Laws of civil-law systems usually keep a role for the 'settlor' in the life of 'trusts', which is the same as that which the settlor usually reserves for

---

[243] See, nonetheless, specifically targeting banks, Liechtenstein, Personen- und Gesellschaftsrecht, article 922, paragraph 4: '[banks] sind verpflichtet, das Treugut vom übrigen Vermögen streng abzusondern.'

[244] Japan, Trust Law 1922 (in the English translation), article 28.

[245] Ethiopia, civil code (French edition), article 525.

[246] In addition to laws already cited, see Venezuela, Ley de fideicomisos, article 14 no. 2: 'Mantener los bienes fideicomitidos debidamente separados de sus demás bienes y de los correspondientes a otros fideicomisos'; Colombia, Código de Comercio, article 1234 no. 2: 'Mantener los bienes objeto de la fiducia separados de los suyos y de los que correspondan a otros negocios fiduciarios'; Israel, Trust Law (in the English translation), s. 3(c): 'A trustee shall hold the trust property separately from any other property or so that it can be distinguished therefrom'; Louisiana, Trust Code, §2094: 'A trustee shall keep the trust property separate from his individual property, and, so far as reasonable, keep it separate from other property not subject to the trust, and see that the property is designated as property of the trust, unless the trust instrument provides otherwise.'

[247] Cf. above, pp. 271.

himself in English and international trust practice (this is the emerging contractuality to which I have drawn attention on more than one occasion). This role has no influence over the powers which naturally attach to the fiduciary, but it varies from the English and international models where it includes a right in favour of the person creating a 'trust' *inter vivos* to take action against the fiduciary for his failure to perform the obligations with which he was charged in the document creating the 'trust'.

In these cases, the basis of the relationship is undoubtedly contractual, and it would appear to be difficult to deprive one contracting party of the right to take action against the other (above all if one considers that the relationship we are describing here, as we shall see below, does not necessarily contemplate the existence of a beneficiary: for this reason, the alternative theoretical possibility, which is that of granting the beneficiaries the right to take action against a non-performing fiduciary, is unavailable). This is a difference with respect to English law which may not be resolved in any other manner.

For purposes of homology I believe that the key question is another, which relates not to the right to an action for non-performance but to the existence, or lack thereof, of a relationship between settlor and trustee as a result of which the former may guide the latter in the performance of the duties with which he has been charged. If this were the case, everything we have learnt of civil-law 'trusts' thus far would lose all substance.[248]

The legislators of Liechtenstein, who are among the most precise in the transposition of structures and rules from the English law of trusts, understood this concept very well.

Der Treugeber kann im übrigen keine Bestimmungen aufstellen, welche den Treuhänder an fortlaufende Weisungen des Treugebers binden. Soweit solche Bestimmungen aufgestellt werden, liegt gewöhnichler Auftrag im Sinne des Obligationenrechts vor.[249]

Provisions this clear were lacking in other laws until the recent Russian decree, where the systematic care commanded by the English and American

---

[248] In Seychelles law, co-owners of real property are obliged by law to appoint a fiduciary, who must sell the property and divide the proceeds. The co-owners are, therefore, both settlors and beneficiaries as in the English trust for sale, and the only interference with the fiduciary's activity which they can justify is postponing the sale (if everyone agrees to postpone it: article 819 civil code). A co-owner may, nonetheless, request a division where 'the property may be conveniently and profitably divided in kind'.

In trusts of movables outside the area of co-ownership, the rules of agency apply, if they have not been waived (article 824 civil code): it is unclear whether this causes the fiduciary to be subject to the principal's instructions.

[249] Liechtenstein, Personen- und Gesellschaftsrecht, article 918, paragraph 1 and the first part of paragraph 2.

drafters and, above all, their desire that anyone coming to such a new institution should have a clear understanding the relationship between settlor and trustee, probably took precedence:

The founder does not have the right to communicate instructions to the owner–trustee, nor to interfere in any way in the methods by which he exercises his rights and performs his obligations.[250]

No other law imposes limits on the powers which a settlor may wish to reserve to himself in the trust instrument: most describe this reservation of rights on various occasions as a limit to the otherwise free exercise of the fiduciary's powers,[251] and thus in a context which sees the fiduciary as full owner, who is, of course, subject not to instructions or other kinds of interference on the part of the settlor, but to the fiduciary purpose of the relationship and therefore to the particular 'charter' of the fiduciary ownership. This concept is well expressed in the law of Panama:

El fiduciario tendrá todas las acciones y derechos inherentes al dominio, pero quedará sujeto a los fines del fideicomiso y a las condiciones y a las obligaciones que le impongan la Ley y el instrumento de fideicomiso.[252]

Most recently, the Argentinean law has provided:

El fiduciario podrá disponer o gravar los bienes fideicomitidos cuando lo requiran los fines del fideicomiso, sin que para ello sea necesario el consentimiento del fiduciante o del beneficiario, a menos que se hubiere pactado lo contrario.[253]

But the same concept, with a certain redundancy which was probably due to the newness of the subject in legislation by a civil-law system in the nineteen twenties, appears in the law of Liechtenstein:

Der Treuhänder ist unter Vorbehalt seiner Verpflichtungen aus der Treuhand durkunde berechtigt, über das Treuhandgut gleich einem selbständingen Träger von Rechten und Pflichten . . . zu verfügen, für das Treugut vor allen Behörden und in allen Verfahren in eigenen Namen . . . aufzutreten, die zu ihm gehörigen Rechte gegen alle Dritte gemäss der Treuhandurkunde zu verwalten und aus-zuüben und soweit nötig, zu versilbern und neu anzulegen, wenn es sich aus dem Treuhandzweck nicht anders ergibt.[254]

Rights and obligations of the fiduciary are inextricably linked, and mutually directed towards the attainment of the purpose for which the relationship was created. The fullness of the fiduciary's position, and the consequence of the entrusting, as illustrated ('los fines del fideicomiso' or

---

[250] Russia, Decree of 24 December 1993, article 18.

[251] For example: Colombia, Código de Comercio, article 1236: 'Al fiduciante corresponderán los siguientes derechos: 1°) Los que se hubiere reservado para ejercerlos directamente sobre los bienes fideicomitidos'.   [252] Panama, Law no. 1 1984, article 25.

[253] Argentina, Ley 24.441, article 17.

[254] Liechtenstein, Personen- und Gesellschaftsrecht, article 919 paragraph 3.

the 'Treuhandzweck' or the 'affectation'[255]) are 'entrusted' to the fiduciary, and he has to decide the actual way in which they will be activated, and to exercise the rights transferred to him in that way.

The extent of the entrusting ordained by law is to some extent tied to the manner in which the instrument is customarily used. This is clear from the rules relating to the duty of a fiduciary to provide an accounting which, while it may uniformly be discharged once a year,[256] is required more frequently by those laws which consider the principal purpose of the institution to be in the area of financial investment.[257]

We cannot leave the topic of powers retained by the settlor without acknowledging the granting of powers by the settlor to a third party. Nothing prevents a settlor from transferring the exercise of powers to a third party which he would have had the right to retain for himself, or to make the transfer subject to the condition subsequent of his death. This is especially true of relationships which are forecast to have a long duration. This is the same legal concept as that of the protector, but it is probable that in this case there has been a convergence of rules borrowed from trusts and rules borrowed from foundations.[258]

e Fiduciary components and conflicts of interest

This is the fifth of the 'basic data' I listed at the beginning of our research. Out of the imposition of a fiduciary component on the exercise of the rights emerges a distinctive economic consequence: the trustee may not profit

[255] This last reference is to Quebec, code civil, article 1278: 'Le fiduciaire a la maîtrise et l'administration exclusive du patrimoine fiduciaire et les titres relatifs aux biens qui le composent sont établis à son nom; il exerce tous les droits afférents au patrimoine et peut prendre toute mesure propre à en assurer l'affectation.'

[256] Japan, Trust Law 1922, article 39.2; Liechtenstein, Personen- und Gesellschaftsrecht, article 923, paragraph 1; Venezuela, Ley de fideicomisos, article 14 no. 3; Ethiopia, civil code, article 535(1); Israel, Trust Law (in the English translation), s. 7(b); Panama, Law no. 1 1984, article 28; Argentina, Ley 24.441, article 7 paragraph 2.

[257] Colombia, Decree no. 663 of 1993, article 155e; Peru, Ley general de bancos, article 332(f); Russia, Decree of 24 December 1993, article 19, paragraph 2.

[258] See, as an example, Japan, Trust Law 1922, article 8 (a person who acts for the protection of the interests of the beneficiaries where they are undetermined or as yet unborn); Ethiopia, civil code, article 520 (the settlor may indicate a person in the trust instrument to whom he grants the power to appoint the fideicommissary or his successor and – *per* article 522 – to take action to revoke his appointment); Panama, Law no. 1 of 1984, article 21: 'En los fideicomisos revocables, el fiduciario podrá ser reemplazado o podrán nombrarse nuevos fiduciarios en cualcuier tiempo por el fideicomitente o por la persona a quien éste haya autorizado para hacer el reemplazo o el nombramiento'; Mauritius, Trusts Act 1989, s. 34 (8): '*Every power conferred under this section shall be exercised according to the discretion of the trustee, but subject to any consent or discretion required under the trust deed* . . .'; Quebec, code civil, articles 1282–3: a person who may appoint the beneficiaries, provided that they belong to the class indicated by the settlor.

from the trust purpose, and profits which he obtains from it belong to the beneficiaries.

There seems to be no point in investigating this 'basic datum' further, since all the relationships we have been discussing are, by their very nature, fiduciary. Furthermore, others belong to the *genus* of *comisiones de confianza* and are, therefore, fiduciary *par excellence*. This being the case, the fifth 'basic datum' is an indisputable fact. It is, however, worth making the observation that the Argentinean law, which is not limited to commercial dealings, but has the aim of creating a general parallel to the trust, also asserts the fiduciary nature of the relationship in its definition of the obligations of the 'trustee':

El fiduciario deberá cumplir las obligaciones impuestas por la ley o la convención con la prudencia y diligencia del buon hombre de negocios que actuá sobre la base de la confianza depositada en él.[259]

Others impose a significant duty of loyalty or diligence on the fiduciary.[260] The rules on conflict of interest[261] and the requirement that the duties of a

---

[259] Argentina, Ley 24.441, article 6.

[260] Louisiana, Trust code, §2082: 'A trustee shall administer the trust solely in the interest of the beneficiary'; Peru, Ley general de bancos, article 332 [duties of the fiduciary] (a): 'Cuidar y administrar los bienes y derechos que constituyen el patrimonio fideicometido con la diligencia y dedicación de un ordenado comerciante y leal administrador'; Israel, Trust Law (in the English translation), s. 10(b): 'In carrying out his functions, a trustee shall exercise such loyalty and diligence as a reasonable person would exercise in the circumstances'; Colombia, Código de Comercio, article 1235: '[rights of the beneficiary] 1°) exigir al fiduciario el fiel cumplimiento de sus obligaciones.' On the expansion of the fiduciary dimension into the area of loyalty, see J. Hennrichs, 'Treupflichten im Aktienrecht', in [1995] AfcP 221; cf. Seychelles, civil code, article 825, which introduces the adverb 'honestly': 'The functions of the fiduciary shall be to hold, manage and administer the property, honestly, diligently and in a business-like manner as if he were the sole owner of the property.'

The Mauritius rule, Trusts Act 1989, s. 25, has no equivalent: 'A trustee shall explain to the beneficiary all his rights and obligations.'

[261] See, for example Ethiopia, civil code (French edition), article 531: 'Le fidéicommissaire ne doit tirer aucun profit personal du fidéicommis, en dehors des avantages qui lui sont consentis expressément par l'acte de constitution du fidéicommis'; Liechtenstein, Personen- und Gesellschaftsrecht, article 925: 'Der Treuhänder ist . . . nicht berechtig, irgend welche Vorteile aus dem Treuhandverhältnis zu ziehen'; Colombia, Decree no. 663 of 1993, article 151.6 and 156.1; Israel, Trust Law (in the English translation), s. 13(a): 'A trustee shall not acquire for himself or any of his relatives any property of the trust or a right in any such property or derive for himself or any of his relatives any other benefit from the property or activities of the trust and shall do nothing involving a conflict of interests between the trust and himself or his relatives.' The law continues by indicating what is intended by 'relatives': the list is very long, and includes companies in which a relative has a share exceeding 5%.

See again Mauritius, Trusts Act 1989, s. 22: 'Duty of trustee not to profit for himself';

fiduciary be carried out personally[262] should also be interpreted in the context of a fiduciary relationship.

To conclude, it appears to me that thirteen of the fifteen systems reviewed[263] recognize institutions which are homologous to the trust.[264] In the other two (Ethiopia and Quebec), homology is only possible if one should hold that the lack of the first 'basic datum' I proposed (the transfer of the right to the trustee) is not relevant, and that the second (segregation) is therefore unimportant.

f Peculiarities of civil-law systems

We may now give some attention to certain other aspects, which translate into *regulae* which are different from those set forth for the English or international trust models, or which bring to light the existence of *regulae* which are consistent with them. Our review will be extremely rapid, since I shall very often identify rules which are easy to comprehend. Having concluded with the homology of civil-law institutions considered with the trust, I shall make liberal use the terms 'settlor', 'trust' and 'trustee' with reference to the homologous *figurae iuris* of the systems under review.

1. Sources

Except for the special case of the Seychelles, where a trust of immovable property held subject to co-ownership is established by law,[265] the sources

s. 23: 'Duty of trustee or agent not to buy trust property'; Peru, Ley general de bancos, article 334, which extends the prohibition 'al cónyuge y a los parentes de las personas indicadas, así como a las personas jurídicas en quel el cónyuge y los parientes, en conjunto, tengan personalmente una participación superior al cincuenta por ciento.'

[262] Japan, Trust Law 1922 (in the English translation), article 26.1, except for unavoidable cases; Venezuela, Ley de fideicomisos, article 15: 'En ningun caso podrá delegar sus funciones' (allowed for single acts); Israel, Trust Law (in the English translation), s. 10 (6); Mauritius, Trusts Act 1989, s. 66.

[263] In §2 I have listed eighteen legal systems, but, for the reasons I gave there, the review undertaken in this section did not include the Philippines, Mexico or St Lucia.

[264] I believe that the Seychelles trust relating to co-owned assets is homologous. I am less sure of the situation regarding the general structure of the fiduciary relationship (article 824 civil code), because I am not able to evaluate the effects of the reference to the law of agency.

[265] Seychelles, civil code, article 818: 'If the property subject to co-ownership is immovable, the rights of the co-owners shall be held on their behalf by a fiduciary through whom only they may act.' This rule should be read together with article 817.1: 'When property, whether movable or immovable, is transferred to two or more persons, the right of co-ownership shall be converted into a claim to a like share in the proceeds of sale of any such property.'

of the trust are a contract or a will.[266] Nonetheless, the law of Liechtenstein mentions the 'Treuhandbrief', which is a unilateral *negotium inter vivos*, on more than one occasion.

Ist ein Treuhänder nicht durch einen Vertrag unter Lebenden, sondern durch Treuhandbrief oder Testament, bestellt worden . . .[267]

It is probable that we are in the presence of a *contaminatio* between the ancient structures of the *Treuhand* and the unilateral nature of the act of transfer, which operates with respect to them, favoured by the attention with which the legislator has followed as far as possible the structure of the English model (where, as we know, the *negotium* by which the trust is created is unilateral).

Article 1262 of the Québec civil code provides that a trust may be established by operation of law or by judgment: it probably refers to constructive or resulting trusts, for which, however, there is little space in a codified system.[268]

It should be noted that on more than one occasion it is provided that acceptance by the trustee may take place by a separate act. It seems obvious to say that acceptance by a separate act does not affect the contractual nature of the relationship which is created by trusts *inter vivos*, but the provision for acceptance by a separate act is too close to the similar mechanism in the area of gifts to pass unnoticed, and not to bring to mind the conceptual artificiality which in many civil-law systems has pushed the gift into the area of contracts rather than into that of unilateral *negotia*. It would be as well to use the word 'trusts' in the plural in the case of civil-law trusts too, because trusts which are evidently contractual, such as those made with financial or investment companies, have no connection with those of Ecuador which, although they may be commercial acts, can have their origin in an 'instrumento público cerrado', so that the relevant dispositions remain unknown to the trustee until the moment arrives, or

---

[266] For the testamentary source, see Japan, Trust Law 1922, article 2; Ethiopia, civil code, article 517(1): gifts or will; Venezuela, Ley de fideicomisos, article 4; Panama, Law no. 1 of 1984, article 10, paragraph 2; Louisiana Trust Code, §1733; Peru, Ley general de bancos, article 319; Quebec, civil code, article 1262; Argentina, Ley 24.441, article 3.

Venezuela, Ley de fideicomisos, article 4, paragraph 2 and Peru, Ley general de bancos, article 330, state that the fiduciary may accept a testamentary trust only if he is provided with an inventory of the assets.

[267] Liechtenstein, Personen- und Gesellschaftsrecht, article 903; see also articles 907 and 917.

[268] The law of Israel also mentions the law as a source of a trust: Trust Law (in the English translation), s. 2: 'A trust is created by Law, by a contract with a trustee or by an instrument of endowment.'

the necessary condition is satisfied, for the opening of the sealed docu-ment.[269] They also have no connection with trusts for which the judge may appoint the trustee if the one appointed by the settlor does not accept, as is the case in Louisiana.[270]

2. Judicial intervention

This call for intervention by a court in the life of a trust opens the way for other considerations which illustrate for us an important aspect of fiduci-ary ownership. Article 693 of the Italian civil code stated as follows[271]

If the appointee fails to perform his duties, the court may appoint an administra-tor, even without a motion.

and article 694 gives a court the power to permit the first appointee to alienate the assets which form the subject of the *fideicommissum*.

In our discussions of both the English and the international models, on a number of occasions we have drawn attention to the close ties which exist between a trustee and the court. The latter may give instructions to a trustee (where the trustee requests them), may revoke the trust, and may modify provisions of the trust instrument. The view of the trustee as the holder of an office, expressly adopted in South Africa and in other laws adhering to the international model,[272] demonstrates the public interest in the regulation of fiduciary ownership and in the enforcement of the 'char-ter' of the fiduciary owner. The Italian rules cited above were in force at a time when the *fideicommissum* was not subject to the limits introduced in 1975. The requirement that a substitute trustee would be a descendant of the initial trustee meant he was disadvantaged with respect to the initial trustee when it came to the protection of his own interests. This situation was not, however, the reason for the introduction of the new rule. Judicial intervention has a more general basis, and is tied to the nature of the charter of fiduciary ownership.

I believe that proof of the accuracy of what I am stating may be found in rules relating to *inter vivos* civil-law trusts. If they were ordinary contracts (and I must apologize for the vagueness of the category), it would not be possible to understand why the trustee could be authorized to obtain a modification of the trust from a court, or why he would have to turn to a court when unforeseen circumstances arose and the trustee was not sure how to act. In fact, he should be able to refer to the settlor (as with an

---

[269] Ecuador, Código de Comercio, article 410 and the Regulation of 26 August 1993, article 41.   [270] Louisiana Trust Code, §§1822–4.
[271] Up until the repeal of this paragraph pursuant to article 198 of the Law of 19 May 1975, no. 151.   [272] See above, chapter 4 §4.h.

agency) or to the beneficiaries, and recourse to the court would only be justified in the case of trusts for purposes. The direction taken by the law of Venezuela is as follows:

cuando el fiduciario tenga que apartase de las instrucciones contenidas en el acto constitutivo del fideicomiso, por un cambio en las circunstancias no previstas por el fideicomitente, deberá pedir instrucciones al Juez del fideicomiso.[273]

and this is typical of the general orientation.[274]

3. Form

As we have already seen, the trust instrument, which involves a simultaneous transfer of the right to the trustee, follows the form required for the transfer.[275] Furthermore, trusts whose purpose is not investments in securities very often require specific formalities, no matter what assets are involved.[276]

4. Trusts for purposes; duration and early termination

The topic of trusts for purposes needs to be considered together with that of duration, since civil-law trusts tend to follow the criterion of the international model, which is to impose a maximum duration on non-purpose trusts, to tie the duration of trusts for purposes in with the attainment of

---

[273] Venezuela, Ley de fideicomisos, article 17.

[274] For various provisions, some of which relate to modifications to the trust instrument or the replacement of a fiduciary, see Japan, Trust Law 1922, articles 23 and 47; Liechtenstein, Personen- und Gesellschaftsrecht, articles 904 and 919, paragraph 6; Venezuela, Ley de fideicomisos, articles 13 and 16; Ethiopia, civil code, articles 522 and 528(2); Colombia, Código de Comercio, article 1239; Seychelles, civil code, article 829; Panama, Law no. 1 of 1984, article 30; Louisiana Trust Code, §1786, §§2064–6; Mauritius, Trusts Act 1989, s. 99; Quebec, code civil, article 1277; Argentina, Ley 24.441, article 9a.

Colombia, Código de Comercio, article 1234, gives banks the powers to give instructions: 'Son deberes indelegables del fiduciario . . .: 5°) Pedir instrucciones al superintendente bancario cuando tenga fundadas dudas acerca la naturaleza y alcance de sus obligaciones o deba apartarse de las autorizaciones contenidas en el acto constitutivo, cuando así lo exijan las circunstancias.'

[275] For all, see Argentina, Ley 24.441; see article 12: 'las formalidades exigibles de acuerdo a la naturaleza de los bienes respectivos'.

[276] Venezuela, Ley de fideicomisos, article 3: notarial act; Seychelles, civil code, articles 823 and 824: a notarial act is required; Louisiana Trust Code, §1752 notarial act with two witnesses; Mauritius, Trusts Act 1989, s. 7(1): public document and registration in the trusts register; Ecuador, Código de Comercio, article 410, paragraph 1: '. . . se establece por instrumento abierto o cerrado'; Seychelles, civil code, articles 823 and 824; Peru, Ley general de bancos, article 319: 'escritura publica'; Russia, Decree of 24 December 1993, article 17, paragraph 1: notarial act. See also Panama, Law no. 1 of 1984, article 4: the oral or implied fideicommissum is prohibited.

the purpose, and, where the purpose appears to be permanent, to permit unlimited duration.

Trusts for purposes are widely recognized in civil-law legislation. They are, of course, recognized in Ethiopia[277] and Quebec,[278] where the legal structure consists of an autonomous patrimony with a particular purpose (and is, as I have already said, outside the domain of the trust as that term is understood in this book). By means of general provisions or special dispositions in legislation they are also recognized in those legislations which provide for institutions homologous to the trust. An example of special regulations may be found in the law of Peru:

fideicomiso cultural, que tenga por objeto el establecimiento de museos, bibliotecas . . . c): fideicomiso filantrópico, que tenga por objeto aliviar la situación de los privados de la razón, los huérfanos, los ancianos abandonados y personas menesterosas . . .[279]

where the 'personas menesterosas' perfectly describe the 'impotentes' of the High Medieval period and the 'impotent' of the Elizabethan law of 1601.[280] Trusts for purposes are identified without further clarification in many other laws, usually in the definitions.[281] With the customary terminological punctiliousness of its English ancestor, the law of Liechtenstein speaks of trusts without beneficiaries.[282]

The civil code of the Seychelles, as we know, recognizes two forms of trust: the first is compulsory for every kind of co-ownership of immovable property which has as its purpose the sale of the property and the division

---

[277] Ethiopia, civil code (French edition), article 518: 'Le fidéicommis peut être constitué au bénéfice d'une personne, d'une oeuvre ou d'une idée quelconque, pourvu seulement qu'il ne porte attente à l'ordre public ni aux bonnes moeurs.'

[278] Quebec, code civil, articles 1268–71, distinguishes between 'utilité privée' and 'utilité sociale'; on the latter: 'La fiducie d'utilité sociale est celle qui est constituée dans un but d'intérêt général, notamment à caractère culturel, éducatif, philanthropique, religieux ou scientifique' (article 1270). Note the assonance with the definitions which are the object of charitable trusts according to the English model.

[279] Peru, Ley general de bancos, article 325 b). See also Japan, Trust Law 1922 (in the English translation), article 66: 'worship, religion, charity, science, the arts, and other public benefits'; Mauritius, Trusts Act 1989, s. 2: '"charitable trust" means a trust which: (a) is for charitable purposes, including religious, educational, literary, scientific or social purposes'.   [280] See above, chapter 3 §1.i.

[281] Panama, Law no. 1 of 1984, article 5: 'Puede constituirse fideicomiso para cualesquiera fines que no contravengan a la moral, las leyes o el orden público'; Ecuador, Código de Comercio, article 410: the transfer takes place 'por un plazo o para cumplir una finalidad específica'.

[282] Liechtenstein, Personen- und Gesellschaftsrecht, article 927 final paragraph: 'Bei gemeinnützigen oder dergleichen Treuhänderschaften, wo anspruchberechtige Begünstigte fehlen . . .'.

of the proceeds; the second is a voluntary trust, in which the existence of beneficiaries is absorbed by the indication of the purpose:

Irrespective of whether movable property is held in co-ownership or not, the owner or co-owners thereof may entrust the property to a fiduciary to be held by him for some particular purpose or purposes. In such case, the property held by the fiduciary is called a fiduciary fund.[283]

The maximum duration of non-purpose trusts is variously fixed at between twenty and fifty years.[284]

5. Who can be a 'trustee'

The distinction is between trusts linked to a particular qualification requirement on the part of the trustee and those which may be put into effect without such formality.

The former are usually of a financial nature, and the trustee must be either a bank or a finance company, as in Venezuela, Colombia, Ecuador and Peru. The latter, on the other hand, have a wider application, and anyone may be a trustee, except where the functions of the trustee are carried out by professionals addressing the public.[285] In the case of class trusts of a financial nature, provision is made for the issue of certificates which incorporate the rights of the beneficiaries.[286]

6. Indications regarding the position of the beneficiary

As in the English and international model trusts, beneficiaries are not a requirement. In fact, as we have seen, most of the civil-law systems we are examining allow a trust to be created for the attainment of a purpose.

The beneficiary, if one exists, may be the settlor himself.[287] The benefi-

---

[283] Seychelles, civil code, article 824.

[284] 50 years: Mauritius, Trusts Act 1989, s. 5(1); 30 years: Venezuela, Ley de fideicomisos, article 9; Argentina, Ley 24.441, article 4 (c); 20 years: Peru, Ley general de bancos, article 325; Colombia, Código de Comercio, article 1230, paragraph 3; 20 years from the death of the settlor or for so long as the final beneficiary is alive (the rule is rather more complicated): Louisiana Trust Code, §§1831–2, which, however, regulates charitable trusts separately (§§2271–337) and permits them to be of unlimited duration.
    See also Quebec, code civil, article 1272.   [285] Argentina, Ley 24.441, article 5.

[286] For example, Liechtenstein, Personen- und Gesellschaftsrecht, article 928: 'Durch die Treuhandurkunde kann bestimmt werden, das über Treugut Treuhandzertifikate als Wertpapiere an die Begünstigten ausgegeben werden.' The rule continues by listing the connected rights and the circulation of certificates. Peru, Ley general de bancos, article 336: 'el banco fiduciario puede expedir en favor de los fideicomisarios certificados de participación en las inversiones, bienes y derechos del fideicomiso, en proporción a la parte que corresponda a cada uno de ellos'. Argentina, Ley 24.441, articles 19–26: fideicommissum *financiero* with issuance of shares.

[287] Venezuela, Ley de fideicomisos, article 23; Colombia, Código de Comercio, article 1226,

ciary may often be a person not yet born[288] and, except in the case of Colombia, there is nothing to prevent the appointment of successive beneficiaries;[289] in effect, the comparatively short duration of civil-law non-purpose trusts makes this a somewhat unlikely scenario.

Acceptance by the beneficiaries is not required either to perfect the creation of the trust or to render the distribution in their favour irrevocable (expect by the Peruvian law). If the trust is created as a revocable trust, the settlor may, of course, take back the right transferred to the trustee, and may therefore also change the beneficiaries.[290] If, on the other hand, the trust is irrevocable, the irrevocability also applies to the appointment of beneficiaries, unless the trust instrument states otherwise. It would seem, however, that in some cases the position of the residual beneficiary, using this term to describe the person for whom the assets on trust are intended (and therefore not the beneficiaries of the income), is different; namely when he is a party to the trust instrument (and, perhaps, where he accepts by a separate act).[291]

The legal entitlement of the beneficiary, as in the English model, does not involve any direct relationship with the assets on trust. These belong to the trustee, and the beneficiary's creditors may only attack the benefits and other income due to the beneficiary.[292] Only David, when drafting the

---

paragraph 2; Ecuador, Regulation of 26 August 1993, article 41.4.; Peru, Ley general de bancos, article 322; Quebec, code civil, article 1281. In trusts for sale in the Seychelles, settlor and beneficiary must necessarily be one and the same.

[288] Venezuela, Ley de fideicomisos, article 8; Peru, Ley general de bancos, article 323; Panama, Law no. 1 of 1984, article 18; Ecuador, Regulation of 26 August 1993, article 41.4; Russia, Decree of 24 December 1993, article 7; Argentina, Ley 24.441, article 2, paragraph 1.

[289] Colombia, Código de Comercio, article 1230: 'Quedan prohibidos: . . . 2°) [los negocios fiduciarios] en los cuales el beneficio se concede a diversas personas sucesivamente.' Peru, Ley general de bancos, article 323, and Argentina, Ley 24.441, article 2, paragraph 2 expressly provide for later beneficiaries.

[290] Thus, expressly, Panama, Law no. 1 of 1984, article 16.

[291] Peru, Ley general de bancos, article 321, paragraph 1: 'Si el fideicomisario interviene como parte en el contrato, adquiere a título propio los derechos que en él se establezca a su favor, los que no pueden ser alterados sin su consentimiento.'

[292] Thus, expressly, Ethiopia, civil code (French edition), article 536: 'Les créanciers du fidéicommissaire n'ont aucun droit sur les biens qui font l'objet du fidéicommis'; Colombia, Código de Comercio, article 1238: 'Los acreedores del beneficiario solamente podrán perseguir los rendimientos que le reporten dichos bienes'; Peru, Ley general de bancos, article 327: '. . . tratándose de las obligaciones de los fideicomisarios, esa responsabilidad sólo es exigible sobre los frutos o las prestaciones que se encuentren a disposición de ellos'; but the principle may be extracted by interpretation from all the laws under review.

Ethiopian code, had the idea of incorporating within it a kind of protective trust:

Le constituant du fidéicommis peut stipuler que les revenus du fidéicommis ne pourrant être saisis, entre les mains du fidéicommissaire, par les créanciers du bénéficiaire du fidéicommis.[293]

This provision has no equivalent anywhere else.[294]

7. Forced heirs
The general principle is what one would expect it to be: the transfer of assets to the trust cannot prejudice the rights of the forced heirs.[295] The law of Peru provides a clear enunciation:

Los herederos forzosos del fideicomitente pueden exigir la devolución de bienes enajenados por su causante a titulo de fideicomiso, en la parte que hubiere perjudicado sus legitimas.[296]

Louisiana, torn between maintaining rules of succession which did not conform with those in force in most of the other states and the desire to permit the control over the devolution of an estate which is at the root of family-type trusts, took a middle path: the *légitime* due to a forced heir may be placed in trust, provided that the trust terminates after one gener-

---

[293] Ethiopia, civil code (French edition), article 540.

[294] Except in Mauritius, Trusts Act 1989, s. 86, which is similar to the English Trustee Act. In Japan, provisions rendering a trust protective would be void as against public policy: M. Arai, 'Japan', in Glasson, I, ch. 21, A21.25.

[295] Among the extremely rare cases, we see the 1962 Mauritius decision *Austin v. Bailey*, which held that a trust created under English law by a Mauritius citizen was valid, but which declared that provisions which prejudiced the bequest due to the plaintiff were void (the decision reviewed French case law and literature).

[296] Peru, Ley general de bancos, article 317.
  See also Liechtenstein, Personen- und Gesellschaftsrecht, article 907, paragraph 2: 'In allen andern Fällen ist das Treuhandgeschäft unwiderruflich, unter Vorbehalten der Anfechtung seitens Treugebers oder Dritter nach den Vorschriften über Mängel beim Vertragsabschlusse, des Erbrechts oder der Anfechtungsordnung und gegebenenfalls nach Schenkungsrecht.'
  For the law of Mauritius, Trusts Act 1989, s. 4(8) and (9), no trust may distribute more than 25% of the beneficial interest to a person who is not one of a class of persons likely to be the legal personal representatives of the settlor; and, if the beneficiaries are the children, no one may have more than 10% more than any other.
  In Ecuador, Regulation of 26 August 1993, article 41.13, the settlor must declare under oath 'que su valor [that is, the value of the assets transferred to the fiduciary] no excede del que tiene la porción de bienes de la que puede disponer libremente, de conformidad con las disposiciones aplicables a las asignaciones forzosas'.

ation.[297] This is not a *fideicommissum* limited to a single appointment: these are trusts, and who would be the first appointee in *fideicommissum* would be a trustee.

In 1956, Venezuela bred the protective trust with a limited *fideicommissum*:

No obstante lo dispuesto en el Código Civil sobre la legítima, el testador puede disponer la constitución de un fideicomiso respecto de la misma, o parte de ella, en favor de los herederos forzosos siempre que éstos hayan realizado re-iteradamente actos de prodigalidad o se encuentren de tal manera insolventes que sus futuras adquisiciones se vean seriamente amenazadas.[298]

In both Louisiana and Venezuela, an heir has the right to receive the income from those assets on trust (representing his share of the settlor's estate) which will pass to his heirs on the termination of the trust.

8. Claims to transferred assets and tracing

As we have seen, in contrast to what we know to be the rule in English law, civil-law trusts are usually subject to registration with respect to the assets transferred to the trustee, and formal requirements are set forth for the trust instrument.

These requirements clearly simplify the measures to be adopted in the case of alienation by the trustee, since each time the fiduciary nature of the trustee's right is binding on his successors through operation of the rules regarding registration no specific question relating to the fiduciary property can arise.

Where, on the other hand, the assets or rights need not be registered, or where the registration is not in itself effective with respect to the successors of the trustee, or where a legal system does not have a registry system, an action against the trustee for breach might be recognized, or the transfer by the trustee might be voided where, for example, the transferee has knowledge of the transferor's position as a trustee and the transfer was in breach of trust. As will be clear, we are in the area of 'tracing', but with completely different legal weapons at our disposal.

States such as Ethiopia cannot take advantage of registry systems which would lead to the right of action we are discussing. They condition the action upon the knowledge, or potential knowledge, of the provisions of the trust instrument on the part of the third party:

Les dispositions par lesquelles l'acte constitutif du fidéicommis limite les pouvoirs du fidéicommissaire, ou règle la manière dont ces pouvoirs doivent être

---

[297] Louisiana Trust Code, §§1841–54: 'The légitime in trust'.
[298] Venezuela, Ley de fideicomisos, article 10.

exercés, ne peuvent être opposées aux tiers, à moins qu'il ne soit prouvé que ces tiers ont connu ou dû connaître ces dispositions.[299]

Venezuela makes the same provision, limited to transfers not for value:

Son anulables todos los actos efectuados por el fiduciario en violación de sus obligaciones resueltas del fideicomiso, siempre que el acto sea a titulo gratuito o se haya celebrado con terceros que conocieren o deberian conocer las obligaciones del fiduciario.[300]

The law of Venezuela thus identifies voidability as the legal category which describes the defect in the *negotium* carried out by the trustee. It requires two elements, one objective, in that the limits of fiduciary ownership have been exceeded, and the other subjective, which relates to the third party who contracts with the trustee. I think it worth noting that subjective requirement comes directly from English law which, as we know, equates knowledge with wilful ignorance or ignorance arising out of a failure to effect the kind of inquiries which the circumstances would normally require.

The solution which inspired those among the other systems under review which have specific regulations in this area is also based upon the notion of voidability:[301] Japan,[302] Liechtenstein,[303]

---

[299] Ethiopia, civil code (French edition), article 529(1).

[300] Venezuela, Ley de fideicomisos, article 18.

[301] With the exception of Mauritius, which bravely follows the English method, but at the cost of having recourse to terms which are not customary in a civil-law system, and which, as may be foreseen, are not easy to interpret.

Mauritius, Trusts Act, 1989, s. 79: 'Rights to follow trust property'.

(1) Where trust property other than money, bearer bonds and other negotiable instruments, comes into the hands of a third person inconsistently with a trust, the beneficiary may require such third person to admit formally, or may apply for a declaration, that the property is comprised in the trust.

(2) Where a trustee has disposed of trust property and the money or other property which he has received in return can be traced in his hands, or the hands of his legal personal representative or legatee, the beneficiary shall have, in respect thereof, rights as nearly as may be similar to his rights in respect of the original trust property.

(3) Nothing in this section shall affect the rights of a transferee who has obtained trust property or other property received by a trustee as specified in subsection (2)-(a) in good faith; (b) without notice of the trust; and (c) upon giving value.

[302] Japan, Trust Law 1922 (in the English translation), article 31; annulment, at the request of the beneficiary, provided that the required registration procedure has been followed, 'the other party and sub-acquirers had known or failed to know because of gross negligence that the disposition in question was in contravention of the tenor and purport of the trust'.

[303] Liechtenstein, Personen- und Gesellschaftsrecht, article 912, paragraph 3: 'Haben Dritte zum Treugute gehörende Sachen oder Rechte in Kenntnis ihrer Treuhandeigenschaft vom Treuhänder, ohne dass dieser verfügungsberechtigt war, erworben, so kann' the settlor, the beneficiary or a person appointed by the court 'den Herausgabe- oder den Bereicherungsanspruch zu Gunsten des Treuhandvermögens geltend machen'.

Colombia,[304] Israel[305] and Peru.[306] The law of Liechtenstein, although it recognizes an embryonic form of constructive trust,[307] does not apply it in these circumstances, but prefers an action for annulment and the consequent recovery of the asset, or, where this is factually or legally impossible, an action for unjust enrichment. Apart from the latter, which does not appear in the other laws, but which is probably available within the respective legal systems, the solution is the same everywhere. Anyone who should wish to argue as to whether an action for annulment is more or less effective than tracing would be forgetting that tracing is not a remedy, and that the true comparison should be between the effects of the constructive trust and those of the action for annulment. The former has the advantage of extending to any asset into which the third party may have transformed or converted the asset obtained from the trustee; the latter that of producing real effects as a consequence of the annulment of the disposition by the trustee, although they are limited to the asset which is the subject of the *negotium* between the trustee and the third party. The real effects are produced by the constructive trust, only indirectly, in that the constructive trustee is obliged to retransfer the asset. The constructive trust, however, provides further protection for the beneficiary, because the beneficiary precedes all other creditors; more precisely, he acquires a right to terminate the trust and take possession of the assets themselves.

g Conclusion: open and closed systems

The trust, or trusts, may be looked at in many ways. As I have often – perhaps too often – repeated, I see in them an open-ended structure; in

---

[304] Colombia, Código de Comercio, article 1235: '[the beneficiary may] Impugnar los actos anulables por el fiduciario . . . y exigir la devolución de los bienes dados en fideicomiso a quien corresponda.'

[305] Israel, Trust Law (in the English translation), s. 14: 'Where an act is done in violation of duty imposed by the trust and the third party knows or ought to know of the violation or it is done without consideration, the court may invalidate it, and the third party shall incur the responsibility and obligations of a trustee.'

[306] Peru, Ley general de bancos, article 326, paragraph 3: 'Los actos de disposición que efectúe en contravención de lo pactado son anulables, si el adquirente non actuó de buena fe', unless they took place in the Stock Exchange.

[307] Liechtenstein, Personen- und Gesellschaftsrecht, article 898: 'Wo immer jemand . . . ohne ausdrückliche Bestellung zum Treuhänder von einem anderen Vermögenswerte oder Rechte irgendwelcher Art im eigenen Namen aber zu Gunsten des bisherigen Eigentümers oder eines Dritter besitz, ist mangels anderer Bestimmung das zwischen ihm und dem Dritten bestehende Rechtsverhältnis wie ein Treuhandverhältnis zu behandeln.'

  I have already cited (see above, footnote 235) the Israeli provision which states that a trust has effect 'vis-à-vis the whole world', that is, *erga omnes*, but other rules are missing from the Israeli law which would allow the emergence of the general structure of the constructive trust.

truth, it is the common-law systems which are open. Having arrived at this stage of our research, however, we must ask ourselves how far it is true to say that that civil-law systems are closed.

We have just seen that some transfers of the trust property are voidable because a person knows *or should have known* that the other party is entering into a contract in breach of obligations which he has assumed at the moment in which he became the fiduciary owner of the subject matter of the contract. We are beyond the realm of the written word here, and are led towards legal cultural structures which favour actual facts over their consecration in writing, and never permit the latter to preclude an investigation of the former or their legal consequences.

This is the truly explosive effect of the trust. It is not the fact that a special property arrangement, the charter of the fiduciary owner, may be enforced against third parties because that arrangement simply adds a fact-pattern to those already recognized[308] and although it might permit the application of transactional elements which would not otherwise be possible (this is, of course, a result of no little importance), it does not produce innovations at the level of *principia*. This, however, is the level at which the trust operates, by bringing into the foreground *principia* which may have been in hibernation in the civil law, but which have not been invalidated, and extrapolating from them those *regulae* which each legal system then formulates according to its own terminology and conceptual system. It is these *regulae* which give a preceptive content to the otherwise vague notion of 'fiduciary ownership' and which then permit us to compare it with the trust.[309]

We shall look into this further in chapter 7.

---

[308] The fact that situations comparable to the trust were possible in civil law without upsetting the conceptual system has already been pointed out by R. J. Alfaro, *Trust and the Civil Law*, (see above, footnote 12). Alfaro was the pioneer of the trust in Panama, from where it spread into other countries, for example Puerto Rico.

[309] With regard to article 6 of the Argentinean law 24441 ('El fiduciario deberá cumplir las obligaciones impuestas por la ley o la convención con la prudencia y diligencia del buen hombre de negocios que actuá sobre la base de la confianza depositada en él'), the plan for reform of the Argentinean Civil Code turns, instead, to article 1299: 'sobre la base de la confianza y de la buena fe'; as may be read in Reformas al Código Civil, Buenos Aires, 1993. Highton, Iturraspe, Paolantonio and Rivera, *Reformas al derecho privado* (see above, footnote 35), p. 31 observe that it is not 'amistad, familiaridad o compañerismo, sino una confianza que es hija de la experiencia del fiduciario, de su solvencia, de los años de la gestión de asuntos ajenos, de la profesionalidad; this is a position contrary to the bureaucratic stance taken in Italy regarding requirements of 'onorabilità' in new laws in the financial field.

6 The Hague Convention, 1985

1. The general framework of the shapeless trust

a The Convention and civil-law systems

From the Acts of the Fifteenth Session of the Hague Convention, wherein lie the origins of the treaty text which is the subject of this chapter, there emerges an interesting, and evolving, common-law/civil-law dialectic, of which, I believe, it is essential that account be taken. It developed from a head-on confrontation and a mutual misunderstanding of the respective motives and needs of the two systems, and then turned into a synthesis which provoked further confrontations and misunderstandings. As a result (and this will be one of our guidelines for interpretation of the Convention), the resulting text must constantly be read on three levels: the first is linked with the aims expressed by the drafters and other experts and delegates at the Hague; the second, which often leads to results which contrast with those produced by the first, descends from customary hermeneutic canons; and the third takes account of the dialectic I have referred to above, with contributions during the course of the work from the instinctive civilian aversion to a legal structure which is perceived as being strange and menacing, and from the desire of common lawyers to satisfy the representatives of systems which had to grant their consent if the Convention was to see the light of day.[1]

The conflict between civil law and common law characterizes the

---

[1] The common-law delegates frequently proposed the use of expressions which, in their opinion, would be more intelligible to civilians; see, for example, Actes, p. 238, where the US delegate maintained that there was no difference between 'transfer' and 'place under the control' (this is the central element of the notion of trust: the transfer to the trustee), but that the latter would be more easily understood by civil-law systems. There is, of course, a difference, and adhesion to the US proposal contributed to the birth if the shapeless trust.

preliminary report of the Conference[2] and the discussions which took place at the working sessions. The observation which was made from time to time that they do not after all represent two self-contained blocs, and that within each of the so-called families there exist significant variations, left no meaningful trace; on the contrary, surprise was expressed, and objections were raised, when it became evident that the Liechtenstein trust is indistinguishable from the 'Anglo-American' trust, and that the definition worked out for the latter embraces the former without difficulty.[3] It was thus that the idea of 'trust-like institutions' was launched; it represents one of the most significant misunderstandings of the Conference, and when it was introduced in the preliminary report, it led to the distortion of the purpose of the Convention, and thus to the coming into being of the shapeless trust.

The confrontation gave rise to an underlying structure for the discussions which may briefly be defined as the need for civil-law systems to *defend themselves* from trusts. The trust, it was said, subverts the system of real rights,[4] so that if we really must accept that trusts which satisfy the requirements of the Convention should be recognized in civilian countries, we must erect a series of barriers, and routes which must be followed. In the course of the debate on the provision to be included in article 13, the Italian delegate[5] objected to this requirement; his statement deserves to be quoted in full:

Article 14[6] does not deal with fraud ... It does not concern the subject of mandatory rules or *ordre public*. Rather, it attempts to address the subject of purely internal trusts, which could be perfectly clean and moral, but to which he would not like to give effect because he considered it simply too costly. It would require civil-law countries to create statutes, legal documents etc. He did not wish to give Italian citizens a new legal tool with which to reach results achievable under no presently existing institutions.[7]

The inspiration – both juridical and meta-juridical – behind the Italian delegate's declaration is the opposite of that which lies behind the confrontation: purely domestic trusts do not involve questions of unwaivable

---

[2] A. Dyer and H. van Loono, in Actes, pp. 10–108.
[3] Actes, p. 217 (Bank for International Settlements).
    The classification 'Anglo-American trust' was fashionable during the works of the Conference. The 'Anglo-American' trust does not exist.
[4] Actes, p. 236 (Reporter): 'L'introduction du trust bouleverserait en effet tout le système des droits réels'; similarly at p. 218 (Bank for International Settlements).
[5] Professor Antonio Gambaro.
[6] What in the final text was to become article 13 was at this stage article 14.
[7] Actes, pp. 287–8.

rights or public policy;[8] they may well be 'clean and moral'. Whether or not they are desired is, therefore, a question of opportunity.[9]

This is a far-reaching view, and a correct one from a comparative stand-point, but it received no support. A series of grotesque events took place,[10] and the common lawyers took and kept up a condescending attitude towards the civilians,[11] and the civilians did not even take offence when it was said that courts from civil-law jurisdictions did not have the means to exercise a supervisory function over trustees.[12]

b The purposes of the Convention

The condescending attitude referred to above found its institutional home in the transformation of the Convention into a textbook for civilians.

The Reporter wrote as follows:

l'object de la Convention est de donner aux juristes de droit civil un instrument permettant d'appréhender cette figure juridique étrange que constitue le trust[13]

but the special commission had already said as much:

le principal intérêt de l'avant-projet est pour les Etats de common law, de voir les trusts reconnus dans les Etats de civil law, et pour ces derniers de posséder un instrument permettant de saisir le trust[14]

---

[8] By 'internal trusts' is meant those whose objective content refers to a single legal system (in the hypothesis in the text, Italy). By 'objective content' is meant that over which the person creating the trust can have no influence (for example, the location of the assets, the nationality of the settlor or the beneficiaries).

[9] On which everyone may express his opinion. I do not agree with the last sentence of the contribution referred to above, however: I shall show in the next chapter how trusts permit us to attain results which cannot be reached in any other way; in any event, A. Gambaro reaches the same conclusion in 'Il "trust" in Italia e in Francia', in P. Cendon (ed.), *Scritti in onore di Rodolfo Sacco*, Milan, 1994, I, 497, at pp. 513–20 and in A. Gambaro, A. Giardina and G. Ponzanelli, *Convenzione relativa alla legge sui trusts and al loro riconoscimento*, in *Le nuove leggi civili commentate*, 1993, pp. 1211ff., at pp. 1218–20; along the same lines, R. Lener, 'La circolazione del modello del trust nel diritto continentale del mercato mobiliare', in [1989] Riv. soc. 1050.

[10] In the *avant-projet* there was a provision (article 19), which was similar to article 15 of the final text, on mandatory provisions in the area of wills, succession, etc.; it clearly prevailed over article 11, which disciplines the effects of recognition. The Commission held that it would have been pointless and even confusing to insert into article 11 a reference to article 19; nonetheless, 'elle [la référence] a été maintenue comme étant de nature à rassurer les juristes des pays de civil law' [!].

[11] See, for example Actes, p. 232 (United Kingdom): 'with time civil law jurisdictions would feel less need for protection'.

[12] Commission, no. 12: 'les juges de la plupart des pays de civil law paraissent mal outillés pour exercer de telles foncions' (as if Italian judges had not been accustomed for centuries to watch over guardians and tutors).   [13] Actes, p. 236.

[14] Commission, no. 9.

so that the Convention was intended to indicate, for the benefit of civilians who would not otherwise have been able to find out, what is involved in the recognition of trusts.[15]

In any event, the Australian delegate was perfectly clear:

The aim of the Article [the reference is to article 2, which defines the trust] is to give to lawyers and judges in civil-law countries sufficient indication of what constitutes a trust.[16]

It is certain, therefore, that one of the aims of the Convention, which up until now has never been acknowledged publicly, was pedagogic.[17] In fact, according to the Reporter, 'l'intérêt pédagogique est avant tout à la base de cette Convention'.[18]

A second, and equally certain, purpose was the recognition of trusts, initially identified in the 'Anglo-American trust', with special reference to the exercise of a trustee's duties.[19] In this regard, it was observed that civil-law countries would be accepting obligations without a consideration,[20] but then two different considerations were identified – the discovery of what constitutes a trust (this is the pedagogic function described above), and the attainment of a system of rules for the identification of the applicable law of trusts – both of which the civil-law jurisdictions lacked.

In truth, attention was drawn to the fact that civil-law countries lacked this system because they had no need for it, since cases where the recognition of a trust involved decisions on questions of applicable law were extremely rare.[21] From this, the conviction grew that the conflict-of-laws rules of the Convention would also be of use to common-law countries,[22] if for no other reason than because their courts found themselves faced with the need to render decisions on trusts containing an element of foreignness much more frequently than did their civilian colleagues, and they did not have sufficiently clear and complete rules to lean on. In reality, it was of

---

[15] Commission, no. 81; see also no. 37.

[16] Actes, p. 153. The Australian delegate also demonstrated on other occasions his conviction of the ignorance of civilians: see Actes, p. 250: 'not to indicate that a trustee may also be a beneficiary might mislead civil lawyers into thinking that in such a case there is no trust'.

[17] There were also self-inflicted wounds; see the French delegate: 'au cours des précédentes réunions, les juristes de droit civil ont éprouvé le besoin d'une rédaction à caractère pédagogique' (in Actes, p. 250).   [18] Actes, p. 284.

[19] In fact, the very first draft (in Actes, p. 141–3) concentrated on the powers of the trustee: cf. Actes, p. 137, no. 2; no. 9 and A. Gambaro, Il 'trust' (see above, footnote 9), p. 500.

[20] Commission, no. 9, no. 28.

[21] Actes, p. 230 (Austria). The Italian and French experience is the same: trusts which were the subject of pronouncements from case law were clearly regulated by a foreign law.

[22] Commission, no. 22.

primary importance to common lawyers that a set of uniform rules on conflict of laws in the area of trusts be arrived at, and it seems to me to be strange that they only came to this realization when the work was already under way, since, as I have demonstrated above, common-law writing and case law were both fumbling in the dark, and there had been a chorus of complaints about the deplorable state of the law.[23]

While the delegates drafted the various rules with the so-called Anglo-American trust in mind, the Convention eventually had quite another object.

c The motives behind the shapeless trust

The initial discussions of the special commission led to the conclusion that the Convention should also deal with institutions which are 'analogous' to trusts, but the first working document referred exclusively to trusts under the English model.[24] The texts which followed, as we shall see later in our detailed examination, excluded some of the elements identifying the English model, and the special commission noted the fact that although the various rules had been drafted with an eye to the Anglo-American trust, it had not managed to draft the rule containing the definition of 'trust' in such a way as to exclude 'analogous' institutions.[25]

While some opposed an extension of this kind,[26] and others simply took note of it,[27] many delegates requested that the Convention not be limited to the 'Anglo-American' trust,[28] and that the definition to be given in article 2 be expressed in terms which would include civilian institutions.

The final report heeded this request:

La Quinzième session a . . . décidé d'inclure des institutions autres que le trust de common law proprement dit, à condition que ces institutions répondent aux critères de l'article 2.[29]

This was not a last-minute *coup de main*. The earliest document of the Conference read as follows:

---

[23] See above, chapter 3 §2.m.   [24] Actes, pp. 141–4.   [25] Commission, no. 21.
[26] In particular the Netherlands: Actes, p. 144 and p. 212; and the Bank for International Settlements, p. 216.
[27] Actes, p. 159 (International Union of Latin Notaries); see also p. 206 (Germany).
[28] See, for example, Actes, p. 230 (Egypt), p. 232 (Luxembourg, also with reference to Argentina, Japan and Quebec), p. 233 (Czechoslovakia); and cf. the observations of the President at p. 233, the general discussion at pp. 251–2 and the Report, no. 23.
[29] Report, no. 26. See also Report, no. 36: 'Article 2 veut simplement indiquer les caractéristiques que doit présenter une institution – qu'il s'agisse d'un trust d'un pays de common law ou d'une institution analogue d'un autre pays – pour tomber sous le coup de la Convention.'

La définition adaptée par la Convention devrait être basée sur un concept de base du trust et pourrait couvrir d'autres institutions dans la mesure où celles-ci tombent dans la définition fondamentale. Ainsi certaines institutions présentant des analogies structurelles avec le trust porraient être incluses.[30]

The trust which I call 'shapeless'[31] (whether or not the choice of adjective is pleasing) represented a conscious choice by the Conference. It was in line with what had been proposed at the outset, was encouraged on a number of occasions in the course of the work, and was ultimately recognized.[32] The statement that this is contrary to the intention of the drafters of the text of the Convention does not hold water.[33]

The choice was arrived at by degrees, however, and there was no formal revision of the initial drafts.[34] The text of the Convention was discussed and written with no reference whatsoever to 'analogous' institutions of civil-law countries, but turned out to have a different institution as its point of reference: the structure which had dominated the works was confined to the Preamble, which was proposed to the delegates at the last minute.[35]

A comparative study of what these 'analogous' institutions are is nowhere to be found in the materials of the Conference. Although there are

---

[30] Actes, p. 140.

[31] I first proposed this notion in *Introduzione ai trusts*, ch. 4.

[32] See above, footnote 28. On the last day of the Conference, the Reporter expressed himself thus: 'Le préambule précise que la Convention est centrée sur les trusts de common law et qu'elle permet aussi de prendre en compte des institutions analogues dès lors que ces dernières sont conformes à la définition posée par article 2.'

Following the Convention, see the article published by the Reporter, A. E. von Overbeck, 'Law Applicable to, and Recognition of Trusts in Switzerland: the Possible Future under the Hague Convention', in 2 T&T (1996), no. 5, 6 at 7: 'The Convention was not meant to be limited to the common law trust, but to apply also to institutions in other jurisdictions having the main characteristics enumerated in Article 2.'

[33] Gambaro, *Proprietà*, p. 638, states in footnote 69: 'L'intenzione dei redattori fu certamente diversa e trova espressione nell'art. 5 della Convention ai sensi del quale è escluso il riconoscimento ove la legge applicabile non disciplini compiutamente il tipo di trust i cui effetti siano oggetto della istanza di riconoscimento.' On the intention of the drafters, I have cited above the final report and the preliminary works which underpinned it (see also D. Hayton, 'The Hague Convention on the Law Applicable to Trusts and on their Recognition', in 36 ICLQ (1987) 260, at p. 262; on article 5, a reading of it is sufficient (also reviewing, if necessary, the commentary of L. Fumagalli, in Gambaro, Giardina and Ponzanelli, *Convenzione* (see above, footnote 9), p. 1242; in the light of the misunderstandings which may remain, I dedicated my concluding remarks on the validity of 'domestic' trusts to article 5: see below, chapter 6 §2.d.

[34] The final report also continues to speak of equity in the English, but not in the French, text: see, for example, Report, no. 46: 'the beneficiaries have rights against the trustee which they may assert in a court of equity'; 'les bénéficiaires ont contre le trustee des droits qu'ils peuvent faire valoir en justice.'

[35] Working document no. 58 of 17 October 1984 (in Actes, p. 312); the Conference concluded its work on the morning of the 19th.

occasional mentions of functional and structural analogies, they represent nothing more than a vague exercise. The English model was not compared with a series of civil-law structures which it was claimed could be compared with it, nor was a category developed which was feasible from a comparative viewpoint and which included both English-model trusts and other institutions. On the contrary, the huge problems with a task of this nature, and the opportunity to avoid even having to undertake it, were both referred to explicitly.[36] In article 2, therefore, the notion of a trust for all seasons was preferred: the shapeless trust, in addition to being in the minds of the drafters, may be found in article 2 of the Convention.

d The shapeless trust (article 2)

The Convention contains its own set of references, in that, contrary to Hague Convention practice, it defines the legal phenomenon which it regulates in the text itself. If the Convention is to be applied to any fact-pattern, in civil or common law, it must first be determined that the fact-pattern corresponds with the requirements of article 2. If that determination is not made, the fact-pattern will remain outside the scope of the Convention.[37]

Article 2 defines the Convention fact-pattern. We shall now examine it point by point, using the French text.[38]

1. Transfer to the trustee

Article 2.1 holds that in order to find that a trust exists, it is sufficient that 'des biens ont été placés sous le contrôle d'un trustee'.[39] The first draft put it differently: 'lorsque des biens sont transférés à . . . une personne, le trustee'.

There is an evident contrast between these two versions, just as it is clear (as was immediately pointed out[40]) that the former, the definitive text,

---

[36] See the declaration of the president in Actes, p. 251 and the melancholy recognition in Report, no. 26: 'L'inclusion des institutions analogues . . . a finalement été admise sans vote formel.'

[37] For example, a blind trust is not a trust for the Convention, because it does not provide for the duty of the trustee to account for his management. In fact, the requirement of 2.2c is not satisfied by the accounting presented by the trustee on the termination of the trust, since a trust of this type may last for many years and a mere final accounting does not allow any control over the management (to be effective, the control must take place during the management).

[38] I have chosen the French text because the terms used are more appropriate for a comparison with non-common-law trusts, which we reviewed in chapter 5.

[39] See earlier article 2 of the Revised Text: 'Le trust a pour effet de placer des biens sous le controle d'un trustee dans l'intéret d'un bénéficiaire.'

[40] Actes, p. 159 (International Union of Latin Notaries).

opens the door to many civilian legal structures.[41] I do not believe that it is by mere chance that the text under review in article 2 is close to the definition in the Israeli law of 1979 and the conceptual explanation offered in Louisiana;[42] on the contrary, this close connection shows that the Convention sought to use language which is as far as possible from the terminology which is typical of trusts in their systems of origin.[43]

The notion of 'control' is of very little legal importance. The explanation that it was not possible to be more precise for fear of alarming civil-law countries seems to me to be ridiculous (although it is likely true).[44] Here we see an ambivalence which marks the whole interpretive path of the Convention, and which has its origins in the phenomenon described in the previous pages: it was conceived for the English-model trust, was drafted with the collaboration of civilians who had first been put on the defensive, and was finally (and thanks to the very definition we are reviewing here) made to apply not only to trusts, but also to every institution which corresponds to the fact-pattern defined in article 2.

Article 2.1 continues by stating that the transfer of control to the trustee takes place for the benefit of a beneficiary or for a specific purpose. The latter element, which was not present in the first draft, removes us yet further from the English-model trust. As we know, trusts for purposes (with the exception of charitable trusts) are, in principle, void in English law, and charitable trusts have very special limitations with respect to their purpose.

Article 2.1 therefore defines a fact-pattern which moves away from the English trust model: it does away with the transfer to the trustee, which, as

---

[41] In Colombia, circular unica juridica no. 7 of 1996, article 1, defines perfectly the co-existence of structures from the two formulations within the same legal system: 'Para los efectos de esta Circular, se entienden por negocios fiduciarios aquellos actos de confianza en virtud de los cuales una persona entrega a otra uno o más bienes determinados, transfiriendo o no la propiedad de los mismos . . . Si hay transferencia de la propiedad de los bienes estaremos ante la denominada fiducia mercantil . . ., fenómeno que no se presenta en los encargos fiduciarios, también instrumentados con apoyo en las normas relativas al mandato, en lo cuales solo existe la mera entrega de los bienes.'

[42] R. A. Pascal, 'The Trust Concept and Substitution', in 19 LouisianaLR (1959) 273.

[43] The official explanation, that reference to the transfer of the assets to the trustee was omitted (in spite of the fact that it was held to be essential if a trust is to be created) because the identification of the applicable law of the transfer is not a purpose of the trust, is unconvincing. (Commission, no. 30; Report, no. 54). Here we are at the heart of the definition, and article 2 refers to acts *inter vivos* and to wills which place assets under the control of a trustee; it could easily have added that those assets are transferred to the trustee.

[44] C. Jauffret-Spinosi, 'La Convention de la Haye relative à la loi applicable au trust et à sa reconnaissance (1er juillet 1985)', in JdrInt (1987), 23, at 27: 'afin de ne pas effaroucher les pays romanistes'.

we know, is essential,[45] and admits trusts for purposes in general.[46] In this way, the definition of the shapeless trust begins to emerge, and we shall now look at its other characteristics.

2. The settlor as trustee

The first draft read: 'lorsque des biens sont transférées à ou retenus par une personne, le trustee'. The second alternative was immediately deleted; since it is an alternative, it is not possible to understand whom it might have harmed.

The attempts to return to the original version[47] were not successful in bringing about a change of mind, and the proposal for an amendment presented *in extremis* by four delegations met the same fate.[48] The point on which everyone agreed was that a declaration of trust by which a person pronounced himself trustee of a right of which he was already the owner would remain outside the Convention,[49] as would all acts of transfer to the trustee.[50]

In my opinion, there is doubt as to whether *negotia* by which a person declares himself to be the trustee of a right which is his constitute trusts for the Convention.[51] It pre-supposes that trustee and settlor are different persons, which would therefore lead one towards the conclusion that they do not;[52] on the other hand, the reference to the settlor in article 2 was inserted at the request of the civilian delegates, while the common lawyers considered it to be pointless,[53] and demonstrated their conviction that trusts where settlor and trustee are one and the same were within the sphere of the Convention on a number of occasions. On balance, the arguments in favour of extending the Convention to include self-declared trusts seem to me to be convincing.

---

[45] On cases where the settlor appoints himself trustee, see immediately below.

[46] Article 2 has permitted legislation of the international trust model on trusts for purposes, allowed almost without limits, and has thus led practice towards solutions which would otherwise have been impossible.

I refer to the tendency which, thanks to the Convention, has substituted trusts for purposes for offshore holding companies: see above, chapter 4 §4.f.

[47] Actes, p. 214 (Commonwealth Secretariat and Canada); p. 237 (United Kingdom).

[48] In Actes, p. 319: this was an elegant means of returning to the question, because there was a desire to introduce into article 4, on the *negotium* of transfer to the trustee which was excluded from the Convention), a mention that an act by which an asset is 'set aside by a person to be held by himself as a trustee' was to be included.

[49] See, for example, Actes, p. 237 (United Kingdom).   [50] I shall discuss this below.

[51] The doubt was not removed by Report, no. 57.

[52] This emerges clearly from article 21.   [53] Cf. Commission, no. 40.

3. The relationship (fiduciary or otherwise)

On the subject of the duties of a trustee, the first draft read: 'd'utiliser les biens du trust à des fins fiduciaires, dont il est responsable'. Objections were lodged from all sides,[54] the reference was omitted, and no mention was made anywhere in the Convention of the fiduciary nature of the relationship, or of the fiduciary dimension.

This is a significant omission, at least for those who see the essence of the trust in the entrusting. The Convention, notwithstanding declarations to the contrary,[55] did not characterize either the fact-pattern of a conventional trust or the duties of a trustee from a fiduciary angle. There are other omissions which go together with this, one of which seems to me to dominate the others, and to allow the final classification of the shapeless trust: the failure to identify the relationship between the trustee and other parties.

The Convention does not clarify whether the relationship is trilateral (with the possible absence of one of the parties if there are no beneficiaries[56]) or bilateral, or in the latter case whether where one pole is represented by the trustee, the other is represented by the settlor or the beneficiaries.[57] The shapeless trust clearly permits both.

It is easy to understand that to hinge the trust upon a relationship between trustee and settlor expands the boundaries of the shapeless trust to an excessive degree, but there appears to be no reason why this expansion should not take place. In fact, the abandonment of the requirement of a transfer of the right (or, to use the language of the Convention, the assets) to the trustee, and its substitution with the term 'control', opened up a perilous breach; if the settlor may retain the right, and grant only the exercise of it to the trustee (the exclusive exercise of the right by the trustee seems to me to be the equivalent of 'control'), it is easy to identify a lasting relationship between settlor and trustee. This, as we know, is the very antithesis of the English-model trust, and draws us closer to a number of institutions known in various other legal systems. I shall return to this issue later.

---

[54] Actes, pp. 145 (the Netherlands) and 146 (United Kingdom).   [55] Report, nos. 40 and 46.

[56] The only reference to them, which does not negate the subject we are discussing, is in article 8.2g.

[57] Commission, no. 40 states: the settlor was included in the definition because the civilians wished it, but there are three essential elements of a trust: settlor, assets and beneficiaries.

4. The fund, title, management

Article 2.2 lists three further elements of the fact-pattern: the trust assets are a distinct fund, and are not a part of the trustee's estate; title is held in the trustee's name or in the name of another person on behalf of the trustee; and the trustee has powers of management, and the duty to account for his acts (without clarifying to whom: this is another example of the uncertainty which I have just illustrated regarding the persons involved in the relationship).

The French text tends to entify the trust: 'les biens du trust' as opposed to 'the trust assets' of the English text. As a result, it presents a criterion which does not correspond to the English text: 'les biens du trust constituent une masse distincte et ne font pas partie du patrimoine du trustee' as opposed to 'the trust assets constitute a separate fund and are not a part of the trustee's own estate'. This is not at all the same thing: the French text refers to a separate estate, while the English text refers to the phenomenon of segregation. The French text excludes the assets on trust from the trustee's estate, while the English text includes them, but clarifies that they do not belong to the 'trustee's own estate'. Here the significant word is 'own'; this may be understood only within the English-model trust, and in the light of equitable theories (and, possibly, of the theory I have proposed in this book regarding the equitable lack of title of the trustee).

I am not (on this occasion) criticizing the text of the Convention. I merely wish to draw attention to the way the Convention – in this case as in others – does not adhere to the English-model trust. If it had wished to show that it did, it would have been sufficient to make the Preamble – where equity is mentioned – the foundation of the whole Convention.[58] I simply make the point that article 2 concentrates on the 'assets'. This is not a happy solution from a systematic viewpoint; on this subject I would refer the reader to my discussion of the notion of the English-model trust, centred on the concept of 'entitlement' and of 'right' of the trustee.[59]

5. Powers retained by the settlor; the trustee as beneficiary

Article 2.2 was designed to show that the retention by the settlor of 'certaines prérogatives',[60] and, in line with the Australian proposal,[61] the fact that the trustee enjoys 'certains droits en qualité de bénéficiaire',[62] are

---

[58] Not even this point escaped the attention of the president, who declared that if the intention had been to limit the Convention to the 'Anglo-American trust', it would have been necessary to include a clause in the text as well as in the preamble (Actes, p. 251).
[59] See above, chapter 3 §3.d–§3.g.   [60] In the working document no. 8bis (in Actes, p. 149).
[61] Actes, p. 153.   [62] In the working document no. 9 (in Actes, p. 167).

not necessarily incompatible with the existence of a trust.

As to the first point, which was accepted without discussion, the English text speaks of 'rights and powers'. These are two extremely technical words,[63] in comparison with which 'prérogatives' belongs to everyday language. The interpretation of 'prérogatives' will be of enormous significance, because it will tie in with the unhappy definition of the trust as the transfer of 'control' and not of the right, and will once again raise issues which have already been resolved in English law, and, probably, in the international trust model, but which are perfect for expanding the notion of the shapeless trust to an almost infinite degree.

The Report explains that it was felt that it was appropriate to draw attention to untypical aspects of the relationship.[64] Why would this be the case, if the sole result of their existence is to find that incompatibility with the notion of trust is not inevitable? If the Convention provided us with a working definition of the trust, we would have within the concept adopted by the Convention the tools to comprehend the extent to which these two characteristics are in conflict with the notion of trust, if at all. Without this conceptual apparatus, however, we have no way of evaluating whether in any given circumstances where 'prérogatives' are retained by a settlor a legal relationship is a trust or not. Such a decision, in fact, cannot be left to the applicable law of the trust, since to identify the trust it would use its own criteria, which have no application in the context of this self-referencing Convention. The Convention, which did not pretend to establish a uniform substantive law, does not set out to determine what is a trust in the law of States which have ratified it, but only which legal relationships of foreign law must be recognized by those States as a trust.

The court of a State in which a request is made for recognition of a legal relationship governed by a foreign law must first evaluate whether the relationship is a trust. This cannot be achieved by applying the foreign law to the relationship (although it governs it), because for the purposes of recognition it is the Convention which determines whether or not one is in the presence of a trust. The Convention itself therefore introduces a dramatic element of uncertainty, above all in non-marginal cases, because the modern tendency, especially in countries where the trust legislation is recent, is to reserve numerous rights to the settlor. The court in the country where recognition is sought will have no guidance in weighing the incompatibility (which is not necessarily present), since neither the definition which opens article 2 nor the three characteristics listed immediately

---

[63] On 'powers', see above, chapter 3 §1.c.   [64] Report, no. 47.

thereafter provide an explanation. Here we have clear evidence of the dangers which the shapeless trust presents, and we shall now see another crucial example.

6. Lack of separation from the settlor

The Convention lacks a structural element which is characteristic of the English-model trust: the separation between the settlor and the trust.

Article 2 ignores the relationship between the settlor and the subject matter of the trust (except for the transfer of 'control' to the trustee). While it is said that a trustee's creditors may not act against that which the trustee 'controls', no mention is made of the creditors of the settlor (just as, we have already observed, nothing is said about the relationship between settlor and trustee or regarding the identity of the person who has the right to receive an accounting).

Clearly, the omission of any requirement regarding the position of the settlor's creditors permits that vast range of relationships where the transferor has a direct right of supervision over the trustee to be considered to be trusts, for the purposes of the Convention; for example, fiduciary relationships which are not accompanied by a transfer of ownership to the trustee, those which have a right to manage or to act as their sole purpose, or those where the trustee/fiduciary is obliged to transfer the trust assets back to the settlor/principal.

The shapeless trust does not, therefore, require a legal detachment between the settlor and the trust, let alone the radical cut which is typical of the English-model trust.

7. Conclusion: 'systems which recognize the trust'

The term 'shapeless trust' is controversial, and it is precisely for this reason that I have proposed and support its use. By its excess of expression over meaning, and the profound contradiction of postulating a legal structure with no shape, it serves to establish that the Convention deals neither with the English-model trust nor with any other known structure, but with an open-ended series of fact-patterns which belong to both common law and to civil law.

The examination of article 2 which we have just concluded makes the statement that shapeless trusts exist in every legal system extremely plausible.

One interpretative result of the conclusion we have reached lies in emptying the provisions of the Convention referring to systems 'qui ne connaissent pas l'institution du trust', 'which do not have the institution of the trust' of any content.[65] The 'trust' in question is, in fact, the one defined in article 2, which is the shapeless trust. When the drafters at the Hague wrote the various rules, they were thinking of the 'Anglo-American' trust, but they later decided that the Convention should apply to the trust defined in article 2, which, as we have just demonstrated, is clearly not the 'Anglo-American' trust. No other interpretation is open to us: the 'States which do not have the institution of the trust' are limited to those which do not have structures ascribable to article 2 of the Convention. It is probable that none exist.[66]

Illustrious scholars of trusts have expressed puzzlement at the notion of the shapeless trust,[67] and have interpreted it as a criticism of the Hague Convention,[68] or have contested the assertion that the Convention trust is in reality far from the traditional model.[69] The failing which I hold the work of the Convention to be guilty of is not, as they believe, the lack of documentation on legal systems; rather, it is, for the most part, analytical. The latter probably depends on the former; at the beginning of the nine-teen eighties, trusts were still considered to be a peculiarity of common law, and the comparative approach to trusts was still that which I described at the beginning of chapter 5. The Preliminary Report presented to the delegates was, unfortunately, full of omissions and, as I have already pointed out, drawn from second- and third-hand information. No serious research was conducted into non-common-law systems, either before or during the Conference.

The consequences are still to be seen today: even though everyone recog-nizes that the trust which is the subject of the Convention is not the

---

[65] The citation is from article 13; see also articles 5 and 6. It would perhaps have been simpler to take a class of legal systems which does not recognize the trust (either English-model or shapeless) as the general legal structure.

[66] A comparative note before leaving this topic. The thirteen types of trust which we described in chapter 5 are not shapeless trusts; with the minimum data which we used as the basis of our review, we decided whether they are legal structures which may be homologous to traditional English-model trusts. There was, in fact, no need to deviate from a rigid adherence to the model to arrive at this. It is evident that they fall within the definition of the Convention, as do those (Ethiopia and Quebec) which we excluded because they do not conform to the minimum data set forth for the comparison. Scottish and South African trusts and the Dutch *bewind* also undoubtedly fall into this category, as do the systems of tribal lands, pursuant to the customary laws of Ghana and Nigeria although they are in no way comparable to the English-model trust: see S. K. B. Asante, 'Fiduciary Principles in Anglo-American Law and the Customary Law of Ghana – A Comparative Study', in 14 ICLQ (1965) 1144.

[67] This is the terminology employed by English-language writers, with reference to my essay 'The Shapeless Trust', in 1 T&T (1995), no. 3, 15, and in [1995] 1 Vita not. 51.

[68] von Overbeck, 'Law Applicable' (see above, footnote 32).   [69] Waters, *Cours*, pp. 441–3.

English-model trust, only very rarely does one look beyond Scottish law, the Dutch *bewind*, the *fiducie* of Quebec (which, in any event, as I believe I successfully demonstrated in chapter 5, is not comparable to a trust), and a few other foreign institutions.

The failure to conduct a comparative analysis has led to the definition of a legal structure whose relevance was not understood, and which today has problems of acceptance. This is not, however, a criticism; it is an interpretation of the rules of the Convention.

e Voluntary and involuntary trusts (articles 3 and 20)

Article 3 imposes two further requirements for the identification of a 'Convention' trust, one substantive and the other of form.

Article 3: La Convention ne s'applique qu'aux trusts créés volontairement et dont la preuve est apportée par écrit;
The Convention applies only to trusts created voluntarily and evidenced in writing.

From the outset, it was decided that constructive and resulting trusts would remain outside the sphere of the Convention,[70] and article 2.2, which corresponds to the current article 3, limited the scope of the Convention to trusts 'constitués de manière expresse'. The 'voluntary' trust is a category invented at the Hague[71] which in no way corresponds to the 'express' trust. Above all, the former is unknown in English law, and in this book I have used the term 'expressly established trusts'.

On this subject, I should add that I am unable to comprehend why trusts established by law should have been categorically excluded from the Convention.[72] I would recall two examples from among those I set out above:[73] the trust for sale provided for by the law in the case of intestate succession, and the trust (which the law renders equally compulsory) regarding the communion of property rights in real property. In the former case, the trust permits the trustee to transfer the deceased's assets and divide them among the legitimate heirs, while in the second, the trust represents the technical means whereby a co-owner may obtain the division of the assets by means of a sale of the property. It appears to me that in both cases, these

---

[70] Actes, p. 137.

[71] The Dutch delegate opposed this, and proposed that the term 'expressly created trusts' should be used (Actes, p. 246).

[72] Not even the United Kingdom delegation understood this (see Actes, p. 146): 'So much of English property law is bound up with the non-express class of trusts. It is particularly unfortunate if statutorily imposed trusts are to be excluded' (note the use of the correct term 'express').   [73] See above, chapter 2 §1.c.

powers may be exercised abroad, where the assets in question are to be found, without provoking any disorder. Why, then, should these trusts not be included among those which are automatically recognized under the Convention?

The drafters of the Convention have created considerable confusion, which we should now discuss.

The idea that trusts exist which do not have their origin in an express declaration is an old one; opposite the express trust, we have the non-express trust.[74] The term 'non-express' may signify that there is no declaration of will at all, or that there is no declaration of will sufficient to create a trust. This latter distinction follows a very fine line, but it would nonetheless be sustainable if important consequences for the regulation of trusts could be drawn from it: we have already seen in our examination of constructive and resulting trusts in chapter 2 that this is not the case.

The preliminary report on the question is completely inconsistent,[75] and the work was later directed towards the path taken by the United States which considered the constructive trust as a remedy against unjust enrichment,[76] and the traditional concept that resulting trusts give effect to the implicit will of the settlor. Regarding this last point, the (correct) observation that there cannot in any case be written proof of resulting trusts was to no avail,[77] and the (erroneous) conviction was developed which saw resulting trusts falling within the subject matter of the Convention, because they were established voluntarily, whereas constructive trusts remain excluded because they are 'created' by a court.[78]

Which are the trusts which are established *voluntarily* in the system of the Convention? They are certainly the expressly established trusts, but, contrary to the predetermined purpose of the drafters, certain types of constructive trust might be included, while certain types of resulting trust might not.

Constructive trusts which might be included are those which begin with a declaration of will, evidenced in writing, which is insufficient to establish a trust: for example, obligations assumed by the seller of property which are not reproduced in the final document, or those assumed by a testator in the context of mutual wills. In both cases, the will of the settlor is evident, but is not sufficient to create a trust. Contrary to what the drafters of the Convention have stated, it is not at all true that constructive trusts always

---

[74] See the discussion on terminology above, chapter 2 §1.b.
[75] Preliminary Report, nos. 107–10; no English legal text is cited, except for a legal dictionary.   [76] See above, chapter 2 §5.e.   [77] Actes, p. 214 (Commonwealth Secretariat).
[78] Report, nos. 49–51.

operate against the wishes of the constructive trustee;[79] we have seen in chapter 2 that the constructive trust is very often the means by which express will is acted upon, although it had not been expressed to a sufficient degree to give rise to the creation of a trust.

If one makes will the controlling argument ('created voluntarily'), the application of the Convention to resulting trusts might be prejudiced. In fact, the will of the settlor is also lacking in a considerable number of types of resulting trust: consider the purchase of an asset which is put in the name of a third party, and the delivery of a sum of money for a specific purpose. The drafters of the Convention cancelled the original wording of article 2 which referred to 'expressly established' trusts, taking the position that in this way resulting trusts (which they believed to be founded upon the implicit will of the settlor) would have been excluded.[80] As we know, this is not the case, and great confusion has ensued.[81]

At the origin of this confusion there lies another, preliminary one, so to speak, which contrasts voluntary trusts with 'judicial' trusts. We must now discuss this type, which is the subject of article 20 of the Convention (which permits a State to extend the Convention to such trusts[82]). In reality, on the subject of 'judicial' trusts, the French text speaks of trusts 'créés par une décision de justice', while the English text speaks of trusts '*declared by judicial decision*'. Is this the same thing, since one text seems to refer to dispositive judgments, while the other refers to declaratory judgments?[83] Furthermore, is there an exclusive division between trusts established by an act of will and those which 'have their origins'[84] in a judgment?

The problem had become more complex because it had been posed above all in the context of the recognition of foreign judgments. At that time, it was pointed out that the Brussels Convention on jurisdiction and enforcement of decisions in the civil and commercial fields extends to decisions in the area of trusts 'established by application of a law or in writing or by an

---

[79] Commission, no. 34.   [80] Actes, pp. 179–80.

[81] The lack of an in-depth study in the preliminary report and the fact that many of the delegates had an imperfect knowledge of trust law played a part in causing the confusion to which I refer in these pages. The question posed by the Dutch delegate – did anyone among those present know what an implied trust was? (in Actes, p. 246) – is peculiar, as is the confession by one of the authors of the preliminary report that it was the discussion on constructive trusts which had made him realize what they were (in Actes, p. 245).

[82] The rule has its origins in a British and French proposal (working document no. 51).

[83] Here, what was at that time the English, Australian and Canadian view of constructive trusts evidently prevailed; the US view, on the other hand, which had left its mark on all the preparatory work, was recessive.

[84] I use this imprecise term deliberately, in an attempt to unify the French and English texts of article 20.

oral agreement confirmed in writing':[85] the entire spectrum of sources of the trust, in other words. The Lugano Convention takes the same position; eighteen states, almost the whole of geographic Europe, are thus bound.[86] The Hague Convention was not intended to be transformed into a tool for the recognition of foreign judgments, and, after a rule regarding recognition had been drafted,[87] it was eliminated, and trusts of judicial origin were excluded.[88]

The fact is, however, that the Brussels Convention trust,[89] like that of the Rome Convention of 1980 and, later, that of the Hague Convention of 1988 on the law applicable to succession on death (article 14),[90] is the English-model trust. That of the Hague Convention trust, on the other hand, is the shapeless trust. The Rome Convention excludes the trust from its sphere because, looking at the English-model trust, it does not consider it to be contractual.[91] In all probability, however, trusts which belong to different models are included, as, for example, those we looked at in chapter 5, which have an undoubtedly contractual origin. Also included are shapeless trusts which emerge from contracts. Both these types, which the Rome Convention considers to be trusts, are regulated twice in the area of applicable law: by the Hague Convention in that they are shapeless trusts, and by the Rome Convention, since they belong to the field of contractual obligations.[92]

To conclude, it seems to me that the Convention should be interpreted according to the errors which it contains: a trust will be of judicial origin, and therefore will fall outside the sphere of the Convention (in the absence of a declaration of extension such as that described in article 20), not simply because a judgment declares that it exists, but only when the decision *condemns the defendant to behave like a trustee*, usually with the aim of compensating the plaintiff for losses he has suffered. If the basis of the

---

[85] For example, Commission, no. 33; Report, no. 169, with reference to article 5 no. 6: clause added to the Brussels Convention with regard to the ratification of the United Kingdom.

[86] The state of ratifications is not yet complete;; see the *Premessa al Codice del diritto internazionale privato della Comunità Europea* by R. Clerici, F. Mosconi and F. Pocar, Milan, 1992.

[87] Article 13 of the *avant-projet*.

[88] The acts are accompanied by an excellent explanation by the *Bureau Permanent* (Actes, pp. 162–6), which was virtually ignored by the delegates.

[89] On the relationship between the Brussels and Hague Conventions, see L. Fumagalli, 'La Convention dell'Aja sul "trust" and il diritto internazionale privato', in [1992] Dir. comm. int. 533, at 564–5.   [90] The text is in [1989] Riv. dir. int. priv. proc. 446.

[91] See above, chapter 3 §1.a.

[92] For trusts which do not belong to the English-model, and which have their origins in a contract (see chapter 5), the Convention of Rome should prevail on the basis of the postponement of article 57 of the Italian reform of private international law: F. Pocar, 'La scelta della legge regolatrice del trust', in *Atti Milano*, ch. I, §§2–3.

judgment is different, there may or may not be a 'voluntarily created' trust, and the deciding factor for the purposes of recognition will not be the judgment itself, but its *ratio decidendi*.[93] The judge charged with the recognition must decide if the judgment on which the existence of the trust depends shows voluntary conduct – evidenced in writing – on the part of the defendant or not (or, possibly, find the evidence in writing in the judgment which is the subject of the request for recognition).[94] Here the alternative discussed above concerning the purpose of the voluntary conduct makes a second appearance in a different fact-pattern: I believe that it is correct to consider as included within the Convention system only that voluntary conduct which corresponds in civilian terms to the trust which I have called 'expressly established'.

f Conclusions

For all fact-patterns which fall within the definition set forth in article 2, the Convention has enunciated the rules which regulate certain aspects of conflict of laws.

The Convention was created to validate the activities of common-law trustees in civilian systems,[95] and to reach an understanding on the criteria

---

[93] It seems to me that not dissimilar results are obtained by C. Jauffret-Spinosi, 'Convention de la Haye' (see above, footnote 44), 35 and D. Hayton, 'Hague Convention' (see above, footnote 33), at 265–6, although they arrive at them by different paths and for different reasons; cf. Underhill, *Trust*, p. 828 (edited by D. Hayton).

[94] It will be recalled that written proof is required by article 3 of the Convention.

[95] English-model trusts were already recognized by the civil-law systems in which the problem had been raised; in addition to the Italian case law, it should be remembered that pronouncements in favour of recognition had been made in Switzerland, France, Germany, Greece, Luxembourg and Denmark.

  For France, see above all Béraudo, *Trusts*, §§350–71 (there is a large number of French decisions in the area of trusts, especially testamentary trusts; with particular reference to the exercise of trustees' powers, see Cass. 3 novembre 1983, in JdrInt (1985), 115, on the fact that it is not necessary to enter a foreign judgment which validates the appointment of trustees of a testamentary trust); J.-C. Goldsmith, 'Trusts in France', in 2 T&T (1996), no. 6, 6; C. Deneuville, 'Le droit français et le trust', in *Atti Milano*, ch. 31; and previously L. T. Bates, 'Common Law Express Trusts in French Law', in 40 Yale LJ (1930) 34.

  For Switzerland, see C. Reymond, 'Réflexions de droit comparé sur la Convention de la Haye sur le trust', in *Revue de droit international et de droit comparé* (1991), 7 at pp. 9–11; W. Reyser, 'Convention de diligence et trust', in *Société anonyme suisse* (1988) 49; D.-A. Dreyer, *Le trust en droit suisse*, Geneva, 1981; E. Klainguti, 'Trusts in Swiss Law and Banking Practice', in *Atti Milano*, ch. 32; for Denmark see the tax decision described in 1 T&T (1995) no. 1, 4; for Belgium see the precedents, above all in the area of wills, referred to by G. van Hecke and K. Lenaerts, *Internationaal privaatrecht* (2nd edition), E. Story, Scientia, Aalen 1989; for the Netherlands, see J. B. Vegter, *The Anglo-American Trust and Dutch Private Law*, Utrecht, 1995; for precedents from various jurisdictions (Austria, Greece, Luxembourg and Switzerland) see D. Hayton, International Recognition of Trusts, in Glasson, §§C1.29–C1.42.

for resolution of conflicts of laws within common-law systems,[96] but instead it has validated both international model trusts, and trusts from civil-law systems (which probably would have been validated anyway, even if the Convention had been limited to 'Anglo-American' trusts), and an as yet undefinable series of institutions, civilian and otherwise.

2. The applicable law

a *Negotium* of creation and *negotium* of transfer: the law of the trust (article 4)

The transfer to a trustee is an optional element of the shapeless trust; as we have seen, it is sufficient that the trustee should have 'control' of the 'trust assets'.[97] When a transfer takes place, the applicable law of the act of transfer is identified not by the Convention, but by the conflict rules which would also apply in other cases: this is the effect of the provision of article 4 concerning 'preliminary' acts.

From the time of the initial work, the experts had taken a liking to the image of the launch-pad and the missile: the missile is the trust, and the launch-pad is what causes it to come to life, and does not concern the Convention. This figure of speech comes up frequently in the discussions, and is warmly received.[98] It makes me shiver, because it embraces two different legal *negotia* within the 'launch-pad': creation, and transfer. When the president of the session meekly observed that the metaphor of the missile and the launch-pad was understandable in the context of testamentary trusts (where creation and transfer coincide), but that perhaps the subject was more complex with regard to other trusts,[99] the discussion, which was totally dominated by common-law experts and their emphasis on the practical relevance of questions of law, did not change course in the

---

In general, see E. Gaillard and D. T. Trautman, 'Trusts in Non-Trust Countries: Conflict of Laws and the Hague Convention on Trusts', in AJCL (1987), 307, at 315–16; A. Gambaro, 'Problemi in materia di riconoscimento degli effetti dei trusts nei Paesi di civil law', in [1984] 1 Riv. dir. civ. 93, at pp. 95–6 and the works cited above, chapter 5, footnote 3.

[96] And also to carry out a pedagogic function for the benefit of civilian jurists, as we have seen.

[97] I continue to use the terminology of the Convention, although I believe it to be incorrect.

[98] And in the Report, no. 53: 'On a donné l'image du lanceur et de la fusée: il faut toujours un "lanceur", par example un testament, une donation ou autre acte juridique, qui met en marche la "fusée", le trust. L'acte juridique préalable, le "lanceur", ne tombe pas sous le coup de la Convention.'

[99] The president was perfectly correct. As we saw at the beginning of chapter 3, the express testamentary trust is the only one where the *negotium* of creation and the *negotium* of transfer coincide (half-secret testamentary trusts are different, and they fall within the Convention because they may be proved by a writing. Secret trusts are clearly outside, but these matters were not even touched on during the Conference).

slightest.[100] The transfer of an asset to a trustee, however, or the transfer of control over an asset to a trustee, cannot be considered to be in any way a 'preliminary' question, as stated in article 4. Unless the distinction between the *negotia* of creation and transfer is called into question,[101] the very opposite is true: the preliminary question is that which concerns the validity of the *negotium* of creation, not that of transfer.

In the discussions of the text of article 4, a proposal was made to eliminate the adjective 'preliminary',[102] but the majority opposed it on the grounds that the general idea was that a trust could not exist without the transfer of the asset to the trustee.[103] The falsity of this opinion derives from the rules in English law, the international model and many trusts from civil-law jurisdictions, which regulate cases where the trustee designated by the settlor does not accept, or dies before accepting. All these rules state that the trust remains valid, and lay down the procedure for the appointment of another trustee.[104] None of this would be possible if the *negotium* of creation were not autonomous, and did not prevail over the *negotium* of transfer. I would add that the trustee often receives distributions after the original one has been made; it is surely not possible to consider these transfers to be 'preliminary' to the validity of a trust which clearly already exists. Finally, it is possible that the opposite may happen, so that the *negotium* of transfer takes place *before* the *negotium* of creation, or is accompanied by a general indication that the transfer will be followed by an indication of the terms of the trust to which the transfer (which has already taken place) will be subject.[105]

According to the initial proposals, the applicable law of the trust was to govern every aspect of the *negotium* of creation, including its form,[106] but this point was later eliminated, and it was agreed that the 'law of the trust' (as I shall abbreviate the expression 'the law governing the trust') would govern questions of substantial validity, and not validity of form.[107] It is not

---

[100] Note the weakness of the Preliminary Report, no. 55, on this question.

[101] As I have frequently pointed out, the two *negotia* can co-exist in the same document and within the same declaration.

[102] Actes, p. 238 (Greece); at this stage, the article in question was numbered 2.

[103] This conviction was expressed by one and all, and in the final report; notwithstanding this, as we saw above, the requirement of transfer was eliminated in favour of that of control.

[104] Secret trusts represent a case where the *negotium* of creation must necessarily precede the transfer: see above, chapter 3 §1.f.

[105] Where we see once again the essentially unilateral nature of the *negotium* of creation.

[106] Revised text, article 6, final paragraph, in Actes, p. 149: 'Au sens du présent article, le terme "validité" vise la validité du trust en la forme et au fond des dispositions relatives au trust . . .' Article 6 became article 8 in the final version.

[107] See the discussion in Actes, pp. 238–41.

correct to state, as the report seems to me to do, that the law applicable to the *negotium* of creation of the trust is the same as the applicable law of the trust.[108]

Once the relationships between creation and transfer have been clarified in this way, the *negotium* of creation will be governed as to form by the law dictated by the ordinary rules of conflict, and as to its effects by the applicable law of the trust. It is not certain that the latter will extend to questions regarding the capacity of the settlor, the trustee or any beneficiaries.[109]

b The unlimited freedom to choose the applicable law (article 6)

Article 6 provides that the trust will be governed by the law chosen by the settlor: 'Le trust est régi par la loi choisie par le constituant'; 'A trust shall be governed by the law chosen by the settlor'. The settlor is, therefore, the sole arbiter of the law which will regulate the trust which he creates, and the principle of autonomy of will rules.[110]

This provision was not arrived at without a long struggle, because a second position – that the choice of the settlor would not, or might not, be effective in the absence of objective elements of nexus between the choice of law and the trust – had manifested itself from the outset.[111] This position was expressed in a number of proposals, ranging from article 3.3 of the first draft[112] to the Greek proposal, which substantially repeated it,[113] to the Dutch proposal that during the ratification process a State should be permitted to declare that it would not give effect to a choice of law where the objective elements of the trust were not connected to that law,[114] to the proposal of the International Union of Latin Notaries that the choice of law should be limited to a predetermined range of possibilities.[115]

This position, in the various forms outlined above, or more generally

---

[108] Report, no. 54: 'La loi désignée par la Convention ne s'applique qu'à la constitution du trust lui-meme.'

[109] Report, no. 59. On the relationship between natural capacity and *lex causae* see G. Rossolillo, 'Qualche riflessione in tema di incapacità naturale', in [1994] Riv. dir. int. priv. proc. 67, at 74–6.

[110] Report, no. 63. On the general subject, see M. Giuliano, 'La loi d'autonomie: le principe et sa justification théorique', in [1979] Riv. dir. int. priv. proc. 217; S. M. Carbone, 'L'autonomia privata nel diritto internazionale privato delle obbligazioni', in [1982] Dir. comm. sc. int. 15.

[111] See previously preliminary document no. 6, in Actes, p. 139, no. 10b.

[112] 'Il peut ne pas etre tenu compte de ce choix, lorsque ni le constituant ni l'objet du trust n'ont de liens réels avec la loi choisie.'   [113] Working document no. 32.

[114] In Actes, p. 213.

[115] Actes, p. 147: the law of the trust must correspond either to the domestic law of the settlor, or to that of his domicile or residence, or to the place where the trust will be managed, the assets are located or the main purpose will be realized.

expressed in the form of direct opposition to the principle of the autonomy of will of the settlor, was restated on various occasions by different delegations;[116] it was pointed out, for example, that article 6 would allow a French citizen to create a trust in the Bahamas of assets located in France. There was no way out, however, and the unlimited freedom of choice of law was approved by a wide majority.[117]

It was believed by some that the civilian defence forces (it was not yet clear that the subject of the works was no longer the 'Anglo-American' trust, but the shapeless trust) might withdraw and still win the day by taking up a position behind the rules which would regulate the recognition of trusts, and by including limiting provisions at that stage, but the ambiguity of this position is evident, and was expressed by the Greek delegate when he perceived that his proposal to limit freedom of choice of law was not going to be successful.[118]

It should be said that the settlor's absolute freedom of choice is not a major innovation on the international front;[119] it had already been recognized in case law from France, which can certainly not be considered to be liberal in these areas.[120] It had also been adopted by the Hague Conventions of 1955,[121] 1978[122] and 1985[123] and by the Convention of Rome on the law applicable to contractual obligations[124] which, like the later *Convención Interamericana sobre derecho aplicable a los contratos internacionales* of 1994,[125] imposed no limitations on the freedom of the parties; on the contrary, they had no difficulty in recognizing that the chosen law need not have any other material connection with the contract, and that the mere choice of a foreign jurisdiction in place of the local law qualifies as an element of

---

[116] As an example, see Actes, pp. 145 (the Netherlands); 146 (Sweden); 147 (Commonwealth Secretariat); 159 (International Union of Latin Notaries); 211 (Italy); 231 (Greece).

[117] Actes, p. 257; Italy abstained.   [118] Actes, p. 257.

[119] F. Pocar, 'La libertà di scelta' (see above, footnote 92), §4. On international practice in this area, see A. Saravalle, 'Clausole con scelta di legge variabile e la Convenzione di Roma del 1980', in [1995] Riv. dir. int. priv. proc. 17.

[120] Cour d'Appel of Paris, 10 January 1970, in RevCrit (1971), 518, on a trust created by a French citizen of securities in the United States. This could have had some relevance if the question had concerned the effectiveness of the trust over assets located in France, but it was not relevant to the question of freedom to choose the applicable law of the trust (cf. the note by G. A. L. Droz, 528).

[121] Convention sur la loi applicable aux ventes a caractère international d'objets mobiliers corporels, article 2.

[122] Convention on the law applicable to agency, article 5; this Convention is not yet in force.

[123] On international sale of goods.

[124] Article 3.1: 'the contract is governed by the law chosen by the parties.'

[125] On which see L. Pereznieto Castro, 'Introducción a la Convención Interamericana sobre derecho aplicable a los contratos internacionales', in [1994] Riv. dir. int. priv. proc. 765 (771–3 on the choice of applicable law).

internationality, and so serves to place the contract within the ambit of the Convention even though all the other elements of the contract are strictly domestic.[126]

c Other questions of private international law (articles 7, 5, 9, 10 and 8)

There is no need to go into the other rules of the Convention regarding the law of the trust in this book.[127] I would just point out that in the absence of a choice expressed by the settlor (article 7.1), or where the choice falls upon a system which lacks rules for the type of trust in question (article 6.2), the trust will be governed by the law with which it has the closest connection. In order to identify that law, account is taken of the place of administration of the trust, the location of the assets, the residence or domicile of the trustee, and the place where the purpose of the trust is to be fulfilled (article 7.2) (although the list is not all-inclusive and is not in order of importance[128]).

It may be that even the provisions of article 7 do not lead to a law which contains provisions for the type of trust in question, and in this case the Convention cannot be applied (article 5).

A trust may be governed by various laws, in the sense that (per article 9) elements which are susceptible to severability, such as administration, may be subject to different laws from those regulating validity (the law of the trust), if the trust permits (article 10). The law of the trust will determine the possibility of the trust later being subject to a different law (article 10[129]). As we noted in chapter 4, the international trust model has substantially adopted the provisions of the Convention in this area.

The law of the trust, as we have already seen, regulates the validity of the trust and (per article 8) all issues relating to the life of the trust (the missile's course, to follow the figure of speech which we took exception to above).

---

[126] G. Sacerdoti, 'Finalità and caratteri generali della Convenzione di Roma. La volontà delle parti come criterio di collegamento', in G. Sacerdoti amd M. Frigo, *La Convenzione di Roma sul diritto applicabile ai contratti internazionali* (2nd edition), Milan, 1994, pp. 1ff., at p. 14.

[127] On which, in addition to the comments already cited, see F.-E. Klein, 'A propos de la Convention de La Haye du 1er juillet 1985 relative à la loi applicable au trust et à sa reconnaissance', in F. Sturm (ed.), *Mélanges Paul Piotet*, Berne, 1990; H. Kötz, 'Die 15. Haager Konferenz und das Kollisionsrecht des Trusts', in RabelsZ (1986) 562; A. E. von Overbeck, 'La convention de La Haye du 1er juillet 1985 relative à la loi applicable au trust et à sa reconnaissance', in 41 SJIR (1985) 30; V. Salvatore, *Il trust. Profili di diritto internazionale e comparato*, Padua, 1996, pp. 66–70.

[128] Cf. Commission, no. 64 and the prevailing vote to this effect (Actes, p. 266).

[129] For the history of these provisions, see Commission, nos. 72–9; the debate and the vote are in Actes, pp. 275–9.

Duration is one of these issues, and so one of the most frequently debated questions of private international law of trusts in common law is resolved. To borrow terms from corporate English, we are speaking of the 'by-laws' of the trust and its 'organs', submitted to the jurisdiction of the law of the trust.[130]

d The 'domestic' trust (article 5)

The Hague Convention system imposes no limit on the choice of applicable law. There is, therefore, nothing to prevent an Italian citizen from creating a trust which is regulated by the law of his choice; in particular, there is nothing to prevent all the elements of the trust from being concentrated in Italy.

This conclusion, which I first expressed in 1994 in *Introduzione ai trusts*, is a natural result of the explanations provided above, and is irrefutable unless objections are raised to my interpretation of article 6 of the Convention, which I have developed while adhering strictly to the preparatory work, the text of the rule and opinions expressed in the literature.[131] If we consider that even illustrious authors have treated the entire Convention as if it were about *foreign* trusts (and I shall demonstrate in the next section that this is not so), this is an appropriate time to re-state the conventional method for determining the applicable law of a trust.

The main criterion is the choice of law by the settlor. I have already listed the many limits which some delegations attempted to impose on this choice, and we have seen how they were rejected. Those writers who today would tie the choice of applicable law to objective elements of nexus suggest – sometimes brilliantly – positions which can no longer be supported, in that they have already been proposed and expressly rejected.[132]

It may happen, expressly or by implication, as permitted by article 6, that the choice of the settlor falls on a legal system which does not define the *negotium* which he has created as a trust. Even in this case, the choice of the settlor does not lead to the non-application of the Convention, because

---

[130] Recent private international writing has suggested new perspectives in the area of 'competent jurisdiction': see P. Picone, *Ordinamento competente e diritto internazionale privato*, Padua, 1986, pp. 95–102 and 257–6.

[131] Von Overbeck, Law Applicable (see above, footnote 32), 7: 'The choice of the law of a trust jurisdiction is fully valid without other considerations.' The author repeated this position in a presentation at the Seminario del Consiglio Nazionale del Notariato in Rome on 12 July 1996. U. Morello, 'Fiducia e negozio fiduciari: dalla "riservatezza" alla "trasparenza"', in *Atti Milano*, ch. 8, §9, is of the same opinion.

[132] I am referring to G. Broggini, 'Il trust nel diritto internazionale privato italiano', in *Atti Milano*, ch. 2.

article 6.2 provides that in such a case one looks to the system which offers the closest connection (article 7), as in the case where the settlor has made no choice, explicit or implicit. If a trust is not found by this method, the Convention is not applicable (article 5).

This is the system of the Convention. Article 5 means exactly what a literal reading would suggest:

La Convention ne s'applique pas dans la mesure où la loi déterminée par le chapitre 2 [Articles 6 to 10] ne connaît pas l'institution du trust ou la catégorie du trust en cause.

Chapter 2 contains the rule on freedom of choice, express or implied. Only where the choice is lacking, or where it leads to a system which does not regulate such a *negotium* as a trust, does one look to the system with which the *negotium* has the closest connections. Where even this system does not define the *negotium* as a trust, the Convention cannot be applied.[133]

Since this interpretative path has had some difficulty being understood, I have prepared a simple chart of the logical steps required.[134]

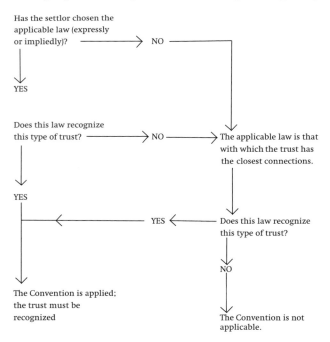

[133] R. Lenzi, 'Operatività dei trusts in Italia', in [1995] Riv. not. 1379, at 1382, agrees that domestic trusts (he, like others, uses this term) are legal, but holds that the choice of applicable law does not operate as a criterion with private-international significance, but as a simple renvoi to foreign law.
[134] The chart is reproduced from my report in *Atti Milano*, ch. 3.

3. Recognition and its effects

a The 'foreign' trust and the universality of the Convention (article 21)

And so we arrive at a fundamental problem regarding the subject of the Convention: as some would have it, the Convention is about 'foreign' trusts. According to how this expression is interpreted, this is either self-evident or a dangerous error.[135] It is self-evident in that one cannot speak of 'recognition' in the presence of a legal relationship, the effects and structure of which belong to the legal system where 'recognition' is sought; recognition presupposes the insertion into the legal system of a phenomenon which would otherwise only operate in a different, and therefore foreign, legal system. It is a dangerous error, on the other hand, if the term 'foreign' is given a different meaning, and is tied, for example, to the nationality or personal law of the settlor, or to the place where the trust is administered or the assets are located, or to other criteria of this kind which we have seen in some modern laws on trusts. *In the system of the Convention, the 'foreign' trust does not exist.*[136]

In fact, article 11.1 of the Convention provides that a trust will be recognized in the Contracting States if it has been created in accordance with chapter 2 (articles 6–10). Article 6, as we have just seen, sanctions the unlimited freedom of the settlor to choose the law of the trust. Contracting States are, therefore, obliged to recognize trusts regulated by a foreign law, and it is here that we find the only *element of foreignness* required.

On this last subject, it would have been perfectly possible, as Italy requested,[137] to limit recognition to trusts governed by the law of a Contracting State. Instead, the majority decided in favour of universality (any foreign law);[138] this universality clearly widens the geographical borders of the shapeless trust.

Having established these principles, the Convention regulates the recognition of the trust (or, perhaps more correctly, the effects which a foreign law which regulates a trust has in the local forum[139]) in clear terms. It

---

[135] Just as he had on the subject of the distinction between voluntary and express trusts, the Dutch delegate once again suggested the correct solution, and once again received no support. His solution was not to speak of recognition, but of the 'effects' of trusts created according to the provisions of the Convention (working document no. 14).

[136] The notion of 'foreign' trusts was expressly contested, without opposition, both by experts (France and Denmark) and by the Reporter (in Actes, pp. 290–1) and was omitted from the final text of article 13 (cf. Report, no. 132).

[137] Actes, p. 304, with the prediction that ratification of the Convention would otherwise be unthinkable.

[138] See the discussion and vote in Actes, pp. 303–5; see also Commission, no. 88, the German proposal (working document no. 62) and the relevant discussion (in Actes, p. 336).

[139] This terminology, as I stated above, was supported by the Netherlands.

firstlists the minimum effects of recognition (articles 11 and 12), and then sets forth a specific limitation (article 13) and a principle of favour (article 14). Finally, it lists general limitations (articles 15, 16 and 18).

b The minimum effects of recognition

Article 11 of the Convention, after declaring that the trust must be recognized, is composed of two sections:

1. Article 11.2: Recognition shall imply, as a minimum, that . . . etc.;
2. Article 11.3: In so far as the law applicable to the trust requires or provides, such recognition shall imply . . . that etc.

The difference between the two provisions is clear: the first is a material rule, while the second is a rule of conflict regarding the basic effects which the applicable law must receive in the local forum.

Article 11.2 lists three apparently obvious rules:

– that the trust assets are separate from the personal assets of the trustee;
– that the trustee may act as plaintiff or defendant;
– that the trustee may appear in that capacity before notaries and public authorities.

These three rules are translated into legal rules of the local forum, in addition to their existence in the applicable law. While we can be certain that the first will find a corresponding rule in the applicable law of the trust, since it belongs to the definition of the trust provided by the Convention (article 2), the other two may or may not correspond to provisions of the foreign law. In this sense, and within these limits, article 11.1 is a rule of uniform material law,[140] and the trustee of a (shapeless) trust may therefore act as plaintiff or defendant, and may appear in his capacity as trustee before notaries and public authorities as a consequence of the ratification of the Convention, even if the law of the trust should make no provision for this.

Article 11.3 indicates other effects of recognition, but only in so far as they correspond to rules of the applicable law of the trust:

(a)–(c) The trust assets may not be attacked by personal creditors of the trustee, even in the event of his bankruptcy, or by his spouse, or by his heirs;
(d) Recovery of the trust assets must be allowed where the trustee, in breach of the trust, has mingled the trust assets with his own, or has (wrongly) disposed of them.

The effects described in (a) to (c) are repetitive and obvious. Apart from the

---

[140] This opinion was earlier expressed by the Greek delegation: Actes, p. 282.

reference to spouse and heirs, they correspond to the fundamental elements of the shapeless trust and the obligatory element of segregation (article 2 of the Convention).

The effects described in (d) are, however, in a completely different category, and clearly refer to tracing in the English trust model. This greatly alarmed some civilian delegates,[141] and absolutely terrified the representative of the Bank for International Settlements, who forecast an unacceptable subversion of banking practice, and the introduction of elements of dangerous uncertainty into the relationship between banks and their customers.[142] Here there was an intersection of considerations which did not relate to tracing as such, but to the responsibility of a banker who had been informed of the existence of a trust and had conducted himself in a manner which prejudiced the rights of the beneficiaries.[143]

Tracing, as we have seen above, is not a legal remedy, but a procedural technique in support of an entitlement.[144] The fact that the third party is or is not a constructive trustee of an asset which is part of or linked to a trust does not arise out of the tracing. Furthermore, since it is a procedural technique, tracing cannot be applied in a foreign action in any fashion; it is prevented from being applied by basic principles of international law.

Article 11.3(d) speaks of 'revendication', which is a civilian term. In the case of shapeless trusts, such as the *bewind*, where there is no transfer of the asset to the trustee, the reference is correct. It is probably also correct in the case of trusts which do not belong to the English model, where the law permits a beneficiary to take action to obtain the annulment of a transfer carried out by the trustee.[145] It is incorrect, on the other hand, in the case of English-model trusts.[146]

Unfortunately, detailed comparative research was lacking also in this case.[147] It was preferred to introduce a note of caution which will provoke serious interpretative problems:

Toutefois, les droits et les obligations d'un tiers détenteur des biens du trust demeurent régis par la loi déterminée par les règles de conflit du for.

---

[141] See, for example, Actes, p. 212 (the Netherlands), p. 233 (Switzerland).

[142] Actes, pp. 215–20.

[143] The Italian delegate correctly pointed out that questions of responsibility would be decided on the basis of the local law, and absolutely not on the basis of the law of the trust (in Actes, p. 281).   [144] See above, pp. 58–65.   [145] See above, chapter 2 §4.b.

[146] I refer the reader to my explanation of the entitlement of the beneficiary: see above, chapter 3 §3.e. The British delegation had proposed a different formulation of the rule: Actes, p. 282 and working document no. 47.

[147] See the debate in Actes, pp. 280–1; 282–3; cf. Report, nos. 111–17.

c The minimum effects of recognition and the form (articles 3 and 12)

We know that in the English-model trust no provision is made for any form of registration, whether in a land registry or any other kind of registry (such as a share register[148]); on the contrary, it is expressly forbidden. We also know that in trusts of non-common-law countries, forms of registration are compulsory.[149]

It was immediately proposed at the Hague Convention that registration be a requirement,[150] and the need for the trust instrument to be in writing, and not simply proved by a writing, was underlined. One of the first drafts provided that 'La présente Convention ne s'applique qu'aux trusts établis par écrit',[151] but immediately after this the text passed to trusts 'dont la preuve est apportée par écrit'.[152] At the same time, as we noted above, the *negotium* of transfer, which is precisely the *negotium* whose registration is the subject of article 12, is excluded from the scope of the Convention.

The formal requirement of article 2 ('evidenced in writing') relates to the *negotium* creating the trust, while article 12 relates to the *negotium* of transfer; there is no contact between the two rules.

Remaining with the second rule for a moment, we see that here too the civilian experts fell prey to irrational fears. Once the Convention had imposed the recognition of trusts, what better guarantee could there be than to impose registration? The Bank for International Settlements, to cite one of the most fearful participants, would surely have obtained the tranquillity it sought if it had understood that legal action is not possible against a bank unless the existence of a trust is formally communicated to it. Instead, refuge was sought in article 15.1(f) (on the protection of third parties acting in good faith) and a further element of uncertainty was thereby introduced. Legal systems where registration is widespread, as is generally the case in civil-law countries, would have been extremely pleased if the Convention, as it did in article 11.2, which we have just discussed, had introduced a material rule on compulsory registration of trusts. Trusts would thus have been assimilated by the system.

Instead, the solution adopted by the Convention was to recognize the right of the trustee to carry out registration formalities as trustee, or 'de telle façon que l'existence du trust apparaisse', unless this is incompatible with, or forbidden by, the *lex loci*. Article 12 is, accordingly, a material rule

---

[148] See above, chapter 3 §3.c; see also Actes, p. 160 (Law Society of England and Wales).
[149] See above, chapter 5 §4.b.   [150] Actes, p. 138.
[151] Revised text, article 1A (in Actes, p. 149).
[152] The English text reads 'evidenced in writing'; this is not the same thing (see above, chapter 3 §1.a); the Preliminary Report, no. 52, states that the requirement is satisfied if the trustee notes down the wishes communicated to him orally by the settlor. This does not seem to me to correspond to the Italian concept of written proof.

like article 11.2. Both the prohibition scenario, which I believe involves many common-law countries, but not civil-law countries which lack rules on the subject, and the question of incompatibility of registration are completely incomprehensible, and lead to false results.

The trust, which must be recognized pursuant to the Convention, requires at the very least that the assets on trust should not be susceptible to attack by the trustee's creditors (article 11.2). How could systems where registration is widespread permit this result without at the same time at least permitting – and I am not saying compelling – the forms of registration to which they are accustomed? The consequence of this would be secrecy of the trust, but this would not result in the failure of segregation, which is imposed by the rules on recognition; the result would be that third parties, or certain categories of third parties, would be immune from the effects of the segregation. If unwaivable rules of the forum (which, as we shall see, are protected by article 15 of the Convention), should prevent trusts which are not publicized from being enforceable against third parties, for example where they comprise assets which would normally be subject to forms of registration, the whole Convention would collapse with respect to these trusts, and one would no longer even be able to discuss recognition. It therefore seems to me that civil-law jurisdictions should do their best to ensure that trusts should be made public, even to the extent of making registration compulsory.[153]

d Optional recognition (article 13)

When we commented on article 6, we noted the many attempts – none of which were successful – to limit the freedom of choice of the applicable law of the trust by the settlor. The civil-law delegates based their final defence on rules relating to recognition. Given the general provision on the duty to recognize trusts created on the basis of a law identified pursuant to articles 6 and 7 of the Convention (article 7: 'Un trust créé conformément à la loi déterminée par le chapitre précédent sera reconnu en tant que trust'), there was a flurry of proposals aimed at preventing recognition in certain cases.[154] It is very important, I believe, to re-trace the path which led to the current article 13, as it will provide us with the key to a correct understanding of the rule.

The first objective of five of the civilian delegations was to deny recognition to a trust of assets located in a State which did not recognize the institution of the trust, or in cases where settlor and beneficiaries were

---

[153] [Since the original Italian edition of this book there have been many instances in Italy of trusts registered in the Land Register.]
[154] Cf. Commission, nos. 115–24.

resident in States which did not recognize it.[155] Supported (albeit tepidly) by Italy alone,[156] this proposal that recognition be *forbidden* was in conflict with the general movement, which preferred a list of cases where the *possibility* of denying recognition was admitted.[157] The proposal of the five delegations was modified to this effect at the moment of the vote, but was rejected anyway.[158]

Once the road towards the option of denial had been taken (instead of the route of prohibition), there was no lack of solutions. The Netherlands wanted to reserve to each State the right to declare whether or not it would recognize trusts where the applicable law was different from the one with which all the other elements of the trust were connected.[159] This proposal was not even voted on, and saw the end of the original structure of the rule. In fact, if a prohibitive rule had been chosen, article 13 would have sanctioned a limit to recognition and thereby to the preceptive sphere of the Convention. All of the later proposals, on the other hand, including the one which was subsequently approved, called for the *right not to recognize*: it is up to the courts to decide on a case-by-case basis whether it would be correct to create an exception to the principle of recognition. Article 13 is, therefore, directed towards the courts.[160]

Italy, which formulated a proposal which did not even reach the voting stage, found the positions taken by the Reporter, and later by the president,

---

[155] Working document no. 33 (Argentina, Egypt, Spain, France, Greece).   [156] Actes, p. 291.
[157] Even the delegates of some of the proposing States were against the prohibition.
[158] The proposal received the votes of the proposers, Denmark and Italy: Actes, p. 292.
[159] Actes, p. 213.
[160] Report, no. 123 expressly states as such: 'La faculté prévue par article 13 est ouverte aux juges de tous les Etats contractants . . . La clause sera surtout utilisée par les juges qui estiment que la situation a été abusivement soustraite à l'application de leur propre loi'; see also D. Hayton, *Hague Convention* (see above, footnote 33), 274. See also the conclusion of this chapter.

S. Tondo, 'Ambientazione del trust nel nostro ordinamento e controllo notarile sul trustee', in *Atti Milano*, ch. 15, asked (seeking an affirmative answer) whether a reading of the rule which made the intended recipient the legislator rather than a judge might not be more appropriate (this is also the opinion of N. Lipari, 'Fiducia statica e trusts', in *Atti Milano*, ch. 7, §3). A reading of the rule lends itself to both interpretations. In the text, I have followed the interpretation closest to the intention of the drafters of the Convention, but since it was not transmitted to article 13, it remains only one of the interpretative data.

Diplomatic practice is in favour of the reading used in the text. The only State which passed a domestic law on trusts when it ratified the Convention (the Netherlands), far from imposing limitations, reinforced the provisions of the Convention on land registration and the segregation of trust assets in the case of the trustee's bankruptcy: law of 4 October 1995, in Staatsblad, 1995, 508; France, as we know, did not even consider passing a law to put article 13 into effect, preferring to go down the no-through road represented by a general domestic law.

which we shall discuss below, to be weak, and formulated its own text, according to which recognition became optional in cases where the State of recognition did not recognize the type of trust in question and did not have a similar institution, the settlor and the beneficiaries were nationals of and resident in that State, and the trust assets were located there.[161]

Attention was concentrated on two other proposals, which then came together in versions A and B of article 14, and were later reformulated by the president.[162] Version A (which was not much different from the Dutch proposal) made it possible to deny recognition where all the elements of the trust were connected to the State of recognition except the applicable law and the trustee, while version B provided for the same result where all the significant elements of the trust (apart from the applicable law, the place of administration and the residence of the trustee – the elements which, in the Convention system, the settlor may choose at his pleasure) were more closely connected with a State whose legal system did not recognize the institution of the trust or the type of trust in question.[163] The latter version was the one approved[164] and became the current article 13.

In the discussions on this subject,[165] once the proposal regarding prohibition of recognition had been discarded, two schools of thought predominated, neither of which was in any way rational or had any comparative basis: one school saw trusts as instruments of fraud, whilst the other saw them as a *negotium* closed to civilians.

As far as the former is concerned, the common-law delegates simply responded that the suspicion that trusts were used for fraudulent purposes lacked any substance,[166] and that in any event the Convention provided

---

[161] 'Aucun Etat n'est tenu de reconnaître un trust si:
  a) le droit de cet Etat ne reconnaît pas la catégorie de trust en cause ou une institution analogue et
  b) le constituant et les bénéficiaires ont la nationalité de cet Etat et la résidence habituelle dans cet Etat, et
  c) le trust porte sur des biens qui sont situés dans le territoire de cet Etat' (working document no. 34; see the illustration of this position in Actes, pp. 210 and 286).

[162] Working document no. 50.

[163] The proposal which was approved included the phrase 'all the significant elements'; the word 'all' was eliminated during the drafting process; the general consensus was that the meaning of the rule had not been changed, and that it included all the significant elements anyway: Actes, pp. 331–2; the proposal which was approved pointed out a separation among the three elements which were declared irrelevant, while the final text pointed out the connection: this, too, was held to be correct: Actes, p. 331.

[164] Italy abstained.

[165] Actes, pp. 285–8; 290–2. See also C. Jauffret-Spinosi, 'Convention de la Haye' (see above, footnote 44), 61–5.

[166] Actes, p. 287 (Australia).

strong defences against this possibility.[167] They could have responded, as one later did off the record, that structures which have a fraudulent purpose are quite another thing, and civil-law jurisdictions have done nothing to defend themselves against them. As for the latter, the delegates made frequent reference to the 'domestic' trust without ever requesting that recognition be prohibited.[168]

This last point deserves explanation. The 'domestic' trust is a trust whose objective elements may not be altered by the settlor, and which are connected to a single legal system (it is not necessary to discuss the objective elements here, or to elaborate, for example, on whether one must take nationality or residence into consideration). Is there any reason to *prohibit* recognition where the system to which the objective elements are connected does not recognize that particular type of trust?[169]

This question is to be asked for *all* kinds of trust. A State which holds that the trust subverts its system of real rights (I have not heard any suggestion which goes so far as to theorize that there may be a breach of public policy[170]) should simply not ratify the Convention. In fact, there would be no legal justification for permitting a foreigner, or a citizen resident abroad, to create trusts of assets situated in a State if this meant breaching that State's system of real rights. Adherence to the Convention, as all the commentators have pointed out, means precisely that trusts do not subvert anything (or, if we prefer, that the level of subversion they produce is acceptable).

To prohibit citizens from doing what foreigners can do in Italy with Italian assets would raise issues of personal status and capacity, and would also, in all probability, be unconstitutional.[171] Perhaps the only person to realize this was the Italian delegate, who, in the contribution referred to at the beginning of this chapter, stated that 'domestic' trusts could not raise

---

[167] Actes, p. 287 (United States) and p. 288 (Canada), with reference to those articles which were to become articles 15, 16 and 18, on which see below.

[168] Cf. L. Fumagalli in (see above, footnote 9), *sub* article 13, at p. 1284.

[169] As I have already warned, legal systems which do not recognize any kind of (shapeless) trust probably do not exist.

[170] The commonly held opinion is, it seems to me, that this question can no longer be asked after ratification of the Convention; see Gambaro, 'Il "trust"' (see above, footnote 9), p. 507; Gambaro *Proprietà*, p. 641; M. E. Corrao in Gambaro, Giardina and Ponzanelli, *Convenzione* (see above, footnote 9), *sub* article 18, pp. 1312–13; P. Piccoli, 'Possibilità operative del trust nell'ordinamento italiano. L'operatività del trustee dopo la Convention de L'Aja', in [1995] 1 Riv. not. 37, at 62.

[171] Why, for example, can houses and farms in Tuscany be the subject of trusts created by rich English people, possibly with Italian trustees, when the villas and farms next door cannot only because they belong to Italians? As we have seen, some supported this, but the position did not prevail; this must be taken into account when interpreting the Convention. See Lipari, *Fiducia statica* (see above, footnote 160), §3.

issues of imperative rules or public policy, and declared that they could be 'perfectly clean and moral'. He preferred them not to be recognized for practical reasons (which, evidently, are on a different level from that of the legal interpretation of the Convention).[172]

Article 13 did not, however, develop out of such a broad view of the terms of the problem;[173] it was a reaction to the unlimited freedom of choice of applicable law permitted by the Convention, but it was placed in an inappropriate context because the rules concerning recognition could hardly restrict the unlimited freedom which the preceding articles of the Convention granted to the settlor to choose the law governing the trust. The context is also inappropriate for a second reason which concerns recognition: something which could have been prohibited directly is now prohibited optionally, and is therefore placed in the area of discretion rather than in the area of principles. I shall return to these issues shortly.

Article 13 does not identify the elements which make denial of recognition possible where they are connected to a State which does not recognize the trust or the type of trust in question. Both the Austrian delegate and the president expressed the view that they should be identified by reference to article 7, where the significant elements for identifying the applicable law of the trust in the absence of choice by the settlor are listed.[174] No other interpretation would seem possible, if one considers that the citizenship or residence of the settlor and beneficiaries, and the relevant personal status and capacity, had been debated twice: first when the rules on choice of law of the trust were formulated (article 6), and again during the formulation of article 13. In both cases, the notion of the 'foreign' trust appeared to be extraneous to the system of the Convention, and these criteria were rejected.[175] An interpretative connection between articles 13 and 7 is, therefore, necessary.

Article 7 lists the following four criteria:

1. The place of administration of the trust;
2. The situs of the assets of the trust;

---

[172] Actes, pp. 287–8.

[173] But the very same Italian delegate, on his return to Italy, fell into the trap he had vigorously fought against: A. Gambaro, 'Il "trust"' (see above, footnote 9), p. 502 and in A. Gambaro, A. Giardina and G. Ponzanelli, *Convenzione* (see above, footnote 9), at p. 1216.

[174] Actes, p. 332 (Austria): 'Les éléments significatifs visés à article 13 sont les mêmes que ceux qui sont pris en considération lors du choix de la loi conformément à article 7, à l'exception de ceux qui sont expressément nommés ensuite.' The president agreed. Lenzi, 'Operatività' (see above, footnote 133), 1380, did not, but gave no reasons.

[175] The creation of a trust 'in a country which recognizes and regulates the kind of trust in question' was never mentioned among the elements of foreignness, to which Gambaro, *Proprietà*, 637–8, refers.

3.   The place of residence or business of the trustee;
4.   The objects of the trust and the places where they are to be fulfilled.

Given that the first and the third of these are declared by article 13 to be irrelevant, it must be concluded that the circumstances ('significant elements') which may impede recognition of a trust are limited to the second and the fourth listed above: the place where the trust assets are located, and the purpose of the trust and the place where it is to be fulfilled.

It is of no little importance in order to understand the system of the Convention, that there was no discussion on the foreignness between these elements and the forum where recognition is requested: that was so because what matters is that they should belong to systems which do not recognize the trust or the category to which the trust in question belongs (we know that the first case is unlikely to arise, so that actual occurrences will concentrate on the second).

The fact that the place where the trust assets are located or where the purposes of the trust are to be fulfilled is in a State which does not recognize the trust or the particular type of trust does not lead to non-recognition, because otherwise it would have been prohibited or subject to a specific exception (and the whole structure of the Convention would have crumbled). The only possible result where denial of recognition is optional is that article 13 be considered to be a closing rule in the system of the Convention, which reflects the general interest and not, as is often claimed, only the interest of civilians.[176] This reading of the rule will perhaps seem more cogent after we have looked at the limits which the Convention imposes in the area of recognition.

e Limits to recognition (article 15)

The purpose of article 15 was to prevent a trust from breaching mandatory provisions of a law designated by the conflict rules of the forum (which will often be the law of the forum itself).[177] The 'mandatory provisions' are defined in article 15 as those which cannot be derogated from by the will of the parties.

This principle of pre-eminence was reformulated more than once,[178] and

---

[176] Take the example of a trust for non-charitable purposes governed by a law other than English law: recognition could be refused in England, since this type of trust is not admitted under English law. We saw other examples of trusts which are valid in one common-law country and not in another above, in chapter 3, footnotes 274 and 294. The United Kingdom did not see these issues at the time of ratification of the Convention, and cancelled article 13 from the ratification instrument. (The text may be reviewed in M. Lupoi, *Trust Laws of the World*, Rome, 1996.)   [177] Commission, no. 135.

[178] No less than five proposals were discussed.

constitutes the systematic limit, so to speak, of the application of the law of the trust. It does not concern the notion of trust, but the *effects* which a specific trust produces.[179] Article 15 contains a partial list of areas:

(a) The protection of minors and incapable parties;
(b) The personal and proprietary effects of marriage;
(c) Wills and succession rights;
(d) The transfer of property and security interests in property;[180]
(e) The protection of creditors[181] in matters of insolvency;[182]
(f) The protection in other respects of third parties acting in good faith.[183]

To read some proposals which were not accepted, article 15 was to have a much wider range, including the exclusion of 'trusts d'affaires',[184] real rights in general,[185] and company law.[186] Other proposals were in favour of preceding the list with a clause limiting its application to exceptional cases.[187]

Article 15 is an extremely wise rule. The creation of a trust cannot lead to the breach of rules which cannot be derogated from 'by voluntary act', and which are imposed by the law which is identified by the conflict rules of the forum. In this way, a careful limit is placed on the latitude which had been granted the settlor in his choice of the law of the trust; this law will, of course, regulate the trust and its 'by-laws', but not necessarily all of the *effects* of the trust. Article 15 regulates certain of these effects, and prevents them from reaching fruition. It makes recognition of trusts simpler, be-

---

[179] Report, nos. 136–8; see also Actes, p. 298 (United Kingdom).
[180] The addition of the term 'real' was proposed by France: Actes, p. 299. It should be noted that the Netherlands excluded both this paragraph and the following one from the law passed with the ratification of the Convention.
[181] The original text was much broader, because it referred generically to 'third parties': see Actes, p. 340.
[182] Among the numerous examples of attitudes taken by civilian delegates which were attributable solely to their lack of understanding of the English-model trust (not to speak of other types), I would mention that of the German delegate, who posed the question of the trustee who, acting in that capacity, carried out business activities and then wanted to limit his responsibility to the trust assets (Actes, p. 301; as we know, the responsibility of the trustee in English law is general, and not limited to the trust assets (from which he can recover what he had to pay): see the contributions by the United Kingdom delegate at pp. 301 and 302 and by the United States delegate at p. 302.
    The question of responsibility of the trustee within the framework of the shapeless trust is completely different, since in both the international trust model and in civilian trusts (as we saw in chapters 4 and 5) there is a tendency to limit the responsibility of the trustee to the trust assets alone.
[183] Inclusion of the requirement of good faith passed with 12 votes in favour and 13 abstentions (including Italy): Actes, p. 301.
[184] Actes, pp. 220 and 235 (Bank for International Settlements).
[185] Actes, pp. 206, 294 and 298 (Germany); cf. Commission, no. 149.
[186] Working document no. 44 (Germany); see the discussion and vote in Actes, pp. 301–2.
[187] Working document no. 42 (United States).

cause it prevents all kinds of abuse right from the outset: in other words, the trust may not be used to get around or avoid mandatory provisions.[188] The scholars of the Convention have frequently placed article 15, like article 13, among the rules which protect civil-law systems. This is not at all the case.[189] Article 15 cannot be seen as protecting interests which are known only by civil-law systems. That is not so even as regards the position of forced heirs, a notion wrongly held to be a peculiarity of civil law: in fact the absolute freedom to bequeath by will does not exist in many States of the United States,[190] and wherever it still exists, the tendency is to reduce it.[191] Article 15 escapes the contrast between civil and common law, and falls completely within the system of the Convention, because every legal

---

[188] For a balanced review of article 15 see M. B. Deli, in Gambaro, Giardina and Ponzanelli, *Convenzione* (see above, footnote 9), *sub* article 15.

[189] Dicey and Morris *On The Conflict of Laws* (12th edition), London, 1993, p. 1092, point out that a trust which breaches the rule against perpetuities would probably not be recognized by the English courts (under article 15 of the Convention).

[190] J. McKnight, 'Spanish Legitim in the United States. Its Survival and Decline', in 44 AJCL (1996) 75, draws an interesting picture of the interference (in Texas, Louisiana, New Mexico, Arizona, Florida and California) between principles of Spanish and French origin on the rights of heirs and the more widespread tendency in the United States in favour of testamentary freedom.

[191] See the extensive historical–comparative review by D. W. M. Waters, 'Invading the Succession on Behalf of the Family – Europe, and Common Law Canada and Québec', in *Mélanges Germain Brière*, Montreal, 1993, 71.

   English law recognized the institution of *legitime* of movable assets until the fourteenth century, and for three more centuries in some regions (such as Yorkshire) and in the customary law of London: see R. H. Helmholz, *Canon Law and the Law of England*, London and Roncesverte, 1987, ch. 13, which illustrates its canon law basis (on the different system of succession to movable and immovable property, which is still the law in Scotland, see Wilson and Duncan, ch. 31). When equity took the place of the ecclesiastical courts, in the absence of rules on an action to recall assets into the estate of the deceased, it declared fraudulent *negotia* which were prejudicial to the heirs: A. Duckworth, Forced Heirship and the Trust, in Glasson, B1, 38–9.

   The English law which protects the relatives is the Inheritance (Provision for Family and Dependants) Act 1975, amended by the Law Reform (Succession) Act 1995 principally in order to recognize the rights of the testator's live-in partner. It provides that the testator must set forth 'reasonable provisions for maintenance' (see A. Miranda, *Il testamento nel diritto inglese*, Padua, 1995, pp. 107–13, 444–6). English case law has not yet provided a complete interpretative framework for the rule, and will never be able to do so, since it is an open-ended rule (regarding testamentary dispositions in favour of offspring, see G. Miller, 'Provisions for Adult Children under the Inheritance (Provision for Family and Dependants) Act 1975', in [1995] Conv 22). Recently, the extreme position has been taken of making a legal distribution to the widow of almost the entire estate of the husband, without taking into consideration that she was ninety years old and that the will already granted her the use of the marital home, as well as making other dispositions in her favour: *Re Krubert* (1996) (for general considerations on the position of the widow, see *Moody v. Stevenson* (1992)).

system has an interest in not allowing a foreign law which is the applicable law of a trust to produce effects other than those which relate to the trust's typical effects.

Article 15 does not impose limits on the Convention as a whole or on recognition of trusts in general, but on the recognition or non-recognition of certain *effects* of *specific* trusts.

f Limits of the Convention (articles 16, 18 and 19)

Article 16 deals with laws of immediate application. These have no connection with the provisions (identified by criteria of conflicts of the forum) which cannot be derogated from, referred to by article 15. The laws of immediate application are similar to the *lois de police* of the Convention of Rome.[192] Hence the rejection of the position taken by those who would have wished to include both types of provision in a single article.[193]

The first draft of article 16 was extremely complex.[194] It was somewhat simplified during the course of the debate. There had been a proposal that, in exceptional cases, laws could be applied of a State other than that of the forum which had to be applied[195] according to the terms of the trust. (Although this was removed during discussions, it re-appeared in the final text.[196]) Article 16 was, in fact, subject to further discussion after it had been formally approved, the aim being to re-introduce this limitation,[197] which is, furthermore, subject to reservation by a State at the time of ratification of the Convention (article 16.3).

Article 18 concerns restrictions dictated by public policy. This conforms with Hague Convention practice,[198] and raises no particular problems.[199]

---

[192] Actes, pp. 294 and 333 (the Reporter); p. 295 (Greece); p. 297 (the President); p. 334 (France). Cf. Report, no. 149.

[193] Law of 31 May 1995, no. 218, article 17: 'Norme di applicazione necessaria. E fatta salva la prevalenza sulle disposizioni che seguono delle norme italiana che, in considerazione del loro oggetto e del loro scopo, debbono essere applicate nonostante il richiamo alla legge straniera.'   [194] It corresponds to article 20 of the *avant-projet*.   [195] Actes, p. 296.

[196] Proposed by the United States, Finland, France and Switzerland (working document no. 59).   [197] Actes, pp. 333–5.

[198] Cf. M. E. Corrao in Gambaro, Giardina and Ponzanelli, *Convenzione* (see above, footnote 9), *sub* article 18, at p. 1308.

An identical formulation is found in article 10 of the Hague Convention on the Recognition of Divorces and Legal Separations, on which see Cass. 18 gennaio 1991 no. 490, in [1991] 1 Nuova giur. civ. commentata 464 (with note by G. Campeis and A. de Pauli): a foreign judgment may not be entered, pursuant to article 10, 'solo quando sia lesiva dei principi fondamentali ed irrinunciabili dell'ordinamento interno'; to give the right significance to this statement it should be considered that the decision cited above held that a foreign divorce judgment could be entered by mutual consent between an Italian and a foreign person.   [199] See the brief discussion in Actes, p. 293.

Article 19 sanctions the obvious exclusion of fiscal matters from the Convention.

g Conclusion: articles 14 and 15.2, and article 13 as a closing provision

Article 14, defined as a provision *in favorem trustis*,[200] was accepted without a word of debate: recognition of a trust may also occur as a result of mechanisms which are more favourable to recognition than those of the Convention.

There was only a short debate on article 15.2. Article 15, as we have just seen, subordinates the effects of every trust to those provisions of the law identified by the conflict rules of the forum which cannot be derogated from. Article 15 does not necessarily refer to a trust as a whole; it may, of course, happen that the effects which contrast with the mandatory provisions are so vital to a trust that failure to recognize them means failing to recognize the trust itself. Article 15.2 therefore provides that the court must seek to give effect to the purpose of the trust by other means. This provision comes from a German proposal[201] and was considered to be equivalent to an appeal to the 'bonne volonté' of a judge.[202] It received wide approval.[203]

We can now conclude with article 13, which I consider to be the closing provision of the system of the Convention.

A court which has the powers set forth in article 13 must seek the criteria which will guide it in the exercise of its discretion not to recognize certain trusts *within the Convention*. It will note that the Convention ignores the notion of 'foreign' trusts, that one of its unfailing principles is the freedom of choice of the law of the trust, that the trust with which it deals is the shapeless trust and not the English-model trust, that nowhere does it impose criteria based on the citizenship, residence or domicile of the settlor or the beneficiaries, that its aim is to facilitate recognition of trusts, and, above all, that it harmonizes the effects of each specific trust with the national law, thanks to the basic provision in article 15. Finally, the court will note that every possible objection to trusts with close links to legal systems which do not recognize them as a generally applicable legal structure was raised during the course of the works, but that no proposal to refuse recognition or to limit the freedom of choice of applicable law of the trust was accepted. There remained the *option* not to recognize a trust

---

[200] Actes, p. 332 (Reporter).   [201] Working document no. 44.   [202] Report, no. 147.
[203] It was approved with 21 votes in favour (including that of Italy), 2 against, and 2 abstentions.

falling within the scope of article 13, which logically leads one to suppose that even in these cases recognition should take place *as a rule*.

The analysis I have conducted in this chapter therefore leads to a consideration of article 13 as the one which provides the ultimate remedy in cases where, notwithstanding articles 18, 16 and 15, the methods or the purposes of the trust are judged by a court to be repugnant in a certain legal system (which is not necessarily that of the forum) which does not recognize that particular type of trust, but in which the trust has its main *effects*: article 13 avoids the risk that a trust might succeed in producing repugnant effects in spite of all the defensive measures of the Convention.[204]

[204] For example, tax evasion or unlawful tax avoidance.

7 Trusts in Italy

1. The civilian approach to trusts

a Introduction

The widespread interest in trusts which developed in Italy (as elsewhere in continental Europe) in the nineteen eighties was not born out of a sense of curiosity about comparative issues or a passing fad. It was the result of the prestige which the institution acquired in the eyes of civilian jurists when they discovered that they did not have the means to control economic phenomena which were developing within gaps in the law. The knowledge which they then acquired, however, was only as deep as the contingent issues which had produced it, and was limited to practical applications which were not backed up by a systematic understanding of foreign law, and which collided with the general inertia of the Italian legal system.

After an initial period notable for the frequently superficial nature of writing on the subject, the ratification of the Hague Convention is at last promoting in-depth analysis. As a result, the absence of 'competitive substitutes' for the trust has now been recognized[1] (a conclusion which had been arrived at outside Italy over half a century earlier[2]), and comparative lawyers have proposed that the 'dogmatic narrow-mindedness' provoked by 'the fossilization of the reference categories' be abandoned, and have urged that scholars not be dazzled by '*idola*', which is the fruit of 'legal provinciality'.[3]

There is certainly a favourable legal environment for the acceptance of

[1] Gambaro, *Proprietà*, pp. 642–7.
[2] Réné Savatier had written of civilian 'inferiority' in 1937.
[3] The first two expressions are Gambaro's, from *Proprietà*, p. 642; the second two are mine (*Introduzione ai trusts*, Milan, 1994, p. 159).

proposals of this kind, and I intend that the considerations which I shall proposes in this chapter should represent an early contribution.

It should be pointed out immediately, I believe, that both the traditional, dogmatic civilian approach and the more modern, functional approach are completely unsuitable, the former because it translates its concepts into a foreign system, and the latter because it underestimates the systematic and structural significance. It may be that on occasion the functional approach might be relegated to second place, or even ignored, but not when it comes time to face a reality which, as is the case with trusts, is distinguished by two elements which might tend to cancel each other out in another context, but which here converge and sustain each other: a high level of underlying technicality and the existence of principles of conscience. Each of these elements presents significant problems of comprehension and 'translation', and the line of least resistance (and the most widely followed route) is undoubtedly that of identifying fictitious heights (such as the scission between ownership and management, or between title and enjoyment), or of attempting to arrive at false *reductiones in unum* (such as the trilateral design of the trust), or, finally, of achieving rapid recognition by bringing into play some of the most significant categories in the history of European law (such as the *fideicommissum* and the right of ownership).

The specificity of the trust lies in the segregation of the right of the trustee, but it is the child of entrusting, and entrusting is the result of *fiducia*, which developed as fiduciary ownership. Each of these three passages contains elements of great importance to the jurist, and I shall attempt to define them briefly in this chapter. The definitions presuppose that the reader has understood the conclusions I have reached in the preceding chapters, and I shall presume that he has (although he may not agree with them).

b *Fiducia, fideicommissum* and trust

Fiducia exists where a party has a moral certainty that his wishes will be carried out; the fiduciary *negotium* lacks the explanations, precautions and attention to detail which a contracting party (or a testator) would not normally omit.

From this moral certainty springs the lack of a clear determination of the programme which has been entrusted to the fiduciary; not of the result (here the fiduciary himself is often the first to seek clarification), but the means by which it will be attained. The entrusting of a right to a fiduciary or the direct acquisition by the fiduciary is what leads him to select the methods he will use to attain the result. Accordingly, the will expressed by the entrusting party prevails over any legal requirements, mandatory or not, and the social value which justifies the *negotium*, the *fiducia*, comes to the fore.

As I see it, these are the three pillars which make up the foundation of the structure of the *fiducia*. It may take different forms, depending on whether one pillar has to bear more weight than the others, depending on actual implementation and on differing social and economic circumstances.

From the first pillar (the moral certainty of performance) we have the discretion of the fiduciary. This is not the power to abuse, to which the parties do not even give a thought, but the absence of those detailed precepts which define what is meant by abuse solely by dint of having been expressed, and thanks to these expressions would be placed in a different class, namely that of suspicion and the search for ways of avoiding them.

The heavy responsibility which the fiduciary bears is a product of the second pillar (the lack of a programme). The fiduciary only has vague indications to follow, and (if he cannot seek assistance from the courts) he accepts the burden of following his conscience to resolve every problem he encounters while realizing the purpose of the *fiducia*, especially those unforeseen questions which the entrusting party, either by necessity or because of the way the relationship has been structured, has not answered.

The third pillar (priority over legal requirements) leads to the fact that the fiduciary will never make a claim against the entrusting party or the beneficiaries that a legal requirement is missing – mandatory or not – which frees him from the obligations he has assumed: not a purpose *contra legem* where he has assumed rights which the beneficiary could not own personally, not lack of form, and not even the period of limitation.[4]

Into this category fall both bilateral *fiduciae* and those where a person claims to be the fiduciary of others for rights which are his. The act of entrusting rights to himself or the reliance he created by his conduct, bring into effect the same relationship as would have developed if these rights had been entrusted to him by a third party who had declared the trust.[5]

---

[4] The role that legal incapacity to acquire played in the Roman *fideicommissum* (cf. Johnston, *Roman Trusts*, pp. 21–9) is well known. It is interesting to note that South African and Italian law are in opposite corners today: the former is in favour of the validity of the fiduciary relationship (as in Andorra: L. puig Ferriol, 'El Prestanoms en el Dret Andorrà', in A. Iglesia Ferreirós (ed.), *Aces del I simposi juridic Principato d'Andorra/República de San Marino*, Andorra, 1994, p. 699), while the latter is in favour of nullity: see, respectively, Honoré, *Trusts*, pp.141–2 (with reference to racial discrimination); Trib. Verona, 23 February 1982, in [1983] 1 Giur. It. 2, 396.

[5] Cf. N. Lipari, *Il negozio fiduciario*, Milan, 1964, pp. 153 *et seq.*, 303 *et seq.*, and 390 *et seq.*, and

This picture includes liberal as well as interested entrustings, the latter in two different forms, depending on whether the interest is the entruster's (for example, entrusting to the fiduciary the duty to pay off the entruster's debts) or the fiduciary's (for example, with regard to a creditor or a third party with an interest that the *fiducia* comes into being). The interested entrustings fall more squarely than others into this category, because a conflict of interest is always round the corner, and the fiduciary's vigilance over his own conduct can touch great heights of moral drama.

One might object that the picture I have just sketched out is ethical rather than legal; the very terms I have used seem to come from outside the legal sphere, and sometimes seem to be against the written law. I would first respond that this picture does belong to a social view of the *fiducia*, and corresponds to the view which the experience of case law provides us. Secondly, I would point out that the most recent Italian case law has shown how the fiduciary *negotium* can be made autonomous, and how it may thus be exempted from requirements of form despite the fact that it relates to assets which require a writing in order to be transferred.[6] This marks the abandonment of a line of case law (recently confirmed[7]) which radically contradicted the line I have taken, and brings about a still unfathomable qualitative leap forward which provides significant support for my position.

It seems to me, therefore, that Italian law is following in the footsteps of Roman law and English law to the extent that, although using different forms and techniques, and with different results, they dragged the *fiducia*, *this view of fiducia*, from the area of conscience and dropped it into the area of law.[8] The underlying issue which I shall deal with in this chapter is the challenge posed to the civilian jurist by the trust, which is, in the first place, to succeed in establishing commercial or business structures which better reflect today's reality (this is an extremely important task, and I shall return to it on a number of occasions), but also to take in hand the values which modern society is discovering once more, and to give effect to them by using the technical tools which the trust offers us and which in the Italian legal system are validated by those *principia* which were created in Roman and English law, one of which is within our reach today.[9]

---

recently 'Fiducia statica e trusts', in *Atti Milano*, ch. 7, §1

[6] Cass. 21 November 1988, no. 6263, in [1991] 1 Foro it. 2495; 28 September 1994, no. 7899, in [1995] 1 Foro it. 1527.

[7] Cass. 16 October 1988 no. 5663, in [1989] 1 Foro it. 101.

[8] Cf. Johnston, *Roman Trusts*, pp. 21–41 and G. Broggini, 'Il trust nel diritto internazionale privato italiano', in *Atti Milano*, ch. 2, §1.

[9] I agree with the words of Johnston, *Roman Trusts*, p. 288, with which he concludes a solid,

Notwithstanding the evident fundamental difference, which consists of the enjoyment of assets for the fiduciary's own use in the first case, and for the use of others in the second, a nexus has often been found between the Roman *fideicommissum* and the trust. If the basis for this belief is sought in the fideicommissary substitution, it is a weak one; the fiduciary vein of the Roman *fideicommissum* was formally extinguished when it was made the equivalent of the legacy in the time of Justinian, and by the abolition of the '*tenebrosissimus error*',[10] which allowed the beneficiary the *in rem missio*,[11] and deprived the beneficiary of the specific form of protection which distinguished him from the legatee.

European common law asserted itself in the centuries immediately following the dissolution of the Roman Empire in the West, and found in the vulgar Roman law (which was practically speaking the Roman law in force[12]), adapted by the Church, the legal structures within which to place social relationships and predominant values. The *fiducia* and entrusting operated in this context, the same which in Lombard law obliged a donor *post obitum* who had remained in possession of the property but did not have sufficient means to maintain it to call upon the donee and tell him: 'ecce vedis, quia necessitate compulsus, res istas vado dare; si tibi vedetur, subveni mihi et istas res conservo in tuam proprietatem'.[13] In another sense, the mingling of *fiducia cum creditore* and *pignus*, with the resulting right of the creditor to sell the property and keep the proceeds, illustrates a junction of great comparative value: on the one hand, the imperial bureaucratic solution, which prohibited the covenant

---

original, well-constructed, and stimulating discussion: 'The trust [a. refers to the fideicommissum] had immense internal strength, granted to it by its procedural and interpretative principles. The barest requirements had to be met to validate a trust: only a formless expression of intention was needed; and this was paralleled by a remarkable procedural flexibility . . . its importance lay in its freedom, the potential it offered the jurists to expand and develop an entire system from a few modest principles.'

[10] C. 6.43.3.2 (531).

[11] C. 6.43.3.1 (529); see G. Impallomeni, 'L'efficacia del fedecommesso pecuniario nei confronti di terzi. La "in rem missio"', in 70 BIDR (1967) 1.

For classical law, see, for example, Pauli sent., 4.1.15: 'Rem fideicommissam si heres vendiderit eamque sciens compararit, nihilo minus in possessionem eius fideicommissarius mitti iure desiderat.' Cf. Johnston, *Roman Trusts*, pp. 256–83.

[12] See my *The Origins of the European Legal Order*, Cambridge, 2000 (*Alle radici del mondo giuridico europeo*, Rome, 1994), ch. 2; E. Cortese, *Il diritto nella storia medievale*, I, Rome, 1995, pp. 96–8; A. Padoa-Schioppa, *Il diritto nella storia d'Europa*, I, Padua, 1995, pp. 42–9.

[13] Roth., 173. Modern contractual practice does not ignore cases where a gratuitous disposition, or which is in any event disproportionate to the consideration received, is effective at the date of death of the donor on the condition that the donor has not in the meantime found himself in a situation of need: see Cass. 11 November no. 6083, in [1989] 1 Foro it. 1163 (with a note by E. Calò), and in [1989] Riv. not. 647.

of forfeiture[14] and which in all likelihood was never heeded by the practitioners,[15] and on the other the equitable solution, which tempers the severity of the covenant,[16] and gives rise to the modern mortgage.[17] If, instead of looking at the law of Justinian, which was of very little relevance for high medieval civilization, one studies that complex and inadequately researched phenomenon represented by the European common law of the high middle ages (Anglo-Saxon law was a part of it), one sees that the structure of the *fiducia* is not found within the fideicomissary substitution, and so in the law of succession, but in the much wider field of the *fideicommissum inter vivos*[18] and the testamentary *fiducia* in the strict sense of the term.[19]

The limited scope of this book does not allow historical detail which might interfere with my treatment of the subject at hand, but it is necessary to suggest the sense of continuity, otherwise reference to the *principia* as the foundation of the civilian response to the challenge represented by trusts would be mere rhetoric.[20]

While in England the trust was developing in equity, other parts of Europe were seeing the development of institutions characterized by recognition of the effects of an entrusting with a contractual basis. The *propiedad*

[14] C. 8, 34(35), 3 (and C. Theod. 3.2.1): Constantine, 326.

[15] The prohibition of the *covenant of forfeiture* cannot work fairly without a court system which protects the legitimate interests of the creditor punctually and correctly. Such a system did not exist in the last century of the Roman Empire, and does not exist in Italy today.

[16] Constantine wrote of *asperitas* in C. 8, 34(35), 3, pr.   [17] See above, chapter 3, §2.g.

[18] For certain Roman law sources concerning the *fideicommissum inter vivos* or fiduciary institutions of heirs, to execute with immediate effect or after a brief period, see D. 26.1.48, D. 26.1.92, and D. 28.2.18. In the first of these, it was explained that a fiduciary could not even receive the yield of the asset which had been transferred to him. South African literature holds that these sources refer to the *fideicommissum purum*: see Honoré, *Trusts*, pp. 46–7; B. Beinart, 'Trusts in Roman and Roman–Dutch Law', in W. A. Wilson (ed.), *Trusts and Trust-like Devices*, London, 1981, 167, at pp. 177–9. The *fideicommissum inter vivos* also exists in Jersey law: see Matthews and Sowden, §§1.17–1.19 (the appendix contains the Loi sur les tenures en fidéicommis of 1862).

On the *fideicommissum* in Roman law, see P. Voci, '*Fedecommesso* (diritto romano)', in *Enc. Dir.*, XVII, Milan, 1968, 103; a simple and lively analysis in A. D. Manfredini, *La volontà oltre la morte*, Turin, 1991, pp. 99–109. For a complete overview of the institution, see A. Palazzo, 'Attribuzioni patrimoniali tra vivi e assetti successori per la trasmissione della ricchezza familiare', in [1993] Vita not. 1228ff., at 1229–44, later in *La trasmissione familiare della ricchezza. Limiti e prospettive di riforma del sistema successorio*, Padua, 1995, 17.

[19] See the clause of a form of will: 'commissari mei volo esse Perum et Iohannem patruos mei, quorum fidei committo vendendi ac disponendi suo arbitrio quecumque voluerint de meis bonis' (published in A. Iglesia Ferreirós (ed.), *Aces del I simposi juridic Principato d'Andorra / República de San Marino*, Andorra, I, 1994, p. 549.

[20] In particular with regard to *amplificatio*: '"Amplificatio" est gravior quaedam affirmatio quae motu animorum conciliat in dicendo fidem': G. Vico, *Institutiones oratoriae*, 31 G. Crifò (ed.), Naples, 1989.

fiduciaria of the new Argentinean legislation[21] is the fulfillment of a long civilian tradition which had been seen in South America, among other examples, by the Chilean civil code of 1857[22] and in South Africa by Roman–Dutch law.[23] The entruster transfers an asset to the fiduciary for a predetermined period or under certain conditions.[24] The legal system recognizes the segregation which results from the transfer, and the fiduciary connotations of the position of the temporary owner.[25] The opportunity which the fiduciary enjoys to transfer or encumber the property is the recognition of his fiduciary position,[26] and stands in contrast to the different line of development, which limits the phenomenon to the area of succession, strips the original fiduciary element from the heir, and prohibits him from transferring the property.

In the *propiedad fiduciaria*, the fiduciary does not normally have an interest in the existence of the trust, and the distinction is made between the beneficiary of the proceeds and the residual beneficiary, who is the final recipient of the property on the termination of the *fideicomiso*. In this way the elements of ownership are exhausted without leaving any for the fiduciary. However, the fiduciary may have an interest, alone or together with the entruster: in this way, we see again the three-way division, which I illustrated at the beginning of this section, among liberal entrusting, entrusting with an interest of the entruster, and entrusting with an interest of the trustee or a third party.

The topic of the relationship between trusts and contracts in favour of third parties must be examined here. In South Africa (and to some extent in

---

[21] I refer to the law of 1995, which I commented on in chapter 5.

[22] Of which article 748 is significant: if the fiduciary comes to be lacking while the condition is in effect 'gozará fiduciariamente de la propiedad el mismo constituyente, si viviere, o sus herederos'; article 807 of the Colombian civil code contains the same provision.

[23] B. Beinart, 'Trusts in Roman and Roman–Dutch Law' (see above, footnote 18), at 180–8; see also R. W. Lee, *An Introduction to Roman-Dutch Law* (5th edition), Oxford, 1953, p. 375.

[24] See also the Brazilian Civil Code, article 1733: the testamentary *fideicommissum* may be in favour of a 'gravado ou fiduciario' not only for the life of the latter, but also until the end of a term or the fulfillment of a condition: we are, therefore, outside the area of the classic fideicommissary practices.

[25] The Chilean civil code (in article 762) identifies the purchase title of the *fideicommissary* (or final beneficiary) in the *fieicomiso*, not in the transfer which the fiduciary makes to him. In the meantime, the *fideicommissary* 'no tiene derecho ninguno sobre el fideicomiso, sino la simple expectativa de adquirirlo' (article 761). This is the classic doctrine of common law.

[26] For example, article 757 of the Chilean civil code provides that the fiduciary, when he imposes burdens on the property, must conduct himself like a tutor or guardian; cf. article 816 of the Colombian civil code; see also article 758 of the Chilean civil code: the fiduciary may modify the assets transferred to him 'pero conservando su integridad y valor'; cf. article 817 of the Colombian civil code.

Scotland), the trust is classified as a *stipulatio alteri*; this occurred, however, in the context of Roman–Dutch law, which, for the reasons we shall now see, does not lend itself to being used as a key to the interpretation of Italian law.[27]

The main analogy between the effects of the trust and those of the contract in favour of third parties seems to be found in the acquisition of the right by the third party. This analogy is not decisive – it may be found in other institutions, for example, the *fideicommissum* – but it is limited to certain types of trusts, since in others (as is the case with discretionary trusts) the beneficiary obtains a benefit only as a result of an act of will on the part of the trustee. It is, furthermore, inapplicable to trusts for purposes, which in South Africa have been compared with the *donatio sub modo*. In any event, the analogy may immediately be contrasted with a fundamental element of the trust structure (as we pointed out when we looked at South Africa[28]), which does not require acceptance by the beneficiary, and, where there has been acceptance, does not attach any importance to it. Finally, the granting of rights to beneficiaries of a trust may be completely lacking, because a trust may lack beneficiaries,[29] and also because, as we have just recalled, the trust may be discretionary in nature even though beneficiaries have been nominated. Where, on the other hand, the granting takes place, it is unilateral in nature, and the beneficiary only has the right to refuse it, if he is so disposed. There is a second analogy between the position of the *stipulating party* and that of the settlor; neither of the two – at least after the third party has been irrevocably identified – has rights in respect of promisor and trustee respectively.[30]

There is, however, a systematic reason why trusts and contracts in favour of third parties cannot be compared. The prevailing opinion in Italy, as is well known, is that the contract in favour of third parties is a *covenant within a contract*, and not a typical contractual structure into which any type of contents may be fitted;[31] the typical elements may be found in the attributive effects of the covenant, which consist of re-directing a contractual

---

[27] In France and Germany, the situation developed completely differently: see A. Guarneri, 'Costituzione di servitù e stipulazione a favore di terzo', in [1980] 2 Riv. dir. comm. 339.

[28] See above, chapter 5, §3.b.

[29] There is, however, no distinction between the contract in favour of third parties and cases where the trust does not yet have beneficiaries either because they are to be identified later or because they do not yet exist: see, respectively, Cass. 6 July 1983 no. 4562, in [1983] 1 Giust. civ. 2589; Cass. 30 March 1982 no. 1990, in Mass.

[30] For Italian law, see U. Majello, *L'interesse dello stipulante nel contratto a favore di terzi*, Naples, 1962, pp. 173–86; M. Giorganni, *L'obbligazione*, Milan, 1968, pp. 64–5.

[31] U. Majello, *L'interesse dello stipulante* (see above, footnote 30), pp. 20–7. A review of this topic must begin with G. Pacchioni, *I contratti a favore di terzi*, Padua, 1933, pp. 181–90.

effect towards the third party.³² The covenant therefore accedes to a contract which already has its *causa* as between the parties.³³ A 'pure' contract in favour of third parties, where the promisor is only a conduit through which the stipulating party effects a grant in favour of a third party, does not belong in Italian law for two reasons. Firstly, the grant which would be seen as taking place between the stipulating party and the third party, whose existence would not by itself serve to afford a causal justification for the grant: the relationship between the stipulating party and the promisor would be a kind of agency. Secondly, unlike the covenant in favour of third parties, what the third party would receive would not be sustained by a bilaterality in the arrangement between the stipulating party and promisor.³⁴ Hence, the benefit would come to the third party from the stipulating party rather than from the promisor, causing the structure of the *negotium* to undergo a fundamental change.³⁵

It seems to me that these considerations introduce insuperable obstacles to the comparison of trusts with contracts in favour of third parties.³⁶

The situation is different in South African law, where the *fideicommissum purum*, of which we have also found traces in Roman law, is accepted. It is essentially an agency relationship, where the fiduciary acquires ownership of the asset which he must later transfer to the third party without enjoying any benefit from it in the meantime.

---

³² G. Gorla, 'Contratto a favore di terzi e nudo patto', in [1955] 1 Riv. dir. civ. 585; cf. C. A. Capo, *Il potere di revoca dello stipulante nel contratto a favore di terzi*, Rome, n.d., pp. 15–18.

³³ Even more so if one considers the contract in favour of third parties to be a contract with alternative obligations, as proposed by P. Caliceti, *Contratto e negozio nella stipulazione a favore di terzi*, Padua, 1994.

  Contra F. Girino, *Studi in tema di stipulazione a favore di terzi*, Milan, 1965, pp. 46–9.

³⁴ It appears to me that the case law has continued to require that the right granted to a third party should be one which would otherwise belong to the stipulating party pursuant to the contract between him and the promisor. See Cass. 1 August 1994, no. 7160, in [1995] 1 Foro it. 2204 (increase of share capital with shares put in the name of a third party); Cass. 4 October 1994, no. 8075, and Cass. 11 June 1983, no. 4012 in Mass.

³⁵ Thus introducing the topic of the cause of the grant to the third party in terms which are radically different from those apparent where there is a simple covenant: on the cause of the grant to third parties, see L. V. Moscarini, *I negozi a favore di terzi*, Milan, 1970, pp. 230–63, and, for the specific case of a grant apparently without consideration, F. Gazzoni, 'Babbo Natale e l'obbligo di dare', in [1991] 1 Giust. civ. 2896. The relationship between the stipulating party and the beneficiary is not insignificant in the executory phase of the relationship between beneficiary and promisor: see U. Majello, *L'interesse dello stipulante* (see above, footnote 30), pp. 208–18.

³⁶ It is on this basis that the case law rejects the idea that an agency undertaken in the interest of a party other than the principal creates any right of the third party towards the agent, 'unlike in the case of the contract in favour of third parties, which has a direct effect on the third party, thereby entitling him to demand performance by the promisor': Trib. Firenze, 9 June 1989, in [1994] 1 Giur. it. 2, 398.

These few brief references give rise to a problem of fundamental importance to all civil-law systems which, without mentioning the best-known examples, has been discussed in detail in Scotland and South Africa: 'I can think of no principle of our law according to which the individual can during his lifetime unilaterally sequester a portion of his estate and dedicate it to certain ends.'[37] Contrary to what is often said, I believe that it is not the principle of the unity of the patrimony which comes into play,[38] but if I am to justify this statement, I will now have to return to the notion of segregation.

c Separation, autonomy and segregation

Italian scholars, who have mainly followed German scholarship, and later, but to a more limited extent, the French, have yet to find a common ground regarding the notions of autonomous and separate patrimonies. What is more, they have been put off by statutory language which (with increased frequency in recent years) takes pleasure in inventing terms without a sufficient conceptual basis,[39] to the point where they belie a sense of impotence which forces the legislature, if you will forgive the expression, to wear both belt and braces.[40] Italian writing has been led astray by the term '*patrimonio*', full as it is of metajuridical shades of meaning and unsuited as it is for use with the adjective 'segregated'. While 'separate' and 'autonomous', on the other hand, are regularly placed together with *patrimonio*, the object of the segregation, as our study of trusts has shown, is often a single right or, more generally, a single entitlement.

The debate in the literature is useful for the comparative scholar, but it is

---

[37] Van der Heever JA in *Crookes v. Watson* (1956). For Scottish studies, see T. B. Smith, *Studies Critical and Comparative*, Edinburgh, 1962, 168; for South African studies, see B. Beinart, 'Trusts' (see above, footnote 18), pp. 180–2; Honoré, *Trusts*, pp. 49–50.

[38] Especially now that the historical origins of article 2740 of the Italian Civil Code in the preparatory works of the Napoleonic *code civil* have been explained as the syncretism between the Romanistic model and the *coutumier* model of the *nantissement*: A. Candian, 'Discussioni napoleoniche sulla responsabilità patrimoniale (alle origini dell'art. 2740 codice civile)', in M. Lupoi, L. Moccia and P. Prosperetti (eds.), *Scintillae Iuris – Studi in memoria di Gino Gorla*, Milan, 1994, III, p. 1085. See, on the other hand, Gambaro, *Proprietà*, p. 649, who holds that it is a 'fetish . . . which has already been greatly corroded by special legislation'.

[39] I am thinking, for example, of the 'distinct' patrimony as in the second paragraph of article 3 of the Law of 23 March 1983 no. 77 on investment funds.

[40] I am referring to D. lgsl. 21 April 1993 no. 14 on pension funds: article 4.2: 'Fondi pensione possono essere costituiti altresì nell'ambito del patrimonio di una singola società o di un singolo ente pubblico anche economico attraverso la formazione con apposita deliberazione di un *patrimonio di destinazione, separato ed autonomo*, nell'ambito del patrimonio della medesima società o ente.'

not binding on him unless it leads to a unanimity which he should then accept as correct.[41] Although we have observed a very wide phenomenology in the previous pages, and I have had the opportunity to illustrate what I mean by segregation, it will still be useful to return to the subject once more, and to compare segregation with autonomy and separation.

The first element of dissimilarity has been noted just above: separation and autonomy generally refer to a complex of entitlements, both active and passive, while segregation may well only refer to a single entitlement of any kind, even a mere *de facto* expectation or (in common law) equitable interest. Finally, if one looks first at that group of elements within which I suggested that we identify the 'heart' of the trust (chapter 2), one will see that segregation may arise out of the rules of equity; discussions on the notion of segregation, therefore, should not be limited to expressly created trusts (and still less to trusts with final beneficiaries).

From a comparative point of view, the notion of 'separate patrimony' would seem to me to refer to a phenomenon which is distinct from segregation. A separate patrimony is made up of entitlements which *belong to a person* but which are nonetheless subject to special rules when it comes to that person's debts, his death, his matrimonial property, and so on.[42] The special rules which follow separation are those which identify the creditors of the separate patrimony; as far as the separate patrimony is concerned, they will prevail over that person's general creditors because they alone may satisfy their claims directly against the separate patrimony, while the general creditors, the spouse and the heirs will look to the right which that person has nonetheless retained in his patrimony, namely the ownership of the separate patrimony. There is, therefore, a displacement, the effect of which may also be to suck out the substance of what remained in that person's general patrimony (i.e., the ownership of the separate patrimony), or else to impose a waiting period to the general creditors until conditions which would lead to the dissolution of the separation may occur.[43] And, of course, the separate patrimony may in the meantime be

---

[41] For an up-to-date bibliography, see A. Zoppini, *Le fondazioni – dalla tipicità alle tipologie*, Naples, 1995, pp. 47–52; G. Ferri Jr, 'Patrimonio e gestione. Spunti per una ricostruzione sistematica dei fondi comuni di investimento', in [1992] 1 Riv. dir. comm. 25, at 25–41.

[42] The distinctive element of these rules with respect to the ordinary rules is simply that the act of transfer, although it has not removed an entitlement from the patrimony, has nonetheless modified the direction or the priorities of the position of third-party creditors; cf., although using different terminology, L. Bigliazzi Geri, under 'Patrimonio autonomo', in *Enc. Dir.*, XXXII, Milan, 1982, s. 6, and the general theory of A. Pino, *Il patrimonio separato*, Padua, 1950.

[43] For conditional testamentary institutions , see Cass. 28 January 1983 no. 808, in Mass.

reduced to zero in order to satisfy the debts which are attributable to it.[44]

The separation does not, therefore, bring about a failing of the *belonging* (the belonging, that is, of what was transferred to the separate patrimony), but places it in an intermediate situation, thanks to which the events relating to the person, who remains the ultimate owner of the separate patrimony, do not affect it generally. Those events may, however, affect the ownership connection between the person and the separate patrimony, possibly with a right under the law to attach it, but without being able to force their way to the assets which make up the separate patrimony. One consequence of the view I am setting forth here is that, besides this indirect route, a channel of one-way communication from the separate to the ordinary patrimony of the person still exists. Through this, the enrichment of the separate patrimony may be passed to the general patrimony, since there is no requirement that it should be confined there; any enrichment belongs to the person who is the owner of both patrimonies, who may dispose of it as he thinks fit.[45]

To remain in the comparative field, I reserve the term 'autonomous patrimony' for cases where no such channel of communication exists in either direction. The management element then comes to the fore, while the ownership of the patrimony is dormant, or even unclear, and is not in any event connected with the person entitled to manage the patrimony (in certain cases one may speak of a patrimony without an owner or temporarily without an owner). This is the case, for example, with vacant succession (*eredità giacente*) and with an estate in bankruptcy (*patrimonio fallimentare*), but also with committees of tenants who are assignees of public or low-cost housing before the transfer of ownership of the housing becomes effective,[46] with the funds of associations and committees,[47] and with funds with

---

[44] As, for example, with assets subject to seizure: Cass. 4 July 1991 no. 7534, in Mass.; Cass. 19 March 1984 no. 1877, in Mass.; assets assigned to creditors: Trib. Reggio Emilia 20 February 1981, in [1982] Riv. dott. comm. 618; activities relating to mathematical reserves of management of life insurance, which '*sono riservate in modo esclusivo all'adempimento delle obbligazioni assunte con i contratti di assicurazione sulla vita*': article 12.20 of D.L. 18 January 1993 no. 8 (included in Law 19 March 1993 no. 68), which supplies the authentic interpretation of L. 22 October 1986 no. 742, article 802; social security funds collected pursuant to article 2117 of the civil code with deposits made by the business alone, in cases where the purpose fails and funds remain unused.

[45] For critical comments on my position, see S. Tondo, 'Ambientazione del trust nel nostro ordinamento e controllo notarile sul trustee', in *Atti Milano*, ch. 15, §2.2.

[46] Cass. 23 September 1991 no. 9896, in *Arch. locazioni* (1992), 300.

[47] The first modern and complete study of this subject may be found in R. Rascio, *Destinazioni dei beni senza personalità giuridica*, Naples, 1971.

For recent case law, see Cass. 12 March 1992, no. 3011, in Mass. and Trib. Milan 5 March 1987, in [1987] Società 819 (*società in nome collettivo*); Trib. Milan 26 September 1988, in

a public purpose.[48] The manager's problems never affect the autonomous patrimony, and vice-versa, because a common ownership is lacking.[49]

With reference to the trust, segregation must be studied from two different perspectives: that of the settlor and that of the trustee. As far as the settlor is concerned, the trust is created out of an act of disposition and the entrusting which it necessarily entails. The settlor has no action against a trustee who is in breach, and what the settlor places in trust is lost to him forever. Alternatively, the trust is born out of the application of a rule of equity, or out of the law (statutory trusts[50]) without an act of disposition.

As far as the separate patrimony is concerned, the distinction from the trust does not lie in the fact that the latter derives from an act of transfer in favour of a trustee, because there is no transfer in a trust created by a person who then appoints himself as trustee, let alone in constructive and implied trusts, as I have pointed out in previous chapters. The real distinction lies in the lack of any channel of communication between what one might consider to be a separate patrimony and its owner. The peculiarity of the trust where settlor and trustee are one and the same, or where there is no settlor (so that in either instance no disposition in favour of the trustee exists), lies in the closure of what would otherwise be a channel between the general patrimony and the subject matter of the trust, for both belong to the same person. On the contrary, the general creditors of the trustee do not find in his patrimony that intermediate situation of belonging following what I termed above 'displacement' which would allow them to look at the ownership of the separate patrimony as an asset pertaining to the general patrimony of their debtor; nor is there any channel by which any enrichment of the separate patrimony to the general one may possibly be directed. There is a total and definitive separation between the two areas.[51]

With respect to the autonomous patrimony, the common element is

[1991] 2 Giur. comm. 824 (assets of the *associazione di base* with respect to those of the *associazione di vertice*); App. Milan 15 May 1981, in [1981] 1 Foro pad. 251 (unrecognized associations).

[48] For case law, see Cass. 29 October 1983 no. 6462, in Mass.; 22 December 1981 no. 6753, in Mass. (city pension fund of Trieste, which was independent from the City Council); Cass. 6 July 1990 no. 7131, in [1991] 1 Giust. civ. 344 (fund for road accident victims). Funds which a council allocates to a local health authority, however, have been held to constitute a separate patrimony (Trib. Rome, 27 June 1988, in [1989] Rass. dir. farmaceutico 756) (this is erroneous, I believe).

[49] Cf. V. Durante, Patrimonio (dir. civ.), in *Enc. giur. Treccani*, XXII, §2.2.

[50] See above, chapter 2 §1.c.

[51] The false functional analogy between separate patrimony and trust, with reference to a company with a single shareholder, has most recently been proposed by Gambaro, *Proprietà*, 649; for a different view which leads to similar results to those in my text, see A. Zoppini, *Le fondazioni* (see above, footnote 42), pp. 154–6.

provided by subrogation, the effects of which, as a result of the segregation, do not go beyond the legal sphere of the trust, and by the lack of relevance attached to the identity of the manager of the patrimony (trust assets, as we know, must be transferred from one trustee to another). The distinction between trusts and separate patrimonies lies in the fact that only in the former case is ownership found in the same hands. In this respect, one must not be distracted by so-called 'typical' classifications which, when compared with the wide typology of trusts, are mere trivialities. On the contrary, it must be emphasized that a trust may have any kind of entitlement as its subject matter, including those which are unconnected with the dynamism and transformability which are the indisputable characteristics of the autonomous patrimony.

The trustee, as we have seen above, exercises every right and power connected to the entitlement which is the subject matter of the trust in a responsible manner because it is *his*,[52] and he therefore has (according to the English model) personal and unlimited responsibility for every obligation he assumes. There is no subjective difference in ownership between the trustee and the patrimony (which is not a legal person). A further consequence of this is that in the trust the problem of juridical antagonism between the trustee and the function of the trust never arises; this is the case, for example, with directors of companies, which are legal persons.[53] If anything, there is the possibility that the trustee may be seen as the holder of an office, similar to the current situation in South Africa.[54]

These considerations introduce us to another specificity of segregation, seen from the genetic point of view: even an express trust, like constructive and resulting trusts, may be created without an act of disposition (either by the settlor or by the settlor/trustee) where the *negotium* of creation precedes the *negotium* of transfer and the trust is stamped on to the right at the same time as the trustee acquires it.[55] This is analogous to the theory relating to foundations: there is an empty vessel into which the contents are poured. The *negotium* of creation of the trust is different from the *negotium* of transfer or, generally, from that of the disposition of the right which is the subject matter of the trust. A trustee who must receive sums from a third

---

[52] This is why, unlike in the case of the manager of an autonomous patrimony, the trustee is never faced with the problem of authorization to carry out an act which affects the patrimony.

[53] The question of alterity may, on the other hand, present itself at the empirical level (conflict of interest).

[54] For the situation in Italy, see C. Licini, 'Una proposta per strutturare in termini monistici l'appartenenza nel rapporto di "fiducia anglosassone" trust', in [1996] 1 Riv. not. 125.

[55] Cf. see above, chapter 3 §1.a.

party for an established purpose segregates them within his own patrimony at the moment he receives them, on the basis of the instrument
which (previously) created the trust.[56] It is not necessary, therefore, for the
right which is the subject matter of the trust to leave the settlor's general
patrimony, and it may never have become a part of it.[57]

Finally, as for the *patrimonio di destinazione*, although it has become a part
of the legislative jargon,[58] it is not a separate legal category: at the most, it
might be considered to be an (unworkable) general concept which embraces the phenomena of separation, autonomy and segregation.

Segregation is not unknown in civilian systems, a current example being
the *fondo patrimoniale*. It was formerly present in *patrimoni familiari* and
dowries,[59] and in non-family matters in the area of purchases of movables
and credits by an undisclosed agent. Those purchases cannot be attacked by
his creditors (subject, in Italian law, to the agent providing ironclad evidence of the date on which he was appointed as agent). Above all, segregation should not be looked on with disfavour, or thought of as exceptional or
as of marginal significance.[60] On the contrary, the use of the concept of
segregation should be extended. At the same time, those formal requirements should be removed, which in Italian law render the proof that a
certain legal event took place on a given date most difficult. They attest to
the existence of a *principium* of legal mistrust in people, and yet they favour
those who are in bad faith and hide behind the lack of formal requirements. The legal disowning of the *fiducia* (the generic kind which, for
example, a principal has in his agent) connotes the aridity of a legal system,
and explains why, failing a written document between principal and agent
instructing the latter to purchase real property, the property is deemed to
be the agent's against the interests of the principal who provided him with
the means to effect the purchase.[61]

---

[56] Take the example of a person who buys a lottery ticket and makes his possible winnings
the subject of a trust. The subject matter of the act of transfer is not the *spes*, but its
possible conversion into winnings or, to be more precise, the winnings themselves which,
if they were to materialize, would belong to the trustee without ever having been the
property of the settlor, and without the settlor's having had more than a mere *spes* of
obtaining them.

[57] Thus we complete the list of the reasons why the view of the trust as a separate patrimony
(which was proposed, among others, by S. Tondo, Sul riconoscimento del trust nel nostro
ordinamento, in Fiducia, trust, mandato ed agency, Milan, 1991, pp. 117ff., at p. 133) does not
provide a complete picture of the legal structure of the trust.

[58] D. Lgsl. 21 April 1993 no. 124 (pension funds), article 4.2.

[59] The *patrimonio familiare* is a modern version of the dowry, and the *fondo patrimoniale* is a
modern version of the *patrimonio familiare*: cf. G. Gabrielli, Patrimonio familiare e fondo
patrimoniale, in Enc. Dir., XXXII, Milan, 1982, 293.

[60] Cf. R. Calvo, La proprietà del mandatario, Padua, 1996, ch. 4.

[61] From this point of view the decision of Trib. Roma 4 March 1986, in [1987] 1 Giur. it. 2, 374

Segregation is an instrument of action, and without it the analytical selection of interests works in contrast with the correct criteria of allocation.[62] If the basic character of modern legal systems, which govern the economy, is to acknowledge the right to make choices with respect to which persons invoke the right to take responsibility for their own actions,[63] the lack of a general mechanism of segregation limits the range of choices and leads to degeneration, simulation and hidden nominee structures.[64] The very extensive Italian literature on the subject of simulation has no parallel in common law;[65] taking an example from everyday life, to make what belongs to Dick appear to belong to Tom becomes a necessity (which negates the possibility of there being a choice) if the legal system offers no alternative. Family relationships suddenly deteriorate when the legal significance of written instruments is discovered and every 'fiduciary' understanding in place up until that moment becomes legally ineffective. This causes moral, social and legal traumas and breakups; the individuals involved have the sensation that they do not belong to *that* legal system, to which they are no longer ready to recognize any axiological validity.[66]

I have already said that segregation is the final result of the *fiducia*, through the entrusting; merely to treat it as one of many techniques, now that we have the chance to raise it to the level of a principle of general application would mean remaining on the fringes of the *orbe comunicante*.

Segregation does not always result from *fiducia*, but *fiducia* always leads to segregation once *fiducia* is legally recognized and sanctioned. This unilat-

---

is reprehensible: 'Il mandato, con o senza rappresentanza, avente ad oggetto l'acquisto di beni immobili deve risultare da forma scritta a pena di nullità con la conseguenza che, in difetto, il mandatario che acquista in nome proprio un immobile ne diventa proprietario, senza che colui che ha conferito l'incarico possa chiederne il ritrasferimento a proprio favore o, in luogo di ciò, ottenere il risarcimento dei danni, competendogli solo quanto prestato per l'esecuzione dell'incarico in base alle norme sull'indebito.'

Fortunately, more open case law also exists, such as Cass. 3 April 1991 no. 3468, in [1991] Corriere giur. 772, with a note by V. Mariconda: 'Nell'ipotesi di mandato ad acquistare immobili nullo per difetto di forma, l'acquisto effettuato dal mandatario, in nome e per conto proprio, concreta una totale inattuazione del contenuto dell'obligazione principale nascente dal contratto ex art. 1703 c.c., che dà luogo a responsabilità risarcitoria a carico del mandatario stesso.'

[62] Cf. G. Zaccaria, *Questioni di interpretazione*, Padua, 1996, pp. 12–17.
[63] N. Irti, 'Persona e mercato', in [1995] Riv. dir. civ. 289, at 295.
[64] Cf., for a different position, N. Lipari, *Il negozio fiduciario* (see above, footnote 5), pp. 317–26.
[65] This is also true for case law.
[66] On this last aspect, see E. Opocher, 'Valore (filosofia del diritto)', in *Enc. Dir.*, XLVI, Milan, 1993, 111; for a completely different, but no less stimulating, view, see G. Calabresi, *Ideals, Beliefs, Attitudes and the Law*, Milan, 1996 (Syracuse, NY, 1985).

eral connection, as I have pointed out above, permits recourse to segregation in order to arrive at the correct choice of the interests to be protected,
as witnessed by a recent decision of the Italian Constitutional Court, which,
in order to protect the interests of the wife to whom maintenance payments were owed, effectively segregated sums in the patrimony of a third
party who owed them to the husband. This was, in fact, the legal outcome
of the judge's order to pay the wife rather than the husband; this effect is
even more evident where the order refers to sums falling due periodically
in the future.[67]

Another fact-pattern concerns the mingling within the patrimony of an
agent of the sums which he holds for the principal and of purchases which
he makes on behalf of the principal without using the principal's name: in
my opinion, there is no justification for the rigid rule laid down in article
1707 of the civil code, which often gives rise to situations where the
principal is treated like any other creditor of an agent, even though the
sums collected and the purchases made are, as one would say in equity, 'his'
and not the agent's.[68] Evidently, the reason for this is that no mechanism
for segregation is available, and it is therefore impossible to select the
interest of the principal over the interests of the agent's general creditors.[69]

Two situations intertwine here: on one hand, the *fiducia*, which produces
segregation, and on the other, the segregation which functions in terms of
the pre-eminence of one interest over other competing interests. In English
law, there is always a trust here: the fact that the second of the two
situations just described is not connected with the *fiducia*, but with fiduciary relationships (agency) and that it concerns a conflict between the
beneficiary and third parties, rather than between beneficiary and trustee,
led us to conclude at the end of chapter 3 that the trust has very little
connection with the *fiducia* as it is commonly understood.

d Conclusions

Drawing conclusions from what has emerged so far, I propose the following
theory of expressly created trusts in civilian terms.

---

[67] Corte Cost. 6 July 1994 no. 278 in [1994] 1 Foro it. 2948. In order for the court order to have
    effect, it must be held that the creditors of the creditor-spouse may not attack the assets
    which are the subject of the order, and that where the sums are physically identifiable
    not even the creditors of the debtor-spouse to whom the order is directed may do so.
[68] The genesis of this rule was shown by P. G. Jaeger, *La separazione del patrimonio fiduciario nel
    fallimento*, Milan, 1968, pp. 338–58.
[69] There is also a role for another of the *idola fori*; see P. Schlesinger, 'L'eguale diritto dei
    creditori di essere soddisfatti sui beni del debitore', in [1995] Riv. dir. proc. 319.

The *negotium* of creation of a trust may be without consideration, gratuitous or interested, or for value.[70]

The cause of the *negotium* of creation is the programme to segregate one or more entitlements, or a group of entitlements taken as one (*trust assets*), which the settlor strips himself of, either by transferring them to a third party (the *trustee*), or by legally isolating them within his patrimony, so as to protect interests which the legal system deems worthy of protection (the *purpose of the trust*).

The *negotium* of creation is a unilateral act (which must be brought to the attention of the trustee, where the trustee and the settlor are not the same person), which the trustee may reject; this rejection does not cause the trust to fail where the *negotium* of creation occurs simultaneously with the *negotium* of transfer to the trustee.

The trust assets are transferred to the trustee, by the settlor or third parties, by means of instruments of transfer, *inter vivos* or on death, which may take place at the same time as, before or after the *negotium* of creation of the trust. These instruments of transfer have their own *causa*, which is the implementation of the *negotium* of creation[71] following their connection with the *negotium* of creation of a trust. Thanks to this connection, the *negotia* of transfer produce another result, in addition to the usual one: the entrusting of the subject matter of the transfer to the trustee to pursue the purpose of the trust and its consequent segregation from the remaining patrimony of the trustee.

The trust assets are transferred by one trustee to his successor by means of *negotia* which are justified (externally) by the *negotium* of creation.

Segregation means that the trust assets always have an owner, the trustee, but that the personal matters of the trustee have no consequences for the trust assets. Moreover, issues relating to the trust assets bring about a liability which concerns the trustee's general patrimony: both with respect to third parties, where he undertakes obligations without limiting his liability to the trust assets, and with regard to the beneficiaries, where he causes the segregation to fail.

The fulfillment of the purpose of the trust is entrusted to the trustee, who selects the methods and the timing, within the limits imposed on him by the *negotium* of creation. In making his choices and putting them into effect, the trustee takes into consideration the freedom offered him by the

---

[70] On the distinction between *gratuità* and *liberalita*, see G. B. Ferri, Negozio giuridico, in *Digesto*, Sez. priv. Civ., XII, Turin, 1995, §8.

[71] U. Morello agrees, I believe, in 'Fiducia e negozio fiduciario: dalla "riservatezza" alla "transparenza"', in *Atti Milano*, ch. 8, §5.

law and the lack of control over his performance which result from his position as full owner of the trust assets, as the means of carrying out his duties. The trustee does not profit from the trust assets or from the position he holds. Except as provided for in the *negotium* of creation, it is up to the trustee to determine on a case-by-case basis whether to present himself as a trustee. The legal system evaluates the trustee's conduct according to criteria of integrity, loyalty and good faith of a fiduciary who takes decisions on his own account in a disinterested and altruistic manner so as to achieve the purposes of the trust in the best possible manner.

The binding nature of the trust has an effect on third parties who, in breach of the *negotium* of creation or of legal rules, acquire trust assets without consideration, or for value with real or imputed knowledge of the existence of the trust. In these cases, the disposition executed by the trustee is, depending on the facts, voidable or revocable, and the third party who has disposed of the asset so that the trust can no longer recover it is responsible for damages suffered by the beneficiaries or the purpose of the trust, possibly jointly with the trustee.

Within the segregated patrimony, the trust assets may be transformed and converted, or may increase or decrease in value, without any modification to the duties of the trustee or the rights of the beneficiaries, where they exist.

The settlor never has the right to sue the trustee. The creditor of the trustee's services is the beneficiary, where there is one, and if there is not, it is the public or private person who has the right, according to the *negotium* of creation or the law, to demand that the trustee perform the obligations arising out of the entrusting. The trustee has an obligation towards the purpose of the trust: in principle, the beneficiaries cannot make him carry out his role in a manner suggested by them.

The remaining sections of the original Italian version of this book have not been translated: they deal with purely Italian aspects of trusts, and I decided that they would be of little interest to non-Italian readers. If I am mistaken, I apologise, and direct the reader's attention to the Italian version.

Index

acceptance, 97, 316, 321
accounting, 170, 172n.
accumulation trusts, 162
acquisitions, and equitable defect, 80, 81
act of disposition, 2, 14, 96, 103, 303
act of transfer *see* transfer to the trustee
actio pauliana, 117–19, 135, 181, 300
actions, 21, 59, 60, 64, 90, 98, 154, 181, 183
    consequences of, 69
    and constructive trusts, 91
    personal, 194, 195
    for restitution, 78, 92
active trusts, 157, 158
administration, 350, 361
administration period, 116, 117
administrative law, 19
advancement, presumption of, 53–5
agents, 24, 33n., 141, 157, 162n., 258, 294, 376, 382, 384
    see also fiduciary relationships
agreements void for defect in form, 43–4, 84
Anglo-Norman law, 21
Anguilla, 205, 206, 221n., 238, 256, 262
animal trusts, 123
anomalous trusts, 123–4, 180
Antigua and Barbuda, 206
'antitrust' laws, 123
'Anton Piller Orders', 72
appeals, 174n.–175n.
applicable law
    English trust model, 149–56
    Hague Convention, 330, 338, 344, 346–52
    international trust model, 222, 240–5
Argentina, 269, 270, 273–4, 287, 305, 312, 314, 316, 326n., 374
asset-protection trusts, 119, 135–6
assets, 40, 140
    beneficiary and, 189–93
    commingling of, 172

immovable, 153, 191n.
and third parties, 53–4
and tracing, 58–9
Attorney General, 129
auctor in rem suam, 168, 296
Australia, 6, 7, 8, 23n., 24n., 41n., 44n., 54n., 116n., 117n., 150, 152n., 154n., 176n., 202
    estoppel, 83n.
    inter vivos trusts, 153
    rights in family home, 47, 48n., 49n.
    unjust enrichment, 87, 88n.
autonomy, 349, 377–84
awe, 39, 40, 84

'back bond', 292, 294, 296
bad faith, 63, 249, 382
Bahamas, 172n., 206, 208, 349
bankruptcy, 20, 31, 33n., 35, 59, 60–1, 77, 99n., 117n., 118–19, 134, 173, 213, 354, 363, 379
banks, 24, 31, 32n., 56, 59n., 99, 139, 148, 172n., 173, 174n., 210, 216, 278, 285, 287, 291, 310, 356
Barbados, 7n., 37n., 53n., 84n., 207, 208, 238
bare trusts, 26n., 74, 147n., 156–62, 163, 176, 89, 191, 197, 263
Belize, 205, 207–8, 219, 226, 227, 228, 233, 234, 238, 247, 253, 258, 259, 262, 264
belonging, 378, 379, 380
beneficial rights, 144
beneficiaries, 84, 100, 107, 110, 113, 144, 167, 168, 170, 180, 183–93, 254, 271, 372, 374, 375, 384, 386
    bare trusts, 157
    civil-law systems, 272, 273, 285ff., 291, 298ff., 320–2
    constructive trusts, 50, 92, 94

beneficiaries (*cont.*)
  and co-ownership, 19
  and creation of a trust, 96–7, 98
  discretionary trusts, 131, 132, 133,
    189–90
  entrusting, 197–8
  and equitable ownership, 3, 189, 192–3
  equitable rights of, 77, 80, 82
  interest of, 192
  lack of, 161
  non-express trusts, 74, 75, 77
  protection of, 26–7, 199–200
  protective trusts, 133–4
  purpose trusts, 123, 124–5, 130
  and reasons for nullity, 121
  resulting trusts, 54
  revocable trusts, 103
  and rights *in rem*, 187, 188–9
  and tracing, 61, 64, 272
Bermuda, 208–9, 238, 243, 246, 247, 248,
    249, 257n., 261
bewind, 188, 297, 341, 355
blind trusts, 333n.
bonus paterfamilias, 226
breach of trust, 77, 78, 227, 230–1, 280, 284,
    323, 326, 386
  constructive trusts, 29–34, 84, 92–3
  and trustee, 175–8, 229–30, 232
bribery, 25–6, 70, 92
British Guyana, 41n.
British Virgin Islands, 208, 209, 210n., 228,
    238, 257, 265
Browne-Wilkinson, Lord, 84n., 93n.
Brussels Convention (1968), 343, 344
  Art.5(6), 155
  Art.16, 193, 194
business trusts, 122–3, 138–44, 217

Canada, 6, 7, 8, 16n., 32n., 33, 41n., 54,
    68n., 122, 150, 202
  charitable trusts, 127n., 128
  creation of the trust, 152n., 153
  fiduciary relationships, 24n.
  rights in family home, 47
  unjust enrichment, 87, 88n., 93n.
canon law, 28, 184–6, 293
capacity, 212
case law, 7, 8, 9, 11, 12, 13, 17, 84, 125, 172,
    173, 177, 204
  innovations in, 4, 28
Catalan law, 112
Cayman Islands, 7n., 32n., 34n., 35n., 168n.,
    205, 208, 209–10, 221, 263n., 265
  foreign laws, 246, 247n., 252
  migration of trusts, 241
  revocatory actions, 248–9, 252
  transfer to the trustee, 244, 245

wilful default, 231–2
certainty, lack of, 131n.
certificates of benefit, 281
cestui que, 2, 183n.
Ceylon, 183n., 192n.
Chancery law, 13, 21, 57, 64
charitable trusts, 2, 123, 124, 125, 126–30,
    160, 161, 166n., 178, 180, 192, 296, 334
  international trust model, 208, 212, 222,
    235, 252–3, 257
Charity Commissioners, 129
children, 108, 134; *see also* minors
Chile, 274n., 374
chose in action, 59n., 125, 190
civil-law systems, 1, 4, 11, 12, 35, 72, 76,
    136, 156, 165, 181, 186, 194, 201, 217,
    218, 220
  beneficiaries, 272, 273, 285, 286, 287,
    291, 298, 299, 300, 301, 320–2
  business trusts, 138, 140
  closed structure of, 326
  comparative data, 269–73, 301–26
  conceptual problems, 9
  conflict of laws, 151–2
  conflicts of interest, 313–15
  contracts, 95, 273, 277, 282, 286, 299,
    304, 311, 316, 317
  definition of a trust, 271–3, 282, 283, 292,
    298, 303
  and English model, 275, 276, 277, 279,
    280, 284, 287, 289, 292ff., 301ff., 311,
    316, 324
  entrusting, 196, 271, 293, 303, 310–13
  exportation of the trust, 301–3
  express trusts, 384–6
  fiduciaries, 198, 274, 275, 276, 279, 282,
    284–7, 288, 289, 291, 293, 294, 297,
    299–300, 303–8, 310, 312, 313–15, 317,
    323
  forced heirs, 322–3
  and foreign law, 8, 301
  form, 318
  and Hague Convention, 327–9, 332–3
  inter-vivos trusts, 278, 279, 299, 303, 311,
    316, 317
  judicial intervention, 317–18
  Latin America, 269, 270, 273–6, 284–7,
    290–2, 304ff.
  legislation, 7, 301–2
  purpose trusts, 318–20
  regulae, 315–25
  segregation, 308–10
  settlor, 271, 281, 283, 293, 294, 304, 305,
    310–13, 315ff.
  sources of a trust, 315–17
  tracing, 272, 273, 323–5
  transfer to the fiduciary, 303–8

trustee, 271, 272, 273ff., 298, 299, 300, 301, 302, 303, 305, 306, 311, 312, 315ff., 320, 323–5
  unjust enrichment, 88
  see also Italian trusts
class actions, 146
client funds, 20
closed structures, 326
cohabitation, 49, 55–6, 82
Colombia, 269, 270, 274–5, 306n., 309, 321, 324, 334n.
colonial laws, 8, 210n.
commerce, 24, 30, 99, 285
committees, 379
common law, 1, 5, 6, 12, 13, 36, 38, 67, 95, 136, 155, 173, 179, 184, 187, 270, 296, 326, 340
  business trusts, 143
  and civil law, 327, 329
  and equity, 4, 26–7, 42, 57, 58–9, 65–6, 71, 73, 96, 111, 137, 186
  'estate', 105, 107, 108
  European, 36, 126n., 201, 202, 216, 230n., 297, 372–4
  and fraud, 21
  and international trust model, 201, 202, 225
  ownership, 185ff., 191
  plurality in, 7
  problems in, 150, 151–2
  rules, 10–11
  and statute law, 66
  and theft, 80
  tracing, 58–60
  unjust enrichment, 88
companies, 23, 24, 25, 40, 126, 136, 138–44, 146, 147, 148, 149, 209, 210, 212n., 244, 255, 275, 288, 291, 298n., 363
  nominee, 217, 218
  see also business trusts; directors of companies; financial trusts; trust companies
comparative law, 1, 7, 8, 11, 12, 16, 35–6, 72, 92n., 150, 174, 267–73, 301–26, 340, 341
compensation, 34, 85, 167–8, 280
condition subsequent, 120–1, 134n.
conduit companies, 159, 161–2
'confidence', 4
confidentiality, 220, 222–3
conflict of laws, 149–52, 153, 154, 210, 330, 345–6
conflicts of interest, 227, 271, 296, 313–15
conscience, 4, 21, 28, 64, 70, 105, 110, 181, 184, 188, 203, 303, 369, 370, 371
  and equity, 65, 80, 81n., 85, 86, 193
consensualism, 95

consideration, 97, 330
  lack of, 79–80
constructive trusts, 8, 9, 16, 17, 18, 22–50, 67, 100, 113, 137n., 155, 166n., 178, 209, 214n., 216, 295, 300, 316, 325, 381
  agreements void for defect in form, 43–4, 84
  in American law, 89–90, 91
  automatic and discretionary, 49
  beneficiaries, 50, 92, 94
  breach of trust, 29–34, 84
  civil-law systems, 277, 280, 281
  dispositions of real property, 50
  distinct from express trusts, 74–7, 85
  donatio mortis causa, 36–7, 84, 121
  entrusting, 76, 198
  and equity, 77–86
  Hague Convention, 238, 341, 342, 343
  improper benefits, 22–6, 84
  influence over will of testator, 41, 84
  and international model, 232, 233–5
  lack of equitable fullness, 3
  lack of form, 84
  law of conversion, 69–70
  mutual wills, 41–3, 84
  notice, 26, 28–9, 30, 31
  oral, 45–6, 47
  'proprietary base' of, 93–4
  and proprietary estoppel, 83n.
  remedial, 90, 91, 92
  and resulting trusts, 55
  rights in the family home, 46–50, 55, 84
  and secret trusts, 111
  and segregation, 40, 77, 199
  seller of land not yet transferred, 34–6
  structure, 15, 74, 90, 121
  theory of, 77–86
  and tracing, 26, 32, 61, 63, 65
  transfer of property, 26–9, 45
  trustee de son tort, 34
  undue influence, 39–41, 84
  undue payment, 38–9, 84, 93
  unjust enrichment, 86–94
contempt of court, 71, 72
contracts, 4, 34, 43, 95, 153, 183, 197, 344, 349, 350
  annulment, 78, 79
  business trusts, 142
  civil-law systems, 95, 277, 286, 299, 311, 316, 317, 374–6
  emerging element of, 162–6, 224, 264–6
  in favour of third parties, 44n., 53, 375–6
  specific performance, 73
  void, 56–7
control, 104, 334, 338, 346
conversion, theory of, 69, 70

conveyance, 34, 35
Cook Islands, 208, 211–12, 219, 223, 237,
    242, 247, 250–1, 252, 253, 257, 258,
    264
co-ownership, 4, 19–20, 55–6, 105, 168,
    172n., 289, 311n., 341
corporations, charitable, 126
Court of Appeal, 25, 36–7, 46n., 53, 55, 62n.,
    63, 99, 137n., 138n., 176
courts, 58, 70, 71, 73–4, 107, 116, 120, 121,
    130, 174, 186, 317–18
covenants, 373, 376
creation of the trust, 2, 4, 14–15, 19, 66, 67,
    179, 209, 306, 373
    applicable law, 152–3, 154, 346–8
    expressions of, 98
    form of, 97, 113
    international trust model, 242–3
    negotium of, 346–8, 381–2, 385
    pursuant to a judgment, 238
    traditional English model, 95–122
    and voidance, 120, 121
creditors, 15, 54, 86, 90, 116, 117–19, 133,
    135, 188, 378, 380
    and bankruptcy, 20
    guarantees to, 138–9
    mortgages, 137–8
    protection, 119, 165, 215, 245, 248, 363
    and tracing, 61, 62
crimes, 209, 211, 221, 222
    benefits derived from, 38, 80–1, 84
Criscuoli, Giovanni, 2n.
culpa lata, 231n., 232
culpa in vigilando, 228
customary form, 182
cy-près, 130, 235–6
Cyprus, 210–11, 270

damages, 34, 59, 71, 85, 86, 91, 175, 386
death, 42, 104, 108, 110, 111, 113, 143
    and constructive trusts, 36–7
debtors, 138, 188, 248
debts, 116, 117
declaration, 1, 68, 99, 202, 217, 220, 271,
    335
    and nullity, 119, 120
defect
    in equity, 79–81, 84, 86, 294
    ex parte accipientis, 80, 81, 84, 86
    ex parte solventis, 79, 84, 113
    of form, 43–5, 84
    of title of trustee, 179–83
defendant
    conscience of, 85
    and tracing, 60–5
degeneration, 383
'delays prejudice equity', 69–70, 72

Denning, Lord, 2n., 8n., 48n., 92n., 102n.,
    118
deposits, 141
desuetude, 66n.
Diplock, Lord, 87n., 166n.
directors of companies, 23n.–24n., 25, 40,
    122, 136, 177, 381
disclosure, 218
discretion, 32
discretionary trusts, 3, 102, 130–3, 134,
    151, 162, 169, 180, 375
    beneficiaries, 131ff., 189–90
    constructive, 49
    international trust model, 259, 262
displacement, 380
disposition see act of disposition;
    testamentary disposition
dissolution, 107
distribution, 3, 102, 141–2
dolus, 21–2, 203n., 232
domestic trusts see internal trusts
domicile, 154, 155–6, 240, 350, 366
    see also residence
dominium, 37
donatio mortis causa, 36–7, 84, 121, 139n.
double-taxation treaties, 158–62, 163, 207,
    211, 218
duration, 104–10, 123, 129, 133n., 134, 147,
    155, 205, 206, 208, 286–7, 351
    civil-law model, 318–20
    international trust model, 205, 206, 208,
    254n., 255–7
    and nullity, 120
duress, 40
Dutch law, 87n., 341
    see also Roman-Dutch law

ecclesiastical law see canon law
Ecuador, 269, 270, 275–6, 306n., 320, 322n.
Eldon, Lord, 37
employee-share schemes, 146
English trust model,
    actio pauliana, 117–19, 135, 181, 300
    applicable law and non-residential
        trusts, 149–56
    asset-protection trusts, 119, 135–6
    beneficiaries, 125, 183–93
    breach of trust, 181
    business trusts, 122–3, 138–44
    case law, 8, 9, 16, 58, 82, 85–6, 125, 173
    charitable trusts, 123, 126–30
    creation of the trust, 14–15, 19, 66, 67,
        95–122, 152–3
    discretionary trusts, 130–3
    duration, 255, 256, 257
    entrusting, 75, 76–7
    'estate' and duration of trusts, 104–10

express trusts, 14–15, 75–7
family trusts, 149
  and Hague Convention, 328, 330, 331,
    333, 337, 339, 340, 344, 355, 356
  inheritance, 120
  and international model, 201, 202–4,
    223–39
  mortgages, 136–8
  non-express trusts, 75–7
  notion of trust, 156–200
  personal representative, 116–17
  powers of appointment, 101–3
  protective trusts, 133–4
  purpose trusts, 123–6
  reasons for nullity, 119–22
  revocable 'grantor' trusts, 103–4
  secret and half-secret trusts, 110–16,
    119–20, 183
  settlor as trustee, 96, 99–100, 101
  trustee, definition of, 178ff., 224, 271
  trustee, obligations of, 75–6, 180, 181
  typology of trusts, 122–56
entitlement, 3, 94, 190n., 197, 272, 381,
    385
  single, 378
  of trustee, 179, 182
entrusting, 75, 76–7, 195–9, 260, 261n., 262,
    263, 271, 303, 370, 371, 372, 374, 385
  civil-law systems, 310–13
  and nullity, 120
  and segregation, 199–200
  and trustee, 182, 183, 198
equitable charge, 139, 140, 141
equitable fullness of title, 189
  lack of, 3, 82–3, 84, 100, 179–83, 302
equitable interests, 3, 18, 27, 28, 29, 56, 77,
    79, 85, 100, 103, 133, 138, 378
  transfer of, 46, 51
equitable obligations, 4, 30, 75–6, 137
  in rem, 59, 60, 64
  of trustee, 180, 181, 182
equitable ownership, 2, 3, 56, 81, 107, 125,
    164, 187–8, 190
  and undue payment, 39, 84
equitable rights, 3, 77, 131, 137, 144, 180
  of third parties, 27, 143
equity, 1, 2, 3, 8–9, 13, 17, 173
  acts in personam, 64, 70–3
  after a perfected purchase, 84
  bribery, 25–6, 70, 92–3
  and common law, 4, 26–7, 42, 65–6, 71,
    73, 96, 111, 137
  and constructive trusts, 22–50
  co-ownership, 19, 84
  creation of the trust, 98
  defects in, 78–82, 179–83
  and delay, 69–70

estates, 105–10
  follows the law, 57–8, 79, 105
  form of trust instrument, 66–9
  and fraud, 20–2, 40, 42–3, 65–6, 68, 79,
    85, 90, 111
  and international trust model, 202–4
  mortgages, 137, 138
  and non-express trusts, 74–94
  oral agreements, 45–6, 84
  ownership, 81–2, 186–7
  restitution, 89
  rights in the family home, 46–50, 55, 84
  in Scotland, 294, 295, 296
  and statute law, 65–6
  transfer of property, 26–9, 84
  see also equitable fullness of title;
    equitable obligations; equitable rights;
    maxims of equity; mere equities
erga omnes, 36
escrow, 143n.
estate agents, 20, 143
estates, 37, 104–10, 157, 163–4, 181, 185,
    186, 190n., 191
  escheat of, 121n.
  mortgages, 138
estoppel, 44, 82n.–83n.
  see also proprietary estoppel
ethics, 21, 28, 29, 30, 119, 120, 121, 370,
    371–2
Ethiopia, 270, 276, 307, 308, 310, 314n.,
    315, 316n., 319, 322, 323
European Community, 217
European Court of Justice, 53, 193–5
European law, 36, 84, 126n., 164, 201, 202,
    216, 292
  see also civil-law systems; common
    law; medieval law
ex lege, 18, 19, 158
exceptio doli generalis, 21
express trusts, 1, 4, 8, 14–15, 44, 111, 113,
    184, 193, 303, 381
  Belize, 234
  and contracts, 95, 96
  entrusting, 197, 198
  failure of, 155
  and Hague Convention, 341–5
  Italian, 384–6
  lack of form, 68, 85
  and non-express trusts, 74–7, 85
  settlor as trustee, 99

family home, rights in, 46–50, 81, 84
family relationships, 20, 53–4, 383
family trusts, 149, 151, 236, 255–6, 322
feudal property, 67, 186
fideicomiso, 269, 274, 275, 276, 284–5, 286–7,
    291, 292, 304, 305, 312, 322, 374

fideicommissum, 112, 186, 192n., 195, 196, 273, 297, 299–300, 301, 303, 317, 323, 369, 372, 373, 375
fides, 186
fiducia, 3–4, 76, 157, 195, 196, 198, 225, 294, 303ff., 369–73, 382, 383–4
fiduciante, 40n.
fiduciaries, 22, 32, 70, 112, 132, 192n., 299, 370, 371
  and constructive trusts, 76
  improper benefit by, 79, 80, 92
  obligations, 145n.
  and ownership, 198–9, 317, 326
  responsibilities of, 4
  transfer to, 303–8
  see also fiduciary relationships
fiduciary relationships, 14, 17, 117, 194, 195–6, 226, 271, 272, 384
  and breach of trust, 29
  civil law, 198, 274, 275, 276, 279, 282, 284ff., 291, 297, 299–300, 303–8, 313–15, 317, 323
  Hague Convention, 336, 339
  improper benefits from, 22–6, 79–80, 84
  and Italian trusts, 369–77
  Japan, 279
  and protector, 259–60
  and tracing, 60
  and undue payment, 39
financial sector, 28–9, 275, 285, 291
Financial Services Act (1986), 20, 231
financial trusts, 145–9, 151, 254, 320
fixed trusts, 131, 161, 162
'flee clause', 241
forced heirs rule, 152, 165, 284, 291, 322–3, 364
foreign law, 5, 8, 10–13, 16, 152, 154n., 208, 209, 214, 245–8, 252, 301, 338, 343–4, 364
  see also conflict of laws
foreign trusts, 210, 212, 217, 218, 281, 351, 353–4, 361–2, 366
form, 14, 15, 111, 279, 347, 370, 371
  civil-law systems, 318
  defect in, 43–5
  lack of, 85, 121–2
  of trust instrument, 66–9, 85, 95–8
  of a will, 113
foundations, 288, 308, 313, 381
fraud, 4, 17, 33n., 41, 42, 43, 54, 68, 79, 111, 113, 115, 132, 135, 178, 359
  actio pauliana, 117–19, 300
  equitable notion of, 20–2, 40, 65–6, 90
  international trust model, 203, 205, 215, 229–30, 248–9
  and written law, 85

French law, 164, 201, 213, 218, 268, 280–1, 289, 290, 349
fumus boni iuris, 72
future interests, 106–8

Gambaro, A., 8n., 328
German law, 43, 140, 281
Ghana, 62n.
Gibraltar, 212–13
gifts, 26, 36, 123n., 301, 316
good faith, 60, 63, 175, 226, 273, 284, 303, 356, 386
Gorla, Gino, 2n.
grantor trusts, 103–4, 135
gross negligence, 230, 231, 279
guarantees, 138–42, 148, 190, 219
Guernsey, 201, 205, 207, 213–14, 218, 220, 225, 303
  breach of trust, 230
  constructive trusts, 233–4
  creation of the trust, 243
  definition of a trust, 238–9
  foreign laws, 245
  obligation of a trustee, 226
  tracing, 235
  transfer to the trustee, 243

Hague Convention (1955), 349
Hague Convention on the Law Applicable to Succession on Death (1988), 344, 349
Hague Convention on the Law Applicable to Trusts and on their Recognition (1985), 5–6, 9, 10, 156, 173, 209, 212, 214, 215, 217, 221, 286
  'analogous' institutions, 332–3
  applicable law, 330, 338, 344, 346–52, 361
  Art.2, 207, 237–9, 265, 333–41, 343, 345, 354, 355, 356
  Art.2.1, 334
  Art.2.2, 337
  Art.3, 341–2, 348, 356
  Art.3.3, 348
  Art.4, 242, 346–8
  Art.5, 350, 351–2
  Art.6, 240–1, 242, 348–50, 351, 352, 353, 357
  Art.6.2, 350, 352
  Art.7, 240, 241, 242, 350, 352, 353, 357, 361
  Art.7.1, 350
  Art.8, 242, 350–1, 353
  Art.9, 241, 242, 350–1, 353
  Art.10, 241, 242, 350–1, 353
  Art.11, 353, 354
  Art.11.1, 353, 354

Art.11.2, 354, 356, 357
Art.11.3, 354–5
Art.11.3(d), 355
Art.12, 354, 356–7
Art.13, 328, 354, 357–62, 364, 366–7
Art.14, 328, 354, 357, 362–4, 366, 367
Art.15, 354, 357, 362–4, 366, 367
Art.15.1(f), 356
Art. 15(2), 366
Art.16, 354, 364, 365, 367
Art.18, 354, 364, 365, 367
Art.19, 366
Art.20, 343–5
Art.21, 353–4
and civil-law systems, 327–9, 332–3
and conflict of laws, 330–1, 345–6
constructive and resulting trusts, 238,
  341–3
creation of the trust, 346–8, 363
definitions, 224, 237–9, 328, 331, 333ff.
domestic trusts, 351–2, 360–1
duties of a trustee, 336
effects of the trust, 363–4, 367
express trusts, 341–4
fiduciary relationship, 336, 339
'foreign trusts', 351, 353–4, 361–2, 366
form of registration, 356–7
fraud, 359–60
fund, 337
'judicial' trusts, 343
law of the trust, 350–1
laws of immediate application, 364–6
management powers of trustee, 337
negotium of creation and transfer,
  346–8
place, 350, 361–2
powers retained by the settlor, 337–8
preliminary report, 17n., 342, 347
purposes of, 151, 329–31
recognition of trusts, 330, 353–67
separation of settlor and trust, 339
settlor as trustee, 335
settlor, choice of law by, 351–2
settlor, unlimited freedom of choice of,
  349
shapeless trusts, 331–41, 344, 346, 355
title, 337
transfer to the trustee, 333–5, 346
trustee as beneficiary, 337–8
universality of, 353–4
voluntary trusts, 14, 341–5
weaknesses of, 339–41
half-secret trusts *see* semi-secret trusts
heirs, 41, 43n., 78–9, 81, 112, 114, 115, 116,
  117, 124, 287, 374, 378
  see also children; forced heirs rule
historical explanations, 12–13

homology, 311, 315, 319
honesty, 29, 30, 40, 177
Hong Kong, 212, 214
House of Lords, 6n., 24n., 42n., 44n., 51, 56,
  57, 72n., 81, 82n., 86, 88n., 127n., 128,
  139n., 176, 293

illegality, 54, 56
immovable property, 67n., 153, 154n., 286,
  289, 315
implied trusts, 14, 16, 18, 19, 48, 209, 277
  settlor as trustee, 99
  structure, 15
importation, 9, 12
improper benefits, 4, 22–60, 79, 84
in pari causa turpitudinis, 56n.
in rem, 59, 60, 64, 187, 188–9, 194, 200,
  249
income, 109–10, 120, 131, 148, 159, 167
incomplete provisions, 82, 84
incorporation by reference, 115
India, 183n., 218
indicia, 77
inheritance law, 120
inheritance tax, 103
injunctions, 70–2
Insolvency Act (1986), 117, 118
intent, 1, 48, 49, 55, 56
  proof of, 118
  testamentary, 115
inter vivos trusts, 4, 78, 96, 97, 113, 135, 151,
  153, 154n., 179, 207, 238, 245
  civil-law model, 278, 279, 299, 303, 311,
    316, 317
interests, 106–8, 133, 134, 371, 374, 384
  determinable, 120–1
  see also equitable interests
intermediaries, sums received by, 20
internal trusts, 10, 328, 351–2, 360–1
international trust model, 7, 76, 109, 136n.,
  151, 166n., 270, 311, 317, 347, 350
  acceptance of trustee, 223–4
  applicable law, 209, 240–5
  companies, 209, 210, 212n., 217, 218,
    244, 255
  constructive trusts, 233–5
  creation of the trust, 242–3
  cy-près, 235–6
  definition of a trust, 214n., 237–9
  definition of a trustee, 224
  delegation of trustee power, 228–9
  duration of a trust, 255–7
  emerging contractual element, 224,
    264–6
  equity, 202–4
  forced heirship, 152
  foreign law, 245–8

international trust model (*cont.*)
  form of trust instrument, 233–5
  and fraud, 203, 205, 215, 229–32, 248–9
  legal status of beneficiary, 224–5
  legal status of trustee, 224
  legislative foundation, 201
  letter of wishes, 262–4
  new *regulae*, 239–66
  obligations of trustee, 225–7
  openness of, 202, 203
  protective trusts, 236
  protector, 101, 206, 212, 217, 254, 257–62
  purpose trusts, 252–5, 257
  regulae from English law, 223–39
  regulation, 243
  responsibilities of trustee, 229–32
  resulting trusts, 236
  revocatory actions, 248–52
  tax exemptions, 204–5
  termination, 237
  theoretical elements, 204
  tracing, 235
  transfer to the trustee, 243–5
  unanimity, 228, 244
interpositio, 156, 157, 162, 184
intestate succession, 19
investments, 100–1, 136, 146–7, 167, 171n.,
    172n., 176n., 177, 202, 207, 208, 215,
    275, 277, 278, 279
Irish law, 115, 124n.
Isle of Man, 215
Israel, 270, 279–80, 307, 325, 334
Italian Civil Code, 44n., 113n., 287
  Art. *167–71*, 303
  Art. *627*, 115–16
  Art. *629*, 130n., 258
  Art. *693*, 317
  Art. *694*, 317
  Art. *1707*, 384
  Art. *2033*, 39n.
  Art. *7002*, 171n.
Italian trusts, 10, 72n., 144, 145n.
  breach of trust, 29n.
  civilian approach, 368–86
  contractual element, 374–6
  creation of the trust, 97
  dual-ownership model, 268
  express trusts, 384–6
  fiduciary relationships, 24n., 369–77
  functional approach, 369
  potestà, 103, 132n.
  segregation, 377–84
  wills, 42n.

Jamaica, 209–10, 221
Japan, 277–9, 301, 304, 306n., 310, 313n.,
    324

Jersey, 7n., 21, 147n., 166n., 201, 202, 203,
    205, 207, 213, 214, 215–17, 221, 228,
    260n., 265, 303
  acceptance of trustee, 223
  breach of trust, 227, 230–1
  constructive trusts, 233, 234
  definition of a trust, 224
  foreign laws, 245
  responsibility of a trustee, 229
  resulting trusts, 236
  tracing, 235
  transfer to trustee, 243
John of Gaunt, 156, 162–3
joint ownership *see* co-ownership
joint purchase, 55–6, 84
judges, 18, 21, 24, 58, 70, 72, 74, 86, 122,
    345
  and remedies, 92
  and written law, 85
judicial intervention, 317–18
judicial trusts, 343–5
Justinian's law, 37, 373

'knowing assistance', 29, 30n,
'knowing receipt', 29–34
knowledge, 30, 31, 207n., 232, 323, 324,
    326, 386

land, 97, 111, 156, 163, 186
  not yet transferred, 34–6
  registration, 27n., 173, 280
  trust of *see* trust for sale
Latin America, 269, 270, 273–6, 284–7,
    290–2, 304ff., 374
Law of Property Act (1925), 19, 67n., 68n.,
    98n., 117, 137n., 173n.
law of the trust, 350, 363
lawyers, 40, 143
  and fiduciary relationship, 23
  sums received by, 20
'legal ownership', 2, 56
legislation, 7, 18, 145n., 170, 270, 301–2,
    338
Lepaulle, P., 269, 275, 288, 300, 302n.
letter of wishes, 262–4
Liechtenstein, 270, 280–1, 304, 307, 309,
    311, 312–13, 316, 319, 320n., 324, 325,
    328
limitations, 58, 101, 109, 110, 161, 162, 164,
    165, 178, 180, 197, 365
'living trusts', 104, 153
local law, 204, 212, 215, 241, 244, 246, 251
Lombard law, 136n., 372
Louisiana, 270, 281–3, 305, 314n., 317, 322,
    323, 334
Lugano Convention, 344
Luxembourg, 145n., 304, 345n.

Macnaghton, Lord, 127, 128
Maitland, F.W., 187, 267
Malta, 201, 217–18, 226, 227, 233, 234, 238, 270, 280
'Mareva injunction', 72, 73n., 251
Massachusetts trust, 122–3
Mauritius, 201, 212n., 218, 220, 226, 234, 238, 243, 270, 301, 305, 307, 314n., 322n., 324n.
maxims of equity, 56n., 57–74, 97
  and common law, 57, 58–9, 65–6
  equity acts *in personam*, 64, 70–3
  equity follows the law, 57–8, 79
  equity looks at that as done which ought to have been done, 69–70
  equity will not assist volunteers, 73
  and fraud, 65–6
  he who seeks equity must do equity, 72
  and tracing, 58–65
medieval law, 36, 112, 136, 163, 292, 373
mental incapacity, 20, 172n.
'mere equities', 27, 77, 78, 85
Mexico, 267, 269, 284–5, 291, 303
minors, 20, 107, 363
mistake of law, 78, 81
mixed funds, 61, 82n., 172
mixed-law systems, 4, 7, 78n.
  see also civil-law systems
money-laundering, 209
mortgages, 50, 106, 136–8, 176, 277, 292n., 373
mortis causa, 43n., 78, 112, 121, 183
  see also donatio mortis causa
movable property, 36n., 58–9, 225, 286, 289
multiple ownership, 144
Muslim law, 208, 283

Napoleonic code, 201, 281, 283, 289, 290, 377n.
natural law, 57
Nauru, 218–19, 253, 256
negotiorum gestio, 34n., 301
negotium, 3–4, 96, 305, 306, 310, 324, 325, 352, 359, 370, 371
  of creation and transfer, 346–8, 381–2
  form of, 66
  form-free, 15
  inter-vivos, 316
Nevis, 212n., 219, 238
New Hebrides *see* Vanuatu
New York law, 38, 152, 158
New Zealand, 6, 7, 8, 31, 43, 51n., 79n., 80n., 202
  business trusts, 141n.
  estoppel, 83n.
  rights in family home, 47
  unjust enrichment, 87, 88n.

Niue, 219, 262
nominee agreements, 157, 159, 162, 163, 197, 217, 218, 383
non-express trusts, 68, 74–94, 193
  compared to express trusts, 74–7
  entrusting, 75, 76–7, 197, 198
  form, 74
  and Hague Convention, 342
  lack of settlor, 2, 74
  problems of, 15
  segregation, 75, 77
  structure, 56
  terminology, 16–19
  theory, 85
  see also constructive trusts; implied trusts; resulting trusts
non-resident trusts, 155–6, 219
Norman law, 201, 213, 265
notice, 26, 28–9, 30, 31, 232, 233, 273
Nottingham, Lord, 15, 67
nullity *see* voidance

obligations, 4, 69, 86, 124, 180, 181, 182, 249, 386
  see also equitable obligations
OECD model, 159–61
offshore trusts, 205, 208, 211n., 217, 252
open structures, 202, 203, 204, 302, 325–6
oral agreements, 45–6, 68n., 84
oral declaration, 37, 97, 98
'owner', notion of, 70
ownership, 1, 2, 196
  beneficial, 161, 187ff., 224
  concept of, 187–9
  'due', 81, 82, 188, 192
  and equity, 81–3
  fiduciary, 198–9, 317, 326
  and Italian trusts, 369
  multiple, 144
  rights, 185, 187, 188, 192–3
  splitting of, 2
  see also co-ownership; equitable ownership

pactum commissorium, 136–8
Panama, 269, 270, 285–6, 306n.
partners, 143, 212n.
patrimony, 15, 40, 57, 303, 385
  by appropriation, 268
  autonomous, 379–81
  separate, 377–84, 386
pension funds, 24, 145–6, 208n., 216, 231
perpetual trusts, 109, 124
perpetuities, rule against, 104, 108–9, 129, 219, 221, 256
persona, 70

personal property, 37, 38, 59, 67, 81, 84,
    97n., 152, 154n., 165, 225
personal representative, 116–17, 120
personal status and capacity, 360, 361
persons, 106, 159–60, 271, 276, 308
    division among several, 143–4
    numbers of, 1–2
    separate patrimony, 378
Peru, 269, 270, 286–7, 306n., 319, 320, 321,
    322, 325
Philippines, 270, 277
place of administration, 350, 361, 362
pledge interest, 145
political purpose, 128–9
power of attorney, 172n., 196
powers, 338
    of administration, 164
    of appointment, 101–3
    to consent, 100–1
    granting of, 132, 133
    theory of, 103
    of trustee, 170–1, 174–5ff.
precatory trusts, 98n., 119
precedents, 18
predecease, 36, 37
presumptions, 53, 54, 55, 56, 61
principia, 11n., 174, 301, 303, 326, 372, 373
principles, 10, 11, 13, 66, 87
private international law, 204, 209, 240,
    243, 245, 350–1
    conflict of laws in, 149–52
private understandings, 120
Privy Council, 6n., 25–6, 32, 62n., 80, 116n.,
    169n., 172n., 192n.
probate, 104
procedural remedies, 21, 34, 78, 82
promises, 73, 82, 303
property, 17, 97, 183
    acquisition of, 26–7, 81
    division, 19–20, 191
    and law of conversion, 69–70
    non-ownership rights, 46–50, 55, 81
    purchased in common, 55–6, 84
    rights, 4, 94, 105
    tracing, 61
    transfer, 2, 26–9, 35
    see also mortgages; personal property;
    real property
proprietary estoppel, 44, 82
proprietary remedy, 64
protection, 21, 26, 27, 32, 73, 198, 199, 307
    creditor, 119, 165, 215, 245, 248, 363
    effects of, 82
    minors and incapable parties, 363
protective trusts, 133–4, 212, 236, 276, 284,
    301, 322
protector, 101, 206, 212, 217, 254, 257–62

public funds, 379–80
Public Trustee, 158n., 167n.
public welfare trusts, 127–8, 130, 296
publicity, 172–3
purchasers, 35, 36, 44, 50, 54, 81, 84, 139,
    141, 156, 382
    conscience of, 27, 28–9
    of merchandise, 99
    and third party obligations, 45
purpose trusts, 2, 123–6, 130, 133n., 151,
    178, 223, 252–5, 257, 259, 262, 271, 273
    Belize, 208, 253, 254
    Bermuda, 208, 253, 254
    civil-law systems, 318–20
    Cook Islands, 253
    and Hague Convention, 334
    Jersey, 216
    Nauru, 219, 253
    see also charitable trusts

quantum, 180, 182
quantum meruit, 89n.
Quebec, 270, 287–8, 290, 307, 308–9, 313n.,
    315, 316, 319, 341
quia timet, 72n.
Quistclose trust, 17n., 51n., 52, 99n., 148n.

Rabel, Ernst, 149
real property, 104, 121, 173, 194
    community of rights in, 19–20
    dispositions of, 50
    feudal, 157, 184
    gift of, 36
    minors, 20
    and ownership, 188–9, 191
    tracing, 61
    transfers, 67, 184
    voidance, 43–4
    see also estates
real rights, 64–5, 184–5, 190, 192, 194, 195,
    328
receipts, 99
receivers, 73–4, 119
recognition, 349, 353–67
Recognition of Trusts Act (1987), 5n.
recovery, 60, 61
redemption, 137, 138
refusal, 97
registration, 27n., 34, 35, 36, 173, 217–18,
    220, 278, 304, 306–7, 323
    compulsory, 129, 239
    form of, 356–7
    of property in favour of third parties, 84
regulae, 10–13, 16, 18, 19, 46, 72, 78, 80–1,
    84ff., 87, 121–2, 301
    civil-law systems, 315–25, 326
    international trust model, 223–66

regulation, 204, 243, 276
religious trusts, 128, 174n., 277
remainder, 105–6
remedial law, 90–4
remedies, 17, 21, 32, 34, 56, 64
  in equity, 72, 77–81, 91, 93
replevin, 59
residence, 156, 159, 160, 162, 210–11, 219,
  240, 350, 361, 366
residual trusts *see* resulting trusts
residuary legatee, 124n.
restitution, 34, 40, 56, 59, 78, 80, 89, 91,
  175
  literature on, 88
resulting trusts, 8, 9, 16, 17–18, 47, 48,
  50–7, 67, 100, 113–14, 118, 125n., 155,
  193, 300, 316
  assets in name of third party, 53–4
  automatic and presumed, 17, 18, 55
  civil-law systems, 277, 280
  delivery of sum for specific purpose,
    51–3, 84
  distinct from express trusts, 74–7, 85
  entrusting, 76–7, 198
  and equity, 77–86
  Hague Convention, 238, 341ff.
  incomplete transfers, 50–1, 52, 54, 84
  international model, 236
  lack of equitable fullness, 3
  lack of form, 85
  lack of settlor, 75
  limitation on, 56–7
  purchase of property in common, 55–6,
    84
  structure, 15
  theory of, 77–86
returning trusts *see* resulting trusts
reversion, 105–6
revocable trusts, 103–4, 111, 121–22, 135,
  162, 321
revocatory actions, 209, 210, 212, 219, 221,
  248–52, 284, 286
  see also actio pauliana
rights, 1, 2, 38, 40, 65, 108, 184–5, 338
  ad rem, 200
  community of, 19
  division of, 143
  in the family home, 46–50, 55
  in personam, 188–9, 191n., 194
  in rem, 187–9, 194, 200
  ownership, 185, 187, 188, 192–3
  transfer of, 96–8
  and trustees, 179–83, 191, 192–3
  see also equitable rights; real rights
Roman-Dutch law, 112n., 188, 297, 298–9,
  375
Roman law, 13, 21–2, 78n., 87, 89n., 112,

184–6, 195, 196, 300, 301, 371, 372
Rome Convention (1980), 344, 349, 364
rules, 4, 10, 21, 58, 84–6, 150–1, 302
  and equity, 66, 70
  improper benefits, 25
  international trust model, 204
  and trustee, 170–1
  see also conflict of laws; maxims of
    equity; *regulae*
Russia, 270, 288–9, 306n., 311–12

St Lucia, 290
St Vincent, 220
sale, 34, 170, 171
  business trusts, 139
  and co-ownership, 19–20
  and equity, 81, 84
Scarman, L. J., 99n.
Scott, A. W., 57, 188
Scottish law, 10, 13n., 36, 81, 154n., 168,
  188, 231n., 292–6, 298, 374
seals, 73
secret trusts, 96, 110–14, 116, 121–22, 163,
  183, 255, 275
securities, 149
segregation, 15, 40, 65, 75, 77, 82, 182,
  199–200, 271, 298, 337, 355, 357, 374,
  385
  civil-law systems, 308–10, 315
  and companies, 142, 254
  Italian trusts, 377–84
semi-secret trusts, 96, 114–16, 119–20, 183
settlors, 1, 4, 14, 15, 73, 101, 152, 153,
  162–6, 183, 184, 198, 216, 375, 385,
  386
  and asset protection, 135–6
  civil-law systems, 271, 281, 283, 293, 294,
    304, 305, 310–13, 315ff.
  and express trusts, 68
  intentions of, 18
  international trust model, 240, 242, 258
  lack of, 2, 380
  loss of entitlement, 197
  and non-express trusts, 74, 75, 342
  resulting trusts, 50–1
  and revocable trusts, 103–4
  in Scottish law, 293, 294, 295
  separation from trust, 339
  as trustees, 95–6, 99–100, 101, 380
  will of, 342, 343, 349, 351, 352
Seychelles, 201, 220, 234, 238, 243, 270,
  289–90, 306n., 311n., 315, 319–20
shareholders, 147, 149, 177, 241, 254
shares, 36n., 143, 146, 147, 149, 165n., 173,
  278
simulation, 165, 166n., 264, 383
Singapore, 40

South Africa, 10, 78n., 130, 153, 162n., 183, 270, 297–301, 317, 374, 375, 376, 377
specific performance, 73
'spendthrift trust', 133
sport, 128
spouses, 134, 245, 248, 378
    purchase of property in common, 55–6
    rights in the family home, 46–50
statute law, 4, 58, 65–6, 122
    see also legislation
Statute of Frauds (1677), 18, 66, 69, 97
    s. 7, 67, 68
    s. 8, 15, 67, 68
Statute of Limitations, 58, 178
Statute of Uses (1535), 156–7, 158
statutory trusts, 18, 19–20
'Stranger', 26n., 29n., 284
structure, 13, 14–16, 90, 121–2, 136
    international trust model, 223–66
    non-express trusts, 56, 74–5
subject matter of the trust, 3, 16, 18, 57, 98, 125, 181, 182, 187, 189, 271, 272, 380
subjective states, 31, 32, 80, 175
substantive law, 53, 63, 90, 91, 103, 125, 151
succession, 19, 35n., 104, 113, 114, 115, 216, 245, 248, 363
sums of money, 38, 384
    business trusts, 139–44
    and equitable defect, 79–80
    and intermediaries, 20
    and law of conversion, 69–70
    paid in error, 92–3
    paid pursuant to void contracts, 56–7
    payments on pledge, 139
    tracing, 61–3
    transferred for specific purpose, 51–3, 84
syndication operations, 148

taxation, 54, 101, 135, 155, 158, 159, 165, 261
    'adverse party', 104
    avoidance, 126
    discretionary trusts, 131n.
    exemptions, 204–5
    and powers of appointment, 102
    rules of, 103
    see also double-taxation treaties
Templeman, Lord, 25n.
termination, 35, 180, 189, 237, 318–20, 325
testamentary disposition, 35, 41, 42, 103, 110, 113, 119–20, 121, 244
    see also wills
testamentary trusts, 95–6, 110, 124, 151, 153, 154, 166n., 286, 299
    secret, 163
testator, influence over will of, 41, 84

theft, 38n., 80–1
third parties, 40, 45, 84, 90, 105, 107, 164, 165, 173, 177–8, 179, 182, 278, 279, 306, 309, 356, 357, 363, 386
    breach of trust, 30–1, 77, 232
    business trusts, 143
    contracts in favour of, 44n., 183, 374–6
    and equitable interests, 77–8
    equitable rights of, 27, 143
    investment of funds by, 100–1
    obligations towards, 86
    powers of appointment, 102–3
    purchasers, 50
    and resulting trusts, 51–4
    and tracing, 60
    trustees and revocable trusts, 103
time-sharing, 144
title, 39, 103, 272
    completeness of, 82
    defect in, 81, 82–3
    of trustee, 179–80
tort, 34, 300
Totten trust, 152n.
tracing, 26, 32, 58–65, 90, 172, 187, 189, 199, 235, 272, 273, 284, 323–5, 355
transactional instruments, 7
transfer to the trustee, 1, 2, 4, 67n., 96, 154, 155, 185, 212, 243–5, 271, 272, 278–9, 303, 323, 385
    Hague Convention, 333–5, 346
transfers, 39, 67, 98, 108, 118, 184, 374, 346–8, 381–2
    to beneficiary, 81, 83
    breach of trust, 78, 79, 84
    and constructive trusts, 26–9, 78, 79
    form of, 66–9
    to fiduciary, 303–8
    incomplete or ineffective, 50–1, 52, 54
    to minors, 20
    of seller's obligations to third parties, 45, 84
translations, 270, 302
travel agents, 141
treaties, 211, 248
    see also double-taxation treaties
Treuhänderschaft, 3–4, 280–1, 313, 316
Trinidad and Tobago, 22n., 68n., 84n.
trust companies, 165–6, 174n.
trust for sale, 19, 168–9, 171, 172n., 341
trust instruments, 69, 103, 153, 170, 171, 174, 176, 180, 181, 212, 265, 296, 300, 318
    discretionary trusts, 130, 131
    form of, 66–9, 233–5
    lack of, 85
    in traditional English model, 95–8, 102
trust of land see trust for sale

Trustee Act (1893), 202, 206
Trustee Act (1925), 133n., 171n., 175, 202,
  207, 215, 276, 280, 284, 290
  s. 3, 100–1
  s. 33, 134n.
  s. 36(1), 102n.
  s. 41(1), 102n.
  s. 61, 177
trustee de son tort, 34
Trustee Investment Act (1961), 202, 215,
  219
trustees, 1, 2, 4, 144, 178–83, 190n., 209,
  266, 320, 381, 385, 386
  acceptance of, 223–4
  and bankruptcy, 20
  and beneficiaries, 198
  breach of trust, 29–34, 84, 175–8, 181,
    229, 230, 232
  constructive trusts, 76, 94
  and co-ownership, 19
  definition of, 178ff., 224, 281
  delegation of powers, 228–9
  discretionary trusts, 130–1, 132, 133, 169
  duty to act together, 171, 173, 228
  entitlement, 179, 197
  equitable defect of title, 179ff.
  equitable obligations of, 75–6
  essential nature of, 178, 179, 182
  exercise of functions, 152, 154–5
  and express trusts, 68
  fiduciary element, 14, 177, 317
  and improper benefits, 22–6, 84
  incomplete transfer, 51, 84
  injunctions against, 71
  and non-express trusts, 74, 75
  non-resident, 102
  obligations of, 225–7
  office of, 166–78
  payments to, 167–8
  pension schemes, 24
  personal liability, 178
  and personal representative, 116–17, 120
  powers to appoint new, 101–3
  powers of sale, 170–1
  and protector, 258, 259–60
  responsibilities, 175–8, 229–32
  and revocable trusts, 103
  rights, 179ff., 191, 192–3
  sale of land not yet transferred, 34–6
  settlors as, 95–6, 99–100, 380
  and subject matter of trust, 16
  substitution of, 74
  and tracing, 60, 62
  and trust investments, 101
  types of, 179
  will of, 17–18
  see also transfer to the trustee

trusts
  administration of, 154, 155
  and contracts, 95, 183
  definitions, 1–4, 5, 6, 183, 214n., 237–9,
    271–3, 282, 283, 291, 298, 303, 304,
    328, 331, 334, 338, 340
  English case law, 85–6
  'families' of, 201, 270, 328
  in plural, 5, 7, 123, 179, 316
  sources of, 14–15, 201–2
  terminology, 16–19
  theory of, 2, 6, 9, 13, 77–86, 126,
    178–200
  see also civil-law systems; English trust
    model; international trust model
Trusts of Land and Appointment of
  Trustees Act (1996), 101, 107, 138,
    169n., 170
  s. 9, 171n.
  s. 19, 102n., 167n.
Turks and Caicos, 202n., 205, 221, 232, 237,
  238, 248, 256

unanimity, 228, 244, 280
unconscionability, 21, 22, 28, 85
undue influence or awe, 39–41, 84
undue payment, 38–9, 84
unilaterality, 4, 96, 164, 183, 184, 186, 193,
  196, 217, 223, 263, 271, 316, 375, 385
unit trusts, 147
United Kingdom, 5n., 159, 194, 209, 212,
  215
  see also English trust model; Scottish
    law
United States, 6, 7, 8, 23n., 38, 68n., 126,
  146, 147n., 150, 158, 171n., 205n., 209,
  212, 269, 285, 286
  benefits from crimes, 38
  business trusts, 122–3, 138, 143
  constructive trusts, 76, 89, 90n., 91, 342
  creditor protection, 119
  double-taxation treaties, 159, 162n.
  estoppel, 83n.
  living trusts, 104
  protective trusts, 133
  'residence', 156
  Restatements of Trusts and of
    Restitution, 6n.–7n., 86–7, 152, 153,
    155n.
  revocable trusts, 103–4
  undue payments, 38–9
  unjust enrichment, 86–7, 89
unjust enrichment, 86–94, 183, 186, 342
uses, 156–7, 184–6
ususfructus, 185, 191, 192n.

vacant succession, 379

validity, 101, 155, 242, 244, 245, 271, 347,
    350
Vanuatu, 221–2
Variation of Trusts Act (1958), 107
Venezuela, 260n., 269, 270, 275, 286, 290–2,
    304, 306n., 307, 318, 320, 323, 324
verbal agreements, 43–4
vesting, remoteness of, 108–9, 129n.
voidance, 50, 54, 56–7, 108, 109, 117, 123,
    152, 168, 323, 324, 325, 326, 386
  charitable trusts, 127
  for defect in form, 43–4, 84
  reasons for, 119–22, 124, 125, 131
voluntary trusts, 1, 14, 15, 320, 341–5
  see also express trusts

volunteers, 26, 63, 73, 97
voting trusts, 147–8, 254

Waters, D. W. M., 271–3
Western Samoa, 217, 218, 222–3
wilful default, 231–2
wills, 4, 36, 67, 96, 110, 114–15, 184n., 244,
    245, 293, 363
  forms of, 113, 122, 286
  incorrect interpretation of, 78–9
  influence over, 41, 84
  mutual, 41–3, 84
writings, 46, 67, 326, 342, 345, 371
  and creation of a trust, 97, 98, 111
written law, 65, 85, 371

Books in the series

1 *Principles of the institutional law of international organisations*
   C. F. Amerasinghe

2 *Fragmentation and the international relations of micro-states*
   Jorri Duursma

3 *The polar regions and the development of international law*
   Donald R. Rothwell

4 *Ethics and authority in international law*
   Alfred P. Rubin

5 *Sovereignty over natural resources*
   Nico Schrijver

6 *Religious liberty and international law in Europe*
   Malcolm Evans

7 *Unjust enrichment: A study of private law and public values*
   Hanoch Dagan

8 *Trade and the environment: A comparative study of EC and US law*
   Damien Geradin

9 *The changing international law of high seas fisheries*
   Francisco Orrego Vicuña

10 *International organizations before national wants*
    August Reinisch

11 *The right to property in commonwealth constitutions*
    Tom Allen

12 *Trusts: A comparative study*
    Maurizio Lupoi